AMERICAN GOVERNMENT

AMERICAN GOVERNMENT

Readings and Cases

Tenth Edition

Peter Woll
Brandeis University

❖❖❖

HarperCollins*Publishers*

Library of Congress Cataloging-in-Publication Data

American government.

  Includes bibliographical references.
  1. United States—Politics and government.
I. Woll, Peter
JK21.A445 1900   320.973   89–24043
ISBN 0–673–52031–5

Artwork, illustrations, and other materials supplied by the publisher.
Copyright © HarperCollins*Publishers*

    4 5 6 – MPC – 94 93 92 91

This book is dedicated to
my mother,
RUTH C. WOLL,
and
to the memory of my father,
JOHN W. WOLL

Preface

American Government, Tenth Edition, provides key classic and contemporary readings and cases that introduce students to the underpinnings and current practices of American government. It also complements regular texts by illustrating and amplifying important issues and concepts, and at the same time, due to the organization and design of the book, is suitable for use as a core text. Extensive notes are included that prepare for, connect, and comment upon the selections and point out their significance within the broader context of American government.

GENERAL SUBJECTS

The basic areas covered in this edition include: the nature and origins of constitutional theory and practice; federalism and intergovernmental relations; civil liberties and civil rights; the organization and functions of political parties; elections and electoral behavior; political campaigning; the media and political consultants; the nature and functions of interest groups; the powers, responsibilities, and limitations of the presidency; the pros and cons of the presidential nominating process; the presidential establishment; presidential character and style; the president, the media, and public opinion; the rise of the bureaucracy, and the implications of the administrative state for constitutional democracy; the role, powers, and functions of Congress; committee chairmen and congressional staffers as part of the powerful Washington political establishment; Congress and the electoral connection, including the power of incumbency; the differences between legislators' homestyles and their Washington careers; a lively account of a day in the life of a United States senator; and the Supreme Court and the role of the judiciary, with focuses on the ebb and flow of judicial activism and self-restraint, and the continuing political debate over "loose" versus "strict" constitutional construction.

Selections for the text have always been chosen to give students not only an understanding of American political institutions and processes, but also to heighten their appreciation of the richness and excitement of politics. The readings introduce students to political theory and political reality.

THE NEW EDITION

The new edition contains up-to-date and relevant material designed to stimulate student interest and discussion and at the same time to show how our government works. As in previous editions, a balance is maintained among classic selections, important historical and current constitutional law cases, and contemporary readings that pinpoint and analyze evolving political trends.

The tenth edition continues to give students a view of their rich political heritage through classic readings from *The Federalist*. Particularly emphasized are Federalist Papers 47, 48, and 51 (on the separation of powers and checks and balances); 10 (on parties and interest groups); 39 (on federalism); 70 (on the Presidency); and 78 (on judicial review).

Following the precedent of previous editions, the text continues to present major Supreme Court cases, including *Marbury v. Madison* (1803), *McCullough v. Maryland* (1819), and key cases that have set the tone of contemporary constitutional law. The Supreme Court and the judiciary continue to be uniquely powerful in our political system, and the new edition has added the Court's important recent decisions on abortion, *Webster v. Reproductive Health Services* (1989), and the historic Pledge of Allegiance case, *West Virginia Board of Education v. Barnette* (1942). Complementing the new cases are those concerning school prayer (*Engel v. Vitale*, [1962]) abortion (*Roe v. Wade* [1973]), and affirmative action (*Regents of the University of California v. Bakke* [1978]).

Also included is an excerpt from and an in-depth discussion of the controversial case *Texas v. Johnson* (1989), in which the Court held that flag-burning was protected political expression under the First and Fourteenth Amendments. The decision stirred political protests throughout the nation, and resulted in calls for a constitutional amendment to overturn the decision. Court decisions concerning the flag are always controversial, as reflected in the sharp divisions in the Court itself as well as in the nation.

Long before the Court's decision in the flag-burning case, its ruling in the Pledge of Allegiance case during World War II caused angry protests and scathing dissents. The 1988 presidential campaign resurrected the Pledge of Allegiance issue when Republican candidate George Bush and Democratic candidate Michael Dukakis locked horns on the issue of the appropriateness and constitutionality of requiring school children to recite the Pledge.

In other areas the new edition is also strengthened with updated, pertinent selections. The text examines the importance of the Reagan era for the 1990s and the significance of the 1988 presidential election. New readings in Chapter 4 include Paul Allen Beck on the Reagan legacy for parties and elections, V.O. Key, Jr.'s classic work on the responsible electorate, and William Schneider on the selling of the president in 1988. Each selection deals with issues that are of particular importance for the 1990s, evaluating whether the Reagan presidency represented short-term political forces or reflected a long-term party realignment. The new readings also analyze the character of the electorate, assess the extent to which voters understand and follow their interests in presidential campaigns, and estimate the effects campaign strategies had on voters and parties in 1988.

Turning from parties to interest groups in Chapter 5, the new edition takes into account the ever-growing importance of political action committees (PACs) with a new selection by Frank Sorauf on money in American elections. Other new selections portray the way in which the media has become an important interest group in its own right, maintaining a powerful Washington lobby, and the way in which the media and government constantly struggle to define and control the political agenda.

The chapters on the formal institutions of government have also been updated in the new edition. Chapter 6, on the presidency, in addition to the classic works by Clinton Rossiter, Richard Neustadt, Thomas Cronin, and James David Barber, now contains an exciting new selection by Michael Barone on the role of public-opinion pollsters in presidential politics. New to Chapter 7, on the bureaucracy, is Aaron Wildavsky's up-to-date analysis of the Office of Management and Budget (OMB) and the way in which the budget deficits of the modern era have affected executive-legislative relations.

Turning to Congress, Lawrence Dodd contributes a major new selection on the importance of the personal power incentive on Capitol Hill, and Hedrick Smith examines congressional staffers as policy entrepreneurs. A new selection by *Newsweek* writers George Hackett and Eleanor Clift colorfully illustrates the power of incumbency, a topic that is also covered by congressional scholars Richard F. Fenno, Jr., Morris P. Fiorina, and David Mayhew in separate readings. Washington insider and congressional scholar Norman Ornstein contributes another new reading that analyzes the effects of congressional reforms on the character of the House and the Senate.

Finally, in Chapter 9, on the judiciary, former Attorney General Edwin Meese and Supreme Court Associate Justice William J. Brennan, Jr. take up the gauntlet for and against strict constitutional construction, respectively, in new selections drawn from their historic debate on the issue.

As in previous editions, an extensive *Instructors Manual* accompanies the text. In addition to being a comprehensive guide to the selections, the manual contains background material and multiple-choice questions. At the instructor's discretion any part of the manual may be reproduced for students as an instructional aid.

ACKNOWLEDGMENTS

Unfortunately, space does not permit me to thank the numerous individuals who over the years have generously given their time, energy, and ideas to help me make this work a major American government source book. Among the many, however, I would especially like to thank Neil Sullivan for his long-standing interest in the book, and his valuable ideas and suggestions. My colleague Shep Melnick gave me helpful and timely advice during the preparation of the new edition. I would also like to thank Martin Northway and Julie Howell, who skillfully edited the text and guided it through the production maze. I am indebted as well to Bruce Nichols, whose editorial acumen helped me update and further improve the book. Once again, I owe a debt of gratitude to Elaine Herrmann, who has word-processed my notes and comments accurately and on time.

Contents

THE JUDICIAL SOURCES OF MAJOR POLITICAL CONTROVERSIES OVER CIVIL LIBERTIES AND RIGHTS

The Pledge of Allegiance to the Flag

The American Flag

Religious Freedom and the Issue of Prayer in Public Schools

The Right to Abortion

THE NATURE OF THE PRESIDENCY: POWER AND PERSUASION

Strong presidential leadership has been necessary since the framing of the Constitution to overcome the forces of disunity within the political system.

The Constitution makes the president more of a clerk than a king. Presidential influence depends upon powers of persuasion. There is never assured support for White House policies. To be effective, the president must persuade constituents—the bureaucracy, Congress, the president's political party, citizens at large, and foreign governments—that presidential policies are in their interests.

PRESIDENTIAL POLITICS

Post-1968 reforms of presidential nominating politics to increase grassroots participation were a necessary response to changing political forces, strengthening rather than weakening parties in the 1980s.

THE PRESIDENTIAL ESTABLISHMENT

The Executive Office of the President has become a dominant force in the White House, often overshadowing the person who occupies the Oval Office. Presidents promise to reduce the size of the presidential bureaucracy, but the political realities that buttress a large presidential establishment have remained unchanged.

PRESIDENTIAL CHARACTER AND STYLE

It is the total character of the person who occupies the White House that is the determinant of presidential performance.

THE PRESIDENT AND THE MEDIA

From the vantage-point of the White House, the press, while a potentially useful conduit of managed news, is seen more as an adversary than an ally.

CONSTITUTIONAL BACKGROUND: REPRESENTATION OF POPULAR, GROUP, AND NATIONAL INTERESTS

The functions of the House and Senate are fundamentally different. The House, popularly elected for a two-year term, stands close to the people and represents popular interests on matters of local concern. Senators, indirectly elected for staggered six-year terms, are more detached, deliberative, and conservative. A primary responsibility of the Senate is to act as a conservative check on the House.

CONGRESS AND THE WASHINGTON POLITICAL ESTABLISHMENT

Congress, always with an eye to the reelection of its members, has created a vast federal bureaucracy to implement programs that ostensibly benefit constituents. Congressmen, who gain credit for establishing the programs in the first place, step in once again to receive credit for handling constituent complaints against the bureaucracy.

COMMITTEE CHAIRMEN AS PART OF THE WASHINGTON ESTABLISHMENT

The power of Jamie Whitten, Chairman of the House Appropriations Subcommittee on Agriculture, illustrates how committee chairmen can singlehandedly control the policies of administrative departments and agencies.

CONGRESSMEN AS POLITICAL ENTREPRENEURS

The pursuit of personal power within Congress supports decentralization and the dispersion of power on Capitol Hill, which is particularly reflected in committee domination of the legislative process. However, presidential assaults on Congress occasionally cause members to subordinate their desire for personal aggrandizement to strengthen Congress as an institution.

CONGRESSIONAL STAFF:
THE SURROGATES OF POWER

CONGRESS AND THE ELECTORAL CONNECTION

A DAY IN THE UNITED STATES SENATE

A Supreme Court justice proclaims that the Court should flexibly interpret the Constitution to make decisions that are in tune with changing popular aspirations.

Appendices

AMERICAN GOVERNMENT

Part One

The Setting of the American System

Chapter 1

Constitutional
Government

The Founding Fathers were consummate politicians, but also brilliant political philosophers in their own right. They did not hesitate to draw upon the rich Western tradition of political philosophy as they searched for an ideal model of government. Above all, they wanted a government responsive to the people but also one of balanced and limited powers.

Constitutional Democracy:
The Rule of Law

The Western political heritage has emphasized the importance of democracy and the rule of law. Aristotle's *Politics* stressed the viability of democracy, provided there are sufficient checks upon unlimited popular rule.

The American constitutional tradition reflects the beliefs of many political philosophers. One of the most dominating figures is John Locke. It is not suggested that Locke was read by most of the colonists, but only that his ideas invariably found their way into many writings of eighteenth-century America, most importantly the Declaration of Independence. In a letter to Henry Lee in 1825, Thomas Jefferson wrote:

"When forced . . . to resort to arms for redress, an appeal to the tribunal of the world was deemed proper for our justification. This was the object of the Declaration of Independence. Not to find out new principles, or new arguments, never before thought of, not merely to say things which had never been said before; but to place before mankind the common sense of the subject, in terms so plain and firm as to command their assent, and to justify ourselves in the independent stand we are compelled to take. Neither aiming at originality of principle or sentiment, nor yet copied from any particular and previous writing, it was intended to be an expression of the American mind, and to give to that expression the proper tone and spirit called for by the occasion. All its authority rests then on the harmonizing sentiments of the day, whether expressed in conversation, in letters, printed essays, or in the elementary books of public right [such] as Aristotle, Cicero, Locke, Sidney, etc. . . .''

In May of 1790, Jefferson wrote: ''Locke's little book on government is perfect as far as it goes.'' Although Jefferson's admiration of Locke was perhaps greater than that of many other colonists, his views did reflect a mood of eighteenth-century America. Locke's *Second Treatise, of Civil Government* attempted to trace the reasons why men enter into political societies in the first place. The eighteenth century, no less than the twentieth, was an era characterized by attempts to be ''scientific'' in political formulations. Locke's *Second Treatise,* first published in 1690, reflected the scientific emphasis that was to prevail so widely beginning in the eighteenth century. To Locke, natural law was objectively valid, and therefore once ascertained, governments based upon it would have a superior claim to legitimacy. Locke is notable for his discussions of natural law, from which he derived the ''best'' form of government. In reading Locke, one should observe how much importance he placed upon property rights and the right of the people to dissolve government once it no longer meets their legitimate expectations.

1

John Locke
SECOND TREATISE,
OF CIVIL GOVERNMENT

OF THE STATE OF NATURE

To understand political power aright, and derive it from its original, we must consider what estate all men are naturally in, and that is, a state of perfect freedom to order their actions, and dispose of their possessions and persons as they think fit, within the bounds of the laws of Nature, without asking leave or depending upon the will of any other man.

A state also of equality, wherein all the power and jurisdiction is reciprocal, no one having more than another, there being nothing more evident than that creatures of the same species and rank, promiscuously born to all the same advantages of Nature, and the use of the same faculties, should also be equal one amongst another, without subordination or subjection, unless the lord and master of them all should, by any manifest declaration of his will, set one above another, and confer on him, by an evident and clear appointment, an undoubted right to dominion and sovereignty. . . .

But though this be a state of liberty, yet it is not a state of license; though man in that state have an uncontrollable liberty to dispose of his person or possessions, yet he had not liberty to destroy himself, or so much as any creature in his possession, but where some nobler use than its bare preservation calls for it. The state of Nature has a law of Nature to govern it, which obliges every one, and reason, which is that law, teaches all mankind who will but consult it, that being all equal and independent, no one ought to harm another in his life, health, liberty or possessions. . . . And, being furnished with like faculties, sharing all in one community of Nature, there cannot be supposed any such subordination among us that may authorize us to destroy one another, as if we were made for one another's uses, as the inferior ranks of creatures are for ours. Every one as he is bound to preserve himself, and not to quit his station wilfully, so by the like reason, when his own preservation comes not in competition, ought he as much as he can to preserve the rest of mankind, and not unless it be to do justice on an offender, take away or impair the life, or what tends to the preservation of life, the liberty, health, limb, or goods of another.

And that all men may be restrained from invading others' rights, and from doing hurt to one another, and the law of Nature be observed, which willeth the peace and preservation of all mankind, the execution of the law of Nature is in that state put into every man's hands, whereby every one has a right to punish the transgressors of that law to such a degree as may hinder its violation. For the law of Nature would, as all other laws that concern men in this world, be in vain if there were nobody that in the state of Nature had a power to execute that law, and thereby preserve the innocent and restrain offenders; and if any one in the state of Nature may punish another for any evil he has done, every one may do so. For in that state of perfect equality, where naturally there is no superiority or jurisdiction of one over another, what any may do in prosecution of that law, every one must needs have a right to do.

And thus, in the state of Nature, one man comes by a power over another, but yet no absolute or arbitrary power to use a criminal, when he has got him in his hands, according to the passionate heats or boundless extravagancy of his own will, but only to retribute to him so far as calm reason and conscience dictate, what is proportionate to his transgression, which is so much as may serve for reparation and restraint. . . .

Every offence that can be committed in the state of Nature may, in the state of Nature, be also punished equally, and as far forth, as it may, in a commonwealth. For—though it would be beside my present purpose to enter here into the particulars of the law of Nature, or its measures of punishment, yet it is certain there is such a law, and that too as intelligible and plain to a rational creature and a studier of that law as the positive laws of commonwealths, nay, possibly plainer; as much as reason is easier to be understood than the fancies and intricate contrivances of men, following contrary and hidden interests put into words. . . .

OF THE ENDS OF POLITICAL SOCIETY AND GOVERNMENT

If man in the state of Nature be so free as has been said, if he be absolute lord of his own person and possessions, equal to the greatest and subject to nobody, why will he part with his freedom, this empire, and subject himself to the dominion and control of any other power? To which it is obvious to answer, that though in the state of Nature he hath such a right, yet the enjoyment of it is very uncertain and constantly exposed to the invasion of others; for all being kings as much as he, every man his equal, and the greater part no strict observers of equity and justice, the enjoyment of the property he has in this state is very unsafe, very insecure. This makes him willing to quit this condition which, however free, is full of fears and continual dangers; and it is not without reason that he seeks out and is willing to join in society with others who are already united, or have a mind to unite for the mutual preservation of their lives, liberties, and estates, which I call by the general name—property.

The great and chief end, therefore, of men uniting into commonwealths, and putting themselves under government, is the preservation of their property; to which in the state of Nature there are many things wanting.

Firstly, there wants an established, settled, known law, received and allowed by common consent to be the standard of right and wrong, and the common measure to decide all controversies between them. For though the law of Nature be plain and intelligible to all rational creatures, yet men, being biased by their interest, as well as ignorant for want of study of it, are not apt to allow of it as a law binding to them in the application of it to their particular cases.

Secondly, in the state of Nature there wants a known and indifferent judge, with authority to determine all differences according to the established law. For every one in that state being both judge and executioner of the law of Nature, men being partial to themselves, passion and revenge is very apt to carry them too far, and with too much heat in their own cases, as well as negligence and unconcernedness, make them too remiss in other men's.

Thirdly, in the state of Nature there often wants power to back and support the sentence when right, and to give it due execution. They who by any injustice offended will seldom fail where they are able by force to make good their injustice. Such resistance many times makes the punishment dangerous, and frequently destructive to those who attempt it.

Thus mankind, notwithstanding all the privileges of the state of Nature, being but in an ill condition while they remain in it are quickly driven into society. Hence it comes to pass, that we seldom find any number of men live any time together in this state. The inconveniences that they are therein exposed to by the irregular and uncertain exercise of the power every man has of punishing the transgressions of others, make them take sanctuary under the established laws of government, and therein seek the preservation of their property. It is this makes them so willingly give up every one his single power of punishing to be exercised by such alone as shall be appointed to it amongst them, and by such rules as the community, or those authorised by them to that purpose, shall agree on. And in this we have the original right and rise of both the legislative and executive power as well as of the governments and societies themselves.

For in the state of Nature to omit the liberty he has of innocent delights, a man has two powers. The first is to do whatsoever he thinks fit for the preservation of himself and others within the permission of the law of Nature; by which law, common to them all, he and all the rest of mankind are one community, make up one society distinct from all other creatures, and were it not for the corruption and viciousness of degenerate men, there would be no need for any other, no necessity that men should separate from this great and natural community, and associate into lesser combinations. The other power a man has in the state of Nature is the power to punish the crimes committed against that law. Both these he gives up when he joins in a private, if I may so call it, or particular political society, and incorporates into any common-wealth separate from the rest of mankind.

The first power—viz., of doing whatsoever he thought fit for the preservation of himself and the rest of mankind, he gives up to be regulated by laws made by the society, so far forth as the preservation of himself and the rest of that society shall require; which laws of the society in many things confine the liberty he had by the law of Nature.

Secondly, the power of punishing he wholly gives up, and engages his natural force, which he might before employ in the execution of the law of Nature, by his own single authority, as he thought fit, to assist the executive power of the society as the law thereof shall require. For being now in a new state, wherein he is to enjoy many conveniences from the labor, assistance, and society of others in the same community, as well as protection from its whole strength, he is to part also with as much of his natural liberty, in providing for himself, as the good, prosperity, and safety of the society shall require, which is not only necessary but just, since the other members of the society do the like.

But though men when they enter into society give up the equality, liberty, and executive power they had in the state of Nature into the hands of the society, to be so far disposed of by the legislative as the good of the society shall require, yet it being only with an intention in every one the better to preserve himself, his liberty and property (for no rational creature can be supposed to change his condition with an intention to be worse), the power of the society or legislative constituted by them can never be supposed to extend farther than the common against those three defects above mentioned that made the state of Nature so unsafe and uneasy. And so, whoever has the legislative or supreme power of any commonwealth, is bound to govern by established standing laws, promulgated and known to the people, and not by extemporary decrees, by indifferent and upright judges, who are to decide controversies by those laws; and to employ the force of the community at home only in the execution of such laws, or abroad to prevent or redress foreign injuries and secure the community from inroads and invasion. And all this to be directed to no other end but the peace, safety, and public good of the people. . . .

OF THE EXTENT OF
THE LEGISLATIVE POWER

The great end of men's entering into society being the enjoyment of their properties in peace and safety, and the great instrument and means of that being the laws established in that society, the first and fundamental positive law of all commonwealths is the establishing of the legislative power, as the first and fundamental natural law, which is to govern even the legislative itself, is the preservation of the society and (as far as will consist with the public good) of every person in it. This legislative is not only the supreme power of the commonwealth, but sacred and unalterable in the hands where the community have once placed it. Nor can any edict of anybody else, in what form soever conceived, or by what power soever backed, have the force and obligation of a law which has not its sanction from that legislative which the public has chosen and appointed; for without this the law could not have that which is absolutely necessary to its being a law, the consent of the society, over whom nobody can have a power to make laws but by their own consent and by authority received from them. . . .

These are the bounds which the trust that is put in them by the society and the law of God and Nature have set to the legislative power of every commonwealth, in all forms of government. First: They are to govern by promulgated established laws, not to be varied in particular cases, but to have one rule for rich and poor, for the favorite at Court and the countryman at plough. Secondly: These laws also ought to be designed for no other end ultimately but the good of the people. Thirdly: They must not raise taxes on the property of the people without the consent of the people given by themselves or their deputies. And this properly concerns only such governments where the legislative is always in being, or at least where the people have not reserved any part of the legislative to deputies, to be from time to time chosen by themselves. Fourthly: Legislative neither must nor can transfer the power of making laws to anybody else, or place it anywhere but where the people have. . . .

OF THE DISSOLUTION
OF GOVERNMENT

The constitution of the legislative [authority] is the first and fundamental act of society, whereby provision is made for the continuation of their union under the direction of persons and bonds of laws, made by persons authorised thereunto, by the consent and appointment of the people, without which no one man, or number of men, amongst them can have authority of making laws that shall be binding to the rest. When any one, or more, shall take upon them to make laws whom the people have not appointed so to do, they make laws without authority, which the people are not therefore bound to obey; by which means they come again to be out of subjection, and may constitute to themselves a new legislative, as they think best, being in full liberty to resist the force of those who, without authority, would impose anything upon them. . . .

Whosoever uses force without right—as every one does in society who does it without law—puts himself into a state of war with those against whom he so uses it, and in that state all former ties are cancelled, all other rights cease, and every one has a right to defend himself, and to resist the aggressor. . . .

Here it is like the common question will be made: Who shall be judge whether the prince or legislative act contrary to their trust? This, perhaps, ill-affected and factious men may spread amongst the people, when the prince only makes use of his due prerogative. To this I reply, The people shall be judge;

for who shall be judge whether his trustee or deputy acts well and according to the trust reposed in him, but he who deputes him and must, by having deputed him, have still a power to discard him when he fails in his trust? If this be reasonable in particular cases of private men, why should it be otherwise in that of the greatest moment, where the welfare of millions is concerned and also where the evil, if not prevented, is greater, and the redress very difficult, dear, and dangerous? . . .

To conclude. The power that every individual gave the society when he entered into it can never revert to the individuals again, as long as the society lasts, but will always remain in the community; because without this there can be no community—no commonwealth, which is contrary to the original agreement; so also when the society hath placed the legislative in any assembly of men, to continue in them and their successors, with direction and authority for providing such successors, the legislative can never revert to the people whilst that government lasts; because, having provided a legislative with power to continue for ever, they have given up their political power to the legislative, and cannot resume it. But if they have set limits to the duration of their legislative, and made this supreme power in any person or assembly only temporary; or else when, by the miscarriages of those in authority, it is forfeited; upon the forefeiture of their rulers, or at the determination of the time set, it reverts to the society, and the people have a right to act as supreme, and continue the legislative in themselves or place it in a new form, or new hands, as they think good.

❖❖   The influence of John Locke goes far beyond his impact on the thinking of the founding fathers of the United States, such as Thomas Jefferson. Some scholars (among them, Louis Hartz, *The Liberal Tradition in America*) have interpreted the American political tradition in terms of the pervasive attachment to the ideas and values set forth in the writings of Locke. There is little question that American political life has been uniquely characterized by widespread adherence to the fundamental principles about the relations among men, society, and government expressed in Locke's writings.

It is not just that we have representative government, with institutions similar in structure and function to those of the constitutional democracy described in Locke's *Second Treatise,* but that through the years we have probably maintained, more than any other society, a widespread agreement about the fundamental human values cherished by Locke. His emphasis upon the sanctity of private property has been paramount in the American political tradition from the very beginning. Moreover, Locke's views on the nature of man are shared by most Americans. All our governmental institutions, processes, and traditions rest upon principles such as the primacy of the individual, man's inborn ability to exercise reason in order to discern truth and higher principles of order and justice, and a political and social equality among men in which no man shall count for more than another in determining the actions of government and their application. We may not have always practiced these ideals, but we have been *theoretically* committed to them.

Framing the Constitution: Elitist or Democratic Process?

A remarkable fact about the United States government is that it has operated for two hundred years on the basis of a written Constitution. Does this suggest unusual sagacity on the part of the Founding Fathers, or exceptional luck? What was involved in framing the Constitution?

In the following selection John P. Roche suggests that the framing of the Constitution was essentially a democratic process involving the reconciliation of a variety of state, political, and economic interests. Roche writes that "The Philadelphia Convention was not a College of Cardinals or a council of Platonic guardians working in a manipulative, predemocratic framework; it was a *nationalist* reform caucus that had to operate with great delicacy and skill in a political cosmos full of enemies to achieve one definitive goal—popular approbation." Roche recognizes that the framers, collectively, were an elite, but he is careful to point out that they were a political elite dedicated for the most part to establishing an effective and at the same time controlled national government that would be able to overcome the weaknesses of the Articles of Confederation. The framers were not, says Roche, a cohesive elite dedicated to a particular set of political or economic assumptions beyond the simple need to create a national government that would be capable of reconciling disparate state interests. The Constitution was "a vivid demonstration of effective democratic political action, and of the forging of a national elite which literally persuaded its countrymen to hoist themselves by their own bootstraps."

2

John P. Roche
THE FOUNDING FATHERS:
A REFORM CAUCUS
IN ACTION

Over the last century and a half, the work of the Constitutional Convention and the motives of the Founding Fathers have been analyzed under a number of different ideological auspices. To one generation of historians, the hand of God was moving in the assembly; under a later dispensation, a dialectic (at various levels of philosophical sophistication) replaced the Deity: "relationships of production" moved into the niche previously reserved for Love of Country. Thus in counterpart to the *zeitgeist*, the framers have undergone miraculous metamorphoses: at one time acclaimed as liberals and bold social engineers, today they appear in the guise of sound Burkean conservatives, men who in our time would subscribe to *Fortune*, look to Walter Lippmann for political theory, and chuckle patronizingly at the antics of Barry Goldwater. The implicit assumption is that if James Madison were among us, he would be President of the Ford Foundation, while Alexander Hamilton would chair the Committee for Economic Development.

The "Fathers" have thus been admitted to our best circles; the revolutionary ferocity which confiscated all Tory property in reach and populated New Brunswick with outlaws has been converted by the "Miltown School" of American historians into a benign dedication to "consensus" and "prescriptive rights." The Daughters of the American Revolution have, through the ministrations of Professors Boorstin, Hartz, and Rossiter, at last found ancestors worthy of their descendants. It is not my purpose here to argue that the "Fathers" were, in fact, radical revolutionaries; that proposition has been brilliantly demonstrated by Robert R. Palmer in his *Age of the Democratic Revolution*. My concern is with the future position that not only were they revolutionaries, but also they were democrats. Indeed, in my view, there is one fundamental truth about the Founding Fathers that *every* generation of zeitgeisters has done its best to obscure: they were first and foremost superb democratic politicians. I suspect that in a contemporary setting, James Madison would be Speaker of the House of Representatives and Hamilton would be the *eminence grise* dominating (*pace* Theodore

From John P. Roche, "The Founding Fathers: A Reform Caucus in Action," *American Political Science Review* (December 1961). Reprinted by permission.

Sorensen or Sherman Adams) the Executive Office of the President. They were, with their colleagues, *political men*—not metaphysicians, disembodied conservatives or Agents of History—and as recent research into the nature of American politics in the 1780s confirms, they were committed (perhaps willy-nilly) to working within the democratic framework, within a universe of public approval. Charles Beard *and* the filiopietists to the contrary notwithstanding, the Philadelphia Convention was not a College of Cardinals or a council of Platonic guardians working within a manipulative, predemocratic framework; it was a *nationalist* reform caucus which had to operate with great delicacy and skill in a political cosmos full of enemies to achieve the one definitive goal—popular approbation.

Perhaps the time has come, to borrow Walton Hamilton's fine phrase, to raise the framers from immortality to mortality, to give them credit for their magnificent demonstration of the art of democratic politics. The point must be reemphasized; they *made* history and did it within the limits of consensus. There was nothing inevitable about the future in 1787; the *zeitgeist*, that fine Hegelian technique of begging causal questions, could only be discerned in retrospect. What they did was to hammer out a pragmatic compromise which would both bolster the "national interest" and be acceptable to the people. What inspiration they got came from their collective experience as professional politicians in a democratic society. As John Dickinson put it to his fellow delegates on August 13, "Experience must be our guide. Reason may mislead us."

In this context, let us examine the problems they confronted and the solutions they evolved. The Convention has been described picturesquely as a counter-revolutionary junta and the Constitution as a coup d'état, but this has been accomplished by withdrawing the whole history of the movement for constitutional reform from its true context. No doubt the goals of the constitutional elite were "subversive" to the existing political order, but it is overlooked that their subversion could only have succeeded if the people of the United States endorsed it by regularized procedures. Indubitably they were "plotting" to establish a much stronger central government than existed under the Articles, but only in the sense in which one could argue equally well that John F. Kennedy was, from 1956 to 1960, "plotting" to become President. In short, on the fundamental *procedural* level, the Constitutionalists had to work according to the prevailing rules of the game. Whether they liked it or not is a topic for spiritualists—and is irrelevant: one may be quite certain that had Washington agreed to play the de Gaulle (as the Cincinnati once urged), Hamilton would willingly have held his horse, but such fertile speculation in no way alters the actual context in which events took place.

I

When the Constitutionalists went forth to subvert the Confederation, they utilized the mechanisms of political legitimacy. And the roadblocks which confronted them were formidable. At the same time, they were endowed with certain potent political assets. The history of the United States from 1786 to 1790 was largely one of a masterful employment of political expertise by the Constitutionalists as against bumbling, erratic behavior by the opponents of reform. Effectively, the Constitutionalists had to induce the states, by democratic techniques of coercion, to emasculate themselves. To be specific, if New York had refused to join the new Union, the project was doomed; yet before New York was safely in, the reluctant state legislature had *suasponte* to take the following steps: (1) agree to send delegates to the Philadelphia Convention; (2) provide maintenance for these delegates (these were distinct stages: New Hampshire was early in naming delegates, but did not provide for their maintenance until July); (3) set up the special ad hoc convention to decide on ratification; and (4) concede to the decision of the ad hoc convention that New York should participate. New York admittedly was a tricky state, with a strong interest in a status quo which permitted her to exploit New Jersey and Connecticut, but the same legal hurdles existed in every state. And at the risk of becoming boring, it must be reiterated that the *only* weapon in the Constitutionalist arsenal was an effective mobilization of public opinion.

The group which undertook this struggle was an interesting amalgam of a few dedicated nationalists with the self-interested spokesmen of various parochial bailiwicks. The Georgians, for example, wanted a strong central authority to provide military protection for their huge, underpopulated state against the Creek Confederacy; Jerseymen and Connecticuters wanted to escape from economic bondage to New York; the Virginians hoped to establish a system which would give that great state its rightful place in the councils of the republic. The dominant figures in the politics of these states therefore cooperated in the call for the Convention. In other states, the thrust towards national reform was taken up by opposition groups who added the "national interest" to their weapons system; in Pennsylvania, for instance, the group fighting to revise the Constitution of 1776 came out four-square behind the Constitutionalists, and in New York, Hamilton and the Schuyler *ambiance* took the same tack against George Clinton. There was, of course, a large element of personality in the affair: there is reason to suspect that Patrick Henry's opposition to the Convention and the Constitution was founded on his conviction that Jefferson was behind both, and a close study of local politics elsewhere would surely reveal that others supported the Constitution for the simple (and politically quite sufficient) reason that the "wrong" people were against it.

To say this is not to suggest that the Constitution rested on a foundation of impure or base motives. It is rather to argue that in politics there are no immaculate conceptions, and that in the drive for a stronger general government, motives of all sorts played a part. Few men in the history of mankind have espoused a view of the "common good" or "public interest" that militated against their private status; even Plato with all his reverence for disembodied reason managed to put philosophers on top of the pile. Thus it is not surprising that a number of diversified private interests joined to push the nationalist public interest; what would have been surprising was the absence of such a pragmatic united front. And the fact remains that, however motivated, these men did demonstrate a willingness to compromise their parochial interests in behalf of an ideal which took shape before their eyes and under their ministrations.

As Stanley Elkins and Eric McKitrick have suggested in a perceptive essay [76 *Political Science Quarterly* 181 (1961)], what distinguished the leaders of the Constitutionalist caucus from their enemies was a "Continental" approach to political, economic and military issues. To the extent that they shared an institutional base of operations, it was the Continental Congress (thirty-nine of the delegates to the Federal Convention had served in Congress), and this was hardly a locale which inspired respect for the state governments. Robert de Jouvenal observed French politics half a century ago and noted that a revolutionary Deputy had more in common with a nonrevolutionary Deputy than he had with a revolutionary non-Deputy; similarly one can surmise that membership in the Congress under the Articles of Confederation worked to establish a continental frame of reference, that a Congressman from Pennsylvania and one from South Carolina would share a universe of discourse which provided them with a conceptual common denominator vis-à-vis their respective state legislatures. This was particularly true with respect to external affairs: the average state legislator was probably about as concerned with foreign policy then as he is today, but Congressmen were constantly forced to take the broad view of American prestige, were compelled to listen to the reports of Secretary John Jay and to the dispatches and pleas from their frustrated envoys in Britain, France and Spain. From considerations such as these, a "Continental" ideology developed which seems to have demanded a revision of our domestic institutions primarily on the ground that only by invigorating our general government could we assume our rightful place in the international arena. Indeed, an argument with great force—particularly since Washington was its incarnation—urged that our very survival in the Hobbesian jungle of world politics depended upon a reordering and strengthening of our national sovereignty.

The great achievement of the Constitutionalists was their ultimate success in convincing the elected representatives of a majority of the white male population that change was imperative. A small group of political leaders with a Continental vision and essentially a consciousness of the United States' *international* impotence, provided the matrix of the movement. To their standard other leaders rallied with their own parallel ambitions. Their great assets were (1) the presence in their caucus of the one authentic American "father figure," George Washington, whose prestige was enormous; (2) the energy and talent of their leadership (in which one must include the towering intellectuals of the time, John Adams and Thomas Jefferson, despite their absence abroad), and their communications "network," which was far superior to anything on the opposition side; (3) the preemptive skill which made "their" issue The Issue and kept the locally oriented opposition permanently on the defensive; and (4) the subjective consideration that these men were spokesmen of a new and compelling credo: *American* nationalism, that ill-defined but nonetheless potent sense of collective purpose that emerged from the American Revolution.

Despite great institutional handicaps, the Constitutionalists managed in the mid-1780s to mount an offensive which gained momentum as years went by. Their greatest problem was lethargy, and paradoxically, the number of barriers in their path may have proved an advantage in the long run. Beginning with the initial battle to get the Constitutional Convention called and delegates appointed, they could never relax, never let up the pressure. In practical terms, this meant that the local "organizations" created by the Constitutionalists were perpetually in movement building up their cadres for the next fight. (The word *organization* has to be used with great caution: a political organization in the United States—as in contemporary England—generally consisted of a magnate and his following, or a coalition of magnates. This did not necessarily mean that it was "undemocratic" or "aristocratic," in the Aristotelian sense of the word: while a few magnates such as the Livingstons could draft their followings, most exercised their leadership without coercion on the basis of popular endorsement. The absence of organized opposition did not imply the impossibility of competition any more than low public participation in elections necessarily indicated an undemocratic suffrage.)

The Constitutionalists got the jump on the "opposition" (a collective noun: oppositions would be more correct) at the outset with demand for a Convention. Their opponents were caught in an old political trap: they were not being asked to approve any specific program of reform, but only to endorse a meeting to discuss and recommend needed reforms. If they took a hard line at the first stage, they were put in the position of glorifying the status quo and of denying the need for *any* changes. Moreover, the Constitutionalists could go to the people with a persuasive argument for "fair play"—"How can you condemn reform before you know precisely what is involved?" Since the state legislatures obviously would have the final say on any proposals that might emerge from the Convention, the Constitutionalists were merely reasonable men asking for a chance. Besides, since they did not make any concrete proposals at that stage, they were in a position to capitalize on every sort of generalized discontent with the Confederation.

Perhaps because of their poor intelligence system, perhaps because of overconfidence generated by the failure of all previous efforts to alter the Articles, the opposition awoke too late to the dangers that confronted them in 1787. Not only did the Constitutionalists manage to get every state but Rhode Island (where politics was enlivened by a party system reminiscent of the "Blues" and the "Greens" in the Byzantine Empire) to appoint delegates to Philadelphia, but when the results were in, it appeared that they dominated the delegations. Given the apathy of the opposition, this was a natural phenomenon: in an ideologically nonpolarized political atmosphere those who get appointed to a special committee are likely to be the men who supported the movement for its creation. Even George Clinton, who seems to have been the first opposition leader to awake to the possibility of trouble, could not prevent the New York legislature from appointing Alexander Hamilton—though he did have the foresight to send two of his henchmen to dominate the delegation. Incidentally, much has been made of the fact that the delegates to Philadelphia were not elected by the people; some have adduced this fact as evidence of the "undemocratic" character of the gathering. But put in the context of the time, this argument is wholly specious: the central government under the Articles was considered a creature of the component states and in all the states but Rhode Island, Connecticut, and New Hampshire, members of the national Congress were chosen by the state legislatures. This was not a consequence of elitism or fear of the mob; it was a logical extension of states' rights doctrine to guarantee that the national institution did not end-run the state legislatures and make direct contact with the people.

II

With delegations safely named, the focus shifted to Philadelphia. While waiting for a quorum to assemble, James Madison got busy and drafted the so-called Randolph or Virginia Plan with the aid of the Virginia delegation. This was a political master-stroke. Its consequence was that once business got underway, the framework of discussion was established on Madison's terms. There was no interminable argument over agenda; instead the delegates took the Virginia Resolutions—"just for purposes of discussion"—as their point of departure. And along with Madison's proposals, many of which were buried in the course of the summer, went his major premise: a new start on a Constitution rather than piecemeal amendment. This was not necessarily revolutionary—but Madison's proposal that this "lump sum" amendment go into effect after approval by nine states (the Articles required unanimous state approval for any amendment) was thoroughly subversive.

Standard treatments of the Convention divide the delegates into "nationalists" and "states' righters" with various improvised shadings ("moderate nationalists," etc.), but these are *a posteriori* categories which obfuscate more than they clarify. What is striking to one who analyzes the Convention as a case study in democratic politics is the lack of clear-cut ideological divisions in the Convention. Indeed, I submit that the evidence—Madison's *Notes*, the correspondence of the delegates, and debates on ratification—indicates that this was a remarkably homogeneous body on the ideological level. Yates and Lansing, Clinton's two chaperones for Hamilton, left in disgust on July 10. (Is there anything more tedious than sitting through endless disputes on matters one deems fundamentally misconceived? It takes an iron will to spend a hot summer as an ideological *agent provocateur*.) Luther Martin, Maryland's bibulous narcissist, left on September 4 in a huff when he discovered that others did not share his self-esteem; others went home for personal reasons. But the hard core of delegates accepted a grinding regimen throughout the attrition of a Philadelphia summer precisely because they shared the Constitutionalist goal.

Basic differences of opinion emerged, of course, but these were not ideological; they were *structural*. If the so-called "states' rights" group had not accepted the fundamental purposes of the Convention, they could simply have pulled out and by doing so have aborted the whole enterprise. Instead of bolting, they returned day after day to argue and to compromise. An interesting symbol of this basic homogeneity was the initial agreement on secrecy: these professional politicians did not want to become prisoners of publicity; they wanted to retain that freedom of maneuver which is only possible when men are not forced to take public stands in the preliminary stages of negotiation. There was no legal means of binding the tongues of the delegates: at any stage in the game a delegate with basic principled objections to the emerging project could have taken the stump (as Luther Martin did after his exit) and denounced the Convention to the skies. Yet Madison did not even inform Thomas Jefferson in Paris of the course of the deliberations and available correspondence indicates that the delegates generally observed the injunction. Secrecy is certainly uncharacteristic of any assembly marked by strong ideological polarization. This was noted at the time: the *New York Daily Advertiser*, August 14, 1787, commented that the "profound secrecy hitherto observed by the Convention [we consider] a happy omen, as it demonstrates that the spirit of party on any great and essential point cannot have arisen to any height."

Commentators on the Constitution who have read *The Federalist* in lieu of reading the actual debates have credited the Fathers with the invention of a sublime concept called "Federalism." Unfortunately *The Federalist* is probative evidence for only one proposition: that Hamilton and Madison were inspired propagandists with a genius for retrospective symmetry. Federalism, as the theory is generally defined, was an improvisation which was later promoted into a political theory. Experts on "federalism" should take to heart the advice of David Hume, who warned in his *Of the Rise and Progress of the Arts and Sciences* that "there is no subject in which we must proceed with more caution than in [history], lest we assign causes which never existed and reduce what is merely contingent to stable and universal principles." In any event, the final balance in the Constitution between the states and the nation must have come as a great disappointment to Madison, while Hamilton's unitary views are too well known to need elucidation.

It is indeed astonishing how those who have glibly designated James Madison the "father" of Federalism have overlooked the solid body of fact which indicates that he shared Hamilton's quest for a unitary central government. To be specific, they have avoided examining the clear import of the Madison-Virginia Plan, and have disregarded Madison's dogged inch-by-inch retreat from the bastions of centralization. The Virginia Plan envisioned a unitary national government effectively freed from and dominant over the states. The lower house of the national legislature was to be elected directly by the people of the states with membership proportional to population. The upper house was to be selected by the lower and two chambers would elect the executive and choose the judges. The national government would be thus cut completely loose from the states.

The structure of the general government was freed from state control in a truly radical fashion, but the scope of the authority of the national sovereign as Madison initially formulated it was breathtaking—it was a formulation worthy of the Sage of Malmesbury himself. The national legislature was to be empowered to disallow the acts of state legislatures, and the central government was vested, in addition to the powers of the nation under the Articles of Confederation, with plenary authority wherever "the separate States are incompetent or in which the harmony of the United States may be interrupted by the exercise of individual legislation." Finally, just to lock the door against state intrusion, the national Congress was to be given the power to use military force on recalcitrant states. This was Madison's "model" of an ideal national government, though it later received little publicity in *The Federalist*.

The interesting thing was the reaction of the Convention to this militant program for a strong autonomous central government. Some delegates were startled, some obviously leery of so comprehensive a project of reform, but nobody set off any fireworks and nobody walked out. Moreover, in the two weeks that followed, the Virginia Plan received substantial endorsement *en principe*; the initial temper of the gathering can be deduced from the approval "without debate or dissent," on May 31, of the Sixth Resolution which granted Congress the authority to disallow state legislation "contravening *in its opinion* the Articles of Union." Indeed, an amendment was included to bar states from contravening national treaties.

The Virginia Plan may therefore be considered, in ideological terms, as the delegates' Utopia, but as the discussions continued and became more specific, many of those present began to have second thoughts. After all, they were not residents of Utopia or guardians in Plato's Republic who could simply impose a philosophical ideal on subordinate strata of the population. They were practical politicians in a democratic society, and no matter what their private dreams might be, they had to take home an acceptable package and defend it—and their own political futures—against predictable attack. On June 14 the breaking point between dream and reality took place. Apparently realizing that under the Virginia Plan, Massachusetts, Virginia, and Pennsylvania could virtually dominate the national government—and probably appreciating that to sell this program to "the folks back home" would be impossible—the delegates from the small states dug in their heels and demanded time for a consideration of alternatives. One gets a graphic sense of the inner politics from John Dickinson's reproach to Madison: "You see the consequences of pushing things too far. Some of the members from the small States wish for two branches in the General Legislature and are friends to a good National Government; but we would sooner submit to a foreign power than . . . be deprived of an equality of suffrage in both branches of the Legislature, and thereby be thrown under the domination of the large States."

The bare outline of the *Journal* entry for Tuesday, June 14, is suggestive to anyone with extensive experience in deliberative bodies. "It was moved by Mr. Patterson [sic, Paterson's name was one of those consistently misspelled by Madison and everybody else] seconded by Mr. Randolph that the further consideration of the report from the Committee of the whole House [endorsing the Virginia Plan] be postponed till tomorrow and before the question for postponement was taken. It was moved by Mr. Randolph seconded by Mr. Patterson that the House adjourn." The House adjourned by obvious prearrangement of the two principals: since the preceding Saturday when Brearley and Paterson of New Jersey had announced their fundamental discontent with the representational features of the Virginia Plan, the informal pressure had certainly been building up to slow down the steamroller. Doubtless there were extended arguments at the Indian Queen between Madison and Paterson, the latter insisting that events were moving rapidly towards a probably disastrous conclusion, towards a political suicide pact. Now the process of accommodation was put into action smoothly—and wisely, given the character and strength of the doubters. Madison had the votes, but this was one of those situations where the enforcement of mechanical majoritarianism could easily have destroyed the objectives of the majority: the Constitutionalists were in quest of a qualitative as well as a quantitative consensus. This was hardly from deference to local Quaker custom; it was a political imperative if they were to attain ratification.

III

According to the standard script, at this point the "states' rights" group intervened in force behind the New Jersey Plan, which has been characteristically portrayed as a reversion to the status quo under the Articles of Confederation with but minor modifications. A careful examination of the evidence indicates that only in a marginal sense is this an accurate description. It is true that the New Jersey Plan put the states back into the institutional picture, but one could argue that to do so was a recognition of political reality rather than an affirmation of states' rights. A serious case can be made that the advocates of the New Jersey Plan, far from being ideological addicts of states' rights, intended to substitute for the Virginia Plan a system which would both retain strong national power and have a chance of adoption in the states. The leading spokesman for the project asserted quite clearly that his views were based more on counsels of expediency than on principle; said Paterson on June 16: "I came here not to speak my own sentiments, but the sentiments of those who sent me. Our object is not such a Governmt. as may be best in itself, but such a one as our Constituents have authorized us to prepare, and as they will approve." This is Madison's version; in Yates's transcription, there is a crucial sentence following the remarks above: "I believe that a little practical virtue is to be preferred to the finest theoretical principles, which cannot be carried into effect." In his preliminary speech on June 9, Paterson had stated "to the public mind we must accommodate ourselves," and in his notes for this and his later effort as well, the emphasis is the same. The *structure* of government under the Articles should be retained:

> 2. Because it accords with the Sentiments of the People
>   [Proof:] 1. Coms. [Commissions from state legislatures defining the juris-
>   diction of the delegates]
> 2. News-papers—Political Barometer. Jersey never would have sent Delegates
>   under the first [Virginia] Plan—
>   Not here to sport Opinions of my own. Wt. [What] can be done. A little
> practicable Virtue preferrable to Theory.

This was a defense of political acumen, not of states' rights. In fact, Paterson's notes of his speech can easily be construed as an argument for attaining the substantive objectives of the Virginia Plan by a sound political route, i.e., pouring the new wine in the old bottles. With a shrewd eye, Paterson queried:

> Will the Operation, and Force of the [central] Govt. depend upon the mode
> of Representn.—No—it will depend upon the Quantum of Power lodged in
> the leg. ex. and judy. Departments—Give [the existing] Congress the same
> Powers that you intend to give the two Branches, [under the Virginia Plan]
> and I apprehend they will act with as much Propriety and more Energy. . . .

In other words, the advocates of the New Jersey Plan concentrated their fire on what they held to be the *political liabilities* of the Virginia Plan—which were matters of institutional structure—rather than on the proposed scope of national authority. Indeed, the Supremacy Clause of the Constitution first saw the light of day in Paterson's Sixth Resolution; the New Jersey Plan contemplated the use of military force to secure compliance with national law; and finally Paterson made clear his view that under either the Virginia or the New Jersey systems, the general government would ". . . act on individuals and not on states." From the states' rights viewpoint, this was heresy: the fundament of that doctrine was the proposition that any central government had as its constituents the states, not the people, and could only reach the people through the agency of the state government.

Paterson then reopened the agenda of the Convention, but he did so within a distinctly nationalist framework. Paterson's position was one of favoring a strong central government in principle, but opposing one which in fact *put the big states in the saddle*. (The Virginia Plan, for all its abstract merits, did very well by Virginia.) As evidence for this speculation, there is a curious and intriguing proposal among Paterson's preliminary drafts of the New Jersey Plan:

> Whereas it is necessary in Order to form the People of the U.S. of America in to a Nation, that the States should be consolidated, by which means all the Citizens thereof will become equally intitled to and will equally participate in the same Privileges and Rights . . . it is therefore resolved, that all the Lands contained within the Limits of each state individually, and of the U.S. generally be considered as constituting one Body or Mass, and be divided into thirteen or more integral parts.
>
> Resolved, That such Divisions or integral Parts shall be styled Districts.

This makes it sound as though Paterson was prepared to accept a strong unified central government along the lines of the Virginia Plan if the existing states were eliminated. He may have gotten the idea from his New Jersey colleague Judge David Brearley, who on June 9 had commented that the only remedy to the dilemma over representation was "that a map of the U.S. be spread out, that all the existing boundaries be erased, and that a new partition of the whole be made into 13 equal parts." According to Yates, Brearley added at this point, "then a government on the present [Virginia Plan] system will be just."

This proposition was never pushed—it was patently unrealistic—but one can appreciate its purpose: it would have separated the men from the boys in the large-state delegations. How attached would the Virginians have been to their reform principles if Virginia were to disappear as a component geographical unit (the largest) for representational purposes? Up to this point, the Virginians had been in the happy position of supporting high ideals with that inner confidence born of knowledge that the "public interest" they endorsed would nourish their private interest. Worse, they had shown little willingness to compromise. Now the delegates from the small states announced that they were unprepared to be offered up as sacrificial victims to a "national interest" which reflected Virginia's parochial ambition. Caustic Charles Pinckney was not far off when he remarked sardonically that "the whole [conflict] comes to this": "Give N. Jersey an equal vote, and she will dismiss her scruples, and concur in the Natl. system." What he rather unfairly did not add was that the Jersey delegates were not free agents who could adhere to their private convictions; they had to take back, sponsor and risk their reputations on the reforms approved by the Convention—and in New Jersey, not in Virginia.

Paterson spoke on Saturday, and one can surmise that over the weekend there was a good deal of consultation, argument, and caucusing among the delegates. One member at least prepared a full length address: on Monday Alexander Hamilton, previously mute, rose and delivered a six-hour oration. It was a remarkably apolitical speech; the gist of his position was that both the Virginia and New Jersey Plans were inadequately centralist, and he detailed a reform program which was reminiscent of the Protectorate under the Cromwellian *Instrument of Government* of 1653. It has been suggested that Hamilton did this in the best political tradition to emphasize the moderate character of the Virginia Plan, to give the cautious delegates something *really* to worry about; but this interpretation seems somehow too clever. Particularly since the sentiments Hamilton expressed happened to be completely consistent with those he privately—and sometimes publicly—expressed throughout his life. He wanted, to take a striking phrase from a letter to George Washington, a "strong well mounted government"; in essence, the Hamilton Plan contemplated an elected life monarch, virtually free of public control, on the Hobbesian ground that only in this fashion could strength and stability be achieved. The other alternatives, he argued, would put policy-making at the mercy of the passions of the mob; only if the sovereign was beyond the reach of selfish influence would it be possible to have government in the interests of the whole community.

From all accounts, this was a masterful and compelling speech, but (aside from furnishing John Lansing and Luther Martin with ammunition for later use against the Constitution) it made little impact. Hamilton was simply transmitting on a different wavelength from the rest of the delegates; the latter adjourned after his great effort, admired his rhetoric, and then returned to business. It was rather as if they had taken a day off to attend the opera. Hamilton, never a particularly patient man or much of a negotiator, stayed for another ten days and then left, in considerable disgust, for New York. Although he came back to Philadelphia sporadically and attended the last two weeks of the Convention, Hamilton played no part in the laborious task of hammering out the Constitution. His day came later when he led the New York Constitutionalists into the savage imbroglio over ratification—an arena in which his unmatched talent for dirty political infighting may well have won the day. For instance, in the New York Ratifying Convention, Lansing threw back into Hamilton's teeth the sentiments the latter had expressed in his June 18 oration in the Convention. However, having since retreated to the fine defensive positions immortalized in the *The Federalist*, the Colonel flatly denied that he had ever been an enemy of the states, or had believed that conflict between states and nation was inexorable! As Madison's authoritative *Notes* did not appear until 1840, and there had been no press coverage, there was no way to verify his assertions, so in the words of the reporter, "a warm personal altercation between [Lansing and Hamilton] engrossed the remainder of the day [June 28, 1788]."

IV

On Tuesday morning, June 19, the vacation was over. James Madison led off with a long, carefully reasoned speech analyzing the New Jersey Plan which, while intellectually vigorous in its criticisms, was quite conciliatory in mood. "The great difficulty," he observed, "lies in the affair of Representation; and if this could be adjusted, all others would be surmountable." (As events were to demonstrate, this diagnosis was correct.) When he finished, a vote was taken on whether to continue with the Virginia Plan as the nucleus for a new constitution: seven states voted "Yes"; New York, New Jersey, and Delaware voted "No"; and Maryland, whose position often depended on which delegates happened to be on the floor, divided. Paterson, it seems, lost decisively; yet in a fundamental sense he and his allies had achieved their purpose: from that day onward, it could never be forgotten that the state governments loomed ominously in the background and that no verbal incantations could exorcise their power. Moreover, nobody bolted the Convention: Paterson and his colleagues took their defeat in stride and set to work to modify the Virginia Plan, particularly with respect to its provisions on representation in the national legislature. Indeed, they won an immediate rhetorical bonus; when Oliver Ellsworth of Connecticut rose to move that the word "national" be expunged from the Third Virginia Resolution ("Resolved that a *national* Government ought to be established consisting of a *supreme* Legislative, Executive and Judiciary"), Randolph agreed and the motion passed unanimously. The process of compromise had begun.

For the next two weeks, the delegates circled around the problem of legislative representation. The Connecticut delegation appears to have evolved a possible compromise quite early in the debates, but the Virginians and particularly Madison (unaware that he would later be acclaimed as the prophet of "federalism") fought obdurately against providing for equal representation of states in the second chamber. There was a good deal of acrimony and at one point Benjamin Franklin—of all people—proposed the institution of a daily prayer; practical politicians in the gathering, however, were meditating more on the merits of a good committee than on the utility of Divine intervention. On July 2, the ice began to break when through a number of fortuitous events—and one that seems deliberate—the majority against equality of representation was converted into a dead tie. The Convention had reached the stage where it was "ripe" for a solution (presumably all the therapeutic speeches had been made), and the South Carolinians proposed a committee. Madison and James Wilson wanted none of it, but with only Pennsylvania dissenting, the body voted to establish a working party on the problem of representation.

The members of this committee, one from each state, were elected by the delegates—and a very interesting committee it was. Despite the fact that the Virginia Plan had held majority support up to that date, neither Madison nor Randolph was selected (Mason was the Virginian) and Baldwin of Georgia, whose shift in position had resulted in the tie, was chosen. From the composition, it was clear that this was not to be a "fighting" committee: the emphasis in membership was on what might be described as "second-level political entrepreneurs." On the basis of the discussions up to that time, only Luther Martin of Maryland could be described as a "bitter-ender." Admittedly, some divination enters into this sort of analysis, but one does get a sense of the mood of the delegates from these choices—including the interesting selection of Benjamin Franklin, despite his age and intellectual wobbliness, over the brilliant and incisive Wilson or the sharp, polemical Gouverneur Morris, to represent Pennsylvania. His passion for conciliation was more valuable at this juncture than Wilson's logical genius, or Morris's acerbic wit.

There is a common rumor that the framers divided their time between philosophical discussions of government and reading the classics in political theory. Perhaps this is as good a time as any to note that their concerns were highly practical, that they spent little time canvassing abstractions. A number of them had some acquaintance with the history of political theory (probably gained from reading John Adams's monumental compilation *A Defense of the Constitutions of Government*, the first volume of which appeared in 1786), and it was a poor rhetorician indeed who could not cite Locke, Montesquieu, or Harrington *in support* of a desired goal. Yet up to this point in the deliberations, no one had expounded a defense of states' rights or the "separation of powers" on anything resembling a theoretical basis. It should be reiterated that the Madison model had no room either for the states or for the "separation of powers": effectively *all* governmental power was vested in the national legislature. The merits of Montesquieu did not turn up until *The Federalist*; and although a perverse argument could be made that Madison's ideal was truly in the tradition of John Locke's *Second Treatise of Government*, the Locke whom the American rebels treated as an honorary president was a pluralistic defender of vested rights, not of parliamentary supremacy.

It would be tedious to continue a blow-by-blow analysis of the work of the delegates; the critical fight was over representation of the states and once the Connecticut Compromise was adopted on July 17, the Convention was over the hump. Madison, James Wilson, and Gouverneur Morris of New York (who was there representing Pennsylvania!) fought the compromise all the way in a last-ditch effort to get a unitary state with parliamentary supremacy. But their allies deserted them and they demonstrated after their defeat the essential opportunist character of their objections—using "opportunist" here in a non-pejorative sense, to indicate a willingness to swallow their objections and get on with the business. Moreover, once the compromise had carried (by five states to four, with one state divided), its advocates threw themselves vigorously into the job of strengthening the general government's substantive powers—as might have been predicted, indeed, from Paterson's early statements. It nourishes an increased respect for Madison's devotion to the art of politics, to realize that this dogged fighter could sit down six months later and prepare essays for *The Federalist* in contradiction to his basic convictions about the true course the Convention should have taken.

V

Two tricky issues will serve to illustrate the later process of accommodation. The first was the institutional position of the Executive. Madison argued for an executive chosen by the national legislature and on May 29 this had been adopted with a provision that after his seven-year term was concluded, the chief magistrate should not be eligible for reelection. In late July this was reopened and for a week the matter was argued from several different points of view. A good deal of desultory speech-making ensued, but the gist of the problem was the opposition from two sources to election by the legislature. One group felt that the states should have a hand in the process; another small but influential circle urged direct election by the people. There were a number of proposals: election by the people, election by state governors, by electors chosen by state legislatures, by the national legislature (James Wilson, perhaps ironically, proposed at one point that an Electoral College be chosen by lot from the national legislature!), and there was some resemblance to three-dimensional chess in the dispute because of the presence of two other variables, length of tenure and reeligibility. Finally, after opening, reopening, and re-reopening the debate, the thorny problem was consigned to a committee for absolution.

The Brearley Committee on Postponed Matters was a superb aggregation of talent and its compromise on the Executive was a masterpiece of political improvisation. (The Electoral College, its creation, however, had little in its favor as an *institution*—as the delegates well appreciated.) The point of departure for all discussion about the presidency in the Convention was that in immediate terms, the problem was nonexistent; in other words, everybody present knew that under any system devised, George Washington would be President. Thus they were dealing in the future tense and to a body of working politicians the merits of the Brearley proposal were obvious: everybody got a piece of cake. (Or to put it more academically, each viewpoint could leave the Convention and argue to its constituents that it had *really* won the day.) First, the state legislatures had the right to determine the mode of selection of the electors; second, the small states received a bonus in the Electoral College in the form of a guaranteed minimum of three votes while the big states got acceptance of the principle of proportional power; third, if the state legislatures agreed (as six did in the first presidential election), the people could be involved directly in the choice of electors; and finally, if no candidate received a majority in the College, the right of decision passed to the national legislature with each state exercising equal strength. (In the Brearley recommendation, the election went to the Senate, but a motion from the floor substituted the House; this was accepted on the ground that the Senate already had enough authority over the executive in its treaty and appointment powers.)

This compromise was almost too good to be true, and the framers snapped it up with little debate or controversy. No one seemed to think well of the College as an *institution*; indeed, what evidence there is suggests that there was an assumption that once Washington had finished his tenure as President, the electors would cease to produce majorities and the Chief Executive would usually be chosen in the House. George Mason observed casually that the selection would be made in the House nineteen times in twenty and no one seriously disputed this point. The vital aspect of the Electoral College was that it got the Convention over the hurdle and protected everybody's interests. The future was left to cope with the problem of what to do with this Rube Goldberg mechanism.

In short, the framers did not in their wisdom endow the United States with a college of Cardinals—the Electoral College was neither an exercise in applied Platonism nor an experiment in indirect government based on elitist distrust of the masses. It was merely a jerry-rigged improvisation which has subsequently been endowed with a high theoretical content. When an elector from Oklahoma in 1960 refused to cast his vote for Nixon (naming Byrd and Goldwater instead) on the ground that the Founding Fathers intended him to exercise his great independent wisdom, he was indulging in historical fantasy. If one were to indulge in counter-fantasy, he would be tempted to suggest that the Fathers would be startled to find the College still in operation—and perhaps even dismayed at their descendants' lack of judgment or inventiveness.

The second issue on which some substantial practical bargaining took place was slavery. The morality of slavery was, by design, not at issue; but in its other concrete aspects, slavery colored the arguments over taxation, commerce, and representation. The "Three-Fifths Compromise," that three-fifths of the slaves would be counted both for representation and for purposes of direct taxation (which was drawn from the past—it was a formula of Madison's utilized by Congress in 1783 to establish the basis of state contributions to the Confederation treasury) had allayed some Northern fears about Southern overrepresentation (no one then foresaw the trivial role that direct taxation would play in later federal financial policy), but doubts still remained. The Southerners, on the other hand, were afraid that Congressional control over commerce would lead to the exclusion of slaves or to their excessive taxation as imports. Moreover, the Southerners were disturbed over "navigation acts," i.e., tariffs, or special legislation providing, for example, that exports be carried only in American ships; as a section depending upon exports, they wanted protection from the potential voracity of their commercial brethren of the Eastern states. To achieve this end, Mason and others urged that the Constitution include a proviso that navigation and commercial laws should require a two-thirds vote in Congress.

These problems came to a head in late August and, as usual, were handed to a committee in the hope that, in Gouverneur Morris's words, "these things may form a bargain among the Northern and Southern States." The Committee reported its measures of reconciliation on August 25, and on August 29 the package was wrapped up and delivered. What occurred can best be described in George Mason's dour version (he anticipated Calhoun in his conviction that permitting navigation acts to pass by majority vote would put the South in economic bondage to the North—it was mainly on this ground that he refused to sign the Constitution):

> The Constitution as agreed to till a fortnight before the Convention rose was such a one as he would have set his hand and heart to. . . . [Until that time] The 3 New England States were constantly with us in all questions . . . so that it was these three States with the 5 Southern ones against Pennsylvania, Jersey and Delaware. With respect to the importation of slaves, [decision-making] was left to Congress. This disturbed the two Southern-most States who knew that Congress would immediately suppress the importation of slaves. Those two States therefore struck up a bargain with the three New England States. If they would join to admit slaves for some years, the two Southern-most States would join in changing the clause which required the ⅔ of the Legislature in any vote [on navigation acts]. It was done.

On the floor of the Convention there was a virtual love-feast on this happy occasion. Charles Pinckney of South Carolina attempted to overturn the committee's decision, when the compromise was reported to the Convention, by insisting that the South needed protection from the imperialism of the Northern states. But his Southern colleagues were not prepared to rock the boat and General C. C. Pinckney arose to spread oil on the suddenly ruffled waters; he admitted that:

> It was in the true interest of the S[outhern] States to have no regulation of commerce; but considering the loss brought on the commerce of the Eastern States by the Revolution, their liberal conduct towards the views of South Carolina [on the regulation of the slave trade] and the interests the weak Southn. States had in being united with the strong Eastern states, he thought it proper that no fetters should be imposed on the power of making commercial regulations; *and that his constituents, though prejudiced against the Eastern States, would be reconciled to this liberality.* He had himself prejudices agst the Eastern States before he came here, but would acknowledge that he had found them as liberal and candid as any men whatever. (Italics added.)

Pierce Butler took the same tack, essentially arguing that he was not too happy about the possible consequences, but that a deal was a deal. Many Southern leaders were later—in the wake of the "Tariff of Abominations"—to rue this day of reconciliation; Calhoun's *Disquisition on Government* was little more than an extension of the argument in the Convention against permitting a Congressional majority to enact navigation acts.

VI

Drawing on their vast collective political experience, utilizing every weapon in the politician's arsenal, looking constantly over their shoulders at their constituents, the delegates put together a Constitution. It was a makeshift affair; some sticky issues (for example, the qualification of voters) they ducked entirely; others they mastered with that ancient instrument of political sagacity, studied ambiguity (for example, citizenship); and some they just overlooked. In this last category, I suspect, fell the matter of the power of the federal courts to determine the constitutionality of acts of Congress. When the judicial article was formulated (Article III of the Constitution), deliberations were still in the stage where the legislature was endowed with broad power under the Randolph formulation, authority which by its own terms was scarcely amenable to judicial review. In essence, courts could hardly determine when "the separate States are incompetent or . . . the harmony of the United States may be interrupted"; the national legislature, as critics pointed out, was free to define its own jurisdiction. Later the definition of legislative authority was changed into the form we know, a series of stipulated powers, *but the delegates never seriously reexamined the jurisdiction of the judiciary under this new limited formulation*. All arguments on the intention of the framers in this matter are thus deductive and *a posteriori*, though some obviously make more sense than others.

The framers were busy and distinguished men, anxious to get back to their families, their positions, and their constituents, not members of the French Academy devoting a lifetime to a dictionary. They were trying to do an important job, and do it in such a fashion that their handiwork would be acceptable to very diverse constituencies. No one was rhapsodic about the final document, but it was a beginning, a move in the right direction, and one they had reason to believe the people would endorse. In addition, since they had modified the impossible amendment provisions of the Articles (the requirement of unanimity which could always be frustrated by "Rogues Island") to one demanding approval by only three-quarters of the states, they seemed confident that gaps in the fabric which experience would reveal could be rewoven without undue difficulty.

So with a neat phrase introduced by Benjamin Franklin (but devised by Gouverneur Morris) which made their decision sound unanimous, and an inspired benediction by the Old Doctor urging doubters to doubt their own infallibility, the Constitution was accepted and signed. Curiously, Edmund Randolph, who had played so vital a role throughout, refused to sign, as did his fellow Virginian George Mason and Elbridge Gerry of Massachusetts. Randolph's behavior was eccentric, to say the least—his excuses for refusing his signature have a factitious ring even at this late date; the best explanation seems to be that he was afraid that the Constitution would prove to be a liability in Virginia politics, where Patrick Henry was burning up the countryside with impassioned denunciations. Presumably, Randolph wanted to check the temper of the populace before he risked his reputation, and perhaps his job, in a fight with both Henry and Richard Henry Lee. Events lend some justification to this speculation: after much temporizing and use of the conditional subjunctive tense, Randolph endorsed ratification in Virginia and ended up getting the best of both worlds.

Madison, despite his reservations about the Constitution, was the campaign manager in ratification. His first task was to get the Congress in New York to light its own funeral pyre by approving the "amendments" to the Articles and sending them on to the state legislatures. Above all, momentum had to be maintained. The anti-Constitutionalists, now thoroughly alarmed and no novices in politics, realized that their best tactic was attrition rather than direct opposition. Thus they settled on a position expressing qualified approval but calling for a second Convention to remedy various defects (the one with the most demagogic appeal was the lack of a Bill of Rights). Madison knew that to accede to this demand would be equivalent to losing the battle, nor would he agree to conditional approval (despite wavering even by Hamilton). This was an all-or-nothing proposition: national salvation or national impotence with no intermediate positions possible. Unable to get Congressional approval, he settled for second best: a unanimous resolution of Congress transmitting the Constitution to the states for whatever action they saw fit to take. The opponents then moved from New York and the Congress, where they had attempted to attach amendments and conditions, to the states for the final battle.

At first the campaign for ratification went beautifully: within eight months after the delegates set their names to the document, eight states had ratified. Only in Massachusetts had the result been close (187–168). Theoretically, a ratification by one more state convention would set the new government in motion, but in fact until Virginia and New York acceded to the new Union, the latter was a fiction. New Hampshire was the next to ratify; Rhode Island was involved in its characteristic political convulsions (the legislature there sent the Constitution out to the towns for decision by popular vote and it got lost among a series of local issues); North Carolina's convention did not meet until July and then postponed a final decision. This is hardly the place for an extensive analysis of the conventions of New York and Virginia. Suffice it to say that the Constitutionalists clearly outmaneuvered their opponents, forced them into impossible political positions, and won both states narrowly. The Virginia Convention could serve as a classic study in effective floor management: Patrick Henry had to be contained, and a reading of the debates discloses a standard two-stage technique. Henry would give a four- or five-hour speech denouncing some section of the Constitution on every conceivable ground (the federal district, he averred at one point, would become a haven for convicts escaping from state authority!); when Henry subsided, "Mr. Lee of Westmoreland" would rise and literally poleax him with sardonic invective (when Henry complained about the militia power, "Lighthorse Harry" really punched below the belt: observing that while the former Governor had been sitting in Richmond during the Revolution, *he* had been out in the trenches with the troops and thus felt better qualified to discuss military affairs). Then the gentlemanly Constitutionalists (Madison, Pendleton, and Marshall) would pick up the matters at issue and examine them in the light of reason.

Indeed, modern Americans who tend to think of James Madison as a rather desiccated character should spend some time with this transcript. Probably Madison put on his most spectacular demonstration of nimble rhetoric in what might be called "The Battle of the Absent Authorities." Patrick Henry in the course of one of his harangues alleged that Jefferson was known to be opposed to Virginia's approving the Constitution. This was clever: Henry hated Jefferson, but was prepared to use any weapon that came to hand. Madison's riposte was superb: First, he said that with all due respect to the great reputation of Jefferson, he was not in the country and therefore could not formulate an adequate judgment; second, no one should utilize the reputation of an outsider—the Virginia Convention was there to think for itself; third, if there were to be recourse to outsiders, the opinions of George Washington should certainly be taken into consideration; and finally, he knew from privileged personal communications from Jefferson that in fact the latter *strongly favored* the Constitution. To devise an assault route into this rhetorical fortress was literally impossible.

VII

The fight was over; all that remained now was to establish the new frame of government in the spirit of its framers. And who were better qualified for this task than the framers themselves? Thus victory for the Constitution meant simultaneous victory for the Constitutionalists; the anti-Constitutionalists either capitulated or vanished into limbo—soon Patrick Henry would be offered a seat on the Supreme Court and Luther Martin would be known as the Federalist "bull-dog." And irony of ironies, Alexander Hamilton and James Madison would shortly accumulate a reputation as the formulators of what is often alleged to be our political theory, the concept of "federalism." Also, on the other side of the ledger, the arguments would soon appear over what the framers "really meant"; while these disputes have assumed the proportions of a big scholarly business in the last century, they began almost before the ink on the Constitution was dry. One of the best early ones featured Hamilton versus Madison on the scope of presidential power, and other framers characteristically assumed positions in this and other disputes on the basis of their political convictions.

Probably our greatest difficulty is that we know so much more about what the framers *should have meant* than they themselves did. We are intimately acquainted with the problems that their Constitution should have been designed to master; in short, we have read the mystery story backwards. If we are to get the right "feel" for their time and their circumstances, we must in Maitland's phrase, "think ourselves back into a twilight." Obviously, no one can pretend completely to escape from the solipsistic web of his own environment, but if the effort is made, it is possible to appreciate the past roughly on its own terms. The first step in this process is to abandon the academic premise that because we can ask a question, there must be an answer.

Thus we can ask what the framers meant when they gave Congress the power to regulate interstate and foreign commerce, and we emerge, reluctantly perhaps, with the reply that they may not have known what they meant, that there may not have been any semantic consensus. The Convention was not a seminar in analytic philosophy or linguistic analysis. Commerce was *commerce*—and if different interpretations of the word arose, later generations could worry about the problem of definition. The delegates were in a hurry to get a new government established; when definitional arguments arose, they characteristically took refuge in ambiguity. If different men voted for the same proposition for varying reasons, that was politics (and still is); if later generations were unsettled by this lack of precision, that would be their problem.

There was a good deal of definitional pluralism with respect to the problems the delegates did discuss, but when we move to the question of extrapolated intentions, we enter the realm of spiritualism. When men in our time, for instance, launch into elaborate talmudic exegesis to demonstrate that federal aid to parochial schools is (or is not) in accord with the intentions of the men who established the Republic and endorsed the Bill of Rights, they are engaging in historical Extra-Sensory Perception. (If one were to join this E.S.P. contingent for a minute, he might suggest that the hard-boiled politicians who wrote the Constitution and Bill of Rights would chuckle scornfully at such an invocation of authority: obviously a politician would chart his course on the intentions of the living, not of the dead, and count the number of Catholics in his constituency.)

The Constitution, then, was not an apotheosis of "constitutionalism," a triumph of architectonic genius; it was a patch-work sewn together under the pressure of both time and events by a group of extremely talented democratic politicians. They refused to attempt the establishment of a strong, centralized sovereignty on the principle of legislative supremacy for the excellent reason that the people would not accept it. They risked their political fortunes by opposing the established doctrines of state sovereignty because they were convinced that the existing system was leading to national impotence and probably foreign domination. For two years, they worked to get a convention established. For over three months, in what must have seemed to the faithful participants an endless process of give-and-take, they reasoned, cajoled, threatened, and bargained amongst themselves. The result was a Constitution which the people, in fact, by democratic processes, did accept, and a new and far better national government was established.

Beginning with the inspired propaganda of Hamilton, Madison, and Jay, the ideological build-up got under way. *The Federalist* had little impact on the ratification of the Constitution, except perhaps in New York, but this volume had enormous influence on the image of the Constitution in the minds of future generations, particularly on historians and political scientists who have an innate fondness for theoretical symmetry. Yet, while the shades of Locke and Montesquieu *may* have been hovering in the background, and the delegates *may* have been unconscious instruments of a transcendent *telos*, the careful observer of the day-to-day work of the Convention finds no overarching principles. The "separation of powers" to him seems to be a by-product of suspicion, and "federalism" he views as a *pis aller*, as the farthest point the delegates felt they could go in the destruction of state power without themselves inviting repudiation.

To conclude, the Constitution was neither a victory for abstract theory nor a great practical success. Well over half a million men had to die on the battlefields of the Civil War before certain constitutional principles could be defined—a baleful consideration which is somehow overlooked in our customary tributes to the farsighted genius of the framers and to the supposed American talent for "constitutionalism." The Constitution was, however, a vivid demonstration of effective democratic political action, and of the forging of a national elite which literally persuaded its countrymen to hoist themselves by their own boot straps. American pro-consuls would be wise not to translate the Constitution into Japanese, or Swahili, or treat it as a work of semi-Divine origin; but when students of comparative politics examine the process of nation-building in countries newly freed from colonial rule, they may find the American experience instructive as a classic example of the potentialities of a democratic elite.

❖❖   John Roche's article on the framing of the Constitution was written as an attack upon a variety of views that suggested the Constitution was not so much a practical political document, as an expression of elitist views based upon political philosophy and economic interests. One such elitist view was that of Charles A. Beard, who published his famous *An Economic Interpretation of the Constitution* in 1913. He suggested that the Constitution was nothing more than the work of an economic elite that was seeking to preserve its property. This elite, according to Beard, consisted of landholders, creditors, merchants, public bondholders, and wealthy lawyers. Beard demonstrated that many of the delegates to the convention fell into one of these categories.

According to Beard's thesis, as the delegates met, the primary concern of most of them was to limit the power of popular majorities and thus protect their own property interests. To Beard, the antimajoritarian attributes that he felt existed in the Constitution were a reflection of the less numerous creditor class attempting to protect itself against incursions by the majority. Specific provisions as well were put into the Constitution with a view towards protecting property, such as the clause prohibiting states from impairing contracts, coining money, or emitting bills of credit. Control over money was placed in the hands of the national government, and in Article VI of the Constitution it was provided that the new government was to guarantee all debts that had been incurred by the national government under the Articles of Confederation.

Ironically, Beard, like Roche, was attempting to dispel the prevailing notions of his time that the Constitution had been formulated by philosopher kings whose wisdom could not be challenged. But while Roche postulates a loosely knit practical political elite, Beard suggests the existence of a cohesive and even conspiratorial economic elite. The limitation on majority rule was an essential component of this economic conspiracy.

The Constitution does contain many provisions that limit majority rule. Beard claimed that the Constitution from initial adoption to final ratification was never supported by the majority of the people. Holding a constitutional convention in the first place was never submitted to a popular vote, nor was the Constitution that was finally agreed upon ratified by a popular referendum. The selection of delegates to state ratifying conventions was not executed through universal suffrage, but on the basis of the suffrage qualifications that applied in the states and that were within the discretion of state legislatures. The limited suffrage in the states severely restricted popular participation in ratification of the Constitution.

Beard's thesis was startling at the time it was published in 1913. As it came under close examination, it was revealed that the evidence simply did not support Beard's hypothesis. Key leaders of the convention, including Madison, were not substantial property owners. Several important opponents to ratification of the Constitution were the very members of the economic elite that Beard said conspired to thrust the Constitution upon an unknowing public.

Before Beard presented his narrow thesis in 1913, he had published in 1912 *The Supreme Court and the Constitution*. The major theme of the book was that the Supreme Court was intended to have the authority to review acts of Congress under the terms of the original Constitution. At the same time, the book presents Beard's elitist view of the framing of the Constitution in a somewhat broader context than it was presented in *An Economic Interpretation of the Constitution* published a year later. But the earlier work clearly contains the economic theme, as in the passage where Beard states that the framers of the Constitution were "anxious above everything else to safeguard the rights of private property against any levelling tendencies on the part of the propertyless masses." The following selection contains Beard's overview of the framing and adoption of the Constitution and highlights his economic theme and his belief in the antimajoritarian attributes of the Constitution.

3

Charles A. Beard
FRAMING THE
CONSTITUTION

As Blackstone[1] shows by happy illustration the reason and spirit of a law are to be understood only by an inquiry into the circumstances of its enactment. The underlying purposes of the Constitution [of the United States], therefore, are to be revealed only by a study of the conditions and events which led to its formation and adoption.

At the outset it must be remembered that there were two great parties at the time of the adoption of the Constitution—one laying emphasis on strength and efficiency in government and the other on its popular aspects. Quite naturally the men who led in stirring up the revolt against Great Britain and in keeping the fighting temper of the Revolutionists at the proper heat were the boldest and most radical thinkers—men like Samuel Adams, Thomas Paine, Patrick Henry, and Thomas Jefferson. They were not, generally speaking, men of large property interests or of much practical business experience. In a time of disorder, they could consistently lay more stress upon personal liberty than upon social control; and they pushed to the extreme limits those doctrines of individual rights which had been evolved in England during the struggles of the small landed proprietors and commercial classes against royal prerogative, and which corresponded to the economic conditions prevailing in America at the close of the eighteenth century. They associated strong government with monarchy, and came to believe that the best political system was one which governed least. A majority of the radicals viewed all government, especially if highly centralized, as a species of evil, tolerable only because necessary and always to be kept down to an irreducible minimum by a jealous vigilance.

Jefferson put the doctrine in concrete form when he declared that he preferred newspapers without government to government without newspapers. The Declaration of Independence, the first state Constitutions, and the Articles of Confederation bore the impress of this philosophy. In their anxiety to defend

Chapter X from *The Economic Basis of Politics and Related Writings by Charles A. Beard*, compiled and annotated by William Beard, Vintage Books, Inc., © 1957 by William Beard and Miriam B. Vagts. Reprinted with permission of William Beard and the Estate of Miriam B. Vagts.

[1]*Compiler's Note:* Blackstone, Sir William (1723–1780). Distinguished commentator on the laws of England, judge, and teacher.

the individual against all federal interference and to preserve to the states a large sphere of local autonomy, these Revolutionists had set up a system too weak to accomplish the accepted objects of government; namely, national defense, the protection of property, and the advancement of commerce. They were not unaware of the character of their handiwork, but they believed with Jefferson that "man was a rational animal endowed by nature with rights and with an innate sense of justice and that he could be restrained from wrong and protected in right by moderate powers confided to persons of his own choice." Occasional riots and disorders, they held, were preferable to too much government.

The new American political system based on these doctrines had scarcely gone into effect before it began to incur opposition from many sources. The close of the Revolutionary struggle removed the prime cause for radical agitation and brought a new group of thinkers into prominence. When independence had been gained, the practical work to be done was the maintenance of social order, the payment of the public debt, the provision of a sound financial system, and the establishment of conditions favorable to the development of the economic resources of the new country. The men who were principally concerned in this work of peaceful enterprise were not the philosophers, but men of business and property and the holders of public securities. For the most part they had had no quarrel with the system of class rule and the strong centralization of government which existed in England. It was on the question of policy, not of governmental structure, that they had broken with the British authorities. By no means all of them, in fact, had even resisted the policy of the mother country, for within the ranks of the conservatives were large numbers of Loyalists who had remained in America, and, as was to have been expected, cherished a bitter feeling against the Revolutionists, especially the radical section which had been boldest in denouncing the English system root and branch. In other words, after the heat and excitement of the War of Independence were over and the new government, state and national, was tested by the ordinary experiences of traders, financiers, and manufacturers, it was found inadequate, and these groups accordingly grew more and more determined to reconstruct the political system in such a fashion as to make it subserve their permanent interests.

Under the state constitutions and the Articles of Confederation established during the Revolution, every powerful economic class in the nation suffered either immediate losses or from impediments placed in the way of the development of their enterprises. The holders of the securities of the Confederate government did not receive the interest on their loans. Those who owned Western lands or looked with longing eyes upon the rich opportunities for speculation there chaffed at the weakness of the government and its delays in establishing order on the frontiers. Traders and commercial men found their plans for commerce on a national scale impeded by local interference with interstate commerce. The currency of the states and the nation was hopelessly muddled. Creditors everywhere were angry about the depreciated paper money which the agrarians had made and were attempting to force upon those from whom they had borrowed specie. In short, it was a war between business and populism. Under the Articles of Confederation populism had a free hand, for majorities in the state legislatures were omnipotent. Anyone who reads the economic history of the time will see why the solid conservative interests of the country were weary of talk about the "rights of the people" and bent upon establishing firm guarantees for the rights of property.

The Congress of the Confederation was not long in discovering the true character of the futile authority which the Articles had conferred upon it. The necessity for new sources of revenue became apparent even while the struggle for independence was yet undecided, and, in 1781, Congress carried a resolution to the effect that it should be authorized to lay a duty of five percent on certain goods. This moderate proposition was defeated because Rhode Island rejected it on the grounds that "she regarded it the most precious jewel of sovereignty that no state shall be called upon to open its purse but by the authority of the state and by her own officers." Two years later Congress prepared another amendment to the Articles providing for certain import duties, the receipts from which, collected by state officers, were to be applied to the payment of the public debt; but three years after the introduction of the measure, four states, including New York, still held out against its ratification, and the project was allowed to drop. At last, in 1786, Congress in a resolution declared that the requisitions for the last eight years had been so irregular in their operation, so uncertain in their collection, and so evidently unproductive, that a reliance on them in the future would be no less dishonorable to the understandings of those who entertained it than it would be dangerous to the welfare and peace of the Union. Congress, thereupon, solemnly added that it had become its duty "to declare most explicitly that the crisis had arrived when the people of the United States, by whose will and for whose benefit the federal government was instituted, must decide whether they will support their rank as a nation by maintaining the public faith at home and abroad, or whether for the want of a timely exertion in establishing a general revenue and thereby giving strength to the Confederacy, they will hazard not only the existence of the Union but those great and invaluable privileges for which they have so arduously and so honorably contended."

In fact, the Articles of Confederation had hardly gone into effect before the leading citizens also began to feel that the powers of Congress were wholly inadequate. In 1780, even before their adoption, Alexander Hamilton proposed a general convention to frame a new constitution, and from that time forward he labored with remarkable zeal and wisdom to extend and popularize the idea of a strong national government. Two years later, the Assembly of the State of New York recommended a convention to revise the Articles and increase the power of Congress. In 1783, Washington, in a circular letter to the governors, urged that it was indispensable to the happiness of the individual states that there should be lodged somewhere a supreme power to regulate and govern the general concerns of the confederation. Shortly afterward (1785), Governor Bowdoin, of Massachusetts, suggested to his state legislature the advisability of calling a national assembly to settle upon and define the powers of Congress; and the legislature resolved that the government under the Articles of Confederation was inadequate and should be reformed; but the resolution was never laid before Congress.

In January, 1786, Virginia invited all the other states to send delegates to a convention at Annapolis to consider the question of duties on imports and commerce in general. When this convention assembled in 1786, delegates from only five states were present, and they were disheartened at the limitations on their powers and the lack of interest the other states had shown in the project. With characteristic foresight, however, Alexander Hamilton seized the occasion to secure the adoption of a recommendation advising the states to choose representatives for another convention to meet in Philadephia the following year "to consider the Articles of Confederation and to propose such changes therein as might render them adequate to the exigencies of the union." This recommendation was cautiously worded, for Hamilton did not want to raise any unnecessary alarm. He doubtless believed that a complete revolution in the old system was desirable, but he knew that, in the existing state of popular temper, it was not expedient to announce his complete program. Accordingly no general reconstruction of the political system was suggested; the Articles of Confederation were merely to be "revised"; and the amendments were to be approved by the state legislatures as provided by that instrument.

The proposal of the Annapolis convention was transmitted to the state legislatures and laid before Congress. Congress thereupon resolved in February, 1787, that a convention should be held for the sole and express purpose of revising the Articles of Confederation and reporting to itself and the legislatures of the several states such alterations and provisions as would when agreed to by Congress and confirmed by the states render the federal constitution adequate to the exigencies of government and the preservation of the union.

In pursuance of this call, delegates to the new convention were chosen by the legislatures of the states or by the governors in conformity to authority conferred by the legislative assemblies.[2] The delegates were given instructions of a general nature by their respective states, none of which, apparently, contemplated any very far-reaching changes. In fact, almost all of them expressly limited their representatives to a mere revision of the Articles of Confederation. For example, Connecticut authorized her delegates to represent and confer for the purpose mentioned in the resolution of Congress and to discuss such measures "agreeable to the general principles of Republican government" as they

---

[2]Rhode Island alone was unrepresented. In all, sixty-two delegates were appointed by the states; fifty-five of these attended sometime during the sessions; but only thirty-nine signed the finished document.

should think proper to render the Union adequate. Delaware, however, went so far as to provide that none of the proposed alterations should extend to the fifth part of the Articles of Confederation guaranteeing that each state should be entitled to one vote.

It was a truly remarkable assembly of men that gathered in Philadelphia on May 14, 1787, to undertake the work of reconstructing the American system of government. It is not merely patriotic pride that compels one to assert that never in the history of assemblies has there been a convention of men richer in political experience and in practical knowledge, or endowed with a profounder insight into the springs of human action and the intimate essence of government. It is indeed an astounding fact that at one time so many men skilled in statecraft could be found on the very frontiers of civilization among a population numbering about four million whites. It is no less a cause for admiration that their instrument of government should have survived the trials and crises of a century that saw the wreck of more than a score of paper constitutions.

All the members had had a practical training in politics. Washington, as commander-in-chief of the Revolutionary forces, had learned well the lessons and problems of war, and mastered successfully the no less difficult problems of administration. The two Morrises had distinguished themselves in grappling with financial questions as trying and perplexing as any which statesmen had ever been compelled to face. Seven of the delegates had gained political wisdom as governors of their native states; and no less than twenty-eight had served in Congress either during the Revolution or under the Articles of Confederation. These were men trained in the law, versed in finance, skilled in administration, and learned in the political philosophy of their own and all earlier times. Moreover, they were men destined to continue public service under the government which they had met to construct—Presidents, Vice-Presidents, heads of departments, Justices of the Supreme Court were in that imposing body. . . .

As Woodrow Wilson has concisely put it, the framers of the Constitution represented "a strong and intelligent class possessed of unity and informed by a conscious solidarity of interests."[3] . . .

The makers of the federal Constitution represented the solid, conservative, commercial and financial interests of the country—not the interests which denounced and proscribed judges in Rhode Island, New Jersey, and North Carolina, and stoned their houses in New York. The conservative interests, made desperate by the imbecilities of the Confederation and harried by state legislatures, roused themselves from their lethargy, drew together in a mighty effort to establish a government that would be strong enough to pay the national debt, regulate interstate and foreign commerce, provide for national defense, prevent fluctuations in the currency created by paper emissions, and control the propensities of legislative majorities to attack private rights. . . . The rad-

---

[3]Woodrow Wilson, *Division and Reunion* (New York: Longmans, Green, & Co., 1893), p. 12.

icals, however, like Patrick Henry, Jefferson, and Samuel Adams, were conspicuous by their absence from the convention.[4] . . .

[The makers of the Constitution were convened] to frame a government which would meet the practical issues that had arisen under the Articles of Confederation. The objections they entertained to direct popular government, and they were undoubtedly many, were based upon their experience with popular assemblies during the immediately preceding years. With many of the plain lessons of history before them, they naturally feared that the rights and privileges of the minority would be insecure if the principle of majority rule was definitely adopted and provisions made for its exercise. Furthermore, it will be remembered that up to that time the right of all men, as men, to share in the government had never been recognized in practice. Everywhere in Europe the government was in the hands of a ruling monarch or at best a ruling class; everywhere the mass of the people had been regarded principally as an arms-bearing and tax-paying multitude, uneducated, and with little hope or capacity for advancement. Two years were to elapse after the meeting of the grave assembly at Philadelphia before the transformation of the Estates General into the National Convention in France opened the floodgates of revolutionary ideas on human rights before whose rising tide old landmarks of government are still being submerged. It is small wonder, therefore, that, under the circumstances, many of the members of that august body held popular government in slight esteem and took the people into consideration only as far as it was imperative "to inspire them with the necessary confidence," as Mr. Gerry frankly put it.[5]

Indeed, every page of the laconic record of the proceedings of the convention preserved to posterity by Mr. Madison shows conclusively that the members of that assembly were not seeking to realize any fine notions about democracy and equality, but were striving with all the resources of political wisdom at their command to set up a system of government that would be stable and efficient, safeguarded on one hand against the possibilities of despotism and on the other against the onslaught of majorities. In the mind of Mr. Gerry, the evils they had experienced flowed "from the excess of democracy," and he confessed that while he was still republican, he "had been taught by experience the danger of the levelling spirit."[6] Mr. Randolph in offering to the consideration of the convention his plan of government, observed "that the general object was to provide a cure for the evils under which the United States labored; that, in tracing these evils to their origin, every man had found it in the turbulence and follies of democracy; that some check therefore was to be sought for against this tendency of our governments; and that a good Senate seemed most likely

---

[4]*Compiler's Note:* The contents of this paragraph have been taken from positions on pp. 75–76 and 88 of the original text of *The Supreme Court and the Constitution* and placed here to emphasize the economic theme.

[5]Jonathan Elliot, *The Debates in the Several State Conventions on the Adoption of the Federal Constitution* (Washington, D.C.: The Editor, 1827–1830), vol. v, p. 160.

[6]*Ibid.*, vol. v, p. 136.

to answer the purpose."[7] Mr. Hamilton, in advocating a life term for Senators, urged that "all communities divide themselves into the few and the many. The first are rich and well born and the other the mass of the people who seldom judge or determine right."

Gouverneur Morris wanted to check the "precipitancy, changeableness, and excess" of the representatives of the people by the ability and virtue of men "of great and established property—aristocracy; men who from pride will support consistency and permanency. . . . Such an aristocratic body will keep down the turbulence of democracy." While these extreme doctrines were somewhat counterbalanced by the democratic principles of Mr. Wilson who urged that "the government ought to possess, not only first, the force, but second the mind or sense of the people at large," Madison doubtless summed up in a brief sentence the general opinion of the convention when he said that to secure private rights against majority factions, and at the same time to preserve the spirit and form of popular government, was the great object to which their inquiries had been directed.[8]

They were anxious above everything else to safeguard the rights of private property against any leveling tendencies on the part of the propertyless masses. Gouverneur Morris, in speaking on the problem of apportioning representatives, correctly stated the sound historical fact when he declared: "Life and liberty were generally said to be of more value than property. An accurate view of the matter would, nevertheless, prove that property was the main object of society. . . . If property, then, was the main object of government, certainly it ought to be one measure of the influence due to those who were to be affected by the government."[9] Mr. King also agreed that "property was the primary object of society"[10]; and Mr. Madison warned the convention that in framing a system which they wished to last for ages they must not lose sight of the changes which the ages would produce in the forms and distribution of property. In advocating a long term in order to give independence and firmness to the Senate, he described these impending changes: "An increase of population will of necessity increase the proportion of those who will labor under all the hardships of life and secretly sigh for a more equal distribution of its blessings. These may in time outnumber those who are placed above the feelings of indigence. According to the equal laws of suffrage, the power will slide into the hands of the former. No agrarian attempts have yet been made in this country, but symptoms of a levelling spirit, as we have understood have sufficiently appeared, in a certain quarter, to give notice of the future danger."[11] And again, in support of the argument for a property qualification on voters, Madison urged: "In future

[7]*Ibid.*, vol. v, p. 138.

[8]*The Federalist*, No. 10.

[9]Elliot's *Debates*, *op. cit.*, vol. v, p. 279.

[10]*Ibid.*, p. 280.

[11]*Ibid.*, p. 243.

times, a great majority of the people will not only be without landed, but any other sort of property. These will either combine, under the influence of their common situation,—in which case the rights of property and the public liberty will not be secure in their hands,—or, what is more probable, they will become the tools of opulence and ambition; in which case there will be equal danger on another side."[12] Various projects for setting up class rule by the establishment of property qualifications for voters and officers were advanced in the convention, but they were defeated. . . .

The absence of such property qualifications is certainly not due to any belief in Jefferson's free-and-equal doctrine. It is due rather to the fact that the members of the convention could not agree on the nature and amount of the qualifications. Naturally a landed qualification was suggested, but for obvious reasons it was rejected. Although it was satisfactory to the landed gentry of the South, it did not suit the financial, commercial, and manufacturing gentry of the North. If it was high, the latter would be excluded; if it was low it would let in the populistic farmers who had already made so much trouble in the state legislatures with paper-money schemes and other devices for "relieving agriculture." One of the chief reasons for calling the convention and framing the Constitution was to promote commerce and industry and to protect personal property against the "depredations" of Jefferson's noble freeholders. On the other hand a personal-property qualification, high enough to please merchant princes like Robert Morris and Nathaniel Gorham would shut out the Southern planters. Again, an alternative of land or personal property, high enough to afford safeguards to large interests, would doubtless bring about the rejection of the whole Constitution by the troublemaking farmers who had to pass upon the question of ratification.[13]. . .

Nevertheless, by the system of checks and balances placed in the government, the convention safeguarded the interests of property against attacks by majorities. The House of Representatives, Mr. Hamilton pointed out, "was so formed as to render it particularly the guardian of the poorer orders of citizens,"[14] while the Senate was to preserve the rights of property and the interests of the minority against the demands of the majority.[15] In the tenth number of *The Federalist*, Mr. Madison argued in a philosophic vein in support of the proposition that it was necessary to base the political system on the actual conditions of "natural inequality." Uniformity of interests throughout the state, he contended, was impossible on account of the diversity in the faculties of men, from

---

[12]*Ibid.*, p. 387.

[13]*Compiler's Note:* This single paragraph from "Whom Does Congress Represent?" *Harper's Magazine*, Jan., 1930, pp. 144–152, has been inserted here because of its value in amplifying the passages from *The Supreme Court and the Constitution*. Reprinting from this article by Beard has been done with the permission of *Harper's Magazine*.

[14]*Elliot's Debates, op. cit.*, vol. v, p. 244.

[15]*Ibid.*, vol. v, p. 203.

which the rights of property originated; the protection of these faculties was the first object of government; from the protection of different and unequal faculties of acquiring property the possession of different degrees and kinds of property immediately resulted; from the influence of these on the sentiments and views of the respective proprietors ensued a division of society into different interests and parties; the unequal distribution of wealth inevitably led to a clash of interests in which the majority was liable to carry out its policies at the expense of the minority; hence, he added, in concluding this splendid piece of logic, "the majority, having such coexistent passion or interest, must be rendered by their number and local situation unable to concert and carry into effect schemes of oppression"; and in his opinion it was the great merit of the newly framed Constitution that it secured the rights of the minority against "the superior force of an interested and overbearing majority."

This very system of checks and balances, which is undeniably the essential element of the Constitution, is built upon the doctrine that the popular branch of the government cannot be allowed full sway, and least of all in the enactment of laws touching the rights of property. The exclusion of the direct popular vote in the election of the President; the creation, again by indirect election, of a Senate which the framers hoped would represent the wealth and conservative interests of the country[16]; and the establishment of an independent judiciary appointed by the President with the concurrence of the Senate—all these devices bear witness to the fact that the underlying purpose of the Constitution was not the establishment of popular government by means of parliamentary majorities.

Page after page of *The Federalist* is directed to that portion of the electorate which was disgusted with the "mutability of the public councils." Writing on the presidential veto Hamilton says: "The propensity of the legislative department to intrude upon the rights, and absorb the powers, of the other departments has already been suggested and repeated. . . . It may perhaps be said that the power of preventing bad laws included the power of preventing good ones; and may be used to the one purpose as well as the other. But this objection will have little weight with those who can properly estimate the mischiefs of that inconstancy and mutability in the laws which form the greatest blemish in the character and genius of our governments. They will consider every institution calculated to restrain the excess of law-making and to keep things in the same state in which they happen to be at any given period, as more likely to do good than harm; because it is favorable to greater stability in the system of legislation. The injury which may be possibly done by defeating a few good laws will be amply compensated by the advantage of preventing a number of bad ones."

---

[16]*Compiler's Note:* Popular election of senators was achieved in 1913 through the Seventeenth Amendment to the Constitution.

When the framers of the Constitution had completed the remarkable instrument which was to establish a national government capable of discharging
effectively certain great functions and checking the propensities of popular
legislatures to attack the rights of private property, a formidable task remained
before them—the task of securing the adoption of the new frame of government
by states torn with popular dissensions. They knew very well that the state
legislatures which had been so negligent in paying their quotas [of money] under
the Articles [of Confederation] and which had been so jealous of their rights,
would probably stick at ratifying such a national instrument of government.
Accordingly they cast aside that clause in the Articles requiring amendments
to be ratified by the legislature of all the states; and advised that the new
Constitution should be ratified by conventions in the several states composed
of delegates chosen by the voters.[17] They furthermore declared—and this is a
fundamental matter—that when the conventions of nine states had ratified the
Constitution the new government should go into effect so far as those states
were concerned. The chief reason for resorting to ratifications by conventions
is laid down by Hamilton in the twenty-second number of *The Federalist:* "It
has not a little contributed to the infirmities of the existing federal system that
it never had a ratification by the people. Resting on no better foundation than
the consent of the several legislatures, it has been exposed to frequent and
intricate questions concerning the validity of it powers; and has in some instances given birth to the enormous doctrine of a right of legislative repeal.
Owing its ratification to the law of a state, it has been contended that the same
authority might repeal the law by which it was ratified. However gross a heresy
it may be to maintain that a party to a compact has a right to revoke that
compact, the doctrine itself has respectable advocates. The possibility of a
question of this nature proves the necessity of laying the foundations of our
national government deeper than in the mere sanction of delegated authority.
The fabric of American empire ought to rest on the solid basis of the consent
of the people. The streams of national power ought to flow immediately from
that pure original fountain of all legitimate authority."

Of course, the convention did not resort to the revolutionary policy of
transmitting the Constitution directly to the conventions of the several states.
It merely laid the finished instrument before the Confederate Congress with
the suggestion that it should be submitted to "a convention of delegates chosen
in each state by the people thereof, under the recommendation of its legislature,
for their assent and ratification; and each convention assenting thereto and
ratifying the same should give notice thereof to the United States in Congress
assembled." The convention went on to suggest that when nine states had

---

[17]*Compiler's Note:* The original text, p. 75, comments: "It was largely because the framers of
the Constitution knew the temper and class bias of the state legislatures that they arranged that
the new Constitution should be ratified by conventions."

ratified the Constitution, the Confederate Congress should extinguish itself by making provision for the elections necessary to put the new government into effect. . . .

After the new Constitution was published and transmitted to the states, there began a long and bitter fight over ratification. A veritable flood of pamphlet literature descended upon the country, and a collection of these pamphlets by Hamilton, Madison, and Jay, brought together under the title of *The Federalist*—though clearly a piece of campaign literature—has remained a permanent part of the contemporary sources on the Constitution and has been regarded by many lawyers as a commentary second in value only to the decisions of the Supreme Court. Within a year the champions of the new government found themselves victorious, for on June 21, 1788, the ninth state, New Hampshire, ratified the Constitution, and accordingly the new government might go into effect as between the agreeing states. Within a few weeks, the nationalist party in Virginia and New York succeeded in winning these two states, and in spite of the fact that North Carolina and Rhode Island had not yet ratified the Constitution, Congress determined to put the instrument into effect in accordance with the recommendations of the convention. Elections for the new government were held; the date March 4, 1789, was fixed for the formal establishment of the new system; Congress secured a quorum on April 6; and on April 30 Washington was inaugurated at the Federal Hall in Wall Street, New York.

❖❖   Charles A. Beard suggests that there is a dichotomy between the values of the Constitution and those of the Declaration of Independence, between Jefferson and his followers on the one hand, and Madison and Hamilton on the other. He suggests that Jefferson and the Revolutionists supported political equality and individual freedom and opposed a strong central government. The spirit of the Revolution, argues Beard, spawned the Articles of Confederation, which purposely created a weak and ineffective government. The Revolutionists, in general, were not men of property and thus did not believe that a strong central government was necessary to protect their interests. By contrast, the framers of the Constitution reflected the spirit of Alexander Hamilton, who ironically was not a man of substantial property himself, but who advocated an energetic and dominant national government. Hamilton, like many of the framers, was a strong proponent of governmental protection of property interests.

Limitation of Governmental Power and of Majority Rule

The most accurate and helpful way to characterize our political system is to call it a constitutional democracy. The term implies a system in which the government is regulated by laws that control and limit the exercise of political power. In a constitutional democracy people participate in government on a limited basis. A distinction should be made between an unlimited democratic government and a constitutional democracy. In the former, the people govern through the operation of a principle such as majority rule without legal restraint; in the latter, majority rule is curtailed and checked through various legal devices. A constitutional system is one in which the formal authority of government is restrained. The checks upon government in a constitutional society customarily include a division or fragmentation of authority that prevents government from controlling all sectors of human life.

Hamilton noted in *Federalist 1*, "It seems to have been reserved to the people of this country, to decide by their conduct and example, the important question, whether societies of men are really capable or not, of establishing good government from reflection and choice, or whether they are forever destined to depend, for their political constitutions, on accident and force." The framers of our Constitution attempted to structure the government in such a way that it would meet the needs and aspirations of the people and at the same time check the arbitrary exercise of political power. The doctrine of the separation of powers was designed to prevent any one group from gaining control of the national governmental apparatus. The selections reprinted here from *The Federalist*, which was written between October 1787 and August 1788, outline the theory and mechanism of the separation of powers.

4

James Madison
FEDERALIST 47

I proceed to examine the particular structure of this government, and the distribution of this mass of power among its constituent parts.

One of the principal objections inculcated by the more respectable adversaries to the constitution, is its supposed violation of the political maxim, that the legislative, executive, and judiciary departments, ought to be separate and distinct. In the structure of the federal government, no regard, it is said, seems to have been paid to this essential precaution in favor of liberty. The several departments of power are distributed and blended in such a manner, as at once to destroy all symmetry and beauty of form; and to expose some of the essential parts of the edifice to the danger of being crushed by the disproportionate weight of other parts.

No political truth is certainly of great intrinsic value, or is stamped with the authority of more enlightened patrons of liberty, than that on which the objection is founded. The accumulation of all powers. legislative, executive, and judiciary, in the same hands, whether of one, a few, or many, and whether hereditary, self-appointed, or elective, may justly be pronounced the very definition of tyranny. Were the federal constitution, therefore, really chargeable with this accumulation of power, or with a mixture of powers, having a dangerous tendency to such an accumulation, no further arguments would be necessary to inspire a universal reprobation of the system. I persuade myself, however, that it will be made apparent to every one, that the charge cannot be supported, and that the maxim on which it relies has been totally misconceived and misapplied.

The oracle who is always consulted and cited on this subject, is the celebrated Montesquieu. If he be not the author of this invaluable precept in the science of politics, he has the merit of at least displaying and recommending it most effectually to the attention of mankind. . . .

From . . . facts, by which Montesquieu was guided, it may clearly be inferred, that in saying, "there can be no liberty, where the legislative and executive powers are united in the same person, or body of magistrates"; or "if the power of judging, be not separated from the legislative and executive powers," he did not mean that these departments ought to have no *partial agency* in, or no *control* over, the acts of each other. His meaning . . . can amount to no more than this, that where the *whole* power of one department is exercised by the same hands which possess the *whole* power of another department, the fundamental principles of a free constitution are subverted. . . .

If we look into the constitutions of the several states, we find, that notwithstanding the emphatical, and, in some instances, the unqualified terms in which this axiom has been laid down, there is not a single instance in which the several departments of power have been kept absolutely separate and distinct. . . .

The constitution of Massachusetts has observed a sufficient, though less pointed caution, in expressing this fundamental article of liberty. It declares, "that the legislative department shall never exercise the executive and judicial powers, or either of them: the executive shall never exercise the legislative and judicial powers, or either of them: the judicial shall never exercise the legislative and executive powers, or either of them." This declaration corresponds precisely with the doctrine of Montesquieu. . . . It goes no farther than to prohibit any one of the entire departments from exercising the powers of another department. In the very constitution to which it is prefixed, a partial mixture of powers has been admitted. . . .

FEDERALIST 48

. . . I shall undertake in the next place to show, that unless these departments be so far connected and blended, as to give to each a constitutional control over the others, the degree of separation which the maxim requires, as essential to a free government, can never in practice be duly maintained.

It is agreed on all sides, that the powers properly belonging to one of the departments ought not to be directly and completely administered by either of the other departments. It is equally evident, that neither of them ought to possess, directly or indirectly, an overruling influence over the others in the administration of their respective powers. It will not be denied, that power is of an encroaching nature, and that it ought to be effectually restrained from passing the limits assigned to it. After discriminating, therefore, in theory, the several classes of power, as they may in their nature be legislative, executive, or judiciary; the next, and most difficult task, is to provide some practical security for each, against the invasion of the others. What this security ought to be, is the great problem to be solved.

Will it be sufficient to mark, with precision, the boundaries of these departments, in the constitution of the government, and to trust to these parchment barriers against the encroaching spirit of power? This is the security which appears to have been principally relied on by the compilers of most American constitutions. But experience assures us, that the efficacy of the provision has been greatly overrated; and that some more adequate defense is indispensably necessary for the more feeble, against the more powerful members of the government. The legislative department is everywhere extending the sphere of its activity, and drawing all power into its impetuous vortex. . . .

In a government where numerous and extensive prerogatives are placed in the hands of an hereditary monarch, the executive department is very justly regarded as the source of danger, and watched with all the jealousy which a zeal for liberty ought to inspire. In a democracy, where a multitude of people exercise in person the legislative functions, and are continually exposed, by their incapacity for regular deliberation and concerted measures, to the ambitious intrigues of their executive magistrates, tyranny may well be apprehended on some favorable emergency, to start up in the same quarter. But in a representative republic, where the executive magistracy is carefully limited, both in the extent and the duration of its power; and where the legislative is exercised by an assembly, which is inspired by a supposed influence over the people, with an intrepid confidence in its own strength; which is sufficiently numerous to feel all the passions which actuate a multitude; yet not so numerous as to be incapable of pursuing the objects of its passions, by means which reason prescribes; it is against the enterprising ambition of this department, that the people ought to indulge all their jealousy and exhaust all their precautions.

The legislative department derives a superiority in our governments from other circumstances. Its constitutional powers being at once more extensive, and less susceptible of precise limits, it can, with the greater facility, mask, under complicated and indirect measures, the encroachment which it makes on the coordinate departments. It is not infrequently a question of real nicety in legislative bodies, whether the operation of a particular measure will, or will not extend beyond the legislative sphere. On the other side, the executive power being restrained within a narrower compass, and being more simple in its nature; and the judiciary being described by landmarks, still less uncertain, projects of usurpation by either of these departments would immediately betray and defeat themselves. Nor is this all: as the legislative department alone has access to the pockets of the people, and has in some constitutions full discretion, and in all a prevailing influence over the pecuniary rewards of those who fill the other departments; a dependence is thus created in the latter, which gives still greater facility to encroachments of the former. . . .

FEDERALIST 51

To what expedient then shall we finally resort, for maintaining in practice the necessary partition of power among the several departments, as laid down in the constitution? The only answer that can be given is, that as all these exterior provisions are found to be inadequate, the defect must be supplied, by so con-triving the interior structure of the government, as that its several constituent parts may, by their mutual relations, be the means of keeping each other in their proper places. . . .

In order to lay a due foundation for that separate and distinct exercise of the different powers of government, which, to a certain extent, is admitted on all hands to be essential to the preservation of liberty, it is evident that each department should have a will of its own; and consequently should be so con-stituted, that the members of each should have as little agency as possible in the appointment of the members of the others. . . .

It is equally evident, that the members of each department should be as little dependent as possible on those of the others, for the emoluments annexed to their offices. Were the executive magistrate, or the judges, not independent of the legislature in this particular, their independence in every other, would be merely nominal.

But the great security against a gradual concentration of the several powers in the same department, consists in giving to those who administer each de-partment, the necessary constitutional means, and personal motives, to resist encroachments of the others. The provision for defense must in this, as in all other cases, be made commensurate to the danger of attack. Ambition must be made to counteract ambition. The interest of the man must be connected with the constitutional rights of the place. It may be a reflection on human nature, that such devices should be necessary to control the abuses of government. But what is government itself, but the greatest of all reflections on human nature? If men were angels, no government would be necessary. If angels were to govern men, neither external not internal controls on government would be necessary. In framing a government, which is to be administered by men over men, the great difficulty lies in this: You must first enable the government to control the governed; and in the next place, oblige it to control itself. A dependence on the people is, no doubt, the primary control on the government; but experience has taught mankind the necessity of auxiliary precautions.

This policy of supplying by opposite and rival interests, the defect of better motives, might be traced through the whole system of human affairs, private as well as public. We see it particularly displayed in all the subordinate distri-butions of power; where the constant aim is, to divide and arrange the several offices in such a manner, as that each may be a check on the other; that the private interest of very individual, may be a sentinel over the public rights. These inventions of prudence cannot be less requisite to the distribution of the supreme powers of the state.

But it is not possible to give to each department an equal power of self-defense. In republican government, the legislative authority necessarily predominates. The remedy for this inconvenience is, to divide the legislature into different branches; and to render them by different modes of election, and different principles of action, as little connected with each other, as the nature of their common functions, and their common dependence on the society will admit. It may even be necessary to guard against dangerous encroachments, by still further precautions. As the weight of the legislative authority requires that it should be thus divided, the weakness of the executive may require, on the other hand, that it should be fortified. An absolute negative on the legislature, appears, at first view, to be the natural defense with which the executive magistrate should be armed. But perhaps it would be neither altogether safe, nor alone sufficient. On ordinary occasions, it might not be exerted with the requisite firmness; and on extraordinary occasions, it might be perfidiously abused. May not this defect of an absolute negative be supplied by some qualified connection between this weaker department, and the weaker branch of the stronger department, by which the latter may be led to support the constitutional rights of the former, without being too much detached from the rights of its own department?

An Overview of the Framing and Purpose of the Constitution

The preceding selections have offered contrasting views on the framing, nature, and purpose of the Constitution. As background, John Locke's political philosophy expressed in his *Second Treatise, Of Civil Government* (1690) supported the political beliefs of many eighteenth-century Americans in government as a social contract between rulers and ruled to protect the natural rights of citizens to life, liberty, and, very importantly, property.

To John Roche, the Constitution was a practical political document reflecting compromises among state delegations with contrasting political and economic interests, and between advocates of strong national power and proponents of states' rights. Charles Beard saw the Constitution as a reflection of the interests of property owners and creditors who feared that the rule of the debtor majority would inflate currency, cancel debts, and deprive creditors of their rightful property. James Madison's selections from *The Federalist* suggest a mistrust of government, a wary view of both political leaders and the people, and an emphasis upon the need for governmental checks and balances to prevent the arbitrary exercise of political power. Madison also distrusted what he termed "faction," by which he meant political parties or special-interest groups, which he considered intrinsically to be opposed to the national interest (see Federalist 10, Chapter 4).

The separation of powers among the executive, legislative, and judicial branches is an outstanding characteristic of our constitutional system. A uniquely American separation of powers incorporated an *independent* executive, pitting the president against Congress and requiring their cooperation to make the government work. The separation of powers was a constitutional filter through which political demands had to flow before they could be translated into public policies.

James Madison clearly saw the separation-of-powers system, incorporating checks and balances among the branches of government, as a process that would help to prevent arbitrary and excessive governmental actions. The three branches of the government, but particularly the president and Congress, would have independent political bases, motivations, and powers that would both enable and encourage them to compete with each other.

While Madison saw the separation of powers as an important limit upon arbitrary government, Alexander Hamilton represented a different point of view. He viewed the independent presidency, a central component of the separation of powers, as an office that could make the national government energetic and effective. "Energy in the executive is the definition of good government," wrote Hamilton in *The Federalist*, No. 70, and the constitutional separation of powers would provide that energy rather than simply making the president a co-equal branch subject to congressional whims or Supreme Court constraints.

History has, at different times, borne out the views of both Madison and Hamilton regarding the effect of the separation of powers. During times of relative political tranquility the president and Congress have often been stalemated in a deadlock of democracy. But Hamilton's imperial presidency has taken charge in times of crisis, such as during the Civil War, Franklin D. Roosevelt's New Deal in the 1930s, and the Second World War in the 1940s.

Is the separation-of-powers and checks-and-balances system, an eighteenth-century concept, the best way to run our government as the twentieth century comes to a close? James MacGregor Burns wrote, in *The Deadlock of Democracy*, that the Madisonian model "was the product of the gifted men who gathered in Philadelphia [in 1787] and it deserves much of the admiration and veneration we have accorded it. But this is also the system of checks and balances and interlocked gears of government that requires the consensus of many groups and leaders before the nation can act; and it is the system that exacts the heavy price of delay and devitalization. . . ."

In the following selection an experienced Washington insider addresses the question of whether or not the separation-of-powers system should be changed.

5

Lloyd N. Cutler
TO FORM A GOVERNMENT

> [On May 10, 1940, Winston Churchill was summoned to Buckingham Palace.] His Majesty received me most graciously and bade me sit down. He looked at me searchingly and quizzically for some moments, and then said: "I suppose you don't know why I have sent for you?" Adopting his mood, I replied: "Sir, I simply couldn't imagine why." He laughed and said: "I want to ask you to form a Government." I said I would certainly do so.
>
> WINSTON S. CHURCHILL
The Gathering Storm (1948)

Our society was one of the first to write a constitution. This reflected the confident conviction of the Enlightenment that explicit written arrangements could be devised to structure a government that would be neither tyrannical nor impotent in its time and to allow for future amendment as experience and change might require.

We are all children of this faith in a rational written arrangement for governing. Our faith should encourage us to consider changes in our Constitution—for which the framers explicitly allowed—that would assist us in adjusting to the changes in the world in which the Constitution must function. Yet we tend to resist suggestions that amendments to our existing Constitutional framework are needed to govern our portion of the interdependent world society we have become and to cope with the resulting problems that all contemporary governments must resolve.

A particular shortcoming in need of a remedy is the structural inability of our government to propose, legislate, and administer a balanced program for governing. In parliamentary terms one might say that under the U.S. Constitution it is not now feasible to "form a government." The separation of powers

Reprinted by permission of *Foreign Affairs*, Fall 1980. Copyright, 1980 by the Council on Foreign Relations, Inc.

between the legislative and executive branches, whatever its merits in 1793, has become a structure that almost guarantees stalemate today. As we wonder why we are having such a difficult time making decisions we all know must be made and projecting our power and leadership, we should reflect on whether this is one big reason.

We elect one presidential candidate over another on the basis of our judgment of the overall program he presents, his ability to carry it out, and his capacity to adapt his program to new developments as they arise. We elected President Jimmy Carter, whose program included, as one of its most important elements, the successful completion of the SALT II negotiations that his two predecessors had been conducting since 1972. In June 1979 President Carter did complete and sign a SALT II treaty, which he and his cabinet regarded as very much in the national security interests of the United States. Notwithstanding subsequent events, the president and his cabinet continued to hold that view—indeed they believed the mounting intensity of our confrontation with the Soviet Union made it even more important for the two superpowers to adopt and abide by explicit rules about the size and quality of each side's strategic nuclear arsenal and how each side can verify what the other side is doing. Because we do not form a government, however, it was not possible for President Carter to carry out this major part of his program.

Of course the constitutional requirement of Senate advice and consent to treaties presents a special situation. The case for the two-thirds rule was much stronger in 1793, when events abroad rarely affected this isolated continent and when "entangling foreign alliances" were viewed with a skeptical eye. Whether it should be maintained in an age when most treaties deal with such subjects as taxation and trade is open to question. No parliamentary regime anywhere in the world has a similar provision. But in the United States—at least for major issues like SALT—there is merit to the view that treaties should indeed require the careful bipartisan consultation essential to win a two-thirds majority. This is the principle that Woodrow Wilson fatally neglected in 1919. But it has been carefully observed by recent presidents, including President Carter for the Panama Canal treaties and the SALT II treaty. For each of these there was a clear record of support by previous Republican administrations, and there would surely have been enough votes for fairly rapid ratification if the president could have counted on the total or nearly total support of his own party—if, in short, he had truly formed a government, with a legislative majority that took the responsibility for governing.

Treaties may indeed present special cases, and I do not argue here for any change in the two-thirds requirement. But our inability to form a government able to ratify SALT II is replicated regularly over the whole range of legislation required to carry out any president's overall program, foreign and domestic. Although the enactment of legislation takes only a simple majority of both houses, that majority is very difficult to achieve. Any part of the president's legislative program may be defeated or amended into an entirely different meas-

ure, so that the legislative record of any presidency may bear little resemblance
to the overall program the president wanted to carry out. Energy and the budget
are two critical examples. Indeed, SALT II itself could have been presented for
approval by a simple majority of each house under existing arms control legislation, but the administration deemed this task even more difficult than achieving a two-thirds vote in the Senate. This difficulty is of course compounded
when the president's party does not even hold the majority of the seats in both
houses, as from 1946 to 1948, from 1954 to 1960, and from 1968 to 1976—or
almost half the duration of the seven administrations between 1946 and 1980.

In such a case the Constitution does not require or even permit the holding
of a new election, in which those who oppose the president can seek office to
carry out their own program. Indeed, the opponents of the various elements of
the president's program usually have a different makeup from one element to
another. They would probably be unable to get together on any overall program
of their own or to obtain the congressional votes to carry it out. As a result
the stalemate continues, and because we do not form a government, we have
no overall program at all. We cannot fairly hold the president accountable for
the success or failure of his program, because he lacks the constitutional power
to put that program into effect.

Compare this system with the structure of parliamentary governments. A
parliamentary government may have no written constitution, as in the United
Kingdom. Or it may have a written constitution, as in West Germany, Japan,
and Ireland, that in other respects—such as an independent judiciary and an
entrenched Bill of Rights—closely resembles our own. Although it may have a
ceremonial president or, as in Japan, an emperor, its executive consists of those
members of the legislature chosen by the elected legislative majority. The majority elects a premier or prime minister from among its number, and he or she
selects other leading members of the majority as members of the cabinet. The
majority as a whole is responsible for forming and conducting the government.
If any key part of its program is rejected by the legislature or if a vote of no
confidence is carried, the government must resign, and either a new government
must be formed out of the existing legislature, or a new legislative election must
be held. If the program *is* legislated, the public can judge the result and can
decide at the next regular election whether to reelect the majority or turn it
out. At all times the voting public knows who is in charge and whom to hold
accountable for success or failure.

Operating under a parliamentary system, Chancellor Helmut Schmidt
formed a West German government with a majority of only four, but he succeeded in carrying out his overall program. In 1979 Margaret Thatcher won a
majority of some thirty to forty in the British Parliament. She had a very radical
program, one that could make fundamental changes in the economy, social
fabric, and foreign policy of the United Kingdom. There was room for legitimate
doubt whether her overall program would achieve its objectives and, even if it
did, whether it would prove popular enough to reelect her government at the

next election. There was not the slightest doubt, however, that she would be able to legislate her entire program, including any modifications she made to meet new problems. In a parlimentary system it is the duty of each majority member of the legislature to vote for each element of the government's program, and the government possesses the means to punish members if they do not. Each member's political and electoral future is tied to the fate of the government his majority has formed. Politically speaking, he lives or dies by whether that government lives or dies.

President Carter's party had a much larger majority percentage in both houses of Congress than Chancellor Schmidt or Prime Minister Thatcher had. But this comfortable majority did not even begin to ensure that he or any other president could rely on that majority to vote for each element of his program. No member of that majority had the constitutional duty or the practical political need to do so. Neither the president nor the leaders of the legislative majority had the means to punish him if he did not. In the famous phrase of Joe Jacobs, the fight manager, "it's every man for theirself."

Let me cite one example. In the British House of Commons, just as in our own House, some of the majority leaders are called whips. In the Commons the whips do just what their title implies. If the government cares about the pending vote, they "whip" the fellow members of the majority into compliance, under pain of party discipline if a member disobeys. On the most important votes, the leaders invoke what is called a three-line whip, which must be obeyed on pain of resignation or expulsion from the party.

In our House a Democratic majority whip can himself feel free to leave his Democratic president and the rest of the House Democratic leadership on a crucial vote if he believes it important to his constituency and his conscience to vote the other way. When he does so, he is not expected or required to resign his leadership post; indeed he is back a few hours later whipping his fellow members of the majority to vote with the president and the leadership on some other issue. All other members are equally free to vote against the president and the leadership when they feel it important to do so. The president and the leaders have a few sticks and carrots they can use to punish or reward, but nothing even approaching the power that a British government or a German government can wield against any errant member of the majority.

I am hardly the first to notice this fault. As Judge Carl McGowan has reminded us, that "young and rising academic star in the field of political science, Woodrow Wilson—happily unaware of what the future held for him in terms of successive domination of, and defeat by, the Congress—despaired in the late 19th century of the weakness of the Executive Branch vis-à-vis the Legislative, so much so that he concluded that a coalescence of the two in the style of English parliamentary government was the only hope."

As Wilson put it, [in his famous book *Congressional Government*,] "power and strict accountability for its use are the essential constituents of good Government." Our separation of executive and legislative power fractions power and prevents accountability.

In drawing this comparison, I am not blind to the proven weaknesses of parliamentary government or to the virtues that our forefathers saw in separating the executive from the legislature. In particular, the parliamentary system lacks the ability of a separate and vigilant legislature to investigate and curb the abuse of power by an arbitrary or corrupt executive. Our own recent history has underscored this virtue of separating these two branches.

Moreover, our division of executive from legislative responsibility also means that a great many more voters are represented in positions of power, rather than as mere members of a "loyal opposition." If I am a Democrat in a Republican district, my vote in the presidential election may still give me a proportional effect. If my party elects a president, I do not feel—as almost half the voters in a parliamentary constituency like Oxford must feel—wholly unrepresented. One result of this division is a sort of permanent centrism. While this means that no extreme or Thatcher-like program can be legislated, it also means fewer wild swings in statutory policy.

This is also a virtue of the constitutional division of responsibility. It is perhaps what John Adams had in mind when, at the end of his life, he wrote to his old friend and adversary Thomas Jefferson that "checks and ballances, Jefferson, . . . are our only Security, for the progress of Mind, as well as the Security of Body."

These virtues of separation are not without their costs. I believe that the costs have been mounting in the past half-century and that it is time to examine whether we can reduce the costs of separation without losing its virtues.

During this century other nations have adopted written constitutions, sometimes with our help, that blend the virtues of our system with those of the parliamentary system. The Irish constitution contains a replica of our Bill of Rights, an independent Supreme Court that can declare acts of the government unconstitutional, a figurehead president, and a parliamentary system. The postwar German and Japanese constitutions, which we helped to draft, are essentially the same. Although the Gaullist French constitution contains a Bill of Rights somewhat weaker than ours, it provides for a strong president who can dismiss the legislature and call for new elections. But it also retains the parliamentary system and its blend of executive and legislative power achieved by forming a government out of the elected legislative majority. The president, however, appoints the premier or first minister.

THE NEED TO GOVERN
MORE EFFECTIVELY

We are not about to revise our own Constitution so as to incorporate a true parliamentary system. We do need to find a way, however, of coming closer to the parliamentary concept of forming a government under which the elected majority is able to carry out an overall program and is held accountable for its success or failure.

For several reasons it is far more important in the 1980s than it was in 1940, 1900, or 1800 for our government to have the ability to formulate and carry out an overall program.

1. The first reason is that government is now constantly required to make a different kind of choice than was common in the past, a kind for which it is difficult to obtain a broad consensus. That kind of choice, which may be called allocative, has become the fundamental challenge to government today. As a newspaper article put it:

> The domestic programs of the last two decades are no longer seen as broad campaigns to curb pollution or end poverty or improve health care. As these programs have filtered down through an expanding network of regulation, they single out winners and losers. The losers may be workers who blame a lost promotion on equal employment programs; a chemical plant fighting a tough pollution control order; a contractor who bids unsuccessfully for a government contract, or a gas station owner who wants a larger fuel allotment.

This is a way of recognizing that, in giving government great responsibilities, we have forced a series of choices among those responsibilities.

During the second half of this century, our government has adopted a wide variety of national goals. Many of these goals—checking inflation, spurring economic growth, reducing unemployment, protecting our national security, ensuring equal opportunity, increasing social security, cleaning up the environment, improving energy efficiency—conflict with one another, and all of them compete for the same resources. There may have been a time when we could simultaneously pursue all these goals to the utmost. Even in a country as rich as this one, however, that time is now past. One of the central tasks of modern government is to make wise balancing choices among courses of action that pursue one or more of our many conflicting and competing objectives.

Furthermore, as new economic or social problems are recognized, a responsible government must *adjust* its priorities. In formulating energy policy, the need to accept realistic oil prices had to be balanced against the immediate effect of dramatic price increases on consumers and affected industries and on the overall rate of inflation. To cope with the energy crisis, earlier objectives of policy had to be accommodated along the way. Reconciling one goal with another is a continuous process. A critical regulatory goal of 1965 (automobile safety) had to be reconciled with an equally critical regulatory goal of 1970 (clean air) long before the safety goal had been achieved, just as both those critical goals had to be reconciled with 1975's key goal (closing the energy gap) long before either automobile safety or clean air had lost its importance. Reconciliation was needed because many automobile safety regulations increased vehicle size and weight and therefore increased gasoline consumption and undesirable emission and also because auto emission control devices tend to increase gasoline consumption. Moreover, throughout this fifteen-year period, we had to reconcile all three goals with another critical national objective—wage and price stability—when in pursuit of these other goals we made vehicles more costly to purchase and to operate.

In 1980 we found our automobile industry at a serious competitive disadvantage vis-à-vis Japanese and European imports, making it necessary to limit those regulatory burdens that aggravated the extent of the disadvantage. A responsible government must be able to adapt its programs to achieve the best balance among its conflicting goals as each new development arises.

For balancing choices like these, a kind of political triage, it is almost impossible to achieve a broad consensus. Every group will be against some part of the balance. If the losers on each item are given a veto on that part of the balance, a sensible balance cannot be struck.

2. The second reason is that we live in an increasingly interdependent world. What happens in distant places is now just as consequential for our security and our economy as what happens in Seattle or Miami. No one today would use the term "Afghanistanism," as the opposition benches did in the British Parliament a century ago, to deride the government's preoccupation with a war in that distant land. No one would say today, as President Wilson said in 1914, that general European war could not affect us and is no concern of ours. We are now an integral part of a closely interconnected world economic and political system. We have to respond as quickly and decisively to what happens abroad as to what happens within the portion of this world system that is governed under our Constitution.

New problems requiring new adjustments come up even more frequently over the foreign horizon than over the domestic one. Consider the rapid succession of events and crises after President Carter took up the relay baton for his leg of the SALT II negotiations in 1977: the signing of the Egyptian-Israeli peace treaty over Soviet and Arab opposition, the Soviet-Cuban assistance to guerrilla forces in Africa and the Arabian peninsula, the recognition of the People's Republic of China, the final agreement on the SALT II terms and the signing of the treaty in Vienna, the revolution in Iran and the seizure of our hostages, the military coup in Korea, the Soviet-supported Vietnamese invasion of Kampuchea, our growing dependence on foreign oil from politically undependable sources, the affair of the Soviet brigade in Cuba, the polarization of rightist and leftist elements in Central America, and finally the Soviet invasion of Afghanistan and the added threat it posed to the states of Southwest Asia and to the vital oil supplies of Europe, Japan, and the United States.

Each of these portentous events required a prompt reaction and response from our government, including in many cases a decision about how it would affect our position on the SALT II treaty. The government must be able to adapt its overall program to deal with each such event as it arises, and it must be able to execute the adapted program with reasonable dispatch. Many of these adaptations—such as changes in the levels and direction of military and economic assistance—require joint action by the president and the Congress, something that is far from automatic under our system. When Congress does act, it is prone to impose statutory conditions or prohibitions that fetter the president's discretion to negotiate an appropriate assistance package or to adapt it to fit even later developments. The congressional bans on military assistance to Turkey, any form of assistance to the contending forces in Angola, and any aid to Argentina if it did not meet our human rights criteria are typical examples.

Indeed, the doubt that Congress will approve a presidential foreign policy initiative has seriously compromised our ability to make binding agreements with nations that form a government. Given the fate of SALT II and lesser treaties and the frequent congressional vetoes of other foreign policy actions, other nations now realize that our executive branch commitments are not as binding as theirs, that Congress may block any agreement at all, and that at the very least they must hold something back for a subsequent round of bargaining with the Congress.

3. The third reason is the change in Congress and its relations with the executive. When the Federalist and Democratic Republican parties held power, a Hamilton or a Gallatin would serve in the cabinet but continue to lead rather than report to their party colleagues in the houses of Congress. Even when the locus of congressional leadership shifted from the cabinet to the leaders of Congress itself in the early nineteenth century, it was a congressional leadership capable of collaboration with the executive. This was true until very recently. The Johnson-Rayburn collaboration with Eisenhower a generation ago is an instructive example. But now Congress itself has changed.

There have been well-intended democratic reforms of Congress and an enormous growth of the professional legislative staff. The former ability of the president to sit down with ten or fiteen leaders in each house and agree on a program those leaders could carry through Congress has virtually disappeared. The committee chairmen and the leaders no longer have the instruments of power that once enabled them to lead. A Lyndon Johnson would have a much harder time getting his way as majority leader today than when he did hold and pull those strings of power in the 1950s. When Senator Mike Mansfield became majority leader in 1961, he changed the practice of awarding committee chairmanships on the basis of seniority. He declared that all senators are created equal. He gave every Democratic senator a major committee assignment and then a subcommittee chairmanship, adding to the sharing of power by reducing the leadership's control.

In the House the seniority system was scrapped. Now the House majority caucus—not the leadership—picks the committee chairmen and the subcommittee chairmen as well. The House parliamentarian has lost the critical power to refer bills to a single committee selected by the Speaker. Now bills like the energy bills go to several committees, which then report conflicting versions to the floor. Now markup sessions take place in public; indeed, even the House-Senate joint conference committees, at which differing versions of the same measure are reconciled, must meet and barter in public.

The conference committees on the Synthetic Fuels Corporation and the Energy Mobilization Board, for example, were so big and their procedures so cumbersome that they took six months to reach agreement, and then the agreement on the board was rejected by the House. All this means that there are no longer a few leaders with power who *can* collaborate with the president. Power is further diffused by the growth of legislative staffs, sometimes making it difficult for the members even to collaborate with one another. From 1975 to 1980 the Senate alone hired 700 additional staff members, an average of seven per member.

Party discipline and the political party itself have also declined. Presidential candidates are no longer selected as Adlai Stevenson was, by the leaders or bosses of their party. Who are the party leaders today? There are no such people. The party is no longer the instrument that selects the candidate. Indeed, the party today, as a practical matter, is no more than a neutral open forum that holds the primary or caucus in which candidates for president and for Congress may compete for favor and be elected. The party does not dispense most of the money needed for campaigning, as European and Japanese parties do. The candidates raise most of their own money. To the extent that money influences legislative votes, it comes not from a party with a balanced program but from a variety of single-interest groups.

We now have a great many diverse and highly organized interest groups—not just broad-based agriculture, labor, business, and ethnic groups interested in a wide variety of issues affecting their members. We now have single-issue groups—environmental, consumer, abortion, right to life, pro- and anti-SALT, pro- and anti-nuclear—that stand ready to lobby for their single issue and to reward or punish legislators, both in cash and at the ballot box, according to how they respond on the single issue that is the group's raison d'être. On many specific foreign policy issues involving particular countries, exceptionally strong voting blocs in this wonderful melting pot of a nation exert a great deal of influence on individual senators and representatives.

WHY THE STRUCTURE
SOMETIMES WORKS

It is useful to compare this modern failure of our governmental structure with its earlier classic successes. There can be no structural fault, it might be said, so long as Franklin Roosevelt could put through an entire antidepression program in 100 days or Lyndon Johnson could enact a broad program for social justice three decades later. These infrequent exceptions, however, confirm the general rule of stalemate.

If we look closely, we will find that in this century the system has succeeded only on the rare occasions when an unusual event has brought us together and created substantial consensus throughout the country on the need for a whole new program. Roosevelt had such a consensus in the early days of the New Deal and from Pearl Harbor to the end of World War II. But we tend to forget that in 1937 his court-packing plan was justifiably rejected by Congress—a good point for those who favor complete separation of the executive from the legislature—and that as late as August 1941, when Roosevelt called on Congress to pass a renewal of the Selective Service Act, passage was gained by a single vote in the House. Johnson had such a consensus for both his domestic and his Vietnam initiatives during the first three years after the shock of John Kennedy's assassination brought us together, but it was gone by 1968. Carter had it for his responses to the events in Iran and Afghanistan and to the belated realization of our need for greater energy self-sufficiency, but he did not hold it for long. Yet the consensus on Afghanistan was marred by the long congressional delay in appropriating the small amounts needed to register nineteen- and twenty-year-olds under the Selective Service Act—a delay that at least blurred the intended effect of this signal to the world of our determination to oppose further Soviet aggression.

When the great crisis and the resulting large consensus are not there—when the country is divided somewhere between 55–45 and 45–55 on each of a wide set of issues and the makeup of the majority is different on every issue—it has not been possible for any modern president to form a government that could legislate and carry out his overall program.

Yet modern government has to respond promptly to a wide range of new challenges. Its responses cannot be limited to those for which there is a large consensus induced by some great crisis. Modern government also has to work in every presidency, not just in one presidency out of four, when a Wilson, a Roosevelt, or a Johnson comes along. It also has to work for the president's full time in office, as it did not even for Wilson and Johnson. When they needed congressional support for the most important issue of their presidencies, they could not get it.

When the president gets only half a loaf of his overall program, it is not necessarily better than none, because it may lack the essential quality of balance. Half a loaf leaves both the president and the public in the worst of all possible worlds. The public—and the press—still expect the president to govern. But the president cannot achieve his overall program, and the public cannot fairly blame the president because he does not have the power to legislate and execute his program. Nor can the public fairly blame the individual members of Congress, because the Constitution allows them to disclaim any responsibility for forming a government and hence any accountability for its failures.

Of course the presidency always has been and will continue to be what Theodore Roosevelt called "a bully pulpit"—not a place from which to bully in the sense of intimidating the Congress and the public, but in the idiom of Roosevelt's day a marvelous place from which to exhort and lift up Congress and the public. All presidents have used the bully pulpit in this way, and this is one reason why the American people continue to revere the office and almost always revere its incumbent. Television has probably amplified the power of the bully pulpit, but it has also shortened the time span of power; few television performers can hold their audiences for four consecutive years. In any event, a bully pulpit, though a glorious thing to have and to employ, is not a government, and it has not been enough to enable any postwar president to form a government for his entire term.

Finally, the myth persists that the existing system can be made to work satisfactorily if only the president will take the trouble to consult closely with the Congress. During the period between 1947 and 1965 there were indeed remarkable cases, at least in foreign policy, where such consultation worked to great effect, even across party lines. The relations between Senator Arthur Vandenberg and Secretaries George Marshall and Dean Acheson and between Senator Walter George and Secretary of State John Foster Dulles come readily to mind. But these examples were in an era of strong leadership within the Congress and of unusual national consensus on the overall objectives of foreign policy and the measures needed to carry them out.

Even when these elements have not been present, every president has indeed tried to work with the majority in Congress, and the majority in every Congress has tried to work with the president. When there was a large consensus in response to the crises in Afghanistan and Iran, a notable achievement was a daily private briefing of congressional leaders by the secretary of state and weekly private briefings with all Senate and House members who wanted to attend—a step that helped to keep that consensus in being. Another achievement of recent times is the development of the congressional budget process, exemplified by the cooperation between the congressional leadership and the president in framing the 1981 budget.

The jury is still out, however, on how long such a large consensus will hold. Except on the rare issues where there is such a consensus, the structural problems usually prove too difficult to overcome. In each administration it becomes more difficult to make the present system work effectively on the range of issues, both domestic and foreign, that the United States must now manage even though there is no large consensus.

CHANGING THE STRUCTURE THROUGH CONSTITUTIONAL AMENDMENT

If we decide we want the ability to form a government, the only way to get it is to amend the Constitution. That, of course, is extremely difficult. Since 1793, when the Bill of Rights was added, we have amended the Constitution only sixteen times. Some of these amendments were structural, such as the direct election of senators, votes for women and eighteen-year-olds, the two-term limit for presidents, and the selection of a successor vice president. But none has touched the basic separation of executive and legislative powers.

The most we can hope for is a set of modest changes that would make our structure work somewhat more in the manner of a parliamentary system, with somewhat less separation between the executive and the legislature than now exists. There are several proposals. Here are some of the more interesting ideas.

1. We now vote for a presidential candidate and a vice-presidential candidate as an inseparable team. We could require that in presidential election years voters in each congressional district vote for a trio of candidates, as a team, for president, vice president, and member of Congress. This would tie the political fortunes of the party's presidential and congressional candidates to one another and give them some incentive for sticking together after they are elected. Such a proposal could be combined with a four-year term for members of the House of Representatives. This would tie the presidential and congressional candidates even more closely and has the added virtue of giving members greater protection against the pressures of single-issue political groups. This combination was the brainchild of Representative Jonathan Bingham of New York.

In our bicameral legislature the logic of the Bingham proposal would suggest that the inseparable trio of candidates for president, vice president, and member of Congress be expanded to a quintet including the two senators, who would also have the same four-year term. But no one has challenged the gods of the Olympian Senate by advancing such a proposal.

2. Another idea is to permit or require the president to select 50 percent of his cabinet from among the members of his party in the Senate and the House, who would retain their seats while serving in the cabinet. This would be only a minor infringement on the constitutional principle of separation of powers, but it would require a change in Article I, Section 6, which provides that "no person holding any office under the United States shall be a member of either house during his continuance in office." It would tend to increase the intimacy between the executive and the legislature and add to their sense of collective responsibility. The 50 percent test would leave the president adequate room to bring other qualified persons into his cabinet, even though they did not hold elective office.

3. A third intriguing suggestion is to provide the president with the power, to be exercised not more than once in his term, to dissolve Congress and call for new congressional elections. This is the power now vested in the president under the French constitution. It would provide the opportunity that does not now exist to break an executive-legislative impasse and to let the public decide whether it wishes to elect senators and representatives who *will* legislate the president's overall program.

For obvious reasons, the president would invoke such a power only as a last resort, but his ability to do so could have a powerful influence on congressional responses to his initiatives. This would of course be a radical and highly controversial proposal, and it raises a number of technical difficulties relating to the timing and conduct of the new election, the staggering of senatorial terms, and similar matters. But it would significantly enhance the president's power to form a government.

The experience of presidents—such as Nixon in 1970—who sought to use the midterm election as a referendum on their programs suggests that any such dissolution and new election would be as likely to continue the impasse as to break it. Perhaps any exercise of the power to dissolve Congress should automatically require a new presidential election as well. Even then, the American public might be perverse enough to reelect all the incumbents to office.

4. Another variant on the same idea is that in addition to empowering the president to call for new congressional elections, we might empower a majority or two-thirds of both houses to call for new presidential elections. This variant was scathingly attacked in a series of conversations between Professor Charles Black of the Yale Law School and Representative Bob Eckhardt of Texas, published in 1975, because they think that such a measure would vitally diminish the president's capacity to lead.

5. Another proposal that deserves consideration is a single six-year presidential term, an idea with many supporters, among them Presidents Eisenhower, Johnson, and Carter, to say nothing of a great many political scientists. (The French constitution provides a seven-year term for the president but permits reelection.) Of course, presidents would like to be elected and then forget about politics and get to the high ground of saving the world. But if first-term presidents did not have the leverage of reelection, we might institutionalize for every presidency the lame duck impotence we now see when a president is not running for reelection.

6. It may be that one combination of elements of the third, fourth, and fifth proposals would be worthy of further study. It would be roughly as follows:

• The president, vice president, senators, and representatives would all be elected for simultaneous six-year terms.

• On one occasion each term the president could dissolve Congress and call for new congressional elections for the remainder of the term. If he did so, Congress, by majority vote of both houses within thirty days of his action, could call for simultaneous new elections for president and vice president for the remainder of the term.

• All state primaries and state conventions for any required midterm elections would be held 60 days after the first call for new elections. Any required national presidential nominating conventions would be held 30 days later. The national elections would be held 60 days after the state primary elections and state conventions. The entire cycle would take 120 days. The dissolved Congress would be free to remain in session for part or all of this period.

• Presidents would be allowed to serve only one full six-year term. If a midterm presidential election were called, the incumbent would be eligible to run and, if reelected, to serve the balance of his six-year term.

Limiting each president to one six-year term would enhance the objectivity and public acceptance of the measures he urges in the national interest. He would not be regarded as a lame duck, because of his continuing power to dissolve Congress. Our capacity to form a government would be enhanced if the president could break an impasse by calling for a new congressional election and by the power of Congress to respond by calling for a new presidential election.

Six-year terms for senators and representatives would diminish the power of single-interest groups to veto balanced programs for governing. Because any midterm elections would have to be held promptly, a single national primary, a shorter campaign cycle, and public financing of congressional campaigns— three reforms with independent virtues of their own—would become a necessity for the midterm election. Once tried in a midterm election, they might well be adopted for regular elections as well.

7. One final proposal may be mentioned. It would be possible, through constitutional amendment, to revise the legislative process in the following way. Congress would first enact broad mandates, declaring general policies and directions and leaving the precise allocative choices, within a congressionally approved budget, to the president. All agencies would be responsible to the president. By dividing tasks among them and making the difficult choices of fulfilling some congressional directions at the expense of others, the president would fill in the exact choices, the allocative decisions. Then any presidential action would be returned to Congress, where it would await a two-house legislative veto. If not so vetoed within a specified period, the action would become law.

If the legislative veto could be overturned by a presidential veto—subject in turn to a two-thirds override—this proposal would go a long way toward enhancing the president's ability to form a government. In any event, it should enable the elected president to carry out the program he ran on, subject to congressional oversight, and end the stalemate over whether to legislate the president's program in the first instance. It would let Congress and the president each do what they have shown they now do best.

Such a resequencing, of course, would turn the present process on its head. But it would bring much closer to reality the persisting myth that it is up to the president to govern—something he now lacks the constitutional power to do.

CONCLUSION

How can these proposals be evaluated? How can better proposals be devised? Above all, how can the public be educated to understand the costs of the present separation between our executive and legislative branches, to weigh those costs against the benefits, and to decide whether a change is needed?

One obvious possibility is the widely feared constitutional convention—something for which the Constitution itself provides—to be called by Congress itself or two-thirds of the states. Jefferson expected one to occur every generation. Conventions are commonplace to revise state constitutions. But Congress has never even legislated the applicable rules for electing and conducting a national constitutional convention, even though more than thirty states have called for one to adopt an amendment limiting federal taxes and expenditures. Because of the concern generated by this proposal, any idea of a national constitutional convention on the separation of powers is probably a nonstarter.

A more practicable first step would be the appointment of a bipartisan presidential commission to analyze the issues, compare how other constitutions work, hold public hearings, and make a full report. The commission could include ranking members of the House and Senate, or Congress could establish a parallel joint commission of its own.

The point of this article is not to persuade the reader of the virtue of any particular amendment. I am far from persuaded myself. But I am convinced of these propositions:

- We need to do better than we have in forming a government for this country, and the need is becoming more acute.
- The structure of our Constitution prevents us from doing significantly better.
- It is time to start thinking and debating about whether and how to correct this structural fault.

Chapter 2

Federalism

The United States government utilizes a "federal" form to secure certain political and economic objectives. This chapter identifies both the traditional and modern goals of American federalism from the writings of important theorists who have examined general and specific problems in national-state relationships. The validity of federalism is also analyzed.

Constitutional Background: National v. State Power

No subject attracted greater attention or was more carefully analyzed at the time of the framing of the Constitution than federalism. *The Federalist* devoted a great deal of space to proving the advantages of a federal form of government relative to a confederacy, since the Constitution was going to take some of the power traditionally within the jurisdiction of state governments and give it to a newly constituted national government.

The victory of the nationalists at the Constitutional Convention of 1787, which resulted in sovereign states giving up a significant portion of their authority to a new national government, is remarkable by any standard of measurement. Today, when the creation of the Union is largely taken for granted, it is difficult to appreciate the environment of the Revolutionary period, a time when the states wanted at all costs to protect their newly won freedom from an oppressive British government. The constitution of 1787 was accepted as a matter of necessity as much as desire.

It was against the background of the Articles of Confederation that Hamilton wrote in *The Federalist* about the advantages of the new "federal" system that would be created by the Constitution. The Articles of Confederation had been submitted to the states in 1777 and was finally ratified by all of the states in 1781, Maryland being the only holdout after 1779. The "League of Friendship" that had been created among the states by the Articles had proved inadequate to meeting even the minimum needs of union. The government of the Articles of Confederation had many weaknesses, for it was essentially a league of sovereign states, joined together more in accordance with principles of international agreement than in accordance with the rules of nation states. Most of the provisions of the Articles of Confederation concerned the foreign relations of the new government, and matters of national defense and security. For this purpose a minimum number of powers were granted to the national government, which, however, had no executive or judicial authority and was therefore incapable of independent enforcement. National actions were dependent upon the states for enforcement, and under Article Two "each state retains its sovereignty, freedom and independence, and every power, jurisdiction and right, which is not by this confederation expressly delegated to the United States, in Congress assembled." The paucity of authority delegated to the central government under the Articles left the sovereignty of the states intact. And the national government was totally dependent upon the states as agents of enforcement of what little authority it could exercise. The government of the Articles of Confederation then, without an executive or judicial branch, and without such crucial authority as the power to tax and regulate commerce, required a drastic overhaul if it was to become a national government in fact as well as in name.

In the following selections from *The Federalist* Alexander Hamilton argues the advantages of the new federal Constitution, and at the same time attempts to alleviate the fears of his opponents that the new government would intrude upon and possibly eventually destroy the sovereignty of the states. The national government, he wrote, must be able to act directly upon the citizens of the states to regulate the common concerns of the nation. He found the system of the Articles of Confederation too weak, allowing state evasion of national power. Augmenting the authority of the national government would not destroy state sovereignty, because of the inherent strength of the individual states (which at the time Hamilton wrote were singly and collectively far more powerful than any proposed national government). Moreover, there would be no incentives for ambitious politicians to look to the states to realize their goals, for the scope of national power was sufficient to occupy temptations for political aggrandizement.

6

Alexander Hamilton
FEDERALIST 16

The . . . death of the confederacy . . . is what we now seem to be on the point of experiencing, if the federal system be not speedily renovated in a more substantial form. It is not probable, considering the genius of this country, that the complying states would often be inclined to support the authority of the union, by engaging in a war against the non-complying states. They would always be more ready to pursue the milder course of putting themselves upon an equal footing with the delinquent members, by an imitation of their example. And the guilt of all would thus become the security of all. Our past experience has exhibited the operation of this spirit in its full light. There would, in fact, be an insuperable difficulty in ascertaining when force would with propriety be employed. In the article of pecuniary contribution, which would be the most usual source of delinquency, it would often be impossible to decide whether it had proceeded from disinclination, or inability. The pretense of the latter would always be at hand. And the case must be very flagrant in which its fallacy could be detected with sufficient certainty to justify the harsh expedient of compulsion. It is easy to see that this problem alone, as often as it should occur, would open a wide field to the majority that happened to prevail in the national council, for the exercise of factious views, of partiality, and of oppression.

It seems to require no pains to prove that the states ought not to prefer a national constitution, which could only be kept in motion by the instrumentality of a large army, continually on foot to execute the ordinary requisitions or decrees of the government. And yet this is the plain alternative involved by those who wish to deny it the power of extending its operations to individuals. Such a scheme, if practicable at all, would instantly degenerate into a military despotism; but it will be found in every light impracticable. The resources of the union would not be equal to the maintenance of any army considerable enough to confine the larger states within the limits of their duty; nor would the means ever be furnished of forming such an army in the first instance. Whoever considers the populousness and strength of several of these states singly at the present juncture, and looks forward to what they will become, even at the distance of half a century, will at once dismiss as idle and visionary any scheme which aims at regulating their movements by laws, to operate upon them in their collective capacities, and to be executed by a coercion applicable to them in the same capacities. A project of this kind is little less romantic than the monster-taming spirit attributed to the fabulous heroes and demigods of antiquity. . . .

The result of these observations to an intelligent mind must clearly be this, that if it be possible at any rate to construct a federal government capable of regulating the common concerns, and preserving the general tranquillity, it must be founded, as to the objects committed to its case, upon the reverse of the principle contended for by the opponents of the proposed constitution [i.e., a confederacy]. It must carry its agency to the persons of the citizens. It must stand in need of no intermediate legislations; but must itself be empowered to employ the arm of the ordinary magistrate to execute its own resolutions. The majesty of the national authority must be manifested through the medium of the courts of justice. The government of the union, like that of each state, must be able to address itself immediately to the hopes and fears of individuals; and to attract to its support, those passions which have the strongest influence upon the human heart. It must, in short, possess all the means, and have a right to resort to all the methods, of executing the powers with which it is entrusted, that are possessed and exercised by the governments of the particular states.

To this reasoning it may perhaps be objected, that if any state should be disaffected to the authority of the union, it could at any time obstruct the execution of its laws, and bring the matter to the same issue of force, with the necessity of which the opposite scheme is reproached.

The plausibility of this objection will vanish the moment we advert to the essential difference between a mere NONCOMPLIANCE and a DIRECT and ACTIVE RESISTANCE. If the interposition of the state legislatures be necessary to give effect to a measure of the union [as in a confederacy], they have only NOT TO ACT, OR TO ACT EVASIVELY, and the measure is defeated. This neglect of duty may be disguised under affected but unsubstantial provisions so as not to appear, and of course not to excite any alarm in the people for the safety of the constitution. The state leaders may even make a merit of their surreptitious invasions of it, on the ground of some temporary convenience, exemption, or advantage.

But if the execution of the laws of the national government should not require the intervention of the state legislatures; if they were to pass into immediate operation upon the citizens themselves, the particular governments could not interrupt their progress without an open and violent exertion of an unconstitutional power. No omission, nor evasions, would answer the end. They would be obliged to act, and in such a manner, as would leave no doubt that they had encroached on the national rights. An experiment of this nature would always be hazardous in the face of a constitution in any degree competent to its own defense, and of a people enlightened enough to distinguish between a legal exercise and an illegal usurpation of authority. The success of it would require not merely a factious majority in the legislature, but the concurrence of the courts of justice, and of the body of the people. . . .

FEDERALIST 17

An objection, of a nature different from that which has been stated and answered in my last address, may, perhaps, be urged against the principle of legislation for the individual citizens of America. It may be said, that it would tend to render the government of the union too powerful, and to enable it to absorb those residuary authorities, which it might be judged proper to leave with the states for local purposes. Allowing the utmost latitude to the love of power, which any reasonable man can require, I confess I am at a loss to discover what temptation the persons entrusted with the administration of the general government could ever feel to divest the states of the authorities of that description. The regulation of the mere domestic police of a state, appears to me to hold out slender allurements to ambition. Commerce, finance, negotiation, and war, seem to comprehend all the objects which have charms for minds governed by that passion; and all the powers necessary to those objects, ought, in the first instance, to be lodged in the national depository. The administration of private justice between the citizens of the same state; the supervision of agriculture, and of other concerns of a similar nature; all those things, in short, which are proper to be provided for by local legislation, can never be desirable cares of a general jurisdiction. It is therefore improbable, that there should exist a disposition in the federal councils, to usurp the powers with which they are connected; because the attempt to exercise them would be as troublesome as it would be nugatory; and the possession of them, for that reason, would contribute nothing to the dignity, to the importance, or to the splendor, of the national government.

But let it be admitted, for argument's sake, that mere wantonness, and lust of domination, would be sufficient to beget that disposition; still, it may be safely affirmed, that the sense of the constituent body of the national representatives, or in other words, of the people of the several states, would control the indulgence of so extravagant an appetite. It will always be far more easy for the state governments to encroach upon the national authorities, than for the national government to encroach upon the state authorities. The proof of this proposition turns upon the greater degree of influence which the state governments, if they administer their affairs with uprightness and prudence, will generally possess over the people; a circumstance which at the same time teaches us, that there is an inherent and intrinsic weakness in all federal constitutions; and that too much pain cannot be taken in their organization, to give them all the force which is compatible with the principles of liberty.

The superiority of influence in favor of the particular governments, would result partly from the diffusive construction of the national government; but chiefly from the nature of the objects to which the attention of the state administrations would be directed.

It is a known fact in human nature, that its affections are commonly weak in proportion to the distance of diffusiveness of the object. Upon the same principle that a man is more attached to his family than to his neighborhood, to his neighborhood than to the community at large, the people of each state would be apt to feel a stronger bias towards their local governments, than towards the government of the union, unless the force of that principle should be destroyed by a much better administration of the latter.

This strong propensity of the human heart, would find powerful auxiliaries in the objects of state regulation.

The variety of more minute interests, which will necessarily fall under the superintendence of the local adminstrations, and which will form so many rivulets of influence, running through every part of the society, cannot be particularized, without involving a detail too tedious and uninteresting to compensate for the instruction it might afford.

There is one transcendent advantage belonging to the province of the state governments, which alone suffices to place the matter in a clear and satisfactory light—I mean the ordinary administration of criminal and civil justice. This, of all others, is the most powerful, most universal and most attractive source of popular obedience and attachment. It is this, which, being the immediate and visible guardian of life and property; having its benefits and its terrors in constant activity before the public eye; regulating all those personal interests, and familiar concerns, to which the sensibility of individuals is more immediately awake; contributes, more than any other circumstance, to impress upon the minds of the people affection, esteem, and reverence towards the government. This great cement of society, which will diffuse itself almost wholly through the channels of the particular governments, independent of all other causes of influence, would insure them so decided an empire over their respective citizens, as to render them at all times a complete counterpoise, and not infrequently dangerous rivals to the power of the union.

❖❖   In *Federalist 39*, James Madison stated that the new Constitution was both federal and national. He attempted to answer arguments that the Constitution destroyed the confederacy of sovereign states and replaced it with a national government. In answering this argument Madison used the term "federal" as it was used by the objectors to the Constitution he was attempting to answer. They essentially used "federal" and "confederacy" interchangeably, each term referring to a system requiring agreement among the states before certain actions could be taken. Because agreement was required among the states for ratification, for example, Madison referred to the establishment of the Constitution as a *federal* and not a national act. Madison suggested that the character of the House of Representatives, which derives its powers from the people, was national rather than federal. Conversely, the Senate, representing the states equally, was federal, not national. With regard to the powers of the national government, Madison claimed that in operation they are national because they allow the national government to act directly upon the people, but in extent they are federal because they are limited, the states having agreed to delegate only a certain number of powers to the national government. A truly national government would not be limited in the scope of its powers.

7

James Madison
FEDERALIST 39

The last paper having concluded the observations which were meant to introduce a candid survey of the plan of government reported by the convention, we now proceed to the execution of that part of our undertaking.

The first question that offers itself is whether the general form and aspect of the government be strictly republican. It is evident that no other form would be reconcilable with the genius of the people of America; with the fundamental principles of the Revolution; or with that honorable determination which animates every votary of freedom to rest all our political experiments on the capacity of mankind for self-government. If the plan of the convention, therefore, be found to depart from the republican character, its advocates must abandon it as no longer defensible.

What, then, are the distinctive characters of the republican form? Were an answer to this question to be sought, not by recurring to principles but in the application of the term by political writers to the constitutions of different States, no satisfactory one would ever be found. Holland, in which no particle of the supreme authority is derived from the people, has passed almost universally under the denomination of a republic. The same title has been bestowed on Venice, where absolute power over the great body of the people is exercised in the most absolute manner by a small body of hereditary nobles. Poland, which is a mixture of aristocracy and of monarchy in their worst forms, has been dignified with the same appellation. The government of England, which has one republican branch only, combined with an hereditary aristocracy and monarchy, has with equal impropriety been frequently placed on the list of republics. These examples, which are nearly as dissimilar to each other as to a genuine republic, show the extreme inaccuracy with which the term has been used in political disquisitions.

If we resort for a criterion to the different principles on which different forms of government are established, we may define a republic to be, or at least may bestow that name on, a government which derives all its powers directly or indirectly from the great body of the people, and is administered by persons holding their offices during pleasure for a limited period, or during good behavior. It is *essential* to such a government that it be derived from the great body of the society, not from an inconsiderable proportion or a favored class of it; otherwise a handful of tyrannical nobles, exercising their oppressions by a delegation of their powers, might aspire to the rank of republicans and claim for their government the honorable title of republic. It is *sufficient* for such a government that the persons administering it be appointed, either directly or indirectly, by the people; and that they hold their appointments by either of the tenures just specified; otherwise every government in the United States, as well as every other popular government that has been or can be well organized or well executed, would be degraded from the republican character. According to the constitution of every State in the Union, some or other of the officers of government are appointed indirectly only by the people. According to most of them, the chief magistrate himself is so appointed. And according to one, this mode of appointment is extended to one of the co-ordinate branches of the legislature. According to all the constitutions, also, the tenure of the highest offices is extended to a definite period, and in many instances, both within the legislative and executive departments, to a period of years. According to the provisions of most of the constitutions, again, as well as according to the most respectable and received opinions on the subject, the members of the judiciary department are to retain their offices by the firm tenure of good behavior.

On comparing the Constitution planned by the convention with the standard here fixed, we perceived at once that it is, in the most rigid sense, comformable to it. The House of Representatives, like that of one branch at least of all the State legislatures, is elected immediately by the great body of the people. The Senate, like the present Congress and the Senate of Maryland, derives its appointment indirectly from the people. The President is indirectly derived from the choice of the people, according to the example in most of the States. Even the judges, with all other officers of the Union, will, as in the several States, be the choice, though a remote choice, of the people themselves. The duration of the appointments is equally conformable to the republican standard and to the model of State constitutions. The House of Representatives is periodically elective, as in all the States; and for the period of two years, as in the State of South Carolina. The Senate is elective for the period of six years, which is but one year more than the period of the Senate of Maryland, and but two more than that of the Senates of New York and Virginia. The

President is to continue in office for the period of four years; as in New York and Delaware the chief magistrate is elected for three years, and in South Carolina for two years. In the other States the election is annual. In several of the States, however, no explicit provision is made for the impeachment of the chief magistrate. And in Delaware and Virginia he is not impeachable till out of office. The President of the United States is impeachable at any time during his continuance in office. The tenure by which the judges are to hold their places is, as it unquestionably ought to be, that of good behavior. The tenure of the ministerial offices generally will be a subject of legal regulation, conformable to the reason of the case and the example of the State constitutions.

Could any further proof be required of the republican complexion of this system, the most decisive one might be found in its absolute prohibition of titles of nobility, both under the federal and the State governments; and in its express guaranty of the republican form to each of the latter.

"But it was not sufficient," say the adversaries of the proposed Constitution, "for the convention to adhere to the republican form. They ought with equal care to have preserved the *federal* form, which regards the Union as a *Confederacy* of sovereign states; instead of which they have framed a *national* government, which regards the Union as a *consolidation* of the States." And it is asked by what authority this bold and radical innovation was undertaken. The handle which has been made of this objection requires that it should be examined with some precision.

Without inquiring into the accuracy of the distinction on which the objection is founded, it will be necessary to a just estimate of its force, first, to ascertain the real character of the government in question; secondly, to inquire how far the convention were authorized to propose such a government; and thirdly, how far the duty they owed to their country could supply any defect of regular authority.

First.—In order to ascertain the real character of the government, it may be considered in relation to the foundation on which it is to be established; to the sources from which its ordinary powers are to be drawn; to the operation of those powers; to the extent of them; and to the authority by which future changes in the government are to be introduced.

On examining the first relation, it appears, on one hand, that the Constitution is to be founded on the assent and ratification of the people of America, given by deputies elected for the special purpose; but, on the other, that this assent and ratification is to be given by the people, not as individuals composing one entire nation, but as composing the distinct and independent States to which they respectively belong. It is to be the assent and ratification of the several States, derived from the supreme authority in each State—the authority of the people themselves. The act, therefore, establishing the Constitution will not be a *national* but a *federal* act.

That it will be a federal and not a national act, as these terms are understood by the objectors—the act of the people, as forming so many independent

States, not as forming one aggregate nation—is obvious from this single consideration: that it is to result neither from the decision of a *majority* of the people of the Union, nor from that of a *majority* of the States. It must result from the *unanimous* assent of the several States that are parties to it, differing not otherwise from their ordinary assent than in its being expressed, not by the legislative authority, but by that of the people themselves. Were the people regarded in this transaction as forming one nation, the will of the majority of the whole people of the United States would bind the minority, in the same manner as the majority in each State must bind the minority; and the will of the majority must be determined either by a comparison of the individual votes, or by considering the will of the majority of the States as evidence of the will of a majority of the people of the United States. Neither of these rules has been adopted. Each State, in ratifying the Constitution, is considered as a sovereign body independent of all others, and only to be bound by its own voluntary act. In this relation, then, the new Constitution will, if established, be a *federal* and not a *national* constitution.

The next relation is to the sources from which the ordinary powers of government are to be derived. The House of Representatives will derive its powers from the people of America; and the people will be represented in the same proportion and on the same principle as they are in the legislature of a particular State. So far the government is *national*, not *federal*. The Senate, on the other hand, will derive its powers from the States as political and coequal societies; and these will be represented on the principle of equality in the Senate, as they now are in the existing Congress. So far the government is *federal*, not *national*. The executive power will be derived from a very compound source. The immediate election of the President is to be made by the States in their political characters. The votes allotted to them are in a compound ratio, which considers them partly as distinct and coequal societies, partly as unequal members of the same society. The eventual election, again, is to be made by that branch of the legislature which consists of the national representatives; but in this particular act they are to be thrown into the form of individual delegations from so many distinct and co-equal bodies politic. From this aspect of the government it appears to be of a mixed character, presenting at least as many *federal* as *national* features.

The difference between a federal and national government, as it relates to the *operation of the government,* is by the adversaries of the plan of the convention supposed to consist in this, that in the former the powers operate on the political bodies composing the confederacy in their political capacities; in the latter, on the individual citizens composing the nation in their individual capacities. On trying the Constitution by this criterion, it falls under the *national* not the *federal* character; though perhaps not so completely as has been understood. In several cases, and particularly in the trial of controversies to which States may be parties, they must be viewed and proceeded against in their collective and political capacities only. But the operation of the government on the people in their individual capacities, in its ordinary and most essential proceedings, will, in the sense of its opponents, on the whole, designate it, in this relation, a *national* government.

But if the government be national with regard to the *operation* of its powers, it changes its aspect again when we contemplate it in relation to the extent of its powers. The idea of a national government involves in it not only an authority over the individual citizens, but an indefinite supremacy over all persons and things, so far as they are objects of lawful government. Among a people consolidated into one nation, this supremacy is completely vested in the national legislature. Among communities united for particular purposes, it is vested partly in the general and partly in the municipal legislatures. In the former case, all local authorities are subordinate to the supreme; and may be controlled, directed, or abolished by it at pleasure. In the latter, the local or municipal authorities form distinct and independent portions of the supremacy, no more subject, within their respective spheres, to the general authority than the general authority is subject to them, within its own sphere. In this relation, then, the proposed government cannot be deemed a *national* one; since its jurisdiction extends to certain enumerated objects only, and leaves to the several States a residuary and inviolable sovereignty over all other objects. It is true that in controversies relating to the boundary between the two jurisdictions, the tribunal which is ultimately to decide is to be established under the general government. But this does not change the principle of the case. The decision is to be impartially made, according to the rules of the Constitution; and all the usual and most effectual precautions are taken to secure this impartiality. Some such tribunal is clearly essential to prevent an appeal to the sword and a dissolution of the compact; and that it ought to be established under the general rather than under the local governments, or, to speak more properly, that it could be safely established under the first alone, is a position not likely to be combated.

If we try the Constitution by its last relation to the authority by which amendments are to be made, we find it neither wholly *national* nor wholly *federal*. Were it wholly national, the supreme and ultimate authority would reside in the *majority* of the people of the Union; and this authority would be competent at all times, like that of a majority of every national society to alter or abolish its established government. Were it wholly federal, on the other hand, the concurrence of each State in the Union would be essential to every alteration that would be binding on all. The mode provided by the plan of the convention is not founded on either of these principles. In requiring more than a majority, and particularly in computing the proportion by *States*, not by *citizens*, it departs from the national and advances towards the *federal* character; in rendering the concurrence of less than the whole number of States sufficient, it loses again the *federal* and partakes of the *national* character.

The proposed Constitution, therefore, even when tested by the rules laid down by its antagonists, is, in strictness, neither a national nor a federal Constitution, but a composition of both. In its foundation it is federal, not national; in the sources from which the ordinary powers of the government are drawn, it is partly federal and partly national; in the operation of these powers, it is national, not federal; in the extent of them, again, it is federal, not national; and, finally in the authoritative mode of introducing amendments, it is neither wholly federal nor wholly national.

PUBLIUS

❖❖   In *The Federalist,* Alexander Hamilton and James Madison were careful to point out the advantages of the federal form of government that would be established by the Constitution, both over the government that had existed under the Articles of Confederation and in general terms. Because many state political leaders were highly suspicious of the national government that would be created by the new Constitution, much of the efforts of Hamilton and Madison were directed toward allaying their fears. Above all, they both stated, the energy of the national government would never be sufficient to coerce the states into giving up any portion of their sovereignty. Moreover, Hamilton stated in *Federalist 17* that there would be no incentive for national politicians to take away the reserved powers of the states. The sphere of national power, although limited, was considered entirely adequate to absorb even the most ambitious politicians. And James Madison, *Federalist 39,* was careful to point out that the jurisdiction of the national government extended only to certain enumerated objects, implying that the residual sovereignty of the states was in fact greater than the sovereignty of the national government.

Alexis de Tocqueville, an aristocratic French observer of the American political and social scene in the early 1830s, acknowledged his debt to the writers of *The Federalist* in helping him to understand American government. Many of the sanguine views of Hamilton and Madison about the prospects for the new Constitution were echoed in Tocqueville's analysis of American institutions forty years later.

Tocqueville had set out for the United States in 1831, with his friend Gustave de Beaumont, ostensibly to examine the American prison system with a view toward prison reform in France. Tocqueville was a French judicial officer, who after the July Revolution of 1830 became disenchanted with the new government of Louis Philippe, and, in a broader context, with the continual turmoil that he saw in French political institutions. While the investigation of prisons served as a ready excuse for a leave of absence from governmental duties, Tocqueville and Beaumont's real interest was in

studying American society and government. It was their feeling that democracy was probably the wave of the future and that whatever lessons
could be learned from the American experiment would undoubtedly be a
useful guide to the future of European society.

Tocqueville was in the United States for only nine months, from May
1831 until February 1832, but during this time he traveled over most of the
country east of the Mississippi, staying long enough in various places to
gain wide knowledge of local customs and institutions. Most of Tocqueville's observations about the United States were objectively optimistic
about the future of democracy, yet his most hopeful expectations were not
always realized. In particular, after leaving the United States, he became
concerned with the possibility of what he called "tyranny of the majority,"
which he wrote would be an inevitable consequence of egalitarian tendencies in democratic societies such as the United States. The framers of the
Constitution, too, were worried about unbridled majority rule in government, and felt that governmental tyranny by the majority would be curtailed
by such institutional devices as the separation of powers, checks and balances, and federalism, the latter being a division of authority between the
national government and the states. While the framers of the Constitution
felt that the possibility of the tyranny of the majority was primarily a governmental problem, Tocqueville saw it as a societal dilemma, produced by
the egalitarian ethic. Therefore, to Tocqueville, constitutional devices by
themselves would not be sufficient to control the inevitable tendency toward
majority despotism in an egalitarian society.

The following selection is taken from Tocqueville's discussion of the
characteristics of federalism as he saw it in operation in 1831. In his discussion Tocqueville uses the terms "confederation" and "federalism" interchangeably. To him, the American federal system was one type of confederation. This is important to note because Hamilton, in his discussion of
federalism in *The Federalist,* spoke of federalism in the new Constitution as
replacing the "confederacy," by which he meant the government that existed under the Articles of Confederation. Most American writers on politics
distinguish federalism and confederacy in the same way that Hamilton did,
essentially by identifying federalism with the system of the Constitution, and
a confederacy with the system of the Articles of Confederation. Under this
more common definition of federalism, a federal system is one in which
the national government has authority that is separate and distinct from that
of the constituent states, an authority that operates directly upon the citizens
of the states rather than upon the states as entities. Dual sovereignty is a
characteristic of American federalism, whereas under the Articles of Confederation the national government had no authority distinct from the states,
and it could not operate without their consent.

The breadth of Tocqueville's analytical method is revealed in his discussion of American federalism. He examines the broad social and political

forces operating in society, refers to historical and comparative experience, and analyzes constitutional forms and institutional characteristics. His approach is both empirical and analytical. Tocqueville recognizes that while the theory of federalism may be clear, it is very difficult to apply it without some further clarification. This has certainly been true of the American federal system. As Tocqueville noted: "The sovereignty of the union is so involved in that of the states that it is impossible to distinguish its boundaries at the first glance. The whole structure of the government is artificial and conventional, and it would be ill adapted to a people which has not been long accustomed to conduct its own affairs, or to one in which the science of politics has not descended to the humblest classes of society. I have never been more struck by the good sense and the practical judgment of the Americans than in the manner in which they elude the numberless difficulties resulting from their federal constitution." Tocqueville implied that after all is said and done, federalism as well as other constitutional forms worked because of the good sense and pragmatism of the American people, which overcame constitutional ambiguity. This is why federalism worked in the United States, but, according to Tocqueville, failed in other countries that attempted to imitate the United States Constitution.

In reading the following selection, students should look for Tocqueville's views on (1) the outstanding characteristics of American federalism; (2) the major advantages of federalism; (3) significant disadvantages of the federal form of government. What evidence does Tocqueville use to buttress his arguments for the advantages and disadvantages of federalism? What changes have occurred since 1831 that might lead to a different perspective on federalism today?

8

Alexis de Tocqueville
DEMOCRACY IN AMERICA: THE FEDERAL CONSTITUTION

CHARACTERISTICS OF THE FEDERAL CONSTITUTION OF THE UNITED STATES OF AMERICA AS COMPARED WITH ALL OTHER FEDERAL CONSTITUTIONS

The United States of America does not afford the first or the only instance of a confederation, several of which have existed in modern Europe, without referring to those of antiquity. Switzerland, the Germanic Empire, and the Republic of the Low Countries either have been or still are confederations. In studying the constitutions of these different countries one is surprised to see that the powers with which they invested the federal government are nearly the same as those awarded by the American Constitution to the government of the United States. They confer upon the central power the same rights of making peace and war, of raising money and troops, and of providing for the general exigencies and the common interests of the nation. Nevertheless, the federal government of these different states has always been as remarkable for its weakness and inefficiency as that of the American Union is for its vigor and capacity. Again, the first American Confederation perished through the excessive weakness of its government; and yet this weak government had as large rights and privileges as those of the Federal government of the present day, and in some respects even larger. But the present Constitution of the United States contains certain novel principles which exercise a most important influence, although they do not at once strike the observer.

This Constitution, which may at first sight be confused with the federal constitutions that have preceded it, rests in truth upon a wholly novel theory, which may be considered as a great discovery in modern political science. In all the confederations that preceded the American Constitution of 1789, the states allied for a common object agreed to obey the injunctions of a federal government; but they reserved to themselves the right of ordaining and enforcing the execution of the laws of the union. The American states which combined in 1789 agreed that the Federal government should not only dictate the laws, but execute its own enactments. In both cases the right is the same, but the exercise of the right is different; and this difference produced the most momentous consequences.

In all the confederations that preceded the American Union the federal government, in order to provide for its wants, had to apply to the separate governments; and if what it prescribed was disagreeable to any one of them, means were found to evade its claims. If it was powerful, it then had recourse to arms; if it was weak, it connived at the resistance which the law of the union, its sovereign, met with, and did nothing, under the plea of inability. Under these circumstances one of two results invariably followed: either the strongest of the allied states assumed the privileges of the federal authority and ruled all the others in its name;[1] or the federal government was abandoned by its natural supporters, anarchy arose between the confederates, and the union lost all power of action.[2]

In America the subjects of the Union are not states, but private citizens: the national government levies a tax, not upon the state of Massachusetts, but upon each inhabitant of Massachusetts. The old confederate governments presided over communities, but that of the Union presides over individuals. Its force is not borrowed, but self-derived; and it is served by its own civil and military officers, its own army, and its own courts of justice. It cannot be doubted that the national spirit, the passions of the multitude, and the provincial prejudices of each state still tend singularly to diminish the extent of the Federal authority thus constituted and to facilitate resistance to its mandates; but the comparative weakness of a restricted sovereignty is an evil inherent in the federal system. In America each state has fewer opportunities and temptations to resist; nor can such a design be put in execution (if indeed it be entertained) without an open violation of the laws of the Union, a direct interruption of the ordinary course of justice, and a bold declaration of revolt; in a word, without taking the decisive step that men always hesitate to adopt.

In all former confederations the privileges of the union furnished more elements of discord than of power, since they multiplied the claims of the nation without augmenting the means of enforcing them; and hence the real weakness of federal governments has almost always been in the exact ratio of their nominal power. Such is not the case in the American Union, in which, as in ordinary governments, the Federal power has the means of enforcing all it is empowered to demand. . . .

---

[1] This was the case in Greece when Philip undertook to execute the decrees of the Amphictyons; in the Low Countries, where the province of Holland always gave the law; and in our own time in the Germanic Confederation, in which Austria and Prussia make themselves the agents of the Diet and rule the whole confederation in its name.

[2] Such has always been the situation of the Swiss Confederation, which would have perished ages ago but for the mutual jealousies of its neighbors.

ADVANTAGES OF THE FEDERAL SYSTEM IN GENERAL, AND ITS SPECIAL UTILITY IN AMERICA

. . . In small states, the watchfulness of society penetrates everywhere, and a desire for improvement pervades the smallest details; the ambition of the people being necessarily checked by its weakness, all the efforts and resources of the citizens are turned to the internal well-being of the community and are not likely to be wasted upon an empty pursuit of glory. The powers of every individual being generally limited, his desires are proportionally small. Mediocrity of fortune makes the various conditions of life nearly equal, and the manners of the inhabitants are orderly and simple. Thus, all things considered, and allowance being made for the various degrees of morality and enlightenment, we shall generally find more persons in easy circumstances, more contentment and tranquillity, in small nations than in large ones.

When tyranny is established in the bosom of a small state, it is more galling than elsewhere, because, acting in a narrower circle, everything in that circle is affected by it. It supplies the place of those great designs which it cannot entertain, by a violent or exasperating interference in a multitude of minute details; and it leaves the political world, to which it properly belongs, to meddle with the arrangements of private life. Tastes as well as actions are to be regulated; and the families of the citizens, as well as the state, are to be governed. This invasion of rights occurs but seldom, however, freedom being in truth the natural state of small communities. The temptations that the government offers to ambition are too weak and the resources of private individuals are too slender for the sovereign power easily to fall into the grasp of a single man; and should such an event occur, the subjects of the state can easily unite and overthrow the tyrant and the tyranny at once by a common effort.

Small nations have therefore always been the cradle of political liberty; and the fact that many of them have lost their liberty by becoming larger shows that their freedom was more a consequence of their small size than of the character of the people.

The history of the world affords no instance of a great nation retaining the form of republican government for a long series of years;[3] and this has led to the conclusion that such a thing is impracticable. For my own part, I think it imprudent for men who are every day deceived in relation to the actual and the present, and often taken by surprise in the circumstances with which they are most familiar, to attempt to limit what is possible and to judge the future. But it may be said with confidence, that a great republic will always be exposed to more perils than a small one.

All the passions that are most fatal to republican institutions increase with an increasing territory, while the virtues that favor them do not augment in

---

[3] I do not speak of a confederation of small republics, but of a great consolidated republic.

the same proportion. The ambition of private citizens increases with the power of the state; the strength of parties with the importance of the ends they have in view; but the love of country, which ought to check these destructive agencies, is not stronger in a large than in a small republic. It might, indeed, be easily proved that it is less powerful and less developed. Great wealth and extreme poverty, capital cities of large size, a lax morality, selfishness, and antagonism of interests are the dangers which almost invariably arise from the magnitude of states. Several of these evils scarcely injure a monarchy, and some of them even contribute to its strength and duration. In monarchical states the government has its peculiar strength; it may use, but it does not depend on, the community; and the more numerous the people, the stronger is the prince. But the only security that a republican government possesses against these evils lies in the support of the majority. This support is not, however, proportionably greater in a large republic than in a small one; and thus, while the means of attack perpetually increase, in both number and influence, the power of resistance remains the same; or it may rather be said to diminish, since the inclinations and interests of the people are more diversified by the increase of the population, and the difficulty of forming a compact majority is constantly augmented. It has been observed, moreover, that the intensity of human passions is heightened not only by the importance of the end which they propose to attain, but by the multitude of individuals who are animated by them at the same time. Everyone has had occasion to remark that his emotions in the midst of a sympathizing crowd are far greater than those which he would have felt in solitude. In great republics, political passions become irresistible, not only because they aim at gigantic objects, but because they are felt and shared by millions of men at the same time.

It may therefore be asserted as a general proposition that nothing is more opposed to the well-being and the freedom of men than vast empires. Nevertheless, it is important to acknowledge the peculiar advantages of great states. For the very reason that the desire for power is more intense in these communities than among ordinary men, the love of glory is also more developed in the hearts of certain citizens, who regard the applause of a great people as a reward worthy of their exertions and an elevating encouragement to man. If we would learn why great nations contribute more powerfully to the increase of knowledge and the advance of civilization than small states, we shall discover an adequate cause in the more rapid and energetic circulation of ideas and in those great cities which are the intellectual centers where all the rays of human genius are reflected and combined. To this it may be added that most important discoveries demand a use of national power which the government of a small state is unable to make: in great nations the government has more enlarged ideas, and is more completely disengaged from the routine of precedent and the selfishness of local feeling; its designs are conceived with more talent and executed with more boldness.

In time of peace the well-being of small nations is undoubtedly more general and complete; but they are apt to suffer more acutely from the calamities of war than those great empires whose distant frontiers may long avert the presence of the danger from the mass of the people, who are therefore more frequently afflicted than ruined by the contest.

But in this matter, as in many others, the decisive argument is the necessity of the case. If none but small nations existed, I do not doubt that mankind would be more happy and more free; but the existence of great nations is unavoidable.

Political strength thus becomes a condition of national prosperity. It profits a state but little to be affluent and free if it is perpetually exposed to be pillaged or subjugated; its manufactures and commerce are of small advantage if another nation has the empire of the seas and gives the law in all the markets of the globe. Small nations are often miserable, not because they are small, but because they are weak; and great empires prosper less because they are great than because they are strong. Physical strength is therefore one of the first conditions of the happiness and even of the existence of nations. Hence it occurs that, unless very peculiar circumstances intervene, small nations are always united to large empires in the end, either by force or by their own consent. I do not know a more deplorable condition than that of a people unable to defend itself or to provide for its own wants.

The federal system was created with the intention of combining the different advantages which result from the magnitude and the littleness of nations; and a glance at the United States of America discovers the advantages which they have derived from its adoption.

In great centralized nations the legislator is obliged to give a character of uniformity to the laws, which does not always suit the diversity of customs and of districts; as he takes no cognizance of special cases, he can only proceed upon general principles; and the population are obliged to conform to the requirements of the laws, since legislation cannot adapt itself to the exigencies and the customs of the population, which is a great cause of trouble and misery. This disadvantage does not exist in confederations; Congress regulates the principal measures of the national government, and all the details of the administration are reserved to the provincial legislatures. One can hardly imagine how much this division of sovereignty contributes to the well-being of each of the states that compose the Union. In these small communities, which are never agitated by the desire of aggrandizement or the care of self-defense, all public authority and private energy are turned towards internal improvements. The central government of each state, which is in immediate relationship with the citizens, is daily apprised of the wants that arise in society; and new projects are proposed every year, which are discussed at town meetings or by the legislature, and which are transmitted by the press to stimulate the zeal and to excite the interest of the citizens. This spirit of improvement is constantly alive in the American republics, without compromising their tranquillity; the ambition of power yields to the less refined and less dangerous desire for well-being. It is generally believed in America that the existence and the permanence of the republican form of government in the New World depend upon the existence and the duration of the federal system; and it is not unusual to attribute a large share of the misfortunes that have befallen the new states of South America to the injudicious erection of great republics instead of a divided and confederate sovereignty.

It is incontestably true that the tastes and the habits of republican government in the United States were first created in the townships and the provincial assemblies. In a small state, like that of Connecticut, for instance, where cutting a canal or laying down a road is a great political question, where the state has no army to pay and no wars to carry on, and where much wealth or much honor cannot be given to the rulers, no form of government can be more natural or more appropriate than a republic. But it is this same republican spirit, it is these manners and customs of a free people, which have been created and nurtured in the different states, that must be afterwards applied to the country at large. The public spirit of the Union is, so to speak, nothing more than an aggregate or summary of the patriotic zeal of the separate provinces. Every citizen of the United States transfers, so to speak, his attachment to his little republic into the common store of American patriotism. In defending the Union he defends the increasing prosperity of his own state or county, the right of conducting its affairs, and the hope of causing measures of improvement to be adopted in it which may be favorable to his own interests; and these are motives that are wont to stir men more than the general interests of the country and the glory of the nation.

On the other hand, if the temper and the manners of the inhabitants especially fitted them to promote the welfare of a great republic, the federal system renders their task less difficult. The confederation of all the American states presents none of the ordinary inconveniences resulting from large associations of men. The Union is a great republic in extent, but the paucity of objects for which its government acts assimilates it to a small state. Its acts are important, but they are rare. As the sovereignty of the Union is limited and incomplete, its exercise is not dangerous to liberty; for it does not excite those insatiable desires for fame and power which have proved so fatal to great republics. As there is no common center to the country, great capital cities, colossal wealth, abject poverty, and sudden revolutions are alike unknown; and political passion, instead of spreading over the land like a fire on the prairies, spends its strength against the interests and the individual passions of every state.

Nevertheless, tangible objects and ideas circulate throughout the Union as freely as in a country inhabited by one people. Nothing checks the spirit of enterprise. The government invites the aid of all who have talents or knowledge to serve it. Inside of the frontiers of the Union profound peace prevails, as within the heart of some great empire; abroad it ranks with the most powerful nations of the earth: two thousand miles of coast are open to the commerce of the world; and as it holds the keys of a new world, its flag is respected in the most remote seas. The Union is happy and free as a small people, and glorious and strong as a great nation.

WHY THE FEDERAL SYSTEM IS NOT PRACTICABLE FOR ALL NATIONS, AND HOW THE ANGLO-AMERICANS WERE ENABLED TO ADOPT IT

. . . I have shown the advantages that the Americans derive from their federal system; it remains for me to point out the circumstances that enabled them to adopt it, as its benefits cannot be enjoyed by all nations. The accidental defects of the federal system which originate in the laws may be corrected by the skill of the legislator, but there are evils inherent in the system which cannot be remedied by any effort. The people must therefore find in themselves the strength necessary to bear the natural imperfections of their government.

The most prominent evil of all federal systems is the complicated nature of the means they employ. Two sovereignties are necessarily in presence of each other. The legislator may simplify and equalize as far as possible the action of these two sovereignties, by limiting each of them to a sphere of authority accurately defined; but he cannot combine them into one or prevent them from coming into collision at certain points. The federal system, therefore, rests upon a theory which is complicated at the best, and which demands the daily exercise of a considerable share of discretion on the part of those it governs. . . .

In examining the Constitution of the United States, which is the most perfect federal constitution that ever existed, one is startled at the variety of information and the amount of discernment that it presupposes in the people whom it is meant to govern. The government of the Union depends almost entirely upon legal fictions; the Union is an ideal nation, which exists, so to speak, only in the mind, and whose limits and extent can only be discerned by the understanding.

After the general theory is comprehended, many difficulties remain to be solved in its application; for the sovereignty of the Union is so involved in that of the states that it is impossible to distinguish its boundaries at the first glance. The whole structure of the government is artificial and conventional, and it would be ill adapted to a people which has not been long accustomed to conduct its own affairs, or to one in which the science of politics has not descended to the humblest classes of society. I have never been more struck by the good sense and the practical judgment of the Americans than in the manner in which they elude the numberless difficulties resulting from their Federal Constitution. I scarcely ever met with a plain American citizen who could not distinguish with surprising facility the obligations created by the laws of Congress from those created by the laws of his own state, and who, after having discriminated between the matters which come under the cognizance of the Union and those which the local legislature is competent to regulate, could not point out the exact limit of the separate jurisdictions of the Federal courts and the tribunals of the state.

The Constitution of the United States resembles those fine creations of human industry which ensure wealth and renown to their inventors, but which are profitless in other hands. . . .

The second and most fatal of all defects, and that which I believe to be inherent in the federal system, is the relative weakness of the government of the Union. The principle upon which all confederations rest is that of a divided sovereignty. Legislators may render this partition less perceptible, they may even conceal it for a time from the public eye, but they cannot prevent it from existing; and a divided sovereignty must always be weaker than an entire one. The remarks made on the Constitution of the United States have shown with what skill the Americans, while restraining the power of the Union within the narrow limits of a federal government, have given it the semblance, and to a certain extent the force, of a national government. By this means the legislators of the Union have diminished the natural danger of confederations, but have not entirely obviated it.

The American government, it is said, does not address itself to the states, but transmits its injunctions directly to the citizens and compels them individually to comply with its demands. But if the Federal law were to clash with the interests and the prejudices of a state, it might be feared that all the citizens of that state would conceive themselves to be interested in the cause of a single individual who refused to obey. If all the citizens of the state were aggrieved at the same time and in the same manner by the authority of the Union, the Federal government would vainly attempt to subdue them individually; they would instinctively unite in a common defense and would find an organization already prepared for them in the sovereignty that their state is allowed to enjoy. Fiction would give way to reality, and an organized portion of the nation might then contest the central authority.

The same observation holds good with regard to the Federal jurisdiction. If the courts of the Union violated an important law of a state in a private case, the real though not the apparent contest would be between the aggrieved state represented by a citizen and the Union represented by its courts of justice.

He would have but a partial knowledge of the world who should imagine that it is possible by the aid of legal fictions to prevent men from finding out and employing those means of gratifying their passions which have been left open to them. The American legislators, though they have rendered a collision between the two sovereignties less probable, have not destroyed the causes of such a misfortune. It may even be affirmed that, in case of such a collision, they have not been able to ensure the victory of the Federal element. The Union is possessed of money and troops, but the states have kept the affections and the prejudices of the people. The sovereignty of the Union is an abstract being, which is connected with but few external objects; the sovereignty of the states is perceptible by the senses, easily understood, and constantly active. The former is of recent creation, the latter is coeval with the people itself. The sovereignty of the Union is factitious, that of the states is natural and self-existent, without effort, like the authority of a parent. The sovereignty of the nation affects a few of the chief interests of society; it represents an immense but remote country, a vague and ill-defined sentiment. The authority of the states controls every individual citizen at every hour and in all circumstances; it protects his property, his freedom, and his life; it affects at every moment his well-being or his misery. When we recollect the traditions, the customs, the prejudices of local and familiar attachment with which it is connected, we cannot doubt the superiority of a power that rests on the instinct of patriotism, so natural to the human heart.

Since legislators cannot prevent such dangerous collisions as occur between the two sovereignties which coexist in the Federal system, their first object must be, not only to dissuade the confederate states from warfare, but to encourage such dispositions as lead to peace. Hence it is that the Federal compact cannot be lasting unless there exists in the communities which are leagued together a certain number of inducements to union which render their common dependence agreeable and the task of the government light. The Federal system cannot succeed without the presence of favorable circumstances added to the influence of good laws. All the nations that have ever formed a confederation have been held together by some common interests, which served as the intellectual ties of association. . . .

The circumstance which makes it easy to maintain a Federal government in America is not only that the states have similar interests, a common origin, and a common language, but they have also arrived at the same stage of civilization, which almost always renders a union feasible. I do not know of any European nation, however small, that does not present less uniformity in its different provinces than the American people, which occupy a territory as extensive as one half of Europe. The distance from Maine to Georgia is about one thousand miles; but the difference between the civilization of Maine and that of Georgia is slighter than the difference between the habits of Normandy and those of Brittany. Maine and Georgia, which are placed at the opposite extremities of a great empire, have therefore more real inducements to form a confederation than Normandy and Brittany, which are separated only by a brook.

The geographical position of the country increased the facilities that the American legislators derived from the usages and customs of the inhabitants; and it is to this circumstance that the adoption and the maintenance of the Federal system are mainly attributable.

The most important occurrence in the life of a nation is the breaking out of a war. . . . A long war almost always reduces nations to the wretched alternative of being abandoned to ruin by defeat or to despotism by success. War therefore renders the weakness of a government most apparent and most alarming; and I have shown that the inherent defect of federal governments is that of being weak.

The federal system not only has no centralized administration, and nothing that resembles one, but the central government itself is imperfectly organized, which is always a great cause of weakness when the nation is opposed to other countries which are themselves governed by a single authority. In the Federal Constitution of the United States, where the central government has more real force than in any other confederation, this evil is extremely evident. . . .

How does it happen, then, that the American Union, with all the relative perfection of its laws, is not dissolved by the occurrence of a great war? It is because it has no great wars to fear. Placed in the center of an immense continent, which offers a boundless field for human industry, the Union is almost as much insulated from the world as if all its frontiers were girt by the ocean. . . .

The great advantage of the United States does not, then, consist in a Federal Constitution which allows it to carry on great wars, but in a geographical position which renders such wars extremely improbable.

No one can be more inclined than I am to appreciate the advantages of the federal system, which I hold to be one of the combinations most favorable to the prosperity and freedom of man. I envy the lot of those nations which have been able to adopt it; but I cannot believe that any confederate people could maintain a long or an equal contest with a nation of similar strength in which the government is centralized. A people which, in the presence of the great military monarchies of Europe, should divide its sovereignty into fractional parts would, in my opinion, by that very act abdicate its power, and perhaps its existence and its name. But such is the admirable position of the New World that man has no other enemy than himself, and that, in order to be happy and to be free, he has only to determine that he will be so.

The Supremacy of National Law

Tracing the historical development of nation-state relationships, one finds that there has been constant strife over the determination of the boundaries of national power in relation to the reserved powers of the states. The Civil War did not settle once and for all the difficult question of national versus state power. The Supreme Court has played an important role in the development of the federal system, and some of its most historic opinions have upheld national power at the expense of the states. In the early period of the Court, Chief Justice John Marshall in *McCulloch* v. *Maryland*, 4 Wheaton 316 (1819), stated two doctrines that have had a profound effect upon the federal system: (1) the doctrine of implied powers; (2) the doctrine of the supremacy of national law. The former enables Congress to expand its power into numerous areas affecting states directly. By utilizing the commerce clause, for example, Congress may now regulate what is essentially *intrastate* commerce, for the Court has held that this is implied in the original clause giving Congress the power to regulate commerce among the several states. The immediate issues in *McCulloch* v. *Maryland* were, first, whether or not Congress had the power to incorporate, or charter, a national bank; second, if Congress did have such a power, although nowhere stated in the Constitution, did the existence of such a bank prevent state action that would interfere in its operation?

9

McCULLOCH v. MARYLAND
4 WHEATON 316 (1819)

Mr. Chief Justice Marshall delivered the opinion of the Court, saying in part:

In the case now to be determined, the defendant, a sovereign state, denies the obligation of a law enacted by the legislature of the Union; and the plaintiff, on his part, contests the validity of an act which has been passed by the legislature of that state. The Constitution of our country, in its most interesting and vital parts, is to be considered; the conflicting powers of the government of the Union and of its members, as marked in that Constitution, are to be discussed; and an opinion given, which may essentially influence the great operations of the government. . . .

If any one proposition could command the universal assent of mankind, we might expect it would be this: that the government of the Union, though limited in its powers, is supreme within its sphere of action. This would seem to result necessarily from its nature. It is the government of all; its powers are delegated by all; it represents all, and acts for all. Though any one state may be willing to control its operations, no state is willing to allow others to control them. The nation, on those subjects on which it can act, must necessarily bind its component parts. But this question is not left to mere reason: the people have, in express terms, decided it, by saying, "this Constitution, and the laws of the United States, which shall be made in pursuance thereof," "shall be the supreme law of the land," and by requiring that the members of the state legislatures, and the officers of the executive and judicial departments of the states, shall take the oath of fidelity to it. . . .

A constitution, to contain an accurate detail of all the subdivisions of which its great powers will admit, and of all the means by which they may be carried into execution, would partake of the prolixity of a legal code, and could scarcely be embraced by the human mind. It would probably never be understood by the public. Its nature, therefore, requires that only its great outlines should be marked, its important objects designated, and the minor ingredients which compose those objects be deduced from the nature of the objects themselves. That this idea was entertained by the framers of the American Constitution, is not only to be inferred from the nature of the instrument, but from the language. . . .

Although, among the enumerated powers of government, we do not find the word "bank," or "incorporation," we find the great powers to lay and collect taxes; to borrow money; to regulate commerce; to declare and conduct a war; and to raise and support armies and navies. The sword and the purse, all the external relations, and no inconsiderable portion of the industry of the nation, are entrusted to its government. It can never be pretended that these vast powers draw after them others of inferior importance, merely because they are inferior. Such an idea can never be advanced. But it may, with great reason, be contended, that a government, entrusted with such ample powers, on the due execution of which the happiness and prosperity of the nation so vitally depends, must also be entrusted with ample means for their execution. The power being given, it is the interest of the nation to facilitate its execution. It can never be their interest, and cannot be presumed to have been their intention, to clog and embarrass its execution by withholding the most appropriate means. Throughout this vast republic, from the St. Croix to the Gulf of Mexico, from the Atlantic to the Pacific, revenue is to be collected and expended, armies are to be marched and supported. The exigencies of the nation may require, that the treasure raised in the North should be transported to the South, that raised in the East conveyed to the West, or that this order should be reversed. Is that construction of the Constitution to be preferred which would render these operations difficult, hazardous, and expensive? Can we adopt that construction (unless the words imperiously require it) which would impute to the framers of that instrument, when granting these powers for the public good, the intention of impeding their exercise by withholding a choice of means? If, indeed, such be the mandate of the Constitution, we have only to obey; but that instrument does not profess to enumerate the means by which the powers it confers may be executed; nor does it prohibit the creation of a corporation, if the existence of such a being be essential to the beneficial exercise of those powers. It is, then, the subject of fair inquiry, how far such means may be employed. . . .

We admit, as all must admit, that the powers of the government are limited, and that its limits are not to be transcended. But we think the sound construction of the Constitution must allow to the national legislature that discretion, with respect to the means by which the powers it confers are to be carried into execution, which will enable that body to perform the high duties assigned to it, in the manner most beneficial to the people. Let the end be legitimate, let it be within the scope of the Constitution, and all means which are appropriate, which are plainly adapted to that end, which are not prohibited, but consist with the letter and spirit of the Constitution, are constitutional. . . .

It being the opinion of the court that the act incorporating the bank is constitutional; and that the power of establishing a branch in the state of Maryland might be properly exercised by the bank itself, we proceed to inquire:

Whether the state of Maryland may, without violating the Constitution, tax that branch? . . .

That the power of taxation is one of vital importance; that it is retained by the states; that it is not abridged by the grant of a similar power to the government of the Union; that it is to be concurrently exercised by the two governments: are truths which have never been denied. But, such is the paramount character of the Constitution, that its capacity to withdraw any subject from the action of even this power, is admitted. The states are expressly forbidden to lay any duties on imports or exports, except what may be absolutely necessary for executing their inspection laws. If the obligation of this prohibition must be conceded—if it may restrain a state from the exercise of its taxing power on imports and exports; the same paramount character would seem to restrain, as it certainly may restrain, a state from such other exercise of this power, as is in its nature incompatible with, and repugnant to, the constitutional laws of the Union. A law, absolutely repugnant to another, as entirely repeals that other as if express terms of repeal were used.

On this ground the counsel for the bank place its claim to be exempted from the power of a state to tax its operations. There is no express provision for the case, but the claim has been sustained on a principle which so entirely pervades the Constitution, is so intermixed with the materials which compose it, so interwoven with its web, so blended with its texture, as to be incapable of being separated from it, without rending it into shreds.

This great principle is, that the Constitution and the laws made in pursuance thereof are supreme; that they control the Constitution and laws of the respective states, and cannot be controlled by them. From this, which may be almost termed an axiom, other propositions are deduced as corollaries, on the truth or error of which, and on their application to this case, the cause has been supposed to depend. These are, 1. That a power to create implies a power to preserve. 2. That a power to destroy, if wielded by a different hand, is hostile to, and incompatible with, these powers to create and preserve. 3. That where this repugnancy exists, that authority which is supreme must control, not yield to that over which it is supreme. . . .

If we apply the principle for which the state of Maryland contends, to the Constitution generally, we shall find it capable of changing totally the character of that instrument. We shall find it capable of arresting all the measures of the government, and of prostrating it at the foot of the states. The American people have declared their Constitution, and the laws made in pursuance thereof, to be supreme; but this principle would transfer the supremacy, in fact, to the states. . . .

The court has bestowed on this subject its most deliberate consideration. The result is a conviction that the states have no power, by taxation or otherwise, to retard, impede, burden, or in any manner control, the operations of the constitutional laws enacted by Congress to carry into execution the powers vested in the general government. That is, we think, the unavoidable consequence of that supremacy which the Constitution has declared. . . .

❖❖ Constitutional doctrine regarding the power of the national government to regulate commerce among the states to promote general prosperity has been clarified in a series of Supreme Court cases. At issue is the interpretation of the power to "regulate commerce with foreign nations, and among the several States," granted to Congress in Article 1. Some of these cases have emphasized the role of the national government as umpire, enforcing certain rules of the game within which the free enterprise system functions; others have emphasized the positive role of the government in regulating the economy.

A key case supporting the supremacy of the national government in commercial regulation was *Gibbons* v. *Ogden,* 9 Wheaton 1 (1824). The New York legislature, in 1798, granted Robert R. Livingston the exclusive privilege to navigate by steam the rivers and other waters of the state, provided he could build a boat that would travel at four miles an hour against the current of the Hudson River. A two-year time limitation was imposed, and the conditions were not met; however, New York renewed its grant for two years in 1803 and again in 1807. In 1807 Robert Fulton, who now held the exclusive license with Livingston, completed and put into operation a steamboat which met the legislative conditions. The New York legislature now provided that a five-year extension of their monopoly would be given to Livingston and Fulton for each new steamboat they placed into operation on New York waters. The monopoly could not exceed thirty years, but during that period anyone wishing to navigate New York waters by steam had first to obtain a license from Livingston and Fulton, who were given the power to confiscate unlicensed boats. New Jersey and Connecticut passed retaliatory laws, the former authorizing confiscation of any New York ship for each ship confiscated by Livingston and Fulton, the latter prohibiting boats licensed in New York from entering Connecticut waters. Ohio also passed retaliatory legislation. Open commercial warfare seemed a possibility among the states of the union.

In 1793 Congress passed an act providing for the licensing of vessels engaged in the coasting trade, and Gibbons obtained under this statute a license to operate boats between New York and New Jersey. Ogden was engaged in a similar operation under an exclusive license issued by Livingston and Fulton, and thus sought to enjoin Gibbons from further operation. The New York court upheld the exclusive grants given to Livingston and Fulton, and Gibbons appealed to the Supreme Court. Chief Justice Marshall made it quite clear that (1) states cannot interfere with a power granted to Congress by passing conflicting state legislation, and (2) the commerce power includes anything affecting "commerce among the states" and thus may include *intrastate* as well as interstate commerce. In this way the foundation was laid for broad national control over commercial activity.

❖❖   Over its history the Supreme Court has interpreted the commerce clause both to expand and contract the authority of the national government. After Chief Justice John Marshall's era ended in 1836, the Court gradually adopted a more restrictive view of the national commerce power, protecting state sovereignty over many areas of commercial regulation that Marshall clearly would have allowed Congress to regulate. The Supreme Court did not fully return to the broad commerce clause interpretation of the *Gibbons* case until 1937, when it reluctantly capitulated to Franklin D. Roosevelt's New Deal and the centralized government it represented. The restoration of the Marshall Court's definition of the commerce power removed constitutional restraints upon Congress.

Since 1937 the Supreme Court has essentially upheld congressional interpretations of its own authority under the commerce clause. While the commerce power is generally used to support economic regulation, Congress turned to the commerce clause for the legal authority to enact the Civil Rights Act of 1964. The public accommodations section of the bill, Title II, proscribed discrimination in public establishments, including inns, hotels, motels, restaurants, motion-picture houses, and theaters. The law declared that the "operations of an establishment affects commerce . . . if . . . it serves or offers to serve interstate travelers or a substantial portion of the food which it serves or gasoline or other products which it sells, has moved in commerce . . . [or if] it customarily presents films, performances, athletic teams, exhibitions, or other sources of entertainment which move in commerce." In *Heart of Atlanta Motel, Inc. v. United States*, 379 US 241 (1964), the Supreme Court upheld the law under the commerce clause. The motel-plaintiff contended that it was in no way involved in interstate commerce, arguing that while some of its guests might be occasionally engaged in commerce, "persons and people are not part of trade or commerce . . . people conduct commerce and engage in trade, but people are not part of commerce and trade." But the Court accepted the government's argument that racial discrimination in public accommodations impedes interstate travel by those discriminated against, causing disruption of interstate commerce which Congress has the authority to prevent.

The Supreme Court did briefly resurrect the commerce clause as a limit on congressional power over the states in *National League of Cities* v. *Usery,* 426 US 833 (1976). A sharply divided Court held that Congress could not regulate governmental activities that were an integral part of state sovereignty. The decision overturned provisions of the Fair Labor Standards Act that governed state employees. The Court's majority opinion argued that states had traditionally controlled their employees, a responsibility within state sovereignty because the states through their own democratic processes should have the autonomy to decide for themselves how they would manage their public sector.

It was not long, however, before the Court reversed the *National League of Cities* decision, holding in *Garcia* v. *San Antonio Metropolitan Transit Authority,* 83L Ed. 2d 10 16 (1985), that Congress could apply minimum-wage requirements to the states and their localities. Again the vote was closely divided, 5–4, and this time the majority opinion struck a distinct note of judicial self-restraint, concluding: "We doubt that courts ultimately can identify principled constitutional limitations on the scope of Congress' commerce clause powers over the states merely by relying on a *priori* definitions of state sovereignty." The Court found nothing in the Fair Labor Standards Act that violated state sovereignty, implying that it was up to Congress and not the courts to determine the extent of its power under the commerce clause. Sharp dissents were registered in the case, possibly indicating that in the future the issue once again may be joined and a more conservative Supreme Court majority uphold some commerce clause restraints against national regulation of state governments. The *Garcia* decision is directly in line with Court precedents since 1937 that have supported virtually unlimited congressional authority under the commerce clause.

A Perspective on Federalism: Present and Future

In the following selection, the role of the states in the political system is discussed from the perspective that the nature of intergovernmental relations reflects underlying political conditions and realities. As James Madison pointed out in *Federalist 39,* the original constitutional scheme of federalism represented a delicate balance between national and state ("federal") interests. But, under the original constitutional design, the national government was not to intervene directly in the affairs of state governments; and the problems of subsidiary local governments within states were not considered to be separate from the problems of the states themselves, and therefore, they were a proper matter for resolution by the individual state governments.

Morton Grodzins points out that strict separation of national and state functions has never really existed, and that even before the Constitution of 1787 a national statute passed by the Continental Congress gave grants-in-aid of land to the states for public schools. Tocqueville also comments on the difficulties of formally separating, in theory, the responsibilities of national, state, and local governments. The history of the federal system has seen the ebb and flow of national dominance over the states; centralization and decentralization have been the cyclical themes of federalism and intergovernmental relations. The thrust of the New Deal was toward centralization through the use of federal grant-in-aid programs, a philosophy that dominated the government until the emergence of the "New Federalism" of the Nixon administration, which supported decentralization of power from the national to the state governments. The move toward decentralization was broadly supported by the Republican party. Revenue-sharing was inaugurated by President Nixon to transfer national funds to the states, without stipulation of how the money was to be spent. The revenue-sharing procedure was in direct contrast to the grant-in-aid programs, which allowed for state receipt of federal money upon the condition of state adherence to national standards. President Reagan's New Federalism proposed the merging of grant-in-aid programs into block grants to the states leading eventually to a reduced federal role in financing state and local governments. The continuing conflict between the themes and realities of centralization and decentralization are examined in the following selection.

10

Morton Grodzins
THE FEDERAL SYSTEM

Federalism is a device for dividing decisions and functions of government. As the constitutional fathers well understood, the federal structure is a means, not an end. The pages that follow are therefore not concerned with an exposition of American federalism as a formal, legal set of relationships. The focus, rather, is on the purpose of federalism, that is to say, on the distribution of power between central and peripheral units of government.

I. THE SHARING OF FUNCTIONS

The American form of government is often, but erroneously, symbolized by a three-layer cake. A far more accurate image is the rainbow or marble cake, characterized by an inseparable mingling of differently colored ingredients, the colors appearing in vertical and diagonal strands and unexpected whirls. As colors are mixed in the marble cake, so functions are mixed in the American federal system. Consider the health officer, styled "sanitarian," of a rural county in a border state. He embodies the whole idea of the marble cake of government.

The sanitarian is appointed by the state under merit standards established by the federal government. His base salary comes jointly from state and federal funds, the county provides him with an office and office amenities and pays a portion of his expenses, and the largest city in the county also contributes to his salary and office by virtue of his appointment as a city plumbing inspector. It is impossible from moment to moment to tell under which governmental hat the sanitarian operates. His work of inspecting the purity of food is carried out under federal standards; but he is enforcing state laws when inspecting commodities that have not been in interstate commerce; and somewhat perversely he also acts under state authority when inspecting milk coming into the county from producing areas across the state border. He is a federal officer when impounding impure drugs shipped from a neighboring state; a federal-state officer when distributing typhoid immunization serum; a state officer when enforcing standards of industrial hygiene; a state-local officier when inspecting the city's water supply; and (to complete the circle) a local officer when insisting that

From Morton Grodzins, ed., *Goals for Americans: The Report of the President's Commission on National Goals*, pp. 265–282. New York, The American Assembly. Reprinted by permission.

the city butchers adopt more hygienic methods of handling their garbage. But he cannot and does not think of himself as acting in these separate capacities. All business in the county that concerns public health and sanitation he considers his business. Paid largely from federal funds, he does not find it strange to attend meetings of the city council to give expert advice on matters ranging from rotten apples to rabies control. He is even deputized as a member of both the city and county police forces.

The sanitarian is an extreme case, but he accurately represents an important aspect of the whole range of governmental activities in the United States. Functions are not neatly parceled out among the many governments. They are shared functions. It is difficult to find any governmental activity which does not involve all three of the so-called "levels" of the federal system. In the most local of local functions—law enforcement or education, for example—the federal and state governments play important roles. In what, a priori, may be considered the purest central government activities—the conduct of foreign affairs, for example—the state and local governments have considerable responsibilities, directly and indirectly.

The federal grant programs are only the most obvious example of shared functions. They also most clearly exhibit how sharing serves to disperse governmental powers. The grants utilize the greater wealth-gathering abilities of the central government and establish nationwide standards, yet they are "in aid" of functions carried out under state law, with considerable state and local discretion. The national supervision of such programs is largely a process of mutual accommodation. Leading state and local officials, acting through their professional organizations, are in considerable part responsible for the very standards that national officers try to persuade all state and local officers to accept.

Even in the absence of joint financing, federal-state-local collaboration is the characteristic mode of action. Federal expertise is available to aid in the building of a local jail (which may later be used to house federal prisoners), to improve a local water purification system, to step up building inspections, to provide standards for state and local personnel in protecting housewives against dishonest butchers' scales, to prevent gas explosions, or to produce a land use plan. States and localities, on the other hand, take important formal responsibilities in the development of national programs for atomic energy, civil defense, the regulation of commerce, and the protection of purity in foods and drugs; local political weight is always a factor in the operation of even a post office or a military establishment. From abattoirs and accounting through zoning and zoo administration, any governmental activity is almost certain to involve the influence, if not the formal administration, of all three planes of the federal system.

II. ATTEMPTS TO UNWIND
THE FEDERAL SYSTEM

[From 1947 to 1960] there [were] four major attempts to reform or reorganize
the federal system: the first (1947–49) and second (1953–55) Hoover Commissions on Executive Organization; the Kestnbaum Commission on Intergovernmental Relations (1953–55); and the Joint Federal-State Action Committee
(1957–59). All four of these groups . . . aimed to minimize federal activities.
None of them . . . recognized the sharing of functions as the characteristic way
American governments do things. Even when making recommendations for
joint action, these official commissions [took] the view (as expressed in the
Kestnbaum report) that "the main tradition of American federalism [is] the
tradition of separateness." All four . . . in varying degrees, worked to separate
functions and tax sources.

The history of the Joint Federal-State Action Committee is especially instructive. The committee was established at the suggestion of President Eisenhower, who charged it, first of all, "to designate functions which the States are
ready and willing to assume and finance that are now performed or financed
wholly or in part by the Federal Government." He also gave the committee
the task of recommending "Federal and State revenue adjustments required to
enable the States to assume such functions."[1]

The committee subsequently established seemed most favorably situated to
accomplish the task of functional separation. It was composed of distinguished
and able men, including among its personnel three leading members of the
President's Cabinet, the director of the Bureau of the Budget, and ten state
governors. It had the full support of the President at every point, and it worked
hard and conscientiously. Excellent staff studies were supplied by the Bureau of
the Budget, the White House, the Treasury Department, and, from the state
side, the Council of State Governments. It had available to it a large mass of
research data, including the sixteen recently completed volumes of the Kestnbaum Commission. There existed no disagreements on party lines within
the committee and, of course, no constitutional impediments to its mission.
The President, his Cabinet members, and all the governors (with one possible
exception) on the committee completely agreed on the desirability of de-

---

[1]The President's third suggestion was that the committee "identify functions and responsibilities likely to require state or federal attention in the future and . . . recommend the level of state
effort, or federal effort, or both, that will be needed to assure effective action." The committee
initially devoted little attention to this problem. Upon discovering the difficulty of making separatist
recommendations, i.e., for turning over federal functions and taxes to the states, it developed a
series of proposals looking to greater effectiveness in intergovernmental collaboration. The committee was succeeded by a legislatively based, 26-member Advisory Commission on Intergovernmental Relations, established September 29, 1959.

centralization-via-separation-of-functions-and-taxes. They were unanimous in wanting to justify the committee's name and to produce action, not just another report.

The committee worked for more than two years. It found exactly two programs to recommend for transfer from federal to state hands. One was the federal grant program for vocational education (including practical-nurse training and aid to fishery trades); the other was federal grants for municipal waste treatment plants. The programs together cost the federal government less than $80 million in 1957, slightly more than two percent of the total federal grants for that year. To allow the states to pay for these programs, the committee recommended that they be allowed a credit against the federal tax on local telephone calls. Calculations showed that this offset device, plus an equalizing factor, would give every state at least 40 percent more from the tax than it received from the federal government in vocational education and sewage disposal grants. Some states were "equalized" to receive twice as much.

The recommendations were modest enough, and the generous financing feature seemed calculated to gain state support. The President recommended to Congress that all points of the program be legislated. None of them was, none has been since, and none is likely to be.

III. A POINT OF HISTORY

The American federal system has never been a system of separated governmental activities. There has never been a time when it was possible to put neat labels on discrete "federal," "state," and "local" functions. Even before the Constitution, a statute of 1785, reinforced by the Northwest Ordinance of 1787, gave grants-in-land to the states for public schools. Thus the national government was a prime force in making possible what is now taken to be the most local function of all, primary and secondary education. More important, the nation, before it was fully organized, established by this action a first principle of American federalism: the national government would use its superior resources to initiate and support national programs, principally administered by the states and localities.

The essential unity of state and federal financial systems was again recognized in the earliest constitutional days with the assumption by the federal government of the Revolutionary War debts of the states. Other points of federal-state collaboration during the Federalist period concerned the militia, law enforcement, court practices, the administration of elections, public health measures, pilot laws, and many other matters.

The nineteenth century is widely believed to have been the preeminent period of duality in the American system. Lord Bryce at the end of the century described (in *The American Commonwealth*) the federal and state governments as "distinct and separate in their action." The system, he said, was "like a great factory wherein two sets of machinery are at work, their revolving wheels apparently intermixed, their bands crossing one another, yet each set doing its own work without touching or hampering the other." Great works may contain gross errors. Bryce was wrong. The nineteenth century, like the early days of the republic, was a period principally characterized by intergovernmental collaboration.

Decisions of the Supreme Court are often cited as evidence of nineteenth-century duality. In the early part of the century the Court, heavily weighted with Federalists, was intent upon enlarging the sphere of national authority; in the later years (and to the 1930s) its actions were in the direction of paring down national powers and indeed all governmental authority. Decisions referred to "areas of exclusive competence" exercised by the federal government and the states; to their powers being "separated and distinct"; and to neither being able "to intrude within the jurisdiction of the other."

Judicial rhetoric is not always consistent with judicial action, and the Court did not always adhere to separatist doctrine. Indeed, its rhetoric sometimes indicated a positive view of cooperation. In any case, the Court was rarely, if ever, directly confronted with the issue of cooperation versus separation as such. Rather it was concerned with defining permissible areas of action for the central government and the states; or with saying with respect to a point at issue whether any government could take action. The Marshall Court contributed to intergovernmental cooperation by the very act of permitting federal operations where they had not existed before. Furthermore, even Marshall was willing to allow interstate commerce to be affected by the states in their use of the police power. Later courts also upheld state laws that had an impact on interstate commerce, just as they approved the expansion of the national commerce power, as in statutes providing for the control of telegraphic communication or prohibiting the interstate transportation of lotteries, impure foods and drugs, and prostitutes. Similar room for cooperation was found outside the commerce field, notably in the Court's refusal to interfere with federal grants-in-land or cash to the states. Although research to clinch the point has not been completed, it is probably true that the Supreme Court from 1800 to 1936 allowed far more federal-state collaboration than it blocked.

Political behavior and administrative action of the nineteenth century provide positive evidence that, throughout the entire era of so-called dual federalism, the many governments in the American federal system continued the close administrative and fiscal collaboration of the earlier period. Governmental activities were not extensive. But relative to what governments did, intergovernmental cooperation during the last century was comparable with that existing today.

Occasional presidential vetoes (from Madison to Buchanan) of cash and land grants are evidence of constitutional and ideological apprehensions about the extensive expansion of federal activities which produced widespread intergovernmental collaboration. In perspective, however, the vetoes are a more important evidence of the continuous search, not least by state officials, for ways and means to involve the central government in a wide variety of joint programs. The search was successful.

Grants-in-land and grants-in-services from the national government were of first importance in virtually all the principal functions undertaken by the states and their local subsidiaries. Land grants were made to the states for, among other purposes, elementary schools, colleges, and special educational institutions; roads, canals, rivers, harbors, and railroads; reclamation of desert and swamp lands; and veterans' welfare. In fact whatever was at the focus of state attention became the recipient of national grants. (Then, as today, national grants established state emphasis as well as followed it.) If Connecticut wished to establish a program for the care and education of the deaf and dumb, federal money in the form of a land grant was found to aid that program. If higher education relating to agriculture became a pressing need, Congress could dip into the public domain and make appropriate grants to states. If the need for swamp drainage and flood control appeared, the federal government could supply both grants-in-land and, from the Army's Corps of Engineers, the services of the only trained engineers then available.

Aid also went in the other direction. The federal government, theoretically in exclusive control of the Indian population, relied continuously (and not always wisely) on the experience and resources of state and local governments. State militias were an all-important ingredient in the nation's armed forces. State governments became unofficial but real partners in federal programs for homesteading, reclamation, tree culture, law enforcement, inland waterways, the nation's internal communications system (including highway and railroad routes), and veterans' aid of various sorts. Administrative contacts were voluminous, and the whole process of interaction was lubricated, then as today, by constituent-conscious members of Congress.

The essential continuity of the collaborative system is best demonstrated by the history of the grants. The land grant tended to become a cash grant based on the calculated disposable value of the land, and the cash grant tended to become an annual grant based upon the national government's superior tax powers. In 1887, only three years before the frontier was officially closed, thus signaling the end of the disposable public domain, Congress enacted the first continuing cash grants.

A long, extensive, and continuous experience is therefore the foundation of the present system of shared functions characteristic of the American federal system, what we have called the marble cake of government. It is a misjudgment of our history and our present situation to believe that a neat separation of governmental functions could take place without drastic alterations in our society and system of government.

IV. DYNAMICS OF SHARING: THE POLITICS OF THE FEDERAL SYSTEM

Many causes contribute to dispersed power in the federal system. One is the simple historical fact that the states existed before the nation. A second is in the form of creed, the traditional opinion of Americans that expresses distrust of centralized power and places great value in the strength and vitality of local units of government. Another is pride in locality and state, nurtured by the nation's size and by variations of regional and state history. Still a fourth cause of decentralization is the sheer wealth of the nation. It allows all groups, including state and local governments, to partake of the central government's largesse, supplies room for experimentation and even waste, and makes unnecessary the tight organization of political power that must follow when the support of one program necessarily means the deprivation of another.

In one important respect, the Constitution no longer operates to impede centralized government. The Supreme Court since 1937 has given Congress a relatively free hand. The federal government can build substantive programs in many areas on the taxation and commerce powers. Limitations of such central programs based on the argument, "it's unconstitutional," are no longer possible as long as Congress (in the Court's view) acts reasonably in the interest of the whole nation. The Court is unlikely to reverse this permissive view in the foreseeable future.

Nevertheless, some constitutional restraints on centralization continue to operate. The strong constitutional position of the states—for example, the assignment of two Senators to each state, the role given the states in administering even national elections, and the relatively few limitations on their lawmaking powers—establishes the geographical units as natural centers of administrative and political strength. Many clauses of the Constitution are not subject to the same latitude of interpretation as the commerce and tax clauses. The simple, clearly stated, unambiguous phrases—for example, the President "shall hold his office during the term of four years"—are subject to change only through the formal amendment process. Similar provisions exist with respect to the terms of Senators and Congressmen and the amendment process. All of them have the effect of retarding or restraining centralizing action of the federal government. The fixed terms of the President and members of Congress, for example, greatly impede the development of nationwide, disciplined political parties that almost certainly would have to precede continuous large-scale expansion of federal functions.

The constitutional restraints on the expansion of national authority are less important and less direct today than they were in 1879 or in 1936. But to say that they are less important is not to say that they are unimportant.

The nation's politics reflect these decentralizing causes and add some of their own. The political parties of the United States are unique. They seldom perform the function that parties traditionally perform in other countries, the function of gathering together diverse strands of power and welding them into one. Except during the period of nominating and electing a President and for the essential but nonsubstantive business of organizing the houses of Congress, the American parties rarely coalesce power at all. Characteristically they do the reverse, serving as a canopy under which special and local interests are represented with little regard for anything that can be called a party program. National leaders are elected on a party ticket, but in Congress they must seek cross-party support if their leadership is to be effective. It is a rare President during rare periods who can produce legislation without facing the defection of substantial numbers of his own party. (Wilson could do this in the first session of the Sixty-Third Congress; but Franklin D. Roosevelt could not, even during the famous hundred days of 1933.) Presidents whose parties form the majority of the Congressional houses must still count heavily on support from the other party.

The parties provide the pivot on which the entire governmental system swings. Party operations, first of all, produce in legislation the basic division of functions between the federal government, on the one hand, and state and local governments, on the other. The Supreme Court's permissiveness with respect to the expansion of national powers has not in fact produced any considerable extension of exclusive federal functions. The body of federal law in all fields has remained, in the words of Henry M. Hart, Jr., and Herbert Wechsler, "interstitial in its nature," limited in objective and resting upon the principal body of legal relationships defined by state law. It is difficult to find any area of federal legislation that is not significantly affected by state law.

In areas of new or enlarged federal activity, legislation characteristically provides important roles for state and local governments. This is as true of Democratic as of Republican administrations and true even of functions for which arguments of efficiency would produce exclusive federal responsibility. Thus the unemployment compensation program of the New Deal and the airport program of President Truman's administration both provided important responsibilities for state governments. In both cases attempts to eliminate state participation were defeated by a cross-party coalition of pro-state votes and influence. A large fraction of the Senate is usually made up of ex-governors, and the membership of both houses is composed of men who know that their reelection depends less upon national leaders or national party organization than upon support from their home constituencies. State and local officials are key members of these constituencies, often central figures in selecting candidates and in turning out the vote. Under such circumstances, national legislation taking state and local views heavily into account is inevitable.

Second, the undisciplined parties affect the character of the federal system as a result of Senatorial and Congressional interference in federal administrative programs on behalf of local interests. Many aspects of the legislative involvement in administrative affairs are formalized. The Legislative Reorganization Act of 1946, to take only one example, provided that each of the standing committees "shall exercise continuous watchfulness" over administration of laws within its jurisdiction. But the formal system of controls, extensive as it is, does not compare in importance with the informal and extralegal network of relationships in producing continuous legislative involvement in administrative affairs.

Senators and Congressmen spend a major fraction of their time representing problems of their constituents before administrative agencies. An even larger fraction of Congressional staff time is devoted to the same task. The total magnitude of such "case work" operations is great. In one five-month period of 1943 the Office of Price Administration received a weekly average of 842 letters from members of Congress. If phone calls and personal contacts are added, each member of Congress on the average presented the OPA with a problem involving one of his constituents twice a day in each five-day work week. Data for less vulnerable agencies during less intensive periods are also impressive. In 1958, to take only one example, the Department of Agriculture estimated (and underestimated) that it received an average of 159 Congressional letters per working day. Special Congressional liaison staffs have been created to service this mass of business, though all higher officials meet it in one form or another. The Air Force in 1958 had, under the command of a major general, 137 people (55 officers and 82 civilians) working in its liaison office.

The widespread, consistent, and in many ways unpredictable character of legislative interference in administrative affairs has many consequences for the tone and character of American administrative behavior. From the perspective of this paper, the important consequence is the comprehensive, day-to-day, even hour-by-hour, impact of local views on national programs. No point of substance or procedure is immune from Congressional scrutiny. A substantial portion of the entire weight of this impact is on behalf of the state and local governments. It is a weight that can alter procedures for screening immigration applications, divert the course of a national highway, change the tone of an international negotiation, and amend a social security law to accommodate local practices or fulfill local desires.

The party system compels administrators to take a political role. This is a third way in which the parties function to decentralize the American system. The administrator must play politics for the same reason that the politician is able to play in administration: the parties are without program and without discipline.

In response to the unprotected position in which the party situation places him, the administrator is forced to seek support where he can find it. One ever-present task is to nurse the Congress of the United States, that crucial constituency which ultimately controls his agency's budget and program. From the administrator's view, a sympathetic consideration of Congressional requests (if not downright submission to them) is the surest way to build the political support without which the administrative job could not continue. Even the completely task-oriented administrator must be sensitive to the need for

Congressional support and to the relationship between case work requests, on one side, and budgetary and legislative support, on the other. "You do a good job handling the personal problems and requests of a Congressman," a White House officer said, "and you have an easier time convincing him to back your program." Thus there is an important link between the nursing of Congressional requests, requests that largely concern local matters, and the most comprehensive national programs. The administrator must accommodate to the former as a price of gaining support for the latter.

One result of administrative politics is that the administrative agency may become the captive of the nationwide interest group it serves or presumably regulates. In such cases no government may come out with effective authority: the winners are the interest groups themselves. But in a very large number of cases, states and localities also win influence. The politics of administration is a process of making peace with legislators who for the most part consider themselves the guardians of local interests. The political role of administrators therefore contributes to the power of states and localities in national programs.

Finally, the way the party system operates gives American politics their overall distinctive tone. The lack of party discipline produces an openness in the system that allows individuals, groups, and institutions (including state and local governments) to attempt to influence national policy at every step of the legislative-administrative process. This is the "multiple-crack" attribute of the American government. "Crack" has two meanings. It means not only many fissures or access points; it also means, less statically, opportunities for wallops or smacks at government.

If the parties were more disciplined, the result would not be a cessation of the process by which individuals and groups impinge themselves upon the central government. But the present state of the parties clearly allows for a far greater operation of the multiple crack than would be possible under the conditions of centralized party control. American interest groups exploit literally uncountable access points in the legislative-administrative process. If legislative lobbying, from committee stages to the conference committee, does not produce results, a Cabinet secretary is called. His immediate associates are petitioned. Bureau chiefs and their aids are hit. Field officers are put under pressure. Campaigns are instituted by which friends of the agency apply a secondary influence on behalf of the interested party. A conference with the President may be urged.

To these multiple points for bringing influence must be added the multiple voices of the influencers. Consider, for example, those in a small town who wish to have a federal action taken. The easy merging of public and private interest at the local level means that the influence attempt is made in the name of the whole community, thus removing it from political partisanship. The Rotary Club as well as the City Council, the Chamber of Commerce and the mayor, eminent citizens and political bosses—all are readily enlisted. If a conference in a Senator's office will expedite matters, someone on the local scene can be found to make such a conference possible and effective. If technical information is needed, technicians will supply it. State or national professional organizations of local officials, individual Congressmen and Senators, and not infrequently whole state delegations will make the local cause their own. Federal field officers, who service localities, often assume local views. So may elected and appointed state officers. Friendships are exploited, and political mortgages called due. Under these circumstances, national policies are molded by local action.

In summary, then, the party system functions to devolve power. The American parties, unlike any other, are highly responsive when directives move from the bottom to the top, highly unresponsive from top to bottom. Congressmen and Senators can rarely ignore concerted demands from their home constituencies; but no party leader can expect the same kind of response from those below, whether he be a President asking for Congressional support or a Congressman seeking aid from local or state leaders.

Any tightening of the party apparatus would have the effect of strengthening the central government. The four characteristics of the system, discussed above, would become less important. If control from the top were strictly applied, these hallmarks of American decentralization might entirely disappear. To be specific, if disciplined and program-oriented parties were achieved: (1) It would make far less likely legislation that takes heavily into account the desires and prejudices of the highly decentralized power groups and institutions of the country, including the state and local governments. (2) It would to a large extent prevent legislators, individually and collectively, from intruding themselves on behalf of non-national interests in national administrative programs. (3) It would put an end to the administrator's search for his own political support, a search that often results in fostering state, local, and other non-national powers. (4) It would dampen the process by which individuals and groups, including state and local political leaders, take advantage of multiple cracks to steer national legislation and administration in ways congenial to them and the institutions they represent.

Alterations of this sort could only accompany basic changes in the organization and style of politics which, in turn, presuppose fundamental changes at the parties' social base. The sharing of functions is, in fact, the sharing of power. To end this sharing process would mean the destruction of whatever measure of decentralization exists in the United States today.

V. GOALS FOR THE SYSTEM OF SHARING

The Goal of Understanding. Our structure of government is complex, and the politics operating that structure are mildly chaotic. Circumstances are ever-changing. Old institutions mask intricate procedures. The nation's history can be read with alternative glosses, and what is nearest at hand may be furthest from comprehension. Simply to understand the federal system is therefore a difficult task. Yet without understanding there is little possibility of producing desired changes in the system. Social structures and processes are relatively impervious to purposeful change. They also exhibit intricate interrelationships so that change induced at point "A" often produces unanticipated results at point "Z." Changes introduced into an imperfectly understood system are as likely to produce reverse consequences as the desired ones.

This is counsel of neither futility nor conservatism for those who seek to make our government a better servant of the people. It is only to say that the first goal for those setting goals with respect to the federal system is that of understanding it.

Two Kinds of Decentralization. The recent major efforts to reform the federal system have in large part been aimed at separating functions and tax sources, at dividing them between the federal government and the states. All of these attempts have failed. We can now add that their success would be undesirable.

It is easy to specify the conditions under which an ordered separation of functions could take place. What is principally needed is a majority political party, under firm leadership, in control of both Presidency and Congress, and, ideally but not necessarily, also in control of a number of states. The political discontinuities, or the absence of party links, (1) between the governors and their state legislatures, (2) between the President and the governors, and (3) between the President and Congress clearly account for both the picayune recommendations of the Federal-State Action Committee and for the failure of even those recommendations in Congress. If the President had been in control of Congress (that is, consistently able to direct a majority of House and Senate votes), this alone would have made possible some genuine separation and devolution of functions. The failure to decentralize by order is a measure of the decentralization of power in the political parties.

Stated positively, party centralization must precede governmental decentralization by order. But this is a slender reed on which to hang decentralization. It implies the power to centralize. A majority party powerful enough to bring about ordered decentralization is far more likely to choose in favor of ordered centralization. And a society that produced centralized national parties would, by that very fact, be a society prepared to accept centralized government.

Decentralization by order must be contrasted with the different kind of decentralization that exists today in the United States. It may be called the decentralization of mild chaos. It exists because of the existence of dispersed power centers. This form of decentralization is less visible and less neat. It rests on no discretion of central authorities. It produces at times specific acts that many citizens may consider undesirable or evil. But power sometimes wielded even for evil ends may be desirable power. To those who find value in the dispersion of power, decentralization by mild chaos is infinitely more desirable than decentralization by order. The preservation of mild chaos is an important goal for the American federal system.

Oiling the Squeak Points. In a governmental system of genuinely shared responsibilities, disagreements inevitably occur. Opinions clash over proximate ends, particular ways of doing things become the subject of public debate, innovations are contested. These are not basic defects in the system. Rather, they are the system's energy-reflecting life blood. There can be no permanent "solutions" short of changing the system itself by elevating one partner to absolute supremacy. What can be done is to attempt to produce conditions in which conflict will not fester but be turned to constructive solutions of particular problems.

A long list of specific points of difficulty in the federal system can be easily identified. No adequate congressional or administrative mechanism exists to review the patchwork of grants in terms of national needs. There is no procedure by which to judge, for example, whether the national government is justified in spending so much more for highways than for education. The working force in some states is inadequate for the effective performance of some nationwide programs, while honest and not-so-honest graft frustrates efficiency in others. Some federal aid programs distort state budgets, and some are so closely supervised as to impede state action in meeting local needs. Grants are given for programs too narrowly defined, and overall programs at the state level consequently suffer. Administrative, accounting and auditing difficulties are the consequence of the multiplicity of grant programs. City officials complain that the states are intrusive fifth wheels in housing, urban redevelopment, and airport building programs.

Some differences are so basic that only a demonstration of strength on one side or another can solve them. School desegregation illustrates such an issue. It also illustrates the correct solution (although not the most desirable method of reaching it): in policy conflicts of fundamental importance, touching the nature of democracy itself, the view of the whole nation must prevail. Such basic ends, however, are rarely at issue, and sides are rarely taken with such passion that loggerheads are reached. Modes of settlement can usually be found to lubricate the squeak points of the system.

A pressing and permanent state problem, general in its impact, is the difficulty of raising sufficient revenue without putting local industries at a competitive disadvantage or without an expansion of sales taxes that press hardest on the least wealthy. A possible way of meeting this problem is to establish a state-levied income tax that could be used as an offset for federal taxes. The maximum level of the tax which could be offset would be fixed by federal law. When levied by a state, the state collection would be deducted from federal taxes. But if a state did not levy the tax, the federal government would. An additional fraction of the total tax imposed by the states would be collected directly by the federal government and used as an equalization fund, that is, distributed among the less wealthy states. Such a tax would almost certainly be imposed by all states since not to levy it would give neither political advantage to its public leaders nor financial advantage to its citizens. The net effect would be an increase in the total personal and corporate income tax.

The offset has great promise for strengthening state governments. It would help produce a more economic distribution of industry. It would have obvious financial advantages for the vast majority of states. Since a large fraction of all state income is used to aid political subdivisions, the local governments would also profit, though not equally as long as cities are underrepresented in state legislatures. On the other hand, such a scheme will appear disadvantageous to some low-tax states which profit from the in-migration of industry (though it would by no means end all state-by-state tax differentials). It will probably excite the opposition of those concerned over governmental centralization, and they will not be assuaged by methods that suggest themselves for making both state and central governments bear the psychological impact of the tax. Although the offset would probably produce an across-the-board tax increase, wealthier persons, who are affected more by an income tax than by other levies, can be expected to join forces with those whose fear is centralization. (This is a common alliance and, in the nature of things, the philosophical issue rather than financial advantage is kept foremost.)

Those opposing such a tax would gain additional ammunition from the certain knowledge that federal participation in the scheme would lead to some federal standards governing the use of the funds. Yet the political strength of the states would keep these from becoming onerous. Indeed, inauguration of the tax offset as a means of providing funds to the states might be an occasion for dropping some of the specifications for existing federal grants. One federal standard, however, might be possible because of the greater representation of urban areas in the constituency of Congress and the President than in the constituency of state legislatures: Congress might make a state's participation in the offset scheme dependent upon a periodic reapportionment of state legislatures.

The income tax offset is only one of many ideas that can be generated to meet serious problems of closely meshed governments. The fate of all such schemes ultimately rests, as it should, with the politics of a free people. But much can be done if the primary technical effort of those concerned with improving the federal system were directed not at separating its interrelated parts but at making them work together more effectively. Temporary commissions are relatively inefficient in this effort, though they may be useful for making general assessments and for generating new ideas. The professional organizations of government workers do part of the job of continuously scrutinizing programs and ways and means of improving them. A permanent staff, established in the President's office and working closely with state and local officials, could also perform a useful and perhaps important role.

The Strength of the Parts. Whatever governmental "strength" or "vitality" may be, it does not consist of independent decision-making in legislation and administration. Federal-state interpenetration here is extensive. Indeed, a judgment of the relative domestic strength of the two planes must take heavily into account the influence of one on the other's decisions. In such an analysis the strength of the states (and localities) does not weigh lightly. The nature of the nation's politics makes federal functions more vulnerable to state influence than state offices are to federal influence. Many states, as the Kestnbaum Commission noted, live with "self-imposed constitutional limitations" that make it difficult for them to "perform all of the services that their citizens require." If this has the result of adding to federal responsibilities, the states' importance in shaping and administering federal programs eliminates much of the sting.

The geography of state boundaries, as well as many aspects of state internal organization, are the products of history and cannot be justified on any grounds of rational efficiency. Who, today, would create major governmental subdivisions the size of Maryland, Delaware, New Jersey, or Rhode Island? Who would write into Oklahoma's fundamental law an absolute state debt limit of $500,000? Who would design (to cite only the most extreme cases) Georgia's and Florida's gross underrepresentation of urban areas in both houses of the legislature?

A complete catalogue of state political and administrative horrors would fill a sizeable volume. Yet exhortations to erase them have roughly the same effect as similar exhortations to erase sin. Some of the worst inanities—for example, the boundaries of the states, themselves—are fixed in the national constitution and defy alteration for all foreseeable time. Others, such as urban underrepresentation in state legislatures, serve the overrepresented groups, including some urban ones, and the effective political organization of the deprived groups must precede reform.

Despite deficiencies of politics and organizations that are unchangeable or slowly changing, it is an error to look at the states as static anachronisms. Some of them—New York, Minnesota, and California, to take three examples spanning the country—have administrative organizations that compare favorably in many ways with the national establishment. Many more in recent years have moved rapidly towards integrated administrative departments, statewide budgeting, and central leadership. The others have models-in-existence to follow, and active professional organizations (led by the Council of State Governments) promoting their development. Slow as this change may be, the states move in the direction of greater internal effectiveness.

The pace toward more effective performance at the state level is likely to increase. Urban leaders, who generally feel themselves disadvantaged in state affairs, and suburban and rural spokesmen, who are most concerned about national centralization, have a common interest in this task. The urban dwellers want greater equality in state affairs, including a more equitable share of state financial aid; nonurban dwellers are concerned that city dissatisfactions should not be met by exclusive federal, or federal-local, programs. Antagonistic, rather than amiable, cooperation may be the consequence. But it is a cooperation that can be turned to politically effective measures for a desirable upgrading of state institutions.

If one looks closely, there is scant evidence for the fear of the federal octopus, the fear that expansion of central programs and influence threatens to reduce the states and localities to compliant administrative arms of the central government. In fact, state and local governments are touching a larger proportion of the people in more ways than ever before; and they are spending a higher fraction of the total national product than ever before. Federal programs have increased, rather than diminished, the importance of the governors; stimulated professionalism in state agencies; increased citizen interest and participation in government; and, generally, enlarged and made more effective the scope of state action.[2] It may no longer be true in any significant sense that the states and localities are "closer" than the federal government to the people. It is true that the smaller governments remain active and powerful members of the federal system.

Central Leadership: The Need for Balance. The chaos of party processes makes difficult the task of presidential leadership. It deprives the President of ready-made Congressional majorities. It may produce, as in the chairmen of legislative committees, power-holders relatively hidden from public scrutiny and relatively protected from presidential direction. It allows the growth of administrative agencies which sometimes escape control by central officials. These are prices paid for a wide dispersion of political power. The cost is tolerable because the total results of dispersed power are themselves desirable and because, where clear national supremacy is essential, in foreign policy and military affairs, it is easiest to secure.

Moreover, in the balance of strength between the central and peripheral governments, the central government has on its side the whole secular drift towards the concentration of power. It has on its side technical developments that make central decisions easy and sometimes mandatory. It has on its side potent purse powers, the result of superior tax-gathering resources. It has potentially on its side the national leadership capacities of the presidential office. The last factor is the controlling one, and national strength in the federal system has shifted with the leadership desires and capacities of the Chief Executive. As these have varied, so there has been an almost rhythmic pattern: periods of central strength put to use alternating with periods of central strength dormant.

Following a high point of federal influence during the early and middle years of the New Deal, the postwar years have been, in the weighing of central-

[2]See the valuable report, *The Impact of Federal Grants-in-Aid on the Structure and Functions of State and Local Governments*, submitted to the Commission on Intergovernmental Relations by the Governmental Affairs Institute (Washington, 1955).

peripheral strength, a period of light federal activity. Excepting the Supreme Court's action in favor of school desegregation, national influence by design or default has not been strong in domestic affairs. The danger now is that the central government is doing too little rather than too much. National deficiencies in education and health require the renewed attention of the national government. Steepening population and urbanization trend lines have produced metropolitan area problems that can be effectively attacked only with the aid of federal resources. New definitions of old programs in housing and urban redevelopment, and new programs to deal with air pollution, water supply, and mass transportation are necessary. The federal government's essential role in the federal system is that of organizing, and helping to finance, such nationwide programs.

The American federal system exhibits many evidences of the dispersion of power not only because of formal federalism but more importantly because our politics reflect and reinforce the nation's diversities-within-unity. Those who value the virtues of decentralization, which writ large are virtues of freedom, need not scruple at recognizing the defects of those virtues. The defects are principally the danger that parochial and private interests may not coincide with, or give way to, the nation's interest. The necessary cure for these defects is effective national leadership.

The centrifugal force of domestic politics needs to be balanced by the centripetal force of strong presidential leadership. Simultaneous strength at center and periphery exhibits the American system at its best, if also at its noisiest. The interests of both find effective spokesmen. States and localities (and private interest groups) do not lose their influence opportunities, but national policy becomes more than the simple consequence of successful, momentary concentrations of non-national pressures: it is guided by national leaders.

Chapter 3

Civil Liberties and
Civil Rights

Civil liberties and civil rights cover a very broad area. Among the most
fundamental civil liberties are those governing the extent to which individuals can speak, write, and read what they choose. The democratic process
requires the free exchange of ideas. Constitutional government requires the
protection of minority rights and, above all, the right to dissent.

The Nationalization
of the Bill of Rights

It is clear from the debate over the inclusion of the Bill of Rights in the
Constitution of 1787 that its provisions were certainly never intended to be
prohibitions upon state action. The Bill of Rights was added to the Constitution to satisfy state governments that the same rights which they generally
accorded to their own citizens under state constitutions would apply with
respect to the national government, and act as a check upon abridgments
by the national government of civil liberties and civil rights. Proponents of
a separate bill of rights wanted specific provisions to limit the powers of
the national government which, *in its own sphere*, could act directly upon
citizens of the state.

Article Ten, which is not so much a part of the Bill of Rights as an expression of the balance of authority that exists between the national government and the states in the Constitution, provides that "the powers not delegated to the United States by the Constitution, nor prohibited by it to the states are reserved to the states respectively, or to the people." Under the federal system each member of the community is both (1) a citizen of the United States and (2) a citizen of the particular state in which he resides. The rights and obligations of each citizenship class are determined by the legal divisions of authority set up in the Constitution. Apart from specific limits upon state power to abridge civil liberties and civil rights, as for example the prohibitions of Section Ten against state passage of any bills of attainder or ex post facto laws, there is nothing in the main body of the Constitution or the Bill of Rights that controls state action. Originally it was up to the states to determine the protections they would give to their own citizens against state actions. The applicability of the Bill of Rights to national action only was affirmed in *Barron* v. *Baltimore,* 7 Peters 243 (1833).

The adoption of the Fourteenth Amendment in 1868 potentially limited the discretion that the states had possessed to determine the civil liberties and rights of citizens within their sphere of authority. The Fourteenth Amendment provided that:

> 1. All persons born or naturalized in the United States, and subject to the jurisdiction thereof, are citizens of the United States and of the state wherein they reside. No state shall make or enforce any law which shall abridge the privileges or immunities of citizens of the United States; nor shall any state deprive any person of life, liberty, or property, without due process of law; nor deny to any person within its jurisdiction the equal protection of the laws. . . .
>
> 5. The Congress shall have power to enforce, by appropriate legislation, the provisions of this article.

Although the Fourteenth Amendment appeared to be a tough restriction upon state action, its provisions were equivocal and required clarification by the Supreme Court before they could take effect. The history of the Fourteenth Amendment suggested that it was designed to protect the legal and political rights of blacks against state encroachment, and was not to have a broader application. In the *Slaughterhouse Cases,* 16 Wallace 36 (1873), the Supreme Court held that the privileges and immunities clause of the Fourteenth Amendment did nothing to alter the authority of the states to determine the rights and obligations of citizens subject to state action. Under this doctrine the Bill of Rights could not be made applicable to the states.

It was not until *Gitlow* v. *New York,* 268 U.S. 652 (1925), that the Court finally announced that the substantive areas of freedom of speech and of press of the First Amendment are part of the "liberty" protected by the

Fourteenth Amendment due process clause; however, in Gitlow's case the Court found that the procedures that had been used in New York to restrict his freedom of speech did not violate due process. In *Near v. Minnesota,* 283 U.S. 697 (1931), the Court for the first time overturned a state statute as a violation of the Fourteenth Amendment due process clause because it permitted prior censorship of the press. *Gitlow* and *Near* were limited because they incorporated only the freedom of speech and press provisions of the First Amendment under the due process clause of the Fourteenth Amendment. The cases marked the beginning of a slow and tedious process of "incorporation" of most of the provisions of the Bill of Rights as part of the due process clause of the Fourteenth Amendment. The process of incorporation did not begin in earnest until the Warren Court, and then not until the 1960s. By the late 1970s all of the Bill of Rights was incorporated as protections against state action, with the exceptions of the rights to grand jury indictment, trial by jury in *civil* cases, the right to bear arms, protection against excessive bail and fines, and protection against involuntary quartering of troops in private homes.[1]

The following case presents an example of incorporation of the right to counsel under the due process clause of the Fourteenth Amendment. In cases prior to *Gideon v. Wainwright,* decided in 1963, the Court had upheld an ad hoc right to counsel in individual cases. That is, it had held that the facts of a particular case warranted granting the right to counsel as part of due process under the Fourteenth Amendment for that particular case only. By such ad hoc determinations, the Court was able to exercise self-restraint in relation to federal-state relations, by not requiring a general right to counsel in all state criminal cases. *Powell v. Alabama,* 287 U.S. 45 (1932), was an example of such an ad hoc inclusion of the right to counsel in a specific case, where, in a one-day trial, seven blacks had been convicted of raping two white girls, and sentenced to death. The Court held that under the circumstances of the case the denial of counsel by the Alabama courts to the defendants violated the due process clause of the Fourteenth Amendment. In *Powell,* however, the Court did not incorporate the right to counsel in all criminal cases under this due process clause. It only provided that "in a capital case, where the defendant is unable to employ counsel, and is incapable adequately of making his own defense because of ignorance, feeblemindedness, illiteracy, or the like, it is the duty of the court, whether requested or not, to assign counsel for him as a necessary requisite of due process of law. . . ." The *Powell* case was widely interpreted as nationalizing (incorporating) the right to counsel in all *capital* cases. The Court reaffirmed its refusal to incorporate the right to counsel in all criminal cases

---

[1]For an excellent discussion of the incorporation of most of the Bill of Rights under the due process clause of the Fourteenth Amendment, see Henry J. Abraham, *Freedom and the Court* (3rd edition, New York: Oxford University Press, 1977), Chapter 3.

in *Betts* v. *Brady*, 316 U.S. 455 (1942). There the Court held that the Sixth Amendment applies only to trials in federal courts and that the right to counsel is not a fundamental right, essential to a fair trial, and therefore is not required in all cases under the due process clause of the Fourteenth Amendment. The Court emphasized that whether or not the right to counsel would be required depended upon the circumstances of the case in which it was requested.

In *Gideon* v. *Wainwright* the Court finally nationalized the right to counsel in all criminal cases under the due process clause of the Fourteenth Amendment. The case represented, in 1963, an important step in the progression toward nationalization of most of the Bill of Rights. While Justice Roberts, writing for the majority of the Court in the *Betts* case in 1942, found that the right to counsel was not fundamental to a fair trial, Justice Black, who had dissented in the *Betts* case, writing for the majority in *Gideon* v. *Wainwright* in 1962, held that the right to counsel was fundamental and essential to a fair trial and therefore was protected by the due process clause of the Fourteenth Amendment. In *Gideon*, Justice Black noted:

> We accept that the *Brady* assumption, based as it was on our prior cases, that a provision of the Bill of Rights which is "fundamental and essential to a fair trial" is made obligatory upon the states by the Fourteenth Amendment. We think the Court in *Betts* was wrong, however, in concluding that the Sixth Amendment's guarantee of counsel is not one of the fundamental rights.

The history of Supreme Court interpretation of the Fourteenth Amendment due process clause reveals the Court acting both politically and ideologically. In the period from 1868 to 1925 the Court was careful to exercise judicial self-restraint in interpreting the Fourteenth Amendment, in part because of the conservative views of most of the justices that the Court should not impose national standards of civil liberties and civil rights upon the states. The Court did not believe in self-restraint in all areas, as is demonstrated by its use of the due process clause of the Fourteenth Amendment to impose its own views on the proper relationship between the states and business. The Court read the Fourteenth Amendment due process clause in such a way as to protect the property interests of business against state regulation. Many such laws were found to be taking the liberty or property of business without due process. Beginning with *Gitlow* v. *New York* in 1925, the Court for the first time added substance to the due process clause of the Fourteenth Amendment in the area of civil liberties by including First Amendment freedoms of speech and press as part of the "liberty" of the due process clause.

While the Supreme Court is sensitive to the political environment in which it functions, the ways in which it has interpreted the due process clause of the Fourteenth Amendment suggest that ideological convictions are more important than pressure from political majorities. During the era of economic substantive due process under the Fourteenth Amendment, which ended in 1937, the Court was really taking an elitist position that did not agree with the political majorities in many states that were behind the regulatory laws that the Court struck down. Nor can it be said that when the Court began to add substance in civil liberties and civil rights to the due process clause and extend procedural protection that it was supported by political majorities. In fact, the Warren Court's extension of the Fourteenth Amendment due process clause, particularly in the area of criminal rights, caused a political outcry among the states and their citizens who felt that law-enforcement efforts would be unduly impeded. When the Court, in *Griswold* v. *Connecticut* in 1965, went beyond the explicit provisions of the Bill of Rights to find a right of privacy to strike down Connecticut's birth control statute that prevented the use of contraceptives in the state, even Justice Black, a strong supporter of incorporating the Bill of Rights under the due process clause, took objection. He found in the *Griswold* decision a return to substantive due process in a form that was unacceptable, because it was adding substance to the clause that was not explicitly provided for in the intent of the Fourteenth Amendment, which he had held in *Adamson* v. *California* in 1946 to be total inclusion of the Bill of Rights. The *Griswold* decision was not unpopular politically, but when the Court in *Roe* v. *Wade* in 1973 used the right of privacy to strike down a Texas abortion statute, and in effect declare all state laws that absolutely prohibited abortion to be unconstitutional, a nationwide anti-abortion movement was organized to overturn the decision by mobilizing political support behind a constitutional amendment. The Supreme Court has certainly not, in the area of interpretation of the Fourteenth Amendment, acted solely out of political motives.[2]

The following case presents an example of the way in which the Supreme Court gradually incorporated the Bill of Rights under the Fourteenth Amendment. Behind the decision to nationalize the right to counsel in *Gideon* v. *Wainwright* a fascinating series of events had occurred.[3] By the time the *Gideon* case was called up the Court was purposely looking for an appropriate case from which it could incorporate the right to counsel under the due process clause of the Fourteenth Amendment. The Court felt that Gideon's case presented the kind of circumstances that would be publicly accepted as requiring the right to counsel to ensure fairness. In granting certiorari to Gideon's *in forma pauperis* petition ("in the manner of the pauper," a permission to sue without incurring liability for costs) the Court

---

[2]The forces affecting Supreme Court decision-making are discussed in the selections by William J. Brennan, Jr., and John P. Roche in Chapter 9.

[3]The story of the case is brilliantly told by Anthony Lewis, in *Gideon's Trumpet* (New York: Random House, 1964).

had in effect already made up its mind about the decision. By the appointment of Attorney Abe Fortas, later to become a member of the Court (although eventually forced to resign because of conflict-of-interest charges), one of the most distinguished lawyers in the country, the Court guaranteed an eloquent and persuasive brief for the petitioner, Earl Gideon. The Court felt that the right to counsel was a right whose time had come by 1963.

11

GIDEON v. WAINWRIGHT
372 U.S. 335 (1963)

. . . Mr. Justice Black delivered the opinion of the Court, saying in part:

Petitioner was charged in a Florida state court with having broken and entered a poolroom with intent to commit a misdemeanor. This offense is a felony under Florida law. Appearing in court without funds and without a lawyer, petitioner asked the court to appoint counsel for him, whereupon the following colloquy took place:

> The COURT: Mr. Gideon, I am sorry, but I cannot appoint Counsel to represent you in this case. Under the laws of the State of Florida, the only time the Court can appoint Counsel to represent a Defendant is when that person is charged with a capital offense. I am sorry, but I will have to deny your request to appoint Counsel to defend you in this case.
>
> The DEFENDANT: The United States Supreme Court says I am entitled to be represented by Counsel.

Put to trial before a jury, Gideon conducted his defense about as well as could be expected from a layman. He made an opening statement to the jury, cross-examined the State's witnesses, presented witnesses in his own defense, declined to testify himself, and made a short argument "emphasizing his innocence to the charge contained in the Information filed in this case." The jury returned a verdict of guilty, and petitioner was sentenced to serve five years in the state prison. Later, petitioner filed in the Florida Supreme Court this habeas corpus petition attacking his conviction and sentence on the ground that the trial court's refusal to appoint counsel for him denied him rights "guaranteed by the

Constitution and the Bill of Rights by the United States Government."[1] Treating the petition for habeas corpus as properly before it, the State Supreme Court, "upon consideration thereof" but without an opinion, denied all relief. Since 1942, when *Betts v. Brady*, 316 U.S. 455 . . . was decided by a divided Court, the problem of a defendant's federal constitutional right to counsel in a state court has been a continuing source of controversy and litigation in both state and federal courts. To give this problem another review here, we granted certiorari. 370 U.S. 908. . . . Since Gideon was proceeding *in forma pauperis*, we appointed counsel to represent him and requested both sides to discuss in their briefs and oral arguments the following: "Should this Court's holding in *Betts v. Brady* . . . be reconsidered?"

I.

The facts upon which Betts claimed that he had been unconstitutionally denied the right to have counsel appointed to assist him are strikingly like the facts upon which Gideon here bases his federal constitutional claim. Betts was indicted for robbery in a Maryland state court. On arraignment, he told the trial judge of his lack of funds to hire a lawyer and asked the court to appoint one for him. Betts was advised that it was not the practice in that county to appoint counsel for indigent defendants except in murder and rape cases. He then pleaded not guilty, had witnesses summoned, cross-examined the State's witnesses, examined his own, and chose not to testify himself. He was found guilty by the judge, sitting without a jury, and sentenced to eight years in prison. Like Gideon, Betts sought release by habeas corpus, alleging that he had been denied the right to assistance of counsel in violation of the Fourteenth Amendment. Betts was denied any relief, and on review this Court affirmed. It was held that a refusal to appoint counsel for an indigent defendant charged with a felony did not necessarily violate the Due Process Clause of the Fourteenth Amendment, which for reasons given the Court deemed to be the only applicable federal constitutional provision. The Court said:

> Asserted denial [of due process] is to be tested by an appraisal of the totality of facts in a given case. That which may, in one setting, constitute a denial of fundamental fairness, shocking to the universal sense of justice, may, in other circumstances, and in the light of other considerations, fall short of such denial. 316 U.S., at 462. . . .

Treating due process as "a concept less rigid and more fluid than those envisaged in other specific and particular provisions of the Bill of Rights," the Court held that refusal to appoint counsel under the particular facts and circumstances in

---

In this selection some footnotes are omitted; all are renumbered.

[1]Later in the petition for habeas corpus, signed and apparently prepared by the petitioner himself, he stated, "I, Clarence Earl Gideon, claim that I was denied the rights of the 4th, 5th and 14th amendments of the Bill of Rights."

the Betts case was not so "offensive to the common and fundamental ideas of fairness" as to amount to a denial of due process. Since the facts and circumstances of the two cases are so nearly indistinguishable, we think the *Betts v. Brady* holding if left standing would require us to reject Gideon's claim that the Constitution guarantees him the assistance of counsel. Upon full reconsideration we conclude that *Betts v. Brady* should be overruled.

II.

The Sixth Amendment provides, "In all criminal prosecutions, the accused shall enjoy the right . . . to have the Assistance of Counsel for his defence." We have construed this to mean that in federal courts counsel must be provided for defendants unable to employ counsel unless the right is competently and intelligently waived. Betts argued that this right is extended to indigent defendants in state courts by the Fourteenth Amendment. In response the Court stated that, while the Sixth Amendment laid down "no rule for the conduct of the states, the question recurs whether the constraint laid by the amendment upon the national courts expresses a rule so fundamental and essential to a fair trial, and so, to due process of law, that it is made obligatory upon the states by the Fourteenth Amendment." 316 U.S., at 465. . . . In order to decide whether the Sixth Amendment's guarantee of counsel is of this fundamental nature, the Court in Betts set out and considered "[r]elevant data on the subject . . . afforded by constitutional and statutory provisions subsisting in the colonies and the states prior to the inclusion of the Bill of Rights in the national Constitution, and in the constitutional, legislative, and judicial history of the states to the present date." 316 U.S., at 465. . . . On the basis of this historical data the Court concluded that "appointment of counsel is not a fundamental right, essential to a fair trial." 316 U.S. at 471. . . . It was for this reason the Betts Court refused to accept the contention that the Sixth Amendment's guarantee of counsel for indigent federal defendants was extended to or, in the words of that Court, "made obligatory upon the states by the Fourteenth Amendment." Plainly, had the Court concluded that appointment of counsel for an indigent criminal defendant was "a fundamental right, essential to a fair trial," it would have held that the Fourteenth Amendment requires appointment of counsel in a state court, just as the Sixth Amendment requires in a federal court.

We think the Court in Betts had ample precedent for acknowledging that those guarantees of the Bill of Rights which are fundamental safeguards of liberty immune from federal abridgment are equally protected against state invasion by the Due Process Clause of the Fourteenth Amendment. This same principle was recognized, explained, and applied in *Powell v. Alabama*, 287 U.S. 45 (1932), a case upholding the right of counsel, where the Court held that despite sweeping language to the contrary in *Hurtado v. California*, 110 U.S. 516 (1884), the Fourteenth Amendment "embraced" those "fundamental principles of liberty and justice which lie at the base of all our civil and political institutions,' " even though they had been "specifically dealt with in another part of the Federal Constitution." 287 U.S., at 67. . . . In many cases other than Powell and Betts, this Court has looked to the fundamental nature of original Bill of Rights guarantees to decide whether the Fourteenth Amendment makes them obligatory on the States. Explicitly recognized to be of this "fundamental nature" and therefore made immune from state invasion by the Fourteenth, or some part of it, are the First Amendment's freedoms of speech, press, religion, assembly, association, and petition for redress of grievances. For the same reason, though not always in precisely the same terminology, the Court has made obligatory on the States the Fifth Amendment's command that private property shall not be taken for public use without just compensation, the Fourth Amendment's prohibition of unreasonable searches and seizures, and the Eighth's ban on cruel and unusual punishment. On the other hand, this Court in *Palko v. Connecticut*, 302 U.S. 319 . . . (1937), refused to hold that the Fourteenth Amendment made the double jeopardy provision of the Fifth Amendment obligatory on the States. In so refusing, however, the Court, speaking through Mr. Justice Cardozo, was careful to emphasize that "immunities that are valid as against the federal government by force of the specific pledges of particular amendments have been found to be implicit in the concept of ordered liberty, and thus, through the Fourteenth Amendment, become valid as against the states" and that guarantees "in their origin . . . effective against the federal government alone" had by prior cases "been taken over from the earlier articles of the Federal Bill of Rights and brought within the Fourteenth Amendment by a process of absorption." 302 U.S., at 324–325, 326. . . .

We accept *Betts v. Brady*'s assumption, based as it was on our prior cases, that a provision of the Bill of Rights which is "fundamental and essential to a fair trial" is made obligatory upon the States by the Fourteenth Amendment. We think the Court in Betts was wrong, however, in concluding that the Sixth Amendment's guarantee of counsel is not one of these fundamental rights. Ten years before *Betts v. Brady*, this Court, after full consideration of all the historical data examined in Betts, had unequivocally declared that "the right to the aid of counsel is of this fundamental character." *Powell v. Alabama*, 287 U.S. 45 . . . (1932). While the Court at the close of its Powell opinion did by its language, as this Court frequently does, limit its holding to the particular facts and circumstances of that case, its conclusions about the fundamental nature of the right to counsel are unmistakable. Several years later, in 1936, the Court reemphasized what it had said about the fundamental nature of the right to counsel in this language:

> We concluded that certain fundamental rights, safeguarded by the first eight amendments against federal action, were also safeguarded against state action by the due process of law clause of the Fourteenth Amendment, and among them the fundamental right of the accused to the aid of counsel in a criminal prosecution. *Grosjean v. American Press Co.*, 297 U.S. 233 . . . (1936).

And again in 1938 this Court said:

> [The assistance of counsel] is one of the safeguards of the Sixth Amendment
> deemed necessary to insure fundamental human rights of life and liberty. . . .
> The Sixth Amendment stands as a constant admonition that if the constitu-
> tional safeguards it provides be lost, justice will not 'still be done.' *Johnson* v.
> *Zerbst*, 304 U.S. 458 . . . (1938). To the same effect, see *Avery* v. *Alabama*,
> 308 U.S. 444 . . . (1940), and *Smith* v. *O'Grady*, 312 U.S. 329 . . . (1941).

In light of these and many other prior decisions of this Court, it is not
surprising that the Betts Court, when faced with the contention that "one
charged with crime, who is unable to obtain counsel, must be furnished counsel
by the state," conceded that "[e]xpressions in the opinions of this court lend
color to the argument . . ." 316 U.S., at 462–463. . . . The fact is that in
deciding as it did—that "appointment of counsel is not a fundamental right,
essential to a fair trial"—the Court in *Betts* v. *Brady* made an abrupt break with
its own well-considered precedents. In returning to these old precedents, soun-
der we believe than the new, we but restore constitutional principles established
to achieve a fair system of justice. Not only these precedents but also reason
and reflection require us to recognize that in our adversary system of criminal
justice, any person haled into court, who is too poor to hire a lawyer, cannot
be assured a fair trial unless counsel is provided for him. This seems to us to be
an obvious truth. Governments, both state and federal, quite properly spend
vast sums of money to establish machinery to try defendants accused of crime.
Lawyers to prosecute are everywhere deemed essential to protect the public's
interest in an orderly society. Similarly, there are few defendants charged with
crime, few indeed, who fail to hire the best lawyers they can get to prepare and
present their defenses. That government hires lawyers to prosecute and defendants who have the money hire lawyers to defend are the strongest indications
of the widespread belief that lawyers in criminal courts are necessities, not
luxuries. The right of one charged with crime to counsel may not be deemed
fundamental and essential to fair trials in some countries, but it is in ours. From
the very beginning, our state and national constitutions and laws have laid
great emphasis on procedural and substantive safeguards designed to assure fair
trials before impartial tribunals in which every defendant stands equal before
the law. This noble ideal cannot be realized if the poor man charged with crime
has to face his accusers without a lawyer to assist him. A defendant's need for
a lawyer is nowhere better stated than in the moving words of Mr. Justice
Sutherland in *Powell* v. *Alabama*:

> The right to be heard would be, in many cases, of little avail if it did not
> comprehend the right to be heard by counsel. Even the intelligent and edu-
> cated layman has small and sometimes no skill in the science of law. If charged
> with crime, he is incapable, generally, of determining for himself whether the
> indictment is good or bad. He is unfamiliar with the rules of evidence. Left
> without the aid of counsel he may be put on trial without a proper charge,

and convicted upon incompetent evidence, or evidence irrelevant to the issue or otherwise inadmissible. He lacks both the skill and knowledge adequately to prepare his defense, even though he have a perfect one. He requires the guiding hand of counsel at every step in the proceedings against him. Without it, though he be not guilty, he faces the danger of conviction because he does not know how to establish his innocence. 287 U.S., at 68–69. . . .

The Court in *Betts* v. *Brady* departed from the sound wisdom upon which the Court's holding in *Powell* v. *Alabama* rested. Florida, supported by two other States, has asked that *Betts* v. *Brady* be left intact. Twenty-two States, as friends of the Court, argue that Betts was "an anachronism when handed down" and that it should now be overruled. We agree.

The judgment is reversed and the cause is remanded to the Supreme Court of Florida for further action not inconsistent with this opinion.

Reversed.

Chief Justice Warren, and Justices Brennan, Stewart, White, and Goldberg join in the opinion of the Court.

Mr. Justice Douglas joins the opinion, giving a brief historical resume of the relation between the Bill of Rights and the Fourteenth Amendment. Mr. Justice Clark concurs in the result. Mr. Justice Harlan concurs in the result.

Freedom of Speech and Press

There are many reasons why we should support freedom of speech and press. One of these is the impossibility of proving the existence of an Absolute Truth. No person nor group can be infallible. The "best" decisions are those that are made on the basis of the most widespread information available pertaining to the subject at hand. Freedom of information is an integral part of the democratic process. In this selection from John Stuart Mill's famous essay *On Liberty*, published in 1859, the justifications for permitting liberty of speech and press are discussed.

12

John Stuart Mill
LIBERTY OF THOUGHT
AND DISCUSSION

The time, it is to be hoped, is gone by when any defence would be necessary of the "liberty of the press" as one of the securities against corrupt or tyrannical government. No argument, we may suppose, can now be needed, against permitting a legislature or an executive, not identified in interest with the people, to prescribe opinions to them, and determine what doctrines or what arguments they shall be allowed to hear. This aspect of the question, besides, has been so often and so triumphantly enforced by preceding writers, that it needs not be specially insisted on in this place. Though the law of England, on the subject of the press, is as servile to this day as it was in the time of the Tudors, there is little danger of its being actually put in force against political discussion, except during some temporary panic, when fear of insurrection drives ministers and judges from their propriety; and, speaking generally, it is not, in constitutional countries, to be apprehended, that the government, whether completely responsible to the people or not, will often attempt to control the expression of opinion, except when in doing so it makes itself the organ of the general intolerance of the public. Let us suppose, therefore, that the government is entirely at one with the people, and never thinks of exerting any power of coercion unless in agreement with what it conceives to be their voice. But I deny the right of the people to exercise such coercion, either by themselves or by their government. The power itself is illegitimate. The best government has no more title to it than the worst. It is as noxious, or more noxious, when exerted in accordance with public opinion, than when in opposition to it. If all mankind minus one, were of one opinion, and only one person were of the contrary opinion, mankind would be no more justified in silencing that one person, than he, if he had the power, would be justified in silencing mankind. Were an opinion a personal possession of no value except to the owner; if to be obstructed in the enjoyment of it were simply a private injury, it would make some difference whether the injury was inflicted only on a few persons or on many. But the peculiar evil of silencing the expression of an opinion is, that it is robbing the human race; posterity as well as the existing generation; those who dissent from the opinion, still more than those who hold it. If the opinion is right, they are deprived of the opportunity of exchanging error for truth: if wrong, they lose, what is almost as great a benefit, the clearer perception and livelier impression of truth, produced by its collision with error.

It is necessary to consider separately these two hypotheses, each of which has a distinct branch of the argument corresponding to it. We can never be sure that the opinion we are endeavoring to stifle is a false opinion; and if we were sure, stifling it would be an evil still.

First: the opinion which it is attempted to suppress by authority may possibly be true. Those who desire to suppress it, of course deny its truth; but they are not infallible. They have no authority to decide the question for all mankind, and exclude every other person from the means of judging. To refuse a hearing to an opinion, because they are sure that it is false, is to assume that *their* certainty is the same thing as *absolute* certainty. All silencing of discussion is an assumption of infallibility. Its condemnation may be allowed to rest on this common argument, not the worse for being common.

Unfortunately for the good sense of mankind, the fact of their fallibility is far from carrying the weight in their practical judgment, which is always allowed to it in theory; for while every one well knows himself to be fallible, few think it necessary to take any precautions against their own fallibility, or admit the supposition that any opinion, of which they feel very certain, may be one of the examples of the error to which they acknowledge themselves to be liable. Absolute princes, or others who are accustomed to unlimited deference, usually feel this complete confidence in their own opinions on nearly all subjects. People more happily situated, who sometimes hear their opinions disputed, and are not wholly unused to be set right when they are wrong, place the same unbounded reliance only on such of their opinions as are shared by all who surround them, or to whom they habitually defer: for in proportion to a man's want of confidence in his own solitary judgment, does he usually repose, with implicit trust, on the infallibility of "the world" in general. And the world, to each individual, means the part of it with which he comes in contact; his party, his sect, his church, his class of society: the man may be called, by comparison, almost liberal and largeminded to whom it means anything so comprehensive as his own country or his own age. Nor is his faith in this collective authority at all shaken by his being aware that other ages, countries, sects, churches, classes, and parties have thought, and even now think, the exact reverse. He devolves upon his own world the responsibility of being in the right against the dissentient worlds of other people; and it never troubles him that mere accident has decided which of these numerous worlds is the object of his reliance, and that the same causes which make him a Churchman in London, would have made him a Buddhist or a Confucian in Peking. Yet it is as evident in itself, as any amount of argument can make it, that ages are no more infallible than individuals; every age having held many opinions which subsequent ages have deemed not only false but absurd; and it is as certain that many opinions, now general, will be rejected by future ages, as it is that many, once general, are rejected by the present.

The objection likely to be made to this argument, would probably take some such form as the following. There is no greater assumption of infallibility in forbidding the propagation of error, than in any other thing which is done by public authority on its own judgment and responsibility. Judgment is given to men that they may use it. Because it may be used erroneously, are men to be told that they ought not to use it at all? To prohibit what they think pernicious, is not claiming exemption from error, but fulfilling the duty incumbent on them, although fallible, of acting on their conscientious conviction. If we were never to act on our opinions, because those opinions may be wrong, we should leave all our interests uncared for, and all our duties unperformed. An objection which applies to all conduct, can be no valid objection to any conduct in particular. It is the duty of governments, and of individuals, to form the truest opinions they can; to form them carefully, and never impose them upon others unless they are quite sure of being right. But when they are sure (such reasoners may say), it is not conscientiousness but cowardice to shrink from acting on their opinions, and allow doctrines which they honestly think dangerous to the welfare of mankind, either in this life or in another, to be scattered abroad without restraint, because other people, in less enlightened times, have persecuted opinions now believed to be true. Let us take care, it may be said, not to make the same mistake: but governments and nations have made mistakes in other things, which are not denied to be fit subjects for the exercise of authority: they have laid on bad taxes, made unjust wars. Ought we therefore to lay on no taxes, and, under whatever provocation, make no wars? Men, and governments, must act to the best of their ability. There is no such thing as absolute certainty, but there is assurance sufficient for the purposes of human life. We may, and must, assume our opinion to be true for the guidance of our own conduct: and it is assuming no more when we forbid bad men to pervert society by the propagation of opinions which we regard as false and pernicious.

I answer, that it is assuming very much more. There is the greatest difference between presuming an opinion to be true, because, with every opportunity for contesting it, it had not been refuted, and assuming its truth for the purpose of not permitting its refutation. Complete liberty of contradicting and disproving our opinion, is the very condition which justifies us in assuming its truth for purposes of action; and on no other terms can a being with human faculties have any rational assurance of being right.

When we consider either the history of opinion, or the ordinary conduct of human life, to what is it to be ascribed that the one and the other are no worse than they are? Not certainly to the inherent force of the human understanding; for, on any matter not self-evident, there are ninety-nine persons totally incapable of judging of it, for one who is capable; and the capacity of the hundredth person is only comparative; for the majority of the eminent men of every past generation held many opinions now known to be erroneous, and did or approved numerous things which no one will now justify. Why is it, then, that there is on the whole a preponderance among mankind of rational opinions and rational conduct? If there really is this preponderance—which there must be, unless human affairs are, and have always been, in an almost desperate state—it is owing to a quality of the human mind, the source of everything respectable in man either as an intellectual or as a moral being, namely, that his errors are corrigible. He is capable of rectifying his mistakes, by discussion and experience. Not by experience alone. There must be discussion, to show how experience is to be interpreted. Wrong opinions and practices gradually yield to fact and argument: but facts and arguments, to produce any effect on the mind, must be brought before it. Very few facts are able to tell their own story, without comments to bring out their meaning. The whole strength and value, then, of human judgment, depending on the one property, that it can be set right when it is wrong, reliance can be placed on it only when the means of setting it right are kept constantly at hand. In the case of any person whose judgment is really deserving of confidence, how has it become so? Because he has kept his mind open to criticism of his opinions and conduct. Because it has been his practice to listen to all that could be said against him; to profit by as much of it as was just, and expound to himself, and upon occasion to others, the fallacy of what was fallacious. Because he has felt, that the only way in which a human being can make some approach to knowing the whole of a subject, is by hearing what can be said about it by persons of every variety of opinion, and studying all modes in which it can be looked at by every character of mind. No wise man ever acquired his wisdom in any mode but this; nor is it in the nature of human intellect to become wise in any other manner. The steady habit of correcting and completing his own opinion by collating it with those of others, so far from causing doubt and hesitation in carrying it into practice, is the only stable foundation for a just reliance on it: for, being cognizant of all that can, at least obviously, be said against him, and having taken up his position against all gainsayers—knowing that he has sought for objections and difficulties, instead of avoiding them, and has shut out no light which can be thrown upon the subject from any quarter—he has a right to think his judgment better than that of any person, or any multitude, who have not gone through a similar process.

It is not too much to require that what the wisest of mankind, those who are best entitled to trust their own judgment, find necessary to warrant their relying on it, should be submitted to by that miscellaneous collection of a few wise and many foolish individuals, called the public. The most intolerant of churches, the Roman Catholic Church, even at the canonization of a saint, admits, and listens patiently to, a "devil's advocate." The holiest of men, it appears, cannot be admitted to posthumous honors, until all that the devil could say against him is known and weighed. If even the Newtonian philosophy were not permitted to be questioned, mankind could not feel as complete assurance of its truth as they now do. The beliefs which we have most warrant for, have no safeguard to rest on, but a standing invitation to the whole world to prove them unfounded. . . .

We have now recognized the necessity to the mental well-being of mankind (on which all their other well-being depends) of freedom of opinion, and freedom of the expression of opinion, on four distinct grounds; which we will now briefly recapitulate.

First, if any opinion is compelled to silence, that opinion may, for aught we can certainly know, be true. To deny this is to assume our own infallibility.

Secondly, though the silenced opinion be an error, it may, and very commonly does, contain a portion of truth; and since the general or prevailing opinion on any subject is rarely or never the whole truth, it is only by the collision of adverse opinions that the remainder of the truth has any chance of being supplied.

Thirdly, even if the received opinion be not only true, but the whole truth; unless it is suffered to be, and actually is, vigorously and earnestly contested, it will, by most of those who receive it, be held in the manner of a prejudice, with little comprehension of feeling of its rational grounds. And not only this, but fourthly, the meaning of the doctrine itself will be in danger of being lost, or enfeebled, and deprived of its vital effect on the character and conduct: the dogma becoming a mere formal profession, inefficacious for good, but cumbering the ground, and preventing the growth of any real and heartfelt conviction from reason or personal experience.

Before quitting the subject of freedom of opinion, it is fit to take some notice of those who say, that the free expression of all opinions should be permitted, on condition that the manner be temperate, and do not pass the bounds of fair discussion. Much might be said on the impossibility of fixing where these supposed bounds are to be placed; for if the test be offence to those whose opinion is attacked, I think experience testifies that this offence is given whenever the attack is telling and powerful, and that every opponent who pushes them hard, and whom they find it difficult to answer, appears to them, if he shows any strong feeling on the subject, an intemperate opponent. But this, though an important consideration in a practical point of view, merges in a more fundamental objection. Undoubtedly the manner of asserting an opinion, even though it be a true one, may be very objectionable, and may justly incur severe censure. But the principal offences of the kind are such as it is mostly impossible, unless by accidental self-betrayal, to bring home to conviction. The gravest of them is, to argue sophistically, to suppress facts or arguments, to misstate the elements of the case, or misrepresent the opposite opinion. But all this, even to the most aggravated degree, is so continually done in perfect good faith, by persons who are not considered, and in many other respects may not deserve to be considered, ignorant or incompetent, that it is rarely possible on adequate grounds conscientiously to stamp the misrepresentation as morally culpable; and still less could law presume to interfere with this kind of controversial misconduct. With regard to what is commonly meant by intemperate discussion, namely, invective, sarcasm, personality, and the like, the denunciation of these weapons would deserve more sympathy if it were ever proposed to interdict them equally to both sides; but it is only desired to restrain the employment of them against the prevailing opinion: against the unprevailing they may not only be used without general disapproval, but will be likely to obtain for him who uses them the praise of honest zeal and righteous indignation. Yet whatever mischief arises from their use, is greatest when they are employed against the comparatively defenceless; and whatever unfair advantage can be derived by any opinion from this mode of asserting it, accrues almost exclusively to received opinions. The worst offence of this kind which can be committed by a polemic, is to stigmatize those who hold the contrary opinion as bad and immoral men. To calumny of this sort, those who hold any unpopular opinion are peculiarly exposed, because they are in general few and uninfluential, and nobody but themselves feels much interest in seeing justice done them; but this weapon is, from the nature of the case, denied to those who attack a prevailing opinion: they can neither use it with safety to themselves, nor, if they could, would it do anything but recoil on their own cause. In general, opinions contrary to those commonly received can only obtain a hearing by studied moderation of language, and the most cautious avoidance of unnecessary offence, from which they hardly ever deviate even in a slight degree without losing ground: while unmeasured vituperation employed on the side of the prevailing opinion, really does deter people from professing contrary opinions, and from listening to those who profess them. For the interest, therefore, of truth and justice, it is far more important to restrain this employment of vituperative language than the other; and, for example, if it were necessary to choose, there would be much more need to discourage offensive attacks on infidelity, than on religion. It is, however, obvious that law and authority have no business with restraining either, while opinion ought, in every instance, to determine its verdict by the circumstances of the individual case; condemning every one, on whichever side of the argument he places himself, in whose mode of advocacy either want of candor, or malignity, bigotry, or intolerance of feeling manifest themselves; but not inferring these vices from the side which a person takes, though it be the contrary side of the question to our own: and giving merited honor to every one, whatever opinion he may hold, who had calmness to see and honesty to state what his opponents and their opinions really are, exaggerating nothing to their discredit, keeping nothing back which tells, or can be supposed to tell, in their favor. This is the real morality of public discussion; and if often violated, I am happy to think that there are many controversialists who to a great extent observe it, and a still greater number who conscientiously strive towards it.

❖❖   Mill does not justify absolute liberty of speech and press but implies that there are boundaries—although difficult to determine—to public debate. Democratic governments have always been faced with this dilemma: At what point can freedom of speech and press be curtailed? The Supreme Court has had difficulty in making decisions in areas involving censorship and loyalty and security. Freedom of speech and press cannot be used to destroy the very government that protects civil liberties.

Justice Holmes, in *Schenck v. United States,* 249 U.S. 47 (1919), stated his famous "clear and present danger" test, which subsequently was applied at both the national and state levels, for deciding whether or not Congress could abridge freedom of speech under the First Amendment:

"The most stringent protection of free speech would not protect a man in falsely shouting fire in a theatre and causing a panic. It does not protect a man from an injunction against uttering words that may have all the effects of force. . . . The question in every case is whether the words used are used in such circumstances and are of such a nature as to create a clear and present danger that they will bring about the substantive evils that Congress has a right to prevent. It is a question of proximity and degree. When a nation is at war many things that might be said in time of peace are such a hindrance to its efforts that their utterance will not be endured so long as men fight and that no Court could regard them as protected by any constitutional right."

In 1940 Congress passed the Smith Act, Section 2 of which made it unlawful for any person:

"(1) to knowingly or willfully advocate, abet, advise, or teach the duty, necessity, desirability, or propriety of overthrowing or destroying any government in the United States by force or violence . . . ; (2) with intent to cause the overthrow or destruction of any government in the United States, to print, publish, edit, issue, circulate, sell, distribute, or publicly display any written or printed matter advocating, advising, or teaching the duty, necessity, desirability, or propriety of overthrowing or destroying any government in the United States by force or violence; (3) to organize or help to organize any society, group, or assembly of persons who teach, advocate, or encourage the overthrow or destruction of any government in the United States by force or violence; or to be or become a member of, or affiliate with, any such society . . . , knowing the purposes thereof."

The constitutionality of this act was tested in *Dennis v. United States,* 341 U.S. 494 (1951), which contained five opinions. Vinson spoke for the Court, with Frankfurter and Jackson concurring; Black and Douglas dissented.

13

DENNIS v. UNITED STATES
341 U.S. 494 (1951)

Mr. Chief Justice Vinson announced the judgment of the Court, saying in part:

Petitioners were indicted in July, 1948, for violation of the conspiracy provisions of the Smith Act. . . . A verdict of guilty as to all the petitioners was returned by the jury on October 14, 1949. The Court of Appeals affirmed the convictions. . . . We granted certiorari. . . .

. . . Our limited grant of the writ of certiorari has removed from our consideration any question as to the sufficiency of the evidence to support the jury's determination that petitioners are guilty of the offense charged. Whether on this record petitioners did in fact advocate the overthrow of the government by force and violence is not before us, and we must base any discussion of this point upon the conclusions stated in the opinion of the Court of Appeals, which treated the issue in great detail. That court held that the record in this case amply supports the necessary finding of the jury that petitioners, the leaders of the Communist Party in this country, were unwilling to work within our framework of democracy, but intended to initiate a violent revolution whenever the propitious occasion appeared. . . .

I

It will be helpful in clarifying the issues to treat next the contention that the trial judge improperly interpreted the statute by charging that the statute required an unlawful intent before the jury could convict. More specifically, he charged that the jury could not find the petitioners guilty under the indictment unless they found that petitioners had the intent to "overthrow . . . the Government of the United States by force and violence as speedily as circumstances would permit."

. . . The structure and purpose of the statute demand the inclusion of intent as an element of the crime. Congress was concerned with those who advocate and organize for the overthrow of the government. Certainly those who recruit and combine for the purpose of advocating overthrow intend to bring about that overthrow. We hold that the statute requires as an essential element of the crime proof of the intent of those who are charged with its violation to overthrow the government by force and violence. . . .

II

The obvious purpose of the statute is to protect existing government, not from change by peaceable, lawful and constitutional means, but from change by violence, revolution, and terrorism. That it is within the *power* of the Congress to protect the government of the United States from armed rebellion is a proposition which requires little discussion. Whatever theoretical merit there may be to the argument that there is a "right" to rebellion against dictatorial governments is without force where the existing structure of the government provides for peaceful and orderly change. We reject any principle of governmental helplessness in the face of preparation for revolution, which principle, carried to its logical conclusion, must lead to anarchy. No one could conceive that it is not within the power of Congress to prohibit acts intended to overthrow the government by force and violence. The question with which we are concerned here is not whether Congress has such *power*, but whether the *means* that it has employed conflict with the First and Fifth Amendments to the Constitution.

One of the bases for the contention that the means which Congress has employed are invalid takes the form of an attack on the face of the statute on the grounds that by its terms it prohibits academic discussion of the merits of Marxism-Leninism, that it stifles ideas and is contrary to all concepts of a free speech and a free press. Although we do not agree that the language itself has that significance, we must bear in mind that it is the duty of the federal courts to interpret federal legislation in a manner not inconsistent with the demands of the Constitution. . . . This is a federal statute which we must interpret as well as judge. . . .

The very language of the Smith Act negates the interpretation which petitioners would have us impose on the Act. It is directed at advocacy, not discussion. Thus, the trial judge properly charged the jury that they could not convict if they found that petitioners did "no more than pursue peaceful studies and discussions or teaching and advocacy in the realm of ideas." He further charged that it was not unlawful "to conduct in an American college or university a course explaining the philosophical theories set forth in the books which have been placed in evidence." Such a charge is in strict accord with the statutory language, and illustrates the meaning to be placed on those words. Congress did not intend to eradicate the free discussion of political theories, to destroy the traditional rights of Americans to discuss and evaluate ideas without fear of governmental sanction. Rather Congress was concerned with the very kind of activity in which the evidence showed these petitioners engaged.

III

But although the statute is not directed at the hypothetical cases which petitioners have conjured, its application in this case has resulted in convictions for the teaching and advocacy of the overthrow of the government by force and violence, which, even though coupled with the intent to accomplish that overthrow, contains an element of speech. For this reason, we must pay special heed to the demands of the First Amendment marking out the boundaries of speech.

We pointed out in *Douds, supra*, that the basis of the First Amendment is the hypothesis that speech can rebut speech, propaganda will answer propaganda, free debate of ideas will result in the wisest governmental policies. It is for this reason that this Court has recognized the inherent value of free discourse. An analysis of the leading cases in this Court which have involved direct limitations on speech, however, will demonstrate that both the majority of the Court and the dissenters in particular cases have recognized that this is not an unlimited, unqualified right, but that the societal value of speech must, on occasion, be subordinated to other values and considerations. . . .

The rule we deduce from these cases [*Schenck* and others] is that where an offense is specified by a statute in nonspeech or nonpress terms, a conviction relying upon speech or press as evidence of violation may be sustained only when the speech or publication created a "clear and present danger" of attempting or accomplishing the prohibited crime, e.g. interference with enlistment. The dissents . . . in emphasizing the value of speech, were addressed to the argument of the sufficiency of the evidence. . . .

In this case we are squarely presented with the application of the "clear and present danger" test, and must decide what that phrase imports. We first note that many of the cases in which this Court has reversed convictions by use of this or similar tests have been based on the fact that the interest which the state was attempting to protect was itself too insubstantial to warrant restriction of speech. . . . Overthrow of the government by force and violence is certainly a substantial enough interest for the government to limit speech. Indeed, this is the ultimate value of any society, for if a society cannot protect its structure from armed internal attack, it must follow that no subordinate value can be protected. If, then, this interest may be protected, the literal problem which is presented is what has been meant by the use of the phrase "clear and present danger" of the utterances bringing about the evil within the power of Congress to punish.

Obviously, the words cannot mean that before the government may act, it must wait until the *putsch* is about to be executed, the plans have been laid and the signal is awaited. If government is aware that a group aiming at its overthrow is attempting to indoctrinate its members and to commit them to a course whereby they will strike when the leaders feel the circumstances permit, action by the government is required. The argument that there is no need for government to concern itself, for government is strong, it possesses ample powers to put down a rebellion, it may defeat the revolution with ease needs no answer. For that is not the question. Certainly an attempt to overthrow the government by force, even though doomed from the outset because of inadequate numbers or power of the revolutionists, is a sufficient evil for Congress to prevent. The damage which such attempts create both physically and politically to a nation makes it impossible to measure the validity in terms of the probability of success, or the immediacy of a successful attempt. In the instant case the trial judge charged the jury that they could not convict unless they found that petitioners intended to overthrow the government "as speedily as circumstances would permit." This does not mean, and could not properly mean, that they would not strike until there was certainty of success. What was meant was that the revolutionists would strike when they thought the time was ripe. We must therefore reject the contention that success or probability of success is the criterion.

The situation with which Justices Holmes and Brandeis were concerned in *Gitlow* was a comparatively isolated event [involving a conviction for criminal anarchy in New York of one Gitlow for circulating Communist literature], bearing little relation in their minds to any substantial threat to the safety of the community. . . . They were not confronted with any situation comparable to the instant one—the development of an apparatus designed and dedicated to the overthrow of the government, in the context of world crisis after crisis.

Chief Justice Learned Hand, writing for the majority below, interpreted the phrase as follows: "In each case [courts] must ask whether the gravity of the 'evil,' discounted by its improbability, justifies such invasion of free speech as is necessary to avoid the danger." 183 F.2d at 212. We adopt this statement of the rule. . . .

Likewise, we are in accord with the court below, which affirmed the trial court's finding that the requisite danger existed. The mere fact that from the period 1945 to 1948 petitioners' activities did not result in an attempt to overthrow the government by force and violence is of course no answer to the fact that there was a group that was ready to make the attempt. The formation by petitioners of such a highly organized conspiracy, with rigidly disciplined members subject to call when the leaders, these petitioners, felt that the time had come for action, coupled with the inflammable nature of world conditions, similar uprisings in other countries, and the touch-and-go nature of our relations with countries with whom petitioners were in the very least ideologically attuned, convince us that their convictions were justified on this score. And this analysis disposes of the contention that a conspiracy to advocate, as distinguished from the advocacy itself, cannot be constitutionally restrained, because it comprises only the preparation. It is the existence of the conspiracy which creates the danger. . . . If the ingredients of the reaction are present, we cannot bind the government to wait until the catalyst is added. . . .

We hold that § § 2(a) (1), 2(a) (2) and (3) of the Smith Act, do not inherently, or as construed or applied in the instant case, violate the First Amendment and other provisions of the Bill of Rights, or the First and Fifth Amendments because of indefiniteness. Petitioners intended to overthrow the government of the United States as speedily as the circumstances would permit. Their conspiracy to organize the Communist Party and to teach and advocate the overthrow of the government of the United States by force and violence created a "clear and present danger" of an attempt to overthrow the government by force and violence. They were properly and constitutionally convicted for violation of the Smith Act. The judgments of conviction are affirmed. . . .

Mr. Justice Black, dissenting, said in part:

. . . At the outset I want to emphasize what the crime involved in this case is, and what it is not. These petitioners were not charged with an attempt to overthrow the government. They were not charged with overt acts of any kind designed to overthrow the government. They were not even charged with saying anything or writing anything designed to overthrow the government. The charge was that they agreed to assemble and to talk and publish certain ideas at a later date: The indictment is that they conspired to organize the Communist Party and to use speech or newspapers and other publications in the future to teach and advocate the forcible overthrow of the government. No matter how it is worded, this is a virulent form of prior censorship of speech and press, which I believe the First Amendment forbids. . . .

But let us assume, contrary to all constitutional ideas of fair criminal pro-cedure, that petitioners although not indicted for the crime of actual advocacy, may be punished for it. Even on this radical assumption, the other opinions in this case show that the only way to affirm these convictions is to repudiate directly or indirectly the established "clear and present danger" rule. This the Court does in a way which greatly restricts the protections afforded by the First Amendment. The opinions for affirmance indicate that the chief reason for jettisoning the rule is the expressed fear that advocacy of Communist doctrine endangers the safety of the Republic. Undoubtedly, a governmental policy of unfettered communication of ideas does entail dangers. To the Founders of this nation, however, the benefits derived from free expression were worth the risk. They embodied this philosophy in the First Amendment's command that "Con-gress shall make no law . . . abridging the freedom of speech, or of the press. . . ." I have always believed that the First Amendment is the keystone of our government, that the freedoms it guarantees provide the best insurance against destruction of all freedom. At least as to speech in the realm of public matters, I believe that the "clear and present danger" test does not "mark the furthermost constitutional boundaries of protected expression" but does "no more than recognize a minimum compulsion of the Bill of Rights.". . .

So long as this Court exercises the power of judicial review of legislation, I cannot agree that the First Amendment permits us to sustain laws suppressing freedom of speech and press on the basis of Congress's or our own notions of mere "reasonableness." Such a doctrine waters down the First Amendment so that it amounts to little more than an admonition to Congress. The Amendment as so construed is not likely to protect any but those "safe" or orthodox views which rarely need its protection. I must also express my objection to the holding because, as Mr. Justice Douglas's dissent shows, it sanctions the determination of a crucial issue of fact by the judge rather than by the jury. Nor can I let this opportunity pass without expressing my objection to the severely limited grant of certiorari in this case which precluded consideration here of at least two other reasons for reversing these convictions: (1) the record shows a discriminatory selection of the jury panel which prevented trial before a representative cross-section of the community; (2) the record shows that one member of the trial jury was violently hostile to petitioners before and during the trial.

Public opinion being what it now is, few will protest the conviction of these Communist petitioners. There is hope, however, that in calmer times, when present pressure, passions and fears subside, this or some later Court will restore the First Amendment liberties to the high preferred place where they belong in a free society.

Mr. Justice Douglas, dissenting, said in part:

. . . [N]ever until today has anyone seriously thought that the ancient law of conspiracy could constitutionally be used to turn speech into seditious conduct. Yet that is precisely what is suggested. I repeat that we deal here with speech alone, not with speech *plus* acts of sabotage or unlawful conduct. Not a single seditious act is charged in the indictment. . . .

Free speech has occupied an exalted position because of the high service it has given our society. Its protection is essential to the very existence of a democracy. The airing of ideas releases pressures which otherwise might become destructive. When ideas compete in the market for acceptance, full and free discussion exposes the false and they gain few adherents. Full and free discussion even of ideas we hate encourages the testing of our own prejudices and preconceptions. Full and free discussion keeps a society from becoming stagnant and unprepared for the stresses and strains that work to tear all civilizations apart.

Full and free discussion has indeed been the first article of our faith. We have founded our political system on it. It has been the safeguard of every religious, political, philosophical, economic, and racial group amongst us. We have counted on it to keep us from embracing what is cheap and false; we have trusted the common sense of our people to choose the doctrine true to our genius and to reject the rest. This has been the one single outstanding tenet that has made our institutions the symbol of freedom and equality. We have deemed it more costly to liberty to suppress a despised minority than to let them vent their spleen. We have above all else feared the political censor. We have wanted a land where our people can be exposed to all the diverse creeds and cultures of the world.

There comes a time when even speech loses its constitutional immunity. Speech innocuous one year may at another time fan such destructive flames that it must be halted in the interest of the safety of the Republic. That is the meaning of the clear and present danger test. When conditions are so critical that there will be no time to avoid the evil that the speech threatens, it is time to call a halt. Otherwise, free speech which is the strength of the nation will be the cause of its destruction.

Yet free speech is the rule, not the exception. The restraint to be constitutional must be based on more than fear, on more than passionate opposition against the speech, on more than a revolted dislike for its contents. There must be some immediate injury to society that is likely if speech is allowed. . . .

. . . This record . . . contains no evidence whatsoever showing that the acts charged, viz., the teaching of the Soviet theory of revolution with the hope that it will be realized, have created any clear and present danger to the nation. The Court, however, rules to the contrary. . . .

The political impotence of the Communists in this country does not, of course, dispose of the problem. Their numbers; their positions in industry and government; the extent to which they have in fact infiltrated the police, the armed services, transportation, stevedoring, power plants, munition works, and other critical places—these facts all bear on the likelihood that their advocacy of the Soviet theory of revolution will endanger the Republic. But the record is silent on these facts. If we are to proceed on the basis of judicial notice, it is impossible for me to say that the Communists in this country are so potent or so strategically deployed that they must be suppressed for their speech. I could not so hold unless I were willing to conclude that the activities in recent years of committees of Congress, of the Attorney General, of labor unions, of state legislatures, and of Loyalty Boards were so futile as to leave the country on the edge of grave peril. To believe that petitioners and their following are placed in such critical positions as to endanger the nation is to believe the incredible. It is safe to say that the followers of the creed of Soviet Communism are known to the FBI; that in case of war with Russia they will be picked up overnight as were all prospective saboteurs at the commencement of World War II; that the invisible army of petitioners is the best known, the most beset, and the least thriving of any fifth column in history. Only those held by fear and panic could think otherwise. . . .

. . . The political censor has no place in our public debates. Unless and until extreme and necessitous circumstances are shown, our aim should be to keep speech unfettered and to allow the processes of law to be invoked only when the provocateurs among us move from speech to action.

Vishinsky wrote in 1938 in the Law of the Soviet state, "In our state, naturally, there is and can be no place for freedom of speech, press, and so on for the foes of socialism."

Our concern should be that we accept no such standard for the United States. Our faith should be that our people will never give support to those advocates of revolution, so long as we remain loyal to the purposes for which our nation was founded.

❖❖   The Supreme Court applied the clear and present danger test in the *Dennis* case to uphold the constitutionality of the Smith Act of 1940. Significantly, the Court's limited writ of certiorari prevented it from reviewing whether or not the facts of the case warranted a conclusion that a clear and present danger actually existed because of the actions of the Communist party officials involved. The Court accepted the findings of the trial court that such a danger did exist, and concluded that the law under which the defendants were convicted was a reasonable exercise of congressional power to prevent the overthrow of the government by force and violence. Federal prosecutors concluded that the *Dennis* decision gave them carte blanche to seek indictments and convictions of Communist party officials on the ground that their membership in the party per se supported the conclusion that they were forcibly attempting to overthrow the government. Supporting the prosecutors' view was the statement by the *Dennis* majority that "It is the existence of the conspiracy which creates the danger . . . if the ingredients of the reaction are present, we cannot bind the government to wait until the catalyst is added."

The Court modified its *Dennis* doctrine, however, in *Yates v. United States*, 354 U.S. 298 (1957), in which federal prosecutors had obtained convictions against lower-level Communist party officials for conspiring to overthrow the government by force and violence in violation of the Smith Act. The trial court's charge to the jury failed to mention that in order to convict the defendants jurors would have to find that their advocacy of forceful governmental overthrow was intended and likely to bring action to that end. The Supreme Court's opinion stated: "We are . . . faced with the question whether the Smith Act prohibits advocacy and teaching of forcible overthrow as an abstract principle, divorced from any effort to instigate action to that end, so long as such advocacy or teaching is engaged in with evil intent. We hold that it does not."

In the following case the Court reaffirmed its interpretation of the "clear and present danger" doctrine to require more than mere advocacy of violent political change to sustain governmental suppression of freedoms of expression. The state of Ohio had used its outdated Criminal Syndicalism Statute, enacted in 1919, to prosecute and convict a Ku Klux Klan leader in the 1960s for advocating violent and forcible governmental change. The Court held the statute to be unconstitutional because of its punishment of mere advocacy without requiring the demonstration of a clear and present danger that lawless action would result.

14

BRANDENBURG v. OHIO
395 U.S. 444 (1969)

PER CURIAM:

The appellant, a leader of a Ku Klux Klan group, was convicted under the Ohio Criminal Syndicalism statute for "advocat[ing] . . . the duty, necessity, or propriety of crime, sabotage, violence, or unlawful methods of terrorism as a means of accomplishing industrial or political reform" and for "voluntarily assembl[ing] with any society, group, or assemblage of persons formed to teach or advocate the doctrines of criminal syndicalism." Ohio Rev. Code Ann. § 2923.13. He was fined $1,000 and sentenced to one to 10 years' imprisonment. The appellant challenged the constitutionality of the criminal syndicalism statute under the First and Fourth Amendments to the United States Constitution, but the intermediate appellate court of Ohio affirmed his conviction without opinion. The Supreme Court of Ohio dismissed his appeal . . . "for the reason that no substantial constitutional question exists herein." . . .

The record shows that a man, identified at trial as the appellant, telephoned an announcer-reporter on the staff of a Cincinnati television station and invited him to come to a Ku Klux Klan "rally" to be held at a farm in Hamilton County. With the cooperation of the organizers, the reporter and a cameraman attended the meeting and filmed the events. Portions of the films were later broadcast on the local station and on a national network.

The prosecution's case rested on the films and on testimony identifying the appellant as the person who communicated with the reporter and who spoke at the rally. The State also introduced into evidence several articles appearing in the film, including a pistol, a rifle, a shotgun, ammunition, a Bible, and a red hood worn by the speaker in the films.

One film showed 12 hooded figures, some of whom carried firearms. They were gathered around a large wooden cross, which they burned. No one was present other than the participants and the newsmen who made the film. Most of the words uttered during the scene were incomprehensible when the film was projected, but scattered phrases could be understood that were derogatory of Negroes and, in one instance, of Jews. Another scene on the same film showed the appellant, in Klan regalia, making a speech. The speech, in full, was as follows:

> This is an organizers' meeting. We have had quite a few members here today which are—we have hundreds, hundreds of members throughout the State of Ohio. I can quote from a newspaper clipping from the Columbus, Ohio Dispatch, five weeks ago Sunday morning. The Klan has more members in the State of Ohio than does any other organization. We're not a revengent organization, but if our President, our Congress, our Supreme Court, continues to suppress the white, Caucasian race, it's possible that there might have to be some revengeance taken.
>
> We are marching on Congress July the Fourth, four hundred thousand strong. From there we are dividing into two groups, one group to march on St Augustine, Florida, the other group to march into Mississippi. Thank you.

The second film showed six hooded figures one of whom, later identified as the appellant, repeated a speech very similar to that recorded on the first film. The reference to the possibility of "revengeance" was omitted, and one sentence was added: "Personally, I believe the nigger should be returned to Africa, the Jew returned to Israel." Though some of the figures in the films carried weapons, the speaker did not.

The Ohio Criminal Syndicalism Statute was enacted in 1919. From 1917 to 1920, identical or quite similar laws were adopted by 20 States and two territories. E. Dowell, A History of Criminal Syndicalism Legislation in the United States 21 (1939). In 1927, this Court sustained the constitutionality of California's Criminal Syndicalism Act, . . . the text of which is quite similar to that of the laws of Ohio. *Whitney* v. *California* [1927] . . . The Court upheld the statute on the ground that, without more, "advocating" violent means to effect political and economic change involves such danger to the security of the State that the State may outlaw it. . . . But *Whitney* has been thoroughly discredited by later decisions. See *Dennis* v. *United States*. . . . These later decisions have fashioned the principle that the constitutional guarantees of free speech and free press do not permit a State to forbid or proscribe advocacy of the use of force or of law violation except where such advocacy is directed to inciting or producing imminent lawless action and is likely to incite or produce such action. As we said in *Noto* v. *United States* [1961] . . . "the mere abstract teaching . . . of the moral propriety or even moral necessity for a resort to force and violence, is not the same as preparing a group for violent action and steeling it to such action." . . . *Lowry*. A statute which fails to draw this destinction impermissibly intrudes upon the freedoms guaranteed by the First and Fourteenth Amendments. It sweeps within its condemnation speech which our Constitution has immunized from governmental control. . . .

Measured by this test, Ohio's Criminal Syndicalism Act cannot be sustained. The Act punishes persons who "advocate or teach the duty, necessity, or propriety" of violence "as a means of accomplishing industrial or political reform"; or who publish or circulate or display any book or paper containing such advocacy; or who "justify" the commission of violent acts "with intent to exemplify, spread or advocate the propriety of the doctrines of criminal syndicalism"; or who "voluntarily assemble" with a group formed "to teach or advocate the doctrines of criminal syndicalism." Neither the indictment nor the trial judge's instructions to the jury in any way refined the statute's bald definition of the crime in terms of mere advocacy not distinguished from incitement to imminent lawless action.

Accordingly, we are here confronted with a statute which, by its own words and as applied, purports to punish mere advocacy and to forbid, on pain of criminal punishment, assembly with others merely to advocate the described type of action. Such a statute falls within the condemnation of the First and Fourteenth Amendments. The contrary teaching of *Whitney* v. *California* . . . cannot be supported, and that decision is therefore overruled.

Reversed.

Mr. Justice Black, concurring:

I agree with the views expressed by Mr. Justice Douglas in his concurring opinion in this case that the "clear and present danger" doctrine should have no place in the interpretation of the First Amendment. I join the Court's opinion, which, as I understand it, simply cites *Dennis* v. *United States,* . . . but does not indicate any agreement on the Court's part with the "clear and present danger" doctrine on which *Dennis* purported to rely.

Mr. Justice Douglas, concurring:

While I join the opinion of the Court, I desire to enter a *caveat.*

[T]he World War I cases . . . of [*Schenck, Frohwerk, Debs,* and *Abrams*] put the gloss of "clear and present danger" on the First Amendment. Whether the war power—the greatest leveler of them all—is adequate to sustain that doctrine is debatable. The dissents in *Abrams, Schaefer,* and *Pierce* show how easily "clear and present danger" is manipulated to crush what Brandeis [in *Pierce*] called "[t]he fundamental right of free men to strive for better conditions through new legislation and new institutions" by argument and discourse . . . even in time of war. Though I doubt if the "clear and present danger" test is congenial to the First Amendment in time of a declared war, I am certain it is not reconcilable with the First Amendment in days of peace.

The Court quite properly overrules *Whitney* v. *California,* . . . which involved advocacy of ideas which the majority of the Court deemed unsound and dangerous.

Mr. Justice Holmes, though never formally abandoning the "clear and present danger" test, moved closer to the First Amendment ideal when he said in dissent in *Gitlow* v. *New York,* . . . "Every idea is an incitement. . . . "

We have never been faithful to the philosophy of that dissent.

The Court in *Herndon* v. *Lowry* [1937] . . . overturned a conviction for exercising First Amendment rights to incite insurrection because of lack of evidence of incitement. . . . In *Bridges* v. *California* [1941] . . . we approved the "clear and present danger" test in an elaborate dictum that tightened it and confined it to a narrow category. But in *Dennis* v. *United States* [1951] . . . we opened wide the door, distorting the "clear and present danger" test beyond recognition.

. . . I see no place in the regime of the First Amendment for any "clear and present danger" test, whether strict and tight as some would make it, or free-wheeling as the Court in *Dennis* rephrased it.

When one reads the opinions closely and sees when and how the "clear and present danger" test has been applied, great misgivings are aroused. First, the threats were often loud but always puny and made serious only by judges so wedded to the *status quo* that critical analysis made them nervous. Second, the test was so twisted and perverted in *Dennis* as to make the trial of those teachers of Marxism an all-out political trial which was part and parcel of the cold war that has eroded substantial parts of the First Amendment.

Action is often a method of expression and within the protection of the First Amendment.

Suppose one tears up his own copy of the Constitution in eloquent protest to a decision of this Court. May he be indicted?

Suppose one rips his own Bible to shreds to celebrate his departure from one "faith" and his embrace of atheism. May he be indicted?

Last Term the Court held in *United States* v. *O'Brien* [1968] . . . that a registrant under Selective Service who burned his draft card in protest of the war in Vietnam could be prosecuted. The First Amendment was tendered as a defense and rejected. . . .

But O'Brien was not prosecuted for not having his draft card available when asked for by a federal agent. He was indicted, tried, and convicted for burning the card. And this Court's affirmance of that conviction was not, with all respect, consistent with the First Amendment. . . .

The line between what is permissible and not subject to control and what may be made impermissible and subject to regulation is the line between ideas and overt acts.

The example usually given by those who would punish speech is the case of one who falsely shouts fire in a crowded theatre.

This is, however, a classic case where speech is brigaded with action. . . . They are indeed inseparable and a prosecution can be launched for the overt acts actually caused. Apart from rare instances of that kind, speech is, I think, immune from prosecution. Certainly there is no constitutional line between advocacy of abstract ideas as in *Yates* and advocacy of political action as in *Scales*. The quality of advocacy turns on the depth of the conviction; and government has no power to invade that sanctuary of belief and conscience.

Equal Protection of the Laws: School Desegregation

By now most students are thoroughly familiar with the evolution of the "separate but equal" doctrine first enunciated by the Supreme Court in *Plessy* v. *Ferguson*, 163 U.S. 537 (1896). Students should note that what is involved in cases in this area is legal interpretation of the provision in the Fourteenth Amendment that no state may deny "to any person within its jurisdiction the equal protection of the laws." The *Plessy* case stated that separate but equal accommodations, required by state law to be established on railroads in Louisiana, did not violate the equal protection of the laws clause of the Fourteenth Amendment. The Court went on to say that the object of the Fourteenth Amendment:

> . . . was undoubtedly to enforce the absolute equality of the two races before the law, but in the nature of things it could not have been intended to abolish distinction based upon color, or to enforce social, as distinguished from political, equality, or a commingling of the two races upon terms unsatisfactory to either. Laws permitting, and even requiring, their separation in places where they are liable to be brought into contact do not necessarily imply the inferiority of either race to the other, and have been generally, if not universally, recognized as within the competency of the state legislatures in the exercise of their police power. The most common instance of this is connected with the establishment of separate schools for white and colored children, which has been held to be a valid exercise of the legislative power even by courts of States where the political rights of the colored race have been longest and most earnestly enforced.

Both the police power and education are within the reserved powers of the states; they are reserved, however, only insofar as they do not conflict with provisions of the Constitution. The Supreme Court, in *Brown* v. *Board of Education*, 347 U.S. 483 (1954), finally crystallized its interpretation of the equal protection of the laws clause in a way that resulted in a significant decrease in state power in an area traditionally reserved to states, viz., education. In addition, a general principle was established which extended far beyond the field of education.

15

BROWN v. BOARD OF EDUCATION OF TOPEKA
347 U.S. 483 (1954)

Mr. Chief Justice Warren delivered the opinion of the Court, saying in part:

These cases come to us from the states of Kansas, South Carolina, Virginia, and Delaware. They are premised on different facts and different local conditions, but a common legal question justifies their consideration together in this consolidated opinion.

In each of the cases, minors of the Negro race, through their legal representatives, seek the aid of the courts in obtaining admission to the public schools of their community on a nonsegregated basis. In each instance, they had been denied admission to schools attended by white children under laws requiring or permitting segregation according to race. This segregation was alleged to deprive the plaintiffs of the equal protection of the laws under the Fourteenth Amendment. In each of the cases other than the Delaware case, a three-judge federal district court denied relief to the plaintiffs on the so-called "separate but equal" doctrine announced by this Court in *Plessy* v. *Ferguson*. . . .

The plaintiffs contend that segregated public schools are not "equal" and cannot be made "equal," and that hence they are deprived of the equal protection of the laws. Because of the obvious importance of the question presented, the Court took jurisdiction. . . .

In the first cases in this Court construing the Fourteenth Amendment, decided shortly after its adoption, the Court interpreted it as proscribing all state-imposed discriminations against the Negro race. The doctrine of "separate but equal" did not make its appearance in this Court until 1896 in the case of *Plessy* v. *Ferguson*, *supra*, involving not education but transportation. American courts have since labored with the doctrine for over half a century. In this Court, there have been six cases involving the "separate but equal" doctrine in the field of public education. . . . In more recent cases, all on the graduate school level, inequality was found in that specific benefits enjoyed by white students were denied to Negro students of the same educational qualifications. . . . In none of these cases was it necessary to reexamine the doctrine to grant relief to the Negro plaintiff. And in *Sweatt* v. *Painter* [339 U.S. 629 (1950)], the Court expressly reserved decision on the question whether *Plessy* v. *Ferguson* should be held inapplicable to public education.

In the instant cases, that question is directly presented. Here, unlike *Sweatt v. Painter,* there are findings below that the Negro and white schools involved have been equalized, or are being equalized, with respect to buildings, curricula, qualifications and salaries of teachers, and other "tangible" factors. Our decision, therefore, cannot turn on merely a comparison of these tangible factors in the Negro and white schools involved in each of the cases. We must look instead to the effect of segregation itself on public education.

In approaching this problem, we cannot turn the clock back to 1868 when the Amendment was adopted, or even to 1896 when *Plessy v. Ferguson* was written. We must consider public education in the light of its full development and its present place in American life throughout the Nation. Only in this way can it be determined if segregation in public schools deprives these plaintiffs of the equal protection of the laws.

Today, education is perhaps the most important function of state and local governments. Compulsory school attendance laws and the great expenditures for education both demonstrate our recognition of the importance of education to our democratic society. It is required in the perfomance of our most basic public responsibilities, even service in the armed forces. It is the very foundation of good citizenship. Today it is a principal instrument in awakening the child to cultural values, in preparing him for later professional training, and in helping him to adjust normally to his environment. In these days, it is doubtful that any child may reasonably be expected to succeed in life if he is denied the opportunity of an education. Such an opportunity, where the state has undertaken to provide it, is a right which must be made available to all on equal terms.

We come then to the question presented: Does segregation of children in public schools solely on the basis of race, even though the physical facilities and other "tangible" factors may be equal, deprive the children of the minority group of equal educational opportunities? We believe that it does.

In *Sweatt v. Painter, supra,* in finding that a segregated law school for Negroes could not provide them equal educational opportunities, this Court relied in large part on "those qualities which are incapable of objective measurement but which make for greatness in a law school." In *McLaurin v. Oklahoma State Regents, supra* [339 U.S. 637 (1950)], the Court, in requiring that a Negro admitted to a white graduate school be treated like all other students, again resorted to intangible considerations: "his ability to study, to engage in discussions and exchange views with other students, and, in general, to learn his profession." Such considerations apply with added force to children in grade and high schools. To separate them from others of similar age and qualifications solely because of their race generates a feeling of inferiority as to their status in the community that may affect their hearts and minds in a way unlikely ever to be undone. The effect of this separation of their educational opportunities was well stated by a finding in the Kansas case by a court which nevertheless felt compelled to rule against the Negro plaintiffs:

Segregation of white and colored children in public schools has a detrimental effect upon the colored children. The impact is greater when it has the sanction of the law; for the policy of separating the races is usually interpreted as denoting the inferiority of the Negro group. A sense of inferiority affects the motivation of a child to learn. Segregation with the sanction of law, therefore, has a tendency to retard the educational and mental development of Negro children and to deprive them of some of the benefits they would receive in a racially integrated school system.

Whatever may have been the extent of psychological knowledge at the time of *Plessy v. Ferguson,* this finding is amply supported by modern authority. Any language in *Plessy v. Ferguson* contrary to this finding is rejected.

We conclude that in the field of public education the doctrine of "separate but equal" has no place. Separate educational facilities are inherently unequal. Therefore, we hold that the plaintiffs and others similarly situated for whom the actions have been brought are by reason of the segregation complained of, deprived of the equal protection of the laws guaranteed by the Fourteenth Amendment. This disposition makes unnecessary any discussion whether such segregation also violates the Due Process Clause of the Fourteenth Amendment.

Because these are class actions, because of the wide applicability of this decision, and because of the great variety of local conditions, the formulation of decrees in these cases presents problems of considerable complexity. On re-argument, the consideration of appropriate relief was necessarily subordinate to the primary question—the constitutionality of segregation in public education. We have now announced that such segregation is a denial of the equal protection of the laws. In order that we may have the full assistance of the parties in formulating decrees, the cases will be restored to the docket, and the parties are requested to present further argument on Questions 4 and 5 previously propounded by the Court for the re-argument this Term [which deal with the implementation of desegregation]. The Attorney General of the United States is again invited to participate. The Attorneys General of the states requiring or permitting segregation in public education will also be permitted to appear as *amici curiae* upon request to do so by September 15, 1954, and submission of briefs by October 1, 1954. It is so ordered.

❖❖   On the same day the decision was announced in the *Brown* case (1954), the Court held that segregation in the District of Columbia was unconstitutional on the basis of the due process clause of the Fifth Amendment. (See *Bolling v. Sharpe,* 347 U.S. 497 [1954].) This situation reversed the normal one in that a protection explicitly afforded citizens of states was not expressly applicable against the national government, and could be made so only through interpreting it into the concept of due process of law.

After hearing the views of all interested parties in the *Brown* case the Court, on May 31, 1955, announced its decision concerning the implementation of desegregation in public schools.

16

BROWN v. BOARD OF EDUCATION OF TOPEKA
349 U.S. 294 (1955)

Mr. Chief Justice Warren delivered the opinion of the Court, saying in part:

These cases were decided on May 17, 1954. The opinions of that date, declaring the fundamental principle that racial discrimination in public education is unconstitutional, are incorporated herein by reference. All provisions of federal, state, or local law requiring or permitting such discrimination must yield to this principle. There remains for consideration the manner in which relief is to be accorded.

Because these cases arose under different local conditions and their disposition will involve a variety of local problems, we requested further argument on the question of relief. . . . The parties, the United States, and the states of Florida, North Carolina, Arkansas, Oklahoma, Maryland, and Texas filed briefs and participated in the oral argument.

These presentations were informative and helpful to the Court in its consideration of the complexities arising from the transition to a system of public education freed of racial discrimination. The presentations also demonstrated that substantial steps to eliminate racial discrimination in public schools have already been taken, not only in some of the communities in which these cases arose, but in some of the states appearing as *amici curiae*, and in other states as well. Substantial progress has been made in the District of Columbia and in the communities in Kansas and Delaware involved in this litigation. The defendants in the cases coming to us from South Carolina and Virginia are awaiting the decision of this Court concerning relief.

Full implementation of these constitutional principles may require solution of varied local school problems. School authorities have the primary responsibility for elucidating, assessing, and solving these problems; courts will have to consider whether the action of school authorities constitutes good faith implementation of the governing constitutional principles. Because of their proximity to local conditions and the possible need for further hearings, the courts which originally heard these cases can best perform this judicial appraisal. Accordingly, we believe it appropriate to remand the cases to those courts.

In fashioning and effectuating the decrees, the courts will be guided by equitable principles. Traditionally, equity has been characterized by a practical flexibility in shaping its remedies and by a facility for adjusting and reconciling public and private needs. These cases call for the exercise of these traditional attributes of equity power. At stake is the personal interest of the plaintiffs in admission to public schools as soon as practicable on a nondiscriminatory basis. To effectuate this interest may call for elimination of a variety of obstacles in making the transition to school systems operated in accordance with the constitutional principles set forth in our May 17, 1954, decision. Courts of equity may properly take into account the public interest in the elimination of such obstacles in a systematic and effective manner. But it should go without saying that the vitality of these constitutional principles cannot be allowed to yield simply because of disagreement with them.

While giving weight to these public and private considerations, the courts will require that the defendants make a prompt and reasonable start toward full compliance with our May 17, 1954, ruling. Once such a start has been made, the courts may find that additional time is necessary to carry out the ruling in an effective manner. The burden rests upon the defendants to establish such time as is necessary in the public interest and is consistent with good faith compliance at the earliest practicable date. To that end, the courts may consider problems related to administration, arising from the physical condition of the school plant, the school transportation system, personnel, revision of school districts and attendance areas into compact units to achieve a system of determining admission to the public schools on a nonracial basis, and revision of local laws and regulations which may be necessary in solving the foregoing problems. They will also consider the adequacy of any plans the defendants may propose to meet these problems and to effectuate a transition to a racially nondiscriminatory school system. During this period of transition, the courts will retain jurisdiction of these cases.

The judgments below, except that in the Delaware case, are accordingly reversed and the cases are remanded to the District Courts to take such proceedings and enter such orders and decrees consistent with this opinion as are necessary and proper to admit to public schools on a racially nondiscriminatory basis with all deliberate speed the parties to these cases. The judgment in the Delaware case—ordering the immediate admission of the plaintiffs to schools previously attended only by white children—is affirmed on the basis of the principles stated in our May 17, 1954, opinion, but the case is remanded to the Supreme Court of Delaware for such further proceedings as that Court may deem necessary in the light of this opinion.

It is so ordered.

❖ ❖   After the second decision of the Supreme Court in *Brown v. Board of Education* in 1955, it soon became clear that many Southern states would proceed with deliberate speed not to implement the desegregation of public schools but to obstruct the intent of the Supreme Court. The Southern Manifesto, signed by 101 Congressmen from 11 Southern states in 1956, clearly indicated the line that would be taken by many Southern congressmen to justify defiance of the Supreme Court. The gist of the Manifesto was simply that the Supreme Court did not have the constitutional authority to interfere in an area such as education, which falls within the reserved powers of the states.

After the two *Brown* decisions in 1954 and 1955, the implementation for desegregation in the South was very slow. Ten years later, less than 10 percent of the black pupils in the lower educational levels in the Southern states that had had legally segregated education before were enrolled in integrated schools. It was not until 1970 that substantial progress was made in the South. Between 1968 and 1970 the percentage of black students in all-black schools in eleven Southern states decreased from 68.0 percent to 18.4 percent. One device used to circumvent the Supreme Court's decisions was to establish de facto dual school systems, similar to those that exist in most Northern cities, whereby students are assigned to schools on the basis of the neighborhoods in which they live. Such systems are not de jure segregation because they are not based upon a law requiring segregation per se, but simply upon school board regulations assigning pupils on the basis of where they live. De facto school systems can be as segregated as were the de jure systems previously existing in the South, but the question is to what extent can courts interfere to break up de facto segregation patterns since they are not based upon legal stipulations?

In *Swann v. Charlotte-Mecklenburg County Board of Education*, 402 U.S. 1 (1971), the Supreme Court held that in Southern states with a history of legal segregated education the District Courts have broad power to assure "unitary" school systems by requiring: (1) reassignment of teachers, so that each school faculty will reflect a racial balance similar to that which exists in the community as a whole; (2) reassignment of pupils to reflect a racial ratio similar to that which exists within the total community; (3) the use of noncontiguous school zones and the grouping of schools for the purpose of attendance to bring about racial balance; and (4) the use of busing of elementary and secondary school students within the school system to achieve racial balance.

This case and companion cases were referred to at the time as school "busing" cases, and caused tremendous controversy within the South because communities felt they were not being treated on an equal basis with their Northern counterparts, where de facto segregation is for the most part not subject to judicial intervention. The Nixon Administration, which favored neighborhood schools, was firmly opposed to the transportation of students beyond normal geographic school zones to achieve racial balance. Democratic Senator Ribicoff of Connecticut attempted to attach an amendment to an administration-sponsored bill providing $1.5 billion to aid school districts in the South in the desegregation of facilities that would have required nationwide integration of pupils from intercity schools with children from the suburbs. The amendment was defeated on April 21, 1971, by a vote of 51 to 35, with most Republicans voting against it and 13 of 34 Northern Democrats opposed. Busing remains a highly controversial political issue.

Swann v. *Charlotte-Mecklenburg County Board* (1971) held that the courts could order busing of school children within the limits of the city school district if necessary to achieve desegregated educational facilities. In the case of Charlotte-Mecklenburg the limits of the city school district included the surrounding county. However, only eighteen of the country's one hundred largest city school districts contained both the inner city and the surrounding county. In cities such as San Francisco, Denver, Pasadena, and Boston, court-ordered busing plans pertained only to the central city school district. In 1974 the Supreme Court reviewed a busing plan for Detroit ordered by a federal District Court and sustained by the Court of Appeals that would have required the busing of students among fifty-four separate school districts in the Detroit metropolitan area to achieve racially balanced schools. The decision of the lower federal court in the Detroit case set a new precedent that required busing among legally separate school districts. Proponents of the Detroit busing plan argued that the central city of Detroit was 70 percent black and that the only way integration could be achieved would be to link the school district of Detroit with the surrounding white suburban school districts. In *Milliken* v. *Bradley*, 418 U.S. 717 (1974), the Supreme Court held that the court-ordered Detroit busing plan could not be sustained under the equal protection clause of the Fourteenth Amendment, which was the constitutional provision relied upon in the lower court's decision to require busing. The Supreme Court found that there was no evidence of disparate treatment of white and black students among the fifty-three outlying school districts that surround Detroit. The only evidence of discrimination was within the city limits of Detroit itself. Therefore, since the outlying districts did not violate the equal protection clause they could not be ordered to integrate their systems with that of Detroit. Since discrimination was limited to Detroit, the court order to remedy the situation must be limited to Detroit also. The effect of the decision is to leave standing court orders for busing within school districts, but to prevent the forced merger of inner city schools with legally separate suburban school districts.

The Judicial Sources of Major Political Controversies over Civil Liberties and Rights

Chief Justice John Marshall in the early nineteenth century laid the groundwork for Supreme Court involvement in politics when he declared that "it is emphatically the province and duty of the Judicial Department to say what the law is." Ironically, in the same case he invented the doctrine of "political questions," proclaiming that the courts should not become involved in those matters more appropriately decided by legislative bodies. Marshall muted that note of judicial self-restraint, however, by his implicit recognition that the courts and not legislatures ultimately would decide what matters fell within their jurisdiction.

Chief Justice Marshall's proclamation of judicial power in *Marbury* v. *Madison* also incorporated the doctrine of judicial review. The authority to declare what the law is included the power to review acts of Congress and judge their constitutionality. The *Marbury* case, however, did not involve a major confrontation with Congress. The Court merely held that Congress could not grant it the mandamus power in original jurisdiction, which had been done in the Judiciary Act of 1789. Essentially the Court was interpreting the scope of its own powers, not those of Congress.

Inevitably, however, the power of judicial review pushed the Supreme Court and lower federal courts as well into political controversies as they ruled not only on congressional laws but far more importantly on the actions of state legislatures and courts. As of early 1983 the Supreme Court had held only 127 provisions of federal laws to be unconstitutional in whole or in part out of a total of approximately 88,000 public and private bills that had been passed. By contrast, the Court had overturned on constitutional grounds 1,000 state laws and provisions of state constitutions, 900 of these rulings coming after 1870.[1] By far the greatest political controversies have been over Supreme Court rulings affecting the states, as the nation for most of its history struggled over the question of how far national power should intrude upon state sovereignty.

Controversies surrounding Supreme Court decisions on civil liberties and civil rights have almost entirely involved Supreme Court rulings on the permissible scope of state power. In the early nineteenth century Chief Justice John Marshall's decisions in the historic cases of *McCulloch* v. *Maryland* (1819) and *Gibbons* v. *Ogden* (1823) raised the ire of states' rights advocates who widely proclaimed that the Court's actions would bring about the dissolution of the Union. The Supreme Court had unequivocally upheld national supremacy and wide congressional powers over the states.

---

[1]Henry J. Abraham, *The Judiciary: The Supreme Court in the Governmental Process*, 6th edition (Boston: Allyn and Bacon, 1983), p. 164.

Almost a century and a half after the *McCulloch* decision, the Supreme Court was again embroiled in a political controversy, not concerning the extent of congressional power over the states, an issue that had finally been settled in favor of the national government during the New Deal, but over how far national civil liberties and rights standards should be applied to the states. Under the Chief Justiceship of former California governor Earl Warren, an activist and interventionist Supreme Court in the 1960s completed the process of applying most of the provisions of the Bill of Rights to the states under the due process clause of the Fourteenth Amendment. Before the Warren era the Court had been very reluctant to extend parts of the Bill of Rights to the states, weighing heavily against such action considerations of federalism that supported state sovereignty. It nationalized only what in the view of a majority of the justices were fundamental freedoms and rights without which the democratic process and individual liberty could not survive.

The Pledge of Allegiance to the Flag

The 1988 presidential election campaign resurrected an old controversy, the issue of whether or not school children could and should be *compelled* by state law to begin their school day by reciting the pledge of allegiance to the flag. Republican candidate George Bush accused Democrat Michael Dukakis of being unpatriotic because the Massachusetts governor had refused to sign a state law requiring the pledge, on the ground that the Supreme Court had declared mandatory recitation of the pledge to be a violation of First Amendment freedoms of expression.

The pledge issue first confronted the Supreme Court in 1940, a time of national patriotic fervor on the eve of World War II. Walter Gobitis, a Jehovah's Witness, challenged a school board policy in the town of Minersville, Pennsylvania, that required students to participate in a daily flag salute ceremony during which they recited in unison the pledge of allegiance. During the recitation of the words both teachers and pupils extended their right hands chest-high in a salute to the flag. Gobitis claimed the school policy violated his religious principles and sued to enjoin the public schools from requiring the flag salute ceremony as a condition of attendance. The Court voted 8–1 to uphold the Minersville flag salute policy. In his majority opinion Justice Felix Frankfurter emphasized that the "mere possession of religious convictions which contradict the relevant concerns of a political society does not relieve the citizen from the discharge of political responsibilities. We live by symbols," stated Frankfurter, and the "flag is the symbol of our national unity, transcending all internal differences, however large, within the framework of the Constitution."

Frankfurter's Gobitis opinion reflected a strong tone of judicial self-restraint. He emphasized that to "the legislature no less than to the courts is committed the guardianship of deeply-cherished liberties." The Supreme Court, he wrote, should not become the "school board of the country."

Dissenting in the Gobitis case was Justice Harlan F. Stone, but a new Court majority would soon adopt his views. He attacked the Gobitis majority for undermining the essence of liberty, which is "the freedom of the individual from compulsion as to what he shall think and what he shall say, at least where the compulsion is to bear false witness to his religion." While recognizing that liberty is not an absolute, Stone could find no compelling reason to uphold the required flag salute.

Three years after the Gobitis case, the Court again confronted a challenge, this time in West Virginia, to school regulations requiring the flag salute. In the intervening years the composition of the Court had changed. Franklin D. Roosevelt's attorney general, Robert Jackson, replaced the retiring Chief Justice Charles Evans Hughes in 1941, and Roosevelt chose Stone, the sole dissenter in the Gobitis case, to become chief justice. Moreover, when Justice Byrnes resigned in 1942 to become the head of the Office of War and Mobilization, Roosevelt nominated and the Senate confirmed Wiley B. Rutledge to replace him. The expectation was that both Jackson and Rutledge might be more sympathetic to the view Stone had expressed in his Gobitis dissent. The expectations were borne out as Justice Jackson wrote the majority opinion in the historic West Virginia case that overturned the Gobitis decision:

17

WEST VIRGINIA STATE BOARD OF EDUCATION v. BARNETTE
319 U.S. 624 (1943)

Mr. Justice Jackson delivered the opinion of the Court:

Following the decision by this Court on June 3, 1940, in *Minersville School District* v. *Gobitis* . . . , the West Virginia legislature amended its statutes to require all schools therein to conduct courses of instruction in history, civics, and in the Constitutions of the United States and of the State "for the purpose of teaching, fostering and perpetuating the ideals, principles and spirit of Americanism, and increasing the knowledge of the organization and machinery of the government.". . .

The Board of Education on January 9, 1942, adopted a resolution containing recitals taken largely from the Court's *Gobitis* opinion and ordering that the salute to the flag become "a regular part of the program of activities in the public schools," that all teachers and pupils "shall be required to participate in the salute honoring the Nation represented by the Flag; provided, however, that refusal to salute the Flag be regarded as an act of insubordination, and shall be dealt with accordingly."

The resolution originally required the "commonly accepted salute to the Flag" which it defined. Objections to the salute as "being too much like Hitler's" were raised by the Parent and Teachers Association, the Boy and Girl Scouts, the Red Cross, and the Federation of Women's Clubs. Some modification appears to have been made in deference to these objections, but no concession was made to Jehovah's Witnesses. What is now required is the "stiff-arm" salute, the saluter to keep the right hand raised with palm turned up while the following is repeated: "I pledge allegiance to the Flag of the United States of America and to the Republic for which it stands; one Nation, indivisible, with liberty and justice for all."

Failure to conform is "insubordination" dealt with by expulsion. Readmission is denied by statute until compliance. Meanwhile the expelled child is "unlawfully absent" and may be proceeded against as a delinquent. His parents or guardians are liable to prosecution, and if convicted are subject to fine not exceeding $50 and jail term not exceeding thirty days.

Appellees, citizens of the United States and of West Virginia, brought suit in the United States District Court for themselves and others similarly situated asking its injunction to restrain enforcement of these laws and regulations against Jehovah's Witnesses. The Witnesses are an unincorporated body teaching that the obligation imposed by law of God is superior to that of laws enacted by temporal government. Their religious beliefs include a literal version of Exodus, Chapter 20, verses 4 and 5, which says: "Thou shalt not make unto thee any graven image, or any likeness of anything that is in heaven above, or that is in the earth beneath, or that is in the water under the earth; thou shalt not bow down thyself to them nor serve them." They consider that the flag is an "image" within this command. For this reason they refuse to salute it.

Children of this faith have been expelled from school and are threatened with exclusion for no other cause. Officials threaten to send them to reformatories maintained for criminally inclined juveniles. Parents of such children have been prosecuted and are threatened with prosecutions for causing delinquency. . . .

This case calls upon us to reconsider a precedent decision, as the Court throughout its history often has been required to do. Before turning to the *Gobitis* case, however, it is desirable to notice certain characteristics by which this controversy is distinguished.

The freedom asserted by these appellees does not bring them into collision with rights asserted by any other individual. It is such conflicts which most frequently require intervention of the State to determine where the rights of one end and those of another begin. But the refusal of these persons to participate in the ceremony does not interfere with or deny rights of others to do so. Nor is there any question in this case that their behavior is peaceable and orderly. The sole conflict is between authority and rights of the individual. The State asserts power to condition access to public education on making a prescribed sign and profession and at the same time to coerce attendance by punishing both parent and child. The latter stand on a right of self-determination in matters that touch individual opinion and personal attitude.

As the present Chief Justice [Stone] said in dissent in the *Gobitis* case, the State may "require teaching by instruction and study of all in our history and in the structure and organization of our government, including the guaranties of civil liberty, which tend to inspire patriotism and love of country." . . . Here, however, we are dealing with a compulsion of students to declare a belief. They are not merely made acquainted with the flag salute so that they may be informed as to what it is or even what it means. The issue here is whether this slow and easily neglected route to aroused loyalties constitutionally may be short-cut by substituting a compulsory salute and slogan. . . .

There is no doubt that, in connection with the pledges, the flag salute is a form of utterance. Symbolism is a primitive but effective way of communicating ideas. The use of an emblem or flag to symbolize some system, idea, institution, or personality, is a short cut from mind to mind. Causes and nations, political parties, lodges and ecclesiastical groups seek to knit the loyalty of their followings to a flag or banner, a color or design. The State announces rank, function, and authority through crowns and maces, uniforms and black robes; the church speaks through the Cross, the Crucifix, the altar and shrine, and clerical raiment. Symbols of State often convey political ideas just as religious symbols come to convey theological ones. Associated with many of these symbols are appropriate gestures of acceptance or respect: a salute, a bowed or bared head, a bended knee. A person gets from a symbol the meaning he puts into it, and what is one man's comfort and inspiration is another's jest and scorn.

Over a decade ago Chief Justice Hughes led this Court in holding that the display of a red flag as a symbol of opposition by peaceful and legal means to organized government was protected by the free speech guaranties of the Constitution. *Stromberg v. California* [1931]. . . . Here it is the State that employs a flag as a symbol of adherence to government as presently organized. It requires the individual to communicate by word and sign his acceptance of the political ideas it thus bespeaks. Objection to this form of communication when coerced is an old one, well known to the framers of the Bill of Rights.

It is also to be noted that the compulsory flag salute and pledge requires affirmation of a belief and an attitude of mind. It is not clear whether the regulation contemplates that pupils forego any contrary convictions of their own and become unwilling converts to the prescribed ceremony or whether it will be acceptable if they simulate assent by words without belief and by gesture barren of meaning. It is now a commonplace that censorship or suppression of expression of opinion is tolerated by our Constitution only when the expression presents a clear and present danger of action of a kind the State is empowered to prevent and punish. It would seem that involuntary affirmation could be commanded only on even more immediate and urgent grounds than silence. But here the power of compulsion is invoked without any allegation that remaining passive during a flag salute ritual creates a clear and present danger that would justify an effort even to muffle expression. To sustain the compulsory flag salute we are required to say that a Bill of Rights which guards the individual's right to speak his own mind, left it open to public authorities to compel him to utter what is not in his mind.

Whether the First Amendment to the Constitution will permit officials to order observance of ritual of this nature does not depend upon whether as a voluntary exercise we would think it to be good, bad or merely innocuous. Any credo of nationalism is likely to include what some disapprove or to omit what others think essential, and to give off different overtones as it takes on different accents or interpretations. If official power exists to coerce acceptance of any patriotic creed, what it shall contain cannot be decided by the courts, but must be largely discretionary with the ordaining authority, whose power to prescribe would no doubt include power to amend. Hence validity of the asserted power to force an American citizen publicly to profess any statement of belief or to engage in any ceremony of assent to one, presents questions of power that must be considered independently of any idea we may have as to the utility of the ceremony in question.

Nor does the issue as we see it turn on one's possession of particular religious views or the sincerity with which they are held. While religion supplies appellees' motive for enduring the discomforts of making the issue in this case, many citizens who do not share these religious views hold such a compulsory rite to infringe constitutional liberty of the individual. It is not necessary to inquire whether non-conformist beliefs will exempt from the duty to salute unless we first find power to make the salute a legal duty.

The *Gobitis* decision, however, *assumed*, as did the argument in that case and in this, that power exists in the State to impose the flag salute discipline upon school children in general. The Court only examined and rejected a claim based on religious beliefs of immunity from an unquestioned general rule. The question which underlies the flag salute controversy is whether such a ceremony so touching matters of opinion and political attitude may be imposed upon the individual by official authority under powers committed to any political organization under our Constitution. We examine rather than assume existence of this power and, against this broader definition of issues in this case, reëxamine specific grounds assigned for the *Gobitis* decision.

1. It was said that the flag-salute controversy confronted the Court with "the problem which Lincoln cast in memorable dilemma: 'Must a government of necessity be too *strong* for the liberties of its people, or too *weak* to maintain its own existence?' " and that the answer must be in favor of strength. . . .

We think these issues may be examined free of pressure or restraint growing out of such considerations.

It may be doubted whether Mr. Lincoln would have thought that the strength of government to maintain itself would be impressively vindicated by our confirming power of the State to expel a handful of children from school. Such oversimplification, so handy in political debate, often lacks the precision necessary to postulates of judicial reasoning. If validly applied to this problem, the utterance cited would resolve every issue of power in favor of those in authority and would require us to override every liberty thought to weaken or delay execution of their policies.

Government of limited power need not be anemic government. Assurance that rights are secure tends to diminish fear and jealousy of strong government, and by making us feel safe to live under it makes for its better support. Without promise of a limiting Bill of Rights it is doubtful if our Constitution could have mustered enough strength to enable its ratification. To enforce those rights today is not to choose weak government over strong government. It is only to adhere as a means of strength to individual freedom of mind in preference to officially disciplined uniformity for which history indicates a disappointing and disastrous end.

The subject now before us exemplifies this principle. Free public education, if faithful to the ideal of secular instruction and political neutrality, will not be partisan or enemy of any class, creed, party, or faction. If it is to impose any ideological discipline, however, each party or denomination must seek to control, or failing that, to weaken the influence of the educational system. Observance of the limitations of the Constitution will not weaken government in the field appropriate for its exercise.

2. It was also considered in the *Gobitis* case that functions of educational officers in States, counties and school districts were such that to interfere with their authority "would in effect make us the school board for the country."

The Fourteenth Amendment, as now applied to the States, protects the citizen against the State itself and all of its creatures—Boards of Education not excepted. These have, of course, important, delicate, and highly discretionary functions, but none that they may not perform within the limits of the Bill of Rights. That they are educating the young for citizenship is reason for scrupulous protection of Constitutional freedoms of the individual, if we are not to strangle the free mind at its source and teach youth to discount important principles of our government as mere platitudes.

Such Boards are numerous and their territorial jurisdiction often small. But small and local authority may feel less sense of responsibility to the Constitution, and agencies of publicity may be less vigilant in calling it to account. The action of Congress in making flag observance voluntary and respecting the conscience of the objector in a matter so vital as raising the Army contrasts sharply with these local regulations in matters relatively trivial to the welfare of the nation. There are village tyrants as well as village Hampdens, but none who acts under color of law is beyond reach of the Constitution.

3. The *Gobitis* opinion reasoned that this is a field "where courts possess no marked and certainly no controlling competence," that it is committed to the legislatures as well as the courts to guard cherished liberties and that it is constitutionally appropriate to "fight out the wise use of legislative authority in the forum of public opinion and before legislative assemblies rather than to transfer such a contest to the judicial arena," since all the "effective means of inducing political changes are left free."

The very purpose of a Bill of Rights was to withdraw certain subjects from the vicissitudes of political controversy, to place them beyond the reach of majorities and officials and to establish them as legal principles to be applied by the courts. One's right to life, liberty, and property, to free speech, a free press, freedom of worship and assembly, and other fundamental rights may not be submitted to vote; they depend on the outcome of no elections.

In weighing arguments of the parties it is important to distinguish between the due process clause of the Fourteenth Amendment as an instrument for transmitting the principles of the First Amendment and those cases in which it is applied for its own sake. The test of legislation which collides with the Fourteenth Amendment, because it also collides with the principles of the First, is much more definite than the test when only the Fourteenth is involved. Much of the vagueness of the due process clause disappears when the specific prohibitions of the First become its standard. The right of a State to regulate, for example, a public utility may well include, so far as the due process test is concerned, power to impose all of the restrictions which a legislature may have a "rational basis" for adopting. But freedoms of speech and of press, of assembly, and of worship may not be infringed on such slender grounds. They are susceptible of restriction only to prevent grave and immediate danger to interests which the State may lawfully protect. It is important to note that while it is the Fourteenth Amendment which bears directly upon the State it is the more specific limiting principles of the First Amendment that finally govern this case.

Nor does our duty to apply the Bill of Rights to assertions of official authority depend upon our possession of marked competence in the field where the invasion of rights occurs. True, the task of translating the majestic generalities of the Bill of Rights, conceived as part of the pattern of liberal government in the eighteenth century, into concrete restraints on officials dealing with the problems of the twentieth century, is one to disturb self-confidence. These principles grew in soil which also produced a philosophy that the individual was the center of society, that his liberty was attainable through mere absence of governmental restraints, and that government should be entrusted with few controls and only the mildest supervision over men's affairs. We must transplant these rights to a soil in which the *laissez-faire* concept or principle of non-interference has withered at least as to economic affairs, and social advancements are increasingly sought through closer integration of society and through expanded and strengthened governmental controls. These changed conditions often deprive precedents of reliability and cast us more than we would choose upon our own judgment. But we act in these matters not by authority of our competence but by force of our commissions. We cannot, because of modest estimates of our competence in such specialities as public education, withhold the judgment that history authenticates as the function of this Court when liberty is infringed.

4. Lastly, and this is the very heart of the *Gobitis* opinion, it reasons that "National unity is the basis of national security," that the authorities have, "the right to select appropriate means for its attainment," and hence reaches the conclusion that such compulsory measures toward "national unity" are constitutional. Upon the verity of this assumption depends our answer in this case.

National unity as an end which officials may foster by persuasion and example is not in question. The problem is whether under our Constitution compulsion as here employed is a permissible means for its achievement.

Struggles to coerce uniformity of sentiment in support of some end thought essential to their time and country have been waged by many good as well as by evil men. Nationalism is a relatively recent phenomenon but at other times and places the ends have been racial or territorial security, support of a dynasty or regime, and particular plans for saving souls. As first and moderate methods to attain unity have failed, those bent on its accomplishment must resort to an ever-increasing severity. As governmental pressure toward unity becomes greater, so strife becomes more bitter as to whose unity it shall be. Probably no deeper division of our people could proceed from any provocation than from finding it necessary to choose what doctrine and whose program public educational officials shall compel youth to unite in embracing. Ultimate futility of such effort from the Roman drive to stamp out Christianity as a disturber of its pagan unity, the Inquisition as a means to religious and dynastic unity, the Siberian exiles as a means to Russian unity, down to the fast failing efforts of our present totalitarian enemies. Those who begin coercive elimination of dissent soon find themselves exterminating dissenters. Compulsory unification of opinion achieves only the unanimity of the graveyard.

It seems trite but necessary to say that the First Amendment to our Constitution was designed to avoid these ends by avoiding these beginnings. There is no mysticism in the American concept of the State or of the nature or origin of its authority. We set up government by consent of the governed, and the Bill of Rights denies those in power any legal opportunity to coerce that consent. Authority here is to be controlled by public opinion, not public opinion by authority.

The case is made difficult not because the principles of its decision are obscure but because the flag involved is our own. Nevertheless, we apply the limitations of the Constitution with no fear that freedom to be intellectually and spiritually diverse or even contrary will disintegrate the social organization. To believe that patriotism will not flourish if patriotic ceremonies are voluntary and spontaneous instead of a compulsory routine is to make an unflattering estimate of the appeal of our institutions to free minds. We can have intellectual individualism and the rich, cultural diversities that we owe to exceptional minds only at the price of occasional eccentricity and abnormal attitudes. When they are so harmless to others or to the State as those we deal with here, the price is not too great. But freedom to differ is not limited to things that do not matter much. That would be a mere shadow of freedom. The test of its substance is the right to differ as to things that touch the heart of the existing order.

If there is any fixed star in our constitutional constellation, it is that no official, high or petty, can prescribe what shall be orthodox in politics, nationalism, religion, or other matters of opinion or force citizens to confess by word or act their faith therein. If there are any circumstances which permit an exception, they do not now occur to us.

We think the action of the local authorities in compelling the flag salute and pledge transcends constitutional limitations on their power and invades the sphere of intellect and spirit which it is the purpose of the First Amendment to our Constitution to reserve from all official control.

The decision of this Court in *Minersville School District v. Gobitis* . . . [is] overruled, and the judgment enjoining enforcement of the West Virginia Regulation is

Affirmed.

Mr. Justice Black and Mr. Justice Douglas concurred in a separate opinion.

Mr. Justice Murphy wrote a separate concurring opinion.

Justices Roberts and Reed dissented.

Mr. Justice Frankfurter, dissenting:

One who belongs to the most vilified and persecuted minority in history is not likely to be insensible to the freedoms guaranteed by our Constitution. Were my purely personal attitude relevant I should wholeheartedly associate myself with the general libertarian views in the Court's opinion, representing as they do the thought and action of a lifetime. But as judges we are neither Jew nor Gentile, neither Catholic or agnostic. We owe equal attachment to the Constitution and are equally bound by our judicial obligations whether we derive our citizenship from the earliest or the latest immigrants to these shores. . . . As a member of this Court I am not justified in writing my private notions of policy into the Constitution, no matter how deeply I may cherish them or how mischievous I may deem their disregard. The duty of a judge who must decide which of two claims before the Court shall prevail, that of a State to enact and enforce laws within its general competence or that of an individual to refuse obedience because of the demands of his conscience, is not that of the ordinary person. It can never be emphasized too much that one's own opinion about the wisdom or evil of a law should be excluded altogether when one is doing one's duty on the bench. The only opinion of our own even looking in that direction that is material is our opinion whether legislators could in reason have enacted such a law. In the light of all the circumstances, including the history of this question in this Court, it would require more daring than I possess to deny that reasonable legislators could have taken the action which is before us for review. Most unwillingly, therefore, I must differ from my brethren with regard to legislation like this. I cannot bring my mind to believe that the "liberty" secured by the Due Process Clause gives this Court authority to deny to the State of West Virginia the attainment of that which we all recognized as a legitimate legislative end, namely, the promotion of good citizenship, by employment of the means here chosen. . . .

The American Flag:
Constitutional Issues

The Supreme Court has periodically confronted constitutional issues concerning the flag. Forty-eight states have laws that make it a crime to burn the flag. Whether or not such laws violate First Amendment freedoms of expression has been raised in the federal courts. For example, in *Street* v.

New York (1969), the black appellant, who had publicly burned a flag to protest the murder of civil rights leader James Meredith, challenged the New York state law under which he was charged, which made it a misdemeanor "publicly to mutilate, deface, defile, or defy, trample upon, or cast contempt upon either by words or act [a flag of the United States]." A police officer testified at the trial that he had heard Street exclaim, "We don't need no damn flag." When the officer asked him whether or not he had burned the flag, Street replied: "Yes, that is my flag; I burned it. If they let that happen to Meredith we don't need an American flag."

In deciding the case the Court weighed the state's interest in inflicting criminal punishment for burning the flag against the individual's freedom of expression under the First Amendment. Holding that New York had convicted the defendant because of his *words,* not because of his *act* in burning the flag, the Supreme Court's majority held that no state interest in the case justified the suppression of what in effect was political expression protected by the First Amendment which applied to the states under the due process clause of the Fourteenth Amendment.

Four justices dissented in the *Street* case. They found, as did the New York Court of Appeals which had upheld the conviction, that Street had been convicted for burning the flag, not because of what he said. The dissenters argued that had the Court properly confronted the real issue in the case the conviction should have been upheld. They stated that the Court had ducked the real issue, which was whether or not it was constitutionally permissible for states criminally to punish desecration of the flag. Chief Justice Earl Warren, in dissent, stated, "The states and the federal government do have the power to protect the flag from acts of desecration and disgrace." Justice Black agreed, proclaiming, "It passes my belief that anything in the federal Constitution bars a state from making the deliberate burning of the American flag an offense." Another dissenter, Justice Fortas, also supported a state's right to prevent the burning of the flag. "The flag," he wrote, "is a special kind of personality. Its use is traditionally and universally subject to special rules and regulation." Fortas pointed out that historically states have prescribed conditions for displaying the flag, and how it may or may not be used. State prohibitions upon flag-burning in a public place are entirely constitutional, concluded Fortas.

Another state flag desecration statute came under judicial scrutiny in *Spence* v. *Washington* (1974). Spence was a college student who had hung his United States flag upside-down outside the window of his apartment in Seattle. Spence, using removable black tape, had attached a peace symbol to the flag that covered approximately one-half of the flag's surface. The state of Washington, in prosecuting Spence, did not use its flag-desecration statute but an "improper use" statute which provided that no person could publicly display a United States flag that had been painted or marked in any way. Noting that Spence did not "permanently disfigure the flag or destroy it," the Court held that his display of a marked flag was political expression protected by the First and Fourteenth Amendments. Once again the Court did not have to face the issue of the constitutionality of a state law banning the burning of the flag.

The Supreme Court finally tackled the highly charged and politically sensitive issue of the constitutionality of laws banning flag-burning in the case reprinted below. Presidential candidate George Bush had made the Pledge of Allegiance and, by implication, respect for the flag, a major campaign issue in 1988. Now it was the Supreme Court's turn to rule, for the first time, on whether or not states could criminally prosecute flag-burning.

18

TEXAS v. JOHNSON
(1989)

Justice William J. Brennan, Jr., joined by Justices Thurgood Marshall, Harry A. Blackmun, Antonin Scalia, and Anthony M. Kennedy, wrote the majority opinion, saying in part:

After publicly burning an American flag as a means of political protest, Gregory Lee Johnson was convicted of desecrating a flag in violation of Texas law. This case presents the question whether his conviction is consistent with the First Amendment. We hold that it is not.

I

While the Republican National Convention was taking place in Dallas in 1984, respondent Johnson participated in a political demonstration dubbed the "Republican War Chest Tour." As explained in literature distributed by the demonstrators and in speeches made by them, the purpose of this event was to protest the policies of the Reagan administration and of certain Dallas-based corporations. The demonstrators marched through the Dallas streets, chanting political slogans and stopping at several corporate locations to stage "die-ins" intended to dramatize the consequences of nuclear war. On several occasions they spray-painted the walls of buildings and overturned potted plants, but Johnson himself took no part in such activities. He did, however, accept an

American flag handed to him by a fellow protester who had taken it from a flagpole outside one of the targeted buildings.

The demonstration ended in front of Dallas City Hall, where Johnson unfurled the American flag, doused it with kerosene and set it on fire. While the flag burned, the protesters chanted, "America, the red, white and blue, we spit on you." After the demonstrators dispersed, a witness to the flag burning collected the flag's remains and buried them in his backyard. No one was physically injured or threatened with injury, though several witnesses testified that they had been seriously offended by the flag burning.

Of the approximately 100 demonstrators, Johnson alone was charged with a crime. The only criminal offense with which he was charged was the desecration of a venerated object in violation of Texas Penal Code Ann. § 42.09 (a)(3) (1989). After a trial, he was convicted, sentenced to one year in prison, and fined $2,000. . . .

* * *

Johnson was convicted of flag desecration for burning the flag rather than for uttering insulting words. This fact somewhat complicates our consideration of his conviction under the First Amendment. We must first determine whether Johnson's burning of the flag constituted expressive conduct, permitting him to invoke the First Amendment in challenging his conviction. . . .

The First Amendment literally forbids the abridgement only of "speech," but we have long recognized that its protection does not end at the spoken or written word. . . .

In deciding whether particular conduct possesses sufficient communicative elements to bring the First Amendment into play, we have asked whether "[a]n intent to convey a particularized message was present, and [whether] the likelihood was great that the message would be understood by those who viewed it.". . . Hence, we have recognized the expressive nature of students' wearing of black armbands to protest American military involvement in Vietnam; . . . of a sit-in by blacks in a "whites only" area to protest segregation, . . . of the wearing of American military uniforms in a dramatic presentation criticizing American involvement in Vietnam, . . . and of picketing about a wide variety of causes. . . .

Especially pertinent to this case are our decisions recognizing the communicative nature of conduct relating to flags. Attaching a peace sign to the flag, . . . saluting the flag, and displaying a red flag, we have held, all may find shelter under the First Amendment. . . . That we have had little difficulty identifying an expressive element in conduct relating to flags should not be surprising. The very purpose of a national flag is to serve as a symbol of our country; it is, one might say, "the one visible manifestation of two hundred years of nationhood.". . . Pregnant with expressive content, the flag as readily signifies this Nation as does the combination of letters found in "America.". . .

* * *

Texas claims that its interest in preventing breaches of the peace justifies John-son's conviction for flag desecration. However, no disturbance of the peace actually occurred or threatened to occur because of Johnson's burning of the flag. . . .

The State's position, therefore, amounts to a claim that an audience that takes serious offense at particular expression is necessarily likely to disturb the peace and that the expression may be prohibited on this basis. Our precedents do not countenance such a presumption. On the contrary, they recognize that a principal "function of free speech under our system of government is to invite dispute. It may indeed best serve its high purpose when it induces a condition of unrest, creates dissatisfaction with conditions as they are, or even stirs people to anger.". . .

Nor does Johnson's expressive conduct fall within that small class of "fight-ing words" that are "likely to provoke the average person to retaliation, and thereby cause a breach of the peace.". . . No reasonable onlooker would have regarded Johnson's generalized expression of dissatisfaction with the policies of the Federal Government as a direct personal insult or an invitation to exchange fisticuffs. . . .

We thus conclude that the State's interest in maintaining order is not implicated on these facts. The State need not worry that our holding will disable it from preserving the peace. We do not suggest that the First Amendment forbids a State to prevent "imminent lawless action.". . . And, in fact, Texas already has a statute specifically prohibiting breaches of the peace, Texas Penal Code Ann. § 42.01 (1989), which tends to confirm that Texas need not punish this flag desecration in order to keep the peace. . . .

* * *

It remains to consider whether the State's interest in preserving the flag as a symbol of nationhood and national unity justifies Johnson's conviction. . . .

Johnson's political expression was restricted because of the content of the message he conveyed. We must therefore subject the State's asserted interest in preserving the special symbolic character of the flag to "the most exacting scrutiny.". . .

Texas argues that its interest in preserving the flag as a symbol of nationhood and national unity survives this close analysis. Quoting extensively from the writings of this Court chronicling the flag's historic and symbolic role in our society, the State emphasizes the " 'special place' " reserved for the flag in our Nation. . . . According to Texas, if one physically treats the flag in a way that would tend to cast doubt on either the idea that nationhood and national unity are the flag's referents or that national unity actually exists, the message con-veyed thereby is a harmful one and therefore may be prohibited.

If there is a bedrock principle underlying the First Amendment, it is that the Government may not prohibit the expression of an idea simply because society finds the idea itself offensive or disagreeable. . . .

We have not recognized an exception to this principle even where our flag has been involved. . . .

. . . If we were to hold that a State may forbid flag burning wherever it is likely to endanger the flag's symbolic role, but allow it wherever burning a flag promotes that role—as where, for example, a person ceremoniously burns a dirty flag—we would be saying that when it comes to impairing the flag's physical integrity, the flag itself may be used as a symbol—as a substitute for the written or spoken word or a "short cut from mind to mind"—only in one direction. We would be permitting a State to "prescribe what shall be orthodox" by saying that one may burn the flag to convey one's attitude toward it and its referents only if one does not endanger the flag's representation of nationhood and national unity.

We never before have held that the Government may ensure that a symbol be used to express only one view of that symbol or its referents. . . .

. . . To conclude that the Government may permit designated symbols to be used to communicate only a limited set of messages would be to enter territory having no discernible or defensible boundaries. Could the Government, on this theory, prohibit the burning of state flags? Of copies of the Presidential seal? Of the Constitution? In evaluating these choices under the First Amendment, how would we decide which symbols were sufficiently special to warrant this unique status? To do so, we would be forced to consult our own political preferences, and impose them on the citizenry, in the very way that the First Amendment forbids us to do. . . .

There is, moreover, no indication—either in the text of the Constitution or in our cases interpreting it—that a separate juridical category exists for the American flag alone. Indeed, we would not be surprised to learn that the persons who framed our Constitution and wrote the Amendment that we now construe were not known for their reverence for the Union Jack. The First Amendment does not guarantee that other concepts virtually sacred to our Nation as a whole—such as the principle that discrimination on the basis of race is odious and destructive—will go unquestioned in the marketplace of ideas. . . . We decline, therefore, to create for the flag an exception to the joust of principles protected by the First Amendment. . . .

We are fortified in today's conclusion by our conviction that forbidding criminal punishment for conduct such as Johnson's will not endanger the special role played by our flag or the feelings it inspires. To paraphrase Justice Holmes, we submit that nobody can suppose that this one gesture of an unknown man will change our Nation's attitude towards its flag. . . .

We are tempted to say, in fact, that the flag's deservedly cherished place in our community will be strengthened, not weakened, by our holding today. Our decision is a reaffirmation of the principles of freedom and inclusiveness that the flag best reflects, and of the conviction that our toleration of criticism such as Johnson's is a sign and source of our strength. Indeed, one of the proudest images of our flag, the one immortalized in our national anthem, is of the bombardment it survived at Fort McHenry. It is the Nation's resilience, not its rigidity, that Texas sees reflected in the flag—and it is that resilience that we assert today.

The way to preserve the flag's special role is not to punish those who feel differently about these matters. It is to persuade them that they are wrong. "To courageous, self-reliant men, with confidence in the power of free and fearless reasoning applied through the process of popular government, no danger flowing from speech can be deemed clear and present, unless the incidence of the evil apprehended is so imminent that it may befall before there is opportunity for full discussion. If there be time to expose through discussion the falsehood and fallacies, to avert the evil by the processes of education, the remedy to be applied is more speech, not enforced silence.". . . And, precisely because it is our flag that is involved, one's response to the flag-burner may exploit the uniquely persuasive power of the flag itself. We can imagine no more appropriate response to burning a flag than waving one's own, no better way to counter a flag-burner's message than by saluting the flag that burns, no surer means of preserving the dignity even of the flag that burned than by—as one witness here did—according its remains a respectful burial. We do not consecrate the flag by punishing its desecration, for in doing so we dilute the freedom that this cherished emblem represents.

V

Johnson was convicted for engaging in expressive conduct. The State's interest in preventing breaches of the peace does not support his conviction because Johnson's conduct did not threaten to disturb the peace. Nor does the State's interest in preserving the flag as a symbol of nationhood and national unity justify his criminal conviction for engaging in political expression. The judgment of the Texas Court of Criminal Appeals is therefore affirmed.

Justice Anthony M. Kennedy, concurring:

I write not to qualify the words Justice Brennan chooses so well, for he says with power all that is necessary to explain our ruling. I join his opinion without reservation, but with a keen sense that this case, like others before us from time to time, exacts its personal toll. This prompts me to add to our pages these few remarks.

The case before us illustrates better than most that the judicial power is often difficult in its exercise. We cannot here ask another branch to share responsibility, as when the argument is made that a statute is flawed or incomplete. For we are presented with a clear and simple statute to be judged against a pure command of the Constitution. The outcome can be laid at no door but ours.

The hard fact is that sometimes we must make decisions we do not like. We make them because they are right, right in the sense that the law and the Constitution, as we see them, compel the result. And so great is our commitment to the process that, except in the rare case, we do not pause to express distaste for the result, perhaps for fear of undermining a valued principle that dictates the decision. This is one of those rare cases.

Our colleagues in dissent advance powerful arguments why respondent may be convicted for his expression, reminding us that among those who will be dismayed by our holding will be some who have had the singular honor of carrying the flag in battle. And I agree that the flag holds a lonely place of honor in an age when absolutes are distrusted and simple truths are burdened by unneeded apologetics.

With all respect to those views, I do not believe the Constitution gives us the right to rule as the dissenting members of the court urge, however painful this judgment is to announce. Though symbols often are what we ourselves make of them, the flag is constant in expressing beliefs Americans share, beliefs in law and peace and that freedom which sustains the human spirit. The case here today forces recognition of the costs to which those beliefs commit us. It is poignant but fundamental that the flag protects those who hold it in contempt.

For all the record shows, this respondent was not a philosopher and perhaps did not even possess the ability to comprehend how repellent his statements must be to the Republic itself. But whether or not he could appreciate the enormity of the offense he gave, the fact remains that his acts were speech, in both the technical and the fundamental meaning of the Constitution. So I agree with the court that he must go free.

Chief Justice Rehnquist joined by Justices Byron R. White and Sandra Day O'Connor, dissenting:

In holding this Texas statute unconstitutional, the Court ignores Justice Holmes' familiar aphorism that "a page of history is worth a volume of logic.". . . For more than 200 years, the American flag has occupied a unique position as the symbol of our Nation, a uniqueness that justifies a governmental prohibition against flag burning in the way respondent Johnson did here. . . .

The flag symbolizes the Nation in peace as well as in war. It signifies our national presence on battleships, airplanes, military installations, and public buildings from the United States Capitol to the thousands of county courthouses and city halls throughout the country. Two flags are prominently placed in our courtroom. Countless flags are placed by the graves of loved ones each year on what was first called Decoration Day, and is now called Memorial Day. The flag is traditionally placed on the casket of deceased members of the armed forces, and it is later given to the deceased's family. . . . Congress has provided that the flag be flown at half-staff upon the death of the President, Vice President, and other government officials "as a mark of respect to their memory." . . . The flag identifies United States merchant ships, 22 U.S.C. § 454, and "[t]he laws of the Union protect our commerce wherever the flag of the country may float.". . .

No other American symbol has been as universally honored as the flag. In 1931, Congress declared "The Star Spangled Banner" to be our national anthem. In 1949, Congress declared June 14th to be Flag Day. In 1987, John Philip Sousa's "The Stars and Stripes Forever" was designated as the national march. . . . Congress has also established "The Pledge of Allegiance to the Flag" and the manner of its deliverance. . . . The flag has appeared as the principal symbol on approximately 33 United States postal stamps and in the design of at least 43 more, more times than any other symbol. . . .

Both Congress and the States have enacted numerous laws regulating misuse of the American flag. Until 1967, Congress left the regulation of misuse of the flag up to the States. Now, however, Title 18 U.S.C. § 700(a), provides that: "Whoever knowingly casts contempt upon any flag of the United States by publicly mutilating, defacing, defiling, burning, or trampling upon it shall be fined not more than $1,000 or imprisoned for not more than one year, or both.". . .

The American flag, then, throughout more than 200 years of our history, has come to be the visible symbol embodying our Nation. It does not represent the views of any particular political party, and it does not represent any particular political philosophy. The flag is not simply another "idea" or "point of view" competing for recognition in the marketplace of ideas. Millions and millions of Americans regard it with an almost mythical reverence regardless of what sort of social, political, or philosophical beliefs they may have. I cannot agree that the First Amendment invalidates the Act of Congress, and the laws of 48 of the 50 States, which make criminal the public burning of the flag.

. . . [T]he public burning of the American flag by Johnson was no essential part of any exposition of ideas, and at the same time it had a tendency to incite a breach of the peace. Johnson was free to make any verbal denunciation of the flag that he wished; indeed, he was free to burn the flag in private. He could publicly burn other symbols of the government or effigies of political leaders. He did lead a march through the streets of Dallas, and conducted a rally in front of the Dallas City Hall. He engaged in a "die-in" to protest nuclear weapons. He shouted out various slogans during the march, including: "Reagan, Mondale which will it be? Either one means World War III"; "Ronald Reagan, killer of the hour, Perfect example of U.S. power"; and "red, white and blue, we spit on you, you stand for plunder, you will go under.". . . For none of these acts was he arrested or prosecuted; it was only when he proceeded to burn publicly an American flag stolen from its rightful owner that he violated the Texas statute.

. . . As with "fighting words," so with flag burning, for purposes of the First Amendment: It is "no essential part of any exposition of ideas, and [is] of such slight social value as a step to truth that any benefit that may be derived from [it] is clearly outweighed" by the public interest in avoiding a probable breach of the peace. The highest courts of several States have upheld state statutes prohibiting the public burning of the flag on the grounds that it is so inherently inflammatory that it may cause a breach of public order. . . .

. . . The Texas statute deprived Johnson of only one rather inarticulate symbolic form of protest—a form of protest that was profoundly offensive to many—and left him with a full panoply of other symbols and every conceivable form of verbal expression to express his deep disapproval of national policy. Thus, in no way can it be said that Texas is punishing him because his hearers— or any other group of people—were profoundly opposed to the message that he sought to convey. Such opposition is no proper basis for restricting speech or expression under the First Amendment. It was Johnson's use of this particular symbol, and not the idea that he sought to convey by it or by his many other expressions, for which he was punished.

. . . The uniquely deep awe and respect for our flag felt by virtually all of us are bundled off under the rubric of "designated symbols,". . . that the First Amendment prohibits the government from "establishing." But the government has not "established" this feeling; 200 years of history have done that. The government is simply recognizing as a fact the profound regard for the American flag created by that history when it enacts statutes prohibiting the disrespectful public burning of the flag.

The Court concludes its opinion with a regrettably patronizing civics lecture, presumably addressed to the Members of both Houses of Congress, the members of the 48 state legislatures that enacted prohibitions against flag burning, and the troops fighting under that flag in Vietnam who objected to its being burned: "The way to preserve the flag's special role is not to punish those who feel differently about these matters. It is to persuade them that they are wrong." . . . The court's role as the final expositor of the Constitution is well established, but its role as a platonic guardian admonishing those responsible to public opinion as if they were truant school children had no similar place in our system of government. The cry of "no taxation without representation" animated those who revolted against the English Crown to found our Nation— the idea that those who submitted to government should have some say as to what kind of laws would be passed. Surely one of the high purposes of a democratic society is to legislate against conduct that is regarded as evil and profoundly offensive to the majority of people—whether it be murder, embezzlement, pollution, or flag burning.

Our Constitution wisely places limits on powers of legislative majorities to act, but the declaration of such limits by this Court "is, at all times, a question of much delicacy, which ought seldom, if ever, to be decided in the affirmative, in a doubtful case.". . . Uncritical extension of constitutional protection to the burning of the flag risks the frustration of the very purpose for which organized governments are instituted. The Court decides that the American flag is just another symbol, about which not only must opinions pro and con be tolerated, but for which the most minimal public respect may not be enjoined. The government may conscript men into the Armed Forces where they must fight and perhaps die for the flag, but the government may not prohibit the public burning of the banner under which they fight. I would uphold the Texas statute as applied in this case.

Justice Stevens, dissenting:

As the court analyzes this case, it presents the question whether the State of Texas, or indeed the Federal Government, has the power to prohibit the public desecration of the American flag. The question is unique. In my judgment, rules that apply to a host of other symbols, such as state flags, armbands, or various privately promoted emblems of political or commercial identity, are not necessarily controlling. Even if flag burning could be considered just another species of symbolic speech under the logical application of the rules that the Court has developed in its interpretation of the First Amendment in other contexts, this case has an intangible dimension that makes those rules inapplicable.

A country's flag is a symbol of more than "nationhood and national unity.". . . It also signifies the ideas that characterize the society that has chosen that emblem as well as the special history that has animated the growth and power of those ideas. The fleurs-de-lis and the tricolor both symbolized "nationhood and national unity," but they had vastly different meanings. The message conveyed by some flags—the swastika, for example—may survive long after it has outlived its usefulness as a symbol of regimented unity in a particular nation.

So it is with the American flag. It is more than a proud symbol of the courage, the determination, and the gifts of nature that transformed 13 fledgling Colonies into a world power. It is a symbol of freedom, of equal opportunity, of religious tolerance, and of goodwill for other peoples who share our aspirations. The symbol carries its message to dissidents both at home and abroad who may have no interest at all in our national unity or survival.

The value of the flag as a symbol cannot be measured. . . .

The ideas of liberty and equality have been an irresistible force in motivating leaders like Patrick Henry, Susan B. Anthony, and Abraham Lincoln, schoolteachers like Nathan Hale and Booker T. Washington, the Philippine Scouts who fought at Bataan, and the soldiers who scaled the bluff at Omaha Beach. If those ideas are worth fighting for—and our history demonstrates that they are—it cannot be true that the flag that uniquely symbolizes their power is not itself worthy of protection from unnecessary desecration.

I respectfully dissent.

Religious Freedom and the Issue of School Prayer

As early as 1940 the Supreme Court nationalized the *free exercise* clause of the First Amendment, but it was not until 1947 that a majority of justices agreed that the *establishment* clause of the First Amendment was also a fundamental liberty protected by the due process clause of the Fourteenth Amendment.[1]

The First Amendment provision embodying the establishment and free exercise clauses states: "Congress shall make no law respecting an establishment of religion, or prohibiting the free exercise thereof." While little controversy surrounded the Supreme Court's nationalization of these provisions, its 1962 decision in *Engel* v. *Vitale*, given in the following selection, holding that religious freedom required a ban on prayers in public schools, caused a political backlash that continued into the 1980s, one that seemed to grow in intensity as the years passed. As the Moral Majority and the Christian Right became politically active in the 1980s, one of their major goals was the restoration of prayers in public schools. They supported state efforts to pass legislation that would get around the school prayer decision by requiring moments of silence rather than prayers to open school days. However, the Supreme Court held in 1985 that an Alabama moment-of-silence statute authorizing public school teachers to hold a one-minute period of silence for "meditation or voluntary prayer" each school day violated the establishment clause of the First Amendment.[2] Of particular concern to the Court were statements by the sponsors of the legislation that they intended the law to restore prayer to public schools. Even conservative justices, such as Sandra Day O'Connor, who supported completely voluntary moments of silence in public schools during which prayers might be given, agreed that the Alabama statute had no secular effect and was an impermissible official encouragement of prayers. The following case originated the school prayer controversy.

---

[1]The two cases nationalizing the First Amendment free exercise and establishment clauses were respectively *Cantwell* v. *Connecticut*, 310 U.S. 296 (1940) and *Everson* v. *Board of Education*, 330 U.S. 1 (1947).

[2]*Wallace* v. *Jaffree*, 86 L Ed. 2d 29 (1985).

19

ENGEL v. VITALE
370 U.S. 421 (1962)

Mr. Justice Black delivered the opinion of the Court, saying in part:

The respondent Board of Education of Union Free School District No. 9, New Hyde Park, New York, acting in its official capacity under state law, directed the School District's principal to cause the following prayer to be said aloud by each class in the presence of a teacher at the beginning of each school day:

> Almighty God, we acknowledge our dependence upon Thee, and we beg Thy blessings upon us, our parents, our teachers and our country.

This daily procedure was adopted on the recommendation of the State Board of Regents, a governmental agency created by the state Constitution to which the New York Legislature has granted broad supervisory, executive, and legislative powers over the state's public school system. These state officials composed the prayer which they recommended and published as a part of their "Statement on Moral and Spiritual Training in the Schools," saying: "We believe that this Statement will be subscribed to by all men and women of good will, and we call upon all of them to aid in giving life to our program."

Shortly after the practice of reciting the Regents' prayer was adopted by the School District, the parents of ten pupils brought this action in a New York State Court insisting that use of this official prayer in the public schools was contrary to the beliefs, religions, or religious practices of both themselves and their children. Among other things, these parents challenged the constitutionality of both the state law authorizing the School District to direct the use of prayer in public schools and the School District's regulation ordering the recitation of this particular prayer on the ground that these actions of official governmental agencies violate that part of the First Amendment of the federal Constitution which commands that "Congress shall make no law respecting an establishment of religion"—a command which was "made applicable to the state of New York by the Fourteenth Amendment of the said Constitution." The New York Court of Appeals, over the dissents of Judges Dye and Fuld, sustained an order of the lower state courts which had upheld the power of New York to use the Regents' prayer as a part of the daily procedures of its public schools so long as the schools did not compel any pupil to join in the prayer over his or her parents' objection. We granted certiorari to review this important decision involving rights protected by the First and Fourteenth Amendments.

We think that by using its public school system to encourage recitiation of the Regents' prayer, the state of New York has adopted a practice wholly inconsistent with the Establishment Clause. There can, of course, be no doubt that New York's program of daily classroom invocation of God's blessings as prescribed in the Regents' prayer is a religious activity. It is a solemn avowal of divine faith and supplication for the blessings of the Almighty. The nature of such a prayer has always been religious, none of the respondents has denied this and the trial court expressly so found. . . .

The petitioners contend among other things that the state laws requiring or permitting use of the Regents' prayer must be struck down as a violation of the Establishment Clause because the prayer was composed by governmental officials as a part of a governmental program to further religious beliefs. For this reason, petitioners argue, the state's use of the Regents' prayer in its public school system breaches the constitutional wall of separation between church and state. We agree with that contention since we think that the constitutional prohibition against laws respecting an establishment of religion must at least mean that in this country it is no part of the business of government to compose official prayers for any group of the American people to recite as a part of a religious program carried on by government.

It is a matter of history that this very practice of establishing governmentally composed prayers for religious services was one of the reasons which caused many of our early colonists to leave England and seek religious freedom in America. The Book of Common Prayer, which was created under governmental direction and which was approved by Acts of Parliament in 1548 and 1549, set out in minute detail the accepted form and content of prayer and other religious ceremonies to be used in the established, tax-supported Church of England. The controversies over the Book and what should be its content repeatedly threatened to disrupt the peace of that country as the accepted forms of prayer in the established church changed with the views of the particular ruler that happened to be in control at the time. Powerful groups representing some of the varying religious views of the people struggled among themselves to impress their particular views upon the government and obtain amendments of the Book more suitable to their respective notions of how religious services should be conducted in order that the official religious establishment would advance their particular religious beliefs. Other groups, lacking the necessary political power to influence the government on the matter, decided to leave England and its established church and seek freedom in America from England's governmentally ordained and supported religion.

It is an unfortunate fact of history that when some of the very groups which had most strenuously opposed the established Church of England found themselves sufficiently in control of colonial governments in this country to write their own prayers into law, they passed laws making their own religion the official religion of their respective colonies. Indeed, as late as the time of the Revolutionary War, there were established churches in at least eight of the thirteen former colonies and established religions in at least four of the other five. But the successful Revolution against English political domination was shortly followed by intense opposition to the practice of establishing religion by law. . . .

By the time of the adoption of the Constitution, our history shows that there was a widespread awareness among many Americans of the dangers of a union of church and state. . . . The First Amendment was added to the Constitution to stand as a guarantee that neither the power nor the prestige of the federal government would be used to control, support or influence the kinds of prayer the American people can say—that the people's religions must not be subjected to the pressures of government for change each time a new political administration is elected to office. Under that amendment's prohibition against governmental establishment of religion, as reinforced by the provisions of the Fourteenth Amendment, government in this country, be it state or federal, is without power to prescribe by law any particular form of prayer which is to be used as an official prayer in carrying on any program of governmentally sponsored religious activity.

There can be no doubt that New York's state prayer program officially establishes the religious beliefs embodied in the Regents' prayer. The respondents' argument to the contrary, which is largely based upon the contention that the Regents' prayer is "nondenominational" and the fact that the program, as modified and approved by state courts, does not require all pupils to recite the prayer but permits those who wish to do so to remain silent or be excused from the room, ignores the essential nature of the program's constitutional defects. Neither the fact that the prayer may be denominationally neutral, nor the fact that its observance on the part of the students is voluntary can serve to free it from the limitations of the Establishment Clause, as it might from the Free Exercise Clause, of the First Amendment, both of which are operative against the states by virtue of the Fourteenth Amendment. Although these two clauses may in certain instances overlap, they forbid two quite different kinds of governmental encroachment upon religious freedom. The Establishment Clause, unlike the Free Exercise Clause, does not depend upon any showing of direct governmental compulsion and is violated by the enactment of laws which establish an official religion whether those laws operate directly to coerce nonobserving individuals or not. This is not to say, of course, that laws officially prescribing a particular form of religious worship do not involve coercion of such individuals. When the power, prestige and financial support of government is placed behind a particular religious belief, the indirect coercive pressure upon religious minorities to conform to the prevailing officially approved religion is plain. But the purposes underlying the Establishment Clause go much further than that. Its first and most immediate purpose rested on the belief that a union of government and religion tends to destroy government and to degrade religion. The history of governmentally established religion, both in England and in this country, showed that whenever government had allied itself with one particular form of religion, the inevitable result has been that it had incurred the hatred, disrespect and even contempt of those who held contrary beliefs. That same history showed that many people had lost their respect for any religion that had relied upon the support of government to spread its faith. The Establishment Clause thus stands as an expression of principle on the part of the Founders of our Constitution that religion is too personal, too sacred, too holy, to permit its "unhallowed perversion" by a civil magistrate. Another purpose of the Establishment Clause rested upon an awareness of the historical fact that governmentally established religions and religious persecutions go hand in hand. The founders knew that only a few years after the Book of Common Prayer became the only accepted form of religious services in the established Church of England, an Act of Uniformity was passed to compel all Englishmen to attend those services and to make it a criminal offense to conduct or attend religious gatherings of any other kind—a law which was consistently flouted by dissenting religious groups in England and which contributed to widespread persecutions of people like John Bunyan who persisted in holding "unlawful [religious] meetings . . . to the great disturbance and distraction of the good subjects of this kingdom. . . ." And they knew that similar persecutions had received the sanction of law in several of the colonies in this country soon after the establishment of official religions in those colonies. It was in large part to get completely away from this sort of systematic religious persecution that the Founders brought into being our Nation, our Constitution, and our Bill of Rights with its prohibition against any governmental establishment of religion. The New York laws officially prescribing the Regents' prayer are inconsistent with both the purposes of the Establishment Clause and with the Establishment Clause itself.

It has been argued that to apply the Constitution in such a way as to prohibit state laws respecting an establishment of religious services in public schools is to indicate a hostility toward religion or toward prayer. Nothing, of course, could be more wrong. The history of man is inseparable from the history of religion. And perhaps it is not too much to say that since the beginning of that history many people have devoutly believed that "More things are wrought by prayer than this world dreams of." It was doubtless largely due to men who believed this that there grew up a sentiment that caused men to leave the cross-currents of officially established state religions and religious persecution in Europe and come to this country filled with the hope that they could find a place in which they could pray when they pleased to the God of their faith in the language they chose. And there were men of this same faith in the power of prayer who led the fight for adoption of our Constitution and also for our Bill of Rights with the very guarantees of religious freedom that forbid the sort of governmental activity which New York has attempted here. These men knew that the First Amendment, which tried to put an end to governmental control of religion and of prayer, was not written to destroy either. They knew rather that it was written to quiet well-justified fears which nearly all of them felt arising out of an awareness that governments of the past had shackled men's tongues to make them speak only the religious thoughts that government wanted them to speak and to pray only to the God that government wanted them to pray to. It is neither sacrilegious nor antireligious to say that each separate government in this country should stay out of the business of writing or sanctioning official prayers and leave that purely religious function to the people themselves and to those the people choose to look to for religious guidance.

It is true that New York's establishment of its Regents' prayer as an officially approved religious doctrine of that state does not amount to a total establishment of one particular religious sect to the exclusion of all others—that, indeed, the governmental endorsement of that prayer seems relatively insignificant when compared to the governmental encroachments upon religion which were commonplace 200 years ago. To those who may subscribe to the view that because the Regents' official prayer is so brief and general there can be no danger to religious freedom in its governmental establishment, however, it may be appropriate to say in the words of James Madison, the author of the First Amendment:

> [I]t is proper to take alarm at the first experiment on our liberties. . . . Who does not see that the same authority which can establish Christianity, in exclusion of all other Religions, may establish with the same ease any particular sect of Christians, in exclusion of all other Sects? That the same authority which can force a citizen to contribute three pence only of his property for the support of any one establishment, may force him to conform to any other establishment in all cases whatsosever?

The judgment of the Court of Appeals of New York is reversed and the cause remanded for further proceedings not inconsistent with this opinion.

Reversed and remanded.

Mr. Justice Frankfurter took no part in the decision of this case.

Mr. Justice White took no part in the consideration or decision of this case.

Mr. Justice Douglas concurred in a separate opinion.

Mr. Justice Stewart, dissenting:

A local school board in New York has provided that those pupils who wish to do so may join in a brief prayer at the beginning of each school day, acknowledging their dependence upon God and asking His blessing upon them and upon their parents, their teachers, and their country. The court today decides that in permitting this brief nondenominational prayer the school board has violated the Constitution of the United States. I think this decision is wrong.

The Court does not hold, nor could it, that New York has interfered with the free exercise of anybody's religion. For the state courts have made clear that those who object to reciting the prayer must be entirely free of any compulsion to do so, including any "embarrassments and pressure." Cf. *West Virginia State Board of Education* v. *Barnette*, 319 U.S. 624. But the Court says that in permitting school children to say this simple prayer, the New York authorities have established "an official religion."

With all respect, I think the Court has misapplied a great constitutional principle. I cannot see how an "official religion" is established by letting those who want to say a prayer say it. On the contrary, I think that to deny the wish of these school children to join in reciting this prayer is to deny them the opportunity of sharing in the spiritual heritage of our nation.

The Court's historical review of the quarrels over the Book of Common Prayer in England throws no light for me on the issue before us in this case. England had then and has now an established church. Equally unenlightening, I think, is the history of the early establishment and later rejection of an official church in our own states. For we deal here not with the establishment of a state church, which would, of course, be constitutionally impermissible, but with whether school children who want to begin their day by joining in prayer must be prohibited from doing so. Moreover, I think that the Court's task, in this as in all areas of constitutional adjudication, is not responsibly aided by the uncritical invocation of metaphors like the "wall of separation," a phrase nowhere to be found in the Constitution. What is relevant to the issue here is not the history of an established church in sixteenth-century England or in eighteenth-century America, but the history of the religious traditions of our people, reflected in countless practices of the institutions and officials of our government.

At the opening of each day's session of this Court we stand, while one of our officials invokes the protection of God. Since the days of John Marshall our Crier has said, "God save the United States and this Honorable Court." Both the Senate and the House of Representatives open their daily sessions with prayer. Each of our Presidents, from George Washington to John F. Kennedy, has upon assuming his office asked the protection and help of God.

The Court today says that the state and federal governments are without constitutional power to prescribe any particular form of words to be recited by any group of the American people on any subject touching religion. The third stanza of "The Star-Spangled Banner," made our national anthem by Act of Congress in 1931, contains these verses:

> Blest with victory and peace, may the heav'n rescued land
> Praise the Pow'r that hath made and preserved us a nation!

Then conquer we must, when our cause it is just,
And this be our motto, "In God is our Trust."

In 1954 Congress added a phrase to the Pledge of Allegiance to the Flag so that it now contains the words "one Nation *under* God indivisible, with liberty and justice for all." In 1952 Congress enacted legislation calling upon the President each year to proclaim a National Day of Prayer. Since 1865 the words "IN GOD WE TRUST" have been impressed on our coins.

Countless similar examples could be listed, but there is no need to belabor the obvious. It was all summed up by this Court just ten years ago in a single sentence: "We are a religious people whose institutions presuppose a Supreme Being." *Zoarch v. Clauson,* 343 U.S. 306, 313.

I do not believe that this Court, or the Congress, or the President has by the actions and practices I have mentioned established an "official religion" in violation of the Constitution. And I do not believe the state of New York has done so in this case. What each has done has been to recognize and to follow the deeply entrenched and highly cherished spiritual traditions of our nation—traditions which come down to us from those who almost two hundred years ago avowed their "firm reliance on the Protection of Divine Providence" when they proclaimed the freedom and independence of this brave new world.

I dissent.

The Right to Abortion

Ironically, while the "liberal" Warren Court stirred political controversy with its school prayer and many other decisions extending civil liberties and rights to the states, it was the "conservative" Supreme Court under the Chief Justiceship of Warren Burger, who was appointed by Republican President Richard M. Nixon in 1969, that raised an even greater political storm by holding in the following case that the Fourteenth Amendment incorporates a right to privacy that grants women the absolute right to abortion during the first trimester of pregnancy. When the decision was handed down in 1973, a majority of states strictly regulated abortions, which could be performed if at all only to protect the life of the mother. The moral codes of many religions, particularly the Catholic Church, forbid abortions under any circumstances.

Supporters of the abortion decision argued that while the issue was indeed a moral one for most people, women had a constitutionally protected right to decide whether or not they would have an abortion. Opponents not only emphatically opposed abortion on moral grounds, but also attacked the Court for acting as a supra-legislature by imposing its own

values upon democratically elected state legislative bodies that were regulating abortion in response to the demands of popular majorities.

The Supreme Court's abortion decision did seem to resurrect "substantive due process," a doctrine under which the Court had in the past judged
the fairness of state legislation in terms not of explicitly stated constitutional
standards but on the basis of its own values. The Bill of Rights does not
contain a general right of privacy, although it may be fairly implied, as
Justice Douglas wrote for a majority of the Court in *Griswold* v. *Connecticut,*
381 U.S. 479 (1965), from First Amendment freedoms of association, Fourth
Amendment protections against unreasonable searches and seizures, and
the Fifth Amendment shield against self-incrimination.

Whether emanating indirectly from the Bill of Rights or considered to
be part of the liberty protected by the Fourteenth Amendment, the right of
privacy that the Supreme Court applied in its abortion decision is highly
subjective and gives the justices great leeway to impose their own concepts
of privacy rights upon legislative bodies. But judicial decisions, especially
those of the Supreme Court, always express the values of those making
them. The justices did go beyond a strict construction of the Bill of Rights
in upholding a woman's right to abortion. However, they had previously
interpreted the Fourteenth Amendment due process clause just as subjec-
tively in each case in the step-by-step process of nationalization of most of
the provisions of the Bill Rights.

The Anglo-American system of law and jurisprudence has always supported the concept of a higher law that ultimately the courts must interpret
and apply. In Great Britain, however, Parliament became supreme after the
Glorious Revolution of 1688, preventing judicial review of parliamentary
laws. Our Supreme Court, on the other hand, continues to be the final
judge of what the law is, and inevitably its decisions will involve the Court
in major political controversies, as has been the case in the following opinion.

20

ROE v. WADE
410 U.S. 113 (1973)

Mr. Justice Blackmun delivered the opinion of the Court:

V

The principal thrust of appellant's attack on the Texas statutes is that they improperly invade a right, said to be possessed by the pregnant woman, to choose to terminate her pregnancy. Appellant would discover this right in the concept of personal "liberty" embodied in the Fourteenth Amendment's Due Process Clause; or in personal, marital, familial, and sexual privacy said to be protected by the Bill of Rights or its penumbras, see *Griswold v. Connecticut* [1965] . . . *Eisenstadt v. Baird* [1972] . . . (White, J., concurring in result); or among those rights reserved to the people by the Ninth Amendment, *Griswold v. Connecticut*, . . . (Goldberg, J., concurring). Before addressing this claim, we feel it desirable briefly to survey, in several aspects, the history of abortion, for such insight as that history may afford us, and then to examine the state purposes and interests behind the criminal abortion laws.

VI

It perhaps is not generally appreciated that the restrictive criminal abortion laws in effect in a majority of States today are of relatively recent vintage. Those laws, generally proscribing abortion or its attempt at any time during pregnancy except when necessary to preserve the pregnant woman's life, are not of ancient or even of common-law origin. Instead, they derive from statutory changes effected, for the most part, in the latter half of the 19th century. . . .

VII

Three reasons have been advanced to explain historically the enactment of criminal abortion laws in the 19th century and to justify their continued existence.

It has been argued occasionally that these laws were the product of a Victorian social concern to discourage illicit sexual conduct. Texas, however, does not advance this justification in the present case, and it appears that no court or commentator has taken the argument seriously. The appellants and amici contend, moreover, that this is not a proper state purpose at all and suggest that, if it were, the Texas statutes are overbroad in protecting it since the law fails to distinguish between married and unwed mothers.

A second reason is concerned with abortion as a medical procedure. When most criminal abortion laws were first enacted, the procedure was a hazardous one for the woman. This was particularly true prior to the development of antisepsis. Antiseptic techniques, of course, were based on discoveries by Lister, Pasteur, and others first announced in 1867, but were not generally accepted and employed until about the turn of the century. Abortion mortality was high. Even after 1900, and perhaps until as late as the development of antibiotics in the 1940's, standard modern techniques such as dilation and curettage were not nearly so safe as they are today. Thus, it has been argued that a State's real concern in enacting a criminal abortion law was to protect the pregnant woman, that is, to restrain her from submitting to a procedure that placed her life in serious jeopardy.

Modern medical techniques have altered this situation. Appellants and various amici refer to medical data indicating that abortion in early pregnancy, this is, prior to the end of the first trimester, although not without its risk, is now relatively safe. Mortality rates for women undergoing early abortions, where the procedure is legal, appear to be as low as or lower than the rates for normal childbirth. Consequently, any interest of the State in protecting the woman from an inherently hazardous procedure, except when it would be equally dangerous for her to forgo it, has largely disappeared. Of course, important state interests in the area of health and medical standards do remain.

The State has a legitimate interest in seeing to it that abortion, like any other medical procedure, is performed under circumstances that insure maximum safety for the patient. This interest obviously extends at least to the performing physician and his staff, to the facilities involved, to the availability of aftercare, and to adequate provision for any complication or emergency that might arise. The prevalence of high mortality rates at illegal "abortion mills" strengthens, rather than weakens, the State's interest in regulating the conditions under which abortions are performed. Moreover, the risk to the woman increases as her pregnancy continues. Thus, the State retains a definite interest in protecting the woman's own health and safety when an abortion is proposed at a late stage of pregnancy.

The third reason is the State's interest—some phrase it in terms of duty— in protecting prenatal life. Some of the argument for this justification rests on the theory that a new human life is present from the moment of conception. The State's interest and general obligation to protect life then extends, it is argued, to prenatal life. Only when the life of the pregnant mother herself is at stake, balanced against the life she carries within her, should the interest of the embryo or fetus not prevail. Logically, of course, a legitimate state interest in this area need not stand or fall on acceptance of the belief that life begins at conception or at some other point prior to live birth. In assessing the State's interest, recognition may be given to the less rigid claim that as long as at least *potential* life is involved, the State may assert interests beyond the protection of the pregnant woman alone.

Parties challenging state abortion laws have sharply disputed in some courts the contention that a purpose of these laws, when enacted, was to protect prenatal life. . . .

It is with these interests, and the weight to be attached to them, that this case is concerned.

VIII

The Constitution does not explicitly mention any right of privacy. In a line of decisions, however, going back perhaps as far as *Union Pacific R. Co. v. Botsford* [1891] . . . , the Court has recognized that a right of personal privacy, or a guarantee of certain areas or zones of privacy, does exist under the Constitution. In varying contexts, the Court or individual Justices have, indeed, found at least the roots of that right in the First Amendment, *Stanley v. Georgia* [1969] . . . ; in the Fourth and Fifth Amendments, *Terry v. Ohio* [1968] . . . , *Katz v. United States* [1967] . . . ; in the penumbras of the Bill of Rights, *Griswold v. Connecticut* [1965] . . . ; in the Ninth Amendment, id., at 486, . . . (Goldberg, J., concurring); or in the concept of liberty guaranteed by the first section of the Fourteenth Amendment, see *Meyer v. Nebraska* [1923]. . . . These decisions make it clear that only personal rights that can be deemed "fundamental" or "implicit in the concept of ordered liberty," *Palko v. Connecticut* [1937] . . . , are included in this guarantee of personal privacy. They also make it clear that the right has some extension to activities relating to marriage, *Loving v. Virginia* [1967] . . . ; procreation, *Skinner v. Oklahoma* [1942] . . . ; contraception, *Eisenstadt v. Baird* [1972]. . . .

This right of privacy, whether it be founded in the Fourteenth Amendment's concept of personal liberty and restrictions upon state action, as we feel it is, or, as the District Court determined, in the Ninth Amendment's reservation of rights to the people, is broad enough to encompass a woman's decision whether or not to terminate her pregnancy. The detriment that the State would impose upon the pregnant woman by denying this choice altogether is apparent. Specific and direct harm medically diagnosable even in early pregnancy may be involved. Maternity, or additional offspring, may force upon the woman a distressful life and future. Psychological harm may be imminent. Mental and physical health may be taxed by child care. There is also the distress, for all concerned, associated with the unwanted child, and there is the problem of bringing a child into a family already unable, psychologically and otherwise, to care for it. In other cases, as in this one, the additional difficulties and continuing stigma of unwed motherhood may be involved. All these are factors the woman and her responsible physician necessarily will consider in consultation.

On the basis of elements such as these, appellant and some amici argue that the woman's right is absolute and that she is entitled to terminate her pregnancy at whatever time, in whatever way, and for whatever reason she alone chooses. With this we do not agree. Appellant's arguments that Texas either has no valid interest at all in regulating the abortion decision, or no interest strong enough to support any limitation upon the woman's sole determination, is unpersuasive. The Court's decisions recognizing a right of privacy also acknowledge that some state regulation in areas protected by that right is appropriate. As noted above, a State may properly assert important interests in safeguarding health, in maintaining medical standards, and in protecting potential life. At some point in pregnancy, these respective interests become sufficiently compelling to sustain regulation of the factors that govern the abortion decision. The privacy right involved, therefore, cannot be said to be absolute. In fact, it is not clear to us that the claim asserted by some amici that one has an unlimited right to do with one's body as one pleases bears a close relationship to the right of privacy previously articulated in the Court's decisions. The Court has refused to recognize an unlimited right of this kind in the past. *Jacobson* v. *Massachusetts* [1905] . . . (vaccination); *Buck* v. *Bell* [1927] . . . (sterilization).

We, therefore, conclude that the right of personal privacy includes the abortion decision, but that this right is not unqualified and must be considered against important state interests in regulation.

Where certain "fundamental rights" are involved, the Court has held that regulation limiting these rights may be justified only by a "compelling state interest," . . . and that legislative enactments must be narrowly drawn to express only the legitimate state interests at stake. . . .

IX

The District Court held that the appellee failed to meet his burden of demonstrating that the Texas statute's infringement upon Roe's rights was necessary to support a compelling state interest. . . . Appellee argues that the State's determination to recognize and protect prenatal life from and after conception constitutes a compelling state interest. As noted above, we do not agree fully with either formulation.

A. The appellee and certain amici argue that the fetus is a "person" within the language and meaning of the Fourteenth Amendment. In support of this, they outline at length and in detail the well-known facts of fetal development. If this suggestion of personhood is established, the appellant's case, of course, collapses, for the fetus' right to life is then guaranteed specifically by the Amendment. The appellant conceded as much on reargument. On the other hand, the appellee conceded on reargument that no case could be cited that holds that a fetus is a person within the meaning of the Fourteenth Amendment.

The Constitution does not define "person" in so many words. Section 1 of the Fourteenth Amendment contains three references to "person." The first, in defining "citizens," speaks of "persons born or naturalized in the United States." The word also appears both in the Due Process Clause and in the Equal Protection Clause. "Person" is used in other places in the Constitution. . . . But in nearly all these instances, the use of the word is such that it has application only postnatally. None indicates, with any assurance, that it has any possible prenatal application.

All this, together with our observation, supra, that throughout the major portion of the 19th century prevailing legal abortion practices were far freer than they are today, persuades us that the word "person," as used in the Fourteenth Amendment, does not include the unborn. . . .

B. The pregnant woman cannot be isolated in her privacy. She carries an embryo and, later, a fetus, if one accepts the medical definitions of the developing young in the human uterus. . . . The situation therefore is inherently different from marital intimacy, or bedroom possession of obscene material, or marriage, or procreation, or education, with which *Eisenstadt, Griswold, Stanley, Loving, Skinner, Pierce,* and *Meyer* were respectively concerned. As we have intimated above, it is reasonable and appropriate for a State to decide that at some point in time another interest, that of health of the mother or that of potential human life, becomes significantly involved. The woman's privacy is no longer sole and any right of privacy she possesses must be measured accordingly.

Texas urges that, apart from the Fourteenth Amendment, life begins at conception and is present throughout pregnancy, and that, therefore, the State has a compelling interest in protecting that life from and after conception. We need not resolve the difficult question of when life begins. When those trained in the respective disciplines of medicine, philosophy, and theology are unable to arrive at any consensus, the judiciary, at this point in the development of man's knowledge, is not in a position to speculate as to the answer.

It should be sufficient to note briefly the wide divergence of thinking on this most sensitive and difficult question. . . .

X

In view of all this, we do not agree that, by adopting one theory of life, Texas may override the rights of the pregnant woman that are at stake. We repeat, however, that the State does have an important and legitimate interest in preserving and protecting the health of the pregnant woman, whether she be a resident of the State or a nonresident who seeks medical consultation and treatment there, and that it has still *another* important and legitimate interest in protecting the potentiality of human life. These interests are separate and distinct. Each grows in substantiality as the woman approaches term and, at a point during pregnancy, each becomes "compelling."

With respect to the State's important and legitimate interest in the health of the mother, the "compelling" point, in the light of present medical knowledge, is at approximately the end of the first trimester. This is so because of the now-established medical fact, referred to above . . . that until the end of the first trimester mortality in abortion may be less than mortality in normal childbirth. It follows that, from and after this point, a State may regulate the abortion procedure to the extent that the regulation reasonably relates to the preservation and protection of maternal health. Examples of permissible state regulation in this area are requirements as to the qualifications of the person who is to perform the abortion; as to the licensure of that person; as to the facility in which the procedure is to be performed, that is, whether it must be a hospital or may be a clinic or some other place of less-than-hospital status; as to the licensing of the facility; and the like.

This means, on the other hand, that, for the period of pregnancy prior to this "compelling" point, the attending physician, in consultation with his patient, is free to determine, without regulation by the State, that, in his medical judgment, the patient's pregnancy should be terminated. If that decision is reached, the judgment may be effectuated by an abortion free of interference by the State.

With respect to the State's important and legitimate interest in potential life, the "compelling" point is at viability. This is so because the fetus then presumably has the capability of meaningful life outside the mother's womb. State regulation protective of fetal life after viability thus has both logical and biological justifications. If the State is interested in protecting fetal life after viability, it may go so far as to proscribe abortion during that period, except when it is necessary to preserve the life or health of the mother.

Measured against these standards, Art. 1196 of the Texas Penal Code, in restricting legal abortions to those "procured or attempted by medical advice for the purpose of saving the life of the mother," sweeps too broadly. The statute makes no distinction between abortions performed early in pregnancy and those performed later, and it limits to a single reason, "saving" the mother's life, the legal justification for the procedure. The statute, therefore, cannot survive the constitutional attack made upon it here. . . .

XI

To summarize and to repeat:

1. A state criminal abortion statute of the current Texas type, that excepts from criminality only a *lifesaving* procedure on behalf of the mother, without regard to pregnancy stage and without recognition of the other interests involved, is violative of the Due Process Clause of the Fourteenth Amendment.

(a) For the stage prior to approximately the end of the first trimester, the abortion decision and its effectuation must be left to the medical judgment of the pregnant woman's attending physician.

(b) For the stage subsequent to approximately the end of the first trimester, the State, in promoting its interest in the health of the mother, may, if it chooses, regulate the abortion procedure in ways that are reasonably related to maternal health.

(c) For the stage subsequent to viability, the State in promoting its interest in the potentiality of human life may, if it chooses, regulate, and even proscribe, abortion except where it is necessary, in appropriate medical judgment, for the preservation of the life or health of the mother.

2. The State may define the term "physician," as it has been employed in the preceding numbered paragraphs of this Part XI of this opinion, to mean only a physician currently licensed by the State, and may proscribe any abortion by a person who is not a physician as so defined.

In *Doe* v. *Bolton* [1973] . . . procedural requirements contained in one of the modern abortion statutes are considered. That opinion and this one, of course, are to be read together. . . .

Mr. Chief Justice Burger concurred.
Mr. Justice Douglas concurred.

Mr. Justice Stewart, concurring:

In 1963, this Court, in *Ferguson* v. *Skrupa*, . . . purported to sound the death knell for the doctrine of substantive due process, a doctrine under which many state laws had in the past been held to violate the Fourteenth Amendment. As Mr. Justice Black's opinion for the Court in *Skrupa* put it: "We have returned to the original constitutional proposition that courts do not substitute their social and economic beliefs for the judgment of legislative bodies, who are elected to pass laws.". . .

Barely two years later, in *Griswold* v. *Connecticut,* . . . the Court held a Connecticut birth control law unconstitutional. In view of what had been so recently said in *Skrupa*, the Court's opinion in *Griswold* understandably did its best to avoid reliance on the Due Process Clause of the Fourteenth Amendment as the ground for decision. Yet, the Connecticut law did not violate any provision of the Bill of Rights, nor any other specific provision of the Constitution. So it was clear to me then, and it is equally clear to me now, that the *Griswold* decision can be rationally understood only as a holding that the Connecticut statute substantively invaded the "liberty" that is protected by the Due Process Clause of the Fourteenth Amendment. As so understood, *Griswold* stands as one in a long line of pre-Skrupa cases decided under the doctrine of substantive due process, and I now accept it as such.

"In a Constitution for a free people, there can be no doubt that the meaning of 'liberty' must be broad indeed.". . . The Constitution nowhere mentions a specific right of personal choice in matters of marriage and family life, but the "liberty" protected by the Due Process Clause of the Fourteenth Amendment covers more than those freedoms explicitly named in the Bill of Rights. . . .

Several decisions of this Court make clear that freedom of personal choice in matters of marriage and family life is one of the liberties protected by the Due Process Clause of the Fourteenth Amendment. *Loving* v. *Virginia,* . . . *Griswold* v. *Connecticut.* . . . In *Eisenstadt* v. *Baird,* . . . we recognized "the right of the *individual,* married or single, to be free from unwarranted governmental intrusion into matters so fundamentally affecting a person as the decision whether to bear or beget a child." That right necessarily includes the right of a woman to decide whether or not to terminate her pregnancy. "Certainly the interests of a woman in giving of her physical and emotional self during pregnancy and the interests that will be affected throughout her life by the birth and raising of a child are of a far greater degree of significance and personal intimacy than the right to send a child to private school protected in *Pierce* v. *Society of Sisters* [1925] . . . , or the right to teach a foreign language protected in *Meyer* v. *Nebraska.* . . ."

Mr. Justice Rehnquist, dissenting:

. . . I have difficulty in concluding, as the Court does, that the right of "privacy" is involved in this case. Texas, by the statute here challenged, bars the performance of a medical abortion by a licensed physician on a plaintiff such as Roe. A transaction resulting in an operation such as this is not "private" in the ordinary usage of that word. . . .

If the Court means by the term "privacy" no more than that the claim of a person to be free from unwanted state regulation of consensual transactions may be a form of "liberty" protected by the Fourteenth Amendment, there is no doubt that similar claims have been upheld in our earlier decisions on the basis of the liberty. I agree with the statement of Mr. Justice Stewart in his concurring opinion that the "liberty," against deprivation of which without due process the Fourteenth Amendment protects, embraces more than the rights found in the Bill of Rights. But that liberty is not guaranteed absolutely against deprivation, only against deprivation without due process of law. The test traditionally applied in the area of social and economic legislation is whether or not a law such as that challenged has a rational relation to a valid state objective. . . . But the Court's sweeping invalidation of any restrictions on abortion during the first trimester is impossible to justify under that standard, and the conscious weighing of competing factors that the Court's opinion apparently substitutes for the established test is far more appropriate to a legislative judgment than to a judicial one.

The Court eschews the history of the Fourteenth Amendment in its reliance on the "compelling state interest" test. . . . But the Court adds a new wrinkle to this test by transposing it from the legal considerations associated with the Equal Protection Clause of the Fourteenth Amendment to this case arising under the Due Process Clause of the Fourteenth Amendment. Unless I misapprehend the consequences of this transplanting of the "compelling state interest test," the Court's opinion will accomplish the seemingly impossible feat of leaving this area of the law more confused than it found it.

While the Court's opinion quotes from the dissent of Mr. Justice Holmes in *Lochner v. New York*, the result it reaches is more closely attuned to the majority opinion of Mr. Justice Peckham in that case. As in *Lochner* and similar cases applying substantive due process standards to economic and social welfare legislation, the adoption of the compelling state interest standard will inevitably require this Court to examine the legislative policies and pass on the wisdom of these policies in the very process of deciding whether a particular state interest put forward may or may not be "compelling." The decision here to break pregnancy into three distinct terms and to outline the permissible restrictions the State may impose in each one, for example, partakes more of judicial legislation than it does of a determination of the intent of the drafters of the Fourteenth Amendment.

The fact that a majority of the States reflecting, after all the majority sentiment in those States, have had restrictions on abortions for at least a century is a strong indication, it seems to me, that the asserted right to an abortion is not "so rooted in the traditions and conscience of our people as to be ranked as fundamental," *Snyder v. Massachusetts* [1934]. . . . Even today, when society's views on abortion are changing, the very existence of the debate is evidence that the "right" to an abortion is not so universally accepted as the appellant would have us believe.

To reach its result, the Court necessarily has had to find within the scope of the Fourteenth Amendment a right that was apparently completely unknown to the drafters of the Amendment. As early as 1821, the first state law dealing directly with abortion was enacted by the Connecticut Legislature. . . . By the time of the adoption of the Fourteenth Amendment in 1868, there were at least 36 laws enacted by state or territorial legislatures limiting abortion. While many States have amended or updated their laws, 21 of the laws on the books in 1868 remain in effect today. . . .

. . . The only conclusion possible from this history is that the drafters did not intend to have the Fourteenth Amendment withdraw from the States the power to legislate with respect to this matter. . . .

Mr. Justice White, joined by Mr. Justice Rehnquist, dissented.

❖❖   The Court's decision in *Roe* v. *Wade* (1973) almost immediately mobilized pro-life forces who pressured Congress for a constitutional amendment to overturn the *Roe* decision. Elected officials were caught in a political vise on the issue, which they considered a no-win situation. Pro-lifers constituted a powerful political movement but not a majority of the

American people who, after the *Roe* decision, favored the pro-choice position although not necessarily the practice of abortion.

For their part, politicians more often than not ducked the abortion issue by making vague statements such as, "I am personally against abortion but I must uphold and respect the Supreme Court's decision on the matter." Before the *Roe* decision many states were well on their way towards liberalizing their abortion statutes in an environment that was relatively free of political rancor. Ironically, the *Roe* decision galvanized political opposition to abortion and forced politicians, however reluctantly, to deal with the issue. As state statutes regulating abortion were struck down one after the other, the pro-life movement gathered more steam than converts.

While pressing for a constitutional amendment, the pro-lifers knew that their best hope was to convince the Supreme Court to overturn *Roe* v. *Wade.* Litigation had produced the decision, and litigation could overturn it if the Court's composition changed to a more conservative, pro-life viewpoint.

Ronald Reagan's election to the presidency in 1980 gave the pro-lifers renewed hopes for change. Reagan took a strong pro-life position, putting the issue at the top of his social agenda. During his eight years as president he was able to make three conservative appointments to the Supreme Court—Sandra Day O'Connor, Antonin Scalia, and Anthony M. Kennedy. Reagan and the pro-lifers had reason to hope that these new justices might tip the Court's scale in favor of overruling *Roe* v. *Wade.*

The suspense on both sides of the abortion issue was almost unbearable as the Court in 1989 reviewed a circuit court decision that had struck down a Missouri abortion law on the ground that it violated the principles of *Roe* v. *Wade.* The law prohibited the use of public facilities or employees to perform abortions, and prohibited the use of public funds for abortion counseling. The following decision, while not overruling *Roe* v. *Wade,* marked the beginning of a change in the Court's attitude on the abortion issue. A *plurality* of justices, led by Chief Justice William H. Rehnquist, began a process of dismantling *Roe,* but did not take the final step, urged by Justice Scalia, of overturning it. Justice Blackmun, who had written the *Roe* opinion, dissented along with Justices Brennan and Marshall. Blackmun wrote, "The simple truth is that *Roe* would not survive the plurality's analysis, and that the plurality provides no substitute for *Roe's* protective umbrella. I fear for the future. I fear for the liberty and equality of the millions of women who have lived and come of age in the sixteen years since *Roe* was decided. I fear for the integrity of, and public esteem for, this Court." He concluded, "For today, at least, the law of abortion stands undisturbed. For today, the women of this nation still retain the liberty to control their destinies. But the signs are evident and very ominous and a chill wind blows."

21

WEBSTER v. REPRODUCTIVE HEALTH SERVICES (1989)

Mr. Chief Justice Rehnquist, joined by Justices White and Kennedy, delivered the opinion of the Court:

This appeal concerns the constitutionality of a Missouri statute regulating the performance of abortions. The United States Court of Appeals for the Eighth Circuit struck down several provisions of the statute on the ground that they violated this court's decision in *Roe v. Wade,* 410 U.S. 113 (1973), and cases following it.

Decision of this case requires us to address four sections of the Missouri Act: (a) the preamble; (b) the prohibition on the use of public facilities or employees to perform abortions; (c) the prohibition on public funding of abortion counseling; and (d) the requirement that physicians conduct viability tests prior to performing abortions. . . .

The Act's preamble, as noted, sets forth "findings" by the Missouri legislature that "the life of each human being begins at conception," and that "unborn children have protectable interests in life, health, and well-being." The Act then mandates that state laws be interpreted to provide unborn children with "all the rights, privileges, and immunities available to other persons, citizens, and residents of this state," subject to the Constitution and this court's precedents. In invalidating the preamble, the Court of Appeals relied on this court's dictum that "a state may not adopt one theory of when life begins to justify its regulation of abortions. It rejected Missouri's claim that the preamble was "abortion-neutral," and "merely determined when life begins in a non-abortion context, a traditional state prerogative.". . .

In our view, the Court of Appeals misconceived the meaning . . . which was only that a state could not "justify" an abortion regulation otherwise invalid under *Roe v. Wade* on the ground that it embodied the state's view about when life begins. . . .

It will be time enough for federal courts to address the meaning of the preamble should it be applied to restrict the activities of appellees in some concrete way. Until then, this court "is not empowered to decide . . . abstract propositions, or to declare, for the government of future cases, principles or rules of law which cannot affect the result as to the thing in issue before it." We therefore need not pass on the constitutionality of the Act's preamble. . . .

Section 188.210 provides that "it shall be unlawful for any public employee within the scope of his employment to perform or assist an abortion, not necessary to save the life of the mother," while 188.215 makes it "unlawful for any public facility to be used for the purpose of performing or assisting an abortion not necessary to save the life of the mother." The Court of Appeals held that these provisions contravened this Court's abortion decisions. We take the contrary view. . . .

The [appeals] court reasoned that the ban on the use of public facilities "could prevent a woman's chosen doctor from performing an abortion because of his unprivileged status at other hospitals or because a private hospital adopted a similar antiabortion stance." It also thought that "such a rule could increase the cost of obtaining an abortion and delay the timing of it as well."

We think that this analysis is much like that which we rejected in [four other cases]. As in those cases, the state's decision here to use public facilities and staff to encourage childbirth over abortion "places no governmental obstacle in the path of a woman who chooses to terminate her pregnancy.". . .

Missouri's refusal to allow public employees to perform abortions in public hospitals leaves a pregnant woman with the same choices as if the state had chosen not to operate any public hospitals at all. The challenged provisions only restrict a woman's ability to obtain an abortion to the extent that she chooses to use a physician affiliated with a public hospital. This circumstance is more easily remedied, and thus considerably less burdensome than indigency which "may make it difficult—and in some cases, perhaps, impossible—for some women to have abortions" without public funding. Having held that the state's refusal to fund abortions does not violate *Roe* v. *Wade,* it strains logic to reach a contrary result for the use of public facilities and employees. . . .

[Three previous cases] all support the view that the state need not commit any resources to facilitating abortions, even if it can turn a profit by doing so. . . . Thus we uphold the Act's restrictions on the use of public employees and facilities for the performance or assistance of nontherapeutic abortions.

The Missouri Act contains three provisions relating to "encouraging or counseling a woman to have an abortion not necessary to save her life." Section 118.205 states that no public funds can be used for this purpose; 188.210 states that public employees cannot, within the scope of their employment, engage in such speech; and 188.215 forbids such speech in public facilities. The Court of Appeals . . . held that all three of these provisions were unconstitutionally vague and that "the ban on using public funds, employees and facilities to encourage or counsel a woman to have an abortion is an unacceptable infringement of the woman's 14th Amendment right to choose an abortion after receiving the medical information necessary to exercise the right knowingly and intelligently."

Missouri has chosen only to appeal the Court of Appeals' invalidation of the public funding provision . . . A majority of the court agrees with appellees that the controversy . . . is now moot . . . We accordingly direct the Court of

Appeals to vacate the judgment of the District Court with instructions to dismiss the relevant part of the complaint. . . .

Section 188.029 of the Missouri Act provides:

"Before a physician performs an abortion on a woman he has reason to believe is carrying an unborn child of 20 or more weeks gestational age, the physician shall first determine if the unborn child is viable by using and exercising that degree of care, skill, and proficiency commonly exercised by the ordinarily skillful, careful, and prudent physician engaged in similar practice under the same or similar conditions. In making this determination of viability, the physician shall perform or cause to be performed such medical examinations and tests as are necessary to make a finding of the gestational age, weight, and lung maturity of the unborn child and shall enter such findings and determination of viability in the medical record of the mother."

As with the preamble, the parties disagree over the meaning of this statutory provision. . . .

The Court of Appeals read 188.029 as requiring that after 20 weeks "doctors must perform tests to find gestational age, fetal weight and lung maturity." The court indicated that the tests needed to determine fetal weight at 20 weeks are "unreliable and inaccurate" and would add $125 to $250 to the cost of an abortion. . . .

We must first determine the meaning of 188.029 under Missouri law. Our usual practice is to defer to the lower court's construction of a state statute, but we believe the Court of Appeals has "fallen into plain error" in this case. . . .

We think the viability-testing provision makes sense only if the second sentence is read to require only those tests that are useful in making subsidiary findings as to viability. . . .

The viability-testing provision of the Missouri Act is concerned with promoting the state's interest in potential human life rather than in maternal health. . . .

In *Roe* v. *Wade*, the court recognized that the state has "important and legitimate" interests in protecting maternal health and in the potentiality of human life. During the second trimester, the state "may, if it chooses, regulate the abortion procedure in ways that are reasonably related to maternal health."

In the first place, the rigid *Roe* framework is hardly consistent with the notion of a Constitution case in general terms, as ours is, and usually speaking in general principles, as ours does. The key elements of the *Roe* framework— trimesters and viability—are not found in the text of the Constitution or in any place else one would expect to find a constitutional principle. . . .

In the second place, we do not see why the state's interest in protecting potential human life should come into existence only at the point of viability, and that there should therefore be a rigid line allowing state regulation after viability but prohibiting it before viability. . . .

The tests that 188.029 requires the physician to perform are designed to determine viability. . . . We are satisfied that the requirement of these tests

permissibly furthers the state's interests in protecting human life and we therefore believe 188.029 to be constitutional.

The dissent takes us to task for our failure to join in a "great issues" debate
as to whether the Constitution includes an "unenumerated" general right to
privacy. . . .

The dissent also accuses us of cowardice and illegitimacy in dealing with
"the most politically divisive domestic legal issue of our time." There is no
doubt that our holding today will allow some governmental regulation of abortion that would have been prohibited under the language [of other cases]. . . .

Both appellants and the United States have urged that we overrule our
decision in *Roe* v. *Wade*. The facts of the present case, however, differ from
those at issue in *Roe*. Here, Missouri has determined that viability is the point
at which its interest in potential human life must be safeguarded. In *Roe*, on
the other hand, the Texas statute criminalized the performance of all abortions,
except when the mother's life was at stake. This case therefore affords us no
occasion to revisit the holding of *Roe*, which was that the Texas statute unconstitutionally infringed the right to an abortion derived from the due process
clause, and we leave it undisturbed. To the extent indicated in our opinion, we
would modify and narrow *Roe* and succeeding cases.

Because none of the challenged provisions of the Missouri Act properly
before us conflict with the Constitution, the judgment of the Court of Appeals
is reversed.

Justice Sandra Day O'Connor, concurring in part and concurring in the judgment:

Nothing in the record before us or the opinions below indicates that sub-
sections 1 (1) and 1 (2) of the preamble to Missouri's abortion regulation statute
will affect a woman's decision to have an abortion. Justice Stevens . . . suggests
that the preamble may also 'interfere with contraceptive choices' . . . because
certain contraceptive devices act on a female ovum after it has been fertilized
by a male sperm.

The Missouri act defines 'conception' as 'the fertilization of the ovum of a
female by the sperm of a male' . . . and invests 'unborn children' with 'protectable interests in life, health and well-being' . . . from 'the moment of conception.'

Justice Stevens asserts that any possible interference with a woman's right
to use such post-fertilization contraceptive devices would be unconstitutional
under *Griswold* v. *Connecticut* . . . and our subsequent contraception cases. . . .

Similarly, certain amici suggest that the Missouri Act's preamble may prohibit the developing technology of in-vitro fertilization, a technique used to
aid couples otherwise unable to bear children in which a number of ova are
removed from the woman and fertilized by male sperm. This process often
produces excess fertilized ova ['unborn children' under the Missouri act's defi-
nition] that are discarded rather than reinserted into the woman's uterus. . . .

It may be correct that the use of post-fertilization contraceptive devices is constitutionally protected by *Griswold* and its progeny but, as with a woman's abortion decision, nothing in the record of the opinions below indicates that the preamble will affect a woman's decision to practice contraception. . . . Neither is there any indication of the possibility that the preamble might be applied to prohibit the performance of in-vitro fertilization. I agree with the court, therefore, that all of these intimations of unconstitutionality are simply too hypothetical to support the use of declaratory judgment procedures and injunctive remedies in this case. . . .

Similarly, it seems to me to follow directly from our previous decisions concerning state or federal funding of abortions . . . that appellees' facial challenge to the constitutionality of Missouri's ban on the utilization of public facilities and the participation of public employees in the performance of abortions not necessary to save the life of the mother . . . cannot succeed. . . .

I agree with the plurality that it was plain error for the Court of Appeals to interpret the second sentence of [the Missouri statute] . . . as meaning that "doctors must perform tests to find gestational age, fetal weight and lung maturity.". . .

It is clear to me that requiring the performance of examinations and tests useful to determining whether a fetus is viable . . . does not impose an undue burden on a woman's abortion decision. . . .

Justice Scalia, concurring in part and concurring in the judgment:

I share Justice Blackmun's view . . . that [the plurality's reasoning] effectively would overrule *Roe v. Wade* . I think that should be done, but would do it more explicitly. . . .

The outcome of today's case will doubtless be heralded as a triumph of judicial statesmanship. It is not that, unless it is statesmanlike needlessly to prolong this court's self-awarded sovereignty over a field where it has little proper business, since the answers to most of the cruel questions posed are political, not juridical—a sovereignty which therefore quite properly, but to the great damage of the court, makes it the object of the sort of organized public pressure that political institutions in a democracy ought to receive.

Justice O'Connor's assertion . . . that a 'fundamental mental rule of judicial restraint' requires us to avoid reconsidering *Roe*, cannot be taken seriously. By finessing *Roe*, we do not, as she suggests . . . adhere to the strict and venerable rule that we should avoid 'deciding questions of a constitutional nature.'

We have not disposed of this case on some statutory or procedural ground, but have decided—and could not avoid deciding—whether the Missouri statute meets the requirements of the United States Constitution. . . .

The real question, then, is whether there are valid reasons to go beyond the most stingy possible holding today. It seems to me there are not only valid, but compelling ones.

Alone sufficient to justify a broad holding is the fact that our retaining control, through *Roe*, of what I believe to be, and many of our citizens recognize to be, a political issue, continuously distorts the public perception of the role of this court.

We can now look forward to at least another term with carts full of mail from the public and streets full of demonstrators, urging us—their unelected and life-tenured judges who have been awarded those extraordinary, undemocratic characteristics precisely in order that we might follow the law despite the popular will, to follow the popular will.

Indeed, I expect we can look forward to even more of that than before, given our indecisive decision today. And if these reasons for taking the unexceptional course of reaching a broader holding are not enough, then consider the nature of the constitutional question we avoid: In most cases, we do no harm by speaking more broadly than the decision requires. Anyone affected by the conduct that the avoided holding would have prohibited will be able to challenge it himself, and have his day in court to make the argument.

Not so with respect to the harm that many States believed, pre-*Roe*, and many may continue to believe, is caused by largely unrestricted abortion. That will continue to occur if the States have the constitutional power to prohibit it, and would do so, but we skillfully avoid telling them so. Perhaps those abortions cannot constitutionally be proscribed. That is surely an arguable question—the question that reconsideration of *Roe v. Wade* entails.

Justice Blackmun, with whom Justice Brennan and Justice Marshall join, concurring in part and dissenting in part:

Today, *Roe v. Wade*, 410 U.S. 113 (1973), and the fundamental constitutional right of women to decide whether to terminate a pregnancy, survive, but are not secure. Although the court extricates itself from this case without making a single, even incremental change in the law of abortion, the plurality and Justice Scalia would overrule *Roe* . . . and would return to the states virtually unfettered authority to control the quintessentially intimate, personal and life-directing decision whether to carry a fetus to term.

Although today, no less than yesterday, the Constitution and the decisions of this court prohibit a state from enacting laws that inhibit women from the meaningful exercise of that right, a plurality of this court implicitly invites every state legislature to enact more and more restrictive abortion regulations in order to provoke more and more test cases, in the hope that sometime down the line, the court will return the law of procreative freedom to the severe limitations that generally prevailed in this country before Jan. 22, 1973.

Never in my memory has a plurality announced a judgment of this court that so foments disregard for the law and for our standing decisions.

Nor, in my memory, has a plurality gone about its business in such a deceptive fashion. At every level of its review, from its effort to read the real meaning out of the Missouri statute, to its intended evisceration of precedents and its deafening silence about the constitutional protections that it would jettison, the plurality obscures the portent of its analysis.

With feigned restraint, the plurality announces that its analysis leaves *Roe* "undisturbed," albeit "modified and narrowed." But this disclaimer is totally meaningless. The plurality opinion is filled with winks and nods, and knowing glances to those who would do away with *Roe* explicitly, but turns a stone face to anyone in search of what the plurality conceives as the scope of a woman's right under the Due Process Clause to terminate a pregnancy free from the coercive and brooding influence of the State.

The simple truth is that *Roe* would not survive the plurality's analysis, and that the plurality provides no substitute for *Roe's* protective umbrella. I fear for the future. I fear for the liberty and equality of the millions of women who have lived and come of age in the 16 years since *Roe* was decided. I fear for the integrity of, and public esteem for, this court.

No one contests that under the *Roe* framework, the State, in order to promote its interest in potential human life, may regulate and even proscribe nontherapeutic abortions once the fetus becomes viable. . . .

A requirement that a physician make a finding of viability, one way or the other, for every fetus that falls within the range of possible viability, does no more than preserve the State's recognized authority.

Although, as the plurality correctly points out, such a testing requirement would have the effect of imposing additional costs on second-trimester abortions where the tests indicated that the fetus was not viable, these costs would be merely incidental to, and a necessary accommodation of, the State's unquestioned right to prohibit nontherapeutic abortions after the point of viability.

In short, the testing provision, as construed by the plurality, is consistent with the *Roe* framework and could be upheld effortlessly under the current doctrine.

Thus, 'not with a bang, but a whimper,' the plurality discards a landmark case of the last generation and casts into darkness the hopes and visions of every woman in this country who had come to believe that the Constitution guaranteed her the right to exercise some control over her unique ability to bear children.

The plurality does so either oblivious or insensitive to the fact that millions of women and their families have ordered their lives around the right to reproductive choice, and that this right has become vital to the full participation of women in the economic and political walks of American life.

The plurality would clear the way once again for government to force upon women the physical labor and specific and direct medical and psychological harms that may accompany carrying a fetus to term. The plurality would clear the way again for the State to conscript a women's body and to force upon her a "distressful life and future.". . .

The result, as we know from experience . . . would be that, every year, hundreds of thousands of women, in desperation, would defy the law and place their health and safety in the unclean and unsympathetic hands of back-alley abortionists, or they would attempt to perform abortions upon themselves, with disastrous results. Every year, many women, especially poor and minority women, would die or suffer debilitating physical trauma, all in the name of enforced morality or religious dictates or lack of compassion, as it may be.

Of the aspirations and settled understandings of American women, or the inevitable and brutal consequences of what it is doing, the tough-approach plurality utters not a word. This silence is callous. It is also profoundly destructive of this court as an institution.

For today, at least, the law of abortion stands undisturbed. For today, the women of this nation still retain the liberty to control their destinies. But the signs are evident and very ominous, and a chill wind blows.

Justice Stevens concurred in part and dissented in part in a separate opinion.

Affirmative Action

The Supreme Court has unequivocally ruled that racial discrimination by law is unconstitutional. When the law treats *racial* groups differently, it is almost invariably the case that the Court will declare the law to be a violation of the equal protection clause of the Fourteenth Amendment or, where federal action is involved, the standards of equal protection required under the due process clause of the Fifth Amendment.[1]

Before the era of the Warren court, which began in 1953 and led immediately to the *Brown* decision, the Supreme Court applied a "rational-relation" or "conceivable-basis" test to determine if legislative classifications that treated separate groups of people differently constituted a violation of equal protection standards. Generally, under these tests the Court upheld the legislative classifications if it found there was a rational relationship between the classifications and legislative goals. Such classifications were also upheld if the Court found a conceivable basis upon which to support the reasoning of the legislature in creating classifications. These equal protection standards are referred to as the "old equal protection."

The Warren court inaugurated the "new equal protection" standards to apply to legislative classifications based on race or other "suspect" group

---

[1]An important exception to the rigid application of equal protection standards to racial classification was the holding of the Supreme Court in *Korematsu v. United States*, 323 U.S. 214 (1944), which upheld a racial classification that treated Japanese-Americans differently than other citizens. The Court found that the federal government could exclude Japanese-Americans from military zones on the West Coast on the ground of national security, a holding that in effect supported the establishment of relocation centers for Japanese-American citizens during World War II.

classifications. For example, gender-classifications have come to be regarded by the Burger court as at least semi-suspect.[2] The new equal protection standards required the demonstration of a "compelling" governmental interest to uphold the legislative classifications under review. The new equal protection standards also required the demonstration of a compelling governmental interest to sustain legislative classifications that burdened fundamental rights. For example, in *Shapiro* v. *Thompson*, 394 U.S. 618 (1969), the Warren court reviewed challenges to state and District of Columbia laws denying welfare assistance to persons who had not resided within their jurisdictions for at least one year immediately prior to applying for assistance. The Court found that the laws burdened the fundamental right to travel, and therefore could be sustained only upon the demonstration of a compelling governmental interest. The Court found no such compelling interest present and held the laws to be unconstitutional. The application of the new equal protection standard is called *strict judicial scrutiny*. When the Court employs this strict judicial scrutiny, the invariable effect is to declare unconstitutional the classification in the law under review.

In the *Bakke* case, presented below, the opinions of Justices Powell and Brennan discuss the circumstances under which strict judicial scrutiny is required by the equal protection clause of the Fourteenth Amendment. This case arose out of a complex set of circumstances. Title VI of the Civil Rights Act of 1964 provided that no person was to be "subjected to discrimination under any program or activity receiving federal financial assistance." The Department of Health, Education and Welfare found this section to require affirmative action programs by private institutions receiving federal aid, to achieve a racial balance among employees and, in institutions of higher learning, within their student bodies as well. Under pressure from civil rights groups, women, and other minorities, many affirmative action plans were adopted throughout the country that contained racial classifications providing for the favored treatment of racial minorities in school admissions and private employment.

The *Bakke* case was initiated by Allan Bakke, a 36-year-old white engineer who decided that he wanted to become a doctor. In 1973 and 1974 he applied, unsuccessfully, for admission to the University of California Medical School at Davis. The school informed Bakke that there were too many qualified applicants and that it could admit only one out of 26 in 1973, and one out of 37 in 1974. However, 16 of the 100 openings in the Davis medical school were set aside for minority applicants. Bakke's objective qualifications, such as his Medical College Admission Test scores and his undergraduate grades, were better than those of some of the minority applicants that were accepted during the years when he was rejected.

---

[2]See, for example, *Frontiero* v. *Richardson*, 411 U.S. 677 (1973).

The minority applicants competed among themselves for the 16 places reserved for them, making it possible to admit minority students with different qualifications than were required of nonminority applicants. Bakke claimed that the admissions procedures violated the equal protection clause and Title VI of the Civil Rights Act of 1964.

The trial court in the *Bakke* case held that the admissions program established racial quotas in violation of the equal protection clause and Title VI. However, the court refused to order the admission of Bakke to the medical school because of his failure to prove that he would have been admitted in the absence of the special program for minorities. The California Supreme Court sustained the trial court's finding that the program violated the equal protection clause and the Civil Rights Act but overruled the trial court's denial of an order that Bakke be admitted. The United States Supreme Court granted certiorari to the California Supreme Court to review the case.

The California Supreme Court, by a five-four vote, ruled that *Bakke* should be admitted to the Davis Medical School. The majority on the issue of admittance agreed that the racial quota system at the school was not an acceptable means to decide who should be admitted. The majority justices favoring admission and a ban on quotas were Powell, Burger, Stevens, Rehnquist, and Stewart. Brennan, White, Marshall, and Blackmun dissented on these issues, arguing that "Davis's special admissions program cannot be said to violate the Constitution simply because it has set aside a predetermined number of places for qualified minority applicants. . . ."

Justice Louis F. Powell, who was in the majority favoring admission and a ban on quotas, joined with the four justices who dissented from the Court's decision and opinion on those issues to form another majority that held that an applicant's race can be considered in deciding who should be admitted to a university program.

22

REGENTS OF THE
UNIVERSITY OF CALIFORNIA
v. BAKKE
438 U.S. 265 (1978)

Mr. Justice Powell announced the judgment of the Court and wrote an opinion:

For the reasons stated in the following opinion, I believe that so much of the judgment of the California court as holds petitioner's special admissions program unlawful and directs that respondent be admitted to the Medical School must be affirmed. For the reasons expressed in a separate opinion, my Brothers The Chief Justice, Mr. Justice Stewart, Mr. Justice Rehnquist, and Mr. Justice Stevens concur in this judgment.

I also conclude for the reasons stated in the following opinion that the portion of the court's judgment enjoining petitioner from according any consideration to race in its admissions process must be reversed. For reasons expressed in separate opinions, my Brothers Mr. Justice Brennan, Mr. Justice White, Mr. Justice Marshall, and Mr. Justice Blackmun concur in this judgment.

Affirmed in part and reversed in part.

II

B

The language of § 601 [of the Civil Rights Act of 1964], like that of the Equal Protection Clause, is majestic in its sweep:

> No person in the United States shall, on the ground of race, color, or national origin, be excluded from participation in, be denied the benefits of, or be subjected to discrimination under any program or activity receiving Federal financial assistance.

The concept of "discrimination," like the phrase "equal protection of the laws," is susceptible of varying interpretations, for as Mr. Justice Holmes declared, "[a] word is not a crystal, transparent and unchanged, it is the skin of a living thought and may vary greatly in color and content according to the circumstances and the time in which it is used.". . . We must, therefore, seek whatever aid is available in determining the precise meaning of the statute before us. . . . Examination of the voluminous legislative history of Title VI reveals a congressional intent to halt federal funding of entities that violate a prohibition of racial discrimination similar to that of the Constitution. Although isolated statements of various legislators, taken out of context, can be marshaled in support of the proposition that § 601 enacted a purely color-blind scheme, without regard to the reach of the Equal Protection Clause, these comments must be read against the background of both the problem that Congress was addressing and the broader view of the statute that emerges from a full examination of the legislative debates.

The problem confronting Congress was discrimination against Negro citizens at the hands of recipients of federal moneys. Indeed, the color blindness pronouncements [of Congress] generally occur in the midst of extended remarks dealing with the evils of segregation in federally funded programs. Over and over again, proponents of the bill detailed the plight of Negroes seeking equal treatment in such programs. There simply was no reason for Congress to consider the validity of hypothetical preferences that might be accorded minority citizens; the legislators were dealing with the real and pressing problem of how to guarantee those citizens equal treatment.

In addressing that problem, supporters of Title VI repeatedly declared that the bill enacted constitutional principles. . . .

In the Senate, Senator Humphrey declared that the purpose of Title VI was "to insure that Federal funds are spent in accordance with the Constitution and the moral sense of the Nation.". . .

Further evidence of the incorporation of a constitutional standard into Title VI appears in the repeated refusals of the legislation's supporters precisely to define the term "discrimination." Opponents sharply criticized this failure, but proponents of the bill merely replied that the meaning of "discrimination" would be made clear by reference to the Constitution or other existing law. . . .

In view of the clear legislative intent, Title VI must be held to proscribe only those racial classifications that would violate the Equal Protection Clause or the Fifth Amendment.

III

A

Petitioner does not deny that decisions based on race or ethnic origin by faculties and administrations of state universities are reviewable under the Fourteenth Amendment. . . . For his part, respondent does not argue that all racial or ethnic classifications are *per se* invalid. . . . The parties do disagree as to the level of judicial scrutiny to be applied to the special admissions program. Petitioner argues that the court below erred in applying strict scrutiny, as this inexact term has been applied in our cases. . . .

En route to this crucial battle over the scope of judicial review, the parties fight a sharp preliminary action over the proper characterization of the special admissions program. Petitioner prefers to view it as establishing a "goal" of minority representation in the Medical School. Respondent, echoing the courts below, labels it a racial quota.

This semantic distinction is beside the point: The special admissions program is undeniably a classification based on race and ethnic background. To the extent that there existed a pool of at least minimally qualified minority applicants to fill the 16 special admissions seats, white applicants could compete only for 84 seats in the entering class, rather than the 100 open to minority applicants. Whether this limitation is described as a quota or a goal, it is a line drawn on the basis of race and ethnic status.

The guarantees of the Fourteenth Amendment extend to all persons. Its language is explicit: "No State shall . . . deny to any person within its jurisdiction the equal protection of the laws." It is settled beyond question that the "rights created by the first section of the Fourteenth Amendment are, by its terms, guaranteed to the individual. The rights established are personal rights". . . . The guarantee of equal protection cannot mean one thing when applied to one individual and something else when applied to a person of another color. If both are not accorded the same protection, then it is not equal.

Nevertheless, petitioner argues that the court below erred in applying strict scrutiny to the special admissions program because white males, such as respondent, are not a "discrete and insular minority" requiring extraordinary protection from the majoritarian political process. . . . This rationale, however, has never been invoked in our decisions as a prerequisite to subjecting racial or ethnic distinctions to strict scrutiny. Nor has this Court held that discreteness and insularity constitute necessary preconditions to a holding that a particular classification is invidious. . . . These characteristics may be relevant in deciding whether or not to add new types of classifications to the list of "suspect" categories or whether a particular classification survives close examination. . . . Racial and ethnic classifications, however, are subject to stringent examination without regard to these additional characteristics. We declared as much in the first cases explicitly to recognize racial distinctions as suspect:

> Distinctions between citizens solely because of their ancestry are by their very nature odious to a free people whose institutions are founded upon the doctrine of equality. *Hirabayashi* [v. *United States* (1943)].

> [A]ll legal restrictions which curtail the civil rights of a single racial group are immediately suspect. That is not to say that all such restrictions are unconstitutional. It is to say that courts must subject them to the most rigid scrutiny. *Korematsu* [v. *United States* (1944)].

The Court has never questioned the validity of those pronouncements. Racial and ethnic distinctions of any sort are inherently suspect and thus call for the most exacting judicial examination. . . .

Although many of the Framers of the Fourteenth Amendment conceived of its primary function as bridging the vast distance between members of the Negro race and the white "majority". . . the amendment itself was framed in universal terms, without reference to color, ethnic origin, or condition of prior servitude. As this Court recently remarked in interpreting the 1866 Civil Rights Act to extend to claims of racial discrimination against white persons, "the 39th Congress was intent upon establishing in the federal law a broader principle than would have been necessary simply to meet the particular and immediate plight of the newly freed Negro slaves.". . .

Over the past 30 years, this Court has embarked upon the crucial mission of interpreting the Equal Protection Clause with the view of assuring to all persons "the protection of equal laws . . ." in a Nation confronting a legacy of slavery and racial discrimination. . . . Because the landmark decisions in this area arose in response to the continued exclusion of Negroes from the mainstream of American society, they could be characterized as involving discrimination by the "majority" white race against the Negro minority. But they need not be read as depending upon that characterization for their results. It suffices to say that "[o]ver the years, this Court has consistently repudiated '[d]istinctions between citizens solely because of their ancestry' as being 'odious to a free people whose institutions are founded upon the doctrine of equality.' ". . .

Petitioner urges us to adopt for the first time a more restrictive view of the Equal Protection Clause and hold that discrimination against members of the white "majority" cannot be suspect if its purpose can be characterized as "benign." The clock of our liberties, however, cannot be turned back to 1868. . . . It is far too late to argue that the guarantee of equal protection to *all* persons permits the recognition of special wards entitled to a degree of protection greater than that accorded others. "The Fourteenth Amendment is not directed solely against discrimination due to a 'two-class theory'—that is, based upon differences between 'white' and Negro.". . .

Once the artificial line of a "two-class theory" of the Fourteenth Amendment is put aside, the difficulties entailed in varying the level of judicial review according to a perceived "preferred" status of a particular racial or ethnic minority are intractable. The concepts of "majority" and "minority" necessarily reflect temporary arrangements and political judgments. As observed above, the white "majority" itself is composed of various minority groups, most of which can lay claim to a history of prior discrimination at the hands of the State and private individuals. Not all of these groups can receive preferential treatment and corresponding judicial tolerance of distinctions drawn in terms of race and nationality, for then the only "majority" left would be a new minority of white Anglo-Saxon Protestants. There is no principled basis for deciding which groups would merit "heightened judicial solicitude" and which would not. Courts would be asked to evaluate the extent of the prejudice and consequent harm suffered by various minority groups. Those whose societal injury is thought to exceed some arbitrary level of tolerability then would be entitled to preferential classifications at the expense of individuals belonging to other groups. Those classifications would be free from exacting judicial scrutiny. As these preferences began to have their desired effect, and the consequences of past discrimination were undone, new judicial rankings would be necessary. The kind of variable sociological and political analysis necessary to produce such rankings simply does not lie within the judicial competence—even if they otherwise were politically feasible and socially desirable.

Moreover, there are serious problems of justice connected with the idea of preference itself. First, it may not always be clear that a so-called preference is in fact benign. . . . Second, preferential programs may only reinforce common stereotypes holding that certain groups are unable to achieve success without special protection based on a factor having no relationship to individual worth. . . . Third, there is a measure of inequity in forcing innocent persons in respondent's position to bear the burdens of redressing grievances not of their making.

By hitching the meaning of the Equal Protection Clause to these transitory considerations, we would be holding, as a constitutional principle, that judicial scrutiny of classifications touching on racial and ethnic background may vary with the ebb and flow of political forces. Disparate constitutional tolerance of such classifications well may serve to exacerbate racial and ethnic antagonisms rather than alleviate them. . . . Also, the mutability of a constitutional principle, based upon shifting political and social judgments, undermines the chances for consistent application of the Constitution from one generation to the next, a critical feature of its coherent interpretation. . . . In expounding the Constitution, the Court's role is to discern "principles sufficiently absolute to give them roots throughout the community and continuity over significant periods of time, and to lift them above the level of the pragmatic political judgments of a particular time and place.". . .

IV

We have held that in "order to justify the use of a suspect classification, a State must show that its purpose or interest is both constitutionally permissible and substantial, and that its use of the classification is 'necessary . . . to the accomplishment' of its purpose or the safeguarding of its interest.". . . The special admissions program purports to serve the purposes of: (i) "reducing the historic deficit of traditionally disfavored minorities in medical schools and in the medical profession"; (ii) countering the effects of societal discrimination; (iii) increasing the number of physicians who will practice in communities currently underserved; and (iv) obtaining the educational benefits that flow from an ethnically diverse student body. It is necessary to decide which, if any, of these purposes is substantial enough to support the use of a suspect classification.

A

If petitioner's purpose is to assure within its student body some specified percentage of a particular group merely because of its race or ethnic origin, such a preferential purpose must be rejected not as insubstantial but as facially invalid. Preferring members of any one group for no reason other than race or ethnic origin is discrimination for its own sake. This the Constitution forbids. . . .

B

. . . [T]he purpose of helping certain groups whom the faculty of the Davis Medical School perceived as victims of "societal discrimination" does not justify a classification that imposes disadvantages upon persons like respondent, who bear no responsibility for whatever harm the beneficiaries of the special admissions program are thought to have suffered. To hold otherwise would be to convert a remedy heretofore reserved for violations of legal rights into a privilege that all institutions throughout the Nation could grant at their pleasure to whatever groups are perceived as victims of societal discrimination. That is a step we have never approved. . . .

C

Petitioner identifies, as another purpose of its program, improving the delivery of health-care services to communities currently underserved. It may be assumed that in some situations a State's interest in facilitating the health care of its citizens is sufficiently compelling to support the use of a suspect classification. But there is virtually no evidence in the record indicating that petitioner's special admissions program is either needed or geared to promote that goal. . . .

D

The fourth goal asserted by petitioner is the attainment of a diverse student body. This clearly is a constitutionally permissible goal for an institution of higher education. Academic freedom, though not a specifically enumerated constitutional right, long has been viewed as a special concern of the First Amendment. . . .

. . . As the interest of diversity is compelling in the context of a university's admissions program, the question remains whether the program's racial classification is necessary to promote this interest. . . .

V

A

It may be assumed that the reservation of a specified number of seats in each class for individuals from the preferred ethnic groups would contribute to the attainment of considerable ethnic diversity in the student body. But petitioner's argument that this is the only effective means of serving the interest of diversity is seriously flawed. . . . Petitioner's special admissions program, focused *solely* on ethnic diversity, would hinder rather than further attainment of genuine diversity. . . .

The experience of other university admissions programs, which take race into account in achieving the educational diversity valued by the First Amendment, demonstrates that the assignment of a fixed number of places to a minority group is not a necessary means toward that end. . . .

B

In summary, it is evident that the Davis special admissions program involves the use of an explicit racial classification never before countenanced by this Court. It tells applicants who are not Negro, Asian, or Chicano that they are totally excluded from a specific percentage of the seats in an entering class. No matter how strong their qualifications, quantitative and extracurricular, including their own potential for contribution to educational diversity, they are never afforded the chance to compete with applicants from the preferred groups for the special admissions seats. At the same time, the preferred applicants have the opportunity to compete for every seat in the class.

The fatal flaw in petitioner's preferential program is its disregard of individual rights as guaranteed by the Fourteenth Amendment. . . . Such rights are not absolute. But when a State's distribution of benefits or imposition of burdens hinges on ancestry or the color of a person's skin or ancestry, that individual is entitled to a demonstration that the challenged classification is necessary to promote a substantial state interest. Petitioner has failed to carry this burden. For this reason, that portion of the California court's judgment holding petitioner's special admissions program invalid under the Fourteenth Amendment must be affirmed.

C

In enjoining petitioner from ever considering the race of any applicant, however, the courts below failed to recognize that the State has a substantial interest that legitimately may be served by a properly devised admissions program involving the competitive consideration of race and ethnic origin. For this reason, so much of the California court's judgment as enjoins petitioner from any consideration of the race of any applicant must be reversed.

Opinion of Mr. Justice Brennan, Mr. Justice White, Mr. Justice Marshall, and Mr. Justice Blackmun, concurring in the judgment in part and dissenting in part:

The Court today, in reversing in part the judgment of the Supreme Court of California, affirms the constitutional power of Federal and State Governments to act affirmatively to achieve equal opportunity for all. The difficulty of the issue presented—whether government may use race-conscious programs to redress the continuing effects of past discrimination—and the mature consideration which each of our Brethren has brought to it have resulted in many opinions, no single one speaking for the Court. But this should not and must not mask the central meaning of today's opinions: Government may take race into account when it acts not to demean or insult any racial group, but to remedy disadvantages cast on minorities by past racial prejudice, at least when appropriate findings have been made by judicial, legislative, or administrative bodies with competence to act in this area.

The Chief Justice and our Brothers Stewart, Rehnquist, and Stevens, have concluded that Title VI of the Civil Rights Act of 1964, . . . as amended, . . . prohibits programs such as that at the Davis Medical School. On this statutory theory alone, they would hold that respondent Allan Bakke's rights have been violated and he must, therefore, be admitted to the Medical School. Our Brother Powell, reaching the Constitution, concludes that, although race may be taken into account in university admissions, the particular special admissions program used by petitioner, which resulted in the exclusion of respondent Bakke, was not shown to be necessary to achieve petitioner's stated goals. Accordingly, these Members of the Court form a majority of five affirming the judgment of the Supreme Court of California insofar as it holds that respondent Bakke "is entitled to an order that he be admitted to the University.". . .

We agree with Mr. Justice Powell that, as applied to the case before us, Title VI goes no further in prohibiting the use of race than the Equal Protection Clause of the Fourteenth Amendment itself. We also agree that the effect of the California Supreme Court's affirmance of the judgment of the Superior Court of California would be to prohibit the University from establishing in the future affirmative action programs that take race into account. . . . Since we conclude that the affirmative admissions program at the Davis Medical School is constitutional, we would reverse the judgment below in all respects. Mr. Justice Powell agrees that some uses of race in university admissions are permissible and, therefore, he joins with us to make five votes reversing the judgment below insofar as it prohibits the University from establishing race-conscious programs in the future. . . .

D

We disagree with the lower courts' conclusion that the Davis program's use of race was unreasonable in light of its objectives. First, as petitioner argues, there are no practical means by which it could achieve its ends in the foreseeable future without the use of race-conscious measures. With respect to any factor (such as poverty or family educational background) that may be used as a substitute for race as an indicator of past discrimination, whites greatly outnumber racial minorities simply because whites make up a far larger percentage of the total population and therefore far outnumber minorities in absolute terms at every socioeconomic level. . . .

Second, the Davis admissions program does not simply equate minority status with disadvantage. Rather, Davis considers on an individual basis each applicant's personal history to determine whether he or she has likely been disadvantaged by racial discrimination. The record makes clear that only minority applicants likely to have been isolated from the mainstream of American life are considered in the special program; other minority applicants are eligible only through the regular admissions program. . . .

V

Accordingly, we would reverse the judgment of the Supreme Court of California holding the Medical School's special admissions program unconstitutional and directing respondent's admission, as well as that portion of the judgment enjoining the Medical School from according any consideration to race in the admissions process.

Mr. Justice Marshall wrote a separate opinion.

Mr. Justice Blackmun wrote a separate opinion.

Mr. Justice Stevens, with whom the Chief Justice, Mr. Justice Stewart, and Mr. Justice Rehnquist join, concurring in the judgment in part and dissenting in part:

Both petitioner and respondent have asked us to determine the legality of the University's admissions program by reference to the Constitution. Our settled practice, however, is to avoid the decision of a constitutional issue if a case can be fairly decided on a statutory ground. "If there is one doctrine more deeply rooted than any other in the process of constitutional adjudication, it is that we ought not to pass on questions of constitutionality . . . unless such adjudication is unavoidable.". . . The more important the issue, the more force there is to this doctrine. In this case, we are presented with a constitutional question of undoubted and unusual importance. Since, however, a dispositive statutory claim was raised at the very inception of this case, and squarely decided in the portion of the trial court judgment affirmed by the California Supreme Court, it is our plain duty to confront it. Only if petitioner should prevail on the statutory issue would it be necessary to decide whether the University's admissions program violated the Equal Protection Clause of the Fourteenth Amendment.

Section 601 of the Civil Rights Act of 1964 . . . provides:

> No person in the United States shall, on the ground of race, color, or national origin, be excluded from participation in, be denied the benefits of, or be subjected to discrimination under any program or activity receiving Federal financial assistance.

The University, through its special admissions policy, excluded Bakke from participation in its program of medical education because of his race. The University also acknowledges that it was, and still is, receiving federal financial assistance. The plain language of the statute therefore requires affirmance of the judgment below. A different result cannot be justified unless that language misstates the actual intent of the Congress that enacted the statute or the statute is not enforceable in a private action. Neither conclusion is warranted. . . .

. . . [I]t seems clear that the proponents of Title VI assumed that the Constitution itself required a colorblind standard on the part of government, but that does not mean that the legislation only codifies an existing constitutional prohibition. The statutory prohibition against discrimination in federally funded projects contained in § 601 is more than a simple paraphrasing of what the Fifth or Fourteenth Amendment would require. . . .

In short, nothing in the legislative history justifies the conclusion that the broad language of § 601 should not be given its natural meaning. We are dealing with a distinct statutory prohibition, enacted at a particular time with particular concerns in mind; neither its language nor any prior interpretation suggests that its place in the Civil Rights Act, won after long debate, is simply that of a constitutional appendage. In unmistakable terms the Act prohibits the exclusion of individuals from federally funded programs because of their race. As succinctly phrased during the Senate debate, under Title VI it is not "permissible to say 'yes' to one person; but to say 'no' to another person, only because of the color of his skin.". . .

The University's special admissions program violated Title VI of the Civil Rights Act of 1964 by excluding Bakke from the Medical School because of his race. It is therefore our duty to affirm the judgment ordering Bakke admitted to the University.

Accordingly, I concur in the Court's judgment insofar as it affirms the judgment of the Supreme Court of California. To the extent that it purports to do anything else, I respectfully dissent.

❖❖ How do the standards of judicial scrutiny differ in the Powell and Brennan opinions? Justice Powell wrote, "Racial and ethnic distinctions of any sort are inherently suspect and thus call for the most exacting judicial examination." Applying strict judicial scrutiny, Powell found no compelling justification for the use of racial quotas by the Davis Medical School. Powell reasoned that "The purpose of helping certain groups whom the faculty of the Davis Medical School perceived as victims of 'societal discrimination' does not justify a classification that imposes disadvantages upon persons like respondent [Bakke], who bear no responsibility for whatever harm the beneficiaries of the special admissions program are thought to have suffered." While Powell held that racial quotas are banned, he ruled that race may be taken into account in admissions programs because "the state has a substantial [i.e., compelling] interest that legitimately may be served by a properly devised admissions program involving the competitive consideration of race and ethnic origin."

The dissenting opinion of Justice Brennan supported the use of racial quotas in the Davis admissions program. Underlying Brennan's dissenting opinion was the finding that the classification under review was not "suspect," nor did it affect fundamental rights; therefore, strict judicial scrutiny, under which a compelling state interest has to be demonstrated to uphold the classification, was not required. Justice Brennan and his fellow dissenters used an intermediate standard of judicial scrutiny, which required more than the mere demonstration of a rational relationship between the classification and the goals sought but less than the demonstration of a compelling state interest to uphold the classification. The intermediate standard announced by Justice Brennan was that the classification "must serve important governmental objectives and be substantially related to achievement of those objectives." To uphold a racial classification, stated Brennan, "an important and articulated purpose for its use must be shown. In addition, any statute must be stricken that stigmatizes any group or that singles out those least well represented in the political process to bear the brunt of a benign program." Brennan concluded that the court's review should be "strict," but not at the level of strict judicial scrutiny, which, because it requires the demonstration of compelling state interests, is always fatal to the program under review.

❖❖ Affirmative action continued to be a major political issue after the Bakke decision. While the use of quotas was banned, race and gender considerations could still be taken into account in school admissions and employment programs. The push for affirmative action that began with President Lyndon B. Johnson, who issued an executive order requiring it for all government contractors and institutions receiving federal aid, continued unabated for over a decade, even during the Republican administrations of Nixon and Ford. However, President Ronald Reagan viewed affirmative action with suspicion, more as an undesirable government interference in private affairs than as a necessary policy to remedy the effects of past discrimination. Under Reagan affirmative action was muted, and the Justice Department even intervened in some cases on the side of plaintiffs challenging affirmative action programs. Opposition to affirmative action was not simply a conservative position, as many liberals also came to feel that the enforcement of affirmative action, which benefited groups, denied individuals the right to be judged on their merits. However, the Supreme Court rejected blanket attacks on affirmative action, holding in several key cases in 1986 that race-conscious practices and even quotas could be used in employment and promotion to remedy the effects of past discrimination.[1] However, the Court in *City of Richmond* v. *Croson* in 1989 overturned an affirmative action program that set aside 30 percent of city construction projects for minority enterprises. Justice Sandra Day O'Connor, who wrote the majority opinion, applied strict judicial scrutiny, finding that absent a finding of past discrimination the Fourteenth Amendment equal protection clause bans state or city government enforcement of racial quotas.

---

[1] *Firefighters* v. *Cleveland* and *Sheet Metal Workers* v. *Equal Employment Opportunity Commission*, decided July 2, 1986.

Part Two

Political Parties, Electoral Behavior, and Interest Groups

❖ ❖ ❖

Chapter 4

Political Parties and
the Electorate

The political process involves the sources, distribution, and use of power in the state. All the institutions and processes of government relate to this area. The role of political parties and the electoral system in determining and controlling political power is examined in this chapter.

Constitutional Background

Political parties and interest groups have developed outside of the original constitutional framework to channel political power in the community, and for this reason they deserve special consideration from students of American government. The Constitution was designed to structure power relationships in such a way that the arbitrary exercise of political power by any one group or individual would be prevented. One important concept held by the framers of the Constitution was that faction, i.e., parties and interest groups, is inherently dangerous to political freedom and stable government. This is evident from *Federalist 10*.

23

James Madison
FEDERALIST 10

Among the numerous advantages promised by a well constructed Union, none deserves to be more accurately developed than its tendency to break and control the violence of faction. The friend of popular governments never finds himself so much alarmed for their character and fate as when he contemplates their propensity to this dangerous vice. He will not fail, therefore, to set a due value on any plan which, without violating the principles to which he is attached, provides a proper cure for it. The instability, injustice, and confusion, introduced into the public councils, have, in truth been the mortal diseases under which popular governments have everywhere perished; as they continue to be the favorite and fruitful topics from which the adversaries to liberty derive their most specious declamations. The valuable improvements made by the American constitutions on the popular models, both ancient and modern, cannot certainly be too much admired; but it would be an unwarrantable partiality, to contend that they have as effectually obviated the danger on this side, as was wished and expected. Complaints are everywhere heard from our most considerate and virtuous citizens, equally the friends of public and private faith, and of public and personal liberty, that our governments are too unstable; that the public good is disregarded in the conflicts of rival parties; and that measures are too often decided, not according to the rules of justice, and the rights of the minor party, but by the superior force of an interested and overbearing majority. However anxiously we may wish that these complaints had no foundation, the evidence of known facts will not permit us to deny that they are in some degree true. It will be found, indeed, on a candid review of our situation, that some of the distresses under which we labor, have been erroneously charged on the operation of our governments; but it will be found, at the same time, that other causes will not alone account for many of our heaviest misfortunes; and, particularly, for the prevailing and increasing distrust of public engagements, and alarm for private rights, which are echoed from one end of the continent to the other. These must be chiefly, if not wholly, effects of the unsteadiness and injustice, with which a factious spirit has tainted our public administrations.

By a faction, I understand a number of citizens, whether amounting to a majority or minority of the whole, who are united and actuated by some common impulse of passion, or of interest, adverse to the rights of other citizens, or to the permanent and aggregate interest of the community.

There are two methods of curing the mischiefs of faction: The one, by removing its causes; the other, by controlling its effects.

There are again two methods of removing the causes of faction: the one, by destroying the liberty which is essential to its existence; the other, by giving to every citizen the same opinions, the same passions, and the same interests.

It could never be more truly said, than of the first remedy, that it was worse than the disease. Liberty is to faction what air is to fire, an aliment, without which it instantly expires. But it could not be a less folly to abolish liberty, which is essential to political life because it nourishes faction, than it would be to wish the annihilation of air, which is essential to animal life, because it imparts to fire its destructive agency.

The second expedient is as impracticable, as the first would be unwise. As long as the reason of man continues fallible, and he is at liberty to exercise it, different opinions will be formed. As long as the connection subsists between his reason and his self-love, his opinions and his passions will have a reciprocal influence on each other; and the former will be objects to which the latter will attach themselves. The diversity in the faculties of men, from which the rights of property originate, is not less an insuperable obstacle to a uniformity of interests. The protection of those faculties is the first object of government. From the protection of different and unequal faculties of acquiring property, the possession of different degrees and kinds of property immediately results; and from the influence of these on the sentiments and views of the respective proprietors, ensues a division of the society into different interests and parties.

The latent causes of faction are thus sown in the nature of man; and we see them everywhere brought into different degrees of activity, according to the different circumstances of civil society. A zeal for different opinions concerning religion, concerning government, and many other points, as well of speculation as of practice; an attachment to different leaders, ambitiously contending for preeminence and power; or to persons of other descriptions, whose fortunes have been interesting to the human passions, have, in turn, divided mankind into parties, inflamed them with mutual animosity, and rendered them much more disposed to vex and oppress each other, than to cooperate for their common good. So strong is this propensity of mankind, to fall into mutual animosities, that where no substantial occasion presents itself, the most frivolous and fanciful distinctions have been sufficient to kindle their unfriendly passions, and excite their most violent conflicts. But the most common and durable source of factions has been the various and unequal distribution of property. Those who hold, and those who are without property, have even formed distinct interests in society. Those who are creditors, and those who are debtors, fall under a like discrimination. A landed interest, a manufacturing interest, a mercantile interest, a moneyed interest, with many lesser interests, grow up of necessity in civilized nations, and divide them into different classes, actuated by different sentiments and views. The regulation of these various and interfering interests forms the principle task of modern legislation, and involves the spirit of party and faction in the necessary and ordinary operations of government.

No man is allowed to be a judge in his own cause; because his interest will certainly bias his judgment, and, not improbably, corrupt his integrity. With equal, nay, with greater reason, a body of men are unfit to be both judges and parties at the same time; yet what are many of the most important acts of legislation, but so many judicial determinations, not indeed concerning the rights of single persons, but concerning the rights of large bodies of citizens? And what are the different classes of legislators, but advocates and parties to the cause which they determine? Is a law proposed concerning private debts? It is a question to which the creditors are parties on one side, and the debtors on the other. Justice ought to hold the balance between them. Yet the parties are, and must be, themselves the judges; and the most numerous party, or, in other words, the most powerful faction, must be expected to prevail. Shall domestic manufactures be encouraged, and in what degree, by restrictions on foreign manufactures? are questions which would be differently decided by the landed and the manufacturing classes; and probably by neither with a sole regard to justice and the public good. . . .

It is in vain to say, that enlightened statesmen will be able to adjust these clashing interests, and render them all subservient to the public good. Enlightened statesmen will not always be at the helm; nor, in many cases, can such an adjustment be made at all, without taking into view indirect and remote considerations, which will rarely prevail over the immediate interest which one party may find in disregarding the rights of another, or the good of the whole.

The inference to which we are brought is, that the *causes* of faction cannot be removed; and that relief is only to be sought in the means of controlling its *effects*.

If a faction consists of less than a majority, relief is supplied by the republican principle, which enables the majority to defeat its sinister views, by regular vote. It may clog the administration, it may convulse the society; but it will be unable to execute and mask its violence under the forms of the constitution. When a majority is included in a faction, the form of popular government, on the other hand, enables it to sacrifice to its ruling passion or interest, both the public good and the rights of other citizens. To secure the public good, and private rights, against the danger of such a faction, and at the same time to preserve the spirit and the form of popular government, is then the great object to which our inquiries are directed. Let me add, that it is the great desideratum, by which alone this form of government can be rescued from the opprobrium under which it has so long labored, and be recommended to the esteem and adoption of mankind.

By what means is this object attainable? Evidently by one of two only. Either the existence of the same passion or interest in a majority, at the same time must be prevented; or the majority, having such coexistent passion or interest, must be rendered, by their number and local situation, unable to concert and carry into effect schemes of oppression. If the impulse and the opportunity be suffered to coincide, we well know, that neither moral nor religious motives can be relied on as an adequate control. They are not found to be such on the injustice and violence of individuals, and lose their efficacy in proportion to the number combined together; that is, in proportion as their efficacy becomes needful.

From this view of the subject, it may be concluded, that a pure democracy, by which I mean a society consisting of a small number of citizens, who assemble and administer the government in person, can admit of no cure from the mischiefs of faction. A common passion or interest will, in almost every case, be felt by a majority of the whole; a communication and concert, results from the form of government itself; and there is nothing to check the inducements to sacrifice the weaker party, or an obnoxious individual. Hence it is, that such democracies have ever been spectacles of turbulence and contention; have ever been found incompatible with personal security, or the rights of property; and have, in general, been as short in their lives, as they have been violent in their deaths. Theoretic politicians, who have patronized this species of government, have erroneously supposed that by reducing mankind to a perfect equality in their political rights, they would, at the same time, be perfectly equalized and assimilated in their possessions, their opinions, and their passions.

A republic, by which I mean a government in which the scheme of representation takes place, opens a different prospect, and promises the cure for which we are seeking. Let us examine the points in which it varies from pure democracy, and we shall comprehend both the nature of the cure and the efficacy which it must derive from the union.

The two great points of difference, between a democracy and a republic, are, first, the delegation of the government, in the latter, to a small number of citizens elected by the rest; secondly, the greater number of citizens, and greater sphere of country, over which the latter may be extended.

The effect of the first difference is on the one hand, to refine and enlarge the public views, by passing them through the medium of a chosen body of citizens, whose wisdom may best discern the true interest in their country, and whose patriotism and love of justice, will be least likely to sacrifice it to temporary or partial considerations. Under such a regulation, it may well happen, that the public voice, pronounced by the representatives of the people, will be more consonant to the public good, than if pronounced by the people themselves, convened for the purpose. On the other hand, the effect may be inverted. Men of factious tempers, of local prejudices, or of sinister designs, may by intrigue, by corruption, or by other means, first obtain the suffrages, and then betray the interest of the people. The question resulting is, whether small or extensive republics are most favorable to the election of proper guardians of the public weal; and it is clearly decided in favor of the latter by two obvious considerations.

In the first place, it is to be remarked, that however small the republic may be, the representatives must be raised to a certain number, in order to guard against the cabals of a few; and that however large it may be, they must be limited to a certain number, in order to guard against the confusion of a multitude. Hence, the number of representatives in the two cases not being in proportion to that of the constituents, and being proportionally greatest in the small republic, it follows that if the proportion of fit characters be not less in the large than in the small republic, the former will present a greater option, and consequently a greater probability of a fit choice.

In the next place, as each representative will be chosen by a greater number of citizens in the large than in the small republic, it will be more difficult for unworthy candidates to practice with success the vicious arts, by which elections are too often carried; and the suffrages of the people being more free, will be more likely to center in men who possess the most attractive merit, and the most diffusive and established characters. . . .

The other point of difference is, the greater number of citizens, and extent of territory, which may be brought within the compass of republican, than of democratic government; and it is this circumstance principally which renders factious combinations less to be dreaded in the former, than in the latter. The smaller the society, the fewer probably will be the distinct parties and interests composing it; the fewer the distinct parties and interests, the more frequently will a majority be found of the same party; and the smaller the number of individuals composing a majority, and the smaller the compass within which they are placed, the more easily they will concert and execute their plans of oppression. Extend the sphere, and you take in a greater variety of parties and interests; you make it less probable that a majority of the whole will have a common motive to invade the rights of other citizens; or if such a common motive exists, it will be more difficult for all who feel it to discover their own strength, and to act in unison with each other. . . .

Hence, it clearly appears, that the same advantage, which a republic has over a democracy, in controlling the effects of faction, is enjoyed by a large over a small republic—is enjoyed by the union over the states composing it. Does this advantage consist in the substitution of representatives, whose enlightened views and virtuous sentiments render them superior to local prejudices, and to schemes of injustice? It will not be denied, that the representation of the union will be most likely to possess these requisite endowments. Does it consist in the greater security afforded by a greater variety of parties, against the event of any one party being able to outnumber and oppress the rest? In an equal degree does the increased variety of parties, comprised within the union, increase this security? Does it, in fine, consist in the greater obstacles opposed to the concert and accomplishment of the secret wishes of an unjust and interested majority? Here, again, the extent of the union gives it the most palpable advantage.

The influence of factious leaders may kindle a flame within their particular states, but will be unable to spread a general conflagration through the other states; a religious sect may degenerate into a political faction in a part of the confederacy; but the variety of sects dispersed over the entire face of it, must secure the national councils against any danger from that source; a rage for paper money, for an abolition of debts, for an equal division of property, or for any other improper or wicked project, will be less apt to pervade the whole body of the union, than a particular member of it; in the same proportion as such a malady is more likely to taint a particular county or district, than an entire state.

In the extent and proper structure of the union, therefore, we behold a republican remedy for the diseases most incident to republican government. And according to the degree of pleasure and pride we feel in being republicans, ought to be our zeal in cherishing the spirit, and supporting the character of Federalists.

❖❖   The following selection is taken from E. E. Schattschneider's classic treatise, *Party Government*. In this material he examines both the implications of *Federalist 10* and counter-arguments to the propositions stated by Madison, with regard to political parties and interest groups.

24

E. E. *Schattschneider*
PARTY GOVERNMENT

The Convention at Philadelphia produced a constitution with a dual attitude: it was proparty in one sense and antiparty in another. The authors of the Constitution refused to suppress the parties by destroying the fundamental liberties in which parties originate. They or their immediate successors accepted amendments that guaranteed civil rights and thus established a system of party tolerance, i.e., the right to agitate and to organize. This is the proparty aspect of the system. On the other hand, the authors of the Constitution set up an elaborate division and balance of powers within an intricate governmental structure designed to make parties ineffective. It was hoped that the parties would lose and exhaust themselves in futile attempts to fight their way through the labyrinthine framework of the government, much as an attacking army is expected to spend itself against the defensive works of a fortress. This is the antiparty part of the constitution scheme. To quote Madison, the "great object" of the Constitution was "to preserve the public good and private right against the danger of such a faction [party] and at the same time to preserve the spirit and form of popular government."

In Madison's mind the difference between an autocracy and a free republic seems to have been largely a matter of the precise point at which parties are stopped by the government. In an autocracy parties are controlled (suppressed) at the source; in a republic parties are tolerated but are invited to strangle themselves in the machinery of government. The result in either case is much the same, sooner or later the government checks the parties but *never do the parties control the government.* Madison was perfectly definite and unmistakable in his disapproval of party government as distinguished from party tolerance. In the opinion of Madison, parties were intrinsically bad, and the sole issue for discussion was the means by which bad parties might be prevented from becoming dangerous. What never seems to have occurred to the authors of the Constitution, however, is that parties might be *used* as beneficent instruments of popular government. It is at this point that the distinction between the modern and the antique attitude is made.

The offspring of this combination of ideas was a constitutional system having conflicting tendencies. The Constitution made the rise of parties inevitable yet was incompatible with party government. This scheme, in spite of its subtlety, involved a miscalculation. Political parties refused to be content with the role assigned to them. The vigor and enterprise of the parties have therefore made American political history the story of the unhappy marriage of the parties and the Constitution, a remarkable variation of the case of the irresistible force and the immovable object, which in this instance have been compelled to live together in a permanent partnership . . .

THE RAW MATERIALS OF POLITICS

People who write about interests sometimes seem to assume that all interests are special and exclusive, setting up as a result of this assumption a dichotomy in which the interests on the one side are perpetually opposed to the public welfare on the other side. But there are common interests as well as special interests, and common interests resemble special interests in that they are apt to influence political behavior. The raw materials of politics are not all antisocial. Alongside of Madison's statement that differences in wealth are the most durable causes of faction there should be placed a corollary that the common possessions of the people are the most durable cause of unity. To assume that people have merely conflicting interests and nothing else is to invent a political nightmare that has only a superficial relation to reality. The body of agreement underlying the conflicts of a modern society ought to be sufficient to sustain the social order provided only that the common interests supporting this unity are mobilized. Moreover, not all differences of interest are durable causes of conflict. Nothing is apt to be more perishable than a political issue. In the democratic process, the nation moves from controversy to agreement to forgetfulness; politics is not a futile exercise like football, forever played back and forth over the same ground. The government creates and destroys interests at every turn.

There are, in addition, powerful factors inhibiting the unlimited pursuit of special aims by any organized minority. To assume that minorities will stop at nothing to get what they want is to postulate a degree of unanimity and concentration within these groups that does not often exist in real life. If every individual were capable of having only one interest to the exclusion of all others, it might be possible to form dangerous unions of monomaniacs who would go to great extremes to attain their objectives. In fact, however, people have many interests leading to a dispersion of drives certain to destroy some of the unanimity and concentration of any group. How many interests can an individual have? Enough to make it extremely unlikely that any two individuals will have the same combination of interests. Anyone who has ever tried to promote an association of people having some special interest in common will realize, first, that there are marked differences of enthusiasm within the group and, second, that interests compete with interests for the attention and enthu-siasm of every individual. Every organized special interest consists of a group of busy, distracted individuals held together by the efforts of a handful of specialists and enthusiasts who sacrifice other matters in order to concentrate on one. The notion of resolute and unanimous minorities on the point of violence is largely the invention of paid lobbyists and press agents.

The result of the fact that every individual is torn by the diversity of his own interests, the fact that he is a member of many groups, is *the law of the imperfect political mobilization of interests.* That is, it has never been possible to mobilize any interest 100 percent. . . .

It is only another way of saying the same thing to state that conflicts of interests are not cumulative. If it were true that the dividing line in every conflict (or in all major conflicts) split the community identically in each case so that individuals who are opposed on one issue would be opposed to each other on all other issues also, while individuals who joined hands on one oc-casion would find themselves on the same side on all issues, always opposed to the same combination of antagonists, the cleavage created by the cumulative effect of these divisions would be fatal. But actually conflicts are not cumulative in this way. In real life the divisions are not so clearly marked, and the alignment of people according to interests requires an enormous shuffling back and forth from one side to the other, tending to dissipate the tensions created.

In view of the fact, therefore, (1) that there are many interests, including a great body of common interests, (2) that the government pursues a multiplicity of policies and creates and destroys interests in the process, (3) that each individual is capable of having many interests, (4) that interests cannot be mobilized perfectly, and (5) that conflicts among interests are not cumulative, it seems reasonable to suppose that the government is not the captive of blind forces from which there is no escape. There is nothing wrong about the raw materials of politics.

Functions and Types of Elections

Most people transmit their political desires to government through elections. Elections are a critical part of the democratic process, and the existence of *free* elections is a major difference between democracies and totalitarian or authoritarian forms of government. Because elections reflect popular atti-tudes toward governmental parties, policies, and personalities, it is useful to attempt to classify different types of elections on the basis of changes and trends that take place within the electorate. Every election is not the same. For example, the election of 1932 with the resulting Democratic landslide was profoundly different from the election of 1960, in which Kennedy won by less than 1 percent of the popular vote.

Members of the Center for Political Studies at the University of Michigan, as well as V. O. Key, Jr., have developed a typology of elections that is useful in analyzing the electoral system. The most prevalent type of election can be classified as a "maintaining election," "one in which the pattern of partisan attachments prevailing in the preceding period persists and is the primary influence on the forces governing the vote."[1] Most elections fall into the maintaining category, a fact significant for the political system because such elections result in political continuity and reflect a lack of serious upheavals within the electorate and government. Maintaining elections result in the continuation of the majority political party.

At certain times in American history, what V. O. Key, Jr., has called "critical elections" take place. He discusses this type of election, which results in permanent realignment of the electorate and reflects basic changes in political attitudes.

Apart from maintaining and critical elections, a third type, in which only temporary shifts take place within the electorate, occurs, which can be called "deviating elections." For example, the Eisenhower victories of 1952 and 1956 were deviating elections for several reasons, including the personality of Eisenhower and the fact that voters could register their choice for President without changing their basic partisan loyalties at congressional and state levels. Deviating elections, with reference to the office of president, are probable when popular figures are running for the office.

In "reinstating elections," a final category that can be added to typology of elections, there is a return to normal voting patterns. Reinstating elections take place after deviating elections as a result of the demise of the temporary forces that caused the transitory shift in partisan choice. The election of 1960, in which most of the Democratic majority in the electorate returned to the fold and voted for John F. Kennedy,[2] has been classified as a reinstating election.

---

[1]Angus Campbell, Philip E. Converse, Warren E. Miller, and Donald E. Stokes, *The American Voter* (New York: John Wiley & Sons, 1960), Chap. 19.

[2]See Philip E. Converse, Angus Campbell, Warren E. Miller, and Donald E. Stokes, "Stability and Change in 1960: A Reinstating Election," *The American Political Science Review,* vol. 55 (June 1961), pp. 269–80.

25

V. O. Key, Jr.
A THEORY OF CRITICAL ELECTIONS

Perhaps the basic differentiating characteristic of democratic order consists in the expression of effective choice by the mass of the people in elections. The electorate occupies, at least in the mystique of such orders, the position of the principal organ of governance; it acts through elections. An election itself is a formal act of collective decision that occurs in a stream of connected antecedent and subsequent behavior. Among democratic orders elections, so broadly defined, differ enormously in their nature, their meaning, and their consequences. Even within a single nation the reality of election differs greatly from time to time. A systematic comparative approach, with a focus on variations in the nature of elections would doubtless be fruitful in advancing the understanding of the democratic governing process. In behavior antecedent to voting, elections differ in the proportions of the electorate psychologically involved, in the intensity of attitudes associated with campaign cleavages, in the nature of expectations about the consequences of the voting, in the impact of objective events relevant to individual political choice, in individual sense of effective connection with community decision, and in other ways. These and other antecedent variations affect the act of voting itself as well as subsequent behavior. An understanding of elections and, in turn, of the democratic process as a whole must rest partially on broad differentiations of the complexes of behavior that we call elections.

While this is not the occasion to develop a comprehensive typology of elections, the foregoing remarks provide an orientation for an attempt to formulate a concept of one type of election—based on American experience—which might be built into a more general theory of elections. Even the most fleeting inspection of American elections suggests the existence of a category of elections in which voters are, at least from impressionistic evidence, unusually deeply concerned, in which the extent of electoral involvement is relatively quite high, and in which the decisive results of the voting reveal a sharp alteration of the preexisting cleavage within the electorate. Moreover, and perhaps this is the truly differentiating characteristic of this sort of election,

From V. O. Key, Jr., "A Theory of Critical Elections," *The Journal of Politics*, 17:1 (February 1955). Reprinted by permission.

the realignment made manifest in the voting in such elections seems to persist for several succeeding elections. All these characteristics cumulate to the conception of an election type in which the depth and intensity of electoral involvement are high, in which more or less profound readjustments occur in the relations of power within the community, and in which new and durable electoral groupings are formed. These comments suppose, of course, the existence of other types of complexes of behavior centering about formal elections, the systematic isolation and identification of which, fortunately, are not essential for the present discussion.

I

The presidential election of 1928 in the New England states provides a specific case of the type of critical election that has been described in general terms. In that year Alfred E. Smith, the Democratic presidential candidate, made gains in all the New England states. The rise in Democratic strength was especially notable in Massachusetts and Rhode Island. When one probes below the surface of the gross election figures it becomes apparent that a sharp and durable realignment also occurred within the electorate, a fact reflective of the activation by the Democratic candidate of low-income, Catholic, urban voters of recent immigrant stock. In New England, at least, the Roosevelt revolution of 1932 was in large measure an Al Smith revolution of 1928, a characterization less applicable to the remainder of the country.

The intensity and extent of electoral concern before the voting of 1928 can only be surmised, but the durability of the realignment formed at the election can be determined by simple analyses of election statistics. An illustration of the new division thrust through the electorate by the campaign of 1928 is provided by the graphs in Figure A, which show the Democratic percentages of the presidential vote from 1916 through 1952 for the city of Somerville and the town of Ashfield in Massachusetts. Somerville, adjacent to Boston, had a population in 1930 of 104,000 of which 28 percent was foreign born and 41 percent was of foreign-born or mixed parentage. Roman Catholics constituted a large proportion of its relatively low-income population. Ashfield, a farming community in western Massachusetts with a 1930 population of 860, was predominantly native born (8.6 percent foreign born), chiefly rural-farm (66 percent), and principally Protestant.

The impressiveness of the differential impact of the election of 1928 on Somerville and Ashfield may be read from the graphs in Figure A. From 1920 the Democratic percentage in Somerville ascended steeply while the Democrats in Ashfield, few in 1920, became even less numerous in 1928. Inspection of graphs also suggests that the great reshuffling of voters that occurred in 1928 was perhaps the final and decisive stage in a process that had been under way for some time. That antecedent process involved a relatively heavy support in 1924 for La Follette in those towns in which Smith was subsequently to find

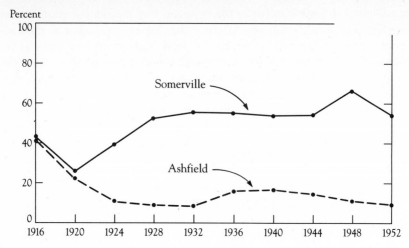

Figure A   Democratic Percentages of Major-Party Presidential Vote, Somerville and Ashfield, Massachusetts, 1916–1952

special favor. Hence, in Figure A, as in all the other charts, the 1924 figure is the percentage of the total accounted for by the votes of both the Democratic and Progressive candidates rather than the Democratic percentage of the two-party vote. This usage conveys a minimum impression of the size of the 1924–1928 Democratic gain but probably depicts the nature of the 1920–1928 trend.

For present purposes, the voting behavior of the two communities shown in Figure A after 1928 is of central relevance. The differences established between them in 1928 persisted even through 1952, although the two series fluctuated slightly in response to the particular influences of individual campaigns. The nature of the process of maintenance of the cleavage is, of course, not manifest from these data. Conceivably the impress of the events of 1928 on individual attitudes and loyalties formed partisan attachments of lasting nature. Yet it is doubtful that the new crystallization of 1928 projected itself through a quarter of a century solely from the momentum given it by such factors. More probably subsequent events operated to reenforce and to maintain the 1928 cleavage. Whatever the mechanism of its maintenance, the durability of the realignment is impressive.

Somerville and Ashfield may be regarded more or less as samples of major population groups within the electorate of Massachusetts. Since no sample survey data are available for 1928, about the only analysis feasible is inspection of election returns for geographic units contrasting in their population composition. Lest it be supposed, however, that the good citizens of Somerville and Ashfield were aberrants simply unlike the remainder of the people of the Commonwealth, examination of a large number of towns and cities is in order. In the interest of both compression and comprehensibility, a mass of data is telescoped into Figure B. The graphs in that figure compare over the period 1916–

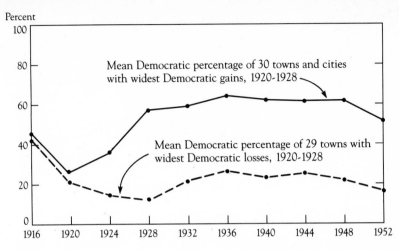

Figure B   Persistence of Electoral Cleavage of 1928 in Massachusetts: Mean Democratic Percentage of Presidential Vote in Towns with Sharpest Democratic Gains, 1920–1928, and in Towns of Widest Democratic Losses, 1920–1928

1952 the voting behavior of the 29 Massachusetts towns and cities having the sharpest Democratic increases, 1920–1928, with that of the 30 towns and cities having the most marked Democratic loss, 1920–1928. In other words, the figure averages out a great many Ashfields and Somervilles. The data of Figure B confirm the expectation that the pattern exhibited by the pair of voting units in Figure A represented only a single case of a much more general phenomenon. Yet by virtue of the coverage of the data in the figure, one gains a stronger impression of the difference in the character of the election of 1928 and the other elections recorded there. The cleavage confirmed by the 1928 returns persisted. At subsequent elections the voters shifted to and fro within the outlines of the broad division fixed in 1928.

Examination of the characteristics of the two groups of cities and towns of Figure B—those with the most marked Democratic gains, 1920–1928, and those with the widest movement in the opposite direction—reveals the expected sorts of differences. Urban, industrial, foreign-born, Catholic areas made up the bulk of the first group of towns, although an occasional rural Catholic community increased its Democratic vote markedly. The towns with a contrary movement tended to be rural, Protestant, native born. The new Democratic vote correlated quite closely with a 1930 vote on state enforcement of the national prohibition law.

Melancholy experience with the eccentricities of data, be they quantitative or otherwise, suggests the prudence of a check on the interpretation of 1928. Would the same method applied to any other election yield a similar result, i.e., the appearance of a more or less durable realignment? Perhaps there can be no doubt that the impact of the events of any election on many individuals

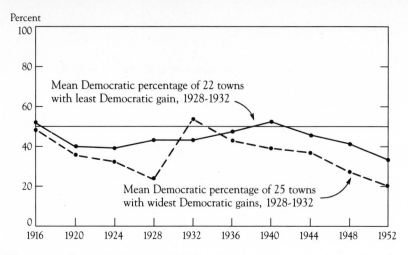

Figure C   Impact of Election of 1932 in New Hampshire: Mean Democratic Percentage of Presidential Vote of Towns with Sharpest Democratic Gain, 1928–1932, Compared with Mean Vote of Towns at Opposite Extreme of 1928–1932 Change

forms lasting party loyalties; yet not often is the number so affected so great as to create sharp realignment. On the other hand, some elections are characterized by a large-scale transfer of party affection that is quite short-term, a different sort of phenomenon from that which occurs in elections marked by broad and durable shifts in party strength. The difference is illustrated by the data on the election of 1932 in New Hampshire in Figure C. The voting records of the twenty-five towns with the widest Democratic gains from 1928 to 1932 are there traced from 1916 to 1952. Observe that Democratic strength in these towns shot up in 1932 but fairly quickly resumed about the same position in relation to other towns that it had occupied in 1928. It is also evident from the graph that this group of towns has on the whole been especially strongly repelled by the Democratic appeal of 1928. Probably the depression drove an appreciable number of hardened Republicans of these towns to vote for a change in 1932, but they gradually found their way back to the party of their fathers. In any case, the figure reflects a type of behavior differing markedly from that of 1928. To the extent that 1932 resembled 1928 in the recrystallization of party lines, the proportions of new Democrats did not differ significantly among the groups of towns examined. In fact, what probably happened to a considerable extent in New England was that the 1928 election broke the electorate into two new groups that would have been formed in 1932 had there been no realignment in 1928.

The Massachusetts material has served both to explain the method of analysis and to present the case of a single state. Examinations of the election of 1928 in other New England states indicate that in each a pattern prevailed similar to that of Massachusetts. The total effect of the realignment differed, of course, from state to state. In Massachusetts and Rhode Island the number of people affected by the upheaval of 1928 was sufficient to form a new majority coalition. In Maine, New Hampshire, and Vermont the same sort of reshuffling of electors occurred, but the proportions affected were not sufficient to overturn the Republican combination, although the basis was laid in Maine and New Hampshire for later limited Democratic success. To underpin these remarks the materials on Connecticut, Maine, New Hampshire, and Rhode Island are presented in Figure D. The data on Vermont, excluded for lack of space, form a pattern similar to that emerging from the analysis of the other states.

In the interpretation of all these 1928 analyses certain limitations of the technique need to be kept in mind. The data and the technique most clearly reveal a shift when voters of different areas move in opposite directions. From 1928 to 1936 apparently a good deal of Democratic growth occurred in virtually all geographic units, a shift not shown up sharply by the technique. Hence, the discussion may fail adequately to indicate the place of 1928 as the crucial stage in a process of electoral change that began before and concluded after that year.

II

One of the difficulties with an ideal type is that no single actual case fits exactly its specifications. Moreover, in any system of categorization the greater the number of differentiating criteria for classes, the more nearly one tends to create a separate class for each instance. If taxonomic systems are to be of analytical utility, they must almost inevitably group together instances that are unlike at least in peripheral characteristics irrelevant to the purpose of the system. All of which serves to warn that an election is about to be classified as critical even though in some respects the behavior involved differed from that of the 1928 polling.

Central to our concept of critical elections is a realignment within the electorate both sharp and durable. With respect to these basic criteria the election of 1896 falls within the same category as that of 1928, although it differed in other respects. The persistence of the new division of 1896 was perhaps not so notable as that of 1928; yet the Democratic defeat was so demoralizing and so thorough that the party could make little headway in regrouping its forces until 1916. Perhaps the significant feature of the 1896 contest was that, at least in New England, it did not form a new division in which partisan lines became more nearly congruent with lines separating classes, religions, or other such social groups. Instead, the Republicans succeeded in drawing new support, in about the same degree, from all sorts of economic and social classes. The result was an electoral coalition formidable in mass but which required both good fortune and skill in political management for its maintenance, given its latent internal contradictions.

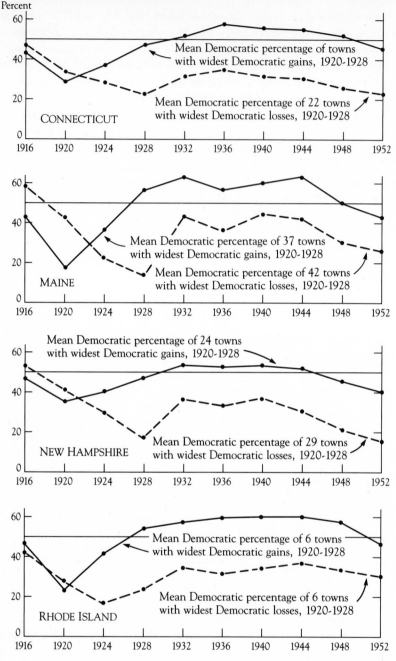

Figure D   Realignment of 1928 in Connecticut, Maine, New Hampshire, and Rhode Island

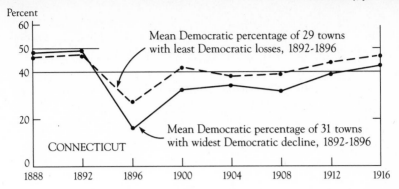

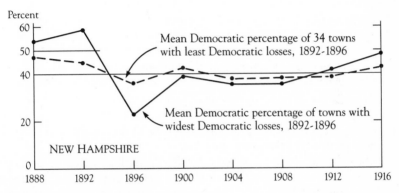

Figure E   Realignment of 1896 in Connecticut and New Hampshire

If the 1896 election is described in our terms as a complex of behavior preceding and following the formal voting, an account of the action must include the panic of 1893. Bank failures, railroad receiverships, unemployment, strikes, Democratic championship of deflation and of the gold standard, and related matters created the setting for a Democratic setback in 1894. Only one of the eight New England Democratic Representatives survived the elections of 1894. The two 1892 Democratic governors fell by the wayside and in all the states the Democratic share of the gubernatorial vote fell sharply in 1894. The luckless William Jennings Bryan and the free-silver heresy perhaps did not contribute as much as is generally supposed to the 1892–1896 decline in New England Democratic strength; New England Democrats moved in large numbers over to the Republican ranks in 1894.

The character of the 1892–1896 electoral shift is suggested by the data of Figure E, which presents an analysis of Connecticut and New Hampshire made by the technique used earlier in examining the election of 1928. The graphs make plain that in these states (and the other New England states show the same pattern) the rout of 1896 produced a basic realignment that persisted at

Table 1   Contrasts between Elections of 1896 and 1928 in Massachusetts: Shifts in Democratic Strength, 1892–1896 and 1920–1928, in Relation to Population Size of Towns

Population size group	Mean Democratic percentage		Mean change	Mean Democratic percentage		Mean change
	1892	1896	1892–96	1920	1928	1920–28
1–999	34.0	14.7	− 19.3	16.5	18.6	+ 2.1
2000–2999	38.8	18.3	− 20.5	21.0	33.1	+12.1
10,000–14,999	46.7	26.9	− 19.8	25.8	43.7	+17.9
50,000 +	47.7	30.1	− 17.6	29.5	55.7	+26.2

least until 1916. The graphs in Figure E also make equally plain that the 1892–1896 realignment differed radically from that of 1928 in certain respects. In 1896 the net movement in all sorts of geographic units was toward the Republicans; towns differed not in the direction of their movement but only in the extent. Moreover, the persistence of the realignment of 1896 was about the same in those towns with the least Democratic loss from 1892 to 1896 as it was in those with the most marked decline in Democratic strength. Hence, the graphs differ from those on 1928 which took the form of opening scissors. Instead, the 1896 realignment appears as a parallel movement of both groups to a lower plateau of Democratic strength.

If the election of 1896 had had a notable differential impact on geographically segregated social groups, the graphs in Figure E of towns at the extremes of the greatest and least 1892–1896 change would have taken the form of opening scissors as they did in 1928. While the election of 1896 is often pictured as a last-ditch fight between the haves and the have-nots, that understanding of the contest was, at least in New England, evidently restricted to planes of leadership and oratory. It did not extend to the voting actions of the electorate. These observations merit some buttressing, although the inference emerges clearly enough from Figure E.

Unfortunately the census authorities have ignored the opportunity to advance demographic inquiry by publishing data of consequence about New England towns. Not much information is available on the characteristics of the populations of these small geographic areas. Nevertheless, size of total population alone is a fair separator of towns according to politically significant characteristics. Classification of towns according to that criterion groups them roughly according to industrialization and probably generally also according to religion and national origin. Hence, with size of population of towns and cities as a basis, Table 1 contrasts the elections of 1896 and 1928 for different types of towns. Observe from the table that the mean shift between 1892 and 1896 was about the same for varying size groups of towns. Contrast this lack of association between size and political movement with the radically different 1920–1928 pattern which also appears in the table.

Table 1 makes clear that in 1896 the industrial cities, in their aggregate vote at least, moved toward the Republicans in about the same degree as did the rural farming communities. Some of the misinterpretations of the election of 1896 flow from a focus on that election in isolation rather than in comparison with the preceding election. In 1896, even in New England cities, the Democrats tended to be strongest in the poor, working-class, immigrant sections. Yet the same relation had existed, in a sharper form, in 1892. In 1896 the Republicans gained in the working-class wards, just as they did in the silk-stocking wards, over their 1892 vote. They were able to place the blame for unemployment upon the Democrats and to propagate successfully the doctrine that the Republican Party was the party of prosperity and the "full dinner pail." On the whole, the effect apparently was to reduce the degree of coincidence of class affiliation and partisan inclination. Nor was the election of 1896, in New England at least, a matter of heightened tension between city and country. Both city and country voters shifted in the same direction. Neither urban employers nor industrial workers could generate much enthusiasm for inflation and free trade; rather they joined in common cause. Instead of a sharpening of class cleavages within New England the voting apparently reflected more a sectional antagonism and anxiety, shared by all classes, expressed in opposition to the dangers supposed to be threatening from the West.

Other contrasts between the patterns of electoral behavior of 1896 and 1928 could be cited but in terms of sharpness and durability of realignment both elections were of roughly the same type, at least in New England. In these respects they seem to differ from most other elections over a period of a half century, although it may well be that each round at the ballot boxes involves realignment within the electorate similar in kind but radically different in extent.

III

The discussion points toward the analytical utility of a system for the differentiation of elections. A concept of critical elections has been developed to cover a type of election in which there occurs a sharp and durable electoral realignment between parties, although the techniques employed do not yield any information of consequence about the mechanisms for the maintenance of a new alignment, once it is formed. Obviously any sort of system for the gross characterization of elections presents difficulties in application. The actual election rarely presents in pure form a case fitting completely any particular concept. Especially in a large and diverse electorate a single polling may encompass radically varying types of behavior among different categories of voters; yet a dominant characteristic often makes itself apparent. Despite such difficulties, the attempt to move toward a better understanding of elections in the terms here employed could provide a means for better integrating the study of electoral behavior with the analysis of political systems. In truth, a considerable proportion of the study of electoral behavior has only a tenuous relation to politics.

The sorts of questions here raised, when applied sufficiently broadly on a comparative basis and carried far enough, could lead to a consideration of basic problems of the nature of democratic orders. A question occurs, for example, about the character of the consequences for the political system of the temporal frequency of critical elections. What are the consequences for public administration, for the legislative process, for the operation of the economy of frequent serious upheavals within the electorate? What are the correlates of that pattern of behavior? And, for those disposed to raise such questions, what underlying changes might alter the situation? Or, when viewed from the contrary position, what consequences flow from an electorate which is disposed, in effect, to remain largely quiescent over considerable periods? Does a state of moving equilibrium reflect a pervasive satisfaction with the course of public policy? An indifference about matters political? In any case, what are the consequences for the public order? Further, what are the consequences when an electorate builds up habits and attachments, or faces situations, that make it impossible for it to render a decisive and clear-cut popular verdict that promises not to be upset by caprice at the next round of polling? What are the consequences of a situation that creates recurring, evenly balanced conflict over long periods? On the other hand, what characteristics of an electorate or what conditions permit sharp and decisive changes in the power structure from time to time? Such directions of speculation are suggested by a single criterion for the differentiation of elections. Further development of an electoral typology would probably point to useful speculation in a variety of directions.

Voting Behavior:
Rational or Irrational?

Parties are supposed to bridge the gap between the people and their government. Theoretically they are the primary vehicles for translating the wishes of the electorate into public policy, sharing this role with interest groups and other governmental instrumentalities in varying degrees. If parties are to perform this aspect of their job properly, the party system must be conducive to securing meaningful debate and action. Party organization and procedure profoundly affect the ability of parties to act in a democratically responsible manner. It should also be pointed out, however, that the electorate has a responsibility in the political process—the responsibility to act rationally, debate the issues of importance, and record a vote for one party or the other at election time. These, at least, are electoral norms traditionally discussed. But does the electorate act in this manner? Is it desirable to have 100 percent electoral participation considering the char-

acteristics of voting behavior? What are the determinants of electoral behavior? These questions are discussed in the following selection.

26

Bernard R. Berelson, Paul F. Lazarsfeld, and William N. McPhee
DEMOCRATIC PRACTICE AND DEMOCRATIC THEORY

REQUIREMENTS FOR THE INDIVIDUAL

Perhaps the main impact of realistic research on contemporary politics has been
to temper some of the requirements set by our traditional normative theory for
the typical citizen. "Out of all this literature of political observation and analysis, which is relatively new," says Max Beloff, "there has come to exist a picture
in our minds of the political scene which differs very considerably from that
familiar to us from the classical texts of democratic politics."

Experienced observers have long known, of course, that the individual
voter was not all that the theory of democracy requires of him. As [British Lord
James] Bryce put it [in his 1888 treatise, *The American Commonwealth*]:

> How little solidity and substance there is in the political or social beliefs of
> nineteen persons out of every twenty. These beliefs, when examined, mostly
> resolve themselves into two or three prejudices and aversions, two or three
> prepossessions for a particular party or section of a party, two or three phrases
> or catch-words suggesting or embodying arguments which the man who repeats
> them has not analyzed.

While our data [from the Elmira study] do not support such an extreme statement, they do reveal that certain requirements commonly assumed for the
successful operation of democracy are not met by the behavior of the "average"
citizen. The requirements, and our conclusions concerning them, are quickly
reviewed.

Interest, Discussion, Motivation. The democratic citizen is expected to be interested and to participate in political affairs. His interest and participation can take such various forms as reading and listening to campaign materials, working for the candidate or the party, arguing politics, donating money, and voting. In Elmira the majority of the people vote, but in general they do not give evidence of sustained interest. Many vote without real involvement in the election, and even the party workers are not typically motivated by ideological concerns or plain civic duty.

If there is one characteristic for a democratic system (besides the ballot itself) that is theoretically required, it is the capacity for and the practice of discussion. "It is as true of the large as of the small society," says [A.D.] Lindsay, "that its health depends on the mutual understanding which discussion makes possible; and that discussion is the only possible instrument of its democratic government." How much participation in political discussion there is in the community, what it is, and among whom—these questions have been given answers . . . earlier. . . . In this instance there was little true discussion between the candidates, little in the newspaper commentary, little between the voters and the official party representatives, some within the electorate. On the grass roots level there was more talk than debate, and, at least inferentially, the talk had important effects upon voting, in reinforcing or activating the partisans if not in converting the opposition.

An assumption underlying the theory of democracy is that the citizenry has a strong motivation for participation in political life. But it is a curious quality of voting behavior that for large numbers of people motivation is weak if not almost absent. It is assumed that this motivation would gain its strength from the citizen's perception of the difference that alternative decisions made to him. Now when a person buys something or makes other decisions of daily life, there are direct and immediate consequences for him. But for the bulk of the American people the voting decision is not followed by any direct, immediate, visible personal consequences. Most voters, organized or unorganized, are not in a position to foresee the distant and indirect consequences for themselves, let alone the society. The ballot is cast, and for most people that is the end of it. If their side is defeated, "it doesn't really matter."

Knowledge. The democratic citizen is expected to be well informed about political affairs. He is supposed to know what the issues are, what their history is, what the relevant facts are, what alternatives are proposed, what the party stands for, what the likely consequences are. By such standards the voter falls short. Even when he has the motivation, he finds it difficult to make decisions on the basis of full information when the subject is relatively simple and proximate; how can he do so when it is complex and remote? The citizen is not highly informed on details of the campaign, nor does he avoid a certain misperception of the political situation when it is to his psychological advantage to do so. The electorate's perception of what goes on in the campaign is colored by emotional feeling toward one or the other issue, candidate, party, or social group.

Principle. The democratic citizen is supposed to cast his vote on the basis of principle—not fortuitously or frivolously or impulsively or habitually, but with reference to standards not only of his own interest but of the common good as well. Here, again, if this requirement is pushed at all strongly, it becomes an impossible demand on the democratic electorate.

Many voters vote not for principle in the usual sense but "for" a group to which they are attached—their group. The Catholic vote or the hereditary vote is explainable less as principle than as a traditional social allegiance. The ordinary voter, bewildered by the complexity of modern political problems, unable to determine clearly what the consequences are of alternative lines of action, remote from the arena, and incapable of bringing information to bear on principle, votes the way trusted people around him are voting. . . .

On the issues of the campaign there is a considerable amount of "don't know"—sometimes reflecting genuine indecision, more often meaning "don't care." Among those with opinions the partisans *agree* on most issues, criteria, expectations, and rules of the game. The supporters of the different sides disagree on only a few issues. Nor, for that matter, do the candidates themselves always join the issue sharply and clearly. The partisans do not agree overwhelmingly with their own party's position, or, rather, only the small minority of highly partisan do; the rest take a rather moderate position on the political consideration involved in an election.

Rationality. The democratic citizen is expected to exercise rational judgment in coming to his voting decision. He is expected to have arrived at his principles by reason and to have considered rationally the implications and alleged consequences of the alternative proposals of the contending parties. Political theorists and commentators have always exclaimed over the seeming contrast here between requirement and fulfillment. . . . The upshot of this is that the usual analogy between the voting "decision" and the more or less carefully calculated decisions of consumers or businessmen or courts, incidentally, may be quite incorrect. For many voters political preferences may better be considered analogous to cultural tastes—in music, literature, recreational activities, dress, ethics, speech, social behavior. Consider the parallels between political preferences and general cultural tastes. Both have their origin in ethnic, sectional, class, and family traditions. Both exhibit stability and resistance to change for individuals but flexibility and adjustment over generations for the society as a whole. Both seem to be matters of sentiment and disposition rather than "reasoned preferences." While both are responsive to changed conditions and unusual stimuli, they are relatively invulnerable to direct argumentation and vulnerable to indirect social influences. Both are characterized more by faith than by conviction and by wishful expectation rather than careful prediction or con-sequences. The preference for one party rather than another must be highly similar to the preference for one kind of literature or music rather than another, and the choice of the same political party every four years may be parallel to the choice of the same old standards of conduct in new social situations. In short, it appears that a sense of fitness is a more striking feature of political preference than reason and calculation.

REQUIREMENTS FOR THE SYSTEM

If the democratic system depended solely on the qualifications of the individual voter, then it seems remarkable that democracies have survived through the centuries. After examining the detailed data on how individuals misperceive political reality or respond to irrelevant social influences, one wonders how a democracy ever solves its political problems. But when one considers the data in a broader perspective—how huge segments of the society adapt to political conditions affecting them or how the political system adjusts itself to changing conditions over long periods of time—he cannot fail to be impressed with the total result. Where the rational citizen seems to abdicate, nevertheless angels seem to tread. . . .

That is the paradox. *Individual voters* today seem unable to satisfy the re-quirements for a democratic system of government outlined by political theo-rists. But the *system of democracy* does meet certain requirements for a going political organization. The individual members may not meet all the standards, but the whole nevertheless survives and grows. This suggests that where the classic theory is defective is in its concentration on the *individual citizen*. What are undervalued are certain collective properties that reside in the electorate as a whole and in the political and social system in which it functions.

The political philosophy we have inherited, then, has given more consid-eration to the virtues of the typical citizen of the democracy than to the working of the *system* as a whole. Moreover, when it dealt with the system, it mainly considered the single constitutive institutions of the system, not those general features necessary if the institutions are to work as required. For example, the rule of law, representative government, periodic elections, the party system, and the several freedoms of discussion, press, association, and assembly have all been examined by political philosophers seeking to clarify and to justify the idea of political democracy. But liberal democracy is more than a political system in which individual voters and political institutions operate. For political de-mocracy to survive, other features are required: the intensity of conflict must be limited, the rate of change must be restrained, stability in the social and economic structure must be maintained, a pluralistic social organization must exist, and a basic consensus must bind together the contending parties.

Such features of the system of political democracy belong neither to the constitutive institutions nor to the individual voter. It might be said that they form the atmosphere or the environment in which both operate. In any case, such features have not been carefully considered by political philosophers, and it is on these broader properties of the democratic political system that more reflection and study by political theory is called for. In the most tentative fashion let us explore the values of the political system, as they involve the electorate, in the light of the foregoing considerations.

Underlying the paradox is an assumption that the population is homogeneous socially and should be homogeneous politically: that everybody is about the same in relevant social characteristics; that, if something is a political virtue (like interest in the election), then everyone should have it; that there is such a thing as "the" typical citizen on whom uniform requirements can be imposed. The tendency of classic democratic literature to work with an image of "the" voter was never justified. For, as we will attempt to illustrate here, some of the most important requirements that democratic values impose on a system require a voting population that is not homogeneous but heterogeneous in its political qualities.

The need for heterogeneity arises from the contradictory functions we expect our voting system to serve. We expect the political system to adjust itself and our affairs to changing conditions; yet we demand too that it display a high degree of stability. We expect the contending interests and parties to pursue their ends vigorously and the voters to care; yet, after the election is over, we expect reconciliation. We expect the voting outcome to serve what is best for the community; yet we do not want disinterested voting unattached to the purposes and interests of different segments of that community. We want voters to express their own free and self-determined choices; yet, for the good of the community, we would like voters to avail themselves of the best information and guidance available from the groups and leaders around them. We expect a high degree of rationality to prevail in the decision; but were all irrationality and mythology absent, and all ends pursued by the most coldly rational selection of political means, it is doubtful if the system would hold together.

In short, our electoral system calls for apparently incompatible properties— which, although they cannot all reside in each individual voter, can (and do) reside in a heterogeneous electorate. What seems to be required of the electorate as a whole is a *distribution* of qualities along important dimensions. We need some people who are active in a certain respect, others in the middle, and still others passive. The contradictory things we want from the total require that the parts be different. This can be illustrated by taking up a number of important dimensions by which an electorate might be characterized.

Involvement and Indifference. How could a mass democracy work if all the people were deeply involved in politics? Lack of interest by some people is not without its benefits, too. True, the highly interested voters vote more, and know more about the campaign, and read and listen more, and participate more; however, they are also less open to persuasion and less likely to change.

Extreme interest goes with extreme partisanship and might culminate in rigid fanaticism that could destroy democratic processes if generalized throughout the community. Low affect toward the election—not caring much—underlies the resolution of many political problems; votes can be resolved into a two-party split instead of fragmented into many parties (the splinter parties of the left, for example, splinter because their advocates are *too* interested in politics). Low interest provides maneuvering room for political shifts necessary for a complex society in a period of rapid change. Compromise might be based upon sophisticated awareness of costs and returns—perhaps impossible to demand of a mass society—but it is more often induced by indifference. Some people are and should be highly interested in politics, but not everyone is or needs to be. Only the doctrinaire would deprecate the moderate indifference that facilitates compromise.

Hence, an important balance between action motivated by strong sentiments and action with little passion behind it is obtained by heterogeneity within the electorate. Balance of this sort is, in practice, met by a distribution of voters rather than by a homogeneous collection of "ideal" citizens.

Stability and Flexibility. A similar dimension along which an electorate might be characterized is stability-flexibility. The need for change and adaptation is clear, and the need for stability ought equally to be (especially from observation of current democratic practice in, say, certain Latin American countries). . . . [I]t may be that the very people who are most sensitive to changing social conditions are those most susceptible to political change. For, in either case, the people exposed to membership in overlapping strata, those whose former life-patterns are being broken up, those who are moving about socially or physically, those who are forming new families and new friendships— it is they who are open to adjustments of attitudes and tastes. They may be the least partisan and the least interested voters, but they perform a valuable function for the entire system. Here again is an instance in which an individual "inadequacy" provides a positive service for society: The campaign can be a reaffirming force for the settled majority and a creative force for the unsettled minority. There is stability on both sides and flexibility in the middle.

Progress and Conservation. Closely related to the question of stability is the question of past versus future orientation of the system. In America a progressive outlook is highly valued, but, at the same time, so is a conservative one. Here a balance between the two is easily found in the party system and in the distribution of voters themselves from extreme conservatives to extreme liberals. But a balance between the two is also achieved by a distribution of political dispositions through time. There are periods of great political agitation (i.e., campaigns) alternating with periods of political dormancy. Paradoxically, the former—the campaign period—is likely to be an instrument of conservatism, often even of historial regression. . . .

Again, then, a balance (between preservation of the past and receptivity to the future) seems to be required of a democratic electorate. The heterogeneous electorate in itself provides a balance between liberalism and conservatism; and so does the sequence of political events from periods of drifting change to abrupt rallies back to the loyalities of earlier years.

Consensus and Cleavage. . . . [T]here are required *social* consensus and cleavage—in effect pluralism—in politics. Such pluralism makes for enough consensus to hold the system together and enough cleavage to make it move. Too much consensus would be deadening and restrictive of liberty; too much cleavage would be destructive of the society as a whole. . . . Thus again a requirement we might place on an electoral system—balance between total political war between segments of the society and total political indifference to group interests of that society—translates into varied requirements for different individuals. With respect to group or bloc voting, as with other aspects of political behavior, it is perhaps not unfortunate that "some do and some do not."

Individualism and Collectivism. Lord Bryce pointed out the difficulties in a theory of democracy that assumes that each citizen must himself be capable of voting intelligently:

> Orthodox democratic theory assumes that every citizen has, or ought to have, thought out for himself certain opinions, i.e., ought to have a definite view, defensible by argument, of what the country needs, of what principles ought to be applied in governing it, of the man to whose hands the government ought to be entrusted. There are persons who talk, though certainly very few who act, as if they believed this theory, which may be compared to the theory of some ultra-Protestants that every good Christian has or ought to have . . . worked out for himself from the Bible a system of theology.

In the first place, however, the information available to the individual voter is not limited to that directly possessed by him. True, the individual casts his own personal ballot. But, as we have tried to indicate . . . that is perhaps the most individualized action he takes in an election. His vote is formed in the midst of his fellows in a sort of group decision—if, indeed, it may be called a decision at all—and the total information and knowledge possessed in the group's present and past generations can be made available for the group's choice. Here is where opinion-leading relationships, for example, play an active role.

Second, and probably more important, the individual voter may not have a great deal of detailed information, but he usually has picked up the crucial *general* information as part of his social learning itself. He may not know the parties' position on the tariff, or who is for reciprocal trade treaties, or what are the differences on Asiatic policy, or how the parties split on civil rights, or how many security risks were exposed by whom. But he cannot live in an American community without knowing broadly where the parties stand. He has learned that the Republicans are more conservative and the Democrats more liberal—and he can locate his own sentiments and cast his vote accordingly. After all, he must vote for one or the other party, and, if he knows the big thing about the parties, he does not need to know all the little things. The basic role a party plays as an institution in American life is more important to his voting than a particular stand on a particular issue.

It would be unthinkable to try to maintain our present economic style of life without a complex system of delegating to others what we are not competent to do ourselves, without accepting and giving training to each other about what each is expected to do, without accepting our dependence on others in many spheres and taking responsibility for their dependence on us in some spheres. And, like it or not, to maintain our present political style of life, we may have to accept much the same interdependence with others in collective behavior. We have learned slowly in economic life that it is useful not to have everyone a butcher or a baker, any more than it is useful to have no one skilled in such activities. The same kind of division of labor—as repugnant as it may be in some respects to our individualistic tradition—is serving us well today in mass politics. There is an implicit division of political labor within the electorate.

Party Realignment in the 1990s

"Critical" elections, as V. O. Key, Jr., points out in selection 25, reflect a long-term shift in party alignment as a majority of the electorate changes sides. In a stable two-party system the opposition party of the past becomes the dominant party of the future. It is difficult if not impossible to identify critical elections reflecting important changes in party identification unless parties themselves effectively aggregate and represent different political interests and public opinions.

Increasingly, American parties have been difficult to define in terms of contrasting interests and ideologies. Party identification among the electorate is not sharply focused. While a majority of voters call themselves either Democrats or Republicans, ticket-splitting in the voting booth is a common practice as the electorate seems to assess candidates more in terms of their personalities and styles than their party affiliations. The voting fickleness of party members and the growing number of voters who label themselves as independents reflect an electorate that does not consider parties to be all that important.

However serious party decline may be, political analysis continues to give parties a central explanatory role. Parties are the only handles we have to get a grip on the broader aspects of politics and political change. Making generalizations about politics requires reference to political parties because they are the only collective and aggregative organizations that represent a wide political spectrum. If electoral shifts cannot be measured in terms of parties they cannot be meaningfully identified.

The following selection assesses Democratic and Republican party fortunes in the Reagan era, and the impact the Reagan presidency had on the party system. The author addresses the important question of whether or not Reagan represented or caused a party realignment that, at least at the presidential level, indicates a long-term electoral shift to the Republican party.

27

Paul Allen Beck
INCOMPLETE REALIGNMENT: THE REAGAN LEGACY FOR PARTIES AND ELECTIONS

IDENTIFYING THE REAGAN LEGACY

As Ronald Reagan retires from public life, he leaves behind a Republican party far stronger than the one he inherited in 1980. The party has regained the ground it lost in the aftermath of the Watergate affair and appears to be stronger in the late 1980s than it has been in decades. How much Reagan personally has contributed to the turnabout in GOP fortunes, however, is far from clear.

Even without Reagan, several forces were working to retrieve the party from the depths to which it sank after Watergate. The twin troubles of the Carter Presidency—inflation and Iran—virtually handed the White House to the GOP in 1980, perhaps no matter who had been their candidate. Indeed, because of the conservative ideological baggage he carried, Reagan may have been less well positioned to take advantage of the anti-Carter backlash than

From Charles O. Jones, *The Reagan Legacy: Promise and Performance* (Chatham, N.J.: Chatham House Publishers, 1988), pp. 160–169. Reprinted by permission.

some other GOP nominee. The party simultaneously was enjoying a growing organizational vitality, especially through the building of a grassroots donor base and a capability to aid its candidates in campaigns. Over the longer haul there has been the seemingly inexorable weakening of the Democratic party coalition—from which the Republicans, as the opposition in a two-party system, could only gain. The Watergate affair may have stalled this pro-Republican momentum only temporarily. To some degree at least, then, President Reagan inherited a party with considerable electoral opportunity. His primary accomplishment may have been the full exploitation of it to his and his party's advantage.

But this is no mean accomplishment. Political history is strewn with examples of leaders who failed to take advantage of favorable circumstances. Richard Nixon frittered away the standing he had won in a landslide victory by his deepening involvement in Watergate. Just before him, Lyndon Johnson saw his Presidency erode under the force of urban riots and Vietnam. What has distinguished Ronald Reagan has been his ability to seize the opportunities presented by an unpopular predecessor, an energized party, and a debilitated opposition. While the Iran-*contra* affair, corruption charges against high administration officials, and the October 1987 stock market decline all threaten to undermine his considerable achievements, there is good reason to believe that President Reagan will leave the White House with his party well along the way toward a partisan realignment.

The Reagan contributions to the Republican resurgence derive mostly from his leadership and the generally positive responses it has evoked from the American public. The Presidency is a powerful pulpit from which to steer the course of American politics. Presidential successes typically redound to the benefit of their party by enhancing public images of its performance capabilities. In the 1980s, in comparison to the immediate post-Watergate period, about twice as many Americans have seen the GOP as the party better able to handle the nation's most important problems, and the primary reason is the Reagan Presidency. By the mid-1980s, in fact, the Republicans had closed the party image gap with the Democrats, a gap that had been as high as 28 percent in 1975.

Reagan's leadership has had an equally important, if more subtle, effect on the agenda of politics—the issues, controversies, even premises that structure political debate. His assault on big government put liberalism on the defensive and lent such respectability to conservative ideas that they permeated the public more deeply than ever before. The 1980s were a time of federal tax cuts, reduced growth in domestic programs, increases in defense spending, and a new surge of conservative moralism in policy making. Reagan's leadership played the major role in bringing these matters to the top of the political agenda. Ironically, even in the traditionally conservative concern for a balanced budget, which was swept aside in the early 1980s and continues to represent a major policy failure of the administration, the President's power to shape debate is illustrated: Who would have thought, before the 1980s, that today many liberal Democrats would be decrying the nation's unprecedented budget deficit or that a bipartisan consensus would emerge around the proposition that the deficit should be reduced?

The Reagan legacy is perhaps best measured by changes during the 1980s in the partisan loyalties of the electorate. The troubles of Carter and his party, as much as they may have affected the electoral fortunes of the Democrats, could not alone create greater numbers of Republican loyalists. Nor did the enhanced organizational effectiveness of the party materially affect its loyalist base; it merely improved its ability to mobilize this base and attract votes beyond it in constructing an electoral majority. Indeed, to increase its partisan strength, the GOP had to become attractive to the electorate in its own right.

. . . [B]y the early 1980s, the percentage of the electorate professing Republican loyalties had regained the ground it had lost after the Watergate affair. The first GOP surge came in the early months of the first Reagan term, a time of spectacular Reagan successes with the Congress. Reagan's landslide reelection in 1984 was accompanied by additional growth in GOP loyalists. By the end of 1984, these two GOP surges had reduced the gap in party loyalists between the parties to about half what it had been little more than a decade before— and to its lowest level since reliable measurements first were available in the early 1950s. The fact that both these surges are readily linked to presidential accomplishments supports the inference that they are attributable to Ronald Reagan. Because partisan loyalties are lasting components of many Americans' political outlooks, rather than momentary responses to temporary political stimuli, the Republican gains registered in them should endure well beyond the Reagan years. This has to count as potentially the most significant Reagan legacy.

The Reagan years have promoted GOP prospects for the future in yet another important way. Eight years of conservative Republican rule have developed a new cadre of Republican party leaders. President Reagan's conservative preachings drew a new generation of ideological activists to the party and encouraged conservative activists already in it. Moreover, with the appointment of his people to some 3000 top policy-making positions in the federal government, the President created a large talent pool of now experienced and credentialed partisans from which his party can recruit for subsequent political activity. Quite consciously applying an ideological litmus test in addition to the usual party loyalty requirements, the Reagan administration has drawn into government large numbers of conservatives. This recruitment, and the grassroots activation that accompanied it, should have an impact on party politics for many years to come. An inadequate supply of good talent has been a perennial problem for the GOP, what with its historic weakness in the South and the natural aversion of conservatives to governmental careers. For the foreseeable future, this problem appears to have been solved.

Not only has the Reagan Presidency been good to his party by developing new talent, but the ideological bias in the effort has turned the GOP in a substantially more conservative direction. The once formidable liberal-moderate wing of the party has been virtually silenced during the Reagan years; its conservative wing has been emboldened. Familiar GOP candidates have refashioned their political appeals to attract more conservative support. These things are hard to gauge with any precision, but the intraparty center of gravity seems to have moved decidedly to the right. This too promises to be a durable part of the Reagan legacy, but it is potentially less propitious to a bright GOP future.

THE INCOMPLETE REALIGNMENT

The real test of the Reagan legacy, indeed the criterion Ronald Reagan might most want to invoke, is whether the partisanship gains under his leadership have constituted a pro-Republican realignment of the American electorate. A realignment occurs when there is a significant and enduring change in the party coalitions—that is, in the partisan loyalties of the electorate. Such a change would most likely displace the Democratic party from its position, since the New Deal realignment, as the dominant party in American politics. Echoing a common refrain of the late 1960s and early 1970s, before the Watergate affair silenced it, many observers have called the Republican resurgence . . . during the Reagan years "an emerging Republican realignment." If they are correct, then Ronald Reagan has left a legacy equaled by only a handful of American Presidents.

Signs of partisan realignment have abounded in the 1980s. Most conspicuously, the South has moved from a dependably Democratic to a dependably Republican region in presidential voting. Clear majorities of white southerners have consistently backed GOP presidential nominees in recent years, including 1976 and 1980 when fellow southerner Jimmy Carter was on the Democratic ticket. They flocked to the Reagan banner in 1984, giving him a full 70 percent of their vote. Aside from Carter, Democratic presidential candidates have carried only one southern state (Texas by Humphrey in 1968) since the Johnson landslide in 1964. The changes in this region alone spell trouble for the Democrats because their majority status cannot be retained if they regularly lose all or most southern states.

With his conservative political philosophy dominating the political agenda, moreover, Ronald Reagan has been able to unite economic and social conservatives behind his party. Economic conservatives have been the bedrock of Republican strength throughout the twentieth century. Until lately, social conservatives, especially Protestant fundamentalists, were not especially attracted to the GOP. In the early years of the century, their natural home was the Democratic party of William Jennings Bryan, thrice Democratic nominee for President and himself a religious fundamentalist who defended the Tennessee ban on the teaching of evolution in the famous Scopes trial of the 1920s. Especially in the South, religious fundamentalists continued to prefer the Democrats during the New Deal years, when the pains of depression submerged the social conservatism of many under a populist economic liberalism. By joining together these two strains of conservatism, Reagan laid the foundation for a majority Republican party.

But past voting patterns and presidential coalition-building successes do not necessarily spell realignment. Instead, realignment requires enduring changes in the party coalitions—a lasting alteration in party loyalties, not just temporary switches in candidate preferences. The question, then, is whether the pro-Republican forces of the post-Watergate resurgence have been powerful enough to dislodge the electorate from the Democratic leanings it has held since the 1930s and then to move it significantly in a Republican direction.

This question has two separate parts, involving first the decay of Democratic loyalties and then the acquisition of Republican loyalties. Because the American political tradition offers voters a legitimate alternative to partisanship, called *independence,* a decline in the loyalist base of one party does not have to be reciprocated by growth in the other party. Two different processes, in fact, are involved: one is appropriately termed *dealignment,* symbolizing the decay of one or both existing party coalitions, and the other of course is *realignment.* Even though dealignment is likely to be followed by realignment, and even may be a necessary condition for realignment, dealignment and realignment are different political phenomena.

The evidence is undeniable that the American electorate underwent a dealignment from 1964 to 1974. Fewer members of the electorate professed Democratic or Republican party loyalties, however measured, in the years after 1965 than during the preceding decade. Among partisans, fewer claimed to be strong Democrats or Republicans. Correspondingly more Americans said that they were independents or had no preference for a party. The percentage of the electorate without either Democratic or Republican party loyalties, measured as 100 percent minus the partisan totals, . . . consequently was about 10 percent higher in 1972–78 than it had been from 1952 to 1964. While both parties lost ground in this dealignment, the majority Democrats, with more to lose, suffered disproportionately more.

In the 1980s, there have been signs that this dealignment may be turning into a realignment. . . . [T]he partisan share of the electorate has grown (albeit slightly and unevenly) throughout the decade. This growth has favored the GOP. Ronald Reagan has figured prominently in this movement, as new high points of Republican loyalty were achieved in the immediate aftermath of each of his two election victories—26 percent in January 1981 and 30 percent in December 1984 and January 1985 in the Times/CBS poll. . . .

Other evidence of Republican partisan gains has surfaced in some, but by no means all, of the states. Interviews with voters as they were exiting the polls on election day in 1980 and 1984 show Republican gains and Democratic losses of party identifiers in eight of nine pivotal states (California, Connecticut, Illinois, Michigan, New Jersey, New York, Pennsylvania, and Texas) and Democratic losses with no corresponding GOP gains in a ninth (Ohio). The Republican surge was particularly large in Texas, and the results of statewide polling show similarly handsome GOP gains in Florida.

A similar story of Republican gains, although even less uniform, is told by changes in party registration figures. Of the twenty-five states that reported such declarations in both 1980 and 1986, the net GOP share of registered voters grew in fifteen; the net Democratic share grew in only five. . . .

Over the longer 1972–86 period, the number of states with Republican gains (13) is almost equaled by the number with Democratic gains (9), but again the largest state gains benefited the Republicans. The largest Democratic net increase, a total of 13 percent in Maine, was exceeded by Republican increases in six states: Arizona (14 percent), Florida (20 percent), Louisiana (29 percent), Nevada (18 percent), Oklahoma (16 percent), and Wyoming (21 percent). Except for Arizona, where 1980 party registration figures were not available, these states were leaders in Republican growth in the most recent period as well.

The most auspicious signs of realignment, though, came around the time of the 1984 election. Not only did Ronald Reagan appear to be the first Republican presidential candidate in over fifty years to outpoll his Democratic opponent among voters under thirty years of age, but these young voters also were more likely to claim Republican than Democratic party loyalties, again for the first time in over fifty years.

In the last realignment of the American party system, the New Deal realignment of the 1930s, new voters led the way. The Democrats were successful in mobilizing into their partisan ranks overwhelmingly disproportionate numbers of young people, who had just attained voting age, and of older citizens who had not been induced to participate in previous contests. So important was this skewed mobilization for the creation of the new Democratic majority that some scholars have concluded that new voters, most of whom are young, hold the key to prospects for enduring party shifts. Lacking previous experience with electoral politics, they are more open to party recruitment and to the retention of their new loyalties for the remainder of their lives. Older voters, by contrast, may defect to opposition candidates favored by contemporary forces, but they typically return to their old habits in succeeding elections. Therefore, the recent change in the partisan behavior of young adults is especially auspicious for the GOP.

Yet alongside these indicators of Republican party ascendancy are others that signal caution in trumpeting a realignment. Most ominous for the Republicans is the fact that elected officials beyond the White House remain predominantly Democratic in 1987 and 1988 . . . in spite of the party's resurgence in recent years. The Democrats still hold about 60 percent of the legislative seats at the state and national levels. Even Republican control of the Senate from 1981 through 1986, exceeding two years for the first time since the New Deal realignment, was broken in the 1986 elections.

The Republican failure to penetrate below the presidential level has been must conspicuous in the South, where Republican presidential success has been most notable. At the beginning of 1987, as has been true for more than a century, southern state legislatures were dominated by Democrats. The greatest GOP representation in either chamber of the eleven southern states was a feeble 37 percent in Tennessee's lower house. Moreover, Republicans held only 39 of 116 southern seats in the U.S. House of Representatives and 6 of 22 southern seats in the U.S. Senate. The only bright spot for the GOP in the South after the 1986 elections was that five of the eleven states now had Republican governors. What kind of realignment leaves so little imprint beyond the presidential level?

By contrast, the shock waves of previous realignments have quickly reverberated throughout the nation. Signs of the New Deal realignment, for example, appeared in congressional elections even before Roosevelt's 1932 presidential victory. In the pre-realignment 71st Congress, elected in 1928, both houses were comfortably under Republican control. By the time the dust had settled after the onset of the depression of 1929 and the Roosevelt victory in 1932, these Republican majorities had been dramatically overturned. The party lost 150 House and 21 Senate seats in the 1930 and 1932 elections! Republican ranks were thinned even further in the next two elections, which left the party with only 89 of 433 seats in the lower chamber and 16 of 96 seats in the Senate during the 75th Congress, elected in 1936.

The New Deal realignment did not sweep as quickly through state politics as previous realignments had. Even so, the 1930 elections destroyed the Republican majority in governors (which they held by a margin of 30 to 18, with most of the Democrats from the South, on the eve of the elections). By 1935 only nine Republicans occupied the governor's mansions in the forty-eight states. There are no reliable data on party loyalties from that period, but party registration figures changed abruptly in many locales in the early 1930s, and by the 1940s, the Democratic party could claim more loyalists than the GOP— undoubtedly just the reverse of the situation in the 1920s.

By the standards of previous realignments, then, the 1980s fail to qualify as a realigning era. The curious dissonance in recent years between pro-Republican presidential preferences and pro-Democratic voting for Congress and in the states signifies instead an electorate that has failed to generalize its support for Republican presidential candidates and its loss of confidence in the Democratic party into broader support for the Republican party. Recent presidential coalitions, in short, are not party coalitions. Furthermore, even though the GOP can claim more self-identified party loyalists than it has enjoyed in decades, its gains remain marginal and leave the party still somewhat short of the Democratic totals. Because these gains have been based on Democratic losses and short-term rallies to a popular President, they also seem highly fragile.

Some scholars, though, have concluded that the United States has experienced a pro-Republican realignment in recent years. But theirs is a realignment devoid of meaning, based on partisan loyalties that cannot hold together across elections and thereby cease to serve as enduring guides to voting behavior. Surely no realignment has occurred if it is based on new "reconstructed parti-sans" who do not follow up their Republican presidential preferences by sup-porting candidates of the same party for other offices. Partisanship is a loyalty to a party, not to a candidate, and as such should serve as an enduring guide to voting behavior. If the politics of the 1980s greatly diminishes its role, then it is a politics of dealignment rather than realignment.

What we have as the Reagan years draw to a close is an incomplete re-alignment—some movement toward Republican ascendancy, but no consoli-dation of this movement by Republican successes beyond the presidential level or in enduring partisan loyalties. That such a process has begun surely is heart-ening to GOP stalwarts. It has given their party powerful momentum, as im-portant in politics as it is in sports. That the process has not yet culminated in a pro-GOP realignment when temporary conditions have been so strongly in its favor (a popular President, a fractured opposition, no foreign policy catas-trophes, and real economic growth), though, does not augur well for the future of the GOP. Opportunities not seized in time may be foregone.

The principal Reagan legacy, then, is a Republican party that has recovered the ground it lost in the Watergate era and seems better positioned than at any time since the New Deal years to become the leading party in America's two-party system. Ronald Reagan's leadership, his skilled use of the opportunities provided a President for redefining political debate, is largely what has brought the GOP this far. In spite of his considerable efforts in behalf of his party, however, he has not been able to leave a more lasting imprint on the American party system. Perhaps there was not enough time for him to consolidate his party's position. Perhaps the absence of a traumatic event, something like the Great Depression, has contained the pressures for realignment-scale changes. Or perhaps, having rejected Democratic loyalties, many voters still cannot bring themselves to make a standing commitment to the GOP. Whatever the reason, it is now apparent that the Republican leaders who follow Reagan will not inherit a dominant party or a realigned party system. Instead, it will be up to them to fulfill—or break—the Reagan era promise of "an emerging Repub-lican majority."

In this continuing quest for realignment, the Republicans enjoy several important advantages. Their national party organization is far better financed and more resourceful in campaigning than that of the Democrats. This enables them to convert close races into victories and thereby make the most of their electoral base, but it does not much affect the size of this base. GOP candidates for the 1988 presidential nomination also are more familiar and experienced than their Democratic counterparts, which may prove more advantageous this time than it did a decade earlier when Washington "outsiders" proved popular. Finally, if the economy overcomes the recent Wall Street scares, a continuation of prosperity on its "watch" should continue to benefit the GOP.

Nonetheless, the prospects for fulfillment of the realignment that seems so near depend primarily, as they always do, on presidential leadership. Ronald Reagan has carried his party up to the brink of realignment. The Twenty-second Amendment to the Constitution, if not his age, prevents him from taking the GOP any further. If Franklin Roosevelt had been similarly limited from running for a third term in 1940 and had turned over the leadership of the Democrats to John Nance Garner, Henry Wallace, or Jim Farley, might not the New Deal realignment have been derailed?

So the prospects for an emerging Republican majority depend on the ability of Reagan's successors to hold together their party's presidential coalition and then to accomplish what eluded even Reagan—the extension of that coalition to other offices or its institutionalization in GOP party loyalties. At this time, these prospects do not seem bright. It is questionable that the party can find another leader with Ronald Reagan's ability to unite social and economic conservatives with moderates in presidential politics, much less erect a grand, majoritarian coalition. A leader who is less appealing to the party's various constituencies threatens its fragile electoral base. It also is doubtful, if only because of the normal twists and turns of fate, that the economic and foreign situations can remain so favorable to the GOP. Without a new Ronald Reagan and uninterrupted good fortune, the best bet for now is that the potential pro-Republican realignment will remain incomplete and that the dealignment-style politics that have characterized the past twenty years will continue.

Political Campaigning

The voice of the people is always heard in the electoral process, but it is not always clear exactly what the people have chosen. The candidates and their political consultants concentrate upon the projection of images rather than on the serious discussion of public issues. The media, interested in gaining as wide an audience as possible, encourage candidates to be brief in the presentation of their programs and to act with an eye to what is newsworthy in the view of television producers and newspaper editors. A maze confronts the electorate, which must be able to peer through the smoke screen of electoral politics in order to be able to vote intelligently. The following selection, from Key's oft-quoted book, *The Responsible Electorate*, argues that voters are not the fools that many politicians and their advisers often take them to be. The electorate, concludes the author, "behaves about as rationally and responsibly as we should expect, given the clarity of the alternatives presented to it and the character of the information available to it."

28

V. O. Key, Jr.
THE VOICE OF THE PEOPLE:
AN ECHO

In his reflective moments even the most experienced politician senses a nagging curiosity about why people vote as they do. His power and his position depend upon the outcome of the mysterious rites we perform as opposing candidates harangue the multitudes who finally march to the polls to prolong the rule of their champion, to thrust him, ungratefully, back into the void of private life, or to raise to eminence a new tribune of the people. What kinds of appeals enable a candidate to win the favor of the great god, The People? What circumstances move voters to shift their preferences in this direction or that? What clever propaganda tactic or slogan led to this result? What mannerism of oratory or style of rhetoric produced another outcome? What band of electors rallied to this candidate to save the day for him? What policy of state attracted the devotion of another bloc of voters? What action repelled a third sector of the electorate?

The victorious candidate may claim with assurance that he has the answers to all such questions. He may regard his success as vindication of his beliefs about why voters vote as they do. And he may regard the swing of the vote to him as indubitably a response to the campaign positions he took, as an indication of the acuteness of his intuitive estimates of the mood of the people, and as a ringing manifestation of the esteem in which he is held by a discriminating public. This narcissism assumes its most repulsive form among election winners who have championed intolerance, who have stirred the passions and hatreds of people, or who have advocated causes known by decent men to be outrageous or dangerous in their long-run consequences. No functionary is more repugnant or more arrogant than the unjust man who asserts, with a color of truth, that he speaks from a pedestal of popular approbation.

It thus can be a mischievous error to assume, because a candidate wins, that a majority of the electorate shares his views on public questions, approves his past actions, or has specific expectations about his future conduct. Nor does victory establish that the candidate's campaign strategy, his image, his television style, or his fearless stand against cancer and polio turned the trick. The election

From V.O. Key, Jr., *The Responsible Electorate* (Cambridge, Mass.: Belknap Press of Harvard Univ. Press, 1966), pp. 1–8. Reprinted by permission.

returns establish only that a winner attracted a majority of votes—assuming the existence of a modicum of rectitude in election administration. They tell us precious little about why the plurality was his.

For a glaringly obvious reason, electoral victory cannot be regarded as necessarily a popular ratification of a candidate's outlook. The voice of the people is but an echo. The output of an echo chamber bears an inevitable and invariable relation to the input. As candidates and parties clamor for attention and vie for popular support, the people's verdict can be no more than a selective reflection from among the alternatives and outlooks presented to them. Even the most discriminating popular judgment can reflect only ambiguity, uncertainty, or even foolishness if those are the qualities of the input into the echo chamber. A candidate may win despite his tactics and appeals rather than because of them. If the people can choose only from among rascals, they are certain to choose a rascal.

Scholars, though they have less at stake than do politicians, also have an abiding curiosity about why voters act as they do. In the past quarter of a century they have vastly enlarged their capacity to check the hunches born of their curiosities. The invention of the sample survey—the most widely known example of which is the Gallup poll—enabled them to make fairly trustworthy estimates of the characteristics and behaviors of large human populations. This method of mass observation revolutionized the study of politics—as well as the management of political campaigns. The new technique permitted large-scale tests to check the validity of old psychological and sociological theories of human behavior. These tests led to new hunches and new theories about voting behavior, which could in turn, be checked and which thereby contributed to the extraordinary ferment in the social sciences during recent decades.

The studies of electoral behavior by survey methods cumulate into an imposing body of knowledge which conveys a vivid impression of the variety and subtlety of factors that enter into individual voting decisions. In their first stages in the 1930s the new electoral studies chiefly lent precision and verification to the working maxims of practicing politicians and to some of the crude theories of political speculators. Thus, sample surveys established that people did, indeed, appear to vote their pocketbooks. Yet the demonstration created its embarrassments because it also established that exceptions to the rule were numerous. Not all factory workers, for example, voted alike. How was the behavior of the deviants from "group interest" to be explained? Refinement after refinement of theory and analysis added complexity to the original simple explanation. By introducing a bit of psychological theory it could be demonstated that factory workers with optimistic expectations tended less to be governed by pocketbook considerations than did those whose outlook was gloomy. When a little social psychology was stirred into the analysis, it could be established that identifications formed early in life, such as attachments to political parties, also reinforced or resisted the pull of the interest of the moment. A sociologist, bringing to play the conceptual tools of his trade, then could show that those factory workers who associate intimately with like-minded persons on the average vote with greater solidarity than do social isolates. Inquiries conducted with great ingenuity along many such lines have enormously broadened our knowledge of the factors associated with the responses of people to the stimuli presented to them by political campaigns.

Yet, by and large, the picture of the voter that emerges from a combination of the folklore of practical politics and the findings of the new electoral studies is not a pretty one. It is not a portrait of citizens moving to considered decision as they play their solemn role of making and unmaking governments. The older tradition from practical politics may regard the voter as an erratic and irrational fellow susceptible to manipulation by skilled humbugs. One need not live through many campaigns to observe politicians, even successful politicians, who act as though they regarded the people as manageable fools. Nor does a heroic conception of the voter emerge from the new analyses of electoral behavior. They can be added up to a conception of voting not as a civic decision but as an almost purely deterministic act. Given knowledge of certain characteristics of a voter—his occupation, his residence, his religion, his national origin, and perhaps certain of his attitudes—one can predict with a high probability the direction of his vote. The actions of persons are made to appear to be only predictable and automatic responses to campaign stimuli.

Most findings of the analysts of voting never travel beyond the circle of the technicians; the popularizers, though, give wide currency to the most bizarre—and most dubious—theories of electoral behavior. Public-relations experts share in the process of dissemination as they sell their services to politicians (and succeed in establishing that politicians are sometimes as gullible as businessmen). Reporters pick up the latest psychological secret from campaign managers and spread it through a larger public. Thus, at one time a goodly proportion of the literate population must have placed some store in the theory that the electorate was a pushover for a candidate who projected an appropriate "father image." At another stage, the "sincere" candidate supposedly had an overwhelming advantage. And even so kindly a gentleman as General Eisenhower was said to have an especial attractiveness to those of authoritarian personality within the electorate.

Conceptions and theories of the way voters behave do not raise solely arcane problems to be disputed among the democratic and antidemocratic theorists or questions to be settled by the elegant techniques of the analysts of electoral behavior. Rather, they touch upon profound issues at the heart of the problem of the nature and workability of systems of popular government. Obviously the perceptions of the behavior of the electorate held by political leaders, agitators, and activists condition if they do not fix, the types of appeals politicans employ as they seek popular support. These perceptions—or theories—affect the nature of the input to the echo chamber, if we may revert to our earlier figure, and thereby control its output. They may govern, too, the kinds of actions that governments take as they look forward to the next election.

If politicians perceive the electorate as responsive to father images, they will give it father images. If they see voters as most certainly responsive to nonsense, they will give them nonsense. If they see voters as susceptible to delusion, they will delude them. If they see an electorate receptive to the cold, hard realities, they will give it the cold, hard realities.

In short, theories of how voters behave acquire importance not because of their effects on voters, who may proceed blithely unaware of them. They gain significance because of their effects, both potentially and in reality, on candidates and other political leaders. If leaders believe the route to victory is by projection of images and cultivation of styles rather than by advocacy of policies to cope with the problems of the country, they will project images and cultivate styles to the neglect of the substance of politics. They will abdicate their prime function in a democratic system, which amounts, in essence, to the assumption of the risk of trying to persuade us to lift ourselves by our bootstraps.

Among the literary experts on politics there are those who contend that, because of the development of tricks for the manipulation of the masses, practices of political leadership in the management of voters have moved far toward the conversion of election campaigns into obscene parodies of the models set up by democratic idealists. They point to the good old days when politicans were deep thinkers, eloquent orators, and farsighted statemen. Such estimates of the course of change in social institutions must be regarded with reserve. They may be only manifestations of the inverted optimism of aged and melancholy men who, estopped from hope for the future, see in the past a satisfaction of their yearning for greatness in our political life.

Whatever the trends may have been, the perceptions that leadership elements of democracies hold of the modes of response of the electorate must always be a matter of fundamental significance. Those perceptions determine the nature of the voice of the people, for they determine the character of the input into the echo chamber. While the output may be governed by the nature of the input, over the longer run the properties of the echo chamber may themselves be altered. Fed a steady diet of buncombe, the people may come to expect and to respond with highest predictability to buncombe. And those leaders most skilled in the propagation of buncombe may gain lasting advantage in the recurring struggles for popular favor.

[My] perverse and unorthodox argument . . . is that voters are not fools. To be sure, many individual voters act in odd ways indeed; yet in the large the electorate behaves about as rationally and responsibly as we should expect, given the clarity of the alternatives presented to it and the character of the information available to it. In American presidential campaigns of recent decades the portrait of the American electorate that develops from the data is not one of an electorate straitjacketed by social determinants or moved by subconscious urges triggered by devilishly skillful propagandists. It is rather one of an electorate moved by concern about central and relevant questions of public policy, of governmental performance, and of executive personality. Propositions so uncompromisingly stated inevitably represent overstatements. Yet to the extent that they can be shown to resemble the reality, they are propositions of basic importance for both the theory and the practice of democracy. . . .

❖❖   The late V. O. Key, Jr., suggested in the previous selection that the voice of the people is not capable of being manipulated by skillful politicians, nor is it apathetic. Rather, his sanguine view was that individuals are indeed aware of government decisions affecting their lives and are capable of rendering rational judgments on the actions of political leaders. At the same time, Key pointed out that voter rationality depends upon the rationality of political campaigns, although he argued that in many instances voters are clever enough to see through political propaganda. Joe McGinniss described in his book *The Selling of the President 1968* how public-relations experts and political propagandists view the electorate and also demonstrated how these views affected the management of President Nixon's campaign in 1968. Readers should ask themselves how a rational democratic electorate can be maintained if the political leadership holds voters in such low esteem.

29

Joe McGinniss
THE SELLING OF THE
PRESIDENT 1968

Politics, in a sense, has always been a con game.

The American voter, insisting upon his belief in a higher order, clings to his religion, which promises another, better life; and defends passionately the illusion that the men he chooses to lead him are of finer nature than he.

It has been traditional that the successful politician honor this illusion. To succeed today, he must embellish it. Particularly if he wants to be President.

"Potential presidents are measured against an ideal that's a combination of leading man, God, father, hero, pope, king, with maybe just a touch of the avenging Furies thrown in," an adviser to Richard Nixon wrote in a memorandum late in 1967. Then, perhaps aware that Nixon qualified only as father, he discussed improvements that would have to be made—not upon Nixon himself, but upon the image of him which was received by the voter.

That there is a difference between the individual and his image is human nature. Or American nature, at least. That the difference is exaggerated and exploited electronically is the reason for this book.

Advertising, in many ways, is a con game, too. Human beings do not need new automobiles every third year; a color television set brings little enrichment of the human experience; a higher or lower hemline no expansion of consciousness, no increase in the capacity to love.

It is not suprising, then, that politicians and advertising men should have discovered one another. And, once they recognized that the citizen did not so much vote for a candidate as make a psychological purchase of him, not surprising that they began to work together.

The voter, as reluctant to face political reality as any other kind, was hardly an unwilling victim. "The deeper problems connected with advertising," Daniel Boorstin has written in the *The Image*, "come less from the unscrupulousness of our 'deceivers' than from our pleasure in being deceived, less from the desire to seduce than from the desire to be seduced. . . .

"In the last half-century we have misled ourselves . . . about men . . . and how much greatness can be found among them. . . . We have become so ac-

From Joe McGinniss, *The Selling of the President 1968*, Chapter 2. Copyright © 1969, by Joemac, Inc. Reprinted by permission of Simon & Schuster, Inc.

customed to our illusions that we mistake them for reality. We demand them. And we demand that there be always more of them, bigger and better and more vivid."

The presidency seems the ultimate extension of our error.

Advertising agencies have tried openly to sell presidents since 1952. When Dwight Eisenhower ran for reelection in 1956, the agency of Batton, Barton, Durstine and Osborn, which had been on a retainer throughout his first four years, accepted his campaign as a regular account. Leonard Hall, national Republican chairman, said: "You sell your candidates and your programs the way a business sells its products."

The only change over the past twelve years has been that, as technical sophistication has increased, so has circumspection. The ad men were removed from the parlor but were given a suite upstairs.

What Boorstin says of advertising: "It has meant a reshaping of our very concept of truth," is particularly true of advertising on TV.

With the coming of television, and the knowledge of how it could be used to seduce voters, the old political values disappeared. Something new, murky, undefined started to rise from the mists. "In all countries," Marshall McLuhan writes, "the party system has folded like the organization chart. Policies and issues are useless for election purposes, since they are too specialized and hot. The shaping of a candidate's integral image has taken the place of discussing conflicting points of view."

Americans have never quite digested television. The mystique which should fade grows stronger. We make celebrities not only of the men who cause events but of the men who read reports of them aloud.

The televised image can become as real to the housewife as her husband, and much more attractive. Hugh Downs is a better breakfast companion, Merv Griffin cozier to snuggle with on the couch.

Television, in fact, has given status to the "celebrity" which few real men attain. And the "celebrity" here is the one described by Boorstin: "Neither good nor bad, great nor petty . . . the human pseudoevent . . . fabricated on purpose to satisfy our exaggerated expectations of human greatness."

This is, perhaps, where the twentieth century and its pursuit of illusion have been leading us. "In the last half-century," Boorstin writes, "the old heroic human mold has been broken. A new mold has been made, so that marketable human models—modern 'heroes'—could be mass-produced, to satisfy the market, and without any hitches. The qualities which now commonly make a man or woman into a 'nationally advertised' brand are in fact a new category of human emptiness."

The television celebrity is a vessel. An inoffensive container in which someone else's knowledge, insight, compassion, or wit can be presented. And we respond like the child on Christmas morning who ignores the gift to play with the wrapping paper.

Television seems particularly useful to the politician who can be charming but lacks ideas. Print is for ideas. Newspapermen write not about people but policies; the paragraphs can be slid around like blocks. Everyone is colored gray. Columnists—and commentators in the more polysyllabic magazines—concentrate on ideology. They do not care what a man sounds like; only how he thinks. For the candidate who does not, such exposure can be embarrassing. He needs another way to reach the people.

On television it matters less that he does not have ideas. His personality is what the viewers want to share. He need be neither statesman nor crusader, he must only show up on time. Success and failure are easily measured: How often is he invited back? Often enough and he reaches his goal—to advance from "politician" to "celebrity," a status jump bestowed by grateful viewers who feel that finally they have been given the basis for making a choice.

The TV candidate, then, is measured not against his predecessors—not against a standard of performance established by two centuries of democracy—but against Mike Douglas. How well does he handle himself? Does he mumble, does he twitch, does he make me laugh? Do I feel warm inside?

Style becomes substance. The medium is the massage and the masseur gets the votes.

In office, too, the ability to project electronically is essential. We were willing to forgive John Kennedy his Bay of Pigs; we followed without question the perilous course on which he led us when missiles were found in Cuba; we even tolerated his calling of reserves for the sake of a bluff about Berlin.

We forgave, followed, and accepted because we liked the way he looked. And he had a pretty wife. Camelot was fun, even for the peasants, as long as it was televised to their huts.

Then came Lyndon Johnson, heavy and gross, and he was forgiven nothing. He might have survived the sniping of the displaced intellectuals had he only been able to charm. But no one taught him how. Johnson was syrupy. He stuck to the lens. There was no place for him in our culture.

"The success of any TV performer depends on his achieving a low-pressure style of presentation," McLuhan has written. The harder a man tries, the better he must hide it. Television demands gentle wit, irony, understatement: the qualities of Eugene McCarthy. The TV politician cannot make a speech; he must engage in intimate conversation. He must never press. He should suggest, not state; request, not demand. Nonchalance is the key word. Carefully studied nonchalance.

Warmth and sincerity are desirable but must be handled with care. Unfiltered, they can be fatal. Television did great harm to Hubert Humphrey. His excesses—talking too long and too fervently, which were merely annoying in an auditorium—became lethal in a television studio. The performer must talk to one person at a time. He is brought into the living room. He is a guest. It is improper for him to shout. Humphrey vomited on the rug.

It would be extremely unwise for the TV politician to admit such knowledge of his medium. The necessary nonchalance should carry beyond his appearance while *on* the show; it should rule his attitude *toward* it. He should express distaste for television; suspicion that there is something "phony" about it. This guarantees him good press, because newspaper reporters, bitter over their loss of prestige to the television men, are certain to stress anti-television remarks. Thus, the sophisticated candidate, while analyzing his own on-the-air technique as carefully as a golf pro studies his swing, will state frequently that there is no place for "public relations gimmicks" or "those show business guys" in his campaign. Most of the television men working for him will be unbothered by such remarks. They are willing to accept anonymity, even scorn, as long as the pay is good.

Into this milieu came Richard Nixon: grumpy, cold, and aloof. He would claim privately that he lost elections because the American voter was an adolescent whom he tried to treat as an adult. Perhaps. But if he treated the voter as an adult, it was as an adult he did not want for a neighbor.

This might have been excused had he been a man of genuine vision. An explorer of the spirit. Martin Luther King, for instance, got by without being one of the boys. But Richard Nixon did not strike people that way. He had, in Richard Rovere's words, "an advertising man's approach to his work," acting as if he believed "policies [were] products to be sold the public—this one today, that one tomorrow, depending on the discounts and the state of the market."

So his enemies had him on two counts: his personality, and the convictions—or lack of such—which lay behind. They worked him over heavily on both.

Norman Mailer remembered him as "a church usher, of the variety who would twist a boy's ear after removing him from church."

McLuhan watched him debate Kennedy and thought he resembled "the railway lawyer who signs leases that are not in the best interests of the folks in the little town."

But Nixon survived, despite his flaws, because he was tough and smart, and—some said—dirty when he had to be. Also, because there was nothing else he knew. A man to whom politics is all there is in life will almost always beat one to whom it is only an occupation.

He nearly became President in 1960, and that year it would not have been by default. He failed because he was too few of the things a President had to be—and because he had no press to lie for him and did not know how to use television to lie about himself.

It was just Nixon and John Kennedy and they sat down together in a television studio and a little red light began to glow and Richard Nixon was finished. Television would be blamed but for all the wrong reasons.

They would say it was makeup and lighting, but Nixon's problem went deeper than that. His problem was himself. Not what he said but the man he was. The camera portrayed him clearly. America took its Richard Nixon straight and did not like the taste.

The content of the programs made little difference. Except for startling lapses, content seldom does. What mattered was the image the viewers received, though few observers at the time caught the point.

McLuhan read Theodore White's *The Making of the President* book and was appalled at the section on the debates. "White offers statistics on the number of sets in American homes and the number of hours of daily use of these sets, but not one clue as to the nature of the TV image or its effects on candidates or viewers. White considers the 'content' of the debates and the deportment of the debaters, but it never occurs to him to ask why TV would inevitably be a disaster for a sharp intense image like Nixon's and a boon for the blurry, shaggy texture of Kennedy." In McLuhan's opinion: "Without TV, Nixon had it made."

What the camera showed was Richard Nixon's hunger. He lost, and bitter, confused, he blamed it on his beard.

He made another, lesser thrust in 1962, and that failed, too. He showed the world a little piece of his heart the morning after and then he moved East to brood. They did not want him, the hell with them. He was going to Wall Street and get rich.

He was afraid of television. He knew his soul was hard to find. Beyond that, he considered it a gimmick; its use in politics offended him. It had not been part of the game when he had learned to play, he could see no reason to bring it in now. He half suspected it was an eastern liberal trick: one more way to make him look silly. It offended his sense of dignity, one of the truest senses he had.

So his decision to use it to become President in 1968 was not easy. So much of him argued against it. But in his Wall Street years, Richard Nixon had traveled to the darkest places inside himself and come back numbed. He was, as in the Graham Greene title, a burnt-out case. All feeling was behind him; the machine inside had proved his hardiest part. He would run for President again and if he would have to learn television to run well, then he would learn it.

America still saw him as the 1960 Nixon. If he were to come at the people again, as candidate, it would have to be as something new; not this scarred, discarded figure from their past.

He spoke to men who thought him mellowed. They detected growth, a new stability, a sense of direction that had been lacking. He would return with fresh perspective, a more unselfish urgency.

His problem was how to let the nation know. He could not do it through the press. He knew what to expect from them, which was the same as he had always gotten. He would have to circumvent them. Distract them with coffee and doughnuts and smiles from his staff and tell his story another way.

Television was the only answer, despite its sins against him in the past. But not just any kind of television. An uncommitted camera could do irreparable harm. His television would have to be controlled. He would need experts. They would have to find the proper settings for him, or if they could not be found, manufacture them. These would have to be men of keen judgment and flawless taste. He was, after all, Richard Nixon, and there were certain things he could not do. Wearing love beads was one. He would need men of dignity. Who believed in him and shared his vision. But more importantly, men who knew television as a weapon: from broadest concept to most technical detail. This would be Richard Nixon, the leader, returning from exile. Perhaps not beloved, but respected. Firm but not harsh; just but compassionate. With flashes of warmth spaced evenly throughout.

Nixon gathered about himself a group of young men attuned to the political uses of television. They arrived at his side by different routes. One, William Gavin, was a thirty-one-year-old English teacher in a suburban high school outside Philadelphia in 1967, when he wrote Richard Nixon a letter urging him to run for President and base his campaign on TV. Gavin wrote on stationery borrowed from the University of Pennsylvania because he thought Nixon would pay more attention if the letter seemed to be from a college professor.

Dear Mr. Nixon:
  May I offer two suggestions concerning your plans for 1968?
  1. Run. You can win. Nothing can happen to you, politically speaking, that is worse than what has happened to you. Ortega y Gasset in his *The Revolt of the Masses* says: "These ideas are the only genuine ideas: the ideas of the shipwrecked. All the rest is rhetoric, posturing, farce. He who does not really feel himself lost, is lost without remission . . . " You, in effect, are "lost"; that is why you are the only political figure with a vision to see things the way they are and not as Leftist or Rightist kooks would have them be. Run. You will win.
  2. A tip for television: instead of those wooden performances beloved by politicians, instead of a glamorboy technique, instead of safety, be bold. Why not have live press conferences as your campaign on television? People will see you daring all, asking and answering questions from reporters, and not simply answering phony "questions" made up by your staff. This would be dynamic; it would be daring. Instead of the medium using you, you would be using the medium. Go on "live" and risk all. It is the only way to convince people of the truth: that you are beyond rhetoric, that you can face reality, unlike your opponents, who will rely on public relations. Television hurt you because you were not yourself; it didn't hurt the "real" Nixon. The real Nixon can revolutionize the use of television by dynamically going "live" and answering everything, the loaded and the unloaded question. Invite your opponents to this kind of a debate.
  Good luck, and I know you can win if you see yourself for what you are; a man who had been beaten, humiliated, hated, but who can still see the truth.

A Nixon staff member had lunch with Gavin a couple of times after the letter was received and hired him.

William Gavin was brought to the White House as a speech writer in January of 1969.

Harry Treleaven, hired as creative director of advertising in the fall of 1967, immediately went to work on the more serious of Nixon's personality problems. One was his lack of humor.

"Can be corrected to a degree," Treleaven wrote, "but let's not be too obvious about it. Romney's cornball attempts have hurt him. If we're going to be witty, let a pro write the words."

Treleaven also worried about Nixon's lack of warmth, but decided that "he can be helped greatly in this respect by how he is handled. . . . Give him words to say that will show his *emotional* involvement in the issues. . . . Buchanan wrote about RFK talking about the starving children in Recife. *That's* what we have to inject. . . .

"He should be presented in some kind of 'situation' rather than cold in a studio. The situation should look unstaged even if it's not."

Some of the most effective ideas belonged to Raymond K. Price, a former editorial writer for the *New York Herald Tribune*, who became Nixon's best and most prominent speech writer in the campaign. Price later composed much of the inaugural address.

In 1967, he began with the assumption that, "The natural human use of reason is to support prejudice, not to arrive at opinions." Which led to the conclusion that rational arguments would "only be effective if we can get the people to make the *emotional* leap, or what theologians call [the] 'leap of faith.' "

Price suggested attacking the "personal factors" rather than the "historical factors" which were the basis of the low opinion so many people had of Richard Nixon.

"These tend to be more a gut reaction," Price wrote, "unarticulated, non-analytical, a product of the particular chemistry between the voter and the *image* of the candidate. *We have to be very clear on this point: that the response is to the image, not to the man.* . . . It's not what's *there* that counts, it's what's projected—and carrying it one step further, it's not what *he* projects but rather what the voter receives. It's not the man we have to change, but rather the *received impression.* And this impression often depends more on the medium and its use than it does on the candidate himself."

So there would not have to be a "new Nixon." Simply a new approach to television.

"What, then, does this mean in terms of our uses of time and of media?" Price wrote.

"For one thing, it means investing whatever time RN needs in order to work out firmly in his own mind that vision of the nation's future that he wants to be identified with. This is crucial. . . . "

So, at the age of fifty-four, after twenty years in public life, Richard Nixon was still felt *by his own staff* to be in need of time to "work out firmly in his own mind that vision of the nation's future that he wants to be identified with."

"Secondly," Price wrote, "it suggests that we take the time and the money to experiment, in a controlled manner, with film and television techniques, with particular emphasis on pinpointing those *controlled* uses of the television medium that can *best* convey the *image* we want to get across. . . .

"The TV medium itself introduces an element of distortion, in terms of its effect on the candidate and of the often subliminal ways in which the image is received. And it inevitably is going to convey a partial image—thus ours is the task of finding how to control its use so the part that gets across is the part we want to have gotten across. . . .

"Voters are basically lazy, basically uninterested in making an *effort* to understand what we're talking about . . . ," Price wrote. "Reason requires a high degree of discipline, of concentration; impression is easier. Reason pushes the viewer back, it assaults him, it demands that he agree or disagree; impression can envelop him, invite him in, without making an intellectual demand. . . . When we argue with him we demand that he make the effort of replying. We seek to engage his intellect, and for most people this is the most difficult work of all. The emotions are more easily roused, closer to the surface, more malleable. . . . "

So, for the New Hampshire primary, Price recommended "saturation with a film, in which the candidate can be shown better than he can be shown in person because it can be edited, so only the best moments are shown; then a quick parading of the candidate in the flesh so that the guy they've gotten intimately acquainted with on the screen takes on a living presence—not saying anything, just being seen. . . .

"[Nixon] has to come across as a person larger than life, the stuff of legend. People are stirred by the legend, including the living legend, not by the man himself. It's the aura that surrounds the charismatic figure more than it is the figure itself, that draws the followers. Our task is to build that aura. . . .

"So let's not be afraid of television gimmicks . . . get the voters to like the guy and the battle's two-thirds won."

So this was how they went into it. Trying, with one hand, to build the illusion that Richard Nixon, in addition to his attributes of mind and heart, considered, in the words of Patrick J. Buchanan, a speech writer, "communicating with the people . . . one of the great joys of seeking the Presidency"; while with the other they shielded him, controlled him, and controlled the atmosphere around him. It was as if they were building not a President but an Astrodome, where the wind would never blow, the temperature never rise or fall, and the ball never bounce erratically on the artificial grass.

They could do this, and succeed, because of the special nature of the man. There was, apparently, something in Richard Nixon's character which sought this shelter. Something which craved regulation, which flourished best in the darkness, behind clichés, behind phalanxes of antiseptic advisers. Some part of him that could breathe freely only inside a hotel suite that cost a hundred dollars a day.

And it worked. As he moved serenely through his primary campaign, there was new cadence to Richard Nixon's speech and motion; new confidence in his heart. And, a new image of him on the television screen.

TV both reflected and contributed to his strength. Because he was winning he looked like a winner on the screen. Because he was suddenly projecting well on the medium he had feared, he went about his other tasks with assurance. The one fed upon the other, building to an astonishing peak in August as the Republican convention began and he emerged from his regal isolation, traveling to Miami not so much to be nominated as coronated. On live, but controlled, TV.

❖❖ The entrance of the professional public-relations person into politics, the extensive use of television to "sell" the candidate, all of which began in 1952, has changed the landscape of presidential politics. The advertising of presidential candidates has changed little over the years, because their public-relations advisers basically take the same approach to the campaign and the electorate. The images of candidates are to be shaped to optimize their appeal to the voters. The loss of elections is now blamed as much on media advisers as on the candidates and their public policy stances. Joe McGinniss, in the preceding selection, puts this idea in its most cynical form in his comment on President Nixon's campaign in 1960: "He nearly became President in 1960, and that year it would not have been by default. He failed because he was too few of the things that a President had to be— and because he had no press to lie for him and did not know how to use television to lie about himself." Nixon's defeat in 1960 is often said to have been caused by deficiencies in his popular image, including his *physical* appearance in the first television debate with John F. Kennedy. Thus, his television advisers in 1968 were very careful to structure the television environment in such a way as to project a favorable Nixon image.

The McGinniss description of the 1968 election could, with very few changes, have been applied to later presidential elections. The candidates were different, but the public-relations advisers took the same approach to selling them to the public. On the whole, the emphasis was on *images*, not issues. One seeks in vain through the verbiage of presidential campaigns to find many concrete statements on public policy. And, as is always the case, what public issues were highlighted were largely selected on the basis of their supposed appeal to the electorate.

Public relations continued to dominate presidential campaigning in 1988. Republican George Bush defeated Democrat Michael Dukakis by a popular vote margin of 54–46 percent and an electoral college sweep of 426–112 votes. Political consultants and media advisors for both candidates, but particularly in the Bush camp, pushed major public policy issues to the background as they concentrated upon images. Bush's advisors tried to portray their candidate as a political Clint Eastwood, "a read-my-lips" man who would not tolerate crime or new taxes. At the same time they attacked the "liberal governor from Massachusetts," virtually accusing him of being unpatriotic because of his opposition to the Pledge of Allegiance, and soft on crime, because of the Massachusetts furlough program under which a particularly notorious criminal, Willy Horton, had been released only to commit yet another heinous crime. Dukakis was put on the defensive from the outset of his campaign and never recovered.

An American Enterprise Institute scholar who closely follows elections analyzes the 1988 presidential campaign in the following selection. He advises candidates in the future to pay attention to issues, particularly those that might help to unite their loosely-knit parties.

30

William Schneider
TOUGH LIBERALS WIN, WEAK LIBERALS LOSE

It could have been a lot worse, say Democrats. Michael Dukakis got 112 electorial votes. That's a 750 percent improvement over Walter Mondale! Dukakis's 46 percent of the popular vote is the highest losing percentage the Democrats have gotten since 1964. Not only that, but the Democrats gained Senate seats, House seats, state legislative seats, and a governorship. That is a rare achievement for a losing party in a presidential race. "Coattails?" observed Representative Patricia Schroeder. "Bush got elected in a bikini."

On the other hand, think of it this way: the Democrats lost to George Bush and Dan Quayle. Last year a Democratic senator quipped, "If we can't beat George Bush, we'd better find another country." Well, they didn't beat George Bush. But there's an election in Canada later this month.

From *The New Republic*, Dec. 5, 1988. Reprinted by permission.

How's this for an irony? Democrats used to wear buttons saying, "The gender gap will get you." The gender gap turned out to be slightly wider this year than it was in 1980 and 1984. In the last two elections, however, it didn't make any difference. Both men and women voted for Ronald Reagan. This year it made a difference. According to the exit polls, women were either evenly split or gave a slight edge to Dukakis. Men voted for Bush by a wide margin. In other words, men elected Bush. The gender gap got the Democrats.

Here are three explanations for what happened to the Democrats this year: (a) Dukakis lost because he ran a lousy campaign. Implication: If Dukakis had run a better campaign, or if the party had put up a better candidate, the Democrats would have won. Not to worry. (b) Dukakis lost because of peace and prosperity. Implication: The Democrats lose because they always seem to run at the wrong time (like every four years). Just wait for things to get really bad under the Bush administration. Not to worry. (c) Dukakis lost because the country doesn't want to buy what the Democrats have to sell. You just can't market liberalism these days. Implication: The Democrats can't win for the foreseeable future. Start worrying.

The correct answer is all three. The Dukakis campaign really didn't have anything to sell the voters. So it was forced to sell off Dukakis as a liberal. He was the first remaindered candidate in the history of American politics.

The Republicans knew from the outset that if the election were a referendum on Bush, they would lose. Bush just had too many negatives: the wimp image, his upperclass origins, his repeated lapses of judgment (Marcos, Noriega, Iran-*contra*, Quayle), and the normal desire for change after eight years. So the Republicans turned the election into a referendum on Dukakis. The central issue in the campaign became Dukakis's values instead of Bush's judgment. Bush called Dukakis a Massachusetts liberal. Dukakis had a hard time denying it. He *is* a Massachusetts liberal. It just wasn't anything he planned on talking about during the campaign.

The fact is, Michael Dukakis never had to defend his values before this year. Liberal values are not controversial in the Democratic Party. And they are no big deal in the Commonwealth of Massachusetts, where the Republican Party is a joke. Suddenly last summer, Dukakis came face to face with real Republicans. And like Sebastian Venable, he got eaten alive.

Bush used the Pledge of Allegiance and the "tank commercial" to convey the idea that Dukakis was weak on defense (with, perhaps, a subliminal message that a son of Greek immigrants was not a real American). Bush used the ACLU issue and the furlough ad to portray Dukakis as soft on crime (with, perhaps, a subliminal appeal to white racism). Dukakis's chosen theme of competence got sunk in Boston Harbor. How did Dukakis respond? By doing nothing. Which confirmed what Bush was saying: "I'm not the wimp. *He's* the wimp."

Dukakis thought he could win the presidency the same way he won the Democratic nomination—by being the "remainderman." During the primaries, he watched the other candidates either self-destruct (Hart, Biden) or destroy one another (Gephardt, Gore, Jackson). Dukakis just picked up the pieces and walked away with the nomination. He thought he could summer in the Berkshires and wait for George Bush to destroy himself.

In March, a week after Super Tuesday, when Dukakis won Florida and Texas, he came in an embarrassing third in Illinois. The next week Jesse Jackson beat him in Michigan. Everyone started screaming advice at Dukakis, but the governor refused to panic. He knew that if he stayed cool, he wasn't going to lose to Jesse Jackson. That's exactly how Dukakis responded when the same thing happened to him in August. After Bush went negative on Dukakis, Democrats started pressuring him to fight back. Dukakis remained cool. He had heard it all before. No one would believe those preposterous commercials anyway. "We used to read this stuff and laugh and say, 'How can this be? Why would people take this seriously?' " his chief secretary recalled to the *New York Times*.

If Dukakis refused to take Bush seriously enough, Bush took Dukakis far too seriously. His anti-Dukakis commercials had an ominous, threatening quality. Bush depicted the governor of Massachusetts as a menace to the republic. Over *Jaws*-like theme music, the ads closed with the line, "America can't afford that risk." It worked. Dukakis's unfavorable ratings doubled from 25 percent in July to 50 percent in October, according to the NBC News-*Wall Street Journal* poll. The view that Dukakis would do a better job than Bush of maintaining a strong national defense dropped by ten points. In July, Dukakis beat Bush, 40 percent to 24 percent, as the candidate who would be tougher on crime. By October, Bush was ahead, 56 percent to 27 percent. In June, 30 percent of the public labeled Dukakis a liberal. In October, the figure reached 51 percent.

Dukakis's great weakness was his total inability to sustain a theme. He started out with competence, until his campaign proved otherwise. Then he told people that the 17 million added jobs under Reagan were not "good jobs at good wages." How many people like to be told that their jobs stink? He ran television commercials talking about the nation's "sham prosperity." But to most people, sham prosperity is a lot better than what they had under Jimmy Carter.

Dukakis spent a week or so on the "middle-class squeeze," during which he came up with approximately one new program a day. In the second debate with Bush, he hit upon the worst theme of all. "Tough choices will be required," he told the nation, "choices I am prepared to make and Mr. Bush is not prepared to make." Bush said, "I am optimistic and I think we can keep this long expansion going." The American people were asked to choose between a candidate whose theme was "We're all right, Jack," and a candidate who said, "Eat your broccoli."

Finally, Mr. Competence became Mr. "On-Your-Side." We got a dash of Gephardt nationalism and some warmed-over Mondale populism. The Dukakis campaign could never decide what it wanted to sell. So the Republicans took over the marketing. "Even though [Dukakis] avoided the interest group endorsements," a GOP strategist told the *Los Angeles Times*, "we were able to define him as a liberal because he did not have any overall theme or identity of his own."

Why has liberalism become such a scare word? The reason is that Reagan has changed the shape of American politics. He has created a powerful political coalition that brings together a variety of interests united by one thing—a distaste for big government. The key constituency in the Reagan coalition is middle-class voters who want low taxes. Thirty years ago, these voters thought of themselves as beneficiaries of government services. Now they think of themselves as taxpayers. Three things happened to change their view of government. In the 1960s the War on Poverty ended up in controversy and failure. As a result, social welfare programs began to lose their middle-class constituency. In the 1970s the inflation crisis gave rise to tax revolt. The wrath of the middle class was aimed at big government, which was seen as poisoning the nation's economy. And in the 1980s Reagan's anti-government program produced, or at least coincided with, a six-year economic recovery.

Look at how Dukakis and Bush approached middle-class voters. When Dukakis talked about "the middle-class squeeze," he was dealing with middle-class voters the same way Democrats have always dealt with constituencies: "You've got a problem. We've got a program." He had a program to help with college tuition expenses, a program to meet child-care needs, a program to provide health insurance for all employees, and a program to encourage affordable home mortgages. These programs were all ingeniously designed to be "self-financing." Middle-class voters tend to be suspicious of government programs. They are afraid that the programs are going to end up costing them money and helping other people. Bush addressed middle-class voters quite differently. He said, "You're in a financial squeeze? Here's what we're going to do for you. We're going to keep the recovery going." The solution middle-class voters want isn't programs. It's prosperity. And that is exactly Bush's mandate—to keep the recovery going. If he does that, he will be a fine president. If he doesn't, he will be in deep doo-doo.

The Reagan coalition also includes business interests that favor a deregulated business environment. It includes religious conservatives who oppose judicial activism. It includes neoconservatives who want a more aggressive foreign policy. And it includes white voters motivated by racial fear and resentment. The two constituencies in which the Democrats have lost the most support over the last 25 years are Southern whites and Northern urban ethnics (formerly called the Archie Bunker vote, now the Morton Downey Jr. vote). These voters see the federal government as the protector of black interests and the promoter of the civil rights agenda.

FDR brought together a coalition of interests who wanted something from government. The Reagan coalition is its mirror image—groups that want less from government. To the amazement of many observers, the coalition held together this year for George Bush. What keeps it together is the perception of a common threat, namely, liberalism. Reagan voters fear that liberals will regain control of the federal government and use it, as they did in the past, to carry out an agenda that includes taxes, regulations, social reforms, and anti-military policies. Bush kept the coalition together because he succeeded in dramatizing the liberal threat.

At the very end of the campaign, Dukakis used economic populism to rally the Democratic Party base. It worked. No Republican since 1952 has done as badly among Democrats as George Bush did this year. In the end, Dukakis pulled the Democratic Party together better than either Carter in 1980 or Mondale in 1984. Then why didn't he win?

Because the Democratic base has shrunk. You can't win elections any more just by holding the Democratic Party together. Exit polls show Democrats and Republicans evenly balanced among 1988 voters. In fact, Dukakis reclaimed a majority of Reagan Democrats. But they comprised less than ten percent of the electorate. Former Democrats who voted for Reagan are still around, of course. It's just that a lot of them no longer call themselves Democrats.

The class-warfare strategy worked for Harry Truman in 1948. It almost worked for Hubert Humphrey in 1968. But it didn't work for Michael Dukakis in 1988. Like Nixon and Reagan before him, Bush used social populism to undercut the Democrats' economic populism. Bush countered Dukakis's claim "I'm on your side" by asserting, "Values are the thing the working man is going to decide on. I've got those values on our side."

National Journal has produced a map of county-by-county results for the 1988 presidential election. Dukakis carried the black belt counties of the South. He carried the liberal belt along the Northern tier—New England, New York, the upper Midwest, and the Pacific Coast from Seattle to San Francisco. He carried the Hispanic belt in south Texas and New Mexico. He carried Hawaii, which is an Asian archipelago. He carried a scattering of farm belt counties in Missouri, Illinois, and Iowa. And he carried Appalachia, where there are a lot of poor whites but few blacks.

In presidential voting, the Democratic Party is now close to becoming a party of blacks and white liberals. In other words, the Jackson constituency and the Dukakis constituency. The two together are far from a national majority. And they don't even get along with each other.

Then why do the Democrats still do so well below the presidential level? Because races below the presidential level are rarely ideological. Challengers, who are often unknown to the voters, find it hard to engage incumbents on the issues. Since most incumbents are Democrats, the Democratic Party has a continuing advantage—so long as it can keep ideology from seeping into state and local voting.

There are two ways Democrats try to keep this from happening. One is to run on competence. Democrats are generally rated better at providing the kinds of benefits and services people want from government. The other is to exploit the advantages of incumbency. This means maintaining a good, and well-publicized, record of constituency service. "We do better the closer we get to people's garbage," one Democratic consultant told the *Washington Post*. Dukakis ran for president on competence—as if he were running for governor. Only it didn't work. You can't exclude values from a presidential election.

Democrats have been engaged in "rethinking" what their party stands for ever since the shock of 1980, and what have they come up with? Pragmatism. 1988 proves that pragmatism is not enough.

Dukakis, of course, is the ultimate pragmatist. He represents the post-ideological generation of Democrats, those who grew up with the civil rights and anti-war movements and remain loyal to those values, but have mastered a new, technocratic style of politics. By putting Lloyd Bentsen on the ticket, Dukakis forged the ultimate pragmatic coalition. Bentsen is a Tory Democrat, a remnant of the *pre*-ideological tradition of the Democratic Party. Like Dukakis, Bentsen sees the Democrats as a governing party, not as a party of activists. With Dukakis and Bentsen on the ticket, the pre-ideological and post-ideological traditions joined forces. And it made lots of liberals nervous.

Jesse Jackson, for one. Jackson went along with the ticket, but he never quite concealed his reservations about it. How could the Democrats win if they didn't *say* anything? In agreeing to support the ticket, Jackson said, in essence, "Go ahead. Do it your way. I'll do what I can to help." But there was another message: "This had better work." It didn't. When a party loses over and over again, as the Democrats have now done in five out of the last six presidential elections, it faces the likelihood of a fundamentalist revolt. At every Democratic convention, someone delivers the party's revival speech. Jackson gave the speech this year, just as Edward Kennedy did in 1980 and Mario Cuomo did in 1984. Each of them defined the party's traditions, ideals, and values. The delegates cried and cheered. Their souls were saved. The party then compromised its traditions, ideals, and values by nominating someone else. Now Jackson is saying that the "centrists" have had their chance. They got Super Tuesday, superdelegates, Dukakis, Bentsen, a meaningless platform, and a timid campaign. Enough compromises, says the left. Next time we want a real Democrat. The moderates have had their chance, and they failed.

The moderate position—pragmatism—has collapsed. So there is nothing between those who want to reaffirm the party's old-time religion and those who want to turn to the right. The problem is that both positions are unrealistic. By moving to the left, the Democrats are only going to make things worse for themselves. Whenever they put up a liberal ticket, the Democrats get locked out of the South. It wasn't supposed to happen this year, not with Bentsen on the ticket and Dukakis running on competence rather than ideology. But the minute Dukakis was exposed as a liberal, the lock closed. The South was lost. It was not quite as bad as in previous years, however. Forty-six percent is better than 40 percent.

It is equally unrealistic to argue that the Democrats should abandon liberalism. The Democratic Party is a liberal party. That is not likely to change, nor should it. The country does not need two Republican parties, even if liberalism is currently out of fashion. After all, conservatives nurtured their anti-government doctrines for 50 years until the Great Inflation of the 1970s finally brought them to ascendancy.

In any case, the nominating process will not allow for much backsliding. No matter how many superdelegates there are, primary voters and caucus participants still control the outcome. And Democrats who choose to participate in those activities are strongly tilted to the left. This does not mean that the most liberal candidate will necessarily win the nomination. It means that the Democratic nominee must be acceptable to liberals, just as the Republican nominee must be acceptable to conservatives.

Jimmy Carter, for instance, was widely distrusted by liberals. But he was legitimized by the civil rights issue. No Democrat who got all those black votes could be considered outside the tent. When Lloyd Bentsen ran for president in 1976, he was very far outside the tent; he ended up with just 4,000 votes. Today there is good reason to believe that Bentsen would be acceptable to liberals. He has done his service for the cause.

The lesson of 1988 is that the Democrats have to run a thematic campaign. But the theme cannot be liberalism. There are plenty of themes a good Democrat can run on without repudiating liberalism. Paul Kirk is right when he says, "I don't think we need to go back and try to rediscover the soul of the Democratic Party." The Democrats need three things to regain the White House—the right opportunity, the right campaign, and the right candidate.

The right opportunity comes when there is a strong desire for change. Watergate created a powerful market for change in 1976, for instance, as did inflation and the hostage crisis in 1980. A lot of Democrats thought the Iran-*contra* scandal and the stock market crash would do the same thing this year. But peace and prosperity prevailed, and the tide for change receded as the campaign went on.

The right campaign means finding out what the voters want that they are not getting. And then selling it to them. After eight years of Eisenhower, youth, dynamism, and vigor sold very well. In 1968, when the country was being torn to pieces, the voters desperately wanted order. After Watergate, 1976 saw a big market for morality. And in 1980, after Jimmy Carter, people were looking for leadership. None of these themes was ideological. They were based on a shrewd assessment of the times. The right theme for 1988 might have been competence, given Reagan's failings as a manager. But it never really sold. When things are going well, who worries about competence?

The right candidate is the biggest problem of all. What the Democrats need is a tough liberal. That is not an oxymoron. It is what Dukakis meant when he said, "I'm a liberal in the tradition of Franklin Roosevelt and Harry Truman and John Kennedy." It is also what Bush meant when he said, "No, you're not. You're a liberal in the tradition of George McGovern and Jimmy Carter and Walter Mondale."

What's the difference between FDR, Truman, and Kennedy on the one hand, and McGovern, Carter, and Mondale on the other? To begin with, the first three aren't around anymore. Ben Wattenberg calls this the "dead liberal" syndrome. Dead liberals are good. Living liberals are bad. But there is another difference. Roosevelt, Truman, and Kennedy (as well as LBJ) were all tough guys. They couldn't be pushed around by the Russians or by the special interests in Washington. McGovern, Carter, and Mondale (and, for that matter, Adlai Stevenson and Hubert Humphrey) had the image of weak liberals. All of them were respected for their integrity. But none was considered tough enough for the job.

Tough liberals win. Weak liberals lose. What happened to Dukakis this year is that his image changed. He started out looking tough when he took on the Democratic field and went the distance with Jesse Jackson. But the Republican campaign turned him into a wimp. His support dropped to 40 percent—about the same as where McGovern, Carter, and Mondale ended up. Only when he came back swinging did Dukakis begin to rise again in the polls.

Ideology is a problem, but one that can easily be overcome. Just find the right theme. That's what Reagan did in 1980. The polls showed that his right-wing views frightened most voters. They were afraid he would start a war or throw old people out in the snow. Reagan was elected in spite of, not because of, his ideology. He offered people something they wanted—leadership. No Democrat is going to win the presidency these days *because* he is a liberal. But with the right campaign, he can win *despite* being a liberal.

Chapter 5

Interest Groups

Interest groups are vital cogs in the wheels of the democratic process. Although *Federalist 10* suggests that one major purpose of the separation-of-powers system is to break and control the "evil effects" of faction, modern political theorists take a much more sanguine view of the role that political interest groups as well as parties play in government. No longer are interest groups defined as being opposed to the "public interest." They are vital channels through which particular publics participate in the governmental process. This chapter examines the nature of interest groups and shows how they function.

The Nature and Functions of Interest Groups

Group theory is an important component of democratic political theory. The essence of group theory is that in the democratic process interest groups interact naturally and properly to produce public policy. In American political thought, the origins of this theory can be found in the theory of concurrent majority in John C. Calhoun's *Disquisition on Government*.

It is very useful to discuss the operation of interest groups within the framework of what can best be described as a concurrent majority system. In contemporary usage the phrase "concurrent majority" means a system in which major government policy decisions must be approved by the dominant interest groups directly affected. The word *concurrent* suggests that each group involved must give its consent before policy can be enacted. Thus a concurrent majority is a majority of each group considered separately. If we take as an example an area such as agricultural policy, in which three or four major private interest groups can be identified, we can say that the concurrent majority is reached when each group affected gives its approval before agricultural policy is passed. The extent to which such a system of concurrent majority is actually functioning is a matter that has not been fully clarified by empirical research. Nevertheless, it does seem tenable to conclude that in many major areas of public policy, it is necessary at least to achieve a concurrent majority of the *major* or *dominant* interests affected.

The *theory* of concurrent majority originated with John C. Calhoun. Calhoun, born in 1781, had a distinguished career in public service at both the national and state levels. The idea of concurrent majority evolved from the concept of state nullification of federal law. Under this states' rights doctrine, states would be able to veto any national action. The purpose of this procedure, theoretically, was to protect states in a minority from encroachment by a national majority that could act through Congress, the President, and even the Supreme Court. Those who favored this procedure had little faith in the separation-of-powers doctrine as an effective device to prevent the arbitrary exercise of national power. At the end of his career Calhoun decided to incorporate his earlier views on state nullification into a more substantial theoretical treatise in political science; thus he wrote his famous *Disquisition on Government* (New York: D. Appleton & Co., 1853) in the decade between 1840 and 1850. He attempted to develop a general theory of constitutional (limited) government, the primary mechanism of which would be the ability of the major interest groups (states in Calhoun's time) to veto legislation adverse to their interests. Students should overlook some of the theoretical inconsistencies in Calhoun and concentrate upon the basic justification he advances for substituting his system of concurrent majority for the separation-of-powers device. Under the latter, group interests are not necessarily taken into account, for national laws can be passed on the basis of a numerical majority. And even though this majority may reflect the interests of some groups, it will not necessarily reflect the interests of all groups affected. Calhoun argued that a system in which the major interest groups can dominate the policy process is really more in accord with constitutional democracy than the system established in our Constitution and supported in *Federalist 10*.

The group theory of John C. Calhoun has been updated and carried over into modern political science by several writers, one of the most important being David B. Truman. David Truman's selection, taken from *The Governmental Process* (1951), contains (1) a definition of the term "interest group" and (2) a brief outline of the frame of reference within which the operations of interest groups should be considered. A fairly articulate interest-group theory of the governmental process is sketched by Truman. It will become evident to the student of American government that interest groups, like political parties, form an integral part of our political system. Further, interest-group theory suggests an entirely new way of looking at government.

31

David B. Truman
THE GOVERNMENTAL PROCESS

INTEREST GROUPS

Interest group refers to any group that, on the basis of one or more shared attitudes, makes certain claims upon other groups in the society for the establishment, maintenance, or enhancement of forms of behavior that are implied by the shared attitudes. . . . [F]rom interaction in groups arise certain common habits of response, which may be called norms, or shared attitudes. These afford the participants frames of reference for interpreting and evaluating events and behaviors. In this respect all groups are interest groups because they are shared-attitude groups. In some groups at various points in time, however, a second kind of common response emerges, in addition to the frame of reference. These are shared attitudes toward what is needed or wanted in a given situation, as demands or claims upon other groups in the society. The term "interest group" will be reserved here for those groups that exhibit both aspects of the shared attitudes. . . .

Definition of the interest group in this fashion . . . permits the identification of various potential as well as existing interest groups. That is, it invites examination of an interest whether or not it is found at the moment as one of the characteristics of a particular organized group. Although no group that makes claims upon other groups in society will be found without an interest or interests, it is possible to examine interests that are not at a particular point in time the basis of interactions among individuals, but that may become such. . . .

GROUPS AND GOVERNMENT: DIFFICULTIES IN A GROUP INTERPRETATION OF POLITICS

Since we are engaged in an effort to develop a conception of the political process in the United States that will account adequately for the role of groups, particularly interest groups, it will be appropriate to take account of some of the factors that have been regarded as obstacles to such a conception and that have caused such groups to be neglected in many explanations of the dynamics of government. Perhaps the most important practical reason for this neglect is that the significance of groups has only fairly recently been forced to the attention of political scientists by the tremendous growth in the number of formally organized groups in the United States within the last few decades. It is difficult and unnecessary to attempt to date the beginning of such attention, but Herring in 1929, in his groundbreaking book, *Group Representation Before Congress*, testified to the novelty of the observations he reported when he stated: "There has developed in this government an extra-legal machinery of as integral and of as influential a nature as the system of party government that has long been an essential part of the government. . . ." Some implications of this development are not wholly compatible with some of the proverbial notions about representative government held by specialists as well as laymen. . . . This apparent incompatibility has obstructed the inclusion of group behaviors in an objective description of the governmental process.

More specifically, it is usually argued that any attempt at the interpretation of politics in terms of group patterns inevitably "leaves something out" or "destroys something essential" about the processes of "our" government. On closer examination, we find this argument suggesting that two "things" are certain to be ignored: the individual, and a sort of totally inclusive unity designated by such terms as "society" and "the state."

The argument that the individual is ignored in any interpretation of politics as based upon groups seems to assume a differentiation or conflict between "the individual" and some such collectivity as the group. . . .

Such assumptions need not present any difficulties in the development of a group interpretation of politics, because they are essentially unwarranted. They simply do not square with . . . evidence concerning group affiliations and individual behavior. . . . We do not, in fact, find individuals otherwise than in groups; complete isolation in space and time is so rare as to be an almost hypothetical situation. It is equally demonstrable that the characteristics of any interest group, including the activities by which we identify it, are governed by the attitudes and the circumstances that gave rise to the interactions of which it consists. There are variable factors, and, although the role played by a particular individual may be quite different in a lynch mob from that of the same individual in a meeting of the church deacons, the attitudes and behaviors involved in both are as much a part of his personality as is his treatment of his family. "The individual" and "the group" are at most merely convenient ways of classifying behavior, two ways of approaching the same phenomena, not different things.

The persistence among nonspecialists of the notion of an inherent conflict between "the individual" and "the group" or "society" is understandable in view of the doctrines of individualism that have underlain various political and economic conflicts over the past three centuries. The notion persists also because it harmonizes with a view of the isolated and independent individual as the "cause" of complicated human events. The personification of events, quite apart from any ethical considerations, is a kind of shorthand convenient in everyday speech and, like supernatural explanations of natural phenomena, has a comforting simplicity. Explanations that take into account multiple causes, including group affiliations, are difficult. The "explanation" of a national complex like the Soviet Union wholly in terms of a Stalin or the "description" of the intricacies of the American government entirely in terms of a Roosevelt is quick and easy. . . .

The second major difficulty allegedly inherent in any attempt at a group interpretation of the political process is that such an explanation inevitably must ignore some greater unity designated as society or the state. . . .

Many of those who place particular emphasis upon this difficulty assume explicitly or implicitly that there is an interest of the nation as a whole, universally and invariably held and standing apart from and superior to those of the various groups included within it. This assumption is close to the popular dogmas of democratic government based on the familiar notion that if only people are free and have access to "the facts," they will all want the same thing in any political situation. It is no derogation of democratic preferences to state that such an assertion flies in the face of all that we know of the behavior of men in a complex society. Were it in fact true, not only the interest group but even the political party should properly be viewed as an abnormality. The differing experiences and perceptions of men not only encourage individuality but also . . . inevitably result in differing attitudes and conflicting group affiliations. "There are," says Bentley in his discussion of this error of the social whole, "always some parts of the nation to be found arrayed against other parts." [From *The Process of Government* (1908).] Even in war, when a totally inclusive interest should be apparent if it is ever going to be, we always find pacifists, conscientious objectors, spies, and subversives, who reflect interests opposed to those of "the nation as a whole."

There is a political significance in assertions of a totally inclusive interest within a nation. Particularly in times of crisis, such as an international war, such claims are a tremendously useful promotional device by means of which a particularly extensive group or league of groups tries to reduce or eliminate opposing interests. Such is the pain attendant upon not "belonging" to one's "own" group that if a normal person can be convinced that he is the lone dissenter to an otherwise universally accepted agreement, he usually will conform. This pressure accounts at least in part for the number of prewar pacifists who, when the United States entered World War II, accepted the draft or volunteered. Assertion of an inclusive "national" or "public interest" is an effective device in many less critical situations as well. In themselves, these claims are part of the data of politics. However, they do not describe any actual or possible political situation within a complex modern nation. In developing a group interpretation of politics, therefore, we do not need to account for a totally inclusive interest, because one does not exist.

Denying the existence of an interest of the nation as a whole does not completely dispose of the difficulty raised by those who insist that a group interpretation must omit "the state." We cannot deny the obvious fact that we are examining a going political system that is supported or at least accepted by a large proportion of the society. We cannot account for such a system by adding up in some fashion the National Association of Manufacturers, the Congress of Industrial Organizations, the American Farm Bureau Federation, The American Legion, and other groups that come to mind when "lobbies" and "pressure groups" are mentioned. Even if the political parties are added to the list, the result could properly be designated as "a view which seems hardly compatible with the relative stability of the political system. . . ." Were such the exclusive ingredients of the political process in the United States, the entire system would have torn itself apart long since.

If these various organized interest groups more or less consistently reconcile their differences, adjust, and accept compromises, we must acknowledge that we are dealing with a system that is not accounted for by the "sum" of the organized interest groups in the society. We must go further to explain the operation of such ideals or traditions as constitutionalism, civil liberties, representative responsibility, and the like. These are not, however, a sort of disembodied metaphysical influence, like Mr. Justice Holmes's "brooding omnipresence." We know of the existence of such factors only from the behavior and the habitual interactions of men. If they exist in this fashion, they are interests. We can account for their operation and for the system by recognizing such interests as representing what . . . we called potential interest groups in the "becoming" stage of activity. "It is certainly true," as Bentley has made clear, "that we must accept a . . . group of this kind as an interest group itself." It makes no difference that we cannot find the home office and the executive secretary of such a group. Organization in this formal sense, as we have seen, represents merely a stage or degree of interaction that may or may not be significant at any particular point in time. Its absence does not mean that these interests do not exist, that the familiar "pressure groups" do not operate as if such potential groups were organized and active, or that these interests may not move from the potential to the organized stage of activity.

It thus appears that the two major difficulties supposedly obstacles to a group interpretation of the political process are not insuperable. We can employ the fact of individuality and we can account for the existence of the state without doing violence to the evidence available from the observed behaviors of men and groups. . . .

INTEREST GROUPS AND
THE NATURE OF THE STATE

Men, wherever they are observed, are creatures participating in those established patterns of interaction that we call groups. Excepting perhaps the most casual and transitory, these continuing interactions, like all such interpersonal relationships, involve power. This power is exhibited in two closely interdependent ways. In the first place, the group exerts power over its members; an individual's group affiliations largely determine his attitudes, values, and the frames of reference in terms of which he interprets his experiences. For a measure of conformity to the norms of the group is the price of acceptance within it. . . . In the second place, the group, if it is or becomes an interest group, which any group in society may be, exerts power over other groups in the society when it successfully imposes claims upon them.

Many interest groups, probably an increasing proportion in the United States, are politicized. That is, either from the outset or from time to time in the course of their development they make their claims through or upon the institutions of government. Both the forms and functions of government in turn are a reflection of the activities and claims of such groups. . . .

The institutions of government are centers of interest-based power; their connections with interest groups may be latent or overt and their activities range in political character from the routinized and widely accepted to the unstable and highly controversial. In order to make claims, political interest groups will seek access to the key points of decision within these institutions. Such points are scattered throughout the structure, including not only the formally established branches of government but also the political parties in their various forms and the relationships between governmental units and other interest groups.

The extent to which a group achieves effective access to the institutions of government is the resultant of a complex of interdependent factors. For the sake of simplicity these may be classified in three somewhat overlapping categories: (1) factors relating to a group's strategic position in the society; (2) factors associated with the internal characteristics of the group; and (3) factors peculiar to the governmental institutions themselves. In the first category are: the group's status or prestige in the society, affecting the ease with which it commands deference from those outside its bounds; the standing it and its activities have when measured against the widely held but largely unorganized interests or "rules of the game"; the extent to which government officials are formally or informally "members" of the group; and the usefulness of the group as a source of technical and political knowledge. The second category includes:

the degree and appropriateness of the group's organization; the degree of cohesion it can achieve in a given situation, especially in the light of competing group demands upon its membership; the skills of the leadership; and the group's resources in numbers and money. In the third category are: the operating structure of the government institutions, since such established features involve relatively fixed advantages and handicaps; and the effects of the group life of particular units or branches of the government. . . .

A characteristic feature of the governmental system in the United States is that it contains a multiplicity of points of access. The federal system establishes decentralized and more or less independent centers of power, vantage points from which to secure privileged access to the national government. Both a sign and a cause of the strength of the constituent units in the federal scheme is the peculiar character of our party system, which has strengthened parochial relationships, especially those of national legislators. National parties, and to a lesser degree those in the states, tend to be poorly cohesive leagues of locally based organizations rather than unified and inclusive structures. Staggered terms for executive officials and various types of legislators accentuate differences in the effective electorates that participate in choosing these officers. Each of these different, often opposite, localized patterns (constituencies) is a channel of independent access to the larger party aggregation and to the formal government. Thus, especially at the national level, the party is an electing-device and only in limited measure an integrated means of policy determination. Within the Congress, furthermore, controls are diffused among committee chairmen and other leaders in both chambers. The variety of these points of access is further supported by relationships stemming from the constitutional doctrine of separation of powers, from related checks and balances, and at the state and local level from the common practice of choosing an array of executive officials by popular election. At the federal level the formal simplicity of the executive branch has been complicated by a Supreme Court decision that has placed a number of administrative agencies beyond the removal power of the President. The position of these units, however, differs only in degree from that of many that are constitutionally within the Executive Branch. In consequence of alternative lines of access available through the legislature and the Executive and of divided channels for the control of administrative policy, many nominally executive agencies are at various times virtually independent of the Chief Executive.

. . . Within limits, therefore, organized interest groups, gravitating toward responsive points of decision, may play one segment of the structure against another as circumstances and strategic considerations permit. The total pattern of government over a period of time thus presents a protean complex of crisscrossing relationships that change in strength and direction with alternations in the power and standing of interests, organized and unorganized.

❖❖   From Truman's definition *any* group, organized or unorganized, that has a shared attitude toward goals and methods for achieving them should be classified as an interest group. Truman is essentially saying that, since people generally function as members of groups, it is more useful and accurate for the political observer to view the governmental process as the interaction of political interest groups. If one accepts the sociologist's assumption that people act and interact only as members of groups, then it is imperative that the governmental process be viewed as one of interest-group interaction.

Within the framework of Truman's definition it is possible to identify both *public* and *private* interest groups. In the political process, governmental groups sometimes act as interest groups in the same sense as private organizations. In many public policies, governmental groups may have more at stake than private organizations. Thus administrative agencies, for example, may lobby as vigorously as their private counterparts to advance their own interests.

Theodore Lowi refers to group theory as "interest-group liberalism." The following selection is taken from his well-known book *The End of Liberalism* (1969), in which he severely criticizes group theory and its pervasive influence upon governmental decision makers. In reading the following selection, remember that the author does not use the term "liberal" in its ordinary sense. The political "liberal" in Lowi's terminology is much like the "economic Liberal" of the early nineteenth century. Just as economic liberalism preached that the public good emerged automatically from the free clash of private interests, the political liberal (in Lowi's terms) supports group theory which holds that the public interest in government is automatically achieved through the interaction of pressure groups.

32

Theodore J. Lowi
THE END OF LIBERALISM:
THE INDICTMENT

The corruption of modern democratic government began with the emergence of interest-group liberalism as the public philosophy. Its corrupting influence takes at least four important forms, four counts, therefore, of an indictment for which most of the foregoing chapters are mere documentation. Also to be indicted, on at least three counts, is the philosophic component of the ideology, pluralism.

SUMMATION 1:
FOUR COUNTS AGAINST
THE IDEOLOGY

1. Interest-group liberalism as public philosophy corrupts democratic government because it deranges and confuses expectations about democratic institutions. Liberalism promotes popular decision-making but derogates from the decisions so made by misapplying the notion to the implementation as well as the formulation of policy. It derogates from the processes by treating all values in the process as equivalent interests. It derogates from democratic rights by allowing their exercise in foreign policy, and by assuming they are being exercised when access is provided. Liberal practices reveal a basic disrespect for democracy. Liberal leaders do not wield the authority of democratic government with the resoluteness of men certain of the legitimacy of their positions, the integrity of their institutions, or the justness of the programs they serve.

2. Interest-group liberalism renders government impotent. Liberal governments cannot plan. Liberals are copious in plans but irresolute in planning. Nineteenth-century liberalism was standard without plans. This was an anachronism in the modern state. But twentieth-century liberalism turned out to be plans without standards. As an anachronism it, too, ought to pass. But doctrines are not organisms. They die only in combat over the minds of men, and no doctrine yet exists capable of doing the job. All the popular alternatives are so very irrelevant, helping to explain the longevity of interest-group liberalism.

Reprinted from *The End of Liberalism: Ideology, Policy, and the Crisis of Public Authority*, by Theodore J. Lowi, with the permission of W. W. Norton & Company, Inc. Copyright © 1969 by W. W. Norton & Company, Inc.

Barry Goldwater most recently proved the irrelevance of one. The *embour-geoisement* of American unions suggests the irrelevance of others.

The Departments of Agriculture, Commerce, and Labor provide illustrations, but hardly exhaust illustrations, of such impotence. Here clearly one sees how liberalism has become a doctrine whose means are its ends, whose combatants are its clientele, whose standards are not even those of the mob but worse, are those the bargainers can fashion to fit the bargain. Delegation of power has become alienation of public domain—the gift of sovereignty to private satrapies. The political barriers to withdrawal of delegation are high enough. But liberalism reinforces these through the rhetoric of justification and often even permanent legal reinforcement: Public corporations—justified, oddly, as efficient planning instruments—permanently alienate rights of central coordination to the directors and to those who own the corporation bonds. Or, as Walter Adams finds, the "most pervasive method . . . for alienating public domain is the certificate of convenience and necessity, or some variation thereof in the form of an exclusive franchise, license or permit. . . . [G]overnment has become increasingly careless and subservient in issuing them. The net result is a general legalization of private monopoly. . . ." While the best examples still are probably the 10 self-governing systems of agriculture policy, these are obviously only a small proportion of all the barriers the interest-group liberal ideology has erected to democratic use of government.

3. Interest-group liberalism demoralizes government, because liberal governments cannot achieve justice. The question of justice has engaged the best minds for almost as long as there have been notions of state and politics, certainly ever since Plato defined the ideal as one in which republic and justice were synonymous. And since that time philosophers have been unable to agree on what justice is. But outside the ideal, in the realms of actual government and citizenship, the problem is much simpler. We do not have to define justice at all in order to weight and assess justice in government, because in the case of liberal policies we are prevented by what the law would call a "jurisdictional fact." In the famous jurisdictional case of *Marbury* v. *Madison* Chief Justice Marshall held that even if all the Justices hated President Jefferson for refusing to accept Marbury and the other "midnight judges" appointed by Adams, there was nothing they could do. They had no authority to judge President Jefferson's action one way or another because the Supreme Court did not possess such jurisdiction over the President. In much the same way, there is something about liberalism that prevents us from raising the question of justice at all, no matter what definition of justice is used.

Liberal governments cannot achieve justice because their policies lack the *sine qua non* of justice—that quality without which a consideration of justice cannot even be initiated. Considerations of the justice in or achieved by an action cannot be made unless a deliberate and conscious attempt was made by the actor to derive his action from a general rule or moral principle governing such a class of acts. One can speak personally of good rules and bad rules, but a homily or a sentiment, like liberal legislation, is not a rule at all. The best rule is one which is relevant to the decision or action in question and is general in the sense that those involved with it have no direct control over its operation. A general rule is, hence, *a priori*. Any governing regime that makes a virtue of avoiding such rules puts itself totally outside the context of justice.

Take the homely example of the bull and the china shop. Suppose it was an op art shop and that we consider op worthy only of the junk pile. That being the case, the bull did us a great service, the more so because it was something we always dreamed of doing but were prevented by law from entering and breaking. But however much we may be pleased, we cannot judge the act. We can only like or dislike the consequences. The consequences are haphazard; the bull cannot have intended them. The act was a thoughtless, animal act which bears absolutely no relation to any aesthetic principle. We don't judge the bull. We only celebrate our good fortune. Without the general rule, the bull can reenact his scenes of creative destruction daily and still not be capable of achieving, in this case, aesthetic justice. The whole idea of justice is absurd.

The general rule ought to be a legislative rule because the United States espouses the ideal of representative democracy. However, that is merely an extrinsic feature of the rule. All that counts is the character of the rule itself. Without the rule we can only like or dislike the consequences of the governmental action. In the question of whether justice is achieved, a government without good rules, and without acts carefully derived therefrom, is merely a big bull in an immense china shop.

4. Finally, interest-group liberalism corrupts democratic government in the degree to which it weakens the capacity of governments to live by democratic formalisms. Liberalism weakens democratic institutions by opposing formal procedure with informal bargaining. Liberalism derogates from democracy by derogating from all formality in favor of informality. Formalism is constraining; playing it "by the book" is a role often unpopular in American war films and sports films precisely because it can dramatize personal rigidity and the plight of the individual in collective situations. Because of the impersonality of formal procedures, there is inevitably a separation in the real world between the forms and the realities, and this kind of separation gives rise to cynicism, for informality means that some will escape their collective fate better than others. There has as a consequence always been a certain amount of cynicism toward public objects in the United States, and this may be to the good, since a little cynicism is the father of healthy sophistication. However, when the informal is elevated to a positive virtue, and hard-won access becomes a share of official authority, cynicism becomes distrust. It ends in reluctance to submit one's fate to the governmental process under any condition, as is the case in the United States in the mid-1960s.

Public officials more and more frequently find their fates paradoxical and their treatment at the hands of the public fickle and unjust when in fact they are only reaping the results of their own behavior, including their direct and informal treatment of the public and the institutions through which they serve the public. The more government operates by the spreading of access, the more public order seems to suffer. The more public men pursue their constituencies, the more they seem to find their constituencies alienated. Liberalism has promoted concentration of democratic authority but deconcentration of democratic power. Liberalism has opposed privilege in policy formulation only to foster it, quite systematically, in the implementation of policy. Liberalism has consistently failed to recognize, in short, that in a democracy forms are important. In a medieval monarchy all formalisms were at court. Democracy proves, for better or worse, that the masses like that sort of thing too.

Another homely parable may help. In the good old days, everyone in the big city knew that traffic tickets could be fixed. Not everyone could get his ticket fixed, but nonetheless a man who honestly paid his ticket suffered in some degree a dual loss: his money, and his self-esteem for having so little access. Cynicism was widespread, violations were many, but perhaps it did not matter, for there were so few automobiles. Suppose, however, that as the automobile population increased a certain city faced a traffic crisis and the system of ticket fixing came into ill repute. Suppose a mayor, victorious on the Traffic Ticket, decided that, rather than eliminate fixing by universalizing enforcement, he would instead reform the system by universalizing the privileges of ticket fixing. One can imagine how the system would work. One can imagine that some sense of equality would prevail, because everyone could be made almost equally free to bargain with the ticket administrators. But one would find it difficult to imagine how this would make the total city government more legitimate. Meanwhile, the purpose of the ticket would soon have been destroyed.

Traffic regulation, fortunately, was not so reformed. But many other government activities were. The operative principles of interest-group liberalism possess the mentality of a world of universalized ticket fixing: Destroy privilege by universalizing it. Reduce conflict by yielding to it. Redistribute power by the maxim of each according to his claim. Reserve an official place for every major structure of power. Achieve order by worshiping the processes (as distinguished from the forms and the procedures) by which order is presumed to be established.

If these operative principles will achieve equilibrium—and such is far from proven—that is all they will achieve. Democracy will have disappeared, because all of these maxims are founded upon profound lack of confidence in democracy. Democracy fails when it lacks confidence in its own authority.

Democratic forms were supposed to precede and accompany the formulation of policies so that policies could be implemented authoritatively and firmly. Democracy is indeed a form of absolutism, but ours was fairly well contrived to be an absolutist government under the strong control of consent-building prior to taking authoritative action in law. Interest-group liberalism fights the absolutism of democracy but succeeds only in taking away its authoritativeness.

Whether it is called "creative federalism" by President Johnson, "cooperation" by the farmers, "local autonomy" by the Republicans, or "participatory democracy" by the New Left, the interest-group liberal effort does not create democratic power but rather negates it.

❖❖   The following discussion by V. O. Key, Jr., concentrates on private pressure groups and the extent to which they are links between public opinion and government. One interesting conclusion is that the elites of interest groups are not able to influence their members' attitudes to anywhere near the degree commonly thought possible. Pressure-group participation in government more often than not reflects highly limited participation by the active elements of the groups. Public policy is often hammered out by very small numbers of individuals both in the government and in the private sphere. Political leaders can never stray too far beyond the boundaries of consent, but these are often very broad.

33

V. O. Key, Jr.
PRESSURE GROUPS

Pressure groups occupy a prominent place in analyses of American politics. In a regime characterized by official deference to public opinion and by adherence to the doctrine of freedom of association, private organizations may be regarded as links that connect the citizen and government. They are differentiated in both composition and function from political parties. Ordinarily they concern themselves with only a narrow range of policies, those related to the peculiar interests of the group membership. Their aim is primarily to influence the content of public policy rather than the results of elections. Those groups with a mass membership, though, may oppose or support particular candidates; in that case they are treated as groups with power to affect election results and,

From *Public Opinion and American Policy* by V. O. Key, Jr. Copyright © 1961 by V. O. Key, Jr. Reprinted by permission of the Trustees of the Luella Gettys Key Estate.

thereby, with capacity to pressure party leaders, legislators, and others in official position to act in accord with their wishes. . . .

PUZZLES OF PRESSURE POLITICS

. . . [There is] a series of puzzles as we seek to describe the role of pressure groups as links between opinion and government. Clearly the model of the lobbyist who speaks for a united following, determined in its aims and prepared to reward its friends and punish its enemies at the polls, does not often fit reality. Nor is it probable that the unassisted effort of pressure organizations to mold public opinion in support of their position has a large effect upon mass opinion. Yet legislators listen respectfully to representations of the spokesmen of private groups, which in turn spend millions of dollars every year in propagandizing the public. Leaders of private groups articulate the concerns of substantial numbers of persons, even though they may not have succeeded in indoctrinating completely the members of their own groups. All this activity must have some functional significance in the political system. The problem is to identify its functions in a manner that seems to make sense. In this endeavor a distinction of utility is that made . . . between mass-membership organizations and nonmass organizations, which far outnumber the former.

Representation of Mass-Membership Groups. Only the spokesmen for mass-membership organizations can give the appearance of representing voters in sufficient numbers to impress (or intimidate) government. The influence of nonmass groups, which often have only a few hundred or a few thousand members, must rest upon something other than the threat of electoral retribution. As has been seen, the reality of the behavior of members of mass organizations is that in the short run they are not manipulable in large numbers by their leaders. Their party identification anchors many of them to a partisan position, and over the longer run they seem to be moved from party to party in presidential elections by the influences that affect all types and classes of people.

The spokesmen of mass-membership groups also labor under the handicap that they may be made to appear to be unrepresentative of the opinions of their members. When the president of an organization announces to a Congressional committee that he speaks for several million people, the odds are that a substantial proportion of his members can be shown to have no opinion or even to express views contrary to those voiced by their spokesmen. This divergency is often explained as a wicked betrayal of the membership or as a deliberate departure from the mass mandate. Yet it is not unlikely that another type of explanation more often fits the facts. Opinions, as we have seen in many contexts, do not fall into blacks and whites. It may be the nature of mass groups that attachment to the positions voiced by the peak spokesmen varies with attachment to and involvement in the group. At the leadership level the group position is voiced in its purest and most uncompromising form. A substantial layer of group activitists subscribes to the official line, but among those with less involvement the faith wins less general acceptance. At the periphery of the group, though, the departure from the official line may be more a matter of indifference than of dissent. Leadership policy is often pictured as the consequence of interaction between leadership and group membership, which may be only partially true. Leaders may be more accurately regarded as dedicated souls who bid for group support of their position. Almost invariably they receive something less than universal acquiescence. This may be especially true in mass organizations in which political endeavor is to a degree a side issue—as, for example, in trade unions and farm organizations. As one traces attitudes and opinions across the strata of group membership, the clarity of position and the extremeness of position become more marked at the level of high involvement and activism.

If it is more or less the nature of mass organizations to encompass a spectrum of opinion rather than a single hue, much of the discussion of the representativeness of group leadership may be beside the point. However that may be, circumstances surrounding the leadership elements of mass organizations place them, in their work of influencing government, in a position not entirely dissimilar to that of leaders of nonmass groups. They must rely in large measure on means not unlike those that must be employed by groups with only the smallest membership. The world of pressure politics becomes more a politics among the activists than a politics that involves many people. Yet politics among the activists occurs in a context of concern about public opinion, a concern that colors the mode of action if not invariably its substance.

Arenas of Decision and Norms of Action. The maneuvers of pressure-group politics thus come ordinarily to occur among those highly involved and immediately concerned about public policy; the connection of these maneuvers with public opinion and even with the opinions of mass-membership organizations tends to be tenuous. Many questions of policy are fought out within vaguely bounded arenas in which the activists concerned are clustered. A major factor in the determination of the balance of forces within each arena is party control of the relevant governmental apparatus. Included among the participants in each issue-cluster of activists are the spokesmen for the pressure groups concerned, the members of the House and Senate committees with jurisdiction, and the officials of the administrative departments and agencies concerned. In the alliances of pressure politics those between administrative agencies and private groups are often extremely significant in the determination of courses of action. The cluster of concerned activists may include highly interested persons, firms, and organizations scattered over the country, though the boundaries delimiting those concerned vary from question to question, from arena to arena. In short, pressure politics among the activists take something of the form that it would take if there were no elections or no concern about the nature of public opinion; that is, those immediately concerned make themselves heard in the process of decision.

In the give and take among the activists, norms and values with foundations in public opinion are conditioning factors. The broad values of the society determine to a degree who will be heard, who can play the game. Those who claim to speak for groups that advocate causes outside the range of consensus may be given short shrift. Some groups advocating perfectly respectable causes may be heard with less deference than others. Subtle standards define what David Truman calls "access" to the decision makers. To some extent this is a party matter: an AFL-CIO delegation does not expect to be heard with much sympathy by a committee dominated by right-wing Republicans. The reality of access, too, may provide an index to the tacit standards in definition of those interests regarded as having a legitimate concern about public policy. The spokesmen of groups both large and small are often heard with respect, not because they wield power, but because they are perceived as the representatives of interests entitled to be heard and to be accorded consideration as a matter of right.

Within the range of the permissible, the process of politics among the activists is governed to some extent by the expectation that all entitled to play the game shall get a fair deal (or at least a fair hearing before their noses are rubbed in the dirt). Doubtless these practices parallel a fairly widespread set of attitudes within the population generally. Probably those attitudes could be characterized as a disposition to let every group—big business and labor unions as well—have its say, but that such groups should not be permitted to dominate the government. In the implementation of these attitudes the legalism of American legislators plays a role. Frequently Congressional committeemen regard themselves as engaged in a judicial role of hearing the evidence and of arriving at decisions based on some sort of standards of equity.

Rituals of the Activists. The maneuvers of group spokesmen, be they spokesmen for mass or nonmass organizations, are often accompanied by rituals in obeisance to the doctrine that public opinion governs. The belief often seems to be that Congressmen will be impressed by a demonstration that public opinion demands the proposed line of action or inaction. Hence, groups organize publicity campaigns and turn up sheaves of editorials in support of their position. They stimulate people to write or to wire their Congressmen; if the labor of stimulation is too arduous, they begin to sign to telegrams names chosen at random from the telephone directory. They solicit the endorsement of other organizations for their position. They lobby the American Legion and the General Federation of Women's Clubs for allies willing to permit their names to be used. On occasion they buy the support of individuals who happen to hold official positions in other organizations. They form fraudulent organizations with impressive letterheads to advance the cause. They attempt to anticipate and to soften the opposition of organizations that might be opposed to their position.

Groups of similar ideological orientation tend to "run" together or to form constellations in confederation for mutual advantage.

All these maneuvers we have labeled "rituals"; that is, they are on the order of the dance of the rainmakers. They may be too brutal a characterization, for sometimes these campaigns have their effects—just as rain sometimes follows the rainmakers' dance. Yet the data make it fairly clear that most of these campaigns do not affect the opinion of many people and even clearer that they have small effect by way of punitive or approbative feedback in the vote. Their function in the political process is difficult to divine. The fact that organizations engage in these practices, though, is in itself a tribute to the importance of public opinion. To some extent, too, these opinion campaigns are not so much directed to mass opinion as to other activists who do not speak for many people either but have access to the arena of decision-making and perhaps have a viewpoint entitled to consideration. In another direction widespread publicity, by its creation of the illusion of mass support, may legitimize a position taken by a legislator. If a legislator votes for a measure that seems to arouse diverse support, his vote is not so likely to appear to be a concession to a special interest.

Barnums among the Businessmen. An additional explanation that apparently accounts for a good deal of group activity is simply that businessmen (who finance most of the campaigns of public education by pressure groups) are soft touches for publicity men. The advertising and public-relations men have demonstrated that they can sell goods; they proceed on the assumption that the business of obtaining changes in public policy is analogous to selling soap. They succeed in separating businessmen from large sums of money to propagate causes, often in a manner that sooner or later produces a boomerang effect.

Professional bureaucrats of the continuing and well-established organizations practice restraint in their public-relations campaigns. They need to gain the confidence of Congressmen and other officials with whom they also need to be able to speak the next time they meet. The fly-by-night organization or the business group that falls into the clutches of an unscrupulous public relations firm is more likely to indulge in the fantastic public relations and pressure campaign. Thus the National Tax Equality Association raised some $600,000 to finance a campaign against the tax exemptions of cooperatives, the most important of which are farm coops. Contributions came from concerns as scattered as the Central Power & Light Co., of Corpus Christi, Texas; Fairmont Foods Co., of Omaha, Nebraska; Central Hudson Gas Electric Corporation, of Poughkeepsie, New York; and the Rheem Manufacturing Co., of San Francisco. The late Representative Reed, of New York, who was not one to attack business lightly, declared:

> Mr. Speaker, an unscrupulous racket, known as the National Tax Equality Association, has been in operation for some time, directing its vicious prop-

aganda against the farm co-operatives. To get contributions from businessmen, this racketeering organization has propagandized businessmen with false statements to the effect that if farm co-operatives were taxed and not exempted the revenue to the government would mount annually to over $800,000,000. [The treasury estimate was in the neighborhood of $20,000,000.] This is, of course, absolutely false and nothing more nor less than getting money under false pretenses. . . . This outfit of racketeers known as the Tax Equality Association has led honest businessmen to believe that their contributions were deductible from gross income as ordinary and necessary business expense with reference to their Federal income-tax return.

The Tax Equality Association provided its subscribers with the following form letter to send to their Congressmen:

Dear Mr. Congressman: You raised my income taxes. Now I hear you are going to do it again. But you still let billions in business and profits escape. How come you raise my taxes, but let co-ops, mutuals, and other profit-making corporations get off scot free, or nearly so? I want a straight answer—and I want these businesses fully taxed before you increase my or anyone else's income taxes again.

Letters so phrased are not well designed to produce favorable Congressional response. The ineptness of this sort of campaign creates no little curiosity about the political judgment of solvent businessmen who put their money or their corporation's money into the support of obviously stupidly managed endeavors.

Autonomous Actors or Links? This review of the activities of pressure groups may raise doubts about the validity of the conception of these groups as links between public opinion and government. The reality seems to be that the conception applies with greater accuracy to some groups than to others. Certainly group spokesmen may represent a shade of opinion to government even though not all their own members share the views they express. Yet to a considerable degree the work of the spokesmen of private groups, both large and small, proceeds without extensive involvement of either the membership or a wider public. Their operations as they seek to influence legislation and administration, though, occur in a milieu of concern about opinion, either actual or latent. That concern also disposes decision makers to attend to shades of opinion and preference relevant to decision though not necessarily of great electoral strength—a disposition of no mean importance in the promotion of the equitable treatment of people in a democratic order. The chances are that the effects of organized groups on public opinion occur mainly over the long run rather than in short-run maneuvers concerned with particular congressional votes. Moreover, group success may be governed more by the general balance of partisan strength than by the results of group endeavors to win friends in the mass public. An industry reputed to be led by swindlers may not expect the most cordial reception from legislative committees, especially at times when the balance of strength is not friendly to any kind of business. If the industry can modify its public image, a task that requires time, its position as it maneuvers on particulars (about which few of the public can ever know anything) may be less unhappy. That modification may be better attained by performance than by propaganda.

Case Studies in Pressure-group Politics

Ironically, the campaign finance laws of the 1970s, which were designed to restrict the influence of money in politics by limiting contributions to political campaigns, spawned PACs, or political action committees. The laws explicitly allowed corporations, labor unions, and any other group to create political action committees that would voluntarily solicit funds from employees, shareholders, union and group members to build war chests that could be used directly and indirectly to help finance congressional campaigns. PACs focused primarily on congressional elections, because presidential campaigns are publicly financed when the candidates, as they always do, accept public funds. Even in presidential races, however, political action committees can make their presence felt by indirectly spending money in behalf of candidates of their choice.

While a political action committee can contribute directly only $10,000 to a candidate—$5,000 each for the primary and general elections—there is no limit on the amount of money that can be indirectly spent, for example, for media advertising to elect or defeat candidates. Moreover, some interests have geometrically expanded their political clout by creating and encouraging confederations of PACs who advance a single cause. Labor union PACs, for example, may be created by local union organizations as well as by the national AFL-CIO, Teamsters, and the United Auto Workers. The National Rifle Association, the National Association of Realtors, the American Medical Association, and Right-to-Life groups have encouraged networks of PACs that collectively can have an enormous impact on congressional campaigns. While political action committees are generally pictured as conservative ideologically, liberal groups, particularly labor interests, have created PACs of their own to advance their causes.

It has become fashionable in the rhetoric of American politics to picture PACs as an unhealthy if not evil influence, creating a Congress that is the "best that money can buy." The term "PAC" has developed a pejorative connotation. The contemporary rhetoric of PACs reflects a strand in American political thought that originated with James Madison's skeptical view of "faction" that he expressed in *Federalist 10*. The popular press has throughout history given interest groups an evil coloration, helping to perpetuate a suspicious popular view of their influence in the political process. James Madison set a theme that has recurred consistently in political commentary since his day.

The following selection describes how political action committees have become an integral part of interest-group and electoral politics.

34

Walter Isaacson
RUNNING WITH THE PACs

Like electronic images gobbling dots across a video screen, the PAC-men darted among the elegant rooms of the National Republican Club on Capitol Hill. At a fund raiser for Congressman Eldon Rudd of Arizona, they dropped their checks into a basket by the door or pressed them into the candidate's palm, before heading for the shrimp rolls and meatballs. Downstairs, other PAC-men crowded into a reception for Delaware Congressman Tom Evans, which featured piano music and White House luminaries. A few stopped in at the party for Deborah Cochran of Massachusetts. Because she is a long-shot challenger, they mainly left business cards rather than checks. But still she came out ahead; the cost of the event was picked up by the National Rifle Association.

Although Congress has adjourned and most members have headed home for the final stretch of the 1982 campaign, candidates can still be found buzzing back to Capitol Hill. They know that Washington is where the money is these days, or at least where one dips into the honeypot of contributions from political action committees (PACs). In a circular chase that is dominating congressional politics as never before, the candidates are courting the PACs, and the PAC-men are courting the candidates. "Harry Truman said that some people like government so much that they want to buy it," says Democratic Congressman David Obey of Wisconsin. "The 1982 elections will see Truman proved right."

There is nothing inherently evil about PACs: they are merely campaign committees established by organizations of like-minded individuals to raise money for political purposes, a valid aspect of the democratic process. In the wake of Watergate, Congress amended the federal election laws in 1974 to limit the role of wealthy contributors and end secretive payoffs by corporations and unions. The new law formalized the role of PACs, which were supposed to provide a well-regulated channel for individuals to get together and support candidates. But as with many well-intended reforms, there were unintended consequences. Instead of solving the problem of campaign financing, PACs became the problem. They proliferated beyond any expectation, pouring far more money into campaigns than ever before. Today the power of PACs threatens to undermine America's system of representative democracy.

This year there are 3,149 PACs placing their antes into the political pot, up from 2,551 in 1980 and 113 in 1972. The estimated total of funds they will dispense for campaigns this year: a staggering $240 million. There is Back Pac, PeacePac and Cigar-Pac. Beer distributors have a committee named—what else?—SixPAC. Whataburger Inc. has one called Whata-Pac. The Concerned Rumanians for a Stronger America has a PAC, as does the Hawaiian Golfers for Good Government. And so do most major corporations and unions.

By law a PAC can give $5,000 to both a candidate's primary and general election campaigns, while an individual contributor can give only $1,000 to each. Presidential elections are financed by federal funds, so most of the money is channeled into congressional, state and local races. Since PACs tend to run in packs, a popular candidate, particularly a powerful incumbent, may raise more than half his war chest from these special-interest groups. One example: Democratic Congressman Thomas Luken of Ohio, who has sponsored numerous special-interest bills and raised some $100,000 from PACs.

During Campaign '82, PACs will directly donate at least $80 million to House and Senate candidates—a leap of more than 45 percent from 1980. Another $160 million may be spent by PACs on local races, independent political advertising, and administrative activities. Says Democrat James Shannon of Massachusetts: "PACs are visibly corrupting the system."

Critics charge that PACs have distorted the democratic process by making candidates beholden to narrow interests rather than to their constituents. "Dependency on PACs has grown so much that PACs, not constituents, are the focus of a Congressman's attention," says Common Cause President Fred Wertheimer, whose citizens' lobby is fighting to reform the system. Special interests, of course, should be able to fight for their own concerns, but the power of PACs has upset the delicate balance between private interests and the public good. Indeed, PAC victories—continued price supports for dairy farmers, the defeat of a proposed fee on commodity trades, a proposed exemption from antitrust laws for shipping companies—often come at taxpayer expense. "It is not surprising there are no balanced budgets," says Republican Jim Leach of Iowa, who is one of fewer than a dozen members of Congress who refuse to take PAC money.

In addition, the close correlation between special-interest donations and legislative votes sometimes makes it seem that Congress is up for sale. Says Republican Senator Robert Dole of Kansas: "When these PACs give money they expect something in return other than good government." Democratic

Congressman Thomas Downey of New York is more blunt: "You can't buy a Congressman for $5,000. But you can buy his vote. It's done on a regular basis." This is one reason why Michigan Democrat William Brodhead decided to quit Congress this year. Says he: "I got sick of feeling indebted to PACs. There is no reason they give money except in the expectation of votes."

Another problem is that PACs have helped raise the cost of campaigning, just as the desire to buy more and more expensive television time increases a candidate's dependency on PACs. Says Democrat Andrew Jacobs of Indiana, a critic of PACs: "It's like getting addicted by a pusher. You become accustomed to lavish campaigns." In 1974 the average cost of campaigning for the House was $50,000; in 1980 the average was $150,000, and this year races costing $500,000 are not uncommon. Says House Republican Leader Robert Michel of Illinois, who has raised more than $220,000 from PACs: "This year I'll pay several hundred thousand dollars for a job that pays $60,000."

Before the sanctioning of PACs in the early 1970s, corporations and unions were generally prohibited from donating to campaigns. Money from large special interests, however, was often funneled secretly in stuffed envelopes; Lyndon Johnson built his power base by serving as a conduit for campaign donations from oil tycoons and construction companies, and one of the key Watergate revelations was the pernicious influence of large corporate payoffs made under the table. But the national parties, and the local political machines, remained the dominant force in the control of campaign funds. By diminishing the role of parties, PACs tend to make elected officials more narrow in their allegiances. This lessens the chance for broad coalitions that balance competing interests. Says Stuart Eizenstat, former domestic affairs adviser to Jimmy Carter: "PACs balkanize the political process."

Labor unions, which organized the first political action committees, will pump some $20 million into the 1982 campaign through 350 separate PACs. Business followed the union lead and soon overtook them: this year 1,497 corporate PACs will give $30 million to the candidates. Trade associations such as the National Association of Realtors and the American Medical Association (A.M.A.) account for 613 PACs, which will chip in another $22 million. An additional 45 PACs are run by cooperatives like the Associated Milk Producers, and will give $2 million this election. By far the greatest, and most worrisome, growth has been among the loose cannons of the PAC arsenal, ideological PACs not connected to any organization. Among them: the National Conservative Political Action Committee (NCPAC) and North Carolina Senator Jesse Helms' Congressional Club. The 644 nonconnected PACs are expected to donate only $6 million directly to candidates. But they will use most of their money for negative propaganda unauthorized by any candidate and for building up direct-mail lists that will help fund future political wars.

PAC money is mainly helping incumbents, since most PACs are guided by the pragmatic desire for access to power. Many corporate PACs that supported successful conservative challengers in 1980 are concentrating this year on so-lidifying Republican gains. Only 15 percent of the PAC money has gone to challengers so far this election. In the past this bias toward incumbents meant that Democrats fared slightly better with PACs than Republicans, but now the increasing strength of corporate PACs (which give 65 percent of their money to Republicans) relative to labor PACs (which channel 90 percent of their funds to Democrats) could mean that G.O.P. candidates receive slightly more money.

The PACs are playing a dominant role in many races around the country. When Ohio Republican Paul Pfeifer launched his challenge against Senator Howard Metzenbaum last spring, he was given so little chance that the prag-matic PACs shunned him. Metzenbaum's $3 million campaign fund, on the other hand, included $350,000 in PAC money by the end of the summer, mainly from unions. But last month, while Metzenbaum was in Washington conducting a maverick crusade against special-interest bills, Pfeifer began showing strength in the polls. Suddenly PAC money started flowing to the challenger. Says a Pfeifer aide: "More than anything else, a poll will speak to the PAC community. They're like a business trying to invest." One-third of Pfeifer's campaign do-nations are now from PACs.

Congressmen Ike Skelton and Wendell Bailey of Missouri have been pitted against each other by redistricting. Such a clash of incumbents inevitably trig-gers heavy PAC spending, and some groups like the A.M.A. have hedged their bets by donating to both. With dairy and labor PACs lining up behind Democrat Skelton, and corporate ones behind Republican Bailey, each side has raised $100,000 from special interests.

Another heated PAC showdown is the California race between Democrat Phillip Burton and Republican Milton Marks. When Marks first flew to Wash-ington to solicit PAC money, he ran into Burton at a restaurant. "I'm here to raise money to run against you," Marks proclaimed jovially. Of his 800 PAC solicitations, Marks hooked 100 donors, raising almost $100,000. Burton piously proclaims he will never take corporate PAC money. But he will take it from labor, progressive groups and conservationist clubs. More than half of his $450,000 reelection fund will come from such PACs.

A far different type of political influence develops when an ideological PAC targets a race. NCPAC, for example, is notorious for mounting negative campaigns against candidates it hopes to see defeated. In these races NCPAC rarely makes direct contributions to a candidate, and thus can spend as much as it wishes. (In 1976 the Supreme Court ruled that parts of the federal election law violated the right of free speech. It said that candidates may personally use as much of their own money as they want, and that unaffiliated groups, like NCPAC, can spend unlimited amounts on their own advocacy campaigns as long as their activity is not authorized by any candidate's official organization.) Moreover, since NCPAC is not affiliated with a candidate, it is less accountable for the tone and content of its campaign. As NCPAC Chairman Terry Dolan has admitted, "A group like ours could lie through its teeth, and the candidate it helps stays clean." NCPAC played a loud but indefinite role in the defeat of four liberal Senators in 1980, but since then it has waned in power if not in dollars.

Liberal groups have responded to NCPAC and other right-wing organizations by forming PACs of their own. Among the new groups is Progressive PAC (ProPAC), which will spend $150,000 in the election, most of it having gone into now abandoned negative campaigns against conservatives. Another is Democrats for the '80s (nicknamed PamPAC for Founder Pamela Harriman), which is spending $500,000. One of the richest ideological PACs is that of the National Organization for Women, which hopes to donate more than $2 million this year to candidates who support its feminist positions and who oppose Reaganomics. Says newly elected NOW President Judy Goldsmith: "We will proceed with work on defeating the right wing."

The growing importance of PAC donations means that the scramble for such money has become an integal part of campaigning. "It used to be that lobbyists lobbied congressmen," say PAC Critic Mike Synar, a Democratic Congressman from Oklahoma. "Now, Congressmen lobby lobbyists—for money." When that inevitable creature of the PAC explosion, the National Association for Association PACs, threw a party, 80 Congressmen showed up. "I've never seen such a group grope," says Democrat Dan Glickman of Kansas. Republican James Coyne of Pennsylvania playfully installed five PacMan video games near the bar of one of his Washington fund raisers in honor of the real PAC-men who have donated $126,000 to his 1982 campaign. Other lawmakers shower the PACs with glossy brochures soliciting money.

Republican Senator Orrin Hatch of Utah has already collected an astounding $750,000 from 531 PACs. Over scrambled eggs at a breakfast last Tuesday in Salt Lake City, he graciously accepted $5,000 more from the Association of Trial Lawyers. Such support, his campaign manager says, "shows a level of commitment to Hatch nationwide by thousands of people." It also shows, critics say, that he is intensely pro-business and chairs the powerful Labor and Human Resources Committee.

Indeed, the pursuit of PAC money has given a national flavor to state campaigns. Two Democratic congressional hopefuls from California, Doug Bosco and Barbara Boxer, ran into each other this year in the Washington waiting room of a PAC they were both courting. Says Bosco: "You get kind of bored with yourself going from PAC to PAC to PAC. You get the feeling you are being processed." San Diego's Republican mayor Pete Wilson, running for the Senate, made a pilgrimage to Washington a few weeks ago and met with Bernadette Budde of the Business Industry PAC (BIPAC). He also held a $500-per-PAC-man reception at a hotel near the White House. Total take: $75,000.

Houston and Dallas, where the oil money runs thick, have become hubs of PAC activity. "We had a congressional candidate here from North Carolina recently and gave him a few thousand dollars," says Jack Webb, executive director of the Houston PAC. "Then we took him around and introduced him to other oil folks and I'm pretty sure he left with more than $10,000 in pledges." HouPAC plans to give away $200,000 this year, ten times its donations for 1980.

Deciding how to divvy up their bounty can be a complex process for PACs. The 20 trustees of the Realtors PAC held the last of a dozen strategy sessions in Chicago's downtown Marriott Hotel two weeks ago, working late into the night and through the next day to cull the 150 worthy candidates who would receive the last of the $2.5 million allotted for 1982. Each trustee had a folder on supplicants that included voting records and "campaign intelligence reports" prepared with the aid of eight full-time field specialists. Washington staffers gave briefings on where incumbents stand on such issues as the balanced-budget amendment and the mortgage subsidy bill.

Candidates seeking the Realtors' money must submit answers to a six-page questionnaire. In some cases the "correct" answers are all too obvious. "Do you agree or disagree [that] trade associations have a right and a responsibility to hold members of Congress accountable for their votes?" Others are trickier. One asks candidates to rank what contributes most to high interest rates: record deficits, restrictive monetary policy, excessive tax cuts, etc. (A: The Realtors have fought strongly against high deficits.) "Sometimes candidates plead with me to give them the correct answers," say Political Resources Director Randall Moorhead.

Typical of the Realtors' deliberation was their discussion of the Texas Senate race between Democratic Incumbent Lloyd Bentsen and Challenger Jim Collins. Although Republican Collins was very sympathetic to the Realtors' philosophy and had been a supporter in the House, Bentsen is the incumbent and likely victor. He got the $4,250. Challegers are referred to as "risk capital ventures."

The choices for smaller PACs are simpler. At a meeting this month to hand out the last of its $225,000 congressional donations, the PAC of the Grumman Corp., maker of fighter jets, gave another $1,000 to Democrat William Chappell of Florida, who is on the Defense Appropriations Subcommittee. Says Grumman PAC Chairman Dave Walsh: "We have selfish interests. We dole out money to those on committees dealing with defense and to those whose viewpoint is in line with ours."

Small PACs often look to larger ones for guidance. The Chamber of Commerce, BIPAC and the AFL-CIO publish "opportunity lists" to lead like-minded PAC money where it will do the most good. The Chamber recently produced a video version of its list by broadcasting a four-hour, closed-circuit television show called *See How They Run* to 150 PAC managers in seven cities. It opens with patriotic music and a waving flag as Chamber President Richard Lesher extols "a brighter future for America through political action." Presidential

Assistant Kenneth Duberstein joins Chamber analysts in handicapping 50 key races. One of the Chamber choices, Pennsylvania's Coyne, expresses the sentiment of the rest of the all-Republican lineup: "The key to my race is, Can we marshal the resources?"

An article in *INC.* magazine, which is aimed at independent businessmen, offers advice on "some ways to measure your return" from PAC donations. It explains how to compute the "equity share" and "cost-vote ratio" that can be "bought" for each candidate. "Special interests don't contribute to congressional candidates for the fun of it," the article advises. "They do so to get things done." It dismisses any moral qualms: "If politicians want to sell and the public wants to buy, there is not much you can do to stop the trade."

The question of whether PAC donations actually buy votes or only reward members who tend to vote properly is akin to that of the chicken and the egg. One thing is certain: the combination of chickens and eggs fertilizes the legislative process. The National Automobile Dealers Association, which will contribute more than $850,000 to congressional candidates this election, was able to kill a regulation requiring that buyers be informed of known defects in used cars for sale. The United Auto Workers (U.A.W.) is handing out more than $1 million this year while it lines up support for a "domestic content" bill that requires foreign firms to use a high percentage of American parts and labor in cars they sell in the U.S. Lockheed Corp., like its competitor Boeing, donated heavily to the House and Senate armed services committees as it fought to win a Government contract for its C-5B cargo plane. The National Rifle Association (N.R.A.) will give away $1.3 million this year, some of it to help Senate Judiciary Committee members who approved a law loosening gun-control regulations.

Although lobbyists and Congressmen deny that votes are for sale, the link to donations is often uncomfortably clear. The U.A.W. PAC in New Jersey has long backed Congressman Peter Rodino. But last month Rodino was informed that future support would be contingent on his agreeing to co-sponsor the domestic content bill. When his office said he would, the union publicly announced that its endorsement came "following Rodino's decision to sign on as a co-sponsor" of the bill. The appearance of coercion annoyed Rodino. Said an aide: "He thought it was the most heavyhanded thing he had seen during his career." Rodino withdrew as a co-sponsor, although he is still backing the bill.

An example of how donations and votes go hand in palm is the House passage of a bill that would allow the shipping industry to fix prices, which could raise freight costs by about 20 percent. The Merchant Marine and Fisheries Committee has long been a safe harbor for special interests. "Any bill coming out of the Merchant Marine ought to go straight to the grand jury," jokes one Congressman. Both labor and business groups formed an alliance to pass the price fixing bill, with the Seafarers' Union and Lykes Bros. Steamship Co. leading the lobbying by 13 interested PACs. Their total donations to Merchant Marine Committee members: $47,850. After passing the bill 33 to 0, the committee got the House rules suspended to allow only 40 minutes of debate. Since most Congressmen had little idea of what was in the bill, many voted in response to thumbs-up signs from committee members. The bill passed 350 to 33.

Among other PAC-man specials:

The Professionals Bill. The A.M.A. and American Dental Association have been lobbying for a law that would exempt professionals from Federal Trade Commission regulation and thus permit them to fix prices. The bill is still awaiting House action. Since 1979 the two groups have given $2.3 million to House members, 72 percent of it to 213 co-sponsors of the bill. Each sponsor got an average of $7,598, according to Consumer Advocate Ralph Nader's Congress Watch. Thomas Luken, the prime sponsor, got $14,750. Luken, one of Congress's most notorious PAC-men, also sponsored the bill revoking the used-car regulation.

The Beer Bill. Brewers want to be allowed to designate monopoly territories for their distributors, which could raise the cost of beer 20 percent. The legislation is pending in the House. SixPAC has handed out $35,000 to members of the Judiciary Subcommittee on Monopolies. Democrat Jack Brooks of Texas, the chief sponsor, got a $10,000 contribution, a $1,000 honorarium for a speech and a trip to Las Vegas from SixPAC this year.

The Bankruptcy Bill. The credit industry is pushing for a law that would fundamentally change the legal concept of a "fresh start" for those who go broke. The pending bill would require individual debtors, but not businesses, to pay back debts after declaring bankruptcy. Six credit PACs, led by the American Bankers Association and Household Finance Corp., have donated $704,297 to 255 Congressmen co-sponsoring the bill.

Commodity Traders' Fee. PACs representing three major groups of commodities brokers have been fighting a Reagan Administration proposal to set a 6¢ to 12¢ fee on each trade to finance the Commodity Futures Trading Commission. They have contributed to most members of the House and Senate agriculture committees, both of which voted to reject the fee. "It isn't buying votes," said Michael McLeod, a lobbyist with the Chicago Board of Trade. "It's just how the political system works."

Clean Air. The House Health and the Environment Subcommittee voted this year to weaken considerably the Clean Air Act. The twelve members who voted for the relaxation got a total of $197,325 from the PACs of the seven major industries affected. Republican Senator Steve Symms of Idaho, who got $97,500 during his 1980 campaign from affected industries, dutifully introduced one industry amendment after another. "It was clear he had no idea what was in those amendments," says one Senator. Members of his committee even privately mocked him, asking, "Which campaign check had that amendment attached to it?"

When a bill emerges from commitee, and the debate becomes publicized, it becomes harder for special interests to be effective. Grassroots pressure by those in favor of the Clean Air Act, and perhaps also the growth of environmental PACs, make it likely that the act will pass without being significantly weakened.

Defenders of the PAC system say that contributions are an effect, not a cause; and that they are given to those who are already known to be supportive of a PAC's position. "The idea that there's a *quid pro quo* is balderdash," says Republican Congressman Bill Frenzel of Minnesota. Argues BIPAC's Budde: "Pacs are not buying anyone. They're rewarding." Because a single PAC is limited to $5,000 a race, the power it can command, while large, is not overwhelming. The most you can purchase, proponents claim, is access. Says Grumman PAC Chairman Walsh: "We don't expect contracts because we gave someone $5,000. But the likelihood of us getting in to see the Congressman is much higher."

The backers of PACs point out that, like rivers to the sea, special-interest money will find a way to flow into campaigns, and the PAC channel keeps the process regulated and open to public scrutiny. Small donors, who once felt they had no impact, can now pool their money with like-minded voters. "PACs have redistributed political influence," says Phil Gramm of Texas. "They've taken power away from the smoke-filled room." Agrees Jack Webb of HouPAC: "PACs get people involved who otherwise might not be. They're a damned good thing."

There is no argument about one major PAC fact: within ten years, PACs have become a significant method of financing congressional campaigns, accounting for more than one-fourth of all money raised by candidates, and more than one-third of all money raised by incumbents. The average candidate now gets three times as much money from PACs as from a political party. This year, the national campaign committees of the Republican Party have been revitalized by a surge of donations. Even so, unless the laws are changed, PACs are destined to remain much more important than national parties as a source of funds for candidates. Says Herbert Alexander, a professor at the University of Southern California who has written about campaign finance: "The decline of the parties is, in part, a consequence of election reform gone awry."

PACs have become so important and controversial that they are now an issue of their own on the campaign trail. Their proper role is being debated, for example, in the Senate race in Montana. Democratic Incumbent John Melcher is receiving contributions from a wide array of labor, corporate and association PACs. They have given him more than $350,000, over half his campaign fund. "How can you work for your constituents when you've got $10,000 chits out?" demands Republican Challenger Larry Williams, a self-made millionaire. Melcher is countering by making an issue of the fact that NCPAC has waged an irresponsible $250,000 independent effort to defeat him. One of Melcher's television ads depicts NCPAC operatives flying into the state with money-stuffed briefcases to "defeat Doc Melcher."

Democrat Joseph Kolter is also trying to turn PAC donations into an issue in his bid to unseat Republican Congressman Eugene Atkinson of Pennsylvania. Last year Atkinson made a dramatic switch in party allegiance. As a Democrat, he had piously refused on principle to accept PAC money, but since becoming a Republican he has raised $40,000 from business-oriented PACs. In his campaign speeches, Kolter reels off a list of Atkinson donors, referring to General Public Utilities Corp. as "the people who brought you Three Mile Island" and to a group of major industries as "the filthy five." Kolter has his own PAC sources; he is drawing the maximum donations from the United Steel Workers, the U.A.W. and other unions.

Any attempt to reform the PAC system is vulnerable to the law of unintended consequences. Individuals, groups, corporations and unions will continue to have the desire and resources to support favored candidates. They also have the right, and even the responsibility, to do so. Trying to restrict such efforts too severely could just divert them into other, less worthy approaches, like the one followed by NCPAC. Says Michael Malbin, a political analyst at the American Enterprise Institute: "Unless you repeal the First Amendment, people with private interests in legislation will be active."

Public financing of campaigns would solve many of the problems. The same arguments that were persuasive at the presidential level—the need to lower the role of fat-cat donors and special interests—are at least as compelling when it comes to Congress. (In the primaries, presidential candidates raise money, some of it from PACs, that is matched by federal funds. The general election is fully financed by federal money.) But such a process presents practical difficulties: some districts and states are much more expensive to campaign in than others, and incumbents (who make the laws) are unlikely to vote for a system that removes their own built-in advantage. "It's like sending goats to guard the cabbage patch," says Andrew Jacobs of Indiana, one of the Congressmen who refuse PAC money. Moreover, public financing could be expensive.

Raising the $1,000 limit that an individual can contribute to a campaign would help dilute the power of PACs. The individual limit had stayed the same since 1974 despite inflation. "Individual contributions are far less effective than those from a PAC," says Republican Congresswoman Millicent Fenwick of New Jersey. "The PAC's lobbyist will come and twist arms." In her race for a Senate seat, Fenwick has refused PAC money.

Individual donations from corporate leaders, of course, can exert the same type of influence as money from PACs. Indeed, the PAC-stemious Fenwick has raised $13,650 from the top executives of a Wall Street investment firm, far more than the limit imposed on the firm's PAC. But the greatest threat posed by individual contributions in the past was the secrecy surrounding them and their disproportionate amounts. A new $5,000 limit would seem reasonable in light of today's strict reporting requirements.

Another option would be to limit the total amount a House candidate could raise from PACs. A bill setting a $70,000 limit on the amount a House candidate could raise from PACs passed the House in 1979, but died in the Senate. A new measure has been introduced in the House setting the PAC money ceiling at $75,000.

The ideal reform would incorporate elements of each of these proposals. Partial federal financing, either by direct grants or matching funds, could water down the importance of PACs. So could raising the private contribution limit. Increasing the amount people can donate to the national parties, currently $20,000 each year, could strengthen the role of the parties. Finally, setting a reasonable limit on the amount a candidate can get from PACs, certainly no more than $75,000 an election, would rein in the PAC-men.

The difficulty is not so much finding solutions, but persuading Congressmen, who benefit so handsomely, to change the present situation. "It is a lot easier to raise money from PACs than from other sources," observes PAC Critic Barney Frank, a Democratic Congressman from Massachusetts. "You sit there, somebody hands you a check for $3,000, and you say 'Thank you,' " In the end, it is pressure from the voters that may limit the power of the PACs. Some lawmakers, like Missouri Democrat Richard Gephardt, detect rumblings of reform. Says he: "There is a growing sense that the system is getting out of hand."

Money and Elections

Political campaigning has become increasingly expensive at all levels of government. Only presidential campaigns are publicly funded, although candidates in presidential primaries have to garner a certain amount of private contributions to qualify for federal matching funds. The rise of political action committees (PACs), which the campaign finance laws of the 1970s recognized as legitimate, has enhanced the influence of private money and interest-group power in the political process. The following selection examines the important connection between money and politics.

35

Frank J. Sorauf
MONEY IN AMERICAN ELECTIONS

Eras do not have specific dates of origin. The kind of massive, dramatic change that marks their onset is really a cluster of related changes happening only more or less at the same time. And so it has been with campaign finance in the United States. The stirrings of a new era, the contemporary era, began some time in the 1960s, but it arrived full-blown in the 1970s with the coming together of a number of trends and changes in American politics. It is not, however, the onset of the new era that marks it most indelibly, but rather the ways in which the current era differs from the one that preceded it.

Nothing characterizes the new era as vividly as the increase in the sheer sums of money spent in campaigns for public office. In 1972 all of the candidates for Congress spent a total of $77,305,769 in their campaigns; by 1976 the total had edged up to $115,500,000. By 1986 the total cost of congressional campaigns had jumped dramatically to $450,049,177, an increase of 482 percent since 1972. Even allowing for the increase of 162 percent in the Consumer Price Index from 1972 to 1986—that is, correcting for the effect of inflation—the increase in purchasing power dollars is still a very substantial 122 percent.

Other less visible, but scarcely less fundamental, changes altered American campaign finance in the 1970s and 1980s. In earlier years the large contributor—the fabled "fat cat"—had dominated it. Congress ended that domination in 1974; and at least partially in compensatory response, political action committees (PACs) began a period of unprecedented expansion. At bottom, however, the new system of campaign funding came to rest on the political generosity of millions of individual contributors, whether they gave their money directly to candidates or indirectly through PACs and political parties. Finally, a burgeoning of data and information marked the new era. Congress and a good many states began in the 1970s to require parties, PACs, and candidates to report their financial transactions; and a rich and detailed body of data on money in campaigns resulted. Drawing on those data, the mass media have reported the details of campaign finance for the American public in ways unimaginable in earlier years or eras.

I. THE NEW WAYS OF POLITICS

All of these characteristics of the new era in American campaign finance are evidence of more fundamental changes in American politics. Most especially they are reflections of changes in the American way of campaigning. It is *campaign* finance we are talking about, and changes in American campaigns are bound to have an effect on the ways we fund them.

A very shrewd observer of politicians and campaigns [Stimson Bullitt, in *To Be a Politician*] wrote almost prophetically in 1961:

> The media have done to the campaign system what the invention of accurate artillery did to the feudal kingdom—destroyed the barons and shifted their power to the masses and the prince. A candidate now pays less attention to district leaders than to opinion polls.

What seemed prophetic in 1961 seems commonplace in the 1980s. But in truth it is not only the media that wrought the changes. The technologies that revolutionized campaigning embrace all of the arts of modern communication and persuasion: the sample survey (i.e., the poll), computer-based information and analysis, specialized accountancy and legal advice, systematic fund-raising, and strategic scheduling and planning. The men and women who master these skills have become the new campaign technocrats, the campaign managers and consultants who so dominate contemporary electoral politics.

In the decades after World War II, the major American political party slipped into decline. The fabled urban machines were ailing virtually everywhere; only Mayor Richard Daley's in Chicago survived a few years longer. Party organizations in places other than big cities were never models of vitality or effectiveness and now declined even further. Voters loosened their party loyalties a bit more in each decade after the war. The percentage of self-styled independents rose, and even voters who continued to profess a loyalty to a political party often became more casual about their commitment. Since loyalty to party governed a smaller part of the voting decision for millions of voters, split-ticket voting increased. Party lines in the Congress and many state legislatures also softened after World War II. Disciplined, cohesive legislators of one party faced similarly disciplined legislators of the other party less and less often. So, in a number of ways political parties began to count for less in the politics of the nation.

Inevitably, the political parties were able to control less and less of the campaign for public office. Gone were the days when their ranks of local workers and committeemen canvassed the local voters—the equivalent of polling in those days—and gone, too, were the days in which party publications and party parades and rallies were the stuff and excitement of the campaign. The skills and labor the party mobilized were no longer the main resource of the campaign; they were increasingly replaced by the new media, the new technologies, and the new people with the new skills. In short, a new style of campaigning emerged; and the parties were less and less central to it.

Candidates increasingly found themselves free to run their own campaigns—provided they could raise the money to "rent" the new campaign expertise and media of the campaign. In the days of greater party control, the candidates had come by the resources for their campaigns by bartering their loyalty for the resources the party amassed. Candidates now found themselves in a cash economy. Fund-raising suddenly became a vastly more important part of the business of being a candidate or even of being a potential candidate. But for all this trouble in finding cash, candidates literally "purchased" a kind of political freedom. Campaigns were theirs to manage or, more accurately, to arrange the management of. The need to raise large sums of money was at once a weighty burden and a charter of independence from the party and its claims.

Behind all of these shifts and changes in the resources it takes to mount a campaign, there was also a shift in what one might call the resource constituency. In earlier eras the campaign resources, heavy in manpower from the locality, were mobilized by the political party. The resource constituency was, therefore, largely congruent with the electoral constituency. In the new era, the resource constituency is much more apt to be located outside the party organization and, increasingly, outside of the electoral constituency. Candidates for Congress raise more money nationally or regionally; PACs and parties raise it centrally (i.e., nationally) and disburse it back to the candidates in the states and the congressional districts. The consequences of that divergence of electoral and resource constituencies have been momentous.

When Jesse Unruh, then the Democratic speaker of the California Assembly, laid down his dictum that "money is the mother's milk of politics," it had all the freshness of a new insight. That was in the early 1960s. To be sure, some of the fundamental changes in American politics had begun before then. Extensive TV coverage of campaigns was becoming common in the late 1950s, for example. Other changes were just beginning; the number of independents in the American electorate turned upward in the late 1960s. But by the time all the changes and developments were consolidated and shaped in the 1970s by a major body of regulatory legislation, a new era in campaign finance was upon us; and Unruh's dictum—still the most famous one-liner in campaign finance—had begun to seem almost commonplace.

Campaigns and their funding, in turn, reflect the broader context of the entire political system. Above all, the nature of campaigns and campaign finance reflects the centrality of the individual candidate in American politics. With very few exceptions, Americans nominate candidates not by some internal party process but by an election, a primary election. Especially in the states and localities, we choose public officials, such as public utilities commissioners and local assessors, not by appointment but by election. The resulting proliferation of elections and candidates in them extends campaigning to a scope no other democracy knows. And those campaigns are for candidates, not for a party. In much of the rest of the world, voters choose between or among political parties, largely because either parliamentary institutions or proportional representation in elections frame the combat in terms of party outcomes and party control of government.

Even more broadly than that, American campaign finance reflects American society, especially its voluntarism. Raising money for candidates, parties, and PACs has a great deal in common with raising money for the arts, for hospitals, or for charities. The ease with which a little persuasion can coax money from Americans for a worthy purpose has no parallel in the rest of the world, nor is there any parallel to the extensive and thriving American fund-raising industry. The skills and techniques of that industry—the art of the fund-raising letter and the use of computer-based mailing lists, for example—have nourished the new campaign fund-raising. While campaign finance may not replace apple pie in the American pantheon, it is every bit as indigenously American as a United Way campaign.

II. ACTORS AND EVENTS

The actors, the events, and the transactions in American campaign finance are all defined by legislative fiat. And as with all other things in American electoral politics, that means by 51 legislatures: the Congress and those of the fifty states. Congress regulates its own campaigns and those for the presidency, and the state legislatures regulate those for state and local office. (Some states do permit local councils and other governing authorities to exert some control over campaigns for local office.) But, unhappily, campaign finance is not even that simple. Legislation often defines different funding and regulation for different offices at the same level of government. Just at the national level, for instance, there are three systems of campaign finance: one for the two houses of Congress, a second for presidential candidates before the nominating conventions, and a third for the major party candidates for the presidency after the conventions. There is no public funding for the first, partial public funding for the second, and full public funding available for the third. Given all the options and varieties, no one really knows how many systems exist in the American states and localities.

Certainly the most celebrated, documented, and varied of the campaign finance systems is the one for congressional campaigns. It is the one [we] will explore at greatest length; and it offers, therefore, the most useful "bare bones" model of the actors and events in campaign finance (Figure 1–1). Movement in the model is from left to right, as it is in all such flowcharts of a political process. The flow of money begins at the left with the willing individual. That person may give money to a PAC, to a party, or directly to a candidate; or he or she may decide to spend the money autonomously and independently to urge the election or defeat of a candidate. In reality, individuals spend virtually all of their money in the first three options; and among these three well over half of their money goes directly to candidates.

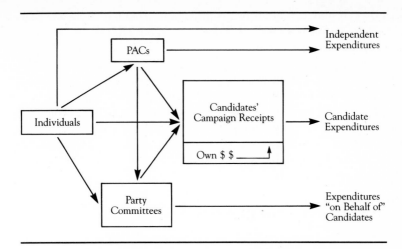

Figure 1–1   Major Actors and Flows of Money in Congressional Campaign Finance

Political parties and PACs, for their part, may contribute funds directly to candidates; they also each have another, though different, political option. PACs may spend "independently"—in TV or newspaper ads or direct mail messages, for example—to urge the election or defeat of candidates, just as individuals may. Political parties may spend directly in the election "on behalf of" candidates; in doing so, they are free to consult and coordinate with those candidates. (They may also spend money generally to promote the party itself.) Finally, of course, the candidates spend what they raise (or most of what they raise) directly in the campaign. In addition, they are free to add their own personal fortune to the funds they raise from individuals, PACs, and parties.

That schema prevails for most campaigns, with one exception: instances of public funding. In the presidential campaigns and various campaigns in less than a fifth of the states, money from some public treasury enters the system if candidates choose to accept the money and, usually, the attendant limit on their expenditures. In those instances one simply adds the treasury as one more source of candidate funds; and if public funds come on a matching basis, one would have to link it to the "trigger" of voluntary contributions from other sources. In the case of presidential campaigns for the general election, public funding is total and shuts out party, PAC, and individual contributions. Public funding in the states, however, is partial; and the public treasury in those campaigns coexists with the other sources of political money.

There are, to be sure, subtle and obscure transactions that so simple a representation cannot suggest. Figure 1–1 does not show, for example, that under federal law PACs may contribute to other PACs or to political party committees. Nor does it show that, in some states, corporations or trade unions may contribute money directly from their main assets to PACs, parties, or candidates. It also does not depict contributions (transfers) from one candidate to another. These, however, are details that do not alter the main contours of this dominant paradigm of American campaign finance.

Patterns of campaign finance vary a bit, then, from nation to state and from state to state; but the general structure is similar and one fundamental fact unites them. There are only five possible sources of the cash resources on which contemporary campaigning depends: a public treasury, individual contributions, party contributions, contributions by a PAC or some similar nonparty organization, and the candidate's own personal resources. That fact is the hard reality no one can escape in thinking either about the status quo in campaign finance or about ways of changing it.

III. JUDGMENT AND REFORM

Most Americans find it difficult, if not impossible, to view the funding of campaigns dispassionately. Small wonder, considering the messages about campaign finance that they regularly receive. Common Cause, the self-styled people's lobby, for instance has mounted a campaign against PACs ("People Against PAC$") in which a major piece of literature proclaims "It's a Disgrace . . . that our United States Congress is on the auction block. UP FOR GRABS to the highest PAC bidders." Much coverage of campaign finance in the mass media is similarly exercised, especially in its treatment of PAC contributions. Nouns like "bribery" and adjectives like "obscene" mark the rhetoric of judgment about campaign finance. It is, in short, not a climate in which detached observation and analysis thrive.

Fear, outrage, and suspicion have, however, always dogged the use of money in American politics. It has always suggested images of bedrock bribery or corruption—the kind in which there is an exchange of favors for money, a quid for the quo. ("If they didn't expect something in return, why would they spend all that money?") It has also symbolized the tyranny of wealth and privilege in government and politics. And in the terms the turn-of-the-century Progressives favored, it has always represented the power of the narrow special interests over the public interests—the power of the greedy few over the many.

Certainly Americans have always been more suspicious of cash contributions than noncash contributions. Somehow we tend to look differently at the $1000 cash contribution than we do at the volunteer who gives $1000 worth of time and skills in the campaign. In fact, federal law makes the same invidious distinction. The $1000 cash contribution must be reported by the candidate as a contribution received, but the $1000 worth of volunteered effort need not be. Moreover, we celebrate the latter as doing one's duty as a citizen and exercising one's First Amendment rights. We do not so celebrate the cash contribution.

All of this is not to suggest a flight from judgment about campaign finance. Judgments about American politics are not merely useful; they are obligatory.

But judgments are rarely useful if they spring from old assumptions and heated arguments rather than evidence and analysis. It is certainly important, for example, to consider what contributors—whether they are individuals, PACs, or parties—expect to gain or achieve by contributing money to candidates. It is equally important to try to gauge the impact of cash expenditures, especially different levels of expenditures, on the outcomes of elections. One could multiply the examples many times over. But, in all cases the effects or consequences of money in campaigns are not as easy to assess as received wisdom would suggest. To assess the motives of individuals, the goals and strategies of groups, and the effects of spending is no easy task, even after one has accumulated a great deal of evidence.

There is in fact no standard or measuring stick for some of the issues that trouble us in campaign finance. Take the question of the magnitudes of the sums spent in campaigns. It is a question of "how much is too much?" The average Democratic or Republican candidate for the House of Representatives in the 1986 general election spent $260,032. Is that too much, too little, or just right? How, in particular, does one decide? By the standards of middle-class personal finance, that total may indeed be appalling. By the standards of public entertainment (in which star baseball or basketball players earn five to ten times that much in a year, not to mention the "take" of rock music stars), the sum seems modest enough. (The salary of the *average* major league baseball player passed $300,000 back in 1984.) All of the Democratic and Republican general election campaigns for the House in 1986 when added together produce a figure ($210,626,146) less than a quarter of the annual advertising budget for Proctor and Gamble.

For many of the issues inherent in the American way of campaign finance, however, there is a clear and powerful standard for judgment: the imperatives and assumptions of democracy. In every sense it is the highest standard of them all. If one argues, for example, that competitive elections with the real possibility of "throwing the rascals out" are essential to a representative democracy, then one has a standard for judging campaign funding if it reduces that competitiveness. (It may not be easy, alas, to conclude if money is in fact reducing the competition.) One's understanding of the nature of representation—certainly a part of one's understanding of popular democracy—will lead one to judgment about the rise of national resource constituencies for members of Congress. Is it desirable or not, that is, that citizens outside of the voting district participate in the politics of the district and possibly win some measure of influence over its elected representative? It is not an easy question to answer, but it would be an impossible one without an underlying concept of representation in democracy.

IV. THE DISCIPLINE OF DATA

Congress's requirement that candidates, parties, PACs, and assorted other spenders report their campaign transactions in considerable detail has produced the most complete data on campaign finance known to modern democracy. Nothing in the states or the rest of the world match them. The Federal Election Commission (FEC) aggregates, publishes, and otherwise makes them available. Its data on congressional and presidential elections sustain the greatest share of the analysis and interpretation in this book. In fact, all data in this book have come from the press releases, printed reports, and computer tapes of the Federal Election Commission unless they are otherwise identified.

The rows and columns of numbers that constitute the data are both a splendid resource and a formidable burden. As a resource they formulate the most complete record available of the campaign finance of a nation. They also have given rise to the largest body of scholarship on campaign finance among the democracies of the world. But they are a burden, too, because they are complex in definition, logic, and structure. They demand a high degree of care and precision even in making simple descriptive statements, and thus they impose a rigorous discipline on both author and reader. Nowhere is it truer that the answer you get depends on the question you ask.

For example, what did a race for the House cost in 1986? Well, the average cost of all campaigns in 1985–86 (the FEC measures in two-year periods called "election cycles") was $148,796. But that figure includes candidates defeated in the primary and even noncandidates who raised and spent money to "test the waters" or send up "trial balloons." (The language of American politics feeds on well-polished cliches.) It even includes candidates from 1984 who raised money in 1985 or 1986 to retire their campaign debts. However, the FEC publishes data limited to the expenditures of the candidates who ran in the general election. The average cost for their campaigns was $218,975, but this includes independent candidates and the candidates of minor parties—candidates who usually spend relatively little and who thus bring down the average. So, what is the figure for major party candidates in the general election? That average is $260,032. For argumentative purposes, critics of the status quo in campaign finance like to cite the average cost of a House campaign for the *winners* in the general election; that average in 1986 was about $355,000. "You pays your money and you takes your choice," but it is supremely important to know exactly what the choice is.

The discipline of the data can also become a tyranny. In one very practical sense, the costs of campaigning for Congress are the costs the participants are required to report by law of Congress. Campaign costs are as Congress does. But it is important to keep in mind that Congress's definition, important as it is, is only one definition. And there are a good many costs it does not include. It assigns no value to the candidate's time and skills or to the time and skills of volunteer supporters, for instance. We tend to count cash costs and not to count noncash costs. Most controversially, federal statutes do not include as campaign expenditures any campaign to register voters or to get them out to vote. These activities are considered to be either nonpartisan or bipartisan. (That position does not convince Republicans who note that it is organized labor that spends the greatest resources on such activities.) That these are *some* part of the costs of contesting the election is less disputable. While some costs of campaigns may go unreported or uncounted, others are often overcounted. National committees of the political parties report total expenditures; for instance, does one wish to assign all the costs of the meetings and travel of the party bureaucrats to the campaigns?

Moreover, reporting—and the data it yields—is not equally demanding for all aspects of campaign finance. PACs must report every campaign contribution, no matter how small; individuals do not themselves have to report any contribution. Candidates must report the name of every PAC from which they receive a contribution; they must report only the names of contributors who give them more than $200. As a result we have far more data about PAC contributions than individual contributions; and given the effects of the "law of available data" on intellectual priorities, scholars and journalists write much more about PACs than they do about individual contributors. Americans thus know much more about PACs.

One could easily multiply the ways in which we become the prisoners of readily available data. Because federal law does not require full reporting about the objects and purposes of candidate expenditures, we know far less about what campaign money buys than we do about those who give it. And when one gets to the far sketchier laws and reporting requirements of many states, one is clutching often at fragments of data and only scattered pieces of the puzzle.

From all of this, one great lesson emerges: master the data or be mastered by them. Unless one understands their definitions and categories and treats them with care and precision, and unless one understands that their definitions are only one among a number of definitions of reality, one runs a great danger of falling victim to their tyranny.

V. CAMPAIGN FINANCE
IN THE BIGGER PICTURE

Depending on the scholarly idiom one prefers, intermediating political organizations such as parties and interest groups aggregate the influence of political individuals and bring those aggregates to bear on the institutions of government; or they link individual citizens to those institutions and the public officials who make policy in them. The process of aggregation or linkage is in fact a number of processes. In representative democracies it is accomplished for the largest number of individuals through the open election of public officials. Others are joined together to exert influence directly on the already chosen officials of government in processes we lump together as lobbying.

In a very rough but important way, political parties and interest groups in American politics long divided the domains of these two great aggregating processes—the parties dominating electoral politics and interest groups dominating the politics of lobbying. To be sure, the division of labor was approximate; but it was very real. And the two different kinds of political organizations seemed remarkably well adapted to their respective domains and to the different organizing tasks in them. Parties, large and omnibus organizations that tried to embrace majorities, were the organizations suited to contest elections. Interest groups, much narrower and more specialized and exclusive rather than inclusive, seemed better suited for the organization of diverse and specialized influence on policy-making.

All of the changes in campaign finance have threatened that great division of labor. Increasingly, interest groups and their offspring, the political action committees, are involved in election politics. And in states where it is legal, corporations, labor unions, and membership organizations are increasingly active directly in funding campaigns. In one sense that incursion is a reflection of the increased weakness of the political parties. But in another, more fundamental way, it reflects also some rudimentary changes in American politics. More and more Americans want to diminish their loyalty to an all-encompassing party; they prefer a more specialized election politics that permits them to pick and choose among candidates and issues. For that more specialized, more selective, more focused politics, the parties are blunter instruments than they want. The very idea of loyally voting a straight party ticket is exactly what the new election politics is *not* about.

The changing roles of the parties and groups have, of course, spawned a new one: the political action committee. PACs had been around in American politics since the 1940s, but only in the 1970s did they grow so dramatically in number and in influence. Most of them, indeed, became the electoral arms of parent organizations directly active in more traditional interest representation before legislatures and executive agencies. Their sharply increased importance reflects both the declining role of the parties in electoral politics and the changes in electoral politics to a politics of issues and volatile coalitions. Political action committees are, moreover, almost uncannily adapted for an election politics that is centered on candidates and that has cash as a medium of exchange.

So, fundamental change in American campaign finance moves forward on two levels. On the most obvious one are the changes in the ways in which we raise and spend resources in campaigns, the changes that mark a new era in campaign finance since the early 1970s. But on another more fundamental level, the changes in campaign finance are part of a broader change in the ways in which we organize influence and consent in the American democracy.

The Media as the Fourth Estate

No one doubts that the media are a powerful political force. The press and the electronic media have been called "the fourth estate," and even the fourth branch of government. In his farewell address, President Ronald Reagan told of his frustration with the media as part of what he called the "Washington colony." "What might be called a triangle of institutions—parts of Congress, the media and special-interest groups—is transforming and placing out of focus our constitutional balance," he said. He observed, "Administrations come and go, but the members of the Iron Triangle endure." Political scientists generally refer to Iron Triangles as including congressional committees, executive agencies, and special interests. By adding the media and eliminating executive agencies Reagan gave a new twist to the term.

The media influence the political process in many ways. Journalists keep the people informed about all kinds of government activities, and help to make complex public policy issues understandable. Reporters also act as important conduits of information within government. Politicians consider a good press essential to their success in both the electoral and governmental arenas.

The media not only influence government through reporting but also as an important interest group in its own right. Publishers and broadcasters are in business to make money, and their economic interests dictate their stands on many important public issues. The following selection describes how the media have become one of Washington's most powerful lobbies.

36

Sheila Kaplan
THE POWERS THAT BE—
LOBBYING

It usually doesn't take much to get a bill introduced in Congress. This past session alone brought proposals to establish Snow White Day, protect kangaroos, and bestow tax breaks on imported cantaloupes. But amid the frivolity, lawmakers never quite found time to consider a slightly riskier proposition: a plan to limit the number of newspapers that media conglomerates can control. Each year, the idea gets pushed by critics concerned about the increasingly concentrated ownership of the press. And each year, the notion gets about as far as, say, a plan to recall every hand gun in America. This year, Rep. Edward Feighan, an Ohio Democrat, actually owned up to "thinking about" introducing a bill. But that's all he's done.

Why the skittishness? Credit one of Washington's most powerful lobbies and one that typically escapes the press's notice: the press itself. Washington's media lobby—broadcasters, publishers, and their trade organizations—has the distinction of being perhaps the most formidable and invisible lobby around. And as the stillborn chain-ownership bill shows, it usually gets what it wants.

How? The media exercises part of its clout in the usual way—giving out donations and honoraria, schmoozing with legislators at resort hot spots. But unlike lobbyists pushing guns or butter, sugar or insurance, the media is its own secret weapon. Every congressman has hometown television stations—and, perhaps even more important, a hometown newspaper that endorses politicians—and none of them wants to anger the people who carry them to the public. The media lobbyist, of course, need never be so vulgar as to raise the specter of editorial retaliation. Even the dullest congressman can catch on to that possibility. "The clout that the newspapers and broadcasters exert is the desire of every elected official to have favorable press attention," says Lionel Van Deerlin, who served as a California representative from 1953–81. "When you hear from these guys, you listen."

So what does the media lobby for—First Amendment safeguards? Open meeting laws? Freer access to public information? Sure, occasionally. But the day-to-day work of a Washington media lobbyist focuses not so much on the front page as the bottom line. That means media muscle gets flexed behind such dubious propositions as giving cigarette companies tax breaks for their nice ads. Or writing loopholes into bills meant to sweep the highways of billboards (owned, often, by media conglomerates). Or freeing the TV stations that control the public's airwaves from the responsibility of providing candidates with the air time they need.

If this behind-the-scenes maneuvering is news to you, there's a reason. For all its skill in portraying the influence of money on politics, the establishment press is less zealous in looking at itself. When *The Washington Post* trained its sleuthing powers on the gun lobby, it detailed the honoraria and campaign contributions the National Rifle Association showered on members of Congress and showed how those congressmen voted to weaken federal gun control. It even profiled the media consultant who designs the NRA's ads. That's precisely the kind of scrutiny the press fails to apply to itself.

THE $175 MYSTERY MEAL

"Follow the money," counseled Deep Throat as modern investigative journalism was born. Lots of good reporters have taken the advice. Large papers like *The Washington Post* even purchase computer tapes from the Federal Election Commission that list campaign contributions. But one of the trails you're unlikely to see reporters follow is the one that leads to the front office. What they would find is the usual bag of Washington tricks. Media corporations—whose holdings include not only newspapers but television and radio stations, magazines, and billboards—peddle their influence with familiar tools: PACS, honoraria, junkets, and revolving-door lobbyists.

FEC records show that executives at most of the top media corporations have written checks as well as editorials. Contributions have come from top executives at Gannett (134 newspapers, ten TV stations, 16 radio stations, billboards); Times Mirror (seven newspapers, 15 magazines, four TV stations); The Washington Post Company (two newspapers, four TV stations, and *Newsweek* magazine); Knight-Ridder (37 newspapers, eight TV stations); Cox Enterprises (20 newspapers, nine TV stations); Time Inc. (17 magazines, HBO, Cinemax, and Cable affiliates in 32 states); *U.S. News and World Report;* Capital Cities/ABC (eight TV stations, 39 newspapers and "about 80 magazines," said a spokesperson); NBC; and many others.

Giving money isn't necessarily improper. Media employees, like others, have the right to make contributions. Where the press goes wrong is in its failure to disclose the contributions it's making. Given the media's role as watchdog of *others'* disclosures, this failure is a pointed one. After all, they're the ones who always decry the insidious influence of money on politics. A *Los Angeles Times* editorial, published last winter, is typical: "In return for their money, contributors clearly get favored treatment. All they get is access, the members always protest, but access is the most important thing that a senator or congressman can provide, short of selling a vote outright."

But many media reps try to obscure their identity on FEC campaign and lobbying forms by failing to identify their employer. From the FEC forms alone, you'd never know that the William F. Gorog who channeled $12,000 to Republican candidates through a fund called "Victory 88" (formerly the Jack Kemp Super Bowl Committee), is the same William F. Gorog who was president of the Magazine Publishers Association and who oversaw its Washington office. Nor would you know that the Fred Drasner who gave $1,000 to Michael Dukakis last year also happens to be Fred Drasner, CEO of *U.S. News and World Report*. You wouldn't know it from calling his office either. Drasner failed to return repeated phone calls in reference to the donation. The final call to his office said *The Washington Monthly* would assume the two Drasners were the same unless he called back. He didn't.

The lobbying forms that media representatives must file show a similar zeal for full disclosure. If a lobbyist spends any money pushing his position, the forms ask for the "name and address of recipient, purpose." It doesn't take a J-school degree to figure out that the point of the form is to disclose the name of the congressman or staff member being feted. Newspaper lobbyists usually comply. (Lobbyist Robert Brinkmann noted that his $49.91 lunch at La Brasserie was with "Chuck Parkinson of Senator Abdnor's staff, re: postal rates and costs.") But not the broadcasters. Media General representative Terese Colling had no problem finding a loophole after her May 22, 1986 night on the town. Her recipients are $122, Theater Guild, Kennedy Center and $174.85—Dominique's. Never heard of old Senator Dominique? It's a restaurant. As for who was there gobbling up that $175 meal, the form gives no clues. Lobbyist Jim May of the National Association of Broadcasters says with a shrug, "That's all we have to do." Keep that in mind the next time you hear a self-righteous, Mike Wallace-type intoning the words "failed to disclose. . . ."

Rather than embrace the responsibility of disclosure, some media moguls grow indignant at the very idea. Hal Brown, a vice president of Gannett's billboard division and chairman of the Outdoor Advertising Association of America, dished out $4,500 to congressional candidates during the 1985–86 election cycle; but a Gannett spokesman huffed at the idea that the donations might be newsworthy. "Employees of the company can make contributions to anyone they like," said the spokesman, Sheila Gibbons. "That's acting in their private interest."

It's a coincidence, no doubt, that Brown's private interests happened to reflect the political interests of the members of the Senate public works committee, which regulates billboards. (Isn't it grand when you and your friends are interested in the same things?) Brown was privately interested in giving $1,000 each to Republican committee members Jim Abdnor and Steve Symms, and $500 to Democrat Patrick Leahy. His private interest also included $500 checks to Republican Bob Dole, then the Senate Majority Leader, and Democrat Jim Wright, House Speaker-to-be. Gannett's interests in billboards may have something to do with the fact that they brought in revenues last year of $200 million, mostly from alcohol and tobacco.

Of course, individual contributions are nickel-and-dime stuff compared to the PAC money and honoraria handed out by the media trade organizations. Ten years ago, there was little media money going into federal elections. But that changed with the advent of cable television. Knowing they'd be heavily regulated by Congress and the FCC, cable operators burst on the scene with a sizable PAC and generous honoraria, starting a bidding war of sorts with broadcasters. Each tried to outdo the other in campaign contributions, speaking fees, and all-expense-paid convention trips for their favorite congressmen to places like Hawaii and Las Vegas—seeking, as it is euphemistically known, to "participate in the political process." Between 1985 and August 1988, the National Cable Television Association donated $446,240 to federal candidates. The NAB gave $307,986 during the same period. Last year, the $114,300 the NAB disbursed in speaking fees was more than any trade group except the American Trucking Associations. A nice sum to chat.

"Where in the past individual broadcasters were reluctant to go to make their cases—or make contributions—as they've watched the realtors and the bankers and everybody else, they've realized that they can't be passive," says NAB lobbyist Susan Alvarado. "Those days are over."

While the American Newspaper Publishers Association has no PAC, many executives at news conglomerates channel contributions through their broadcast divisions or other subsidiaries. Times Mirror doesn't have a PAC, but in April 1988, five Times Mirror cable employees gave $4,000 to the National Cable Television Association's CABLE PAC. Similarly, Knight-Ridder has no PAC, but broadcast executive Daniel E. Gold contributed $2,000 to the NAB's TARPAC, which channeled it to congressional candidates.

The newspaper publishers shy away from honoraria. Then again, they have a more potent weapon: editorial endorsements. "I believe when your local newspaper publisher calls up, no matter how gentle they are, you think 'oh jeez, am I going to get an editorial?' " says Rep. Al Swift, who sits on the House telecommunications subcommittee.

THE LUAU LOBBY

Without that edge broadcasters have to work a little harder. "It's not that they're nicer people," Swift says, "it's just that they don't have editorials." Last spring, NAB brought about 45 members of Congress, key committee staff, and a bevy of FCC officials to their annual meeting in Las Vegas (that nerve center of broadcast journalism). The main attraction was none other than that old broadcaster himself, Ronald Reagan. A few months earlier, it was off to Hawaii for the NAB's "legislative forum" where key players like Strom Thurmond, ranking Republican on the Senate judiciary committee, and House communications subcommittee members Fred Boucher, John Bryant, Dan Coats, Carlos Moorhead, Al Swift, Thomas Tauke, and Billy Tauzin got to mull those First Amendment issues luau-style. Most took home a $1,500 or $2,000 check for the hardship of leaving Washington for Honolulu in January.

To help the industry stay in touch with Congress between those yearly casino-side exchanges on press freedoms, an increasing number of media companies, including Time and Gannett, keep lobbyists on staff. While Times Mirror has two lobbyists on staff, it also orders out for specialists. It hires the firm of Gold and Liebengood, Inc., generally for what it describes as "First Amendment issues." Gold and Liebengood's First Amendment credentials come from its work for the hotbed of constitutional zeal, the Tobacco Institute. Patrick Butler, a vice president in Times Mirror's Washington office, says the company "is quite willing to take a more public position and aggressiveness in the freedom of the press issues." But otherwise, he said, Times Mirror likes to lie low. "On corporate issues, taxes, we are quite low-key and that's why we retain some of our outside people."

BLOWING SMOKE

With the flexing of all that media muscle, you might think the Constitution never had it so good. Sometimes this phalanx of power brokers actually takes on an issue that's good for the Republic—like the successful 1986 effort to save the Freedom of Information Act. But more often, the business of the media is business.

Most shameful is the media lobby's lapdog defense of cigarette ads, under the phony umbrella of First Amendment rights. The only legitimate free speech issue would concern items like the occasional advertorials sponsored by the Tobacco Institute, expressions of a point of view. Newspapers, which regularly refuse ads for products like pornographic films, know they've got no legitimate First Amendment obligation to peddle cigarettes with pictures of a seductive woman who invites readers to "Light My Lucky." The next time one of those publishers starts boasting to the Rotary Club about his "family newspaper," he might think about all the young lungs his glamorous ads help lure into addiction.

But media lobbyists pulled out the stops last year after Reps. Mike Synar and Robert Whittaker tried to extend the ban on televised tobacco ads to cover newspapers and magazines. Another proposal, introduced by Rep. Fortney "Pete" Stark, would have allowed the companies to retain the ads but would have barred them from deducting the ad expense from their taxes. Whittaker received an outpouring of telephone calls and letters from publishers throughout his state, including many on the letterhead of the National Newspaper Association, which represents mostly suburban and rural papers. "They were not very cordial," said one Whittaker aide. Whittaker made a public apology to the Kansas press for implying they were in the pockets of the tobacco lobby. Synar, however, is less circumspect. "The ANPA are the water carriers for the tobacco industry," he said.

Media representatives insist that their interest in the matter is purely constitutional, dismissing the idea that $460 million in newspaper and magazine ads (1986) has quickened their First Amendment concerns. Forget for a moment the irony of those news organizations that take such pride in baring the nation's health hazards throwing their weight behind the country's chief cause of heart disease and lung cancer. And savor instead how the media treats the cherished principle of full disclosure when they're the ones doing the disclosing.

David Starr, publisher of the *Union-News and Republican* in Springfield, Massachusetts and senior editor of Newhouse Newspapers, chairs the ANPA's committee on the First Amendment and freedom of information. Starr introduced what might be called the Red Meat Doctrine, predicting that as cigarette ads go, so go other advertisements: those for beef, which contains cholesterol; contraceptives, "which prevent life"; and wine, since it increases the chances of breast cancer. "Absurd?" Starr asked. "I don't think so." Starr assured Congress that cigarette ads were an insignificant part of newspaper revenues and that his interest was purely constitutional. "We oppose a ban because it threatens free speech," he said.

But what Mr. Freedom of Information failed to mention is that the media companies that own the newspapers usually own magazines, where, as Senator Bill Bradley testified, tobacco conglomerates can account for as much as 30 percent of ad revenues. (Starr also failed to note that the conglomerates that own the top cigarette companies have sometimes punished the enemies of tobacco by withdrawing other ads as well, such as those for food products.) Those economically insignificant tobacco companies spend about $2.4 *billion* a year on tobacco promotion. In 1985, Starr's bosses at Newhouse raked in $3,403,617 in tobacco ads at *Vogue*; $2,666,439 at *Glamour*; $2,902,248 at *Mademoiselle*; and $2,188,192 at *Self*—bastions of First Amendment freedoms, all. But that's just spare change compared to The Washington Post Company's *Newsweek*, which that year inhaled $20.5 million in tobacco ads.

Don't expect Newhouse News's Washington bureau—or virtually any other news agency, for that matter—to clear up Starr's smokescreen. The bureau, which covers D.C. for the 3.5 million people who read the chain's 26 papers, didn't report the issue. It was "just another hearing," says Robert Fichenberg, the D.C. bureau chief. Fichenberg said he knew Starr was in town, but, "I didn't even know what he was testifying on. . . . If indeed there is any [lobbying], we don't know about it until after the fact."

But if the threat to First Amendment freedoms is as dire as the newspaper publishers contend, what accounts for the short shrift that most news organizations gave the hearings? The *Los Angeles Times*, one of the few newspapers that has covered the issue, neglected to note the lobbying role of the ANPA. Jack Nelson, chief of the 40-member bureau, said the omission may have occurred because the story was written by an intern. "The fact is, had I known they were lobbying on it, I would have said, 'Put it in.' " Nelson says he tries to keep a firewall between the Times Mirror business interests and his reporters. But, good intentions notwithstanding, this head-in-the-sand approach won't do; his bureau *ought* to know what the media is lobbying for, and ought to report it.

The *Times* bureau's subsequent stories on the tobacco industry continued to omit the publishers' alliance. "Big Tobacco Buying New Friendships," was the headline over a May 1988 story. The reporter, Myron Levin, is an enterprising critic of the tobacco lobby. He spent a year investigating the industry as an Alicia Patterson fellow (and received a *Washington Monthly* journalism award for one of his thoughtful pieces). But his dispatch on tobacco's new allies failed to mention the role of either the ANPA or Times Mirror itself, which shares one of the Tobacco Institute's lobbying firms. Levin said he thought about including his publisher's role in his research, but recent academic studies and journalism reviews had covered the territory. "It didn't seem new," he said. Speaking of the mainstream press, Levin agreed that "we don't cover ourselves right."

One related story that ought to be considered a textbook case of intelligent reporting belonged to *The Washington Post*'s Morton Mintz. In a story on the refusal of Canadian publishers to accept tobacco ads, he acknowledged the *Post*'s financial interests and pointed out that American papers routinely decline ads for other lawful products, like X-rated films. Where did the *Post* play this piece of work? Page H4.

A BYRD'S-EYE VIEW

Broadcasters, of course, got cut out of the cigarette money years ago when Congress banned televised ads. But the broadcast lobby is no less greedy than the newspaper publishers in pushing for profits while ignoring the public interest. If anything, the broadcasters act more like a typical lobby in their use of junkets, honoraria, and contributions to strengthen their inherently substantial clout. At every turn, the broadcast lobby has done all it can—which is usually quite a lot—to stave off measures that would require a more public-spirited use of the airwaves. They are, after all, the *public's* airwaves. And the licenses to control them are handed out for free. The corporate beneficiaries of this largesse reap huge profits, while voicing indignation at the thought of giving something back.

One recent example concerns the NAB's successful effort to torpedo the Fairness Doctrine, which dates back to the early days of broadcasting, when the FCC required television stations to present balanced views on matters of public concern. Congressmen have typically supported the doctrine since it sets limits on a station's ability to attack them. Ernest Hollings thinks it helped him win his 1959 governor's race in South Carolina, when television stations were required to provide him with a forum while the state's newspapers were arrayed against him.

The broadcasters, eager to run their money machines with no strings attached, argue that with the advent of cable and other sources of information, media voices are sufficiently diverse to render the doctrine obsolete. What this argument ignores is the stunning concentration of media ownership, which leaves fewer corporations calling more shots than anyone could have imagined when the Fairness Doctrine began. In 1982 a study by Ben Bagdikian showed that a scant 52 corporations controlled about half the media outlets in the country; by 1988 he found that number had shrunk to 29. (Not that the broadcasters' free market faith doesn't have its limits: The diversity argument is especially ironic given the broadcasters' zeal to require cable franchises to carry the networks. If it's a competitive, diverse world out there, why the need for special protection?)

There is some merit to a second criticism of the Fairness Doctrine—that it promotes a bland nonpartisanship in which broadcasters quote Longwind Expert Number One and Longwind Expert Number Two, while leaving the dulled viewer no way of knowing who's right. But the assurance of some broadcast balance outweighs that flaw. Since the Reagan FCC repealed the doctrine, broadcasters have had virtually no public obligations in exchange for their public monopoly. (Stations can now renew their licenses merely by sending in a postcard.) Surely this gives the lucrative industry new appreciation for the term free enterprise.

Hollings tried to reinstate the doctrine—and got clobbered. Edward Fritts, president of the NAB, called the lobbying effort "the greatest outpouring of broadcaster concern in modern history," which, sadly enough, may be true. The NAB organized what it calls "a grassroots campaign," flying in TV execs, both network and affiliate, from around the country. Leaving nothing to chance, the NAB called in lobbysits from both sides of the partisan aisle. Reagan vetoed the bill that would have reinstated the doctrine, and, despite its decades of support for the principle, Congress lacked the votes for an override.

"The Fairness Doctrine has such overwhelming support on Capitol Hill, it's a recognition of the tremendous power of electronic media that it didn't go through," said Charles Ferris, a former FCC chairman-turned-lobbyist. Hollings agreed. "Our broadcaster friends are the most powerful I know of . . . ," he told the Senate. "They can change votes right and left, and that is quite understandable. We live and breathe by TV, and that is our reelection. If the local broadcaster calls, you are going to do him a favor. You are not worried about a veto by the president."

If this sounds like blackmail, you won't get the broadcasters to deny it. "There is a lingering apprehension on the part of elected officials, without saying so, that you are wielding a club and could give them some hell," said

Robert Brunner, chairman of the Radio-Television News Directors Association, which lobbied against the doctrine. Brunner, executive news editor of WSAZ-TV in Charleston-Huntington, West Virginia, credits the current success in part to his personal relationship with West Virginia Senator Robert Byrd, the Senate Majority Leader. "I think Byrd would vote the other way," Brunner said, "but partially because of my personal lobbying he's moved it from a high-priority must-do thing to something Congress might not get to . . . a victory [for the broadcasters]." When asked about Brunner's comments, Cindy Huber, a press aide to Byrd, said, "Senator Byrd does know Bob Brunner very well and they do talk, and I'm sure they talked about the Fairness Doctrine." Brunner's not alone in seeking to apply the personal touch. "There are people within our own industry who have personal relationships with members of Congress," said Jim May of the NAB. "We encourage that."

If you expected these cozy relationships to come to light in the brave new world of diverse media, think again. At least *The Washington Post*'s editorial attacking the Fairness Doctrine acknowledged that, with four TV stations, the Post Company is not disinterested. That's more than can be said for the *Atlanta Journal/Constitution*, which ran an editorial entitled "Misnamed Fairness Doctrine is actually anything but fair," while failing to note that its owner, Cox Enterprises, Inc. owns TV stations in Atlanta, Oakland, Pittsburgh, St. Louis, Orlando, and four other cities.

Gannett's *USA Today*, flagship of the 134-newspaper chain and emblem of corporate consolidation, also chirped in about media "diversity." Calling the Fairness Doctrine "stinkweed," the editorial offered some advice: "If you don't like what you see or hear on one channel, flip the dial." It failed to point out that Gannett owns ten TV stations. (If you flip the dial you might still be watching Gannett.) The paper did reassure its readers that the doctrine's demise was nothing to worry about. "No changes for news, broadcasters predict," crooned the headline.

While newspapers disguised their corporate interest, the networks seemed to ignore the issue altogether. *Washington Post* TV critic Tom Shales said he did not see one television story on the Fairness Doctrine battle. "I would call up these guys and say, 'why don't you cover this?' " he said. "They just said that no one could possibly understand this issue and didn't get it on the air."

JUNK-FOOD DEMOCRACY

With that kind of public-mindedness, you can imagine how the broadcast lobby reacted to Rep. Samuel Stratton's proposal to give free air time to political candidates. What's that? You've never even *heard* of such a proposal? Only a cynic could suspect the fact that most major newspapers also own TV stations—which one consultant estimated took in more than $300 million in paid political ads during the 1986 congressional races alone—helps account for the silence.

With an average senator now raising $10,000 a week, every week, the importance of this reform is hard to overstate. The cost of campaigns boosts the role of PACs, strengthens the hands of special interest groups, and deters talented outsiders from running for office. And in the electronic age, nothing drives the campaign inflation like the cost of televised ads.

What to do? Make the stations give free air time to the candidates. The stations are sure *getting* free air time—24 hours of it a day. With political ads accounting for no more than 4 percent of ad time (even in major markets), it's not much to demand of the profit-rich industry in return. It would allow politicians to attend fewer fundraisers and more legislative hearings. It would loosen the grip of PACs. And by allowing challengers to broadcast their message just as much as incumbents, it would help make democracy more democratic.

But rather than give free time (or mere discounts, as one bill proposes), broadcasters typically *hike the rates* 30 days before the ballots are cast.

In response to recent proposals to require discounted time, the broadcast lobby tried to convince Congress that the cost of TV ads wasn't so much after all. "There is nobody up here in this body who runs for political office in a contested race who would believe that for a minute," said Senator Mitchell McConnell to a broadcaster's claim that TV and radio ads account for only 34 percent of a campaign's cost. "I think, with all due respect, it is kind of insulting to our intelligence." Curtis Gans, director of the Committee for the Study of the American Electorate, examined the most competitive Senate races and found the average broadcast expenditure to be about 80 percent.

With their study rebuffed, media lobbyists took a philosophical tack. "Is the cost of campaigning too high?" mused NAB president Ed Fritts before Congress. "In the eyes of some, probably. But when one considers its importance to the functioning of our democracy, others would say, probably not." (Particularly if they own a TV station.) After all, Fritts went on to note in a little consumer products lesson, the $400 million that politicians who made it to the general election spent campaigning in 1986 "is less than what Americans spend each year on popcorn at movie theaters alone. Four hundred million is less than what Americans spend on soft drinks each week of the year. Four hundred million is what Americans spend on candy each quarter." Appealing, no doubt, to the would-be Churchills in the crowd, Fritts concluded reassuringly: "Certainly the value received in our democracy from electing all members of Congress is at least equal to that given by our consumption of popcorn, soft drinks, and candy."

Aside from his jaunt into political theory, Fritts offered some practical advice. Stop worrying about the cost of TV ads, he told the legislators, and "focus . . . [on] improv[ing] the quality of education which voters receive . . ." The broadcast lobby, he said, vigilant citizens ever, was "prepared to make some constructive suggestions to those ends."

McConnell, for one, is on to the game. "Why should we work extra time raising money to make them richer?" he said. "I do think it's excessive greed."

Then again, the senator's not surprised that the broadcasters—with their profits, PACs, and lobbyists—see no problem in the marriage of media, money, and politics.

❖❖   Objectivity is a journalistic standard that reporters widely herald, but the process of news gathering and reporting inevitably has a highly subjective content. What is or is not covered reflects an editor's or reporter's view of what is or is not important, what the public should or should not know. Policies that do not receive publicity have little chance of passage through the intricate maze of government. The press and the media can be important allies of government agencies, politicians, and interest groups in their quest for the enactment of particular public policies.

The following selection describes the constant struggle between the government and the media to define and control the political agenda and the public's view of political reality. Political power often depends upon the result of the combat between the government and the press.

37

Martin Linsky
THE PRESS-GOVERNMENT RELATIONSHIP TODAY

June 6, 1977, 6 a.m. General Alfred Starbird scans the front page of his *Washington Post*. He is stunned to see a 14-paragraph story by Walter Pincus under the headline "Neutron Killer Warhead Buried in ERDA Budget," which reports that "The United States is about to begin production of its first nuclear battlefield weapon specifically designed to kill people through the release of neutrons rather than to destroy military installations through heat and blast." The fourth paragraph of the story, which was to become the most memorable, reads: "According to one nuclear weapons expert, the new warhead 'cuts down on blast and heat and thus total destruction, leaving buildings and tanks standing. But

Reprinted from *Impact: How the Press Affects Federal Policymaking*, by Martin Linsky, with the permission of W. W. Norton & Company, Inc. Copyright © 1986 by The Institute of Politics at Harvard University.

the great quantities of neutrons it releases kill people.' " By the time he gets to the end, Starbird is extremely upset.

Starbird is the assistant administrator for national security at the US Energy Research and Development Administration (ERDA), the agency responsible for the development of all US nuclear weapons. A few days before the story appeared, Pincus had been covering a hearing of the House Appropriations Committee. During a break in the testimony, Pincus began to read a just-published transcript of an earlier committee hearing which included testimony from Starbird on upcoming production in the atomic stockpile. Starbird's testimony contained a reference to enhanced radiation (ER) warheads. When the testimony was declassified, that reference had not been deleted, as it was supposed to have been. As Pincus saw it, this was the first public disclosure of the production of neutron weapons. He knew that a front page article in the *Post* would stir debate, although he says now that he did not foresee the scope of what was to emerge.

The development of the ER warhead, or neutron bomb as it came to be known, had begun over twenty years before. In 1955, as a result of war games which were designed to assess the effects of a "successful" defense of Europe, the NATO allies realized that the existing nuclear warheads then arrayed to repel an invasion by the Soviet Union would in the process also devastate friendly territory and civilian populations, particularly in West Germany. Accordingly, US scientists then set out to develop a "clean" nuclear warhead, one that would limit collateral damage by killing primarily by prompt radiation, rather than by blast or radioactive fallout. A weapon that relied on a concentrated momentary burst of radiation for its effect would have at least the possibility of being able to defend Western Europe without destroying it as well. Before he had left office, President Gerald Ford had signed off on funding for production of the weapon, and Starbird's testimony was defending that appropriations request.

It soon became clear that Starbird was not the only person who was going to be upset by what Pincus had reported. During the next ten months, the list of those who would be concerned about the article and its implications would include many members of the US Senate, most of the leaders of the NATO countries, hundreds of thousands of political activists, and, of course, President Jimmy Carter. As Zbigniew Brzezinski, then the national security adviser, later put it, "The *Post* article touched off a political explosion that reverberated throughout the United States and Europe."

The initial White House reaction to the story on the morning it appeared was to concentrate on finding out more about the weapon and limiting Carter's connection with it. "The president," then-Press Secretary Jody Powell later recalled, "didn't know anything about the weapon at the time, so we initially chased around to get information on it. You could tell by the way the story was played that it was going to be a stinkeroo, although no one anticipated the trouble it eventually caused." White House officials were able to establish quickly that Ford's decision to go ahead with production of the bomb had not been formally reviewed by President Carter. Later that afternoon, Powell told Pincus that Carter would delay the production decision until "he had specifically approved the program."

John Marcum of the NSC staff was asked by Brzezinski to prepare a briefing on the weapon with recommendations for a public response, and he was one of the first to begin to appreciate the dimensions of what was in store. Marcum was worried about the language in the fourth paragraph of Pincus's story, quoting an anonymous weapons expert:

> Our basic recommendation on press guidance was that we ought to provide a more rational perspective on this as an anti-tank weapon. We felt we had to remedy the absurd impression the initial stories created: that this weapon was some weird thing that hit a building, leaving the building intact but killing the people inside.

At the State Department, only a handful of people had even heard of the enhanced radiation weapons, and there was no sense there that the weapons held any great military significance. The typical reaction at State, as Lou Finch, one of the desk officers recalled, was, "Is the neutron bomb a super killer that nobody ever heard of, and have these crazy guys at the Pentagon been hiding this in their back pocket all these years?"

With the White House trying to establish distance and the State Department assuming it was someone else's problem, the task of dealing with the continuing story in the *Post* and with the other interested news organizations and their reporters initially was relegated to the Department of Defense. At Defense, where the neutron bomb was one of its own so to speak, responsibility for dealing with the issue was delegated. Secretary of Defense Harold Brown was not particularly concerned. Brown had once been director of the Livermore Laboratory, where the concept of enhanced radiation had first been worked on; he was thoroughly familiar with the weapons. His knowledge fed his response: "My reaction to the story was just that it cast ER weapons in the worst possible light, saying that they destroyed people and saved property, neglecting to say that the 'people' were Soviet tank crews and the 'property' was the houses in Germany that would fall on civilians and kill them if the property was destroyed. . . . I thought that since it was an incorrect characterization and there was nothing new in it, it wouldn't have a very big effect. Brown's assistant secretary for public affairs, Thomas Ross, had never heard of neutron weapons, so the job of handling the press at the Pentagon was delegated primarily to Donald Cotter, Brown's special assistant for atomic energy. Cotter was a nuclear weapons engineer who was one of those most responsible for assuring that the ER program was fairly represented in the policy and budget process. His guidelines for ERDA and the Department of Defense (DOD) on dealing with the press did no more than confirm that ERDA was working on an enhanced radiation warhead, and had been doing so since the early 1960s.

The strongest and most public reaction in the government came from the US Senate. Senator Mark Hatfield (R–OR) quickly introduced an amendment to the appropriations bill to eliminate funding for ER weapons. The pending fight in the Senate helped Pincus and the *Post* keep the story alive. The *Post* editorialized against the weapon two days after the first Pincus story appeared. For the first ten days, the Senate debate and the *Post* fueled each other to keep the story going until the rest of the media began to get involved on their own. On June 10, the Defense Department drafted a 1½-page rationale for the weapon which tried to minimize the significance of the enhanced radiation warheads. Pincus was still essentially the only reporter covering the story and he saw the press guidance as disingenuous in the extreme: "The Pentagon wanted the money to produce the weapon, and the way they tried to kill the interest was to say 'there's nothing new about this, it's just a modernization program.' That line was passed to the White House, too. Now I had already talked to the people who were convincing the White House that there was nothing new. They had all told me previously that this was a new weapon and they thought it was the greatest thing since sliced bread. I knew they were playing both sides of the issue, so I just began to look for ways to prove what had already been told me by these very same people; that this was a special, new weapon system."

Beginning in mid-June, Cotter began meeting with Pincus on a background basis. The interviews initially were reasonably cordial and constituted a kind of diplomatic minuet. But reaching a meeting of the minds was almost impossible. Cotter's executive officer, who sat in on several of the meetings, remembers it this way: "If Cotter told Pincus something in his story was inaccurate, than the presumption became that the sentence above must be accurate. Moreover, if we said something was inaccurate, then you had to justify what you said. It was very difficult to explain why some of what Pincus wrote was inaccurate without getting into classified information."

One of the turning points in the coverage occurred on June 17, when NBC News ran a film clip, obtained from the Armed Forces Radiology Research Institute, showing what happened to monkeys when they were irradiated with 4,600 rads of neutron radiation. The results, not surprisingly, were quite gruesome. Pincus was then working half-time for NBC. NBC correspondent John Hart told him that the clip had spurred a big viewer reaction and, on June 22, Pincus wrote an article on the clip. ABC ran the clip on June 24, and NBC ran it again several weeks later on the *Today* show. Pincus's June 22 story spawned a phone call from a source who suggested that what Pincus had found in Starbird's testimony was just the tip of the iceberg of a plan to shift most nuclear artillery to an enhanced radiation basis. That information, particularly as it related to specific weapons, was highly classified and on that basis the Defense Department declined to comment when Pincus called to ask for confirmation.

Pincus's article with the new information about the broader implementation of enhanced radiation weaponry led the paper on June 24, and kicked off not only another wave of stories and editorials in the *Post*, but substantially heightened interest among the rest of the press as well. The continuing coverage consistently used some version of the language from Pincus's original story, namely that the bomb "killed people but left buildings intact." There was very little in the news or commentaries which reflected the Defense Department's view of the weapon or any perspective other than what Secretary Brown termed the "incorrect characterization" in that first article.

Cotter and Pincus had scheduled a meeting for June 24, and Cotter let his irritation show. He was deeply annoyed by Pincus's use of the phrase "killer warheads" and by the description of the appropriation as having been "buried" in the ERDA budget. He argued that Pincus knew that the enhanced radiation warheads had gone through normal and required channels so that buried was very misleading, and that all warheads kill. Pincus describes Cotter as "livid" at that session, but defends the coverage: "I had no problem at all with saying that the warheads were 'buried.' I didn't say they were hidden; 99% of the people would not have known to have looked in ERDA's budget to find them. I also had no problem with the 'kills people and leaves buildings standing' tags; that was the beauty of the weapon and that was they way people at the labs talked about it. Those were their terms, not mine. The 'killer warhead' phrase was coined by a *Post* headline writer but I did use it a number of times. It's true that all weapons are killer weapons. To be brutally honest, I'd have to say that it helped people to focus on the weapon, so it didn't hurt the cause. You do develop slogans and it had a nice swing to it."

At the meeting, Cotter tried to convince Pincus that secrecy about the weapons was important because Soviets would have a major re-equipment problem once they were deployed. Pincus went back and wrote a story about that, under the headline "Pentagon Wanted Secrecy On Neutron Bomb Production." The story prompted an editorial in the Sunday *Post* which said, "The whole thing has the look of a black bag job."

Cotter was enraged and called the Pentagon's press expert, Thomas Ross, for advice. Ross discouraged a direct response, but Cotter went ahead anyway: "Ross, I think, regarded me as something of a wild man, running around with these plans to modernize the nuclear weapons that Jimmy Carter said we were going to get rid of. This was a serious $3 billion weapon program these guys were taking cracks at, saying it was being run in a dishonorable fashion. You can't take that shit when you're the guy responsible for the program. These stories were causing all sorts of problems for us, and promised to continue to; the Allies were nervous, the Russians were making hay out of it, and people on the Hill, like Scoop Jackson, were really pissed. With an article coming out every day I finally reached the end of my rope and went in to talk to Charlie Seib, the *Post* ombudsman."

Unbeknownst to Cotter, Seib had already become disturbed by the *Post*'s use of the "killer warhead" phrase, and had written two memos to the paper's top editors questioning its use. Cotter met with Seib with Pincus present. Seib listened and encouraged Cotter to send a letter to the editor. Pincus said nothing at all.

Back at the Pentagon, Ross urged Cotter not to send the letter. After several strongly worded drafts were toned down, Cotter sent a letter which the *Post* eventually published. In it he stated that ERDA had followed all the statutory procedures with regard to the enhanced radiation weapons, including keeping Congress informed, and that the degree of classification for the program was what was required, "no more, no less," to help prevent the spread of the technology to US adversaries.

Early in July, the Defense Department began a low-key media campaign on behalf of the weapons in anticipation of the Senate vote on the Hatfield amendment. Brown was interviewed by NBC. Background briefings on the technical details of the enhanced radiation warhead and on how it compared to existing weapons were provided for Pentagon reporters. Senate supporters of the neutron bomb were worried and pressed for more help, particularly looking to the White House for a clearer commitment. Finally, on July 12, the eve of the Senate vote, President Carter made a crucial intervention. At a televised press conference, he asked for continuing funding while he was making up his mind. All three networks led the news with Carter's comments.

The next day the Senate voted 58–38 against the Hatfield amendment and in favor of a compromise which prohibited funds from being used to build enhanced radiation weapons until the president certified that they were in the national interest. Congress would then have 45 days to disapprove the weapons by a concurrent resolution of both houses. The debate in the Senate featured attacks on the press coverage by the supporters of the neutron bomb and ringing defenses of the press by opponents.

The Senate vote ended the first phase of the neutron bomb story, but the storm was just beginning to stir in Europe. After the Senate debate made it clear that the neutron bomb was to be deployed on European soil, there was increased interest abroad. Egon Bahr was an important figure in the liberal wing of the ruling party in the tenuous coalition government headed by Helmut Schmidt in West Germany. Four days after the vote in the Senate, Bahr published an article on the bomb in *Vorwearts*, the weekly party newspaper. Under the headline "Is Mankind Going Crazy," he picked up the themes of Pincus's original story. Other European columns and editorials echoed the view that the neutron warhead was a singularly perverse invention.

Soon the Soviets got into the act, generating a substantial propaganda campaign against the bomb which helped reinforce growing popular dismay. Beginning right after the Bahr article, one Soviet front organization after another began issuing denunciations of the neutron bomb. TASS and *Izvestia* published a steady diet of critical articles, culminating in a broad statement on

US foreign policy and the bomb in TASS on July 30. It was the first such statement issued by TASS since 1974. The Soviet activity helped stir the pot, intensifying the concern that was already building among many noncommunists in Western European countries.

One of the problems that quickly became apparent was that the arguments which had worked for the Carter administration in the US Senate sounded very different in Europe. At home, the enhanced radiation warheads were justified as providing greater security for the United States by being a more credible threat. The neutron bomb killed people through the release of neutrons rather than heat or blast, thereby inflicting less collateral damage to the countryside than the weapons they were to replace. That would make it more conceivable than before that a Soviet invasion could be repelled without either nuclear escalation or the devastation of Europe. Thus, for example, at one point the Pentagon was distributing diagrams showing the radius of effect of the neutron warheads, with drawings of tanks being blown up and soldiers dying. In Europe that picture looked much less comforting than it did in the US; rather than increased security, the message to many people there reasonably appeared to be that deployment of the neutron bomb would lower the nuclear threshold and increase the chance of a limited nuclear war. To ordinary Europeans, the argument that it was a more credible deterrent because it was believable that it *could* actually be used, meant that it actually *might* be used.

Most allied leaders in Western Europe favored deployment as part of their NATO responsibilities, because the US government had favored it, and because they believed that deterrence was more likely a result than use. But the fuss about the weapon made them look to Washington for a strong commitment to produce the bomb before they tried to defend its deployment. This was particularly true for West German Chancellor Helmut Schmidt; West Germany was one of the three countries, along with Belgium and Holland, where US policymakers actually wanted to deploy the weapons. Schmidt did not believe that he could maintain public support for deploying them, unless he could give the impression that they were being pushed on him by the Americans. Carter, on the other hand, was hoping for clearcut early commitments from the allies. He wanted to be able to say that *he* was the one being pushed, so that the decision to go ahead with production would not seem so harsh in light of his commitment in his inaugural address to "move this year a step toward our ultimate goal—the elimination of all nuclear weapons from this Earth." On September 16, Schmidt and Carter talked about the bomb on the phone. Carter warned that he did not want to proceed with production and "get shot down as an international ogre."

In November, with signs that the debate over the bomb was reviving the European peace movement, the Carter administration finally implemented a comprehensive strategy for building support, even though the president had yet to make his decision. Articles in government publications began to explain the policy considerations behind deployment. The Department of Defense began to generate pro-bomb material for consumption by the allies. There was even an ill-fated effort (exposed and ridiculed by Pincus in the *Post*) to change the name of the bomb from the neutron bomb to the "reduced blast/enhanced radiation weapon."

Both the Soviets and the Americans stepped up propaganda efforts during the beginning of 1978. In January, prompted by the increasing success of Soviet diplomatic pressure against the bomb and the Soviet's covert and semicovert infiltration of the European anti-bomb movement, the US decided to institute its own covert action program. A plan was approved by Brzezinski and Vance which involved asking sympathizers and supporters in the European press corps to give more favorable coverage to the bomb. As explained by Leslie Gelb, then director of politico military affairs at the State Department, it was simply designed to produce some better stories about the bomb: "We weren't trying to disrupt the renting of convention halls [for anti-bomb rallies] or anything like that. This campaign was chosen to supplement our overt activities, like having the embassies talk to European journalists. We thought that more favorable press coverage might help show the European public that we weren't trying to upset the nuclear balance, that the neutron bomb was a legitimate modernization move."

The details of the covert action campaign have remained classified. A sampling of the British and German press coverage from the time indicates that coverage favorable to the neutron bomb and sharply critical of the Soviet propaganda campaign began appearing frequently in February and March. A March 1 report by the United States Information Agency noted that "a trend in Western European media toward the acceptance of the neutron bomb as part of the NATO defense arsenal was intensified in the last two weeks."

The growing media support for neutron warheads seemed to create more latitude for key European leaders in handling the issue. While the US and the USSR were conducting a battle over public opinion and European press coverage of the bomb, the US and its NATO allies were quietly working out an agreement for production and deployment.

The discussions were taking place at the same time that the anti-bomb sentiment was reaching a peak in Europe. The high water mark of the protest movement was probably the International Forum, which was held in Amsterdam on March 18–19. Fifty thousand demonstrators listened to speeches by Daniel Ellsberg, among others, and then marched through the streets of the city in the rain, chanting "Ban the neutron bomb." Organizers of the rally sold 400,000 anti-neutron bomb window bills, stickers, and buttons and collected the signatures of 1.2 million Dutch citizens (there are only about 10 million Dutch voters in all) on anti-bomb petitions.

The US and the Allies worked out what Gelb called an "elaborately choreographed" scenario to make the NATO plan public. It included a commitment to continued production by the US, an effort to make deferral dependent on a Soviet decision to defer the SS–20, and a consensus for deployment from NATO as a whole rather than support from each nation individually. On Saturday, March 18, with the agreement ready to go, Brzezinski sent a two-page decision memo to Carter, who was vacationing in Georgia. Vance says that they decided to send a decision memo rather than an information memo because they "wanted to make absolutely sure, one final time, that the president was really on board."

Carter read the memo and promptly sent word back that he was vetoing the deal. Gelb remembers being awakened early the next morning, Sunday, March 19, by a phone call from the senior NSC aide who was the first one to receive the message from Carter back at the White House. "You won't believe what happened," Gelb recalls him saying, "he checked the wrong box."

Those involved have various theories as to what was the crucial factor in Carter's decision. Vance has speculated that when the president finally saw the memo, committing himself in effect to the deployment of a weapon in Europe that the allies, for whose security it had been developed, would accept but not individually request, his "innermost self rebelled." Brzezinski suggests that Carter "felt that the European governments . . . were attempting to push all the political costs on him." Journalists such as Richard Burt of the *New York Times*, Pincus of the *Post*, and some syndicated columnists speculated in print that Carter was persuaded by UN Ambassador Andrew Young, an opponent of the bomb, that putting it into production would weaken the US position at the upcoming UN Special Session on Disarmament. Yet it is clear that the way the bomb had been characterized was also an influential factor.

Carter returned to Washington and, on March 26, told his dismayed advisers that he was not only against the NATO arrangement, but that he had decided to cancel the bomb. Brzezinski, Vance, and others began preparing a plan for announcing the cancellation as they were simultaneously continuing to try to convince the president to change his mind.

For a week, they had more success at keeping the decision out of the news than they did at convincing Carter to reverse himself. Then, on April 4, the decision to cancel was reported in the *New York Times*. The information had been leaked to *Times* reporter Richard Burt. The White House responded with a wave of official denials that the decision had been made. An anonymous White House source was quoted as saying that the "genuine reappraisal" of the bomb was not yet over. The leak generated a new onslaught of public and private pressure on the president from outside the White House, coming mostly from those in the press and in the Congress who thought it would be a terrible mistake not to go forward with production and deployment.

Finally, on April 7, Carter announced his decision. The characterization of what he was doing was modified; he described it as a deferral rather than outright cancellation of production of the weapon. But the effect was the same. Brzezinski noted at the time that Carter believed that if he had approved the neutron bomb, "his administration would be stamped forever as the administration which introduced bombs that kill people but leave buildings intact."

Those words, of course, came almost verbatim from the anonymous nuclear weapons expert quoted ten months earlier in Walter Pincus's article that started it all.

It was the Pentagon that built the bomb and the government's own expert who coined the description that was so damaging, but it is obvious that the press was central to the policymaking here. It had a powerful influence on the process of decision making and the policy outcome. And the personal and political fallout from Carter's decision was substantial.

The whole saga began in the press, with Walter Pincus's story in the *Washington Post*. Responding to the story was the form that some of the policymaking took. The day it appeared, senior officials in the White House and the Department of Defense concentrated primarily on how to deal with the press, not on the merits or demerits of the neutron bomb. The issue was not what ought to be the administration's position on enhanced radiation warheads, but what ought to be the administration's position on the Pincus story. That pattern continued. The consideration of press strategies became a major focus of policy-makers' time and energy throughout the ten months until the deferral was announced. The development of plans for trying to influence the coverage and thereby influence public perceptions about the issue, was not the exclusive prerogative of Jody Powell and Thomas Ross, whose job descriptions called for management of press relations. It was also given attention at the cabinet secretary level and at the highest levels of the White House staff.

The agreement with the NATO allies that Carter vetoed was as significantly a press strategy as a neutron bomb strategy. The Dutch, the Belgians, the Danes, and the Norwegians were not willing individually to support European deployment. It was all the rest of the allies could do to prevent them from opposing the decision. So the US, in consultation with the Germans and the British, developed the "elaborately choreographed" scenario to create what one of Gelb's aides characterized as "the appearances of a concerted alliance position" when none existed. A carefully worded NATO communique was drafted which stressed that deployment of the neutron bomb was tied to the failure of the Soviets to defer the SS–20; in this way none of the NATO countries, including the US, would appear to be supporting the weapon in and of itself. After the statement was issued, the Americans, Germans, British, and Canadians were to issue their own statements explicitly endorsing it. The rest of the NATO allies would have no comment. Gelb's deputy co-authored the communique. It was, he said later, "more a diplomatic document than a public relations document, but it was all public relations. When I wrote the statement I was considering quite a bit how the press would cover it." The goal was to have the press convey a very specific picture of the policy and its context, a picture which did not capture exactly what had taken place but was a view that the NATO countries were willing to present to the world. The whole plan was, as one senior Defense Department official said, "a sort of theater, where each side, after being rehearsed, would say just enough to satisfy the other side."

It may not be possible to prove that the Pincus story killed the neutron bomb, but without his story there might have been no issue at all. Questions about production and deployment had not yet been raised in the routine course of events by the Senate, the administration, or the allies. As Secretary of Defense Harold Brown later summed it up, "Without the Pincus articles, they [neutron warheads] would have been deployed and nobody would have noticed." Once the coverage began, the dormant neutron bomb policy issue was very much awake. The intensity of the coverage itself made it a major issue. The press attention resonated with the response of some US Senators and among some elements of the public to put the issue high on the agenda for the Carter administration. The more the attention in the press, the less the Defense Department was able to deal with the issue alone and the more the White House, and the president, became directly involved.

The Ford and Carter administrations had done nothing to prepare the public for the neutron bomb debate. After the Pincus story was published, the government could never quite catch up with the momentum that the article created. The image from the initial article had blasted into the consciousness of Senators and the Washington press corps, and seeped its way into public opinion here and abroad. Reframing the issue was a much more difficult job than creating a favorable impression in the first place would have been. Government officials found themselves reacting, unable to seize the initiative. For a long period of time, part of the government, particularly at State and most of the policymakers at DOD except Cotter, adopted a strategy of not responding at all in the hope that the story would simply go away. As Ross reasoned later, "By creating campaigns, giving heavy rebuttals, you prolong the issue rather than get rid of it." They only answered the questions they had to, and only with the minimum amount of information. Later, most of the government turned to a more affirmative but very low-key approach. This involved offering press guidance to other officials who might need to respond, writing articles in government publications laying out the argument in favor of the weapon, and briefing reporters. Only Don Cotter pursued an aggressive press strategy, although all of those involved worried about what to do. Even Cotter's approach was primarily reacting to coverage, rather than trying to influence it in advance. None of the approaches seemed to make much of a difference.

Some of those close to the president believe that one of the consequences of the story was damage to Carter's political future. Brzezinski wrote in his memoirs that as a result of the neutron bomb controversy, "the President's credibility was damaged in Europe and at home." Jody Powell told us that "the neutron bomb fueled what came to be two of our biggest problems in Washington, the appearance of indecisiveness and the notion that Carter was weak on defense." "Politically," Vance wrote in his memoirs, "the costs were extremely high." What makes this question particularly interesting is that a press which saw the whole story in a light different than the one painted by Pincus's original article might have presented Carter in a very different way. Roger Morris, a former NSC aide, made this point in the *Columbia Journalism Review*. Without changing any of the facts, he suggested, "There were elements of another story, a story of Carter striving to discipline an autonomous and insubordinate bureaucracy, of Carter standing up to the Germans and insisting that they take their fair share of responsibility for mutual defense policies, of the President skillfully manipulating opponents at home and abroad."

When Carter finally decided to defer, there were significant consequences beyond his own political future. Brzezinski believes that: "The neutron bomb affair was a major setback in US-European relations, particularly in our relations with West Germany. Personal relations between Carter and Schmidt took a further turn for the worse and never recovered." In the aftermath of the debate about the bomb, officials realized that they had to take the press into account in formulating nuclear weapons policy in Europe. The Reagan administration set up a cabinet-level interagency team for the sole purpose of coordinating the administration's public relations abroad; the team was to give special emphasis to obtaining favorable media coverage and influencing younger Europeans to adopt sympathetic attitudes toward the presence of nuclear weapons and US nuclear policy.

It is impossible to separate the role of the press from the policymaking here. The stakes were high and the press was very much a part of the story. Yet in one form or another, that pattern was repeated throughout our three years of research into how the press affects policymaking.

Finding that the press is central to what goes on in government should not be news, certainly not to those who work in Washington, but it may be an uncomfortable reality for them. Both journalists and reporters have their reasons for hanging on to an unrealistic view of their interaction. For the journalists, acknowledging their influence undermines their felt need to keep their distance from policymaking. Their own ethic demands that they report *on* government, not, in anything more than the most passive sense, be a part *of* it. Not only do journalistic practices, such as the value on objectivity, drive them to that position, but the consequences of understanding their influence are complicating. If they acknowledge to themselves the potential impact of what they are reporting and publishing in a specific case, then they may be said to have contributed to and be held partially responsible for the result. Walter Pincus would not be relieved of some responsibility for the neutron bomb deferral just because he is a reporter. Journalists fear that such a burden, if taken seriously, would undermine what they see as their primary reason for being, namely to tell the people what is going on.

Understanding the impact of the press on policymaking is uncomfortable for the officials as well. It challenges them to internalize that awareness and make it part of the way they conduct themselves in office. It means they can no longer blame the press for their own bad coverage. In the neutron bomb case, it means they cannot blame Pincus for their difficulties with the bomb.

However, the conclusions of our study go well beyond the centrality of the media to government. As viewers or readers, we cannot learn very much about the impact of the press on policymaking just by following the news. We cannot tell what is going on simply by watching. When we see the press and policymakers together on television, they are usually in formal roles and familiar situations, such as at a press conference or on an interview program. Sometimes we see journalists and officials or read about them in conflict at a time of particular tension, such as during the Iranian hostage crises in 1980, the aftermath of the invasion of Grenada in 1983, and the hostage taking at the Beirut airport in 1985. Each of these events generates heated debate about the press-government interaction in times of great moment, but sheds little light on influence of the press on policymaking under less dramatic conditions. Newspapers often comment on the way television covers the news, but very rarely do they comment on other newspapers; television stations almost never cover the print media. Sometimes, but only rarely, newspapers provide a glimpse of behind-the-scenes policymaking activity which shows how decision makers used the press or reacted to coverage.

These random and sporadic images of the press-government connection tend to stick in our minds and shape our opinions, however unrepresentative they might be. In this study we have probed deeper to discover how press and officials really interact, and the effect of their interaction on policymaking.

Overall, we found that the press and policymakers in Washington are engaged in a continuing struggle to control the view of reality that is presented to the American people. The engagement is highly competitive, but collegial nonetheless. When the media's view and the officials' view are more or less shared, the struggle is more like a waltz. When there is a wide gap, or when early on in a particular issue it is not clear which perspective will predominate or even what the perspectives are, toes are stepped on and there is tension between the partners. In either event, the interaction is important to both policymakers and reporters because they believe that the stakes—the goals of governing and the ideals of journalism—are so high.

A minor footnote to recent history captures the essence of this relationship. It involves television, not print, and some of the particular qualities that the electronic media bring to coverage of public affairs, but it is a good metaphor for how press and officials often interact. The incident was reported by James Markham of the *New York Times* on May 4, 1985, as President Ronald Reagan was preparing to leave Washington for his controversial trip to the German military cemetery at Bitburg. White House staff and television newsmen were already at the cemetery site. Markham reported how the White House advance team and network advance teams were negotiating over the placement of the network cameras which would record the visit for posterity . . . and for the nightly news. The issue was whether the cameras would be located on tripods.

CBS had won the draw among the networks and had the preferred position. They wanted to be able to pan in a single shot from the president to an SS grave. The White House people argued that tripods would unduly restrict the already limited space, although they clearly were interested in keeping the president as far away as possible from the SS graves in the eyes of the American people.

The CBS News producer was quoted in the story in the *Times* as acknowledging that the White House staff were trying to "manage the picture. . . . That is their job. Our job is to cope with the story." The CBS crew got their tripod, and the shot they wanted was shown to millions of Americans that night.

The interaction was intense, the interests were professional, and the stakes were high. Government officials representing an administration with a reputation for effective communication spared no details in trying to influence how the news was presented. They knew that without that time and effort, the news would be less reflective of the president's view of reality and more reflective of someone else's view. The journalists for their part, although they accepted the administration's agenda just by covering the trip, were not willing to accept the official perspective on events. They were not only skeptical, they had their own perspective as well and that's the one they wanted to put out on their air.

This was primarily a professional conflict, not a question of right and wrong. It is not at all clear who was right, the White House men or the CBS men. Is it fair to show the president and then pan over to the SS graves? Is it a picture of truth, or is it just good television? Should either CBS or the government have the power to determine how we are going to visualize the event? The struggle over the tripod is an inevitable consequence of both parties aggressively doing their jobs. The press is not disrupting the policymaking any more than the policymakers are disrupting the press. Each is getting in the other's way at the moment, but each needs the other in order to do their own jobs.

Markham acknowledges the influence the press can exert. He concluded that "The way this 10-minute event—and Mr. Reagan's ride through Bitburg to the cemetery—will look on television may determine whether the president's visit is judged a fiasco or a limited damage draw." We cannot know for sure what was the impact of that particular CBS picture; what is significant is that even the *New York Times* reporter thought that the way that little tussle at the Bitburg ceremony was played out had the potential for significant consequences as part of the whole controversy surrounding the trip.

Not only do the press and officials continually bump into each other in the course of doing their work, but the results of their doing so are substantial for the policies and processes of government and, as the neutron bomb case shows, not limited to the location of a tripod and the public assessment of a Presidential trip.

In this study, we sought to find out just what those consequences were. First, we wanted to know in what various ways the press affects the daily routines of senior federal officials: how much time these officials spend with the press and thinking about press matters; to what extent they actively seek coverage and try to influence the coverage they do receive; and how regularly the press covers what they do.

Second, we sought to explore the specific ways in which the press might affect the policies and processes of decisionmaking: what are the circumstances under which the press sets the agenda and frames the issues for the policymakers? Under what conditions can the press impact be expected to be substantial?

Third, we examined how officials deal with the media to see whether there are differences which produce differences in coverage and in press impact. We wanted to understand when and how officials take press considerations into account in making policy, when and how they leak information to the press and aggressively try to manage their press relations, and with what results.

Part Three

NATIONAL GOVERNMENTAL INSTITUTIONS

Chapter 6

The Presidency

The American presidency is the only unique political institution that the United States has contributed to the world. It developed first in this country and later was imitated, usually unsuccessfully, in many nations. In no country and at no time has the institution of the presidency achieved the status and power that it possesses in the United States. This chapter will analyze the basis, nature, and implications of the power of this great American institution.

Constitutional Background: Single v. Plural Executive

The change that has taken place in the presidency since the office was established in 1789 is dramatic and significant. The framers of the Constitution were primarily concerned with the control of the arbitrary exercise of power by the legislature; thus they were willing to give the president broad power since he was not to be popularly elected and would be constantly under attack by the coordinate legislative branch. Although the framers were not afraid of establishing a vigorous presidency, there was a great deal of opposition to a potentially strong executive at the time the Constitution was drafted. In *Federalist 70* Alexander Hamilton attempts to persuade the people of the desirability of a strong presidential office, and while persuading, he sets forth the essential constitutional basis of the office.

38

Alexander Hamilton
FEDERALIST 70

There is an idea, which is not without its advocates, that a vigorous executive is inconsistent with the genius of republican government. The enlightened well-wishers to this species of government must at least hope that the supposition is destitute of foundation; since they can never admit its truth, without, at the same time, admitting the condemnation of their own principles. Energy in the executive is a leading character in the definition of good government. It is essential to the protection of the community against foreign attacks; it is not less essential to the steady administration of the laws, to the protection of property against those irregular and high-handed combinations, which sometimes interrupt the ordinary course of justice, to the security of liberty against the enterprises and assaults of ambition, of faction, and of anarchy. Every man, the least conversant in Roman story, knows how often that republic was obliged to take refuge in the absolute power of a single man, under the formidable title of dictator, as well as against the intrigues of ambitious individuals, who aspired to the tyranny, and the seditions of whole classes of the community, whose conduct threatened the existence of all government, as against the invasions of external enemies, who menaced the conquest and destruction of Rome.

There can be no need, however, to multiply arguments or examples on this head. A feeble executive implies a feeble execution of the government. A feeble execution is but another phrase for a bad execution; and government ill executed, whatever it may be in theory, must be, in practice, a bad government.

Taking it for granted, therefore, that all men of sense will agree in the necessity of an energetic executive, it will only remain to inquire, what are the ingredients which constitute this energy? How far can they be combined with those other ingredients, which constitute safety in the republican sense? And how far does this combination characterize the plan which has been reported by the convention?

The ingredients which constitute energy in the executive are: unity; duration; and adequate provision for its support; competent powers.

The ingredients which constitute safety in the republican sense are: a due dependence on the people; a due responsibility.

Those politicians and statesmen, who have been the most celebrated for the soundness of their principles, and for the justness of their views, have declared in favor of a single executive, and a numerous legislature. They have, with great propriety, considered energy as the most necessary qualification of the former, and have regarded this as most applicable to power in a single hand; while they have, with equal propriety, considered the latter as the best adapted to deliberation and wisdom, and best calculated to conciliate the confidence of the people, and to secure their privileges and interests.

That unity is conducive to energy will not be disputed. Decision, activity, secrecy, and dispatch, will generally characterize the proceedings of one man, in a much more eminent degree than the proceedings of any greater number; and in proportion as the number is increased, these qualities will be diminished.

This unity may be destroyed in two ways; either by vesting the power in two or more magistrates, of equal dignity and authority; or by vesting it ostensibly in one man, subject, in whole or in part, to the control and cooperation of others, in the capacity of counsellors to him. . . .

The experience of other nations will afford little instruction on this head. As far, however, as it teaches anything, it teaches us not to be enamoured of plurality in the executive. . . .

Wherever two or more persons are engaged in any common enterprise or pursuit, there is always danger of difference of opinion. If it be a public trust of office, in which they are clothed with equal dignity and authority, there is peculiar danger of personal emulation and even animosity. From either, and especially from all these causes, the most bitter dissentions are apt to spring. Whenever these happen, they lessen the respectability, weaken the authority, and distract the plans and operations of those whom they divide. If they should unfortunately assail the supreme executive magistracy of a country, consisting of a plurality of persons, they might impede or frustrate the most important measures of the government, in the most critical emergencies of state. And what is still worse, they might split the community into violent and irreconcilable factions, adhering differently to the different individuals who composed the magistracy. . . .

Upon the principles of a free government, inconveniences from the source just mentioned, must necessarily be submitted to in the formation of the legislature; but it is unnecessary, and therefore unwise, to introduce them into the constitution of the executive. It is here, too, that they may be most pernicious. In the legislature, promptitude of decision is oftener an evil than a benefit. The differences of opinion, and the jarrings of parties in that department of the government, though they may sometimes obstruct salutary plans, yet often promote deliberation and circumspection; and serve to check excesses in the majority. When a resolution, too, is once taken, the opposition must be at an end. That resolution is a law, and resistance to it punishable. But no favorable circumstances palliate, or atone for the disadvantages of dissention in the executive department. Here they are pure and unmixed. There is no point at which they cease to operate. They serve to embarrass and weaken the excution of the plan or measure to which they relate, from the first step to the final conclusion of it. They constantly counteract those qualities in the executive, which are the most necessary ingredients in its composition—vigor and expedition; and this without any counterbalancing good. In the conduct of war, in which the energy of the executive is the bulwark of the national security, everything would be to be apprehended from its plurality.

It must be confessed, that these observations apply with principal weight to the first case supposed, that is, to a plurality of magistrates of equal dignity and authority, a scheme, the advocates for which are not likely to form a numerous sect; but they apply, though not with equal, yet with considerable weight, to the project of a council, whose concurrence is made constitutionally necessary to the operations of the ostensible executive. An artful cabal in that council would be able to distract and to enervate the whole system of administration. If no such cabal should exist, the mere diversity of views and opinions would alone be sufficient to tincture the exercise of the executive authority with the spirit of habitual feebleness and dilatoriness.

But one of the weightiest objections to a plurality in the executive, and which lies as much against the last as the first plan, is, that it tends to conceal faults, and destroy responsibility . . . . It often becomes impossible, amidst mutual accusations, to determine on whom the blame or the punishment of a pernicious measure . . . ought really to fall. It is shifted from one to another with so much dexterity, and under such plausible appearances, that the public opinion is left in suspense about the real author. . . .

A little consideration will satisfy us, that the species of security sought for in the multiplication of the executive, is unattainable. Numbers must be so great as to render combination difficult; or they are rather a source of danger than security. The united credit and influence of several individuals must be more formidable to liberty than the credit and influence of either of them separately. When power, therefore, is placed in the hands of so small a number of men, as to admit of their interests and views being easily combined in a common enterprise, by an artful leader, it becomes more liable to abuse, and more dangerous when abused, than if it be lodged in the hands of one man; who, from the very circumstances of his being alone, will be more narrowly watched and more readily suspected, and who cannot unite so great a mass of influence as when he is associated with others. . . .

I will only add, that prior to the appearance of the constitution, I rarely met with an intelligent man from any of the states, who did not admit as the result of experience, that the unity of the executive of this state was one of the best of the distinguishing features of our constitution.

The Nature of the Presidency: Power and Persuasion

What is the position of the presidential office today? There is little doubt that it has expanded far beyond the expectations of the framers of the Constitution. The presidency is the only governmental branch with the necessary unity and energy to meet many of the most crucial problems of twentieth-century government in the United States; people have turned to the president in times of crisis to supply the central direction necessary for survival. In the next selection Clinton Rossiter, one of the leading American scholars of the presidency, gives his view of the role of the office.

39

Clinton Rossiter
THE PRESIDENCY— FOCUS ON LEADERSHIP

No American can contemplate the presidency . . . without a feeling of solemnity and humility—solemnity in the face of a historically unique concentration of power and prestige, humility in the thought that he has had a part in the choice of a man to wield the power and enjoy the prestige.

Perhaps the most rewarding way to grasp the significance of this great office is to consider it as a focus of democratic leadership. Free men, too, have need of leaders. Indeed, it may well be argued that one of the decisive forces in the shaping of American democracy has been the extraordinary capacity of the presidency for strong, able, popular leadership. If this has been true of our past, it will certainly be true of our future, and we should therefore do our best to grasp the quality of this leadership. Let us do this by answering the essential question: For what men and groups does the president provide leadership?

First, the president is *leader of the Executive Branch*. To the extent that our federal civil servants have need of common guidance, he alone is in a position to provide it. We cannot savor the fullness of the president's duties unless we recall that he is held primarily accountable for the ethics, loyalty, efficiency, frugality, and responsiveness to the public's wishes of the two and one-third million Americans in the national administration.

Both the Constitution and Congress have recognized his power to guide the day-to-day activities of the Executive Branch, strained and restrained though his leadership may often be in practice. From the Constitution, explicitly or implicitly, he receives the twin powers of appointment and removal, as well as the primary duty, which no law or plan or circumstances can ever take away from him, to "take care that the laws be faithfully executed."

From Congress, through such legislative mandates as the Budget and Accounting Act of 1921 and the succession of Reorganization Acts, the president has received further acknowledgment of his administrative leadership. Although independent agencies such as the Interstate Commerce Commission and the National Labor Relations Board operate by design outside his immediate area of responsibility, most of the government's administrative tasks are still carried on within the fuzzy-edged pyramid that has the president at its lonely peak; the laws that are executed daily in his name and under his general supervision are numbered in the hundreds.

Many observers, to be sure, have argued strenuously that we should not ask too much of the president as administrative leader, lest we burden him with impossible detail, or give too much to him, lest we inject political considerations too forcefully into the steady business of the civil service. Still, he cannot ignore the blunt mandate of the Constitution, and we should not forget the wisdom that lies behind it. The president has no more important tasks than to set a high personal example of integrity and industry for all who serve the nation, and to transmit a clear lead downward through his chief lieutenants to all who help shape the policies by which we live.

Next, the president is *leader of the forces of peace and war*. Although authority in the field of foreign relations is shared constitutionally among three organs—president, Congress, and, for two special purposes, the Senate—his position is paramount, if not indeed dominant. Constitution, laws, customs, the practice of other nations and the logic of history have combined to place the president in a dominant position. Secrecy, dispatch, unity, continuity, and access to information—the ingredients of successful diplomacy—are properties of his office, and Congress, needless to add, possesses none of them. Leadership in foreign affairs flows today from the president—or it does not flow at all.

The Constitution designates him specifically as "Commander in Chief of the Army and Navy of the United States." In peace and war he is the supreme commander of the armed forces, the living guarantee of the American belief in "the supremacy of the civil over military authority."

In time of peace he raises, trains, supervises and deploys the forces that Congress is willing to maintain. With the aid of the Secretary of Defense, the Joint Chiefs of Staff and the National Security Council—all of whom are his personal choices—he looks constantly to the state of the nation's defenses. He is never for one day allowed to forget that he will be held accountable by the people, Congress and history for the nation's readiness to meet an enemy assault.

In time of war his power to command the forces swells out of all proportion to his other powers. All major decisions of strategy, and many of tactics as well, are his alone to make or to approve. Lincoln and Franklin Roosevelt, each in his own way and time, showed how far the power of military command can be driven by a president anxious to have his generals and admirals get on with the war.

But this, the power of command, is only a fraction of the vast responsibility the modern president draws from the Commander in Chief clause. We need only think back to three of Franklin D. Roosevelt's actions in World War II—the creation and staffing of a whole array of emergency boards and offices, the seizure and operation of more than sixty strike-bound or strike-threatened plants and industries, and the forced evacuation of 70,000 American citizens of Japanese descent from the West Coast—to understand how deeply the president's authority can cut into the lives and liberties of the American people in time of war. We may well tremble in contemplation of the kind of leadership he would be forced to exert in a total war with the absolute weapon.

The president's duties are not all purely executive in nature. He is also intimately associated, by Constitution and custom, with the legislative process, and we may therefore consider him as *leader of Congress*. Congress has its full share of strong men, but the complexity of the problems it is asked to solve by a people who still assume that all problems are solvable has made external leadership a requisite of effective operation.

The president alone is in a political, constitutional, and practical position to provide such leadership, and he is therefore expected, within the limits of propriety, to guide Congress in much of its lawmaking activity. Indeed, since Congress is no longer minded or organized to guide itself, the refusal or inability of the president to serve as a kind of prime minister results in weak and disorganized government. His tasks as leader of Congress are difficult and delicate, yet he must bend to them steadily or be judged a failure. The president who will not give his best thoughts to leading Congress, more so the president who is temperamentally or politically unfitted to "get along with Congress," is now rightly considered a national liability.

The lives of Jackson, Lincoln, Wilson, and the two Roosevelts should be enough to remind us that the president draws much of his real power from his position as *leader of his party*. By playing the grand politician with unashamed zest, the first of these men gave his epic administration a unique sense of cohesion, the second rallied doubting Republican leaders and their followings to the cause of the Union, and the other three achieved genuine triumphs as catalysts of Congressional action. That gifted amateur, Dwight D. Eisenhower, has also played the role for every drop of drama and power in it. He has demonstrated repeatedly what close observers of the presidency know well: that its incumbent must devote an hour or two of every working day to the profession of Chief Democrat or Chief Republican.

It troubles many good people, not entirely without reason, to watch the president dabbling in politics, distributing loaves and fishes, smiling on party hacks, and endorsing candidates he knows to be unfit for anything but immediate delivery to the county jail. Yet if he is to persuade Congress, if he is to achieve a loyal and cohesive administration, if he is to be elected in the first place (and reelected in the second), he must put his hand firmly to the plow of politics. The president is inevitably the nation's No. 1 political boss.

Yet he is, at the same time, if not in the same breath, *leader of public opinion*. While he acts as political chieftain of some, he serves as moral spokesman for all. It took the line of presidents some time to sense the nation's need for a clear voice, but since the day when Andrew Jackson thundered against the Nullifiers of South Carolina, no effective president has doubted his prerogative to speak the people's mind on the great issues of his time, to serve, in Wilson's words, as "the spokesman for the real sentiment and purpose of the country."

Sometimes, of course, it is no easy thing, even for the most sensitive and large-minded presidents, to know the real sentiment of the people or to be bold enough to state it in defiance of loudly voiced contrary opinion. Yet the president who senses the popular mood and spots new tides even before they start to run, who practices shrewd economy in his appearances as spokesman for the nation, who is conscious of his unique power to compel discussion on his own terms and who talks the language of Christian morality and the American tradition, can shout down any other voice or chorus of voices in the land. The president is the American people's one authentic trumpet, and he has no higher duty than to give a clear and certain sound.

The president is easily the most influential leader of opinion in this country principally because he is, among all his other jobs, our Chief of State. He is, that is to say, the ceremonial head of the government of the United States, the *leader of the rituals of American democracy*. The long catalogue of public duties that the Queen discharges in England and the Governor General in Canada is the President's responsibility in this country, and the catalogue is even longer because he is not a king, or even the agent of one, and is therefore expected to go through some rather undignified paces by a people who think of him as a combination of scoutmaster, Delphic oracle, hero of the silver screen, and father of the multitudes.

The role of Chief of State may often seem trivial, yet it cannot be neglected by a president who proposes to stay in favor and, more to the point, in touch with the people, the ultimate support of all his claims to leadership. And whether or not he enjoys this role, no president can fail to realize that his many powers are invigorated, indeed are given a new dimension of authority, because he is the symbol of our sovereignty, continuity and grandeur as a people.

When he asks a senator to lunch in order to enlist his support for a pet project, when he thumps his desk and reminds the antagonists in a labor dispute of the larger interests of the American people, when he orders a general to cease caviling or else be removed from his command, the senator and the disputants and the general are well aware—especially if the scene is laid in the White House—that they are dealing with no ordinary head of government. The framers of the Constitution took a momentous step when they fused the dignity of a king and the power of a prime minister in one elective office— when they made the president a national leader in the mystical as well as the practical sense.

Finally, the president has been endowed—whether we or our friends abroad like it or not—with a global role as *a leader of the free nations*. His leadership in this area is not that of a dominant executive. The power he exercises is in a way comparable to that which he holds as a leader of Congress. Senators and congressmen can, if they choose, ignore the president's leadership with relative impunity. So, too, can our friends abroad; the action of Britain and France in the Middle East is a case in point. But so long as the United States remains the richest and most powerful member of any coalition it may enter, then its president's words and deeds will have a direct bearing on the freedom and stability of a great many other countries.

Having engaged in this piecemeal analysis of the categories of presidential leadership, we must now fit the pieces back together into a seamless unity. For that, after all, is what the presidency is, and I hope this exercise in political taxonomy has not obscured the paramount fact that this focus of democratic leadership is a single office filled by a single man.

The president is not one kind of leader one part of the day, another kind in another part—leader of the bureaucracy in the morning, of the armed forces at lunch, of Congress in the afternoon, of the people in the evening. He exerts every kind of leadership every moment of the day, and every kind feeds upon and into all the others. He is a more exalted leader of ritual because he can guide opinion, a more forceful leader in diplomacy because he commands the armed forces personally, a more effective leader of Congress because he sits at the top of his party. The conflicting demands of these categories of leadership give him trouble at times, but in the end all unite to make him a leader without any equal in the history of democracy.

I think it important to note the qualification: "the history of democracy." For what I have been talking about here is not the Fuehrerprinzip of Hitler or the "cult of personality," but the leadership of free men. The presidency, like every other instrument of power we have created for our use, operates within a grand and durable pattern of private liberty and public morality, which means that the president can lead successfully only when he honors the pattern—by working towards ends to which a "persistent and undoubted" majority of people has given support, and by selecting means that are fair, dignified and familiar.

The president, that is to say, can lead us only in the direction we are accustomed to travel. He cannot lead the gentlemen of Congress to abdicate their functions; he cannot order our civil servants to be corrupt and slothful; he cannot even command our generals to bring off a coup d'état. And surely he cannot lead public opinion in a direction for which public opinion is not prepared—a truth to which our strongest presidents would make the most convincing witnesses. The leadership of free men must honor their freedom. The power of the presidency can move as a mighty host only with the grain of liberty and morality.

The president, then, must provide a steady focus of leadership—of administrators, ambassadors, generals, congressmen, party chieftains, people and men of good will everywhere. In a constitutional system compounded of diversity and antagonism, the presidency looms up as the countervailing force of unity and harmony. In a society ridden by centrifugal forces, it is the only point of reference we all have in common. The relentless progress of this continental republic has made the presidency our truly national political institution.

There are those, to be sure, who would reserve this role to Congress, but, as the least aggressive of our presidents, Calvin Coolidge, once testified, "It is because in their hours of timidity the Congress becomes subservient to the importunities of organized minorities that the president comes more and more to stand as the champion of the rights of the whole country." The more Congress becomes, in Burke's phrase, "a confused and scuffling bustle of local agency" the more the presidency must become a clear beacon of national purpose.

It has been such a beacon at most great moments in our history. In this great moment, too, we may be confident it will burn brightly.

❖❖   The constitutional and statuatory *authority* of the president is indeed extraordinary. However, it is more important to point out that the actual power of the president depends upon his political abilities. The president must act within the framework of a complex and diversified political constituency. He can use the authority of his office to buttress his strength, but this alone is not sufficient. Somehow he must be able to persuade those with whom he deals to follow him; otherside, he will be weak and ineffective.

40

Richard E. Neustadt
PRESIDENTIAL POWER

In the United States we like to "rate" a president. We measure him as "weak" or "strong" and call what we are measuring his "leadership." We do not wait until a man is dead; we rate him from the moment he takes office. We are quite right to do so. His office has become the focal point of politics and policy in our political system. Our commentators and our politicians make a speciality of taking the man's measurements. The rest of us join in when we feel "government" impinging on our private lives. In the third quarter of the twentieth century millions of us have that feeling often.

. . . Although we all make judgments about presidential leadership, we often base our judgments upon images of office that are far removed from the reality. We also use those images when we tell one another whom to choose as president. But it is risky to appraise a man in office or to choose a man for office on false premises about the nature of his job. When the job is the presidency of the United States the risk becomes excessive . . .

We deal here with the president himself and with his influence on governmental action. In institutional terms the presidency now includes 2,000 men and women. The president is only one of them. But *his* performance scarcely can be measured without focusing on *him*. In terms of party, or of country, or the West, so-called, his leadership involves far more than governmental action. But the sharpening of spirit and of values and of purposes is not done in a vacuum. Although governmental action may not be the whole of leadership, all else is nurtured by it and gains meaning from it. Yet if we treat the presidency as the president, we cannot measure him as though he were the government. Not action as an outcome but his impact on the outcome is the measure of the man. His strength or weakness, then, turns on his personal capacity to influence the conduct of the men who make up government. His influence becomes the mark of leadership. To rate a president according to these rules, one looks into the man's own capabilities as seeker and as wielder of effective influence upon the other men involved in governing the country. . . .

"Presidential" . . . means nothing but the president. "Power" means *his* influence. It helps to have these meanings settled at the start.

There are two ways to study "presidential power." One way is to focus on the tactics, so to speak, of influencing certain men in given situations: how to get a bill through Congress, how to settle strikes, how to quiet Cabinet feuds, or how to stop a Suez. The other way is to step back from tactics on those "givens" and to deal with influence in more strategic terms: what is its nature and what are its sources? What can *this* man accomplish to improve the prospect that he will have influence when he wants it? Strategically, the question is not how he masters Congress in a peculiar instance, but what he does to boost his chance for mastery in any instance, looking toward tomorrow from today. The second of these two ways has been chosen for this [selection]. . . .

In form all presidents are leaders, nowadays. In fact this guarantees no more than that they will be clerks. Everybody now expects the man inside the White House to do something about everything. Laws and customs now reflect acceptance of him as the Great Initiator, an acceptance quite as widespread at the Capitol as at his end of Pennsylvania Avenue. But such acceptance does not signify that all the rest of government is at his feet. It merely signifies that other men have found it practically impossible to do *their* jobs without assurance of initiatives from him. Service for themselves, not power for the president, has brought them to accept his leadership in form. They find his actions useful in their business. The transformation of his routine obligations testifies to their dependence on an active White House. A president, these days, is an invaluable clerk. His services are in demand all over Washington. His influence, however, is a very different matter. Laws and customs tell us little about leadership in fact.

Why have our presidents been honored with this clerkship? The answer is that no one else's services suffice. Our Constitution, our traditions, and our politics provide no better source for the initiatives a president can take. Executive officials need decisions, and political protection, and a referee for fights. Where are these to come from but the White House? Congressmen need an agenda from outside, something with high status to respond to or react against. What provides it better than the program of the president? Party politicians need a record to defend in the next national campaign. How can it be made except by "their" Administration? Private persons with a public ax to grind may need a helping hand or they may need a grinding stone. In either case who gives more satisfaction than a president? And outside the United States, in every country where our policies and postures influence home politics, there will be people needing just the "right" thing said and done or just the "wrong" thing stopped in *Washington*. What symbolizes Washington more nearly than the White House?

A modern president is bound to face demands for aid and service from five more or less distinguishable sources: the Executive officialdom, from Congress, from his partisans, from citizens at large, and from abroad. The presidency's clerkship is expressive of these pressures. In effect they are constituency pressures and each president has five sets of constituents. The five are not distinguished by their membership; membership is obviously an overlapping matter. And taken one by one they do not match the man's electorate; one of them, indeed, is outside his electorate. They are distinguished, rather, by their different claims upon him. Initiatives are what they want, for five distinctive reasons. Since government and politics have offered no alternative, our laws and customs turn those wants into his obligations.

Why, then, is the president not guaranteed an influence commensurate with services performed? Constituent relations are relations of dependence. Everyone with any share in governing this country will belong to one (or two, or three) of his "constituencies." Since everyone depends on him why is he not assured of everyone's support? The answer is that no one else sits where he sits, or sees quite as he sees; no one else feels the full weight of his obligations. Those obligations are a tribute to his unique place in our political system. But just because it is unique they fall on him alone. *The same conditions that promote his leadership in form preclude a guarantee of leadership in fact.* No man or group at either end of Pennsylvania Avenue shares his peculiar status in our government and politics. That is why his services are in demand. By the same token, though, the obligations of all other men are different from his own. His Cabinet officers have departmental duties and constituents. His legislative leaders head *Congressional* parties, one in either House. His national party organization stands apart from his official family. His political allies in the states need not face Washington, or one another. The private groups that seek him out are not compelled to govern. And friends abroad are not compelled to run in our elections. Lacking his position and prerogatives, these men cannot regard his obligations as their own. They have their jobs to do; none is the same as his. As they perceive their duty they may find it right to follow him, in fact, or they may not. Whether they will feel obliged *on their responsibility* to do what he wants done remains an open question. . . .

There is reason to suppose that in the years immediately ahead the power problems of a president will remain what they have been in the decades just behind us. If so there will be equal need for presidential expertise of the peculiar sort . . . that has [been] stressed [i.e., political skill]. Indeed, the need is likely to be greater. The president himself and with him the whole government are likely to be more than ever at the mercy of his personal approach.

What may the sixties do to politics and policy and to the place of presidents in our political system? The sixties may destroy them as we know them; that goes without saying. But barring deep depression or unlimited war, a total transformation is the least of likelihoods. Without catastrophes of those dimensions nothing in our past experience suggests that we shall see either consensus of the sort available to F.D.R. in 1933 and 1942, or popular demand for institutional adjustments likely to assist a president. Lacking popular demand, the natural conservatism of established institutions will keep Congress and the party organizations quite resistant to reforms that could give him a clear advantage over them. Four-year terms for congressmen and senators might do it, if the new terms ran with his. What will occasion a demand for that? As for crisis consensus it is probably beyond the reach of the next president. We may have priced ourselves out of the market for "productive" crises on the pattern Roosevelt knew—productive in the sense of strengthening his chances for sustained support *within* the system. Judging from the fifties, neither limited war nor limited depression is productive in those terms. Anything unlimited will probably break the system.

In the absence of productive crises, and assuming that we manage to avoid destructive ones, nothing now forseeable suggests that our next president will have assured support from any quarter. There is no use expecting it from the bureaucracy unless it is displayed on Capitol Hill. Assured support will not be found in Congress unless contemplation of their own electorates keeps a majority of members constantly aligned with him. In the sixties it is to be doubted . . . that pressure from electors will move the same majority of men in either House toward consistent backing for the president. Instead the chances are that he will gain majorities, when and if he does so, by ad hoc coalition-building, issue after issue. In that respect the sixties will be reminiscent of the fifties; indeed, a closer parallel may well be in the late forties. As for "party discipline" in English terms—the favorite cure-all of political scientists since Woodrow Wilson was a youth—the first preliminary is a party link between the White House and the leadership on both sides of the Capitol. But even this preliminary has been lacking in eight of the fifteen years since the Second World War. If ballot-splitting should continue through the sixties it will soon be "un-American" for president and Congress to belong to the same party.

Even if the trend were now reversed, there is no short-run prospect that behind each party label we would find assembled a sufficiently like-minded bloc of voters, similarly aligned in states and districts all across the country, to negate the massive barriers our institutions and traditions have erected against "discipline" on anything like the British scale. This does not mean that a reversal of the ballot-splitting trend would be without significance. If the White House and the legislative leadership were linked by party ties again, a real advantage would accrue to both. Their opportunities for mutually productive bargaining would be enhanced. The policy results might surprise critics of our system. Bargaining "within the family" has a rather different quality than bargaining with members of the rival clan. But we would still be a long way from "party govenment." Bargaining, not "discipline," would still remain the key to Congressional action on a president's behalf. The crucial distinctions between presidential party and Congressional party are not likely to be lost in the term of the next president.

Presidential Politics

Whether the Founding Fathers intended that the president would be a king or a clerk, they clearly did not foresee the deep involvement of the presidency in *partisan* politics. All presidents after George Washington were party chiefs, a role that grew more important as national parties expanded their electoral bases and began to act in a more disciplined fashion to facilitate their control of government. American parties have never been disciplined in the European sense, but they have managed to achieve sufficient organizational unity at both national and more importantly state and local levels to affect and sometimes determine the course of government.

Presidential parties help to identify and translate the political demands of popular majorities into government action. Theoretically at least, presidents should be able to use their role as party chief to bridge the constitutional gap between the presidency and Congress that the separation of powers created. Before becoming party chief, politicians must capture their party's presidential nomination. Whether or not parties should choose their nominees through "brokered" conventions, in which party power brokers and "bosses" dominate, or through a grass-roots process controlled by rank-and-file party members, continues to be hotly debated. Proponents of brokered conventions argue that party leaders tend to choose "better" candidates, those more representative of broad party interests and more likely to appeal to a national electorate, than candidates nominated by a grass-roots process which reflects the views of a relatively narrow party electorate.

The author of the following selection argues that the current grass-roots arrangement for choosing presidential candidates has neither weakened parties nor undermined the president's role as chief of his party. The reforms in presidential nominating politics were, in the author's view, a proper response to a changing political and social environment that required parties to adapt to new electoral forces.

41

Michael Nelson
THE CASE FOR THE CURRENT PRESIDENTIAL NOMINATING PROCESS

The current process by which Americans nominate their parties' candidates for president is the product of nearly two centuries of historical evolution and two decades of deliberate procedural reform. It can be judged successful because it satisfies reasonably well the three main criteria by which any presidential nominating process may be judged:

• Does the process strengthen or weaken the two major parties, which our political system relies on to provide some measure of coherence to a constitutionally fragmented government?

• Does the process foster or impede the selection of presidents who are suitably skilled for the office?

• Is the process regarded as legitimate by the public? Is it seen to be fair and democratic?

POLITICAL PARTIES

Have the two major parties been weakened by the reforms of the presidential nominating process that were instituted by the McGovern-Fraser commission and its successors? Much scholarly talent and energy have been devoted to answering this question in the affirmative. Implicit in such analyses are the beliefs that the parties were basically strong before the post-1968 reforms and that they have been considerably weaker ever since. In truth, neither of these beliefs is fully accurate. The parties were in a state of decline during the 1950s and 1960s, a decline that has been arrested and in most cases reversed during the 1970s and 1980s, as the parties, aided by the reforms, have adapted to the changed social and political environment that underlay their decline. This is true of all three of the components of parties that political scientists, following V.O. Key, have identified as fundamental: the party-in-the-electorate, the party-in-government, and the party organization.

From George Grassmuck (ed.), *Before Nomination: Our Primary Problems* (Washington, DC: The American Enterprise Institute, 1985). Reprinted by permission.

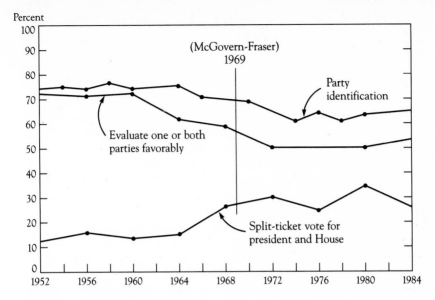

Figure A   Indexes of Party Strength

Sources: Stephen J. Wayne, *The Road to the White House*, 2d ed. (New York: St. Martin's Press, 1984), pp. 57, 59; David E. Price, *Bringing Back the Parties* (Washington, D.C.: Congressional Quarterly Press, 1984), p. 18; and Martin P. Wattenberg, "Realignment without Party Revitalization" (unpublished manuscript).

Party-in-the-Electorate. Americans are no longer as loyal to the parties as they were in the early 1950s, when modern survey research on voting behavior first took form. On this there is little room for dispute: as Figure A indicates, voters are far less likely now than in the past to think of themselves as either Democrats or Republicans, to vote a straight-party ticket (even for presidential and House candidates), or to express a favorable evaluation of one or both political parties.

Natural though the tendency may be to explain dramatic changes by equally dramatic causes, one cannot attribute the decline of the party-in-the-electorate to the reform era that began in 1968. The largest falloff in party identification, which had remained steadily high through the 1950s and early 1960s, came between 1964 and 1966. An additional large drop occurred between 1970 and 1972, but since then the decline in party identification seems to have leveled off or even been reversed. The share of voters who evaluate at least one party favorably, which fell steadily during the 1960s, has stayed very close to 50 percent ever since, rising to 52 percent in 1984. Similarly, split-ticket voting, a more explicitly behavioral indicator of weak voter loyalty to the parties, underwent its greatest increases before the reform era and has declined since 1980.

Whether Ronald Reagan's presidency has reversed the "dealignment" of voters that occurred mainly during the 1960s remains to be seen. But well before 1980 most of the indexes of party strength in the electorate at least had stopped falling.

Party-in-Government. Historically, Americans have used the political parties to join what the Constitution put asunder, namely, the executive and legislative branches. The electorate's habit of straight-ticket voting in twentieth-century elections before 1956 meant that the party that controlled the White House also controlled both houses of Congress in forty-six of fifty-four years.

The rise of split-ticket voting weakened such interbranch aspects of party-in-government: nowadays control by the same party of the presidency and Congress is the exception rather than the rule. As with the party-in-the-electorate, however, the evidence indicates that the party-weakening trend in government began well before the reform era: indeed, it was in 1954 that the new pattern of Republican presidents and divided or Democratic congresses emerged.

Even more significant than the trend in interbranch party strength, perhaps, is the intrabranch trend. During the supposedly halcyon days of parties in the 1950s and 1960s, party unity voting in Congress, as measured by the *Congressional Quarterly*, declined fairly steadily in both parties in both houses, bottoming out in the Ninety-first Congress. During the 1970s and 1980s, in direct contradiction to what the "reform-killed-the-parties" theory would predict, party unity voting has been on the increase. (So has the share of all congressional votes that unite one party against the other.) Nor has this intrabranch development been devoid of interbranch consequences: in 1981 Senate Republicans demonstrated the highest degree of support for a president ever recorded by either party in either house of Congress since the *Congressional Quarterly* began making measurements in 1953.

Party Organization. It is as organizations that the parties were affected most directly by the post-1968 reforms; if party-weakening effects are to be found anywhere, it should be in the realm of party organization. Yet it is here, recent research increasingly is showing, that the opposite is most true: the parties in the 1970s and 1980s are institutionally stronger than they were in the 1950s and 1960s.

The regeneration of the parties as organizations has occurred at all levels of the federal system. In the localities and counties there is now far more party activity in the areas of fund raising, campaign headquarters, voter registration, and get-out-the-vote efforts than during the mid-1960s. About twice as many citizens as in the 1950s (some 24 to 32 percent) report that they have been approached personally by party workers in recent presidential campaigns. The share of state party organizations that have permanent headquarters rose from less than half in 1960 to 95 percent in 1982; the size and professionalism of salaried state party staffs have also grown considerably. Judging from his study of party budgets, political scientist Cornelius Cotter concludes that the percentage of state parties whose organization is "marginal" fell from 69 in 1961 to 31 in 1979; the proportion of highly organized state parties rose from 12 percent to 26 percent.

National party organizations, long the stepchild of the party system, have undergone the most striking transformation of all. Since the mid-1970s, when William Brock became chairman, the Republican National Committee has developed a capacity to recruit candidates to run for local office and provide them with funds and professional assistance in such activities as voter registration and television campaigning; to help state parties enhance their own organizational abilities; to do institutional advertising on a "Vote Republican" theme; and so on. As for the opposition, journalist David Broder reports, "Since 1980 the Democrats have been doing what the Republicans did under Brock: raising money and pumping it back to party-building projects at the state and local level."

The Fall and Rise of the Parties. Political parties in the 1980s have arrested or reversed the decline that they were suffering before the reform era that began in 1968 but only because they are different from what they used to be. The recent reforms have helped the parties to adapt relatively successfully to a changing social and political environment.

Organizationally and procedurally, the parties on the eve of the post-1968 reforms were relics of an earlier era. Virtually since the Andrew Jackson years, party strength had continued to rest on the same foundations. Patronage, in the form of government jobs and contracts, had long been one reliable source of workers and funds for party organizations. Party-sponsored charity work— memorably, the Thanksgiving turkey and the winter bucket of coal—helped to cement the loyalties of many voters. Such tangible inducements aside, voters also found the party label the best device for ordering their choices in elections that involved numerous offices, candidates, and issues.

For some years before 1968, developments in government and society had been weakening these foundations. A merit-based civil service and competitive contracting replaced the patronage system of government hiring and purchasing. Income security programs reduced dependence on charity. After World War II education, income, and leisure time rose rapidly throughout the population— voters now had more ability and opportunity to sort out information for themselves about candidates and issues. During the 1950s, television sets became fixtures in the American home, bringing such information to voters in more accessible (if not always more valuable) form.

From these developments, which eroded some of the main props of the traditional political parties, came others that created the basis for new-style parties. First, the issue basis of political participation intensified, both in the movements of the 1960s (civil rights, antiwar, environmental, feminist, and others), which originated mainly outside the party system, and in the parties themselves. In 1962 James Q. Wilson chronicled the rise during the 1950s of the "amateur Democrat," an upper-middle-class reformer whose main concern was for issues and who saw the party as a vehicle for advancing causes, in opposition to professional party people, who viewed elections mainly as a means of achieving the satisfactions and spoils of victory. In 1964 the amateur Democrat's conservative Republican cousin, whom Aaron Wildavsky dubbed the "purist," seized control of the Republican national convention.

Second, the candidate basis of politics intensified, both in presidential politics, where individual aspirants, following John F. Kennedy in 1960, sought to take their own popular paths to the nomination even if that meant detouring around the party professionals, and in congressional politics, where reelection-oriented incumbents, with increasing success, forged personal bonds with their constituents that freed them from much of their dependency on party. Finally, the media basis of politics intensified. As television, radio, and direct mail became available and highly effective routes for reaching voters, media professionals became more valuable politically, as did fundraising specialists who could help to pay for the expensive new forms of campaigning.

Political parties in all their aspects—in the electorate, in government, and as organizations—were weakened during the 1950s and 1960s by these social and political developments. To recover and thrive the parties had to adapt. To adapt they had to accommodate the rise of four main groups: new-style voters, who by virtue of greater education and leisure no longer needed to depend on parties to order their choices in elections; amateur political activists who regarded the parties mainly as vehicles for political change; entrepreneurial candidates who had ceased to regard party fealty as the necessary or even the most desirable strategy for electoral success; and modern political tacticians who practiced the now essential crafts of polling, advertising, press relations, and fund raising. In sum, the reinvigoration of the parties would have to come on terms that accepted the "new politics" in both that label's common uses: policy as the basis for political participation, and modern campaign professionalism as the incentive to channel such participation through the parties.

What made the transformation and reinvigoration of the parties possible was the organizational and procedural fluidity that was hastened by the post-1968 reforms. Once the lingering hold of party professionals of the *ancien régime* on the nominating process was broken, the new groups of voters, activists, candidates, and campaign professionals were able to establish a new equilibrium of power within the parties that reflected the changed social and political realities. Republicans realized this first and strengthened their party by committing it to conservative political ideology and professional campaign services, which in turn tied the party-in-the-electorate, the party-in-government, and the party organization together. Democrats, preoccupied with the reform process more than with the fruits of reform, were slower to adapt. But, responding to the Republican party's success, they now seem to be following a parallel path: new policies and a new professionalism to rebuild the party.

Perhaps the best evidence of the parties' successful adaptation to change is that the old amateurs have become the new professionals: committed to policy but also to party. Summarizing several studies of delegates to recent Republican and Democratic national conventions, William Crotty and John Jackson conclude that "the new professionals are likely to be college graduates working in a service profession . . . familiar with all the paraphernalia of modern campaigning . . . [and] likely to care deeply about at least some issues. . . . They also care, sometimes passionately, about their party . . . and they see the parties as the best vehicles for advancing both their concept of the public interest and their own political careers."

PRESIDENTS

Many political analysts have argued vigorously that the influence of the presidential nominating process on the selection of suitably skilled presidents, like its influence on the parties, was benign before the post-1968 reforms were instituted but has been malignant ever since. "In the old way," according to Broder, "whoever wanted to run for president of the United States took a couple of months off from public service in the year of the presidential election and presented his credentials to the leaders of his party, who were elected officials, party officials, leaders of allied interest groups, and bosses in some cases. These people had known the candidate over a period of time and had carefully examined his work." As it happened, the qualities those political peers were looking for, argues political scientist Jeane Kirkpatrick, were the very qualities that make for good presidents: "the ability to deal with diverse groups, ability to work out compromises, and the ability to impress people who have watched a candidate over many years." In contrast, under the post-1968 rules, "the skills required to be successful in the nominating process are almost entirely irrelevant to, perhaps even negatively correlated with, the skills required to be successful at governing."

In a real sense, the old nominating process did work reasonably well to increase the chances of selecting skillful presidents. But then so does the new process. The difference underlying this similarity is the contrast between the political and social environment in which contemporary presidents must try to govern and the environment in which their predecessors as recently as the 1950s and 1960s had to operate.

The contrast is most obvious and significant in the nation's capital. As Samuel Kernell notes, the "old" Washington that was described so accurately by Richard Neustadt in his 1960 success manual for presidents, *Presidential Power*, was "a city filled with hierarchies. To these hierarchies were attached leaders or at least authoritative representatives"—committee chairmen and party leaders in Congress, press barons, umbrella-style interest groups that represented broad sectors such as labor, business, and agriculture, and so on. In this setting to lead was to bargain—the same political "whales," to use Harry

MacPhersons's term, who could thwart a president's desires could also satisfy them, and in the same way: by directing the activities of their associates and followers. Clearly a presidential nominating process that placed some emphasis on a candidate's ability to pass muster with Washington power brokers was functional for the governing system.

As the 1960s drew to a close, however, the same social and political changes—and some others as well—that were undermining the foundations of the old party system also were undermining the old ways of conducting the nation's business in Washington. The capital came under the intense and—to many elected politicians—alluring spotlight of television news; a more educated and active citizenry took its heightened policy concerns directly to government officials; interest group activity both flourished and fragmented; and careerism among members of Congress prompted a steady devolution of legislative power to individual representatives and senators and to proliferating committees and subcommittees. From the president's perspective this wave of decentralization meant that Washington had become "a city of free agents" in which "the number of exchanges necessary to secure others' support ha[d] increased dramatically."

What skills do contemporary presidents need if they are to lead in this changed environment, or, to phrase the question more pertinently, what skills should the presidential nominating process foster? Two presidential leadership requirements are familiar and longstanding; first, a strategic sense of the public's disposition to be led during the particular term of office—an ability to sense, shape, and fulfill the historical possibilities of the time; second, some talent for the management of authority, both of lieutenants in the administration who can help the president form policy proposals and of the large organizations in the bureaucracy that are charged with implementing existing programs. Other skills required by presidents are more recent in origin, at least in the form they must take and their importance. Presidents must be able to present themselves and their policies to the public through rhetoric and symbolic action, especially on television. Because reelection-oriented members of Congress "are hypersensitive to anticipated constituent reaction," it is not surprising that the best predictor of a president's success with Congress is his standing in the public opinion polls. Finally, presidents need tactical skills of bargaining, persuasion, and other forms of political gamesmanship to maximize their support among other officials whose help they need to secure their purposes. But in the new Washington these tactical skills must be employed not merely or even mainly on the sort of old-style power brokers who used to be able to help presidents sustain reliable coalitions but on the many elements of a fragmented power system in which tactics must be improvised for new coalitions on each issue.

In several nonobvious and even inadvertent ways, the current nominating process rewards, perhaps requires, most of these skills. The process is, for would-be-presidents, self-starting and complex. To a greater extent than ever before, candidates must raise money, develop appealing issues, devise shrewd campaign strategies, impress national political reporters, attract competent staff, and build active organizations largely on their own. They then must dance through a minefield of staggered and varied state primaries and caucuses, deciding and reevaluating weekly or even daily where to spend their time, money, and other resources. What better test of a president's ability to manage lieutenants and lead in a tactically skillful way in the equally complex, fragmented, and uncertain environment of modern Washington or, for that matter, the modern world?

The fluidity of the current nominating process also has opened it to Washington "outsiders." This development, although much lamented by critics of the post-1968 reforms, has done nothing more than restore the traditional place of those who have served as state governors in the ranks of plausible candidates for the presidency, thus broadening the talent pool to include more than senators and vice-presidents. (From 1960 to 1972 every major party nominee for president was a senator or a vice-president who previously had been a senator.) As chief executives of their states, governors may be presumed to have certain skills in the management of large public bureaucracies that senators do not.

Self-presentational skills also are vital for candidates in the current nominating process—not just "looking good on television" but being able to persuade skeptical journalists and others to accept one's interpretation of the complex reality of the campaign. If it does nothing else, the endless contest, which carries candidates from place to place for months and months in settings that range from living rooms to stadiums, probably sensitizes candidates to citizens in ways that uniquely facilitate the choice of a president who has a strong strategic sense of his time.

No earthly good is unalloyed, of course. The length and complexity of the current nominating process, to which so much good can be ascribed, are nonetheless sources of real distraction to incumbent presidents who face renomination challenges and to other contenders who hold public office. To be sure, the post-1968 rules cannot be blamed for all of this. Unpopular presidents have always had to battle, to some extent, for renomination; popular presidents still do not. (In 1984 Reagan not only was unopposed for his party's nomination— the first such president since 1956—but received millions of dollars in federal matching funds for his renomination "campaign.") Most challengers seem to be able to arrange time to campaign, either while holding office (Gary Hart, Alan Cranston, Ernest Hollings, and others in 1984) or by abandoning office for the sake of pursuing the presidency (Walter Mondale in 1984, Howard Baker in 1988). Still, by any standard, the same nominating process that tests a would-be president's leadership skills so well must be said to carry at least a moderate price tag.

PUBLIC

Ironically, democratic legitimacy, the paramount value sought by the post-1968 reformers, must be judged as the least achieved of the three main criteria for judging the presidential nominating process: strengthened political parties, skilled presidents, and a satisfied public. Everyone, including journalists, decries the responsibility that the hybrid nature of the process places on the media to interpret who is winning and even which candidates will be taken seriously. Few think it proper that voters in the late primary states have their choices circumscribed by the decisions of voters in Iowa, New Hampshire, and other states with early contests.

The characteristic of the current nominating process that is most corrosive of legitimacy is its sheer complexity. As Henry Mayo notes in his *Introduction to Democratic Theory:*

> If the purpose of the election is to be carried out—to enable the voter to share in political power—the voter's job must not be made more difficult and con-fusing for him. It ought, on the contrary, to be made as simple as the electoral machinery can be devised to make it.

Yet nothing could be less descriptive of the way we choose presidential candidates. "No school, no textbook, no course of instruction," writes Theodore H. White, "could tell young Americans how their system worked." Or, as Richard Stearns, chief delegate hunter for Senator George McGovern in 1972 and Senator Edward Kennedy in 1980, put it: "I am fully confident that there aren't more than 100 people in the country who fully understand the rules."

What would the public prefer? Nothing that will prove consoling to those who dislike the current process for its excesses of democracy and absence of "peer review." Overwhelmingly, citizens want to select the parties' nominees for president through national primaries: in the most recent Gallup survey on this issue, which was completed in June 1984, 67 percent were in favor, 21 percent were opposed, and 12 percent were undecided. And there are ample reasons to believe that citizens mean what they are saying. For one, the national primary idea has received consistently high support by margins ranging from two-to-one to six-to-one—in Gallup surveys that date back to 1952. More important, the direct primary is the method by which voters are accustomed to nominating almost all party candidates for almost all other offices in the federal system.

A vigorous case can be made for a national primary, and not solely because of the heightened legitimacy it would bring to the nomination process. Still, there are good reasons to stay with the current arrangement. First, the very constancy of rules rewriting is in itself subversive of legitimacy. Second, it also is distracting to the parties, diverting them from the more important task of deciding what they have to offer voters. Finally, to bring the argument of this essay full circle, to the extent that the current process helps the political parties to grow stronger and the presidency to work more effectively, voters ultimately will grow not just used to it but pleased with it, and the legitimacy problem will take care of itself.

The Presidential Establishment

The expansion of the Executive Office of the President is a major development of the modern presidency. Created in 1939 by an executive order of President Roosevelt under the reorganization authority granted to him by Congress, the Executive Office has expanded over the years and now occupies a pivotal position in government. The Executive Office was devised originally to act as a staff arm of the presidency. It was to consist of his closest personal advisers, as well as a small number of agencies, such as the Bureau of the Budget (now the Office of Management and Budget), and was to function as an aid to him in carrying out his presidential responsibilities.

The Executive Office was not to be an independent bureaucracy but was to be accountable to the president and to act in accordance with his wishes. However, the tremendous expansion that has occurred in the Executive Office has raised the question of whether or not it has become an "invisible presidency," not accountable to anyone within or without government. The relationships between President Nixon and the Executive Office, particularly, raised this question. President Nixon's emphasis upon managerial techniques led him to expand very significantly the number of agencies within the Executive Office. Moreover, he delegated to his personal staff a wide range of responsibilities over which he failed to exercise continuous supervision. Ehrlichman and Haldeman, before they resigned because of their involvement in events surrounding the Watergate affairs, ruthlessly wielded power around Washington in the name of the president. It was the lack of presidential supervision over his own staff that may have accounted for the Watergate break-in in the first place, as well as other questionable activities, including the burglary of Daniel Ellsberg's psychiatrist's office and the solicitation of unreported funds during the 1972 presidential election year.

President Carter came into office with a promise to reduce the presidential bureaucracy, a promise that he made in conjunction with another to reorganize the regular bureaucracy of the federal government. Both of these promises had a ring of great familiarity, as they had been part of the campaigns of many prior presidents. Carter in particular wanted to reinstate the Cabinet as a major policy-making group that would act as a collegial body advising the president directly. He wanted to reverse the flow of power

from the Cabinet to the presidential bureaucracy, reinstating Cabinet secretaries as the primary spokespersons for presidential policy in the areas
under their jurisdiction. President Carter soon found, like presidents before
him, however, that Cabinet government does not work to the advantage of
the president. The only bureaucracy the president can trust is the presidential bureaucracy. Cabinet secretaries tend to develop their own power bases
and soon become independent of, and even antagonistic to, the president.
By the summer of 1979 Carter fully recognized the strains on his leadership
being produced by a weak presidential bureaucracy and by antagonistic
Cabinet secretaries. He fired HEW Secretary Joseph A. Califano, Jr., and
Treasury Secretary W. Michael Blumenthal, both of whom had flouted the
White House staff by going their own ways. At the same time, Carter
strengthened the presidential bureaucracy by centralizing responsibility in
the White House in the hands of his principal adviser, Hamilton Jordan,
whom he made chief of the White House staff. Carter's initial promises to
decentralize power and reduce the size of the presidential bureaucracy
failed. Centralization of power within the White House continued to be the
theme of the Reagan administration. In the following selection Thomas E.
Cronin examines the politics, structure, and responsibilities of the presidential establishment.

42

Thomas E. Cronin
THE SWELLING OF THE
PRESIDENCY: CAN ANYONE
REVERSE THE TIDE?

In 1939 President Franklin D. Roosevelt created the Executive Office of the
President. In his executive order, Roosevelt stated that "in no event shall the
Administrative Assistants to the President be interposed between the President
and the head of any department or agency."

More than forty-five years later, the size and importance of the White
House staff and the Executive Office of the President have been controversial

Table 1   Expanding the White House Staff

Year	President	Full time employees	Employees temporarily detailed to the White House from outside agencies	Total
1937	Franklin D. Roosevelt	45	112 (June 30)	157
1947	Harry S Truman	190	27 (June 30)	217
1957	Dwight D. Eisenhower	364	59 (June 30)	423
1967	Lyndon B. Johnson	251	246 (June 30)	497
1972	Richard M. Nixon	550	34 (June 30)	584
1975	Gerald R. Ford	533	27 (June 30)	560
1980	Jimmy Carter	488	75 (June 30)	570
1984	Ronald Reagan	575*	17 (June 1983)	592

Source: U.S. Budget and White House interviews and letters.

*Two former explicitly White House staff units, the Office of Administration and the Office of Policy Development, are now formally in the Executive Office of the President and not in the White House. But this misleads. These staffs are indeed White House and presidential staffs and thus are included here. The vice-president employs another 22 White House staffers and the National Security Council another 75 to 100, but these are not included in this 575 person staff of President Reagan.

precisely because they seem to be frequently interposed between president and heads of departments and agencies. In campaigning for the presidency in 1976, Jimmy Carter had pledged to reduce the size of the presidential establishment by 30 percent. Further he claimed he would reverse the flow of power away from the White House staffers and back to his cabinet heads. About halfway through his term, however, Carter fired about half his cabinet secretaries and strengthened the hand of his chief White House aides. And though he had tried to reduce somewhat the number of White House aides by one means or another, the size and importance of the presidential establishment was just as great as it had been in the Nixon and Ford years. Nor has Ronald Reagan, that well-known advocate of a slimmer federal government, reduced the size or importance of the White House staff. (See Table 1.) If anything, Reagan centralized political influence even further.

Ronald Reagan came to the White House pledging to cut back on government. He said he would abolish the Departments of Education and Energy. He stated that "government was not the solution, government is the problem." He shied away from saying he would cut the White House staff and its influence. As Governor of California he was decidedly a "delegator," but he delegated to top aides. He also formed a number of cabinet clusters—headed by his top Sacramento aides, William Clark and Edwin Meese.

Reagan followed the same administrative design soon after he came to Washington. In fact, he brought along Ed Meese and later William Clark to perform many of the same "inner circle" responsibilities they had performed back in California. Reagan recruited many able and experienced persons to serve in his cabinet. Plainly, however, he increasingly favored doing business with his small band of White House aides. The White House inner circle of James Baker, William Clark, Michael Deaver, and Edwin Meese became known as the people with clout in the Reagan Administration. They were the ones that would decide that Alexander Haig must go, that Richard Allen, a national security aide, must go, that Anne Gorsuch, the Environmental Protection Agency Administrator, must go, and so on. They increasingly loomed large as both an inner circle and virtually as an inner cabinet. To be sure, the Secretary of Defense, the Secretary of State, the Attorney General and the Secretary of Treasury were regularly consulted—but they seemed "on call" rather than "on top."

Why has the presidential bureaucracy become a problem? Many analysts feel it is too bloated and too top-heavy with aides, counselors, and advisers who invariably intrude themselves between the president and the department heads—thereby breaking FDR's old promise.

A few months after Carter was in office, the White House staff had grown to nearly 700 aides—although perhaps as many as 175 of these were "on loan" from other governmental departments to assist with energy program planning, appointments and the sizeable increase of mail pouring into the Carter White House. In addition to the White House staff there were several support agencies in the Executive Office, such as the National Security Office and the Office of Management and Budget.

Plainly, the cabinet has lost power and the Executive Office has grown in status, in size, and in powers. In light of experience, should Roosevelt's promise be revised? Can the performance of the Executive Office be made to conform to Roosevelt's promise? Can the presidential establishment really be cut back?

After they were elected, some of Carter's and Reagan's aides discounted the importance of staff cutbacks. Improved delivery of services, better public understanding, and fixing accountability are more important than reducing numbers and costs.

We have heard many plans and promises about government reorganization before. President Nixon was genuinely worried that the presidency had "grown like Topsy" so that it weakened rather than strengthened his ability to manage the federal government. Nixon proposed a sweeping consolidation of Cabinet Departments into four functionally oriented super-departments—Community Development, Natural Resources, Human Resources, and Economic Affairs—and at one point wanted to cut the White House workforce in half. But he did not prevent one of the largest expansions of the presidency in history, nor the aggrandizement of power in his White House that contributed to his isolation and downfall. Rather than assisting the president, Nixon's aides often became assistant presidents.

Nixon had little success in these efforts. The Office of the President increased 13 percent during the Eisenhower and Kennedy years, and another 13 percent under LBJ. But it rose approximately another 25 percent under Nixon. Many of President Nixon's cabinet members say they had difficulty in seeing the president. One joked that "Nixon should have told me I was being appointed to a secret mission when I was made Secretary of Commerce." It was said of another that he had to take the public tour of the White House to get in.

Unchecked growth of the White House establishment and its battalion of "faceless ministers" continued to grow even under Gerald Ford. Mr. Ford had always promised to curb bureaucratic growth. His favorite motto was "A government big enough to give you everything you want is a government big enough to take from you everything you have." But Ford was unsuccessful in reversing the trend. Midway through his brief presidential term, one account indicated there were about seventy-five more White House aides on his staff than when Richard Nixon departed.

The expansion of the presidency, it should be emphasized, was by no means only a phenomenon of the Nixon-Ford years. The number of employees directly under the president has been growing steadily since the New Deal days, when only a few dozen people served in the White House entourage at a cost of less than a few hundred thousand dollars annually.

According to the traditional civics textbook picture, the executive branch is more or less neatly divided into Cabinet departments and their secretaries, agencies and their heads, and the president. A more contemporary view takes note of a few prominent presidential aides, and refers to them as the "White House staff." Neither view adequately recognizes the large and growing coterie surrounding the president, which comprises dozens of assistants, hundreds of presidential advisers, and thousands of members of an institutional amalgam called the Executive Office of the President. The men and women in these categories all fall directly under a president in organizational charts—not under the Cabinet departments—and may best be considered by the term the Presidential Establishment (see Figure A).

In the mid-1970s the Presidential Establishment embraced nearly a score of support staffs (the White House Office, National Security Council, Office of Management and Budget, etc.) and advisory office (Council of Economic Advisors, Office of Science and Technology Policy, Office of Telecommunications Policy, etc.). It spawned a vast proliferation of ranks and titles to go with its proliferation of functions (Counsel to the President, Assistant to the President, Special Consultant, Director, Staff Director, etc.). "The White House now has enough people with fancy titles to populate a Gilbert and Sullivan comic opera," Congressman Morris Udall once observed.

Official figures on the size of the Presidential Establishment, and standard body counts vary widely, depending on exactly who is included, but by one frequently used reckoning, between two to two and a half thousand people work directly for the President of the United States. Payroll and maintenance costs

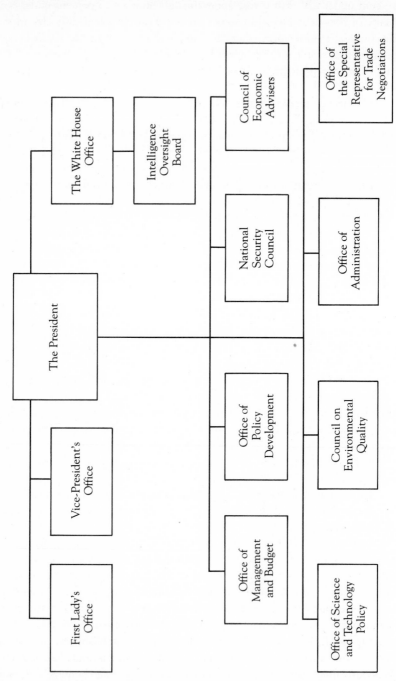

Figure A   The Presidential Establishment, 1984

for this staff run to several hundred million dollars annually. Salary alone for the 488 White House aides in 1980 was estimated at over 22 million dollars.

Under President Nixon, there was a systematic bureaucratization of the Presidential Establishment, in which more new councils and offices were established and more specialization, division of labor, and layers of staffing added than at any time except during World War II. Among the major Nixon additions were the Council of Environmental Quality, the Council on International Economic Policy, the Office of Consumer Affairs, and the Domestic Council. Nixon aide John Ehrlichman wanted the Domestic Council as a base from which to control domestic policy and bypass the Office of Management and Budget as well as the domestic department heads. This may not have been the formal intent exactly, but it was plainly the result.

President Nixon in 1973 moved a number of trusted domestic-policy assistants from the White House rolls and dispersed them to key subCabinet posts across the span of government, virtually setting up White House outposts through the Cabinet departments. One of Nixon's most important staffing actions, after his landslide victory in 1972, was to set up formally a second office, with space and a staff in the White House, for Treasury Secretary George Shultz, as chairman of yet another new presidential body, the Council on Economic Policy. With Schultz as over-secretary of economic affairs, and John Ehrlichman as over-secretary for domestic affairs, Nixon attempted to accomplish the cabinet consolidation that Congress had denied him a year earlier. This super-cabinet was dismantled almost immediately with the Watergate-pressured resignations of Haldeman and Ehrlichman.

President Ford made few changes in the organizational structure of the Executive Office that he inherited from Nixon. He established the Nixon-proposed Council on Wage and Price Stability and a few other councils and boards, most notably an Economic Policy Board that served as a kind of National Security Council and staff for major economic issues. He also allowed the Congress to establish the Office of Science and Technology Policy. Ford continued the Nixon practice of double appointments, such as Kissinger as Secretary of State and head of the National Security Council, and William Simon as Secretary of Treasury and chief spokesman for the White House-based Economic Policy Board.

Carter pledged to cut the White House staff and its importance, and in his first year he earnestly tried to act upon this pledge. He reduced the White House staff by over one hundred persons, but he did so merely by transferring most of the administrative personnel to a newly created Office of Administration within the Executive Office of the President. In fact, many, if not most, of these aides did not even move from their regular offices. They were already located in the Old Executive Office Building, and there they remained. What was labeled a "reduction" was simply a rejuggling of the organizational boxes. Representative Clarence E. Miller of Ohio, who kept tabs on the Carter White House, declared in 1979 that "It appears we are fooling the American people," and he called the Carter reductions "really a shuffling of the deck." White House reporters who studied the growth of the payroll at the White House said appropriations for the White House Office have jumped from $8.3 million in 1971 to a proposed $18.2 million for 1980.

Early in 1980 I had an opportunity to meet with Carter's staff director at the White House, a Mr. Alonzo McDonald. McDonald was a former managing director of McKinsey & Company, the management-consultant firm. He was brought to the Carter White House to reduce the chaos that developed under the decidedly unmanagerial Hamilton Jordan, then the chief of staff. After being in the White House for less than a year, McDonald told me: "Frankly, I would increase the size of the White House staff. It requires more staff. We need larger groups for congressional relations, for dealing with important interest groups; they deserve to be listened to and I now feel that these kinds of staffs can't be cut, they actually should be larger." What did he think, then, of Jimmy Carter's 1976 pledge to cut the White House staff? He diplomatically avoided answering that one.

Carter probably talked more about reorganizing the executive branch than any recent president. Yet, after about two years in office he seemed to have given up. One of his early reorganization aides later summed up Carter's problem as a reorganizer this way:

> For Carter, reorganization was an end in itself, unconnected with the higher purposes of government. He never really linked it together with other policy goals. He gave it up after the first couple of years. Perhaps it was because the rest of government resisted because policy ends and reorganization ends were never discussed or dealt with in any coherent way. Carter, to repeat, had kind of an engineer's notion that organization itself was a policy area. (Personal interview with the writer, February 1980.)

However the names and numbers have changed recently, or may be shifted about in the near future, the Presidential Establishment has not declined in terms of functions, power, or prerogatives; in fact, it has grown.

Does it matter? A number of political analysts have argued recently that it does, and I agree with them. To be sure, the debate about the size of the White House establishment is less important than the purposes to which it is put. But size and purposes are hard to separate. Perhaps the most disturbing aspect of the expansion of the Presidential Establishment is that it has become a powerful inner sanctum of government, isolated from traditional, constitutional checks and balances. It has become common practice for anonymous, unelected, and unratified aides to negotiate sensitive international commitments that are free from congressional oversight. Other aides in the Presidential Establishment wield fiscal authority over billions of dollars in funds that Congress appropriates yet a president refuses to spend, or that Congress assigns to one purpose and the administration routinely redirects to another—all with no semblance of public scrutiny. Such exercises of power pose an important, perhaps vital, question of governmental philosophy: Should a political system that has made a virtue of periodic electoral accountability accord an ever-increasing policy-making role to White House counselors who are neither confirmed by the U.S. Senate nor, because of the doctrine of "executive privilege," subject to questioning by Congress?

Another disquieting aspect of the growth of the Presidential Establishment is that the increase of its powers has been largely at the expense of the traditional sources of executive power and policy-making—the Cabinet members and their departments. When I asked a former Kennedy-Johnson Cabinet member a while ago what he would like to do if he ever returned to government, he said he would rather be a presidential assistant than a Cabinet member. And this is an increasingly familiar assessment of the relative influence of the two levels of the executive branch. In Carter's White House, it was pretty clear from the very beginning that Stuart Eisenstadt, the domestic issues advisor, Hamilton Jordan, the virtual Chief of Staff, and Zbigniew Brzezinski, the National Security Council aide, were among the most powerful members of the Carter administration. Their influence increased the longer Carter kept them.

The Presidential Establishment has become, in effect, a whole layer of government between the president and the Cabinet, and it often stands above the Cabinet in terms of influence with the president. In spite of the exalted position that Cabinet members hold in textbooks and protocol, a number of Cabinet members in recent administrations have complained that they could not even get the President's ear except through a presidential assistant. In his book *Who Owns America?*, former Secretary of the Interior Walter Hickel recounts his combat with a dozen different presidential functionaries and tells how he needed clearance from them before he could get to talk to the president, or how he frequently had to deal with the assistants themselves because the president was "too busy." During an earlier administration, President Eisenhower's chief assistant, Sherman Adams, was said to have told two Cabinet members who could not resolve a matter of mutual concern: "Either make up your mind or else tell me and I will do it. We must not bother the President with this. He is trying to keep the world from war." Several of President Kennedy's Cabinet members regularly battled with White House aides who blocked them from seeing the President. And McGeorge Bundy, as Kennedy's chief assistant for national security affairs, simply side-stepped the State Department in one major area of department communications. He had all important incoming State Department cables transmitted simultaneously to his office in the White House, part of an absorption of traditional State Department functions that visibly continues to this day.

Carter began his presidency by holding weekly Cabinet meetings—two and three hours in length—every Monday morning. He was the first President in recent years to try to get the Cabinet working, talking, and arguing about wide-ranging issues. His intent was not to turn his Cabinet into a parliamentary decision-making collegium, but to establish a team of advisors who could assist and advise him on matters above and beyond the narrow functions of their departments. It was also a recognition by Carter that so many of the problems for a president and for Cabinet members are interdepartmental in character.

Did Carter's Cabinet system work? One White House aide who attended some of these sessions told a *New York Times* reporter that most of the Cabinet members "just sit there, go through their little recitations of what's happening in their departments and nod agreeably when the President speaks." Said another: "These [weekly] meetings . . . are essentially a waste of everybody's time, including the President's."

By his third year, Carter had fired just about half of his Cabinet in the summer of 1978, and he had grown accustomed to relying more heavily than ever on his own proximate White House aides. To his credit, he tried to use the Cabinet more responsibly than his immediate predecessors. He even held more than 60 Cabinet meetings during his first two years. Most of the cabinet meetings had no agendas. The President raised issues that were on his mind, and then solicited the views of those around the table, both on the subjects he had raised and on other matters they thought appropriate. Some of the meetings were criticized as nothing less than adult versions of a grade-school "show-and-tell" session. As the months wore on, several of his Cabinet members, especially Joseph Califano, Michael Blumenthal, Brock Adams, and Andrew Young made their differences of views with the President a public matter. Many of them, from the vantage point of the White House, seemed to be going into business for themselves. Carter and his aides worried about this, and with the tough 1980 elections in mind they decided to "clean house." Secretary of State Cyrus Vance quit somewhat later, in part because he had lost power and influence to his White House counterpart, Zbigniew Brzezinski.

When the Carter Administration is studied in the years to come, the verdict will probably be that the Cabinet failure of his first two years or so was caused more by the president and his aides than by the members of his Cabinet. If Carter had been more experienced in the ways of Washington, if he had been a stronger, more effective coalition builder, he might have molded these talented individuals into a positive force in his Administration. If he had been more popular in the country as a whole, higher in the polls, he would have had greater respect from his Cabinet officers—and they, in turn, would have probably tried fewer end-runs around him in pursuit of their own particular interests.

Perhaps the more things change, the more they stay the same—as the old saying goes.

In a speech in 1971, Senator Ernest Hollings of South Carolina plaintively noted the lowering of Cabinet status. "It used to be," he said, "that if I had a problem with food stamps, I went to see the Secretary of Agriculture, whose department had jurisdiction over that problem. Not anymore. Now, if I want to learn the policy, I must go to the White House to consult John Price [a special assistant]. If I want the latest on textiles, I won't get it from the Secretary of Commerce, who has the authority and responsibility. No, I am forced to go to the White House and see Mr. Peter Flanigan. I shouldn't feel too badly. Secretary Stans [Maurice Stans, then Secretary of Commerce] has to do the same thing."

If Cabinet members individually have been downgraded in influence, the Cabinet as a council of government has become somewhat of a relic, replaced by more specialized policy clusters that as often as not are presided over by White House staffers. The Cabinet's decline has taken place over several administrations. John Kennedy started out his term intending to use the Cabinet as a major policy-making body, but Postmaster General J. Edward Day noted, "After the first two or three meetings, one had the distinct impression that the President felt that decisions on major matters were not made—or even influenced—at Cabinet sessions, and that discussion there was a waste of time. . . . When members spoke up to suggest or to discuss major administration policy, the President would listen with thinly disguised impatience and then postpone or otherwise bypass the question."

President Eisenhower held weekly well-structured Cabinet meetings. Johnson, however, was disenchanted with the Cabinet as a body and characteristically held Cabinet sessions only when the press talked about how the Cabinet was withering away. Under Nixon, the Cabinet was almost never convened at all. Former Nixon counsel John Dean suggested, "I would like to see a more dominant Cabinet. The Nixon Cabinet was totally controllable by the White House staff. A strong Cabinet member should be able to tell a White House staffer, 'Buzz off' or 'Have the President call me himself and I'll tell him why I'm doing what I am.' " Nixon aide John Ehrlichman was very blunt in his description of Nixon's relationship with the Cabinet, "The Cabinet officers are tied closely to the executive, or to put it in extreme terms, when he says jump, they only ask, 'How high?' "

President Ford met with his Cabinet about once a month, using it as a discussion group, not a decision-making body. Ford's Cabinet members have reported that little was accomplished at these sessions and rarely if ever did any arguments take place.

As the Presidential Establishment has taken over policy-making and even some operational functions from the Cabinet departments, the departments have been undercut continuously and the cost has been heavy. These intrusions can cripple the capacity of Cabinet officials to present policy alternatives, and they diminish self-confidence, morale, and initiative within the departments. George Ball, a former undersecretary of state, noted the effects on the State Department: "Able men, with proper pride in their professional skills, will not long tolerate such votes of no-confidence, so it should be no surprise that they are leaving the career service, and making way for mediocrity with the result that, as time goes on it may be hopelessly difficult to restore the Department. . . ."

The irony of this accretion of numbers and functions to the Presidential Establishment is that the presidency has been increasingly afflicted with the very ills of the traditional departments that expansion was intended to remedy. The presidency has become a large, complex bureaucracy itself, rapidly acquiring many dubious characteristics of large bureaucracies in the process: layering, overspecialization, communication gaps, interoffice rivalries, inadequate coordination, and an impulse to become consumed with short-term, urgent operational concerns at the expense of thinking systematically about the consequences of varying sets of policies and priorities and about important long-range problems.

White House aides, in assuming more and more responsibility for the management of government programs, inevitably lose the detachment and objectivity that is so essential for evaluating new ideas. Can a lieutenant vigorously engaged in implementing the presidential will admit the possibility that what the President wants is wrong or not working? Yet a President is increasingly dependent on the judgment of these same staff members, since he seldom sees some of his Cabinet members.

WHY HAS THE PRESIDENCY GROWN BIGGER AND BIGGER?

There is no single villain or systematically organized conspiracy promoting this expansion. A variety of factors is at work. The most significant is the expansion of the role of the presidency itself—an expansion that for the most part has taken place during national emergencies. It should be noted, too, that the business of government has dramatically increased and that the rise of the White House staff is a result of the same forces that have seen a tripling of Congress's staff and a marked increase in law clerks and aides to Supreme Court members. The public and Congress in recent decades have both tended to look to the president for the decisions that were needed in those emergencies. The Great Depression and World War II in particular brought sizeable increases in presidential staffs. And once in place, many stayed on, even after the emergencies that brought them had faded. Smaller national crises have occasioned expansion in the White House entourage, too. After the Russians successfully orbited Sputnik in 1957, President Eisenhower added several science advisors. After the Bay of Pigs, President Kennedy enlarged his national security staff.

Considerable growth in the Presidential Establishment, especially in the post World War II years, stems directly from the belief that critical societal problems require wise men be assigned to the White House to alert the President to appropriate solutions and to serve as the agents for implementing these solutions. Congress has frequently acted on the basis of this belief, legislating the creation of the National Security Council, the Council of Economic Advisors, and the Council on Environmental Quality, among others. Congress has also increased the chores of the presidency by making it a statutory responsibility for the President to prepare more and more reports on critical social areas—annual economic and manpower reports, a biennial report on national growth, etc.

President Nixon responded to a number of troublesome problems that defy easy relegation to any one department—problems like international trade and drug abuse—by setting up special offices in the Executive Office with sweeping authority and sizeable staffs. Once established, these units rarely get dislodged. And an era of permanent crisis ensures a continuing accumulation of such bodies.

Another reason for the growth of the Presidential Establishment is that occupants of the White House frequently distrust members of the permanent government. Nixon aides, for example, viewed most civil servants not only as Democratic but as wholly unsympathetic to such Nixon objectives as decentralization, revenue-sharing, and the curtailment of several Great Society programs. Departmental bureaucracies are viewed from the White House as independent, unresponsive, unfamiliar, and inaccessible. They are suspected again and again of placing congressional, special-interest, or their own priorities ahead of those communicated to them from the White House. Even the President's own Cabinet members soon become viewed in the same light; one of the strengths of Cabinet members, namely their capacity to make a compelling case for their programs, has proved to be their chief liability with presidents.

Presidents may want this type of advocacy initially, but they soon grow weary and wary of it. Efforts by former Interior Secretary Hickel to advance certain environmental programs and by departing Housing and Urban Development Secretary George Romney to promote innovative housing construction methods not only were unwelcome but after a while were viewed with considerable displeasure and suspicion at the White House. Similarly Ronald Reagan asked Alexander Haig, his first Secretary of State, to resign when Haig became too much of an advocate of his own foreign policy views.

Hickel writes poignantly of coming to this recognition during his final meeting with President Nixon, in the course of which the President frequently referred to him as an "adversary." "Initially," writes Hickel, "I considered that a compliment because, to me, an adversary is a valuable asset. It was only after the President had used the term many times and with a disapproving inflection that I realized he considered an adversary an enemy. I could not understand why he would consider me an enemy."

Not only have recent Presidents been suspicious about the depth of the loyalty of those in their Cabinets, but also they invariably become concerned about the possibility that sensitive administration secrets may leak out through the departmental bureaucracies; this is another reason why Presidents have come to rely more on their own personal staff and advisory groups.

Still another reason that more and more portfolios have been given to the presidency is that new federal programs frequently concern more than one federal agency, and it seems reasonable that someone at a higher level is needed to fashion a consistent policy and to reconcile conflicts. Attempts by Cabinet members themselves to solve sensitive jurisdictional questions frequently result in bitter squabbling. At times, too, Cabinet members themselves have recommended that these multidepartmental issues be settled at the White House. Sometimes new presidential appointees insist that new offices for program coordination be assigned directly under the President. Ironically, such was the plea of George McGovern, for example, when President Kennedy offered him the post of director of the Food-for-Peace program in 1961. Later, in his own campaign for the White House, McGovern attacked the buildup of the Presidential Establishment; but back in 1961 he wanted visibility (and no doubt celebrity status), and he successfully argued against his being located outside the White House—in either the State Department or the Department of Agriculture. President Kennedy and his then campaign manager Robert Kennedy felt indebted to McGovern because of his efforts in assisting the Kennedy campaign in South Dakota. Accordingly, McGovern was granted not only a berth in the Executive Office of the President but also the much-coveted title of Special Assistant to the President.

The Presidential Establishment has also been enlarged by the representation of interest groups within its fold. Even a partial listing of staff specializations that have been grafted onto the White House in recent years reveals how interest-group brokerage has become added to the more traditional staff activities of counseling and administration. These specializations form a veritable index of American society: budget and management, national security, economics, congressional matters, science and technology, drug abuse prevention, telecommunications, consumers, national goals, intergovernmental relations, environment, domestic policy, international economics, military affairs, civil rights, disarmament, labor relations, District of Columbia, cultural affairs, education, foreign trade and tariffs, the aged, health and nutrition, physical fitness, volunteerism, intellectuals, Blacks, youth, women, Wall Street, governors, mayors, "ethnics," regulatory agencies and related industry, state party chairmen.

Both President Ford and President Carter, in their efforts to "keep the door of the White House open," maintained a fairly large staff called the Public Liaison Office. William Baroody, Jr., ran Ford's office. Margaret "Midge" Costanza and later Anne Wexler served as Carter's top aides for this operation. Elizabeth Dole and Faith Whittlesey served Reagan in this position. Ford's and Carter's staffs were constantly meeting with ethnic groups, special interest organizations, and with everyone from poet Allen Ginsberg, who wanted to talk about his philosophy on food, to groups opposed to the B-1 bomber and the 1980 Olympic boycott. Reagan's staff tried to win women's support for Reagan's policies and claimed to work with several women's groups. Critics contend that this kind of White House staff is unnecessary, too much of an on-going campaign unit, or merely a staff that engages in "stroking" people who want to say they have taken their cause to the White House. White House aides, of course, claim that ensuring access to the White House for nearly every interest is a requirement of an open presidency.

One of the more fascinating elements in the growth of the Presidential Establishment is the development, particularly under recent administrations, of a huge public-relations apparatus. Scores of presidential aides are now engaged in various forms of press-agentry or public relations, busily selling and reselling the president. This activity—sometimes cynically called the politics of symbolism—is devoted to the particular occupant of the White House, but inevitably, it affects the presidency itself, expanding public expectations about the presidency.

Last, but by no means least, Congress, which has grown increasingly critical of the burgeoning power of the presidency, must itself take some blame for the expansion of the White House. Divided within itself, and often ill-equipped or simply disinclined to make some of the nation's toughest political decisions in recent decades, Congress often has abdicated significant authority to the presidency. In late 1972 Congress almost passed a grant of authority to the president that would have given him the right to determine which programs to cut whenever the budget went beyond the $250 billion ceiling limit—a bill which, in effect, would have handed over to the President some of Congress's long-cherished "power of the purse." Fortunately, Congress could not agree on how to yield this precious power to the executive.

Congress is now making better use of its own General Accounting Office and Congressional Research Service for chores that too often were assigned to the President. Perhaps, also, it might establish in each of its houses special subcommittees on Executive Office operations. Most congressional committees are organized to deal with areas such as labor, agriculture, armed services, or education, paralleling the organization of the Cabinet. What we need now are committees designed explicitly to oversee the White House, to probe how much it costs to run the White House, to probe the size and quality of White House staff arrangements, and to periodically review what might better be removed from the White House and decentralized to the Cabinet secretaries. Can the task of overseeing presidential operations be dispersed among dozens of committees and subcommittees, each of which can look at only small segments of the Presidential Establishment? Since Truman, presidents have had staffs to oversee and lobby the Congress; Congress might want to reciprocate.

While the number of functionaries is the most tangible and dramatic measure of the White House's expansion, its increasing absorption of governmental functions is more disturbing. The White House must understand the dangers inherent in a Presidential Establishment that has become swollen in functions as well as in numbers. The next White House occupant may consider cutting staff or consolidating a number of agencies, but it is yet another thing to reduce the accumulated prerogatives and responsibilities of the presidency.

It is important for presidents not only to criticize the swelling government and its inefficiencies, but also to move to deflate this swelling in the areas where it most needs to be deflated—at home, in the White House, and in the Executive Office of the President. But very likely the attempts to reorganize and reduce the presidential bureaucracy will not succeed, and the forces that buttress the large presidential establishment will remain unchanged.

Presidential Character and Style

The preceding selections in this chapter have focused upon the institutional aspects of the presidency, and the constitutional and political responsibilities of the office. Richard Neustadt does focus upon certain personal dimensions of the power equation, the ability to persuade, but he does not deal with presidential character outside the power context. The following selection is taken from one of the most important and innovative of the recent books dealing with the presidency, in which the author, James David Barber, presents the thesis that it is the *total character* of the person who occupies the White House that is the determinant of presidential performance. As he states, "The presidency is much more than an institution." It is not only the focus of the emotional involvement of most people in politics, but also occupied by an emotional person. How that person is able to come to grips with his feelings and emotions often shapes his orientation toward issues and the way in which he makes decisions. From the very beginning the office was thought of in highly personal terms, for the framers of the Constitution, in part at least, built the office around the character of George Washington, who virtually everyone at the time thought would be the first occupant of the office. And evolution of the office since 1787 has added to its personal quotient. James David Barber provides a framework for the analysis of presidential character and its effect upon performance in the White House.

43

James David Barber
THE PRESIDENTIAL
CHARACTER

When a citizen votes for a presidential candidate he makes, in effect, a prediction. He chooses from among the contenders the one he thinks (or feels, or guesses) would be the best President. He operates in a situation of immense uncertainty. If he has a long voting history, he can recall time and time again when he guessed wrong. He listens to the commentators, the politicians, and his friends, then adds it all up in some rough way to produce his prediction and his vote. Earlier in the game, his anticipations have been taken into account, either directly in the polls and primaries or indirectly in the minds of politicians who want to nominate someone he will like. But he must choose in the midst of a cloud of confusion, a rain of phony advertising, a storm of sermons, a hail of complex issues, a fog of charisma and boredom, and a thunder of accusation and defense. In the face of this chaos, a great many citizens fall back on the past, vote their old allegiances, and let it go at that. Nevertheless, the citizen's vote says that on balance he expects Mr. X would outshine Mr. Y in the presidency.

This [book] is meant to help citizens and those who advise them cut through the confusion and get at some clear criteria for choosing presidents. To understand what actual presidents do and what potential presidents might do, the first need is to see the man whole—not as some abstract embodiment of civic virtue, some scorecard of issue stands, or some reflection of a faction, but as a human being like the rest of us, a person trying to cope with a difficult environment. To that task he brings his own character, his own view of the world, his own political style. None of that is new for him. If we can see the pattern he has set for his political life we can, I contend, estimate much better his pattern as he confronts the stresses and chances of the presidency.

The presidency is a peculiar office. The founding fathers left it extraordinarily loose in definition, partly because they trusted George Washington to invent a tradition as he went along. It is an institution made a piece at a time by successive men in the White House. Jefferson reached out to Congress to put together the beginnings of political parties; Jackson's dramatic force ex-

Excerpted from James David Barber, *The Presidential Character*, 2nd and 3rd Editions (Prentice-Hall, Inc). © 1972, 1977, 1985 by James David Barber. Reprinted by permission of the author.

tended electoral partisanship to its mass base; Lincoln vastly expanded the administrative reach of the office, Wilson and the Roosevelts showed its rhetorical possibilities—in fact every President's mind and demeanor has left its mark on a heritage still in lively development.

But the presidency is much more than an institution. It is a focus of feelings. In general, popular feelings about politics are low-key, shallow, casual. For example, the vast majority of Americans knows virtually nothing of what Congress is doing and cares less. The presidency is different. The presidency is the focus for the most intense and persistent emotions in the American polity. The president is a symbolic leader, the one figure who draws together the people's hopes and fears for the political future. On top of all his routine duties, he has to carry that off—or fail.

Our emotional attachment to presidents shows up when one dies in office. People were not just disappointed or worried when President Kennedy was killed; people wept at the loss of a man most had never even met. Kennedy was young and charismatic—but history shows that whenever a president dies in office, heroic Lincoln or debased Harding, McKinley or Garfield, the same wave of deep emotion sweeps across the country. On the other hand, the death of an ex-president brings forth no such intense emotional reaction.

The president is the first political figure children are aware of (later they add Congress, the Court, and others, as "helpers" of the president). With some exceptions among children in deprived circumstances, the president is seen as a "benevolent leader," one who nurtures, sustains, and inspires the citizenry. Presidents regularly show up among "most admired" contemporaries and forebears, and the president is the "best known" (in the sense of sheer name recognition) person in the country. At inauguration time, even presidents elected by close margins are supported by much larger majorities than the election returns show, for people rally round as he actually assumes office. There is a similar reaction when the people see their president threatened by crisis: if he takes action, there is a favorable spurt in the Gallup poll whether he succeeds or fails.

Obviously the president gets more attention in schoolbooks, press, and television than any other politician. He is one of very few who can make news by doing good things. *His* emotional state is a matter of continual public commentary, as is the manner in which his personal and official families conduct themselves. The media bring across the president not as some neutral administrator or corporate executive to be assessed by his production, but as a special being with mysterious dimensions.

We have no king. The sentiments English children—and adults—direct to the Queen have no place to go in our system but to the president. Whatever his talents—Coolidge-type or Roosevelt-type—the president is the only available object for such national-religious-monarchical sentiments as Americans possess.

The president helps people make sense of politics. Congress is a tangle of committees, the bureaucracy is a maze of agencies. The president is one man trying to do a job—a picture much more understandable to the mass of people who find themselves in the same boat. Furthermore, he is the top man. He ought to know what is going on and set it right. So when the economy goes sour, or war drags on, or domestic violence erupts, the president is available to take the blame. Then when things go right, it seems the president must have had a hand in it. Indeed, the flow of political life is marked off by presidents: the "Eisenhower Era," the "Kennedy Years."

What all this means is that the president's *main* responsibilities reach far beyond administering the Executive Branch or commanding the armed forces. The White House is first and foremost a place of public leadership. That inevitably brings to bear on the president intense moral, sentimental, and quasi-religious pressures which can, if he lets them, distort his own thinking and feeling. If there is such a thing as extraordinary sanity, it is needed nowhere so much as in the White House.

Who the president is at a given time can make a profound difference in the whole thrust and direction of national politics. Since we have only one president at a time, we can never prove this by comparison, but even the most superficial speculation confirms the commonsense view that the man himself weighs heavily among other historical factors. A Wilson reelected in 1920, a Hoover in 1932, a John F. Kennedy in 1964 would, it seems very likely, have guided the body politic along rather different paths from those their actual successors chose. Or try to imagine a Theodore Roosevelt ensconced behind today's "bully pulpit" of a presidency, or Lyndon Johnson as president in the age of McKinley. Only someone mesmerized by the lures of historical inevitability can suppose that it would have made little or no difference to government policy had Alf Landon replaced FDR in 1936, had Dewey beaten Truman in 1948, or Adlai Stevenson reigned through the 1950s. Not only would these alternative presidents have advocated different policies—they would have approached the office from very different psychological angles. It stretches credibility to think that Eugene McCarthy would have run the institution the way Lyndon Johnson did.

The burden of this [argument] is that the crucial differences can be anticipated by an understanding of a potential president's character, his world view, and his style. This kind of prediction is not easy; well-informed observers often have guessed wrong as they watched a man step toward the White House. One thinks of Woodrow Wilson, the scholar who would bring reason to politics; of Herbert Hoover, the Great Engineer who would organize chaos into progress; of Franklin D. Roosevelt, that champion of the balanced budget; of Harry Truman, whom the office would surely overwhelm; of Dwight D. Eisenhower, militant crusader; of John F. Kennedy, who would lead beyond moralisms to achievements; of Lyndon B. Johnson, the Southern conservative; and of Richard M. Nixon, conciliator. Spotting the errors is easy. Predicting with even approximate accuracy is going to require some sharp tools and close attention in their use. But the experiment is worth it because the question is critical and because it lends itself to correction by evidence.

My argument comes in layers.

First, a president's personality is an important shaper of his presidential behavior on nontrivial matters.

Second, presidential personality is patterned. His character, world view, and style fit together in a dynamic package understandable in psychological terms.

Third, a president's personality interacts with the power situation he faces and the national "climate of expectations" dominant at the time he serves. The tuning, the resonance—or lack of it—between these external factors and his personality sets in motion the dynamics of his presidency.

Fourth, the best way to predict a president's character, world view, and style is to see how they were put together in the first place. That happened in his early life, culminating in his first independent political success.

But the core of the argument . . . is that presidential character—the basic stance a man takes toward his presidential experience—comes in four varieties. The most important thing to know about a president or candidate is where he fits among these types, defined according to (a) how active he is and (b) whether or not he gives the impression he enjoys his political life.

Let me spell out these concepts briefly before getting down to cases.

PERSONALITY SHAPES PERFORMANCE

I am not about to argue that once you know a president's personality you know everything. But as the cases will demonstrate, the degree and quality of a president's emotional involvement in an issue are powerful influences on how he defines the issue itself, how much attention he pays to it, which facts and persons he sees as relevant to its resolution, and, finally, what principles and purposes he associates with the issue. Every story of presidential decision-making is really two stories: an outer one in which a rational man calculates and an inner one in which an emotional man feels. The two are forever connected. Any real president is one whole man and his deeds reflect his wholeness.

As for personality, it is a matter of tendencies. It is not that one president "has" some basic characteristic that another president does not "have." That old way of treating a trait as a possession, like a rock in a basket, ignores the universality of aggressiveness, compliancy, detachment, and other human drives. We all have all of them, but in different amounts and in different combinations.

THE PATTERN OF CHARACTER, WORLD VIEW, AND STYLE

The most visible part of the pattern is style. *Style is the president's habitual way of performing his three political roles: rhetoric, personal relations, and homework.* Not to be confused with "stylishness," charisma, or appearance, style is how the president goes about doing what the office requires him to do—to speak, directly or through media, to large audiences; to deal face to face with other politicians, individually and in small, relatively private groups; and to read, write, and calculate by himself in order to manage the endless flow of details that stream onto his desk. No president can escape doing at least some of each. But there are marked differences in stylistic emphasis from president to president. The *balance* among the three style elements varies; one president may put most of himself into rhetoric, another may stress close, informal dealing, while still another may devote his energies mainly to study and cogitation. Beyond the balance, we want to see each president's peculiar habits of style, his mode of coping with and adapting to these presidential demands. For example, I think both Calvin Coolidge and John F. Kennedy were primarily rhetoricians, but they went about it in contrasting ways.

A president's *world view consists of his primary, politically relevant beliefs, particularly his conceptions of social causality, human nature, and the central moral conflicts of the time.* This is how he sees the world and his lasting opinions about what he sees. Style is his way of acting; world view is his way of seeing. Like the rest of us, a president develops over a lifetime certain conceptions of reality—how things work in politics, what people are like, what the main purposes are. These assumptions or conceptions help him make sense of his world, give some semblance of order to the chaos of existence. Perhaps most important: a man's world view affects what he pays attention to, and a great deal of politics is about paying attention. The name of the game for many politicians is not so much "Do this, do that" as it is "Look here!"

"Character" comes from the Greek word for engraving; in one sense it is what life has marked into a man's being. As used here, *character is the way the president orients himself toward life*—not for the moment, but enduringly. Character is the person's stance as he confronts experience. And at the core of character, a man confronts himself. The president's fundamental self-esteem is his prime personal resource; to defend and advance that, he will sacrifice much else he values. Down there in the privacy of his heart, does he find himself superb, or ordinary, or debased, or in some intermediate range? No president has been utterly paralyzed by self-doubt and none has been utterly free of midnight self-mockery. In between, the real presidents move out on life from positions of relative strength or weakness. Equally important are the criteria by which they judge themselves. A president who rates himself by the standard of achievement, for instance, may be little affected by losses of affection.

Character, world view, and style are abstractions from the reality of the whole individual. In every case they form an integrated pattern: the man develops a combination which makes psychological sense for him, a dynamic arrangement of motives, beliefs, and habits in the service of his need for self-esteem.

THE POWER SITUATION AND "CLIMATE OF EXPECTATIONS"

Presidential character resonates with the political situation the president faces. It adapts him as he tries to adapt it. The support he has from the public and interest groups, the party balance in Congress, the thrust of Supreme Court opinion together set the basic power situation he must deal with. An activist president may run smack into a brick wall of resistance, then pull back and wait for a better moment. On the other hand, a president who sees himself as a quiet caretaker may not try to exploit even the most favorable power situation. So it is the relationship between President and the political configuration that makes the system tick.

Even before public opinion polls, the president's real or supposed popularity was a large factor in his performance. Besides the power mix in Washington, the president has to deal with a national climate of expectations, the predominant needs thrust up to him by the people. There are at least three recurrent themes around which these needs are focused.

People look to the president for *reassurance*, a feeling that things will be all right, that the president will take care of his people. The psychological request is for a surcease of anxiety. Obviously, modern life in America involves considerable doses of fear, tension, anxiety, worry; from time to time, the public mood calls for a rest, a time of peace, a breathing space, a "return to normalcy."

Another theme is the demand for a *sense of progress and action*. The president ought to do something to direct the nation's course—or at least be in there pitching for the people. The president is looked to as a take-charge man, a doer, a turner of the wheels, a producer of progress—even if that means some sacrifice of serenity.

A third type of climate of expectations is the public need for a sense of *legitimacy* from, and in, the presidency. The president should be a master politician who is above politics. He should have a right to his place and a rightful way of acting in it. The respectability—even religiosity—of the office has to be protected by a man who presents himself as defender of the faith. There is more to this than dignity, more than propriety. The president is expected to personify our betterness in an inspiring way, to express in what he does and is (not just in what he says) a moral idealism which, in much of the public mind, is the very opposite of "politics."

Over time the climate of expectations shifts and changes. Wars, depressions, and other national events contribute to that change, but there also is a rough cycle, from an emphasis on action (which begins to look too "political") to an emphasis on legitimacy (the moral uplift of which creates its own strains) to an emphasis on reassurance and rest (which comes to seem like drift) and back to action again. One need not be astrological about it. The point is that the climate of expectations at any given time is the political air the President has to breathe. Relating to this climate is a large part of his task.

PREDICTING PRESIDENTS

The best way to predict a President's character, world view, and style is to see how he constructed them in the first place. Especially in the early stages, life is experimental; consciously or not, a person tries out various ways of defining and maintaining and raising self-esteem. He looks to his environment for clues as to who he is and how well he is doing. These lessons of life slowly sink in: certain self-images and evaluations, certain ways of looking at the world, certain styles of action get confirmed by his experience and he gradually adopts them as his own. If we can see that process of development, we can understand the product. The features to note are those bearing on presidential performance.

Experimental development continues all the way to death; we will not blind ourselves to midlife changes, particularly in the full-scale prediction case, that of Richard Nixon. But it is often much easier to see the basic patterns in early life histories. Later on a whole host of distractions—especially the image-making all politicians learn to practice—clouds the picture.

In general, character has its *main* development in childhood, world view in adolescence, style in early adulthood. The stance toward life I call character grows out of the child's experiments in relating to parents, brothers and sisters, and peers at play and in school, as well as to his own body and the objects around it. Slowly the child defines an orientation toward experience; once established, that tends to last despite much subsequent contradiction. By adolescence, the child has been hearing and seeing how people make their worlds meaningful, and now he is moved to relate himself—his own meanings—to those around him. His focus of attention shifts toward the future; he senses that decisions about his fate are coming and he looks into the premises for those decisions. Thoughts about the way the world works and how one might work in it, about what people are like and how one might be like them or not, and about the values people share and how one might share in them too— these are typical concerns for the post-child, pre-adult mind of the adolescent.

These themes come together strongly in early adulthood, when the person moves from contemplation to responsible action and adopts a style. In most biographical accounts this period stands out in stark clarity—the time of emergence, the time the young man found himself. I call it his first independent political success. It was then he moved beyond the detailed guidance of his family; then his self-esteem was dramatically boosted; then he came forth as a person to be reckoned with by other people. The *way* he did that is profoundly important to him. Typically he grasps that style and hangs onto it. Much later, coming into the presidency, something in him remembers this earlier victory and reemphasizes the style that made it happen.

Character provides the main thrust and broad direction—but it does not *determine*, in any fixed sense, world view and style. The story of development does not end with the end of childhood. Thereafter, the culture one grows in and the ways that culture is translated by parents and peers shape the meanings one makes of his character. The going world view gets learned and that learning helps channel character forces. Thus it will not necessarily be true that compulsive characters have reactionary beliefs, or that compliant characters believe in compromise. Similarly for style: historical accidents play a large part in furnishing special opportunities for action—and in blocking off alternatives. For example, however much anger a young may may feel, that anger will not be expressed in rhetoric unless and until his life situation provides a platform and an audience. Style thus has a stature and independence of its own. Those who would reduce all explanation to character neglect these highly significant later channelings. For beyond the root is the branch, above the foundation the superstructure, and starts do not prescribe finishes.

FOUR TYPES OF PRESIDENTIAL CHARACTER

The five concepts—character, world view, style, power situation, and climate of expectations—run through the accounts of presidents in [later chapters of Barber's book], which cluster the presidents since Theodore Roosevelt into four types. This is the fundamental scheme of the study. It offers a way to move past the complexities to the main contrasts and comparisons.

The first baseline in defining presidential types is *activity-passivity*. How much energy does the man invest in his presidency? Lyndon Johnson went at his day like a human cyclone, coming to rest long after the sun went down. Calvin Coolidge often slept eleven hours a night and still needed a nap in the middle of the day. In between the presidents array themselves on the high or low side of the activity line.

The second baseline is *positive-negative affect* toward one's activity—this is, how he feels about what he does. Relatively speaking, does he seem to experience his political life as happy or sad, enjoyable or discouraging, positive or negative in its main effect. The feeling I am after here is not grim satisifaction in a job well done, not some philosophical conclusion. The idea is this: is he someone who, on the surfaces we can see, gives forth the feeling that he has *fun* in political life? Franklin Roosevelt's Secretary of War, Henry L. Stimson, wrote that the Roosevelts "not only understood the *use* of power, they knew the *enjoyment* of power, too. . . . Whether a man is burdened by power or enjoys power; whether he is trapped by responsibility or made free by it; whether he is moved by other people and outer forces or moves them—that is the essence of leadership."

The positive-negative baseline, then, is a general symptom of the fit between the man and his experience, a kind of register of *felt* satisfaction.

Why might we expect these two simple dimensions to outline the main character types? Because they stand for two central features of anyone's orientation toward life. In nearly every study of personality, some form of the active-passive contrast is critical; the general tendency to act or be acted upon is evident in such concepts as dominance-submission, extraversion-introversion, aggression-timidity, attack-defense, fight-flight, engagement-withdrawal, approach-avoidance. In everyday life we sense quickly the general energy output of the people we deal with. Similarly we catch on fairly quickly to the affect dimension—whether the person seems to be optimistic or pessimistic, hopeful or skeptical, happy or sad. The two baselines are clear and they are also independent of one another: all of us know people who are very active but seem discouraged, others who are quite passive but seem happy, and so forth. The activity baseline refers to what one does, the affect baseline to how one feels about what he does.

Both are crude clues to character. They are leads into four basic character patterns long familiar in psychological research. In summary form, these are the main configurations:

Active-positive: There is a congruence, a consistency, between much activity and the enjoyment of it, indicating relatively high self-esteem and relative success in relating to the environment. The man shows an orientation toward productiveness as a value and an ability to use his styles flexibly, adaptively, suiting the dance to the music. He sees himself as developing over time toward relatively well defined personal goals—growing toward his image of himself as he might yet be. There is an emphasis on rational mastery, on using the brain to move the feet. This may get him into trouble; he may fail to take account of the irrational in politics. Not everyone he deals with sees things his way and he may find it hard to understand why.

Active-negative: The contradiction here is between relatively intense effort and relatively low emotional reward for that effort. The activity has a compulsive quality, as if the man were trying to make up for something or to escape from anxiety into hard work. He seems ambitious, striving upward, power-seeking. His stance toward the environment is aggressive and he has a persistent problem in managing his aggressive feelings. His self-image is vague and discontinuous. Life is a hard struggle to achieve and hold power, hampered by the condemnations of a perfectionistic conscience. Active-negative types pour energy into the political system, but it is an energy distorted from within.

Passive-positive: This is the receptive, compliant, other-directed character whose life is a search for affection as a reward for being agreeable and cooperative rather than personally assertive. The contradiction is between low self-esteem (on grounds of being unlovable, unattractive) and a superficial optimism. A hopeful attitude helps dispel doubt and elicits encouragement from others. Passive-positive types help soften the harsh edges of politics. But their dependence and the fragility of their hopes and enjoyments make disappointment in politics likely.

Passive-negative: The factors are consistent—but how are we to account for the man's *political* role-taking? Why is someone who does little in politics and enjoys it less there at all? The answer lies in the passive-negative's character-rooted orientation toward doing dutiful service; this compensates for low self-esteem based on a sense of uselessness. Passive-negative types are in politics because they think they ought to be. They may be well adapted to certain nonpolitical roles, but they lack the experience and flexibility to perform effectively as political leaders. Their tendency is to withdraw, to escape from the conflict and uncertainty of politics by emphasizing vague principles (especially prohibitions) and procedural arrangements. They become guardians of the right and proper way, above the sordid politicking of lesser men.

Active-positive Presidents want most to achieve results. Active-negatives aim to get and keep power. Passive-positives are after love. Passive-negatives emphasize their civic virtue. The relation of activity to enjoyment in a President thus tends to outline a cluster of characteristics, to set apart the adapted from the compulsive, compliant, and withdrawn types.

The first four Presidents of the United States, conveniently, ran through this gamut of character types. (Remember, we are talking about tendencies, broad directions; no individual man exactly fits a category.) George Washington—clearly the most important President in the pantheon—established the fundamental legitimacy of an American government at a time when this was a matter in considerable question. Washington's dignity, judiciousness, his aloof air of reserve and dedication to duty fit the passive-negative or withdrawing type best. Washington did not seek innovation, he sought stability. He longed to retire to Mount Vernon, but fortunately was persuaded to stay on through a second term, in which, by rising above the political conflict between Hamilton and Jefferson and inspiring confidence in his own integrity, he gave the nation time to develop the organized means for peaceful change.

John Adams followed, a dour New England Puritan, much given to work and worry, an impatient and irascible man—an active-negative President, a compulsive type. Adams was far more partisan than Washington; the survival of the system through his presidency demonstrated that the nation could tolerate, for a time, domination by one of its nascent political parties. As President, an angry Adams brought the United States to the brink of war with

France, and presided over the new nation's first experiment in political repression: the Alien and Sedition Acts, forbidding, among other things, unlawful combinations "with intent to oppose any measure or measures of the government of the United States," or "any false, scandalous, and malicious writing or writings against the United States, or the President of the United States, with intent to defame . . . or to bring them or either of them, into contempt or disrepute."

Then came Jefferson. He too had his troubles and failures—in the design of national defense, for example. As for his presidential character (only one element in success or failure), Jefferson was clearly active-positive. A child of the Enlightenment, he applied his reason to organizing connections with Congress aimed at strengthening the more popular forces. A man of catholic interests and delightful humor, Jefferson combined a clear and open vision of what the country could be with a profound political sense, expressed in his famous phrase, "Every difference of opinion is not a difference of principle."

The fourth president was James Madison, "Little Jemmy," the constitutional philosopher thrown into the White House at a time of great international turmoil. Madison comes closest to the passive-positive, or compliant, type; he suffered from irresolution, tried to compromise his way out, and gave in too readily to the "warhawks" urging combat with Britain. The nation drifted into war, and Madison wound up ineptly commanding his collection of amateur generals in the streets of Washington. General Jackson's victory at New Orleans saved the Madison administration's historical reputation; but he left the presidency with the United States close to bankruptcy and secession.

These four Presidents—like all Presidents—were persons trying to cope with the roles they had won by using the equipment they had built over a lifetime. The President is not some shapeless organism in a flood of novelties, but a man with a memory in a system with a history. Like all of us, he draws on his past to shape his future. The pathetic hope that the White House will turn a Caligula into a Marcus Aurelius is as naive as the fear that ultimate power inevitably corrupts. The problem is to understand—and to state understandably—what in the personal past foreshadows the presidential future. . . .

The President and the Media

The media spotlight is on the presidency more than on other governmental institutions. Theodore Roosevelt was the first president to undertake a major effort to co-opt the press, giving Washington reporters space in the White House in order to facilitate his use of them as much as to accommodate the growing presidential press corps. Teddy Roosevelt knew that the press could be an important ally of government, that publicity for presidential policies and actions could help to build public support and ease the job of his administration.

Teddy Roosevelt set a precedent for twentieth-century presidents in recognizing the power of the press and the importance of turning the political reporters' craft to the advantage of the White House by managing the news. Teddy Roosevelt's cousin, Franklin D. Roosevelt, held regular informal press conferences with reporters in the Oval Office, knowing that by keeping them informed of his programs and progress the nation would learn about and, he hoped, support the New Deal.

From the vantage-point of the White House, the press, while potentially a useful conduit of managed news, is seen more as a critic than an ally. Presidents tend to view the press as the enemy with which they have to deal. Charged with the responsibility of coping with the press is the presidential press secretary, who conducts daily briefings apprising White House reporters of the president's actions and plans.

A White House insider, George E. Reedy, now Nieman Professor of Journalism at Marquette University, portrays the world of the White House reporter and the way in which presidents view and treat the press:

44

George E. Reedy
THE PRESS AND THE PRESIDENT

To the leisurely observer of the Washington scene, there is a distinct charm in the startled air of discovery with which the press greets each step in the entirely predictable course of its relationship with the president and the White House staff.

Actually, the patterns are as well-established and as foreseeable as the movements of a Javanese temple dance. The timing will vary as will the alternating degrees of adoration and bitterness. But the sequence of events, at least in modern times, appears to be inexorable. It is only the determination of the press to treat each new day as unprecedented that makes the specific events seem to be news.

Seen from a little distance, cries of outrage from the press over the discovery that Mr. Reagan seeks to "manage the news" have the flavor of an Ed Sullivan rerun show on after-midnight television. They are reminiscent of similar protests in the administrations of Presidents Carter, Nixon, Johnson, Kennedy, Eisenhower, Truman, and Roosevelt. Presidents before that do not offer much material for discussion simply because they served prior to the FDR era, when press-White House relations were put on a daily-contact basis for the first time in history.

The charge of management is a familiar one because it has a strong element of truth. All presidents seek to manage the news and all are successful to a degree. What is not taken into account is that legitimate management of the news from the White House is inescapable and, human nature being what it is, it is hardly surprising that presidents try to bend this necessity for their own ends. Few men will decline an opportunity to recommend themselves highly.

The press would not be happy with a White House that ended all efforts at news management and either threw the mansion wide open for coverage or closed it to outsiders altogether and told journalists to get facts any way they could. Since the early days of the New Deal, reporters have been relying on daily press briefings, prearranged press conferences, and press pools when the president travels. There would be chaos should all this come to an end.

The point is that the White House is covered by journalists through highly developed and formal structures. It is inherent in the nature of such structures that they must be managed by somebody, and the president's office is no exception. Management technique is employed every time the president decides what stories will be released on Monday and what stories will be released on Saturday; every time he decides that some meetings will be open to press coverage and others will not; every time he decides that some visitors will be fed to the press as they walk out of the Oval Office and others will not. Anybody who believes that he will make decisions on the basis of what makes him look bad will believe a hundred impossible things before breakfast.

There are actually times when the press literally does not want news. This became very clear early in the administration of Lyndon Johnson when he inaugurated the custom of unexpected Saturday morning news conferences. This meant disruption of newspaper production schedules all over the United States. Printing pressmen had to be recalled from weekend holidays to work at exorbitant rates; front pages that had been planned in leisurely fashion in the morning had to be scrapped for new layouts; rewrite men who had looked forward to quiet afternoons with their families worked into the evening hours. It was a mess.

After two such conferences, I began getting calls from top bureau chiefs in Washington pleading with me to put an end to them. They made it clear they wanted stories timed so that they would fit conveniently into news slots. It took some doing on my part; Johnson would have enjoyed the discovery that he was putting newspaper publishers to so much expense and trouble. (I think he started these conferences simply because he became lonely on Saturday mornings when there was little to do.) I talked him into dropping the custom by producing figures which showed that the weekend audiences were not large enough to justify the effort.

While it was actually going on, the episode struck me as just another example of the Johnsonian inability to comprehend the press. It was not until later that I realized the deeper significance. The press had not only acquiesced in news management but had actually asked that it be instituted. The fact that nothing was involved except timing was irrelevant. The ability to control the timing of news is the most potent weapon that any would-be news manipulator can have. No absolute line can be drawn between the occasions when he should have it and those when he should not.

This may well account for the indifference of the public to the periodic campaigns against news management. Even to an unsophisticated audience it is apparent that journalists are not objecting to news management per se but only to the kind of news management that makes their professional lives more difficult. However it may look in Washington, at a distance the issue appears as a dispute over control of the news for the convenience of the president or for the convenience of the press. In such a situation, Americans tend to come down on the side of the president.

Of course, if the president is caught in an outright lie—a lie about something in which the public is really concerned—the public will mobilize against him swiftly. But many charges of news management are directed at statements that Americans do not regard as outright lies. Americans have become so accustomed to the kind of exaggeration and misleading facts that are used to sell products on nightly television that a little White House puffery seems quite natural.

There is, of course, another side to the coin. While presidents always try to manipulate the news—and all too often succeed—there is a very real doubt whether the manipulation performs any real service for them, even in the crassest image-building sense. The presidency is a strange institution. The occupant must accept never-ending responsibilities and must act on never-ending problems. It may well be that what a president does speaks so much more loudly than anything he can say that the normal techniques of public relations are completely futile.

In the first place, a president may be able to time his public appearances but he cannot time his acts. He *is* the United States and anything that affects the United States must have a presidential response. He must react to international crises, to domestic disasters, to unemployment, and to inflation; if he chooses to do nothing in any of these instances his inaction will be writ large in the public media.

In the second place, a president may be able to keep his thoughts to himself but he cannot act in any direction without causing waves that sweep through the Washington community. The federal bureaucracy is shot through with holdovers from previous administrations who do not like him; the Congress is loaded with political opponents with whom he must deal; the lobbying offices of the capital are staffed by skilled president-watchers who can interpret his every act and who have sympathetic journalistic listeners. Finally, there is the overwhelming fact that the president has a direct impact on the lives of every citizen and there is a limit to his capacity to mislead. He cannot convince men and women that there is peace when their sons are dying in a war. He cannot hold up images of prosperity (although he will try) when men and women are out of work. He cannot persuade constituents that there is peace and harmony when there is rioting in the streets. There may be instances when he can escape the blame but only when his political opposition is not on its toes.

Against this background, the efficacy of manipulation is dubious at best. It may have a favorable impact on public opinion in the short run. But I know of no persuasive evidence that it helps to build the long-term support a politician needs. Every instance I have studied bears a close parallel to what happened when Lyndon Johnson held his meaningless meeting with the late Soviet premier Alexei Kosygin at Glassboro, New Jersey, in 1967. He was able to maneuver the press into treating it as a major summit conference for a few days, and his poll ratings rose accordingly. But it soon became clear that the meeting had produced nothing of substance and that there had been no reason to expect that it would. The poll ratings went right back down again.

On the other hand, efforts at manipulation invariably challenge the press to dig deeper than journalists ordinarily would. The stories they write about manipulation have little effect. But the stories they write as a result of the digging may have the kind of substance that does make an impact. The whole exercise can well be merely an invitation to trouble on the part of the president.

The bottom line can be simply stated. The president can, within limits, manipulate the press as a whole, and it is probable that his efforts to do so will always backfire.

The President and Public Opinion

Public opinion polling has been part of presidential politics for a long time. President Harry S Truman observed in his memoirs, "Public opinion polls had reached their peak as an American institution during the summer of 1948. Several of these, such as those conducted by George Gallup and Elmo Roper, had established reputations for accuracy that were quite impressive, and many politicians, newspapermen, businessmen and labor leaders begin to look to these surveys as a guide to their actions." Truman never ceased to delight in the inaccuracy of the public-opinion polls which had mistakenly predicted his defeat in 1948.

As with any politician, presidents would like to know public opinion, not simply to follow it but to help them plan their campaign and governing strategies. But "public opinion" is one of the most nebulous concepts in politics. There are simply too many "publics" with contrasting interests and ideas to form a unified public opinion. Presidents both past and present have nevertheless used their public-opinion pollsters in various ways to help them make decisions, as the following selection illustrates.

45

Michael Barone

THE POWER OF THE PRESIDENTS' POLLSTERS

As the president-elect was preparing to enter office, he received some advice from his pollster. Patrick Caddell told Jimmy Carter that, although the president was about to undertake new responsibilities, he should continue "campaigning." He should use fireside chats and town hall meetings, he should eschew the accoutrements of high office and shun the luxuries of the rich. The advice evidently was heeded. In his first act after taking the oath, Carter stepped out of the presidential limousine and walked down Pennsylvania Avenue to the White House. Within weeks he appeared on television before a fire, wearing a sweater and talking unpretentiously to the American people.

Over the next four years, the advice changed, and the president did not always follow it. But Patrick Caddell, seldom seen in Washington in the Carter years without his White House pass dangling from his breast pocket, achieved a level of influence greater than that of any pollster before or since.

It was a precedent not entirely congenial to the polling profession. Political pollsters, after all, earn their fees by helping politicians win elections; Caddell's client saw a big lead wind up as a narrow victory in 1976 and was soundly defeated in 1980. An argument can be made—and I would make it—that Carter did entirely too much "campaigning" in his four years in office and not enough governing, that he spent too much time emphasizing the outsider themes that

"The Power of the Presidents' Pollsters," by Michael Barone, from *Public Opinion*, September/October 1988, published by the American Enterprise Institute, Washington, D.C. Reprinted with the permission of the American Enterprise Institute for Public Policy Research.

had worked for him as an unknown challenger and not enough time establishing himself as an insider who knew how to lead.

Even so, the Carter-Caddell experience did not result in the banishment of pollsters from the White House. Ronald Reagan's pollster, Dr. Richard Wirthlin, has been conducting frequent surveys during the Reagan years (paid for by the national Republican party, as Caddell's were by the national Democratic party, even when Carter had a primary opponent). Wirthlin has been less influential than Caddell, but his work has made an imprint on the Reagan presidency. This year Robert Teeter for George Bush and Irwin "Tubby" Harrison for Michael Dukakis are wearing the "pollsters general" mantle. Pollsters are with us in presidential politics and presidential governing, and they are likely to remain so. All this raises interesting questions: How did they get there? How should they be used now that they're there?

HUMBLE BEGINNINGS

The answer is that pollsters got to the White House even before Dr. George Gallup published his first public opinion survey in October 1935. That was a month after the murder of Huey Long, and so Gallup was not able to give us any results on one of the tantalizing might-have-beens of political history: how much damage would Long have done as a third-party candidate against Franklin Roosevelt in 1936? But Roosevelt himself had already received a report on that, at dinner in June 1935 with James Farley, Joseph Kennedy, and Will Hays, the 1920s Republican national chairman and 1930s movie czar—how one would like to have been a fly on that wall!—plus a statistician named Emil Hurja. Hurja presented results from a poll that showed "the president weaker that [*sic*] at any time since his inauguration" and "showed that [Roosevelt] would carry without difficulty all of the western states with the possible exception of Colorado, including Wisconsin and Minnesota, of course. It showed that in the eastern states he had lost some ground, which, of course, does not worry us because that condition can be corrected in due course." From the results—I have not been able to track down any written version—Farley predicted that Roosevelt would be elected by a five-million-vote plurality, and that Long would win three to four million votes and run uniformly throughout the country. Translated into percentage terms, this comes to something like a 51–39 percent Roosevelt lead over the Republicans, with 10 percent for Long, a drop from Roosevelt's 57–40 percent win over Herbert Hoover in 1932; it would have cost him Massachusetts, New Jersey, and Ohio, and have made New York and Michigan unsure.

Hurja's poll may have done something to inspire Roosevelt's shift to the left in May and June 1935, even though it seems that move started three weeks before, after NRA was declared unconstitutional May 27. Roosevelt had other reasons to believe that Long was a threat. The most sophisticated of the day's polls, Elmo Roper's quarterly surveys that began appearing in *Fortune* in July

1935, had made it clear that most voters were wary of the economic redistributionist politics of some New Dealers and were hostile to the militant new CIO unions. But while this was true of the traditional base each party had held since the Civil War—the Republican northern farmlands and the Democratic Deep South—these policies were popular among the electoral groups that were not firmly attached to either party—the Jews of New York City and the German- and Scandinavian-American Progressives of Wisconsin, Minnesota, and the old Northwest. Roosevelt seems to have understood this without polls, for this was the coalition he had been thinking about assembling since the 1920s. But polls helped convince liberal Republicans to appeal to the swing groups.

Wendell Willkie was surely aware of the *Fortune* polls, since *Fortune* managing editor Russell Davenport was his campaign organizer. Willkie made a point of saying blunt and supposedly impolitic things, which any reader of the *Fortune* polls would have known were widely popular. As Davenport himself wrote in the April 1940 issue, "The fascinating characteristic of Mr. Willkie's position is that most people will agree with it."

The always well-organized and professionally advised Thomas E. Dewey also consulted polls closely. He studied the national polls and even polls in supposedly one-party states such as Florida. "Through Ben Duffey of the New York advertising agency Batten, Barton, Durstine and Osborne," writes Dewey's definitive biographer Richard Norton Smith, "daily telephone conversations were arranged with pollster Archibald Crossley. Both Gallup and Roper offered to make known their findings to Duffey in advance of publication. Gallup did have one question. Why, he asked Duffey, did the Republican campaign want to spend money on polling? The results, after all, were a 'foregone conclusion.' "

So both candidates in 1948 may have appreciated the limits of polling better than the pollsters. Dewey because he didn't seem to trust them (Gallup's last poll was taken October 15–25 and showed Truman with a gain that would certainly prompt any of today's pollsters to stay in the field), Truman because he, like most other Democrats of the times, paid little attention to polls.

POLLS TAKING ROOT

Gallup and other pollsters for years had suggested that polls predicted election results, rather than make the more modest but more accurate claim (accurate probably even in 1948) that they showed opinion at a particular time; and by comparing their final polls to election results, calculated to even tenths of a percentage, they suggested that polls have a greater precision than they can ever realistically claim. Pollsters paid for these sins after 1948, when their final surveys all showed Dewey well ahead.

In the 1952 campaign neither side (even the Eisenhower campaign with its advertising agents) seems to have relied much on pollsters or paid much attention to them. Eisenhower himself overrode the professionals and insisted on campaigning in the South, where he believed correctly that he could carry several states. Among Taft conservatives it had become dogma that there was a huge reservoir of conservative votes among nonvoters—a dogma that surely would not have been supported by polls. Adlai Stevenson's backers quickly developed a distaste for "selling a candidate like soap" and for the survey research associated with such efforts. Most published polls during the campaign showed the race closer than in 1948, with the result that the final 56–44 percent Eisenhower margin came as a great surprise.

When in 1960 the pollster finally became a fixture of a major presidential campaign, the scene was not some high-tech office but a "pink-and-white children's bedroom on the second floor" of one of the Kennedy Hyannis Port houses. It

> had been cleared that evening as a data-analysis section, the beds removed, the baby chairs thrust to the side, a long table set up with mounds of voting statistics; there public opinion analyst Lou Harris was codifying reports received from the communications center downstairs and from the four teletypewriters of the wire agencies installed in the adjacent bedroom.

Back before the networks established reliable voter analysis models—their projections seesawed from a Kennedy landslide to a Nixon landslide on election night—Harris was doing most of this not very useful work himself, for except perhaps in Chicago the votes had already been cast. Harris, however, had done other work in the campaign, sampling opinion nationally, testing responses to issues, looking at poll results in a particular state. This was important in a campaign that was always tightly contested and in which at least the Kennedys (if not the television networks) were aware that past patterns would not obtain. Reactions to new issues and—even more important—the ties of ancestral religion would make all the difference.

The Kennedys' reliance on Lou Harris in the 1960 campaign was the first of several instances in which the Democrats, once so scornful of poll takers, seem to have used them at least as assiduously as the usually better-heeled Republicans. In 1964 Lyndon Johnson was endlessly fascinated with the polls that showed him so popular, and he hired Oliver Quayle as his pollster (Harris having gone out of the candidate polling business in 1963); Barry Goldwater, painfully aware that his was a losing cause, was more interested in being faithful to his principles and his followers than in following any advice that might be suggested by the polls. In 1968 Richard Nixon clearly ran a more organized and deliberate campaign than Hubert Humphrey, whose campaign consultant Joseph Napolitan was typing out his fall campaign plan as Humphrey was being nominated in Chicago in the last week of August. Yet neither campaign, in my view, fully appreciated the insights that sophisticated polling could have provided in that confusing and turbulent year. Humphrey, for example, was clearly out of sync with opinion when he championed, a month after Martin Luther

King was murdered, "the politics of joy." Nixon, who saw Humphrey's support rise while his remained stagnant around the 43 percent level, was not much better.

THE PLAYERS IN
PRESIDENTIAL POLLING

Around this time the pollsters who have dominated presidential polling in most of the years since had begun to emerge. Robert Teeter, of Detroit's Market Opinion Research, is a quiet, calm, thoughtful, ideologically tolerant Republican from the ancestral Republican territory of outstate Michigan, who has played some role in every Republican presidential campaign since 1968. He was the lead pollster in Gerald Ford's very nearly successful attempt to overcome a 62–29 deficit in 1976—a campaign that sounded the themes of national pride and accomplishment that proved so resonant for Ronald Reagan in the 1980s— and he was the lead pollster for George Bush in 1980 and 1988. The other major Republican pollster has been Richard Wirthlin, a Mormon academic from Utah who bridled at supporting Barry Goldwater in 1964 but who has been Ronald Reagan's pollster since 1970. Wirthlin has calmly provided the president with figures and recommended strategies that, over the years, have sometimes pleased and sometimes enraged Reagan's ideological supporters.

On the Democratic side the dominant figure from 1972 until sometime in 1984 was Patrick Caddell. Only twenty-two years old in 1972, a Harvard undergraduate from a career military family in the redneck city of Jacksonville, Florida, he managed to attach himself to George McGovern's longshot campaign. Caddell's great contribution there was the idea, common in academia, of alienation: it was he who counseled McGovern to appeal to supporters of George Wallace on the grounds that they all wanted a change and a removal of the people in power in Washington.

Caddell's problem was that he became a kind of johnny-one-note. A similar alienation theme worked well for Jimmy Carter, as he campaigned in the wake of Watergate in 1975 and 1976 as a candidate who was not from Washington, was not a lawyer, who carried his own suitbag, and who would never lie to you. As late as July 1979, Caddell wrote Carter a memorandum describing a national "malaise" and helped to put together the domestic summit in which Carter ludicrously summoned government officials and national notables up to his mountaintop—as if he were not in charge of the government himself.

Caddell's and Carter's strategy was still to run against Washington and against government—an approach that became unsustainable when Carter was in Washington and headed the government. In contrast, Ronald Reagan once in office used his 1940s movie experience—the best popular culture since Dickens—and identified himself and his political cause with the heart of the country and the concerns that most citizens have at heart.

Caddell's approach was adolescent, always complaining about the grownups in power. Reagan's approach was adult, celebrating the success of those who have worked hard over the years and inviting the next generation to join them. For a moment in the 1970s, when Americans' confidence in their government and their country was low, Caddell's adolescent approach struck a chord. But over the longer haul, as the success of our own country and the weaknesses of our adversaries became harder to hide, Reagan's adult approach summed up the national mood better.

WHAT POLLS CAN'T DO

Do pollsters manipulate politicians who will manipulate voters in turn? These have been the fears of intellectuals ever since the polling profession was born. Actually, the fears go back further. Politicians have always been eager to understand public opinion in any way they can, if only by sampling the opinion of their neighbors and relatives as every American family does at the Thanksgiving dinner table. The fear is that the pollster, being in possession of information so much more reliable and so much more capable of producing political results than anyone else, can become a kind of Svengali.

The history I have recounted does not, I think, substantiate such fears. A Caddell can influence one candidate's campaign, but that influence is still limited in time and place. Politicians are increasingly sophisticated about using pollsters, having learned with the public to understand the limitations of the polling instrument and having observed that following slavishly the implications of any poll at one moment does not guarantee a favorable result in the long run. The ultimate limit is that voters want officeholders who not only campaign effectively but who also govern effectively. And the instincts, the policies, the strategies that produce effective governance are no more discoverable by pollsters than they are by anyone else.

Polling is a tool, not magic; and political pollsters at their best are inspired mechanics, like the guys who without saying an articulate word in English, can get your old Ford Mustang or your old musty refrigerator working again. They are not—certainly they are not yet—our masters.

Judging the Presidency

The presidency, standing as it does at the focal point of our political system and drawing into its vortex the expectations of the American people about government performance, virtually guarantees that presidents will strive to excel in their performance in the White House. In particular, presidents who view the office as the center of political activity and the major source of policy initiative hope to be judged as among the great presidents of history. Before Watergate Richard Nixon, who viewed the presidency as an active-conservative force, hoped to take his place among the great presidents in American history. Presidential "greatness" was almost surely an aspiration of Jimmy Carter and Ronald Reagan, as it is of George Bush.

Running for the position of great president may have an important effect upon performance in the White House. All candidates for greatness are well aware that historians will judge them on the basis of what they have accomplished, the decisions they have made, and the actions they have taken that exhibit leadership. Sometimes presidents feel that the appearance of leadership is as important as the real thing. Style may be substituted for substance. Above all, a president seeking greatness will always strive to aggrandize the presidency in word and deed. This means raising the level of popular expectation about what the president can do to meet and solve national problems, and at the same time demanding support for unilateral presidential actions that may circumvent the carefully constructed constitutional processes of separation of powers and checks and balances. Many "great" presidents have not paid enough attention to constitutional niceties or respected the co-equal role in the governmental process of Congress and the Supreme Court. In the following selection Nelson Polsby argues that while presidential performance may be enhanced because of aspirations to achieve greatness, it is more common for such strivings to produce difficulties and reduce effective leadership.

46

Nelson W. Polsby
AGAINST PRESIDENTIAL
GREATNESS

Until election day is past, candidates for president campaign among their fellow citizens with the simple end in view of being elected. Once they are inaugurated, however, presidents frequently yearn for an even higher office—a niche in the pantheon of "great" presidents. Membership in this exclusive society is, on the whole, not to be achieved through sheer popularity. Was there ever a more popular president than Dwight D. Eisenhower? Yet we all "know" he was not a "great" president, nor even a "near great" one.

How do we know this? Essentially I think the answer is: we know it because historians tell us so. In each generation, or possibly over a shorter span, a consensus arises among the authors of political and historical texts about how well various presidents met the alleged needs of their times. These opinions are in turn the distillate of writings of journalists and other leading opinion-makers who were contemporaries of the various presidents, filtered through the ideological predispositions of the current batch of history writers.

This means that running for great president is a chancy business, since the admissions committee is small and self-conscious, somewhat shifty-eyed, and possibly even harder to please than, let us say, the wonderful folks who guard the lily-white portals of the Chevy Chase Club. Some presidents are smart enough to take out a little insurance. Surely that was one extremely good reason for John Kennedy to invite Arthur Schlesinger, Jr., to join his White House staff and to encourage him to keep notes. Schlesinger's father, also a distinguished historian, was after all the author of two well-publicized surveys of historians—in 1949 and 1962—that ranked presidents for overall greatness.

Lyndon Johnson and, evidently, Richard Nixon, pursued somewhat different strategies. Apparently neither found a court historian wholly to his liking— though after an unsatisfactory experience with Eric Goldman, perhaps Johnson found Doris Kearns more tractable and useful for somewhat similar purposes. Both recent presidents caused their administrations to engage in what might be called over-documentation of their official activities. Johnson hauled tons of stuff down to his museum in Texas where a staff composed "his" memoirs at

From Nelson W. Polsby, "Against Presidential Greatness." Reprinted from *Commentary*, January 1977, by permission; all rights reserved.

leisure. One assumes the Nixon tapes, had they remained undiscovered, would have been employed to some such similar end.

In general, authorized ex-presidential memoirs are pretty awful to read, and nobody takes them seriously as history. At best they can be self-revelatory, and hence grist for the analyst's mill, but they are mostly stale, dull, self-serving documents. By common repute the best ex-presidential memoir ever written was that of Ulysses S. Grant. It was about his Civil War service, not his presidency, and so it is probably too much to expect that it would have saved Grant's presidency from the adverse judgment of "history."

We must conclude that writing memoirs may be a respectable way to fatten the exchequer of an ex-president, but that it is of negligible value in running for great president. Hiring, or charming, a court historian is a somewhat better investment, and especially if, by calculation or misfortune, the court historian's account appears after the death of the president in question. Reflective readers may find it slighty loony that presidents would want to control what people think of them after they have died, but the desire to leave an admiring posterity is surely not all that unusual among Americans. Moreover, among those Americans who land in the White House one can frequently discern an above-average desire to control the rest of the world, future generations, if possible, included.

What is it that historians like to see on the record when they make their ratings? It is impossible to speak with assurance for all future generations of historians. Fads and cross-currents make it difficult even to read the contemporary scene in a perfectly straightforward way. Nevertheless, over the near term, I think it is fair to say that the predominant sentiments of historians about presidents have been shaped by the experience of the New Deal, a longish episode in which presidential leadership was generally perceived to have saved the country not merely in the sense of restoring a modicum of prosperity to the economy, but more fundamentally rescuing the political system from profound malaise and instability.

The evidence that the New Deal actually did either of these things is, as a matter of fact, rather thin. But I shall not argue that attentiveness to evidence is a strong point of the gatekeepers of presidential greatness. They do, however, appear very much to admire presidents who adopt an activist, aggrandizing, constitutional posture toward presidential power. As the senior Schlesinger wrote: "Mediocre Presidents believed in negative government, in self-subordination to the legislative power." My view is that this reflects a New Deal-tutored preference for a particular sort of political structure rather than a statement of constitutional principles about which there can be no two opinions.

William Howard Taft, later a notably activist Chief Justice, put the classic case for the passive presidency when he wrote:

> The true view of the executive function is, as I conceive it, that the President can exercise no power which cannot be fairly and reasonably traced to some specific grant of power or justly implied and included within such express grant

as proper and necessary to its exercise. Such specific grant must be either in the federal Constitution or in an act of Congress passed in pursuance thereof. There is no undefined residuum of power which he can exercise because it seems to him to be in the public interest. . . .

Poor Taft! That sort of argument got him low marks for presidential greatness, and especially since he evidently acted on his beliefs. Says James David Barber, author of the recent study of *The Presidential Character*, " . . . he was from the start a genial, agreeable, friendly, compliant person, much in need of affection. . . . "

Whereas the senior Arthur Schlesinger's 1962 survey rated Taft an "average" sixteenth, between McKinley and Van Buren on the all-time hit parade, Theodore Roosevelt, Taft's friend and patron, comes in a "near great" seventh, just below Andrew Jackson on the list. Roosevelt's theory of the presidency undoubtedly helped him in the sweepstakes. He said:

> I declined to adopt the view that what was imperatively necessary for the Nation could not be done by the President unless he could find some specific authorization to do it. My belief was that it was not only his right but his duty to do anything that the needs of the Nation demanded unless such action was forbidden by the Constitution or by the laws. Under this interpretation of executive power I did and caused to be done many things not previously done by the President and the heads of the departments. I did not usurp power, but I did greatly broaden the use of executive power. In other words, I acted for the public welfare, I acted for the common well-being of all our people, whenever and in whatever manner was necessary, unless prevented by direct constitutional or legislative prohibition. . . .

The beginnings of this conflict in constitutional interpretation and practice have been traced back to the founding of the Republic. In those early years, Leonard White found:

> The Federalists emphasized the necessity for power in government and for energy in the executive branch. The Republicans emphasized the liberties of the citizen and the primacy of representative assemblies. The latter accused their opponents of sympathy to monarchy and hostility to republican institutions. . . . Hamilton . . . insisted on the necessity for executive leadership of an otherwise drifting legislature; Jefferson thought the people's representatives would readily find their way if left alone to educate each other by free discussion and compromise. . . . By 1792 Jefferson thought the executive power had swallowed up the legislative branch; in 1798 Hamilton thought the legislative branch had so curtailed executive power that an able man could find no useful place in the government.

In the present era there is no real conflict at the theoretical level. The last sitting president even half-heartedly to argue against a self-aggrandizing presidency was Eisenhower. To be sure, a few voices—notably Eugene McCarthy's— could be heard proposing structural limitations on presidential powers in the dark days of Vietnam, but the resonance of his argument has faded quickly.

Even the remarkable shenanigans of the Nixon years seem only slightly to have diminished the enthusiasm of opinion leaders for strong presidents. Theodore Sorensen has gone so far as to advance the comforting view that we have nothing to fear from a strong president because Nixon was not in fact a strong president. In the light of such ingenuity one can only conclude that even today the mantle of presidential greatness is available only to those presidents who subscribe to a constitutional theory affording the widest scope for presidential action.

Does the historical record suggest any other helpful hints to the aspiring presidential great? Indeed it does. Crises are good for presidential reputations. Over the short run, as countless public-opinion surveys have shown, a small crisis in foreign affairs followed by a small show of presidential decisiveness is always good for a boost in the president's ratings. These ratings, moreover, are evidently indifferent to the efficacy of the presidential decision; triumph or fiasco, it makes little short-run difference.

Presidential greatness, however, is not decided over the short run. Yet the things that mass publics like today are frequently attractive to historians when painted on a larger canvas. Our three "greatest" presidents were reputedly Washington, Lincoln, and Franklin Roosevelt. The service of all three is intimately associated with three incidents in American history when the entire polity was engaged in total war.

Total war—that is, war engaging some major fraction of the gross national product in its prosecution—creates vastly different conditions of psychological mobilization than the nagging, running sores of limited wars, which, in time, invariably become extremely unpopular. Lyndon Johnson was one president who showed awareness of the irony implicit in the popularity risks of restricting, as well as pursuing, a limited war.

To those scrupulous souls who shrink from manufacturing a war of total mobilization in the service of their future reputations, is there anything left to be said? Surely lessons can be drawn equally from our least successful as well as our most successful presidents. Harding, Grant, and, one surmises, Nixon, lurk somewhere near the bottom of the heap. The smell of very large-scale scandal (not the small potatoes of the Truman era) attaches to the administration of each.

Assuming, for the sake of argument, that presidents want to run an administration untainted by scandal, can they do it? Considering the scale of operations of the United States government, the general absence of corruption in the conduct of its business is an admirable achievement. One doubts that if some illegal and greedy scheme were discovered somewhere in the vast labyrinth of the executive bureaucracies, the president would be held strictly to account. One doubts it unless one of three conditions obtains: the president, once appraised of the scandal, failed to act promptly to set things right, or, second, trusted friends and close associates of the president were involved, or, worse yet, the president himself were involved.

Only Richard Nixon, it will be observed, with his well-known penchant for presidential firsts, hits the jackpot on this list of no-no's. Neither Harding nor Grant escaped blame for the criminal acts of others close to them, but both are commonly held to have been themselves free of wrongdoing.

A final arena in which presidents achieve greatness is in the legislative record. Normally, what is required is a flurry of action, like FDR's hundred days, or Woodrow Wilson's first term. A kindly fate can sweep a new president into office along with a heavy congressional majority of his own party. With a little more luck there can be a feeling abroad in the land that something must be done. Whereupon, for a little while at least, the president and Congress together do something. Great strides in the enactment of public policy are commonly made in this fashion. And it is now settled custom that the president gets the long-run credit.

Thus many of the factors that go into presidential greatness appear to boil down to being in the right place at the right time. Much of the rest consists of having others put the right construction on ambiguous acts. Understandably, quite a lot of White House effort consequently goes into cultivating favorable notice for the incumbent. And here, at this point, a worm begins to emerge from the apple. The scenery, cosmetics, and sound effects that go into good public relations, unless strongly resisted, can begin to overwhelm more substantive concerns. The aspiration to presidential greatness, which under ideal circumstances can provide an incentive for good presidential behavior, under less than ideal circumstances leads to a great variety of diffuculties. For fear of being found out and downgraded, there is the temptation to deny failure, to refuse to readjust course when a program or a proposal doesn't work out. There is the temptation to hoard credit rather than share it with the agencies that actually do the work and produce the results. There is the temptation to export responsibility away from the White House for the honest shortfalls of programs, thus transmitting to the government at large an expectation that loyalty upward will be rewarded with disloyalty down. There is the temptation to offer false hopes and to proclaim spurious accomplishments to the public at large.

As Henry Fairlie and others point out, a presidency that inflates expectations can rarely deliver. Worse yet, such a presidency gives up a precious opportunity to perform essential tasks of civic education, to help ordinary people see both the limitations and the possibilities of democratic government. George Reedy and others have observed that a presidency made of overblown rhetoric and excessive pretension can lose touch with the realities of politics, can waste its resources on trivialities, can fail, consequently, to grasp opportunities to govern well.

This, such as it is, is the case against the pursuit of presidential greatness. It is a case based upon a hope that there can be something approximating a restoration of democratic manners in the presidency. There are, however, good reasons to suppose that such a restoration will be hard to accomplish.

Part of the problem is structural. The complex demands of modern governmental decision-making require that presidents receive plenty of help. They need advice, information, criticism, feedback. They also need people to take care of the endless round of chores that fall to a president's lot: press secretaries, congressional liaison, managers of paper work and the traffic of visitors. Presidents also need to be able to trust the help they are getting, to be able to feel that what is being said and done in their behalf does genuinely place presidential interests first. From these requirements comes the need for an entourage of people whose careers in the limelight are solely the product of presidential favor. And from this entourage invariably comes what I suppose could be called the First Circle of presidential Moonies.

These are the people who "sleep a little better at night," as Jack Valenti so memorably said, because the charisma of their chief powers the machinery of government. During the day, we can be sure, they wear sunglasses to keep from being dazzled by "that special grace" (as members of John Kennedy's entourage frequently put it).

Anybody who doubts Kennedy's impact to this day on his successors should look again at the "great" debates of 1960 and 1976. For his encounter with Richard Nixon, Kennedy was stuffed like a Christmas goose with small discrete facts. In the course of the debates, out they came, two and three at a time. By all accounts, Kennedy "won" the 1960 encounter, albeit by nearly as small a margin as he won the election itself.

This evidently established a standard presidential-candidate debating style which the candidates of 1976 dutifully aped: neither risked the variety of facial expressions that did Nixon in, both spouted facts—not all of them true or relevant—rather than risk explaining their points of view.

It is probably foolish to expect some sort of civic enlightenment to come from debates. They are, rather, as near as our society gets to a trial by ordeal. The debater's central task is neither to inform nor to enlighten, but rather to survive, to avoid saying something that newspaper and television commentators will fix upon as an error or that will require an endless round of "clarifications" and become the "issue" of the following week or two. No wonder both Ford and Carter stood like tethered goats for the twenty-seven-minutes' silence that interrupted their first debate. To have been there at all no doubt temporarily exhausted their capacity to take risks.

The needs of White House staff to bask in reflected glory, plus risk-aversion in the face of the work habits of the mass media, are a potent combination tending to sustain a president's interest in president-worship. Moreover, the mystique of the presidency can be useful politically, vesting the visit in the rose garden, the invitation to breakfast, even a beseeching telephone call to Capitol Hill, with an added value that can spell the difference between political victory and defeat. And of course a president may simply grow fond of being coddled.

Added to these are the powerful factors in the world and in the American political system that have brought the president to the forefront: the increased importance of foreign affairs in the life of the nation, an area in which the president has no serious constitutional rival; the creation and proliferation of federal bureaucracies, all of them subject to presidential influence and supervision; the growth of the mass media with their focus upon the personalities at the center of our national politics, and the decline of political parties as a countervailing force. No wonder the entire political system seems president-preoccupied.

Against this formidable array of forces a plea for modesty of presidential aims, for prudence and moderation in the choice of instruments, for a scaling-down of promises and claims of achievement, seems unlikely to attract widespread agreement, least of all from presidents and their entourages bent on making their mark on History.

Chapter 7

The Bureaucracy

American bureaucracy today is an important fourth branch of the government. Too frequently the administrative branch is lumped under the heading of the "Executive" and is considered to be subordinate to the president. But the following selections will reveal that the bureaucracy is often autonomous, acting outside of the control of Congress, the president, and even the judiciary. This fact raises an important problem for our constitutional democracy: How can the bureaucracy be kept responsible if it does not fit into the constitutional framework that was designed to guarantee limited and responsible government?

Constitutional Background

While the Constitution carefully outlined the responsibilities and powers of the president, Congress, and to a lesser extent the Supreme Court, it did not mention the bureaucracy. The position of the bureaucracy in the separation-of-powers scheme developed by custom and statutory law, rather than by explicit constitutional provisions. The following selection makes it clear that, although the Constitution did not provide for an administrative branch, it did have a bearing upon the development of the bureaucracy. Perhaps the most important result of constitutional bureaucracy is that the administrative agencies have become pawns in the constant power struggle between the president and Congress.

47

Peter Woll
CONSTITUTIONAL DEMOCRACY AND BUREAUCRATIC POWER

The administrative branch today stands at the very center of our governmental process; it is the keystone of the structure. And administrative agencies exercise legislative and judicial as well as executive functions—a fact that is often over-looked . . .

How should we view American bureaucracy? Ultimately, the power of government comes to rest in the administrative branch. Agencies are given the responsibility of making concrete decisions carrying out vague policy initiated in Congress or by the president. The agencies can offer expert advice, closely attuned to the most interested pressure groups, and they often not only determine the policies that the legislature and executive recommend in the first place, but also decisively affect the policy-making process. Usually it is felt that the bureaucracy is politically "neutral," completely under the domination of the president, Congress, or the courts. We will see that this is not entirely the case, and that the president and Congress have only sporadic control over the administrative process.

The bureaucracy is a semi-autonomous branch of the government, often dominating Congress, exercising strong influence on the president, and only infrequently subject to review by the courts. If our constitutional democracy is to be fully analyzed, we must focus attention upon the administrative branch. What is the nature of public administration? How are administration and politics intertwined? How are administrative constituencies determined? What is the relationship between agencies and their constituencies? What role should the president assume in relation to the administrative branch? How far should Congress go in controlling agencies which in fact tend to dominate the legislative process? Should judicial review be expanded? What are the conditions of judicial review? How do administrative agencies perform judicial functions, and how do these activities affect the ability of courts to oversee their actions? These questions confront us with what is called the problem of administrative responsibility: that is, how can we control the activities of the administrative branch? In order to approach an understanding of this difficult problem, it is necessary to appreciate the nature of the administrative process and how it interacts with other branches of the government and with the general public. It is also important to understand the nature of our constitutional system, and the political context within which agencies function.

We operate within the framework of a constitutional democracy. This means, first, that the government is to be limited by the separation of powers and Bill of Rights. Another component of the system, federalism, is designed in theory to provide states with a certain amount of authority when it is not implied at the national level. Our separation of powers, the system of checks and balances, and the federal system help to explain some of the differences between administrative organization here and in other countries. But the Constitution does not explicitly provide for the administrative branch, which has become a new fourth branch of government. This raises the question of how to control the bureaucracy when there are no clear constitutional limits upon it. The second aspect of our system, democracy, is of course implied in the Constitution itself, but has expanded greatly since it was adopted. We are confronted, very broadly speaking, first with the problem of constitutional limitation, and secondly with the problem of democratic participation in the activities of the bureaucracy. The bureaucracy must be accommodated within the framework of our system of constitutional democracy. This is the crux of the problem of administrative responsibility.

Even though the Constitution does not explicitly provide for the bureaucracy, it has had a profound impact upon the structure, functions, and general place that the bureaucracy occupies in government. The administrative process was incorporated into the constitutional system under the heading of "The Executive Branch." But the concept of "administration" at the time of the adoption of the Constitution was a very simple one, involving the "mere execution" of "executive details," to use the phrases of Hamilton in *The Federalist*. The idea, at that time, was simply that the president as Chief Executive would be able to control the Executive Branch in carrying out the mandates of Congress. In *Federalist 72*, after defining administration in this very narrow way, Hamilton stated:

> . . . The persons, therefore, to whose immediate management the different administrative matters are committed ought to be considered as Assistants or Deputies of the Chief Magistrate, and on this account, they ought to derive their offices from his appointment, at least from his nomination, and ought to be subject to his superintendence.

It was clear that Hamilton felt the president would be responsible for administrative action as long as he was in office. This fact later turned up in what can be called the "presidential supremacy" school of thought, which held and still holds that the president is *constitutionally* responsible for the administrative branch, and that Congress should delegate to him all necessary authority for this purpose. Nevertheless, whatever the framers of the Constitution might have planned if they could have foreseen the nature of bureaucratic development, the fact is that the system they constructed in many ways supported bureaucratic organization and functions independent of the president. The role they assigned to Congress in relation to administration assured this result, as did the general position of Congress in the governmental system as a check or balance to the power of the president. Congress has a great deal of authority over the administrative process.

If we compare the power of Congress and the president over the bureaucracy it becomes clear that they both have important constitutional responsibility. Congress retains primary control over the organization of the bureaucracy. It alone creates and destroys agencies, and determines whether they are to be located within the executive branch or outside it. This has enabled Congress to create a large number of *independent* agencies beyond presidential control. Congress has the authority to control appropriations and may thus exercise a great deal of power over the administrative arm, although increasingly the Bureau of the Budget and the president have the initial, and more often than not the final say over the budget. Congress also has the authority to define the jurisdiction of agencies. Finally, the Constitution gives to the legislature the power to interfere in high level presidential appointments, which must be "by and with the advice and consent of the Senate."

Congress may extend the sharing of the appointive power when it sets up new agencies. It may delegate to the president pervasive authority to control the bureaucracy. But one of the most important elements of the separation of power is the electoral system, which gives to Congress a constituency which is different from and even conflicting with that of the president. This means that Congress often decides to set up agencies beyond presidential purview. Only rarely will it grant the president any kind of final authority to structure the bureaucracy. During World War II, on the basis of the War Powers Act, the president had the authority to reorganize the administrative branch. Today he has the same authority, provided that Congress does not veto presidential proposals within a certain time limit. In refusing to give the president permanent reorganization authority, Congress is jealously guarding one of its important prerogatives.

Turning to the constitutional authority of the president over the bureaucracy, it is somewhat puzzling to see that it gives him a relatively small role. He appoints certain officials by and with the advice and consent of the Senate. He has directive power over agencies that are placed within his jurisdiction by Congress. His control over patronage, once so important, has diminished sharply under the merit system. The president is Commander-in-Chief of all military forces, which puts him in a controlling position over the Defense Department and agencies involved in military matters. In the area of international relations, the president is by constitutional authority the "Chief Diplomat," to use [presidential scholar Clinton] Rossiter's phrase. This means that he appoints Ambassadors (by and with the advice and consent of the Senate), and generally directs national activities in the international arena—a crucially important executive function. But regardless of the apparent intentions of some of the framers of the Constitution as expressed by Hamilton in *The Federalist,* and in spite of the predominance of the presidency in military and foreign affairs, the fact remains that we seek in vain for explicit constitutional authorization for the president to be "Chief Administrator."

This is not to say that the president does not have an important responsibility to act as chief of the bureaucracy, merely that there is no constitutional mandate for this. As our system evolved, the president was given more and more responsibility until he became, in practice, Chief Administrator. At the same time the constitutional system has often impeded progress in this direction. The president's Committee on Administrative Management in 1937, and later the Hoover Commissions of 1949 and 1955, called upon Congress to initiate a series of reforms increasing presidential authority over the administrative branch. It was felt that this was necessary to make democracy work. The president is the only official elected nationally, and if the administration is to be held democratically accountable, he alone can stand as its representative. But meaningful control from the White House requires that the president have a comprehensive program which encompasses the activities of the bureaucracy. He must be informed as to what they are doing, and be able to control them. He must understand the complex responsibilities of the bureaucracy. Moreover, he must be able to call on sufficient political support to balance the support which the agencies draw from private clientele groups and congressional committees. This has frequently proven a difficult and often impossible task for the president. He may have the *authority* to control the bureaucracy in many areas, but not enough power.

On the basis of the Constitution, Congress feels it quite proper that when it delegates legislative authority to administrative agencies it can relatively often place these groups outside the control of the president. For example, in the case of the Interstate Commerce Commission . . . Congress has delegated final authority to that agency to control railroad mergers and other aspects of transportation activity, without giving the president the right to veto. The president may feel that a particular merger is undesirable because it is in violation of the antitrust laws, but the Interstate Commerce Commission is likely to feel differently. In such a situation, the president can do nothing because he does not have the *legal authority* to take any action. If he could muster enough political support to exercise influence over the ICC, he would be able to control it, but the absence of legal authority is an important factor in such cases and diminishes presidential power. Moreover, the ICC draws strong support from the railroad industry, which has been able to counterbalance the political support possessed by the president and other groups that have wished to control it. Analogous situations exist with respect to other regulatory agencies.

Besides the problem of congressional and presidential control over the bureaucracy, there is the question of judical review of administrative decisions. The rule of law is a central element in our Constitution. The rule of law means that decisions judicial in nature should be handled by common law courts, because of their expertise in rendering due process of law. When administrative agencies engage in adjudication their decisions should be subject to judicial review—at least, they should if one supports the idea of the supremacy of law. Judicial decisions are supposed to be rendered on an independent and impartial basis, through the use of tested procedures, in order to arrive at the accurate determination of the truth. Administrative adjudication should not be subject to presidential or congressional control, which would mean political determination of decisions that should be rendered in an objective manner. The idea of the rule of law, derived from the common law and adopted within the framework of our constitutional system, in theory limits legislative and executive control over the bureaucracy.

The nature of our constitutional system poses very serious difficulties to the development of a system of administrative responsibility. The Constitution postulates that the functions of government must be separated into different branches with differing constituencies and separate authority. The idea is that the departments should oppose each other, thereby preventing the arbitrary exercise of political power. Any combination of functions was considered to lead inevitably to arbitrary government. This is a debatable point, but the result of the Constitution is quite clear. The administrative process, on the other hand, often combines various functions of government in the same hands. Attempts are made, of course, to separate those who exercise the judicial functions from those in the prosecuting arms of the agencies. But the fact remains that there is a far greater combination of functions in the administrative process than can be accommodated by strict adherence to the Constitution.

It has often been proposed, as a means of alleviating what may be considered the bad effects of combined powers in administrative agencies, to draw a line of control from the original branches of the government to those parts of the bureaucracy exercising similar functions. Congress would control the legislative activities of the agencies, the president the executive aspects, and the courts the judicial functions. This would maintain the symmetry of the constitutional system. But this solution is not feasible, because other parts of the Constitution, giving different authority to these three branches, make symmetrical control of this kind almost impossible. The three branches of the government are not willing to give up whatever powers they may have over administrative agencies. For example, Congress is not willing to give the president complete control over all executive functions, nor to give the courts the authority to review all the decisions of the agencies. At present, judicial review takes place only if Congress authorizes it, except in those rare instances where constitutional issues are involved.

Another aspect of the problem of control is reflected in the apparent paradox that the three branches do not always use to the fullest extent their authority to regulate the bureaucracy, even though they wish to retain their power to do so. The courts, for example, have exercised considerable self-restraint in their review of administrative decisions. They are not willing to use all their power over the bureaucracy. Similarly, both Congress and the president will often limit their dealings with the administrative branch for political and practical reasons.

In the final analysis, we are left with a bureaucratic system that has been fragmented by the Constitution, and in which administrative discretion is inevitable. The bureaucracy reflects the general fragmentation of our political system. It is often the battleground for the three branches of government, and for outside pressure groups which seek to control it for their own purposes.

The Political Roots and
Consequences of Bureaucracy

With the exception of those executive departments that all governments need, such as State, Treasury, and Defense, *private* sector political demands have led to the creation of American bureaucracy. In response to those demands, Congress has over the years created more and more executive departments and agencies to solve economic, political, and social problems. It is important to realize that the bureaucracy is not, as many of its critics have suggested, a conspiracy by government officials to increase their power. The following selection traces the rise of the administrative state and particularly notes how political pluralism has affected the character of the bureaucracy by dividing it into clientele sectors.

48

James Q. Wilson
THE RISE OF THE
BUREAUCRATIC STATE

During its first 150 years, the American republic was not thought to have "bureaucracy," and thus it would have been meaningless to refer to the "problems" of a "bureaucratic state." There were, of course, appointed civilian officials: Though only about 3,000 at the end of the Federalist period, there were about 95,000 by the time Grover Cleveland assumed office in 1881, and nearly half a million by 1925. Some aspects of these numerous officials were regarded as problems—notably, the standards by which they were appointed and the political loyalties to which they were held—but these were thought to be matters of proper character and good management. The great political and constitutional struggles were not over the power of the administrative apparatus, but over the power of the President, of Congress, and of the states.

The Founding Fathers had little to say about the nature or function of the executive branch of the new government. The Constitution is virtually silent on the subject and the debates in the Constitutional Convention are almost devoid of reference to an administrative apparatus. This reflected no lack of concern about the matter, however. Indeed, it was in part because of the Founders' depressing experience with chaotic and inefficient management under the Continental Congress and the Articles of Confederation that they had assembled in Philadelphia. Management by committees composed of part-time amateurs had cost the colonies dearly in the War of Independence and few, if any, of the Founders wished to return to that system. The argument was only over how the heads of the necessary departments of government were to be selected, and whether these heads should be wholly subordinate to the President or whether instead they should form some sort of council that would advise the President and perhaps share in his authority. In the end, the Founders left it up to Congress to decide the matter.

There was no dispute in Congress that there should be executive departments, headed by single appointed officials, and, of course, the Constitution specified that these would be appointed by the President with the advice and consent of the Senate. The only issue was how such officials might be removed.

Reprinted with permission of the author from *The Public Interest*, No. 41 (Fall 1975). © 1975 by National Affairs, Inc.

After prolonged debate and by the narrowest of majorities, Congress agreed that the President should have the sole right of removal, thus confirming that the infant administrative system would be wholly subordinate—in law at least— to the President. Had not Vice-President John Adams, presiding over a Senate equally divided on the issue, cast the deciding vote in favor of presidential removal, the administrative departments might conceivably have become legal dependencies of the legislature, with incalculable consequences for the development of the embryonic government.

THE "BUREAUCRACY PROBLEM"

The original departments were small and had limited duties. The State Department, the first to be created, had but nine employees in addition to the Secretary. The War Department did not reach 80 civilian employees until 1801; it commanded only a few thousand soldiers. Only the Treasury Department had substantial powers—it collected taxes, managed the public debt, ran the national bank, conducted land surveys, and purchased military supplies. Because of this, Congress gave the closest scrutiny to its structure and its activities.

The number of administrative agencies and employees grew slowly but steadily during the 19th and early 20th centuries and then increased explosively on the occasion of World War I, the Depression, and World War II. It is difficult to say at what point in this process the administrative system became a distinct locus of power or an independent source of political initiatives and problems. What is clear is that the emphasis on the sheer *size* of the administrative establishment—conventional in many treatments of the subject—is misleading.

The government can spend vast sums of money—wisely or unwisely— without creating that set of conditions we ordinarily associate with the bureaucratic state. For example, there could be massive transfer payments made under government auspices from person to person or from state to state, all managed by a comparatively small staff of officials and a few large computers. In 1971, the federal government paid out $54 billion under various social insurance programs, yet the Social Security Administration employs only 73,000 persons, many of whom perform purely routine jobs.

And though it may be harder to believe, the government could in principle employ an army of civilian personnel without giving rise to those organizational patterns that we call bureaucratic. Suppose, for instance, that we as a nation should decide to have in the public schools at least one teacher for every two students. This would require a vast increase in the number of teachers and schoolrooms, but almost all of the persons added would be performing more or less identical tasks, and they could be organized into very small units (e.g., neighborhood schools). Though there would be significant overhead costs, most citizens would not be aware of any increase in the "bureaucratic" aspects of education—indeed, owing to the much greater time each teacher would have to devote to each pupil and his or her parents, the citizenry might well conclude that there actually had been a substantial reduction in the amount of "bureaucracy."

To the reader predisposed to believe that we have a "bureaucracy problem," these hypothetical cases may seem farfetched. Max Weber, after all, warned us that in capitalist and socialist societies alike, bureaucracy was likely to acquire an "overtowering" power position. Conservatives have always feared bureaucracy, save perhaps the police. Humane socialists have frequently been embarrassed by their inability to reconcile a desire for public control of the economy with the suspicion that a public bureaucracy may be as immune to democratic control as a private one. Liberals have equivocated, either dismissing any concern for bureaucracy as reactionary quibbling about social progress or embracing that concern when obviously nonreactionary persons (welfare recipients, for example) express a view toward the Department of Health and Human Services indistinguishable from the view businessmen take of the Internal Revenue Service.

POLITICAL AUTHORITY

There are at least three ways in which political power may be gathered undesirably into bureaucratic hands: by the growth of an administrative apparatus so large as to be immune from popular control, by placing power over a governmental bureaucracy of any size in private rather than public hands, or by vesting discretionary authority in the hands of a public agency so that the exercise of that power is not responsive to the public good. These are not the only problems that arise because of bureaucratic organization. From the point of view of their members, bureaucracies are sometimes uncaring, ponderous, or unfair; from the point of view of their political superiors, they are sometimes unimaginative or inefficient; from the point of view of their clients, they are sometimes slow or unjust. No single account can possibly treat of all that is problematic in bureaucracy; even the part I discuss here—the extent to which political authority has been transferred undesirably to an unaccountable administrative realm—is itself too large for a single essay. But it is, if not the most important problem, then surely the one that would most have troubled our Revolutionary leaders, especially those that went on to produce the Constitution. It was, after all, the question of power that chiefly concerned them, both in redefining our relationship with England and in finding a new basis for political authority in the Colonies.

To some, following in the tradition of [Max] Weber, bureaucracy is the inevitable consequence and perhaps necessary concomitant of modernity. A money economy, the division of labor, and the evolution of legal-rational norms to justify organizational authority require the efficient adaptation of means to ends and a high degree of predictability in the behavior of rulers. To this, Georg Simmel added the view that organizations tend to acquire the characteristics of those institutions with which they are in conflict, so that as government becomes more bureaucratic, private organizations—political parties, trade unions, voluntary associations—will have an additional reason to become bureaucratic as well.

By viewing bureaucracy as an inevitable (or, as some would put it, "functional") aspect of society, we find ourselves attracted to theories that explain the growth of bureaucracy in terms of some inner dynamic to which all agencies respond and which makes all barely governable and scarcely tolerable. Bureaucracies grow, we are told, because of Parkinson's Law: Work and personnel expand to consume the available resources. Bureaucracies behave, we believe, in accord with various other maxims, such as the Peter Principle: In hierarchical organizations, personnel are promoted up to that point at which their incompetence becomes manifest—hence, all important positions are held by incompetents. More elegant, if not essentially different, theories have been propounded by scholars. The tendency of all bureaus to expand is explained by William A. Niskanen by the assumption, derived from the theory of the firm, that "bureaucrats maximize the total budget of their bureau during their tenure"—hence, "all bureaus are too large." What keeps them from being not merely too large but all-consuming is that fact that a bureau must deliver to some degree on its promised output, and if it consistently underdelivers, its budget will be cut by unhappy legislators. But since measuring the output of a bureau is often difficult—indeed, even *conceptualizing* the output of the State Department is mind-boggling—the bureau has a great deal of freedom within which to seek the largest possible budget.

Such theories, both the popular and the scholarly, assign little importance to the nature of the tasks an agency performs, the constitutional framework in which it is embedded, or the preferences and attitudes of citizens and legislators. Our approach will be quite different: Different agencies will be examined in historical perspective to discover the kinds of problems—if any, to which their operation give rise, and how those problems were affected—perhaps determined—by the tasks which they were assigned, the political system in which they operated, and the preferences they were required to consult. What follows will be far from a systematic treatment of such matters, and even farther from a rigorous testing of any theory of bureaucratization. Our knowledge of agency history and behavior is too sketchy to permit that.

BUREAUCRACY AND SIZE

During the first half of the 19th century, the growth in the size of the federal bureaucracy can be explained, not by the assumption of new tasks by the government or by the imperialistic designs of the managers of existing tasks, but by the addition to existing bureaus of personnel performing essentially routine, repetitive tasks for which the public demand was great and unavoidable. The principal problem facing a bureaucracy thus enlarged was how best to coordinate its activities toward given and noncontroversial ends.

The increase in the size of the executive branch of the federal government at this time was almost entirely the result of the increase in the size of the Post Office. From 1816 to 1861, federal civilian employment in the executive branch increased nearly eightfold (from 4,837 to 36,672), but 86 percent of this growth was the result of additions to the postal service. The Post Office Department was expanding as population and commerce expanded. By 1869 there were 27,000 post offices scattered around the nation; by 1901, nearly 77,000. In New York alone, by 1894 there were nearly 3,000 postal employees, the same number required to run the entire federal government at the beginning of that century.

The organizational shape of the Post Office was more or less fixed in the administration of Andrew Jackson. The Postmaster General, almost always appointed because of his partisan position, was aided by three (later four) assistant postmaster generals dealing with appointments, mail-carrying contracts, operations, and finance. There is no reason in theory why such an organization could not deliver the mails efficiently and honestly: The task is routine, its performance is measurable, and its value is monitored by millions of customers. Yet the Post Office, from the earliest years of the 19th century, was an organization marred by inefficiency and corruption. The reason is often thought to be found in the making of political appointments to the Post Office. "Political hacks," so the theory goes, would inevitably combine dishonesty and incompetence to the disservice of the nation; thus, by cleansing the department of such persons these difficulties could be avoided. Indeed, some have argued that it was the advent of the "spoils system" under Jackson that contributed to the later inefficiencies of the public bureaucracy.

The opposite is more nearly the case. The Jacksonians did not seek to make the administrative apparatus a mere tool of the Democratic party advantage, but to purify that apparatus not only of what they took to be Federalist subversion but also of personal decadence. The government was becoming not just large, but lax. Integrity and diligence were absent, not merely from government, but from social institutions generally. The Jacksonians were in many cases concerned about the decline in what the Founders had called "republican virtue," but what their successors were more likely to call simplicity and decency. As Matthew Crenson has recently observed in his book *The Federal Machine*, Jacksonian administrators wanted to "guarantee the good behavior of civil servants" as well as to cope with bigness, and to do this they sought both to place their own followers in office and—what is more important—to create a system of depersonalized, specialized bureaucratic rule. Far from being the enemies of bureaucracy, the Jacksonians were among its principal architects.

Impersonal administrative systems, like the spoils system, were "devices for strengthening the government's authority over its own civil servants"; these bureaucratic methods were, in turn, intended to "compensate for a decline in the disciplinary power of social institutions" such as the community, the professions, and business. If public servants, like men generally in a rapidly growing and diversifying society, could no longer be relied upon "to have a delicate regard for their reputations," accurate bookkeeping, close inspections, and regularized procedures would accomplish what character could not.

Amos Kendall, Postmaster General under President Jackson, set about to achieve this goal with a remarkable series of administrative innovations. To prevent corruption, Kendall embarked on two contradictory courses of action: He sought to bring every detail of the department's affairs under his personal scrutiny and he began to reduce and divide the authority on which that scrutiny depended. Virtually every important document and many unimportant ones had to be signed by Kendall himself. At the same time, he gave to the Treasury Department the power to audit his accounts and obtained from Congress a law requiring that the revenues of the department be paid into the Treasury rather than retained by the Post Office. The duties of his subordinates were carefully defined and arranged so that the authority of one assistant would tend to check that of another. What was installed was not simply a specialized management system, but a concept of the administrative separation of powers.

Few subsequent postmasters were of Kendall's ability. The result was predictable. Endless details flowed to Washington for decision, but no one in Washington other than the Postmaster General had the authority to decide. Meanwhile, the size of the postal establishment grew by leaps and bounds. Quickly the department began to operate on the basis of habit and local custom: Since everybody reported to Washington, in effect no one did. As Leonard D. White was later to remark, "the system could work only because it was a vast, repetitive, fixed, and generally routine operation." John Wanamaker, an able businessman who became Postmaster General under President Cleveland, proposed decentralizing the department under 26 regional supervisors. But Wanamaker's own assistants in Washington were unenthusiastic about such a diminution in their authority and, in any event, Congress steadfastly refused to endorse decentralization.

Civil service reform was not strongly resisted in the Post Office; from 1883 on, the number of its employees covered by the merit system expanded. Big-city postmasters were often delighted to be relieved of the burden of dealing with hundreds of place-seekers. Employees welcomed the job protection that civil service provided. In time, the merit system came to govern Post Office personnel almost completely, yet the problems of the department became, if anything, worse. By the mid-20th century, slow and inadequate service, an inability technologically to cope with the mounting flood of mail, and the inequities of its pricing system became all too evident. The problem with the Post Office, however, was not omnipotence but impotence. It was a government monopoly. Being a monopoly, it had little incentive to find the most efficient means to manage its services; being a government monopoly, it was not free to adopt such means even when found—communities, Congressmen, and special-interest groups saw to that.

THE MILITARY ESTABLISHMENT

Not all large bureaucracies grow in response to demands for service. The Department of Defense, since 1941 the largest employer of federal civilian officials, has become, as the governmental keystone of the "military-industrial complex," the very archetype of an administrative entity that is thought to be so vast and so well-entrenched that it can virtually ignore the political branches of government, growing and even acting on the basis of its own inner imperatives. In fact, until recently the military services were a major economic and political force only during wartime. In the late 18th and early 19th centuries, America was a neutral nation with only a tiny standing army. During the Civil War, over two million men served on the Union side alone and the War Department expanded enormously, but demobilization after the war was virtually complete, except for a small Indian-fighting force. Its peacetime authorized strength was only 25,000 enlisted men and 2,161 officers, and its actual strength for the rest of the century was often less. Congress authorized the purchase and installation of over 2,000 coastal defense guns, but barely 6 percent of these were put in place.

When war with Spain broke out, the army was almost totally unprepared. Over 300,000 men eventually served in that brief conflict, and though almost all were again demobilized, the War Department under Elihu Root was reorganized and put on a more professional basis with a greater capacity for unified central control. Since the United States had become an imperial power with important possessions in the Caribbean and the Far East, the need for a larger military establishment was clear; even so, the average size of the army until World War I was only about 250,000.

The First World War again witnessed a vast mobilization—nearly five million men in all—and again an almost complete demobilization after the war. The Second World War involved over 16 million military personnel. The demobilization that followed was less complete than after previous engagements owing to the development of the Cold War, but it was substantial nonetheless— the Army fell in size from over eight million men to only half a million. Military spending declined from $91 billion in the first quarter of 1945 to only slightly more than $10 billion in the second quarter of 1947. For the next three years it remained relatively flat. It began to rise rapidly in 1950, partly to finance our involvement in the Korean conflict and partly to begin the construction of a military force that could counterbalance the Soviet Union, especially in Europe.

In sum, from the Revolutionary War to 1950, a period of over 170 years, the size and deployment of the military establishment in this country was governed entirely by decisions made by political leaders on political grounds. The military did not expand autonomously, a large standing army did not find wars to fight, and its officers did not play a significant role except in wartime and occasionally as presidential candidates. No bureaucracy proved easier to control, at least insofar as its size and purposes were concerned.

A "MILITARY-INDUSTRIAL COMPLEX"?

The argument for the existence of an autonomous, bureaucratically led military-industrial complex is supported primarily by events since 1950. Not only has the United States assumed during this period worldwide commitments that necessitate a larger military establishment, but the advent of new, high-technology weapons has created a vast industrial machine with an interest in sustaining a high level of military expenditures, especially on weapons research, development, and acquisition. This machine, so the argument goes, is allied with the Pentagon in ways that dominate the political officials nominally in charge of the armed forces. There is some truth in all this. We have become a world military force, though that decision was made by elected officials in 1949–1950 and not dictated by a (then nonexistent) military-industrial complex. High-cost, high-technology weapons have become important and a number of industrial concerns will prosper or perish depending on how contracts for those weapons are let. The development and purchase of weapons is sometimes made in a wasteful, even irrational, manner. And the allocation of funds among the several armed services is often dictated as much by inter-service rivalry as by strategic or political decisions.

But despite all this, the military has not been able to sustain itself at its preferred size, to keep its strength constant or growing, or to retain for its use a fixed or growing portion of the Gross National Product. Even during the last two decades, the period of greatest military prominence, the size of the Army has varied enormously—from over 200 maneuver battalions in 1955, to 174 in 1965, rising to 217 at the peak of the Vietnam action in 1969, and then declining rapidly to 138 in 1972. Even military hardware, presumably of greater interest to the industrial side of the military-industrial complex, has often declined in quantity, even though per unit price has risen. The Navy had over 1,000 ships in 1955; it has only 700 today [in 1975]. The Air Force had nearly 24,000 aircraft in 1955; it has fewer than 14,000 today. This is not to say the combat strength of the military is substantially less than it once was, and there is greater firepower now at the disposal of each military unit, and there are various missile systems now in place, for which no earlier counterparts existed. But the total budget, and thus the total force level, of the military has been decided primarily by the President and not in any serious sense forced upon him by subordinates. (For example, President Truman decided to allocate one third of the federal budget to defense, President Eisenhower chose to spend no more than 10 percent of the Gross National Product on it, and President Kennedy strongly supported Robert McNamara's radical and controversial budget revisions.) Even a matter of as great significance as the size of the total military budget for research and development has proved remarkably resistant to inflationary trends: In constant dollars, since 1964 that appropriation has been relatively steady (in 1972 dollars, about $30 billion a year).

The principal source of growth in the military budget in recent years has arisen from Congressionally determined pay provisions. The legislature has voted for more or less automatic pay increases for military personnel with the result that the military budget has gone up even when the number of personnel in the military establishment has gone down.

The bureaucratic problems associated with the military establishment arise mostly from its internal management and are functions of its complexity, the uncertainty surrounding its future deployment, conflicts among its constituent services over mission and role, and the need to purchase expensive equipment without the benefit of a market economy that can control costs. Complexity, uncertainty, rivalry, and monopsony are inherent (and frustrating) aspects of the military as a bureaucracy, but they are very different problems from those typically associated with the phrase "the military-industrial complex." The size and budget of the military are matters wholly within the power of civilian authorities to decide—indeed, the military budget contains the largest discretionary items in the entire federal budget.

If the Founding Fathers were to return to review their handiwork, they would no doubt be staggered by the size of both the Post Office and the Defense Department, and in the case of the latter, be worried about the implications of our commitments to various foreign powers. They surely would be amazed at the technological accomplishments but depressed by the cost and inefficiency of both departments; but they would not, I suspect, think that our Constitutional arrangements for managing these enterprises have proved defective or that there had occurred, as a result of the creation of these vast bureaus, an important shift in the locus of political authority.

They would observe that there have continued to operate strong localistic pressures in both systems—offices are operated, often uneconomically, in some small communities because small communities have influential Congressmen; military bases are maintained in many states because states have powerful Senators. But a national government with localistic biases is precisely the system they believed they had designed in 1787, and though they surely could not have then imagined the costs of it, they just as surely would have said (Hamilton possibly excepted) that these costs were the defects of the system's virtues.

BUREAUCRACY AND CLIENTELISM

After 1861, the growth in the federal administrative system could no longer be explained primarily by an expansion of the postal service and other traditional bureaus. Though these continued to expand, new departments were added that reflected a new (or at least greater) emphasis on the enlargement of the scope of government. Between 1861 and 1901, over 200,000 civilian employees were added to the federal service, only 52 percent of whom were postal workers. Some of these, of course, staffed a larger military and naval establishment stimulated by the Civil War and the Spanish-American War. By 1901 there were over 44,000 civilian defense employees, mostly workers in government-owned arsenals and shipyards. But even those could account for less than one fourth of the increase in employment during the preceding 40 years.

What was striking about the period after 1861 was that the government began to give formal, bureaucratic recognition to the emergence of distinctive interest in a diversifying economy. As Richard L. Schott has written, "whereas earlier federal departments had been formed around specialized governmental functions (foreign affairs, war, finance, and the like), the new departments of this period—Agriculture, Labor, and Commerce—were devoted to the interests and aspirations of particular economic groups."

The original purpose behind these clientele-oriented departments was neither to subsidize nor to regulate, but to promote, chiefly by gathering and publishing statistics and (especially in the case of agriculture) by research. The formation of the Department of Agriculture in 1862 was to become a model, for better or worse, for later political campaigns for government recognition. A private association representing an interest—in this case the United States Agricultural Society—was formed. It made every President from Fillmore to Lincoln an honorary member, it enrolled key Congressmen, and it began to lobby for a new department. The precedent was followed by labor groups, especially the Knights of Labor, to secure creation in 1888 of a Department of Labor. It was broadened in 1903 to be a Department of Commerce and Labor, the parts were separated and the two departments we now know were formed.

There was an early 19th-century precedent for the creation of these client-serving departments: the Pension Office, then in the Department of the Interior. Begun in 1833 and regularized in 1849, the Office became one of the largest bureaus of the government in the aftermath of the Civil War, as hundreds of thousands of Union Army veterans were made eligible for pensions if they had incurred a permanent disability or injury while on military duty; dependent widows were also eligible if their husbands had died in service or of service-connected injuries. The Grand Army of the Republic (GAR), the leading veterans' organization, was quickly to exert pressure for more generous pension laws and for more liberal administration of such laws as already existed. In 1879 Congressmen, noting the number of ex-servicemen living (and voting) in their states, made veterans eligible for pensions retroactively to the date of their discharge from the service, thus enabling thousands who had been late in filing applications to be rewarded for their dilatoriness. In 1890 the law was changed again to make it unnecessary to have been injured in the service—all that was necessary was to have served and then to have acquired a permanent disability by any means other than through "their own vicious habits." And whenever cases not qualifying under existing law came to the attention of Congress, it promptly passed a special act making those persons eligible by name.

So far as is known, the Pension Office was remarkably free of corruption in the administration of this windfall—and why not, since anything an administrator might deny, a legislator was only too pleased to grant. By 1891 the Commissioner of Pensions observed that this was "the largest executive bureau in the world." There were over 6,000 officials supplemented by thousands of local physicians paid on a fee basis. In 1900 alone, the Office had to process 477,000 cases. Fraud was rampant as thousands of persons brought false or exaggerated claims; as Leonard D. White was later to write, "pensioners and their attorneys seemed to have been engaged in a gigantic conspiracy to defraud their own government." Though the Office struggled to be honest, Congress was indifferent—or more accurately, complaisant: The GAR was a powerful electoral force and it was ably and lucratively assisted by thousands of private pension attorneys. The pattern of bureaucratic clientelism was set in a way later to become a familiar feature of the governmental landscape—a subsidy was initially provided, because it was either popular or unnoticed, to a group that was powerfully benefited and had few or disorganized opponents; the beneficiaries were organized to supervise the administration and ensure the funding of the program; the law authorizing the program, first passed because it seemed the right thing to do, was left intact or even expanded because politically it became the only thing to do. A benefit once bestowed cannot easily be withdrawn.

PUBLIC POWER AND PRIVATE INTERESTS

It was at the state level, however, that client-oriented bureaucracies proliferated in the 19th century. Chief among these were the occupational licensing agencies. At the time of Independence, professions and occupations either could be freely entered (in which case the consumer had to judge the quality of service for himself) or entry was informally controlled by the existing members of the profession or occupation by personal tutelage and the management of reputations. The later part of the 19th century, however, witnessed the increased use of law and bureaucracy to control entry into a line of work. The state courts generally allowed this on the grounds that it was a proper exercise of the "police power" of the state, but as Morton Keller has observed, "when state courts approved the licensing of barbers and blacksmiths, but not of horseshoers, it was evident that the principles governing certification were—to put it charitably—elusive ones." By 1952, there were more than 75 different occupations in the United States for which one needed a license to practice, and the awarding of these licenses was typically in the hands of persons already in the occupation, who could act under color of law. These licensing boards—for plumbers, dry cleaners, beauticians, attorneys, undertakers, and the like—frequently have been criticized as particularly flagrant examples of the excesses of a bureaucratic state. But the problems they create—of restricted entry, higher prices, and lengthy and complex initiation procedures—are not primarily the result of some bureaucratic pathology but of the possession of public power by persons who use it for private purposes. Or more accurately, they are the result of using public power in ways that benefited those in the profession in the sincere but unsubstantiated conviction that doing so would benefit the public generally.

The New Deal was perhaps the high water mark of at least the theory of bureaucratic clientelism. Not only did various sectors of society, notably agriculture, begin receiving massive subsidies, but the government proposed, through the National Industrial Recovery Act (NRA), to cloak with public power a vast number of industrial groupings and trade associations so that they might control production and prices in ways that would end the depression. The NRA's Blue Eagle fell before the Supreme Court—the wholesale delegation of public power to private interests was declared unconstitutional. But the piecemeal delegation was not, as the continued growth of specialized promotional agencies attests. The Civil Aeronautics Board, for example, erroneously thought to be exclusively a regulatory agency, was formed in 1938 "to promote" as well as regulate civil aviation and it has done so by restricting entry and maintaining above-market rate fares.

Agriculture, of course, provides the leading case of clientelism. Theodore J. Lowi finds "at least 10 separate, autonomous, local self-governing systems" located in or closely associated with the Department of Agriculture that control to some significant degree the flow of billions of dollars in expeditures and loans. Local committees of farmers, private farm organizations, agency heads, and committee chairmen in Congress dominate policymaking in this area—not, perhaps, to the exclusion of the concerns of other publics, but certainly in ways not powerfully constrained by them.

"COOPERATIVE FEDERALISM"

The growing edge of client-oriented bureaucracy can be found, however, not in government relations with private groups, but in the relations among governmental units. In dollar volume, the chief clients of federal domestic expenditures are state and local government agencies. To some degree, federal involvement in local affairs by the cooperative funding or management of local enterprises has always existed. The Northwest Ordinance of 1784 made public land available to finance local schools and the Morrill Act of 1862 gave land to support state colleges, but what Morton Grodzins and Daniel Elazar have called "cooperative federalism," though it always existed, did not begin in earnest until the passage in 1913 of the 16th Amendment to the Constitution allowed the federal government to levy an income tax on citizens and thereby to acquire access to vast sources of revenue. Between 1914 and 1917, federal aid to states and localities increased a thousandfold. By 1948 it amounted to over one tenth of all state and local spending; by 1970, to over one sixth.

The degree to which such grants, and the federal agencies that administer them, constrain or even direct state and local bureaucracies is a matter of dispute. No general answer can be given—federal support of welfare programs has left considerable discretion in the hands of the states over the size of benefits and some discretion over eligibility rules, whereas federal support of highway construction carries with it specific requirements as to design, safety, and (since 1968) environmental and social impact.

A few generalizations are possible, however. The first is that the states and not the cities have been from the first, and remain today, the principal client group for grants-in-aid. It was not until the Housing Act of 1937 that money was given in any substantial amount directly to local governments and though many additional programs of this kind were later added, as late as 1970 less than 12 percent of all federal aid went directly to cities and towns. The second general observation is that the 1960s mark a major watershed in the way in which the purposes of federal aid are determined. Before that time, most grants were for purposes initially defined by the states—to build highways and airports, to fund unemployment insurance programs, and the like. Beginning in the 1960s, the federal government, at the initiative of the President and his advisors, increasingly came to define the purposes of these grants—not necessarily over the objection of the states, but often without any initiative from them. Federal money was to be spent on poverty, ecology, planning, and other "national" goals for which, until the laws were passed, there were few, if any, well-organized and influential constituencies. Whereas federal money was once spent in response to the claims of distinct and organized clients, public or private, in the contemporary period federal money has increasingly been spent in ways that have *created* such clients.

And once rewarded or created, they are rarely penalized or abolished. What David Stockman has called the "social pork barrel" grows more or less steadily. Between 1950 and 1970, the number of farms declined from about 5.6 million to fewer than three million, but government payments to farmers rose about $283 million to $3.2 billion. In the public sector, even controversial programs have grown. Urban renewal programs have been sharply criticized, but federal support for the program rose from $281 million in 1965 to about $1 billion in 1972. Public housing has been enmeshed in controversy, but federal support for it rose from $206 million in 1965 to $845 million in 1972. Federal financial support for local poverty programs under the Office of Economic Opportunity has actually declined in recent years, but this cut is almost unique and it required the steadfast and deliberate attention of a determined President who was bitterly assailed both in the Congress and in the courts.

SELF-PERPETUATING AGENCIES

If the Founding Fathers were to return to examine bureaucratic clientelism, they would, I suspect, be deeply discouraged. James Madison clearly foresaw that American society would be "broken into many parts, interests and classes of citizens" and that this "multiplicity of interests" would help ensure against "the tyranny of the majority," especially in a federal regime with separate branches of government. Positive action would require a "coalition of a majority"; in the process of forming this coalition, the rights of all would be protected, not merely by self-interested bargains, but because in a free society such a coalition "could seldom take place on any other principles than those of justice and the general good." To those who wrongly believed that Madison thought of men as acting only out of base motives, the phrase is instructive: Persuading men who disagree to compromise their differences can rarely be achieved solely by the parceling out of relative advantage; the belief is also required that what is being agreed to is right, proper, and defensible before public opinion.

Most of the major new social programs of the United States, whether for the good of the few or the many, were initially adopted by broad coalitions appealing to general standards of justice or to conceptions of the public weal. This is certainly the case with most of the New Deal legislation—notably such programs as Social Security—and with most Great Society legislation—notably Medicare and aid to education; it was also conspicuously the case with respect to post-Great Society legislation pertaining to consumer and environmental concerns. State occupational licensing laws were supported by majorities instead in, among other things, the contribution of these statutes to public safety and health.

But when a program supplies particular benefits to an existing or newly created interest, public or private, it creates a set of political relationships that make exceptionally difficult further alteration of that program by coalitions of the majority. What was created in the name of the common good is sustained in the name of the particular interest. Bureaucratic clientelism becomes self-perpetuating, in the absence of some crisis or scandal, because a single interest group to which the program matters greatly is highly motivated and well-situated to ward off the criticisms of other groups that have a broad but weak interest in the policy.

In short, a regime of separated powers makes it difficult to overcome objections and contrary interests sufficiently to permit the enactment of a new program or the creation of a new agency. Unless the legislation can be made to pass either with little notice or at a time of crisis or extraordinary majorities—and sometimes even then—the initiation of new programs requires public interest arguments. But the same regime works to protect agencies, once created, from unwelcome change because a major change is, in effect, new legislation that must overcome the same hurdles as the original law, but this time with one of the hurdles—the wishes of the agency and its client—raised much higher. As a result, the Madisonian system makes it relatively easy for the delegation of public power to private groups to go unchallenged and, therefore, for factional interests that have acquired a supportive public bureaucracy to rule without submitting their interests to the effective scrutiny and modification of other interests.

BUREAUCRACY AND DISCRETION

For many decades, the Supreme Court denied to the federal government any general "police power" over occupations and businesses, and thus most such regulation occurred at the state level and even there under the constraint that it must not violate the notion of "substantive due process"—that is, the view that there were sharp limits to the power of any government to take (and therefore to regulate) property. What clearly was within the regulatory province of the federal government was interstate commerce, and thus it is not surprising that the first major federal regulatory body should be the Interstate Commerce Commission (ICC), created in 1887.

What does cause, if not surprise, then at least dispute, is the view that the Commerce Act actually was intended to regulate railroads in the public interest. It has become fashionable of late to see this law as a device sought by the railroads to protect themselves from competition. The argument has been given its best-known formulation by Gabriel Kolko. Long-haul railroads, facing ruinous price wars and powerless to resist the demands of big shippers for rebates, tried to create voluntary cartels or "pools" that would keep rates high. These pools always collapsed, however, when one railroad or another would cut rates in order to get more business. To prevent this, the railroads turned to the federal government seeking a law to compel what persuasion could not induce. But the genesis of the act was in fact more complex: Shippers wanted protection from high prices charged by railroads that operated monopolistic services in certain communities; many other shippers served by competing lines wanted no legal barriers to prevent competition from driving prices down as far as possible; some railroads wanted regulation to ease competition, while others feared regulation. And the law as finally passed in fact made "pooling" (or cartels to keep prices up) illegal.

The true significance of the Commerce Act is not that it allowed public power to be used to make secure private wealth but that it created a federal commission with broadly delegated powers that would have to reconcile conflicting goals (the desire for higher or lower prices) in a political environment characterized by a struggle among organized interests and rapidly changing technology. In short, the Commerce Act brought forth a new dimension to the problem of bureaucracy: not those problems, as with the Post Office, that resulted from size and political constraints, but those that were caused by the need to make binding choices without any clear standards for choice.

The ICC was not, of course, the first federal agency with substantial discretionary powers over important matter. The Office of Indian Affairs, for a while in the War Department but after 1849 in the Interior Department, coped for the better part of a century with the Indian problem equipped with no clear policy, beset on all sides by passionate and opposing arguments, and infected with a level of fraud and corruption that seemed impossible to eliminate. There were many causes of the problem, but at root was the fact that the government was determined to control the Indians but could not decide toward what end that control should be exercised (extermination, relocation, and assimilation all had their advocates) and, to the extent the goal was assimilation, could find no method by which to achieve it. By the end of the century, a policy of relocation had been adopted *de facto* and the worse abuses of the Indian service had been eliminated—if not by administrative skill, then by the exhaustion of things in Indian possession worth stealing. By the turn of the century, the management of the Indian question had become more or less routine administration of Indian schools and the allocation of reservation land among Indian claimants.

REGULATION VERSUS PROMOTION

It was the ICC and agencies and commissions for which it was the precedent that became the principal example of federal discretionary authority. It is important, however, to be clear about just what this precedent was. Not everything we now call a regulatory agency was in fact intended to be one. The ICC, the Antitrust Division of the Justice Department, the Federal Trade Commission (FTC), the Food and Drug Administration (FDA), the National Labor Relations Board (NLRB)—all these *were* intended to be genuinely regulatory bodies created to handle under public auspices matters once left to private arrangements. The techniques they were to employ varied: approving rates (ICC), issuing cease-and-desist orders (FTC), bringing civil or criminal actions in the courts (the Antitrust Division), defining after a hearing an appropriate standard of conduct (NLRB), or testing a product for safety (FDA). In each case, however, Congress clearly intended that the agency either define its own standards (a safe drug, a conspiracy in restraint of trade, a fair labor practice) or choose among competing claims (a higher or lower rate for shipping grain).

Other agencies often grouped with these regulatory bodies—the Civil Aeronautics Board, the Federal Communications Commission, the Maritime Commission—were designed, however, not primarily to regulate, but to *promote* the development of various infant or threatened industries. However, unlike fostering agriculture or commerce, fostering civil aviation or radio broadcasting was thought to require limiting entry (to prevent "unsafe" aviation or broadcast interference); but at the time these laws were passed few believed that the restrictions on entry would be many or that the choices would be made on any but technical or otherwise noncontroversial criteria. We smile now at their naïveté, but we continue to share it—today we sometimes suppose that choosing an approved exhaust emission control system or a water pollution control system can be done on the basis of technical criteria and without affecting production and employment.

MAJORITARIAN POLITICS

The creation of regulatory bureaucracies has occurred, as is often remarked, in waves. The first was the period between 1887 and 1890 (the Commerce Act and the Antitrust Act), the second between 1906 and 1915 (the Pure Food and Drug Act, the Meat Inspection Act, the Federal Trade Commission Act, the Clayton Act), the third during the 1930s (the Food, Drug, and Cosmetic Act, the Public Utility Holding Company Act, the Securities Exchange Act, the Natural Gas Act, the National Labor Relations Act), and the fourth during the latter part of the 1960s (the Water Quality Act, the Truth in Lending Act, the National Traffic and Motor Vehicle Safety Act, various amendments to the drug laws, the Motor Vehicle Pollution Control Act, and many others).

Each of these periods was characterized by progressive or liberal Presidents in office (Cleveland, T. R. Roosevelt, Wilson, F. D. Roosevelt, Johnson); one was a period of national crisis (the 1930s); three were periods when the President enjoyed extraordinary majorities of his own party in both houses of Congress (1914–1916, 1932–1940, and 1964–1968); and only the first period preceded the emergence of the national mass media of communication. These facts are important because of the special difficulty of passing any genuinely regulatory legislation: A single interest, the regulated party, sees itself seriously threatened by a law proposed by a policy entrepreneur who must appeal to an unorganized majority, the members of which may not expect to be substantially or directly benefited by the law. Without special political circumstances—a crisis, a scandal, extraordinary majorities, an especially vigorous President, the support of media—the normal barriers to legislative innovation (i.e., to the formation of a "coalition of the majority") may prove insuperable.

Stated another way, the initiation of regulatory programs tends to take the form of majoritarian rather than coalition politics. The Madisonian system is placed in temporary suspense: Exceptional majorities propelled by a public mood and led by a skillful policy entrepreneur take action that might not be possible under ordinary circumstances (closely divided parties, legislative-executive checks and balances, popular indifference). The consequence of majoritarian politics for the administration of regulatory bureaucracies is great. To initiate and sustain the necessary legislative mood, strong, moralistic, and sometimes ideological appeals are necessary—leading, in turn, to the granting of broad mandates of power to the new agency (a modest delegation of authority would obviously be inadequate if the problem to be resolved is of crisis proportions) or to the specifying of exacting standards to be enforced (e.g., *no* carcinogenic products may be sold; 95 percent of the pollutants must be eliminated), or to both.

Either in applying a vague but broad rule ("the public interest, convenience, and necessity") or in enforcing a clear and strict standard, the regulatory agency will tend to broaden the range and domain of its authority, to lag behind technological and economic change, to resist deregulation, to stimulate corruption, and to contribute to the bureaucratization of private institutions.

It will broaden its regulatory reach out of a variety of motives: to satisfy the demand of the regulated enterprise that it be protected from competition, to make effective the initial regulatory action by attending to the unanticipated side effects of that action, to discover or stretch the meaning of vague statutory language, or to respond to new constituencies induced by the existence of the agency to convert what were once private demands into public pressures. For example, the Civil Aeronautics Board, out of a desire both to promote aviation and to protect the regulated price structure of the industry, will resist the entry into the industry of new carriers. If a Public Utilities Commission sets rates too low for a certain class of customers, the utility will allow service to those customers to decline in quality, leading in turn to a demand that the Commission also regulate the quality of service. If the Federal Communications Commission cannot decide who should receive a broadcast license by applying the "public interest" standard, it will be powerfully tempted to invest that phrase with whatever preferences the majority of the Commission then entertains, leading in turn to the exercise of control over many more aspects of broadcasting than merely signal interference—all in the name of deciding what the standard for entry shall be. If the Antitrust Division can prosecute conspiracies in restraint of trade, it will attract to itself the complaints of various firms about business practices that are neither conspiratorial nor restraining but merely competitive, and a "vigorous" antitrust lawyer may conclude that these practices warrant prosecution.

BUREAUCRATIC INERTIA

Regulatory agencies are slow to respond to change for the same reason all organizations with an assured existence are slow: There is no incentive to respond. Furthermore, the requirements of due process and of political conciliation will make any response time-consuming. For example, owing to the complexity of the matter and the money at stake, any comprehensive review of the long-distance rates of the telephone company will take years, and possibly may take decades.

Deregulation, when warranted by changed economic circumstances of undesired regulatory results, will be resisted. Any organization, and *a fortiori* any public organization, develops a genuine belief in the rightness of its mission that is expressed as a commitment to regulation as a process. This happened to the ICC in the early decades of this century as it steadily sought both enlarged powers (setting minimum as well as maximum rates) and a broader jurisdiction (over trucks, barges, and pipelines as well as railroads). It even urged incorporation into the Transportation Act of 1920 language directing it to prepare a comprehensive transportation plan for the nation. Furthermore, any regulatory agency will confer benefits on some group or interest, whether intended or not; those beneficiaries will stoutly resist deregulation. (But in happy proof of the fact that there are no iron laws, even about bureaucracies, we note the recent proposals emanating from the Federal Power Commission that the price of natural gas be substantially deregulated.)

The operation of regulatory bureaus may tend to bureaucratize the private sector. The costs of conforming to many regulations can be met most easily— often, *only*—by large firms and institutions with specialized bureaucracies of their own. Smaller firms and groups often must choose between unacceptably high overhead costs, violating the law, or going out of business. A small bakery producing limited runs of a high-quality product literally may not be able to meet the safety and health standards for equipment or to keep track of and administer fairly its obligations to its two employees; but unless the bakery is willing to break the law, it must sell out to a big bakery that can afford to do these things, but may not be inclined to make and sell good bread. I am not aware of any data that measure private bureaucratization or industrial concentration as a function of the economies of scale produced by the need to cope with the regulatory environment, but I see no reason why such data could not be found.

Finally, regulatory agencies that control entry, fix prices, or substantially affect the profitability of an industry create a powerful stimulus for direct or indirect forms of corruption. The revelations about campaign finance in the 1972 presidential election show dramatically that there will be a response to that stimulus. Many corporations, disproportionately those in regulated industries (airlines, milk producers, oil companies), made illegal or hard to justify campaign contributions involving very large sums.

THE ERA OF CONTRACT

It is far from clear what the Founding Fathers would have thought of all this. They were not doctrinaire exponents of laissez-faire, nor were 18th-century governments timid about asserting their powers over the economy. Every imaginable device of fiscal policy was employed by the states after the Revolutionary War. Mother England had, during the mercantilist era, fixed prices and wages, licensed merchants, and granted monopolies and subsidies. (What were the royal grants of American land to immigrant settlers but the greatest of subsidies, sometimes—as in Pennsylvania—almost monopolistically given?) European nations regularly operated state enterprises, controlled trade, and protected industry. But as William D. Grampp has noted, at the Constitutional

Convention the Founders considered authorizing only four kinds of economic controls, and they rejected two of them. They agreed to allow the Congress to regulate international and interstate commerce and to give monopoly protection in the form of copyrights and patents. Even Madison's proposal to allow the federal government to charter corporations was rejected. Not one of the 85 *Federalist* papers dealt with economic regulation; indeed, the only reference to commerce was the value to it of a unified nation and a strong navy.

G. Warren Nutter has speculated as to why our Founders were so restrained in equipping the new government with explicit regulatory powers. One reason may have been the impact of Adam Smith's *Wealth of Nations*, published the same year as the Declaration of Independence, and certainly soon familiar to many rebel leaders, notably Hamilton. Smith himself sought to explain the American prosperity before the Revolution by the fact that Britain, through "salutary neglect," had not imposed mercantilist rules on the colonial economy. "Plenty of good land, and liberty to manage their own affairs in their own way" were the "two great causes" of colonial prosperity. As Nutter observes, there was a spirit of individualistic venture among the colonies that found economic expression in the belief that voluntary contracts were the proper organization principle of enterprise.

One consequence of this view was that the courts in many states were heavily burdened with cases testing the provisions of contracts and settling debts under them. In one rural county in Massachusetts the judges heard over 800 civil cases during 1785. As James Willard Hurst has written, the years before 1875 were "above all else, the years of contract in our law."

The era of contract came to an end with the rise of economic organization so large or with consequences so great that contracts were no longer adequate, in the public's view, to adjust corporate behavior to the legitimate expectations of other parties. The courts were slower to accede to this change than were many legislatures, but in time they acceded completely, and the era of administrative regulation was upon us. The Founders, were they to return, would understand the change in the scale and social significance of enterprise, would approve of many of the purposes of regulation, perhaps would approve of the behavior of some of the regulatory bureaus seeking to realize those purposes, but surely would be dismayed at the political cost resulting from having vested vast discretionary authority in the hands of officials whose very existence—to say nothing of whose function—was not anticipated by the Constitutional Convention and whose effective control is beyond the capacity of the governing institutions which that Convention had designed.

THE BUREAUCRATIC STATE
AND THE REVOLUTION

The American Revolution was not only a struggle for independence but a fundamental rethinking of the nature of political authority. Indeed, until that reformulation was completed the Revolution was not finished. What made political authority problematic for the colonists was the extent to which they believed Mother England had subverted their liberties despite the protection of the British constitution, until then widely regarded in America as the most perfect set of governing arrangements yet devised. The evidence of usurpation is now familiar: unjust taxation, the weakening of the independence of the judiciary, the stationing of standing armies, and the extensive use of royal patronage to reward office-seekers at colonial expense. Except for the issue of taxation, which raised for the colonists major questions of representation, almost all of their complaints involved the abuse of *administrative* powers.

The first solution proposed by Americans to remedy this abuse was the vesting of most (or, in the case of Pennsylvania and a few other states, virtually all) powers in the legislature. But the events after 1776 in many colonies, notably Pennsylvania, convinced the most thoughtful citizens that legislative abuses were as likely as administrative ones: In the extreme case, citizens would suffer from the "tyranny of the majority." Their solution to this problem was, of course, the theory of the separation of powers by which, as brilliantly argued in *The Federalist* papers, each branch of government would check the likely usurpations of the other.

This formulation went essentially unchallenged in theory and unmodified by practice for over a century. Though a sizable administrative apparatus had come into being by the end of the 19th century, it constituted no serious threat to the existing distribution of political power because it either performed routine tasks (the Post Office) or dealt with temporary crises (the military). Some agencies wielding discretionary authority existed, but they either dealt with groups whose liberties were not of much concern (the Indian Office) or their exercise of discretion was minutely scrutinized by Congress (the Land Office, the Pension Office, the Customs Office). The major discretionary agencies of the 19th century flourished at the very period of greatest Congressional domination of the political process—the decades after the Civil War—and thus, though their supervision was typically inefficient and sometimes corrupt, these agencies were for most practical purposes direct dependencies of Congress. In short, their existence did not call into question the theory of the separation of powers.

But with the growth of client-serving and regulatory agencies, grave questions began to be raised—usually implicitly—about the theory. A client-serving bureau, because of its relations with some source of private power, could become partially independent of both the executive and legislative branches—or in the case of the latter, dependent upon certain committees and independent of others and of the views of the Congress as a whole. A regulatory agency (that is to say, a truly regulatory one and not a clientelist or promotional agency hiding behind a regulatory fig leaf) was, in the typical case, placed formally outside the existing branches of government. Indeed, they were called "independent" or "quasi-judicial" agencies (they might as well have been called "quasi-executive" or "quasi-legislative") and thus the special status that clientelist bureaus achieved *de facto*, the regulatory ones achieved *de jure*.

It is, of course, inadequate and misleading to criticize these agencies, as has often been done, merely because they raise questions about the problem of sovereignty. The crucial test of their value is their behavior, and that can be judged only by applying economic and welfare criteria to the policies they produce. But if such judgments should prove damning, as increasingly has been the case, then the problem of finding the authority with which to alter or abolish such organizations becomes acute. In this regard the theory of the separation of powers has proved unhelpful.

The separation of powers makes difficult, in ordinary times, the extension of public power over private conduct—as a nation, we came more slowly to the welfare state than almost any European nation, and we still engage in less central planning and operate fewer nationalized industries than other democratic regimes. But we have extended the regulatory sway of our national government as far as or farther than that of most other liberal regimes (our environmental and safety codes are now models for much of Europe), and the bureaus wielding these discretionary powers are, once created, harder to change or redirect than would be the case if authority were more centralized.

The shift of power toward the bureaucracy was not inevitable. It did not result simply from increased specialization, the growth of industry, or the imperialistic designs of the bureaus themselves. Before the second decade of this century, there was no federal bureaucracy wielding substantial discretionary powers. That we have one now is the result of political decisions made by elected representatives. Fifty years ago, the people often wanted more of government than it was willing to provide—it was, in that sense, a republican government in which representatives moderated popular demands. Today, not only does political action follow quickly upon the stimulus of public interest, but government itself creates that stimulus and sometimes acts in advance of it.

All democratic regimes tend to shift resources from the private to the public sector and to enlarge the size of the administrative component of government. The particularistic and localistic nature of American democracy has created a particularistic and client-serving administration. If our bureaucracy often serves special interests and is subject to no central direction, it is because our legislature often serves special interests and is subject to no central leadership. For Congress to complain of what it has created and it maintains is, to be charitable, misleading. Congress could change what it has devised, but there is little reason to suppose it will.

The Executive Office
of the President

The President has his own bureaucracy, formally called The Executive Office of the President (EOP). President Roosevelt created the EOP in 1939 by executive order to help him deal with the burgeoning New Deal executive branch. A central component of the Executive Office was the Bureau of the Budget, created in 1921 by Congress in the Budget and Accounting Act and placed originally in the Treasury Department.

In 1970, President Richard M. Nixon renamed and reorganized the Bureau of the Budget, calling it the Office of Management and Budget and making it directly accountable to the president for *all* of its activities. Prior to the Nixon reorganization the Bureau of the Budget, although in the Executive Office, derived its authority from Congress and formally carried out congressional responsibilities as well as presidential directives. The Nixon reorganization was subject to a congressional veto, but after acrimonious hearings on Capitol Hill Congress allowed the plan to go into effect. It represented a victory for the imperial presidency over Congress.

To counter dominant executive power in the budgeting arena, Congress passed the Budget and Impoundment Control Act of 1974, creating a Congressional Budget Office (CBO) and Budget committees in both the House and Senate. Congress became an independent force in its own right in the budgeting process. The following selection analyzes the changing role of OMB in budgeting and how this powerful administrative agency deals with the president and Congress in an era of assertive congressional power and growing budget deficits.

49

Aaron Wildavsky
OMB IN AN ERA OF
PERENNIAL BUDGETING

As governing and budgeting became equivalent in the late 1970s and the 1980s, the part played by the Office of Management and Budget (OMB) was bound to be more important than it had been. No matter who was (or is) the director of the budget, the rise of budget resolutions, continuous resolutions, reconciliation, the deficit, the strategic centrality of negotiations over the size and composition of taxing and spending, the ensuing stalemate (and hence the extraordinary degree to which budgeting crowds out other issues)—any, or all, of these would have made OMB more pivotal. David Stockman, a man of exceptional force and talent, and President Reagan's Director of the Budget from 1981 to 1985, speeded up the transformation of OMB from an agency-centered to a congressionally centered presidential adviser-cum-negotiator. Stockman also gave this change an enhanced centralized slant. But under circumstances in which the budget dominated policy making, no one could have prevented OMB from being a key player.

In order to separate cause from effect—OMB as prime mover from OMB as responding to larger trends—we must make a nuanced interpretation of its part in these events. Since its establishment in 1921, when it was cutting small sums, to its revitalization in the late 1930s—and again after the Second World War as presidential staff agency with a cutting bias—OMB (then the Bureau of the Budget) has counted itself (and has been considered by others) to be powerful. Without money of its own, without authority except what the president lends it, and without a large staff (around 200 examiners being the norm), OMB has long been an elite unit. It is one of the best places to be. Service there counts high for promotion elsewhere. The sense of service to the president, upon whose backing all depends, coupled with a belief that this central staff has a national (rather then parochial) viewpoint, has long created a strong esprit de corps.

While it is true that the BOB (and later OMB) participated in a process of budgeting from below (bureau requests, departmental review, submission to and revision by the Director's Review, recommendation to the president, limited agency appeal, final president's budget, congressional validation by use of this budget as its starting point), this was not the whole truth. At least since World War II, when Keynesian doctrines were dominant, BOB–OMB also have worked from the top down. Considerations of fiscal policy, involving the effects of total expenditure and revenue on the economy, mattered. Presidents Truman and Eisenhower believed in (and, to a considerable extent, achieved) balanced budgets. Deeply concerned about inflation, they applied strong downward, or carefully controlled upward, pressure on spending. Although their formulas differed—Truman took revenues, subtracted desirable domestic spending, and left the remainder for defense; Eisenhower subtracted desirable defense from revenues, reserving the rest for domestic purposes—their goals of price and employment stability, reinforced by balanced budgets, were similar. President Kennedy used tax cuts to get a sluggish economy moving without the pain of significant inflation or large deficits.

The usual practice was for OMB to conduct a Spring Preview in which likely spending demands (estimated by OMB staff) were compared to expected revenues; then both were manipulated to achieve desired effects on the economy. Agency spending bids, therefore, were made in a controlled context. Because agencies were told how high they could go, they could accurately translate administration intentions into a loose (ask for more) or tight (keep what you've got) budget request. Agencies could appeal to the president or make an end-run to Congress. But such attempts had to be limited not only because they might fail but also because, given limited time and attention, extra political efforts were better reserved for the most important issues. On run-of-the mill stuff, the guts of agency activities, OMB recommendations were likely to be final.

There is now a pronounced difference. Working largely top down is not the same as working largely bottom up. Once budget examiners used to examine; they went into detail on programs, made field visits, and otherwise kept track of agency programs. Some still do; many do not. Now most examiners deal with aggregates, with total agency spending. Within that total, agencies are freer to spend as they wish (subject, of course, to congressional constraints and clientele demands). The price of this enhanced discretion is increased uncertainty. There may be not only less money but its flow may be interrupted by delay, deferrals, rescissions, the latest continuous round of negotiations, stalemate followed by continuing resolutions, on and on. Budgetary planning is not easy. The decline of the annual budget, early decisions good for a year, is but the other side of the coin of continuous budgeting.

Differences in quantity, if they are large enough, may become differences in quality. BOB-OMB always had relations with Congress. There were always appropriations committees. Since these committees were even more important then than they are today (taking up a larger share of the budget), the director and his chief aides, including top civil servants specializing in public works and other matters of interest to these legislators, had frequent contact with appropriations committees. Failure to pass appropriations on time or the need for supplementals or raising the debt ceiling required OMB to arrange a policy position for the Executive Branch. The difference today lies in the increased frequency of contacts, the institutional arrangements facilitating them, and the character of the interactions.

Today totals dominate all discussion. How much, not what for, is the first question. Nor can there be much room for analysis when the only question of allocation is how much for welfare and how much for defense. Escaping from macro choices over total taxing and spending, moreover, is hardly possible when the Budget Act of 1974 requires an annual resolution to do just that, a requirement reinforced by the establishment of congressional budget committees whose main assignment this is.

"The creation of the budget committees," Bruce Johnson writes, "gave the OMB its own committees to work through. OMB became a client of the budget committees—perhaps their chief client—like the Veterans Administration is a client of the Veterans committees. A similarity of purpose grew, and staff-to-staff contacts developed. The budget committees became a window through which the OMB could view and influence Congress." Given the assumed role of the Senate Budget Committee as spokesman for responsible finance—that is, deficit reduction through increased control over budget authority—it is a natural ally of OMB. OMB also becomes a window through which SBC can obtain information about executive office discussion, and thus leverage in trying to influence executive policies. When the Executive Office of the President reaches out to external constituencies, by the same token, SBC reaches in. For what is going on in Congress then becomes a part of White House deliberation.

Partisanship and ideology also influence executive-legislative relationships. The informal cooperation between SBC and OMB depended in part on the fact that from 1981 to 1986 the Senate was Republican while the House was Democratic. It remains to be seen whether this symbiosis will continue under a Democratically controlled Senate. As policy differences between moderate Senate Republicans and the more conservative Reagan administration deepened, moreover, it became more difficult for OMB and SBC to maintain informal cooperation. OMB and SBC became antagonists, but the early reasons for their cooperation remain and may well reassert themselves.

The existence of the Congressional Budget Office (CBO) has been the scene for another mixed-motive game. Unlike the old days, OMB no longer has carte blanche in manipulating agency estimates. Should events prove CBO's spending estimates more accurate in too many instances, OMB's reputation suffers. Over time, therefore, the staffs of the two agencies have come closer together. This regard is furthered by the substantial presence in both organizations of economists (the two heads of CBO have been economists) with similar perspectives about how to value governmental programs. This does not mean that the two organizations harmoniously coexist. Much of President Reagan's first term was marked by strenuous disagreement between the OMB and CBO over economic assumptions and deficit projections.

Changes in attention (the financial markets, other governments, and congressional budget committees observe total spending) and in process (continuous budgeting) have made the central budget agency more important. Bruce Johnson has it just right:

> To respond immediately to changing financial market reactions to the Federal budget, the Executive branch has to be able to change the budget quickly. Only the OMB can perform this function for the Executive branch. The fine-tuning of fiscal policy is now occurring every 3 to 6 months when it used to be an annual affair.
>
> Not only is the Executive branch, under the guidance of the OMB, formally changing its budget requests to Congress more frequently, but *implicit* Administration budget policy is changing almost monthly as a result of compromises struck with Congress. . . . Each time a new "bipartisan compromise" is announced by the President, the Administration's internal budget estimates change (although for public consumption they may just receive an asterisk to show they are out of date). Various deals are also struck with Congress as the appropriations bills wind their way through committee floor and conference action. OMB is the only Executive branch agency able to sum the totals of all the give and take of the Congressional process to see where the budget estimates are going. The importance of budget "scorekeeping"—keeping track of all these deals—has been increased by the emphasis on budget projections and their importance to the financial community. For this reason alone, the OMB has assumed a leading role in negotiating budget and fiscal policy adjustments with Congress. [*]

Had total spending not become all-important, neither would OMB. It is the concentration on totals, combined with the requirement for annual budget resolutions, together with the possibility of invoking reconciliation, and, so long as it lasts, the necessity of avoiding or following Gramm-Rudman-Hollings sequestration procedure, that make the central budget agency so central. When one budgets all the time, budgeters may indeed get more tired, but also they become more important.

Though any specific starting point must be arbitrary, the recent entry of OMB into congressional negotiations may be traced to the time of James T. McIntyre, Jr., President Carter's budget director, who gradually recognized the need for stronger contact with Congress. He increased his liaison staff from two

---

[*]Bruce Johnson, "The Increasing Role of the Office of Management and Budget in the Congressional Budget Process." Paper prepared for the Fifth Annual Research Conference of Association for Public Policy Analysis and Management, Philadelphia, October 21–22, 1983, pp. 7–8. [This paper later appeared, in revised form, under the title "From Analyst to Negotiator: the OMB's New Role," in *Journal of Policy Analysis and Management*. Copyright © 1984 by the Association for Public Policy Analysis and Management. 3, no. 4 (1984), pp. 501–515. Reprinted by permission of John Wiley & Sons, Inc.]

to six. When Carter submitted his last full budget, the fact that it had a (what, in retrospect, looks like a tiny) $16 billion deficit so discomforted the financial markets and congressional leaders, already down on the president, that it was withdrawn. After a week of negotiation with Democratic Party leaders, McIntyre helped resubmit a new budget. In order to implement the deficit-reduction package (the first of many to follow), McIntyre made novel use of the then-dormant reconciliation procedure. Given the short time available, McIntyre, instead of going through the authorizations, appropriations, and finance committees, dealt only with top party and committee leaders.

As Carter began to squeeze the budget in FY80, OMB took a more active role in lobbying Congress for the president's preferences. The budget negotiations of March 1980 and subsequent continuing resolution difficulties increased the relative influence of OMB. David Mathiasen, Deputy Assistant Director for Budget Review at OMB, has noted that more important than the package of cuts in 1980 was "the way in which this revision took place. Traditionally the American budget has been developed by the executive and presented to the Congress and the public without formal discussions or negotiations. . . . In contrast, the 1981 budget revisions were literally negotiated between executive branch representatives (primarily the Office of Management and Budget and the White House) and the leadership in both houses of the Congress." The emphasis should be on *negotiating* spending legislation.

The 1980 (fiscal 1981) budget battles therefore foreshadowed a situation in which detailed examination of agency performance and estimates by appropriations committee members would have less influence on spending decisions. When "how much" matters more than "what for," agencies and appropriations subcommittees matter less than the actors (presidents and congressional leaders) who negotiate about totals. When these legislative leaders vary from time to time, however, according to who can craft the necessary compromise, the process becomes less predictable. The combination of more intractable problems with more numerous and diverse participants spells trouble.

Stockman institutionalized the ad hoc developments of 1980 and took them a giant step further. He sent a list of proposals for cuts, with accompanying explanations, to Capitol Hill, following them up with personal visits to assess reaction. Earlier, under the Ford administration in the mid-1970s, Director James Lynn had used similar advocacy papers, and Carter's director, McIntyre, had sometimes utilized the requirement under the Budget Impoundment and Control Act for narrative statements explaining how actions met "national needs" to sell the budget. Stockman provided the all-time hard sell. He was able to gauge support from reactions to his proposals, all the while making program supporters feel lucky to get by with cuts that, though modest by Stockman's standards, were considerably larger than agencies otherwise would have contemplated.

Stockman changed OMB's focus from the examining and assembling of agency requests to that of lobbying the administration budget through Congress.

Budget examiners spent far less time in the field getting to know their agencies. Instead, staff was dedicated to tracking budget action through the multiple stages of the congressional process—resolutions were tracked from budget committees to the floor and into conference, out again into appropriations subcommittee and full committee markups, to reappearance on the floor in a continuing resolution, then again in a regular appropriations bill, seemingly settled only to pop up again in markup on a supplemental. To facilitate this tracking, Stockman ordered the development of a computer system that aggregated budget items by both budget function categories and committee jurisdictions, allowing him to trace the spending implications of action at all levels. He also increased the size of the OMB unit that was tracking spending legislation through Congress. Stockman could afford to take this course because there was nothing that he really needed to know about the agencies. For at least a few years he could get by on previous analysis by OMB, the extensive literature produced by GAO, CBO and the think tanks, and his own preferences about what government should and should not do. Ideology provided a substitute for information. The new OMB approach, Hale Champion commented, therefore "almost excluded cabinet departments and agencies from the formulation of the budget."

Since Stockman (and the president) were interested in achieving a preferred set of cuts, not in using the budget to finance agencies, OMB also moved away from the norm of annual budgeting. The annual budget served many needs, but its primary purpose was to regularize the funding, and therefore functioning, of government agencies. Funded for a year in advance, an agency would be able to plan and coordinate its activities. Since in many cases the administration either did not care about these agency functions or was convinced it knew a better (and, not coincidentally, cheaper) way to do the job, in 1981 and 1982 Stockman discarded the norm of annualarity, proposing instead large rescissions—administratively imposed cuts of previously approved appropriations. Basically the budget was under continuous negotiation so that even a place in the formal budget did not guarantee funding at the once-agreed level. Federal agencies, therefore, were whipsawed back and forth, torn between hope and fear that their allocations would be changed during the year. Predictability of spending flows, and whatever short-term planning went with it, were lost.

OMB also gave up its role as protector of agencies against sudden and unreasonable reductions. The place of agencies in the new appropriations process was both precarious and peculiar. Both their budget authority and staffing levels (also partially controlled through that process) were unpredictable. Many agencies were running reduction-in-force (RIF) operations, which were designed to reduce employment while maintaining civil service preferences and protections against political bias. RIFs and a twist called RIF exercises—in which procedures were war-gamed in a drill to determine who would land where in the game of civil-service musical chairs—were spreading fear and chaos in agencies far out of proportion to actual layoffs.

There is no doubt that Stockman was knowledgeable. That matters, partly because information is the medium through which policy is negotiated. It is important as well that staff, allies, and adversaries be made aware that they are dealing with someone who is factually smart. Whether Stockman was also institutionally smart—able to create and sustain social relationships that facilitated his goals—was less certain.

After the congressional elections of 1982 increased Democratic majorities in the House and discomfited the Republican majority in the Senate, reconciliation no longer seemed a viable option to the administration. Nor—considering the liberal Democratic majority in the House and the moderate Republican Party Senate majority, which wanted higher taxes and lower defense spending—was Reagan likely to get acceptable budget resolutions. Therefore, Bruce Johnson explains,

> In the absence of a budget resolution acceptable to the president, the director of the OMB attempted to impose presidential budget targets on the various appropriation bills. Because of the implicit and sometimes explicit threat of a presidential veto, the OMB was successful in exerting such influence in an area of decision normally reserved for an agency and its appropriation subcommittees. Thus, although the process of budget resolution and reconciliation was near collapse in 1983, the OMB continued to be active in the appropriation process, attempting to sell pieces of the president's budget to Congress in that forum.*

One might well say that OMB became the president's lobbyist in Congress.

Within OMB, the realization was growing that the budgetary game had undergone decisive changes. Resolutions did not carry enforcement powers; they could not be counted on to pass; if they did, they often were not enforced. Failing to agree meant only that the real play was in a continuing resolution. Besides, appropriations committees could work without a resolution. Authorizations mattered for entitlements but big ones were unbudgeable and little ones didn't move much. Not much point in talking to authorizers when there are no new programs.

Discovering by 1984 that it could not get authorizations down far enough to bite, OMB concentrated almost entirely on discretionary appropriations and, within that, on the 302(b) allocations under which appropriations committees divided the amount they received from budget committees. Like the old joke about the man who looks for his collar button under the street lamp rather than where he lost it—because the light is better there—OMB concentrated on the pieces of the budget it could do something about. This focus on appropriations accounted for the bulk of time Director Stockman spent negotiating with committee members as well as tracking bills. Before deals could be struck

---

*Bruce Johnson, "From Analyst to Negotiator: The OMB's New Role," *Journal of Policy Analysis and Management*, Vol. 3, No. 4 (1984), p. 504.

on appropriations, it was necessary to estimate how much they were worth and where the bill was located in the process.

OMB expanded its handful of bill trackers to thirteen, one for each of the major committees. Trackers infiltrated hearings, got data wherever they could, and immediately prepared letters to all concerned on Capitol Hill about whether they thought savings were real or illusory. Keeping score is serious business. But why is it necessary?

The appropriations committees can transfer funds from an entitlement to a discretionary account. This maneuver has the effect of increasing discretionary spending while often creating a shortfall in the entitlement, a shortfall that has to be made good in the future. Two examples are transfers of $39 million to the Agriculture Extension Service from food stamps and $66 million from the CCC (Commodity Credit Corporation) reimbursement for prior year losses to the Conservation Service. OMB's bill trackers do not treat such transfers as savings, but the appropriations committees may use them to fit within the budget resolution.

OMB does score as increases in spending transfers from unobligated balances in one account, say, Small Business Administration disaster funds, unlikely to be used, to other accounts, say salary and expenses, that will be used. The amount may be the same—$100 million for the Coast Guard—but the account may differ—a transfer from the navy. Since conflicts occur over the size of defense, OMB wants to charge the amount to domestic, not to defense.

OMB wants to show the amounts authorized in a fiscal year even if they are not spent in that year. Advance appropriations, to be spent in future years, no further action required, and appropriations deferred because they lack authorization, although funds are likely to be provided in a supplemental or continuing resolution, are not scored in that year by Appropriations but they are scored by OMB. Reasonable people might disagree. Similarly, where supplementals are routinely provided, as for fire fighting, or discretionary activities are purposely underfunded in OMB's opinion, it will score the funds as if they had been fully appropriated. There are also occasional adjustments, such as provisions for savings—pay reductions or delayed repayments of loans—that never materialize, which OMB scores as spending.

Among the most important and most controversial scoring choices is the distinction OMB makes (and would like appropriations committees to make) between discretionary and entitlement programs. A cut in appropriations for a discretionary program is indeed a cut. But an apparent reduction in spending for an entitlement "not accompanied," in OMB's words, "by language in appropriations bills to reduce the statutory spending requirements are not scored by OMB as reductions." No doubt there will be disagreement on OMB's promised list of what it considers discretionary versus mandatory for that too would affect scoring.

This emphasis on scoring, reinforced by a cadre of OMB bill trackers, testifies to the importance of the deficit, hence the significance of progress toward reduction and the temptation to appear to be saving more or less depending on the political needs of the moment. For their part, appropriations people figure OMB is cheating when it tells them to cut entitlements that are outside their jurisdiction.

As OMB improved its congressional intelligence, thus being able to intervene in the right subcommittees at the right time, it sought further to streamline its task by combining consideration of appropriations hitherto dealt with separately. The development of continuing resolutions, from stop-gap funding to program changes with future spending implications, provided OMB with another point of entry. OMB was monitoring spending not only in agencies but also in Congress. Would the role of salesman to Congress of spending cuts, the OMB staff wondered, interfere with its tradition of neutral competence and general repository of wisdom about the value of programs?

The Director's use of budget examiners as personal staff or, better still, as research assistants, became well known. According to a civil servant, "It's not uncommon to be called over there—boom, boom—and have him say, 'OK, I've prepared this presentation, I want you to check it and fill in the numbers.' And he'll say, bring it back tomorrow." Not everyone cares for this kind of spot-research role. Observers worry that OMB's stature as an institution to serve presidents and the Executive branch over the long term may decline while its political clout temporarily increases. Hugh Heclo, for instance, is troubled "that the capacity for loyal independence . . . may have diminished over time." Heclo quotes an OMB division director: "He [Stockman] bangs on you for information on the day that he needs it. He doesn't think about how to strengthen the agency's general ability to provide what is wanted. He gets what he wants when he wants it and wherever he can. He doesn't say to himself, I'd better get an organization and process in motion to be able to supply what is needed."

There are, as usual, two sides to this story. OMB had become somewhat demoralized due to low morale in the Carter administration in general, and to disregard of administration recommendations in particular. There is nothing better for restoring high spirits than having a respected director who is on the winning side. OMB under Stockman was an important and exciting place for those staff members to be. His kudos became theirs. The Director could not be expected to overcome presidential opposition to raising taxes or cutting defense; that was part of the old and continuing role of presidential servant. But their Director was a key member of the White House legislative strategy group. He was bright, more than living up to their self-image as being the smarter service. Such strokes made up for a lot.

So far as loss of agency supervision was concerned, it was compensated for by greater OMB influence with Congress. True, examiners whose predecessors had once spent the slow summer months nosing around agencies could no longer do so. Yet, if they were honest with themselves, they knew that the old ways had started to crumble with the new requirements of the 1974 budget reform.

Phenomena like budget resolutions, running totals, even reconciliation, had not been invented, only intensified, by David Stockman. The Central Budget Management System, which records existing spending-decision and projects alternatives, was inevitable in that era of confict over totals and panic over deficits. Whatever else might be attributed to or blamed on Stockman, he was only a reflection, albeit bigger than life, of conflicts that had deep roots in the nation's political life. When he left, dissensus [sic] would remain.

Depending on one's political philosophy, the politicization of OMB began either with its predecessors (BOB as lynchpin of big government under Franklin Roosevelt) or with the Reorganization Plan Number 2 in 1970 under President Nixon, which established a new [stratum] of four Program Associate Directors who were political appointees. President Carter's creation of a new Executive Associate Director for Budget to supervise the earlier four only intensified this practice. Politicization is bipartisan. It may be that more OMB staff than in the past, not just its political appointees, will move with a change of administration. Heclo is rightly interested in maintaining the ethos of OMB, that "It was not a place to be just another bureaucrat. It was a place to work for the presidency broadly understood." But if the presidency is no longer "broadly understood" in the sense of presidential preferences being widely agreed, the politicization of those who serve presidents may be unavoidable.

In a polarized political environment the significance of significance, as it were, also changes. Is it significant to understand the effects on programs of changes in funding? Surely. But it may be deemed more significant to understand the implications of different programs for the size of government. If the Budget Review Division, where the big budget totals are put together, has become the place in OMB where bright young people try to go, as Heclo informs us, that may be because they know where the action is. Unless and until there is consensus rather than dissensus over the size and composition of government, the division that deals with totals is where the action will continue to be.

Chapter 8

Congress

The United States Congress, exercising supreme legislative power, was at the beginning of the nineteenth century the most powerful political institution in the national government. It was feared by the framers of the Constitution, who felt that unless it was closely guarded and limited it would easily dominate both the presidency and the Supreme Court. Its powers were carefully enumerated, and it was made a bicameral body. This latter provision not only secured representation of different interests but also limited the power of the legislature which, when hobbled by two houses often working against each other, could not act as swiftly and forcefully as a single body could. Although still important, the power and prestige of Congress have declined while the powers of the President and the Supreme Court, not to mention those of the vast governmental bureaucracy, have increased. Congressional power, its basis, and the factors influencing the current position of Congress vis-à-vis coordinate governmental departments are discussed in this chapter.

Constitutional Background: Representation of Popular, Group, and National Interests

Article I, Section 1 of the Constitution states that "all legislative powers herein granted shall be vested in a Congress of the United States, which shall consist of a Senate and House of Representatives." Section 8 specifically enumerates congressional powers, and provides that Congress shall have power "to make all laws which shall be necessary and proper for carrying into execution the foregoing powers, and all other powers vested by this Constitution in the government of the United States, or in any department or officer thereof."

Apart from delineating the powers of Congress, Article I provides that the House shall represent the people, and the Senate the states through appointment of members by the state legislatures. The representative function of Congress is written into the Constitution, and at the time of the framing of the Constitution much discussion centered on the nature of representation and what constituted adequate representation in a national legislative body. Further, relating in part to the question of representation, the framers of the Constitution had to determine what the appropriate tasks for each branch of the legislature were, and to what extent certain legislative activities should be within the exclusive or initial jurisdiction of the House or the Senate. All these questions depended to some extent upon the conceptualization the framers had of the House as representative of popular interests on a short-term basis and the Senate as a reflection of conservative interests on a long-term basis. These selections from *The Federalist* indicate the thinking of the framers about the House of Representatives and the Senate.

50

James Madison
FEDERALIST 53

. . . No man can be a competent legislator who does not add to an upright intention and a sound judgment a certain degree of knowledge of the subjects on which he is to legislate. A part of this knowledge may be acquired by means of information, which lie within the compass of men in private, as well as public stations. Another part can only be attained, or at least thoroughly attained, by actual experience in the station which requires the use of it. The period of service ought, therefore, in all such cases, to bear some proportion to the extent of practical knowledge requisite to the due performance of the service. . . .

In a single state the requisite knowledge relates to the existing laws, which are uniform throughout the state, and with which all the citizens are more or less conversant. . . . The great theater of the United States presents a very different scene. The laws are so far from being uniform that they vary in every state; whilst the public affairs of the union are spread throughout a very extensive region, and are extremely diversified by the local affairs connected with them, and can with difficulty be correctly learnt in any other place than in the central councils, to which a knowledge of them will be brought by representatives of every part of the empire. Yet some knowledge of the affairs, and even of the laws of all the states, ought to be possessed by the members from each of the states. . . .

A branch of knowledge which belongs to the acquirements of a federal representative, and which has not been mentioned, is that of foreign affairs. In regulating our own commerce he ought to be not only acquainted with the treaties between the United States and other nations, but also with the commercial policy and laws of other nations. He ought not to be altogether ignorant of the law of nations; for that, as far as it is a proper object of municipal legislation, is submitted to the federal government. And although the House of Representatives is not immediately to participate in foreign negotiations and arrangements, yet from the necessary connection between the several branches of public affairs, those particular subjects will frequently deserve attention in the ordinary course of legislation, and will sometimes demand particular legislative sanction and cooperation. Some portion of this knowledge may, no doubt, be acquired in a man's closet; but some of it also can only be acquired to best effect, by a practical attention to the subject, during the period of actual service in the legislature. . . .

FEDERALIST 56

The . . . charge against the House of Representatives is, that it will be too small to possess a due knowledge of the interests of its constituents.

As this objection evidently proceeds from a comparison of the proposed number of representatives, with the great extent of the United States, the number of their inhabitants, and the diversity of their interests, without taking into view, at the same time, the circumstances which will distinguish the Congress from other legislative bodies, the best answer that can be given to it, will be a brief explanation of these peculiarities.

It is a sound and important principle that the representative ought to be acquainted with the interests and circumstances of his constituents. But this principle can extend no farther than to those circumstances and interests to which the authority and care of the representative relate. An ignorance of a variety of minute and particular objects, which do not lie within the compass of legislation, is consistent with every attribute necessary to a due performance of the legislative trust. In determining the extent of information required in the exercise of a particular authority, recourse then must be had to the objects within the purview of that authority.

What are to be the objects of federal legislation? Those which are of most importance, and which seem most to require knowledge, are commerce, taxation, and the militia.

A proper regulation of commerce requires much information, as has been elsewhere remarked; but as far as this information relates to the laws, and local situation of each individual state, a very few representatives would be sufficient vehicles of it to the federal councils.

Taxation will consist, in great measure, of duties which will be involved in the regulation of commerce. So far the preceding remark is applicable to this object. As far as it may consist of internal collections, a more diffusive knowledge of the circumstances of the state may be necessary. But will not this also be possessed in sufficient degree by a very few intelligent men, diffusively elected within the state? . . .

With regard to the regulation of the militia there are scarcely any circumstances in reference to which local knowledge can be said to be necessary. . . . The art of war teaches general principles of organization, movement, and discipline, which apply universally.

The attentive reader will discern that the reasoning here used, to prove the sufficiency of a moderate number of representatives, does not, in any respect, contradict what was urged on another occasion, with regard to the extensive information which the representatives ought to possess, and the time that might be necessary for acquiring it. . . .

FEDERALIST 57

. . . . The House of Representatives is so constituted as to support in the members an habitual recollection of their dependence on the people. Before the sentiments impressed on their minds by the mode of their elevation, can be effaced by the exercise of power, they will be compelled to anticipate the moment when their power is to cease, when their exercise of it is to be reviewed, and when they must descend to the level from which they were raised; there for ever to remain unless a faithful discharge of their trust shall have established their title to a renewal of it.

I will add, as a . . . circumstance in the situation of the House of Representatives, restraining them from oppressive measures, that they can make no law which will not have its full operation on themselves and their friends, as well as on the great mass of the society. This has always been deemed one of the strongest bonds by which human policy can connect the rulers and the people together. It creates between them that communion of interest, and sympathy of sentiments, of which few governments have furnished examples; but without which every government degenerates into tyranny. If it be asked, what is to restrain the House of Representatives from making legal discriminations in favor of themselves, and a particular class of the society? I answer, the genius of the whole system; the nature of just and constitutional laws; and, above all, the vigilant and manly spirit which actuates the people of America; a spirit which nourishes freedom, and in return is nourished by it.

If this spirit shall ever be so far debased as to tolerate a law not obligatory on the legislature, as well as on the people, the people will be prepared to tolerate anything but liberty.

Such will be the relation between the House of Representatives and their constituents. Duty, gratitude, interest, ambition itself, are the cords by which they will be bound to fidelity and sympathy with the great mass of the people. It is possible that these may all be insufficient to control the caprice and wickedness of men. But are they not all that government will admit, and that human prudence can devise? Are they not the genuine, and the characteristic means, by which republican government provides for the liberty and happiness of the people? . . .

FEDERALIST 58

. . . In this review of the constitution of the House of Representatives . . . one observation . . . I must be permitted to add . . . as claiming, in my judgment, a very serious attention. It is, that in all legislative assemblies, the greater the number composing them may be, the fewer will be the men who will in fact direct their proceedings. In the first place, the more numerous any assembly may be, of whatever characters composed, the greater is known to be the ascendancy of passion over reason. In the next place, the larger the number, the greater will be the proportion of members of limited information and of weak capacities. Now it is precisely on characters of this description that the eloquence and address of the few are known to act with all their force. In the ancient republics, where the whole body of the people assembled in person, a single orator, or an artful statesman, was generally seen to rule with as complete a sway as if a sceptre had been placed in his single hands. On the same principle, the more multitudinous a representative assembly may be rendered, the more it will partake of the infirmities incident to collective meetings of the people. Ignorance will be the dupe of cunning; and passion the slave of sophistry and declamation. The people can never err more than in supposing, that by multiplying their representatives beyond a certain list, they strengthen the barrier against the government of a few. Experience will for ever admonish them, that, on the contrary, after securing a sufficient number for the purposes of safety, of local information, and of diffusive sympathy with the whole society, they will counteract their own views by every addition to their representatives. The countenance of the government may become more democratic; but the soul that animates it will be more oligarchic. The machine will be enlarged, but the fewer, and often the more secret, will be the springs by which its motions are directed. . . .

FEDERALIST 62

Having examined the constitution of the House of Representatives . . . I enter next on the examination of the Senate.

The heads under which this member of the government may be considered are—I. The qualifications of senators; II. The appointment of them by the state legislatures; III. The equality of representation in the Senate; IV. The number of senators, and the term for which they are to be elected; V. The powers vested in the Senate.

I

The qualifications proposed for senators, as distinguished from those of representatives, consist in a more advanced age and a longer period of citizenship. A senator must be thirty years of age at least; as a representative must be twenty-five. And the former must have been a citizen nine years; as seven years are required for the latter. The propriety of these distinctions is explained by the nature of the senatorial trust; which, requiring greater extent of information and stability of character, requires at the same time, that the senator should have reached a period of life most likely to supply these advantages. . . .

II

It is equally unnecessary to dilate on the appointment of senators by the state legislators. Among the various modes which might have been devised for constituting this branch of the government, that which has been proposed by the convention is probably the most congenial with the public opinion. It is recommended by the double advantage of favoring a select appointment, and of giving to the state governments such an agency in the formation of the federal government, as must secure the authority of the former, and may form a convenient link between the two systems.

III

The equality of representation in the Senate is another point, which, being evidently the result of compromise between the opposite pretensions of the large and the small states, does not call for much discussion. If indeed it be right, that among a people thoroughly incorporated into one nation, every district ought to have a *proportional* share in the government: and that among independent and sovereign states bound together by a simple league, the parties, however unequal in size, ought to have an *equal* share in the common councils, it does not appear to be without some reason, that in a compound republic, partaking both of the national and federal character, the government ought to be founded on a mixture of the principles of proportional [as found in the House of Representatives] and equal representation [in the Senate]. . . .

. . . [T]he equal vote allowed to each state, is at once a constitutional recognition of the portion of sovereignty remaining in the individual states, and an instrument for preserving that residuary sovereignty. So far the equality ought to be no less acceptable to the large than to the small states; since they are not less solicitous to guard by every possible expedient against an improper consolidation of the states into one simple republic.

Another advantage accruing from this ingredient in the constitution of the senate is, the additional impediment it must prove against improper acts of legislation. No law or resolution can now be passed without the concurrence, first, of a majority of the people, and then, of a majority of the states. It must be acknowledged that this complicated check on legislation may, in some instances, be injurious as well as beneficial; and that the peculiar defense which it involves in favor of the smaller states, would be more rational, if any interests common to them, and distinct from those of the other states, would otherwise be exposed to peculiar danger. But as the larger states will always be able, by their power over the supplies, to defeat unreasonable exertions of this prerogative of the lesser states; and as the facility and excess of law-making seem to be the diseases to which our governments are most liable, it is not impossible, that this part of the constitution may be more convenient in practice than it appears to many in contemplation.

IV

The number of senators, and the duration of their appointment, come next to be considered. In order to form an accurate judgment on both these points, it will be proper to inquire into the purposes which are to be answered by the Senate; and, in order to ascertain these, it will be necessary to review the inconveniences which a republic must suffer from the want of such an institution.

First. It is a misfortune incident to republican government, though in a lesser degree than to other governments, that those who administer it may forget their obligations to their constituents, and prove unfaithful to their important trust. In this point of view, a senate, as a second branch of the legislative assembly, distinct from, and dividing the power with, a first, must be in all cases a salutary check on the government. It doubles the security to the people by requiring the concurrence of two distinct bodies in schemes of usurpation or perfidy, where the ambition or corruption of one would otherwise be sufficient. . . . [A]s the improbability of sinister combinations will be in proportion to the dissimilarity in the genius of the two bodies, it must be politic to distinguish them from each other by every circumstance which will consist with a due harmony in all proper measures, and with the genuine principles of republican government.

Second. The necessity of a senate is not less indicated by the propensity of all single and numerous assemblies, to yield to the impulse of sudden and violent passions, and to be seduced by factious leaders into intemperate and pernicious resolutions. Examples on this subject might be cited without number; and from proceedings within the United States, as well as from the history of other nations. But a position that will not be contradicted need not be proved. All that need be remarked is, that a body which is to correct this infirmity ought itself to be free from it, and consequently ought to be less numerous. It ought, moreover, to possess great firmness, and consequently ought to hold its authority by a tenure of considerable duration.

Third. Another defect to be supplied by a senate lies in a want of due acquaintance with the objects and principles of legislation. It is not possible that an assembly of men, called, for the most part, from pursuits of a private nature, continued in appointments for a short time, and led by no permanent motive to devote the intervals of public occupation to a study of the laws, the affairs, and the comprehensive interests of their country, should, if left wholly to themselves, escape a variety of important errors in the exercise of their legislative trust. . . .

Fourth. The mutability in the public councils, arising from a rapid succession of new members, however qualified they may be, points out, in the strongest manner, the necessity of some stable institution in the government. Every new election in the states is found to change one-half of the representatives. From this change of men must proceed a change of opinions; and from a change of opinions, a change of measures. But a continual change even of good measures is inconsistent with every rule of prudence, and every prospect of success. . . .

FEDERALIST 63

A *fifth* desideratum, illustrating the utility of a senate, is the want of a due sense of national character. Without a select and stable member of the government, the esteem of foreign powers will not only be forfeited by an unenlightened and variable policy . . . ; but the national councils will not possess that sensibility to the opinion of the world, which is perhaps not less necessary in order to merit, than it is to obtain, its respect and confidence. . . .

I add, as a *sixth* defect, the want in some important cases of a due responsibility in the government to the people, arising from that frequency of elections, which in other cases produces this responsibility. . . .

Responsibility, in order to be reasonable, must be limited to objects within the power of the responsible party, and in order to be effectual, must relate to operations of that power, of which a ready and proper judgment can be formed by the constituents. The objects of government may be divided into two general classes; the one depending on measures, which have singly an immediate and sensible operation; the other depending on a succession of well chosen and well connected measures, which have a gradual and perhaps unobserved operation. The importance of the latter description to the collective and permanent welfare of every country, needs no explanation. And yet it is evident that an assembly elected for so short a term as to be unable to provide more than one or two links in a chain of measures, on which the general welfare may essentially depend, ought not to be answerable for the final result, any more than a steward or tenant, engaged for one year, could be justly made to answer for plans or improvements, which could not be accomplished in less than half a dozen years. Nor is it possible for the people to estimate the *share* of influence, which their annual assemblies may respectively have on events resulting from the mixed transactions of several years. It is sufficiently difficult, at any rate, to preserve a personal responsibility in the members of a *numerous* body, for such acts of the body as have an immediate, detached, and palpable operation on its constituents.

The proper remedy for this defect must be an additional body in the legislative department, which, having sufficient permanency to provide for such objects as require a continued attention, and a train of measures, may be justly and effectually answerable for the attainment of those objects.

Thus far I have considered the circumstances, which point out the necessity of a well constructed senate, only as they relate to the representatives of the people. To a people as little blinded by prejudice, or corrupted by flattery, as those whom I address, I shall not scruple to add, that such an institution may be sometimes necessary, as a defense to the people against their own temporary errors and delusions. As the cool and deliberate sense of the community ought, in all governments, and actually will, in all free governments, ultimately prevail over the views of its rulers; so there are particular moments in public affairs, when the people, stimulated by some irregular passion, or some illicit advantage, or misled by the artful misrepresentations of interested men, may call for measures which they themselves will afterwards be the most ready to lament and condemn. In these critical moments, how salutary will be the interference of some temperate and respectable body of citizens, in order to check the misguided career, and to suspend the blow meditated by the people against themselves, until reason, justice and truth can regain their authority over the public mind? What bitter anguish would not the people of Athens have often avoided, if their government had contained so provident a safeguard against the tyranny of their own passions? Popular liberty might then have escaped the indelible reproach of decreeing to the same citizens the hemlock on one day, and statues on the next.

It may be suggested that a people spread over an extensive region cannot, like the crowded inhabitants of a small district, be subject to the infection of violent passions; or to the danger of combining in the pursuit of unjust measures. I am far from denying that this is a distinction of peculiar importance. I have, on the contrary, endeavored in a former paper to show that it is one of the principal recommendations of a confederated republic. At the same time this advantage ought not to be considered as superseding the use of auxiliary precautions. It may even be remarked that the same extended situation, which will exempt the people of America from some of the dangers incident to lesser republics, will expose them to the inconveniency of remaining for a longer time under the influence of those misrepresentations which the combined industry of interested men may succeed in distributing among them. . . .

Congress and the Washington Political Establishment

The author of the following selection agrees with David Mayhew (see selection No. 56) that the principal goal of members of Congress is reelection. That incentive, the author suggests, has led Congress to create a vast federal bureaucracy to implement programs that ostensibly benefit constituents.

Congress has delegated substantial authority to administrative departments and agencies to carry out programs, inevitably resulting in administrative decisions that frequently step on constituents' toes. Congress, which has gained credit for establishing the programs in the first place, steps in once again to receive credit for handling constituent complaints against the bureaucracy. The author's provocative thesis is that both the establishment and maintenance of a vast federal bureaucracy is explained by the congressional reelection incentive.

51

Morris P. Fiorina
THE RISE OF THE WASHINGTON ESTABLISHMENT

DRAMATIS PERSONAE

In this chapter, the heart of [my] book, I will set out a theory of the Washington establishment(s). The theory is quite plausible from a common-sense standpoint, and it is consistent with the specialized literature of academic political science. Nevertheless, it is still a theory, not proven fact. Before plunging in let me bring out in the open the basic axiom on which the theory rests: the self-interest axiom.

I assume that most people most of the time act in their own self-interest. This is not to say that human beings seek only to amass tangible wealth but rather to say that human beings seek to achieve their own ends—tangible and intangible—rather than the ends of their fellow men. I do not condemn such behavior nor do I condone it (although I rather sympathize with Thoreau's comment that "if I knew for a certainty that a man was coming to my house with the conscious design of doing me good, I should run for my life."). I only claim that political and economic theories which presume self-interested behavior will prove to be more widely applicable than those which build on more altruistic assumptions.

From Morris P. Fiorina, *Congress: Keystone of the Washington Establishment.* Copyright ©1977 by Yale University Press. Reprinted by permission.

What does the axiom imply when used in the specific context of this book, a context peopled by congressmen, bureaucrats, and voters? I assume that the primary goal of the typical congressman is reelection. Over and above the $45,000 salary plus "perks" and outside money, the office of congressman carries with it prestige, excitement, and power. It is a seat in the cockpit of government. But in order to retain the status, excitement, and power (not to mention more tangible things) of office, the congressman must win reelection every two years. Even those congressmen genuinely concerned with good public policy must achieve reelection in order to continue their work. Whether narrowly self-serving or more publicly oriented, the individual congressman finds reelection to be at least a necessary condition for the achievement of his goals.

Moreover, there is a kind of natural selection process at work in the electoral arena. On average, those congressmen who are not primarily interested in reelection will not achieve reelection as often as those who are interested. We, the people, help to weed out congressmen whose primary motivation is not reelection. We admire politicians who courageously adopt the aloof role of the disinterested statesman, but we vote for those politicians who follow our wishes and do us favors.

What about the bureaucrats? A specification of their goals is somewhat more controversial—those who speak of appointed officials as public servants obviously take a more benign view than those who speak of them as bureaucrats. The literature provides ample justification for asserting that most bureaucrats wish to protect and nurture their agencies. The typical bureaucrat can be expected to seek to expand his agency in terms of personnel, budget, and mission. One's status in Washington (again, not to mention more tangible things) is roughly proportional to the importance of the operation one oversees. And the sheer size of the operation is taken to be a measure of importance. As with congressmen, the specified goals apply even to those bureaucrats who genuinely believe in their agency's mission. If they believe in the efficacy of their programs, they naturally wish to expand them and add new ones. All of this requires more money and more people. The genuinely committed bureaucrat is just as likely to seek to expand his agency as the proverbial empire-builder.

And what of the third element in the equation, us? What do we, the voters who support the Washington system, strive for? Each of us wishes to receive a maximum of benefits from government for the minimum cost. This goal suggests maximum government efficiency, on the one hand, but it also suggests mutual exploitation on the other. Each of us favors an arrangement in which our fellow citizens pay for our benefits.

With these brief descriptions of the cast of characters in hand, let us proceed.

TAMMANY HALL GOES
TO WASHINGTON

What should we expect from a legislative body composed of individuals whose first priority is their continued tenure in office? We should expect, first, that the normal activities of its members are those calculated to enhance their chances of reelection. And we should expect, second, that the members would devise and maintain institutional arrangements which facilitate their electoral activities. . . .

For most of the twentieth century, congressmen have engaged in a mix of three kinds of activities: lawmaking, pork barreling, and casework. Congress is first and foremost a lawmaking body, at least according to constitutional theory. In every postwar session Congress "considers" thousands of bills and resolutions, many hundreds of which are brought to a record vote (over 500 in each chamber in the 93rd Congress). Naturally the critical consideration in taking a position for the record is the maximization of approval in the home district. If the district is unaffected by and unconcerned with the matter at hand, the congressman may then take into account the general welfare of the country. (This sounds cynical, but remember that "profiles in courage" are sufficiently rare that their occurrence inspires books and articles.) Abetted by political scientists of the pluralist school, politicians have propounded an ideology which maintains that the good of the country on any given issue is simply what is best for a majority of congressional districts. This ideology provides a philosophical justification for what congressmen do while acting in their own self-interest.

A second activity favored by congressmen consists of efforts to bring home the bacon to their districts. Many popular articles have been written about the pork barrel, a term originally applied to rivers and harbors legislation but now generalized to cover all manner of federal largesse. Congressmen consider new dams, federal buildings, sewage treatment plants, urban renewal projects, etc. as sweet plums to be plucked. Federal projects are highly visible, their economic impact is easily detected by constituents, and sometimes they even produce something of value to the district. The average constituent may have some trouble translating his congressman's vote on some civil rights issue into a change in his personal welfare. But the workers hired and supplies purchased in connection with a big federal project provide benefits that are widely appreciated. The historical importance congressmen attach to the pork barrel is reflected in the rules of the House. That body accords certain classes of legislation "privileged" status: they may come directly to the floor without passing through the Rules Committee, a traditional graveyard for legislation. What kinds of legislation are privileged? Taxing and spending bills, for one: the government's power to raise and spend money must be kept relatively unfettered. But in addition, the omnibus rivers and harbors bills of the Public Works Committee and public lands bills from the Interior Committee share privileged status. The House will allow a civil rights or defense procurement or environmental bill to languish in the Rules Committee, but it takes special precautions to insure that nothing slows down the approval of dams and irrigation projects.

A third major activity takes up perhaps as much time as the other two combined. Traditionally, constituents appeal to their congressman for myriad favors and services. Sometimes only information is needed, but often constituents request that their congressman intervene in the internal workings of federal agencies to affect a decision in a favorable way, to reverse an adverse decision, or simply to speed up the glacial bureaucratic process. On the basis of extensive personal interviews with congressmen, Charles Clapp writes:

> Denied a favorable ruling by the bureaucracy on a matter of direct concern to him, puzzled or irked by delays in obtaining a decision, confused by the administrative maze through which he is directed to proceed, or ignorant of whom to write, a constituent may turn to his congressman for help. These letters offer great potential for political benefit to the congressman since they affect the constituent personally. If the legislator can be of assistance, he may gain a firm ally; if he is indifferent, he may even lose votes.

Actually congressmen are in an almost unique position in our system, a position shared only with high-level members of the executive branch. Congressmen possess the power to expedite and influence bureaucratic decisions. This capability flows directly from congressional control over what bureaucrats value most: higher budgets and new program authorizations. In a very real sense each congressman is a monopoly supplier of bureaucratic unsticking services for his district.

Every year the federal budget passes through the appropriations committees of Congress. Generally these committees make perfunctory cuts. But on occasion they vent displeasure on an agency and leave it bleeding all over the Capitol. The most extreme case of which I am aware came when the House committee took away the entire budget of the Division of Labor Standards in 1947 (some of the budget was restored elsewhere in the appropriations process). Deep and serious cuts are made occasionally, and the threat of such cuts keeps most agencies attentive to congressional wishes. Professors Richard Fenno and Aaron Wildavsky have provided extensive documentary and interview evidence of the great respect (and even terror) federal bureaucrats show for the House Appropriations Committee. Moreover, the bureaucracy must keep coming back to Congress to have its old programs reauthorized and new ones added. Again, most such decisions are perfunctory, but exceptions are sufficiently frequent that bureaucrats do not forget the basis of their agencies' existence. For example, the Law Enforcement Assistance Administration (LEAA) and the Food Stamps Program had no easy time of it this last Congress (94th). The bureaucracy needs congressional approval in order to survive, let alone expand. Thus, when a congressman calls about some minor bureaucratic decision or regulation, the bureaucracy considers his accommodation a small price to pay for the goodwill its cooperation will produce, particularly if he has any connection to the sub-stantive committee or the appropriations subcommittee to which it reports.

From the standpoint of capturing voters, the congressman's lawmaking activities differ in two important respects from his pork-barrel and casework activities. First, programmatic actions are inherently controversial. Unless his district is homogeneous, a congressman will find his district divided on many major issues. Thus when he casts a vote, introduces a piece of nontrivial leg-islation, or makes a speech with policy content he will displease some elements of his district. Some constituents may applaud the congressman's civil rights record, but others believe integration is going too fast. Some support foreign aid, while others believe it's money poured down a rathole. Some advocate economic equality, others stew over welfare cheaters. On such policy matters the congressman can expect to make friends as well as enemies. Presumably he will behave so as to maximize the excess of the former over the latter, but nevertheless a policy stand will generally make some enemies.

In contrast, the pork barrel and casework are relatively less controversial. New federal projects bring jobs, shiny new facilities, and general economic prosperity, or so people believe. Snipping ribbons at the dedication of a new post office or dam is a much more pleasant pursuit than disposing of a consti-tutional amendment on abortion. Republicans and Democrats, conservatives and liberals, all generally prefer a richer district to a poorer one. Of course, in recent years the river damming and stream-bed straightening activities of the Army Corps of Engineers have aroused some opposition among environmen-talists. Congressmen happily reacted by absorbing the opposition and adding environmentalism to the pork barrel: water treatment plants are currently a hot congressional item.

Casework is even less controversial. Some poor, aggrieved constituent be-comes enmeshed in the tentacles of an evil bureaucracy and calls upon Con-gressman St. George to do battle with the dragon. Again Clapp writes;

> A person who has a reasonable complaint or query is regarded as providing an opportunity rather than as adding an extra burden to an already busy office. The party affiliation of the individual even when known to be different from that of the congressman does not normally act as a deterrent to action. Some legislators have built their reputations and their majorities on a program of service to all constituents irrespective of party. Regularly, voters affiliated with the opposition in other contests lend strong support to the lawmaker whose intervention has helped them in their struggle with the bureaucracy.

Even following the revelation of sexual improprieties, Wayne Hays won his Ohio Democratic primary by a two-to-one margin. According to a *Los Angeles Times* feature story, Hays's constituency base was built on a foundation of per-sonal service to constituents:

They receive help in speeding up bureaucratic action on various kinds of federal assistance—black lung benefits to disabled miners and their families, Social Security payments, veterans' benefits and passports.

Some constituents still tell with pleasure of how Hays stormed clear to the seventh floor of the State Department and into Secretary of State Dean Rusk's office to demand, successfully, the quick issuance of a passport to an Ohioan.

Practicing politicians will tell you that word of mouth is still the most effective mode of communication. News of favors to constituents gets around and no doubt is embellished in the process.

In sum, when considering the benefits of his programmatic activities, the congressman must tote up gains and losses to arrive at a net profit. Pork barreling and casework, however, are basically pure profit.

A second way in which programmatic activities differ from casework and the pork barrel is the difficulty of assigning responsibility to the former as compared with the latter. No congressman can seriously claim that he is responsible for the 1964 Civil Rights Act, the ABM, or the 1972 Revenue Sharing Act. Most constituents do have some vague notion that their congressman is only one of hundreds and their senator one of an even hundred. Even committee chairmen may have a difficult time claiming credit for a piece of major legislation, let alone a rank-and-file congressman. Ah, but casework, and the pork barrel. In dealing with the bureaucracy, the congressman is not merely one vote of 435. Rather, he is a nonpartisan power, someone whose phone calls snap an office to attention. He is not kept on hold. The constituent who receives aid believes that his congressman and his congressman alone got results. Similarly, congressmen find it easy to claim credit for federal projects awarded their districts. The congressman may have instigated the proposal for the project in the first place, issued regular progress reports, and ultimately announced the award through his office. Maybe he can't claim credit for the 1965 Voting Rights Act, but he can take credit for Littletown's spanking new sewage treatment plant.

Overall then, programmatic activities are dangerous (controversial), on the one hand, and programmatic accomplishments are difficult to claim credit for, on the other. While less exciting, casework and pork barreling are both safe and profitable. For a reelection-oriented congressman the choice is obvious.

The key to the rise of the Washington establishment (and the vanishing marginals) is the following observation: *the growth of an activist federal government has stimulated a change in the mix of congressional activities.* Specifically, a lesser proportion of congressional effort is now going into programmatic activities and a greater proportion into pork-barrel and casework activities. As a result, today's congressmen make relatively fewer enemies and relatively more friends among the people of their districts.

To elaborate, a basic fact of life in twentieth-century America is the growth of the federal role and its attendant bureaucracy. Bureaucracy is the characteristic mode of delivering public goods and services. Ceteris paribus, the more the government attempts to do for people, the more extensive a bureaucracy it creates. As the scope of government expands, more and more citizens find themselves in direct contact with the federal government. Consider the rise in such contacts upon passage of the Social Security Act, work relief projects and other New Deal programs. Consider the millions of additional citizens touched by the veterans' programs of the postwar period. Consider the untold numbers whom the Great Society and its aftermath brought face to face with the federal government. In 1930 the federal bureaucracy was small and rather distant from the everyday concerns of Americans. By 1975 it was neither small nor distant.

As the years have passed, more and more citizens and groups have found themselves dealing with the federal bureaucracy. They may be seeking positive actions—eligibility for various benefits and awards of government grants. Or they may be seeking relief from the costs imposed by bureaucratic regulations—on working conditions, racial and sexual quotas, market restrictions, and numerous other subjects. While not malevolent, bureaucracies make mistakes, both of commission and omission, and normal attempts at redress often meet with unresponsiveness and inflexibility and sometimes seeming incorrigibility. Whatever the problem, the citizen's congressman is a source of succor. The greater the scope of government activity, the greater the demand for his services.

Private monopolists can regulate the demand for their product by raising or lowering the price. Congressmen have no such (legal) option. When the demand for their services rises, they have no real choice except to meet that demand—to supply more bureaucratic unsticking services—so long as they would rather be elected than unelected. This vulnerability to escalating constituency demands is largely academic, though. I seriously doubt that congressmen resist their gradual transformation from national legislators to errand boy-ombudsmen. As we have noted, casework is all profit. Congressmen have buried proposals to relieve the casework burden by establishing a national ombudsman or Congressman Reuss's proposed Administrative Counsel of the Congress. One of the congressmen interviewed by Clapp stated:

> Before I came to Washington I used to think that it might be nice if the individual states had administrative arms here that would take care of necessary liaison between citizens and the national government. But a congressman running for reelection is interested in building fences by providing personal services. The system is set to reelect incumbents regardless of party, and incumbents wouldn't dream of giving any of this service function away to any subagency. As an elected member I feel the same way.

In fact, it is probable that at least some congressmen deliberately stimulate the demand for their bureaucratic fixit services. (See [Figure A].) Recall that the new Republican in district A travels about his district saying:

> I'm your man in Washington. What are your problems? How can I help you?

NEED HELP WITH A FEDERAL PROBLEM?

Please feel free to communicate with me in person by phone or by mail. Daily from 9 a.m. until 5 p.m. my Congressional District office in Fullerton is open to serve you and your family. The staff will be able to help you with information or assistance on proposed Federal legislation and procedures of Federal agencies. If you are experiencing a problem with Social Security, educational assistance, Veterans Administration, Immigration, Internal Revenue Service, Postal Service, Environmental Protection Agency, Federal Energy Office or any other Federal agency please contact me through this office. If you decide to write to me please provide a telephone number as many times I can call you with information within a day or two.

CONGRESSMAN CHARLES E. WIGGINS
Brashears Center, Suite 103
1400 N. Harbor Boulevard
Fullerton, Ca 92635 (714) 870-7266

My Washington address is
Room 2445 Rayburn Building, Washington, D.C.
20515. Telephone (202) 225-4111.

U S. House of Representatives
WASHINGTON D C 20515
PUBLIC DOCUMENT
OFFICIAL BUSINESS

Charles E. Wiggins
M.C.

POSTAL CUSTOMER - LOCAL
39th District
CALIFORNIA

Figure A   How the Congressman-as-Ombudsman Drums up Business

And in district B, did the demand for the congressman's services rise so much between 1962 and 1964 that a "regiment" of constituency staff became necessary? Or, having access to the regiment, did the new Democrat stimulate the demand to which he would apply his regiment?

In addition to greatly increased casework, let us not forget that the growth of the federal role has also greatly expanded the federal pork barrel. The creative pork barreler need not limit himself to dams and post offices—rather old-fashioned interests. Today, creative congressmen can cadge LEAA money for the local police, urban renewal and housing money for local politicians, educational program grants for the local education bureaucracy. And there are sewage treatment plants, worker training and retraining programs, health services, and programs for the elderly. The pork barrel is full to overflowing. The conscientious congressman can stimulate applications for federal assistance (the sheer number of programs makes it difficult for local officials to stay current with the possibilities), put in a good word during consideration, and announce favorable decisions amid great fanfare.

In sum, everyday decisions by a large and growing federal bureaucracy bestow significant tangible benefits and impose significant tangible costs. Congressmen can affect these decisions. Ergo, the more decisions the bureaucracy has the opportunity to make, the more opportunities there are for the congressman to build up credits.

The nature of the Washington system is now quite clear. Congressmen (typically the majority Democrats) earn electoral credits by establishing various federal programs (the minority Republicans typically earn credits by fighting the good fight). The legislation is drafted in very general terms; so some agency, existing or newly established, must translate a vague policy mandate into a functioning program, a process that necessitates the promulgation of numerous rules and regulations and, incidentally, the trampling of numerous toes. At the next stage, aggrieved and/or hopeful constituents petition their congressman to intervene in the complex (or at least obscure) decision processes of the bureaucracy. The cycle closes when the congressman lends a sympathetic ear, piously denounces the evils of bureaucracy, intervenes in the latter's decisions, and rides a grateful electorate to ever more impressive electoral showings. Congressmen take credit coming and going. They are the alpha and the omega.

The popular frustration with the permanent government in Washington is partly justified, but to a considerable degree it is misplaced resentment. *Congress is the linchpin of the Washington establishment.* The bureaucracy serves as a convenient lightning rod for public frustration and a convenient whipping boy for congressmen. But so long as the bureaucracy accommodates congressmen, the latter will oblige with ever larger budgets and grants of authority. Congress does not just react to big government—it creates it. All of Washington prospers. More and more bureaucrats promulgate more and more regulations and dispense more and more money. Fewer and fewer congressmen suffer electoral defeat. Elements of the electorate benefit from government programs, and all of the electorate is eligible for ombudsman services. But the general, long-term welfare of the United States is no more than an incidental by-product of the system.

Committee Chairmen as Part of the Washington Establishment

In 1885 Woodrow Wilson was able to state categorically in his famous work *Congressional Government:*

> The leaders of the House are the chairmen of the principal Standing Committees. Indeed, to be exactly accurate, the House has as many leaders as there are subjects of legislation; for there are as many Standing Committees as there are leading classes of legislation, and in the consideration of every topic of business the House is guided by a special leader in the person of the chairman of the Standing Committee, charged with the superintendence of measures of the particular class to which that topic belongs. It is this multiplicity of leaders, this many-headed leadership, which makes the organization of the House too complex to afford uninformed people and unskilled observers any easy clue to its methods of rule. For the chairmen

of the Standing Committees do not constitute a cooperative body like a ministry. They do not consult and concur in the adoption of homogeneous and mutually helpful measures; there is no thought of acting in concert. Each Committee goes its own way at its own pace. It is impossible to discover any unity or method in the disconnected and therefore unsystematic, confused, and desultory action of the House, or any common purpose in the measures which its Committees from time to time recommend.

With regard to the Senate he noted:

It has those same radical defects of organization which weaken the House. Its functions also, like those of the House, are segregated in the prerogatives of numerous Standing Committees. In this regard Congress is all of a piece. There is in the Senate no more opportunity than exists in the House for gaining such recognized party leadership as would be likely to enlarge a man by giving him a sense of power, and to steady and sober him by filling him with a grave sense of responsibility. So far as its organization controls it, the Senate . . . proceedings bear most of the characteristic features of committee rule.

The Legislative Reorganization Act of 1946 was designed to streamline congressional committee structure and provide committees and individual congressmen with increased expert staff; however, although the number of standing committees was reduced, subcommittees have increased so that the net numerical reduction is not as great as was originally intended. Further, because Congress still conducts its business through committees: (1) the senior members of the party with the majority in Congress dominate the formulation of public policy through the seniority rule; (2) policy formulation is fragmented, with each committee maintaining relative dominance over policy areas within its jurisdiction; (3) stemming from this fragmentation, party control is weakened, especially when the president attempts to assume legislative dominance.

Although Congress is often pictured as powerless in confrontation with the executive branch, the fact is that the chairmen of powerful congressional committees often dominate administrative agencies over which they have jurisdiction. They are an important part of the broad Washington establishment. This is particularly true of the chairmen of appropriations committees and subcommittees; because of their control of the purse-strings, they are able to wield far more influence over the bureaucracy than are the chairmen of other committees. The appropriations committees have a direct weapon—money—that they can wield against administrative adversaries. And, the chairmen of all committees have seniority that often exceeds that of the bureaucrats with whom they are dealing. The secretaries and assistant secretaries of executive departments are political appointments who rarely stay in government more than two years, whereas powerful congressmen have been around for one or more decades. This gives the congressmen expertise that the political levels of the bureaucracy often lack. Political appointees in the bureaucracy must rely upon their professional staff in order to match the expertise of senior congressmen. The power of the chairmen of the appropriations committees often leads them to interfere directly in administrative operations. They become, in effect, part of the bureaucracy, often dominating it and determining what programs it will implement. The constant interaction between committee chairmen and agencies results in "government without passing laws," to use the phrase of Michael W. Kirst. (See Michael W. Kirst, *Government Without Passing Laws,* Chapel Hill: University of North Carolina Press, 1969.) The following selection deals with this process of legislative influence and describes how one senior Southern congressman established himself as the "permanent secretary of agriculture."[1]

52

Nick Kotz
JAMIE WHITTEN, PERMANENT SECRETARY OF AGRICULTURE

With the sensitive instincts of a successful career bureaucrat, Dr. George Irving scanned the list of states scheduled for the National Nutrition Survey, which was to measure the extent of hunger in America. Halfway down the column his glance froze, and he quickly dialed Congressman Jamie Whitten, the man known in Washington as the "permanent secretary of agriculture."

"Mr. Chairman, they've got Mississippi on that malnutrition study list, and I thought you'd want to know about it," dutifully reported Irving, Administrator of the Agriculture Department's Agricultural Research Service.

For the better part of eighteen years as chairman of the House Appropriations Subcommittee on Agriculture, dapper Jamie L. Whitten has held an iron

---

[1]The selection deals with Mississippi Congressman Jamie Whitten, who has moved into the most powerful position in the House of Representatives since the piece was written—the chairmanship of the Appropriations Committee. At the same time he has retained his position as Chairman of the Appropriations Subcommittee on Agriculture.

From the book *Let Them Eat Promises* by Nick Kotz. © 1969. Used by permission of the publisher, Prentice-Hall, Inc., Englewood Cliffs, NJ.

hand over the budget of the Department of Agriculture (USDA). The entire 107,000-man department is tuned in to the Mississippi legislator's every whim.

"George, we're not going to have another smear campaign against Mississippi, are we?" declared Whitten to his informant. "You boys should be thinking about a *national* survey—and do some studies in Watts and Hough and Harlem!"

Dr. Irving alerted the government's food aid network. "Mr. Whitten wants Mississippi taken off that list," he told Department of Agriculture food administrator Rodney Leonard.

Leonard, in turn, called Dr. George Silver, a Deputy Assistant Secretary of Health, Education, and Welfare, who was responsible for the joint USDA-HEW malnutrition survey.

"Jamie Whitten's found out Mississippi is on the list and is raising hell. I think we'd better drop it," Leonard said.

Silver, recalling HEW Secretary Wilbur Cohen's order to "avoid unnecessary political friction" in choosing the sample states for the hunger survey, called Dr. Arnold Schaefer, the project chief.

"Mississippi's out—politics!" Silver said curtly.

Back at the Department of Agriculture, food administrator Leonard snapped at Jamie Whitten's informant, "You couldn't have killed the project any better if you had planned it!"

Thus, in August, 1967, the Johnson Administration's first meaningful attempt to ascertain the facts about hunger in Mississippi was stopped cold by an executive department's fear of one congressman. This kind of bureaucratic-congressional maneuvering, exercised between the lines of the law, is little understood, seldom given public scrutiny, and far too infrequently challenged. In the quiet process of hidden power, a bureaucrat in the Agriculture Department reacts more quickly to a raised eyebrow from Jamie Whitten than to a direct order from the Secretary himself. Time after time, a few words from Jamie Whitten can harden into gospel at the Department of Agriculture. Indeed, a casual Whitten statement may be so magnified, as it is whispered from official to official, that the response is more subservient than even the Congressman had in mind.

The stocky, 59-year-old Congressman is not shy about his meteoric rise from a country store in Tallahatchie County to a key position in the nation's capital. And his record is impressive—trial lawyer and state legislator at 21, district attorney for five counties at 23, U.S. Congressman at 31 (in 1941), and chairman of an appropriations subcommittee at 36. His steely self-confidence, studied informality, and carefully conservative clothes suggest anything but the stereotype of country-lawyer-come-to-Washington. Only the beginning of a paunch detracts from a physical sense of strength and energy that radiates from Jamie Whitten.

For all his dynamic presence, Whitten has a way of confounding a listener—or potential critic—with silky Southern rhetoric. It is a test of mental agility to remember the original course of a conversation, as one high USDA official noted: "When you check on things with him, Whitten can go all around the barn with you. Often-times you don't fully understand what he meant. So you latch onto the most obvious point you can find and act on that."

With his implicit power, Whitten doesn't *have* to threaten or be specific. In fact, as George Irving pointed out about his conversation with the Congressman that led to dropping Mississippi from the national hunger survey, "He wasn't saying 'don't go to Mississippi,' he was just suggesting that we think about other places."

Bureaucratic officials who are familiar with Whitten's oblique way of expressing his ideas know also that the Mississippian can rattle off complicated economic statistics and arguments with precise logic and organized thought.

Whitten legally holds the power of the purse, and he exercises it shrewdly. His appropriations subcommittee doles out funds for every item in the Agriculture Department's $7 billion budget, and it does not take long for Washington bureaucrats to realize that the chairman's wrath can destroy precious projects and throw hundreds of people out of jobs.

"He's got the most phenomenal information and total recall," one Agriculture official says of Whitten. "Once you fully understand his do's and don't's and establish rapport with him, life is a whole lot easier!"

Jamie Whitten's considerable power is enhanced by his scholarship. He is a conscientious student of every line of the Agriculture budget, and his hawk's-eye is legendary among Department officials. They, in turn, anticipate his scrutiny by checking planned moves with him, thus extending to him a virtual veto on the most minute details. "A suggestion, that's all you have to have in this business," admitted Rodney Leonard.

The key to this phenomenal power—which goes beyond that of budget control—lies in Whitten's network of informants within the Department, and his skill directing their activities and operations. Executive branch officials learn to protect their own jobs, adjusting their loyalties to the legislative branch in a way the Founding Fathers may not have envisioned when they devised their splendid system of checks and balances. Bureaucratic allies of a particular congressman may be able to inject that congressman's political views (or their own) into laws or programs sponsored by the Administration without the consent, or even the knowledge, of the Department head. Secretaries of Agriculture come and go, but Jamie Whitten remains, a product of Mississippi's political oligarchy and the seniority system in Congress.

In theory, an appropriations subcommittee only considers requests for funds to finance programs already approved by Congress. Thus, Whitten shares some power with Bob Poage (D-Tex.), chairman of the House Agriculture Committee. In actuality, a skillful chairman such as Whitten can control policy, alter the original authorizing legislation, and wind up virtually controlling the administration of a department.

In addition to Chairman Whitten, the Agriculture Appropriations Subcommittee has seven members: Democrats William H. Natcher of Kentucky,

W. R. Hull, Jr., of Missouri, George Shipley of Illinois, and Frank Evans of Colorado, and Republicans Odin Langen of Minnesota, Robert H. Michel of Illinois, and Jack Edwards of Alabama. Because a majority of these members share Whitten's outlook on agriculture and his arch-conservative view of social action, the chairman's will becomes the subcommittee's will. As chairman, he also has a hold over staff appointments.

Much of Whitten's power derives from the system within the House of Representatives. Once a subcommittee makes a decision, the full House Appropriations Committee almost always backs it up. This is particularly true with agriculture appropriations, because House Appropriations Chairman George Mahon (D-Tex.) shares Whitten's views on farm policy, welfare spending, and racial issues. For years, Whitten has been in absolute control of all bills before his subcommittee, from the first markup session to the final House vote. "The lines in my face would be deeper except for you" Mahon inscribed on his own portrait in the Mississippian's office.

The House at large rarely has challenged Agriculture budgets because most non-farmbloc members find the subject too complex or dull and rarely take the trouble to inform themselves about it. If some members, or the public, are roused to the point where a challenge develops, the House's committee chairmen generally pull together to defeat the move. Committee members follow to ensure that they will have the chairman's support for their own pet bills—and to keep sacrosanct the whole system of mutual support and protection.

If a challenge happens to get out of hand, the first commandment of a subcommittee chairman is "Never let yourself in for a battle on the House floor if there is any chance for defeat." Part of the power of the chairman stems from his apparent invincibility—and the image must be preserved! Therefore, Whitten went along with the Nixon Administration's full budget request for food aid in 1969, knowing there was sufficient pressure for a much bigger appropriation. Whitten responded here only to the politics of the issue, not the substance, for he still complained to Senator George McGovern that hunger was not a problem, that "Nigras won't work" if you give them free food, and that McGovern was promoting revolution by continuing to seek free food stamps for the poorest Americans.

Where agriculture legislation is concerned, Whitten must share power in some measure with Senator Spessard Holland, a Florida Democrat who chairs the Senate Appropriations Subcommittee on Agriculture. Holland is a blunt man who insists that Section 32 funds—food dollars from customs receipts—should be held in reserve to be used at the proper time to boost prices for his state's citrus, vegetable, and beef industries. When Whitten and Holland act in unison—as they often do—the results are predictable. After the School Lunch Act was liberalized in 1964, they managed to refuse funding free school lunches for more than two years. The Johnson administration had sought only $2–3 million to help some of the estimated 5 million poor children who got no benefits from the lunch program, but all the funds were held back in committee until Senator Philip Hart (D-Mich.) threatened to take the fight to the floor.

Jamie Whitten's power is greater than Holland's, however, not only because appropriations usually originate in the House, but also because in the smaller body of the Senate there is less hesitation to overturn subcommittee decisions than in the tradition-bound House of Representatives. The House system, therefore, assures more *inherent* power for its subcommittee chairmen, and Jamie Whitten has been vigorous and skillful in pursuing it.

GETTING ALONG WITH WHITTEN

Even the Secretary himself feels he must bend to the power of the "permanent secretary." When a delegation headed by Richard Boone of the Citizens' Crusade Against Poverty had asked Orville Freeman to provide free stamps and commodities to help the hungry in Mississippi, the Secretary told them: "I've got to get along with two people in Washington—the President and Jamie Whitten. How can you help me with Whitten?"

Just back from a study of hunger in Mississippi in April, 1967, Dr. Robert Coles and three other doctors also found out about Whitten's influence when they appealed to Orville Freeman. They walked into the Secretary's office feeling that they would be welcomed as helpful, authoritative reporters of the facts, and they left feeling that they had been tagged as troublemakers.

"We were told that we and all the hungry children we had examined and all the other hungry Americans would have to reckon with Mr. Jamie L. Whitten, as indeed must the Secretary of Agriculture, whose funds come to him through the kindness of the same Mr. Whitten. We were told of the problems that the Agriculture Department has with Congress, and we left feeling we ought to weigh those problems as somehow of the same order as the problems we had met in the South—and that we know from our work elsewhere existed all over the country," recalled Coles.

Whitten's power goes beyond the secretary to the presidency itself. In the last year of his administration, President Johnson steadily refused to adopt proposals for broadened food aid that were drafted within his administration. Johnson was then trying to get his income surtax bill through the Congress, and he needed the support of Whitten and the rest of the small group of Southern hierarchs. Johnson declined to risk possible loss of critical votes on the war- and inflation-related surtax.

When Senator Jacob Javits (R-N.Y.) asked Agriculture Secretary Freeman, "What are you afraid of in Mississippi?" (at a July, 1967, hearing on hunger in Mississippi), he wanted to know why Freeman would not modify the food program to reach more of the hungry in Mississippi and elsewhere. The only response he got was ex-marine Freeman's outthrust jaw and a growl that he was not afraid of anyone and would not be intimidated.

Nevertheless, faced with Jamie Whitten's power over his department, and fed information by a Whitten-conscious bureaucracy, Freeman had failed for two years to take measures to feed more of the hungry poor in America. Moreover, the Secretary had stubbornly refused to acknowledge the chasm between his department's efforts and the real needs of the hungry.

From Freeman on down, every Agriculture Department official knew that hunger spelled "hound dog" to Jamie Whitten.

"You've got to understand how Jamie feels about 'hound dog' projects," a career official explained. (In Southern country jargon, a "hound dog" is always hanging around, useless, waiting to be thrown scraps.) Years before, the chairman had killed a small pilot project to teach unemployed Southern Negroes how to drive tractors. "Now, that's a 'hound dog' project, and I don't want to see any more of them" he had said.

Whitten's opposition to any program resembling social welfare—or aid to Negroes—contributed to the failure of War on Poverty programs for rural America. When President Johnson signed an executive order, giving the Agriculture Department responsibility for coordinating the rural war on poverty, Secretary Freeman created a Rural Community Development Service (RCDS) to give the Department a focal point for helping the poor. It was designed to coordinate programs meeting all the needs of the rural poor—housing, education, water, food—not only within the Agriculture Department, but throughout the federal government.

Within a year, the Rural Community Development Service was dead. "Whitten thought the Service smacked of social experimentation and civil rights," a Department of Agriculture official said. In addition, Whitten's brother-in-law, one of many cronies who have filled Agriculture jobs over the years, had clashed with Robert G. Lewis, the idealistic Wisconsin progressive who headed the program. Whitten simply cut off the funds and pigeonholed the coordinating powers of RCDS by placing the responsibility with the docile, conservative Farmers Home Administration. Freeman never fought the issue. There were too many other matters, other appropriations, that were more important to him, so the embryonic effort to coordinate rural poverty programs through the Department of Agriculture ended as little more than a passing idea.

(By assigning the broad rural poverty responsibility to the Department of Agriculture, President Johnson, like President Nixon after him, indicated either a great naïveté about the Department or a lack of seriousness in his proposals. The four congressional committees with which Agriculture must deal undoubtedly are the least receptive of any in Congress to attempts to provide meaningful help to the hard-core rural poor.)

Jamie Whitten has wielded that kind of influence since the mid-1940s, when he killed an emerging Agriculture study that tried to anticipate the social and economic problems of Negro GI's returning from World War II to the feudal cotton South. At the time, the Mississippi Congressman was the youngest chairman of an appropriations subcommittee. By opposing all studies exploring the effects of a changing agriculture upon people, Whitten helped ensure that Agriculture's farm policy would never include serious consideration of the effects of its programs on sharecroppers or farm workers. Whitten and the other powerful Southern congressmen who share his views ensured that the Department would focus only on the cotton planter and his crop. As a result, farm policies that have consistently ignored their toll on millions of black poor have contributed to a rural-urban migration, to a civil rights revolution, and to the ruin of many Americans.

There is no doubt as to the motives of Whitten and the other congressmen who run the Agriculture Department. Testifying on the proposed food stamp law before the Senate Agriculture Committee in 1964, one Department official boldly suggested that it would not help those with little or no income. Committee Chairman Allen J. Ellender (D-La.) indignantly dismissed this complaint against the bill, revealing clearly his own legislative intent.

"I know that in my state we had a number of fishermen who were unable to catch fish," retorted Ellender. "Do you expect the government, because they cannot catch fish, to feed them until the fish are there? In other words, this food stamp program is not to be considered a program just simply to feed people because they cannot get work. This is not what it is supposed to be."

SURPLUS SERFS

What the food stamp program was "supposed to be" was a substitute for a free commodity program that had outlived its usefulness—to Southern plantation owners. Surplus commodities—barely enough to live on—were distributed in the winter when work ceased on the Mississippi plantation of Senator James Eastland (D-Miss.) and on the huge Texas ranches. In the spring, when the $3-a-day planting jobs opened up, the food aid ended. The federal government eased the planter's responsibility by keeping his workers alive during the winter, then permitted the counties that administered the program to withdraw that meager support during planting season—forcing the workers to accept near-starvation wages for survival. When the rural serfs were no longer needed, having been slowly replaced by machines, even that support vanished as the government stopped free commodities in favor of food stamps, which the poorest rural people could not afford. As counties throughout the nation changed from commodities to food stamps, participation fell off by 40 percent; more than 1 million persons, including 100,000 in Mississippi, were forced to drop out of the food program. Whispers of "planned starvation" emerged from the economic crisis of 1967, when the combination of production cutbacks in cotton, automated machinery, and the end of free commodities left the Deep South with thousands of blacks who were unneeded—and hungry. The decisions of the white supremacists in Congress, supported by the subservient Department of Agriculture, contributed to that result.

Whitten's decisions are not always understood by the uninitiated. With his wily ability to juggle figures and cloud ideas, Whitten convinces officials unfamiliar with his technique (and lacking intimate knowledge of the facts) that he is quite a reasonable man—especially when the conversation turns to hunger and the food programs. As he tells it, he was a pioneer on the nutrition issue.

In 1950, he fought for funds for a Department of Agriculture cookbook, and he warned the House it had better concern itself with human as well as animal health. To this day, Whitten insists that the Agriculture Department keep the book in print; he sends a free copy to newlyweds in his district.

The subcommittee chairman also denies that he paralyzed Freeman on the hunger issue: "I *helped* the Secretary by making two points with him," Whitten insists. "I told him he had to charge people what they were accustomed to paying for food stamps because that's what the law says. And I pointed out to him that the law forbids selling food stamps and distributing commodities in the same counties." By making these two helpful points, Whitten blocked the most feasible emergency measures.

"Why, I gave him more money for those food programs than he could spend!" said Whitten.

Actually, the hopelessly inadequate $45 million for food programs Whitten "gave" to Freeman was fought, bought, and paid for by the administration and congressional liberals; this was what was left after Whitten and Holland whittled down the original $100 million, three-year authorization won by liberals on the House floor.

Whitten's explanations of food programs may have appeared perfectly reasonable to Freeman, Sargent Shriver, and many members of Congress, but their total impact was to stop any reform that would get food to the hungry. His own strongly held view is that the food programs should serve the farm programs, not vice versa, and his actions over the years have halted any kind of aid the Agriculture Department might have directed toward the poor. In the early 1960s, when the Kennedy Administration was momentarily concerned for the poor of Appalachia, Agriculture found a way to provide housing grants to aid the hardest-core poor; but once Whitten discovered the grant program in operation, he killed all further appropriations for it.

A few years later, a new cotton program provided advance payments to cotton farmers for withdrawing some of their acreage from production. Sharecroppers, who provided most of the cotton labor force, were supposed to receive their "share" of government payments for idle land. With Whitten's inspiration or blessing, Agriculture adopted a regulation permitting the plantation owner to deduct from the sharecropper's government payments the amount he claimed was owed for the sharecropper's rent, farming expenses, etc. Under the feudal system of the plantation, however, the sharecropper *never* had any legal guarantee that he would receive his fair share of profit for the crop he produced. Blacks who declined to turn over their checks were kicked off hundreds of plantations. The Agriculture Department did not halt the practice.

One of Whitten's sharecropper constituents, trying desperately to find food for her family, gave her own intuitive view of her congressman's attitudes: "He's probably with the bossman's side, don't you know. He's with them. No one's with us but ourselves, and no matter how many of us there are, we don't have what they have."

WINE FOR MISSISSIPPI

Although much of the legislation he favors has enriched American agricultural business with government funds, Whitten's stock answer to any proposed liberalization of the Department of Agriculture food programs is that they are "food programs, not welfare programs." He is adamant about suggestions that food programs be moved to the more liberal Department of Health, Education, and Welfare. "Who'll see to it that [funds for food] don't go for frivolity and wine?" he asks.

Whitten's views on welfare, so strongly felt through the Department of Agriculture, are shared by many Americans. Yet when viewed against the background of Tallahatchie County and its social history, these views, and their interpretations through Agriculture programs, take on a different meaning. Since hunger means poverty, and poverty in Mississippi usually means black, any expanded aid to the hungry means one more threat to the socio-economic order in which the black worker has always been held in absolute dependency upon crumbs from the plantation owner.

The 100,000 or more black Mississippi farm workers who suddenly found themselves with nothing to hold onto in the winter of 1967 were little concerned with frivolity and wine. They had lost their sole supply of food, as Mississippi counties switched over from the inadequate but free surplus commodities to a food stamp program the poor could not afford. "No work, no money, and now, no food," was their outcry, and they desperately sought a reduction in the price of stamps at the very moment when Jamie Whitten was starting his annual review of the Department of Agriculture's budget, with its accompanying discourses on the nature of the poor man. He had heard, the chairman said, that "organized groups" sought to make food stamps free to the poor.

"This is one of the things you always run into," he said to Secretary Freeman. "You make stamps available at 30 percent discount; then they want them at 50, then 75. Now, I have heard reports that some of the organized minority groups are insisting they be provided free of charge. When you start giving people something for nothing, just giving them all they want for nothing, I wonder if you don't destroy character more than you might improve nutrition. I think more and more American people are coming to that conclusion."

They built a lot of character in Mississippi that winter, where the disruption caused by the abrupt changeover to food stamps contributed to the kind of wholesale destitution not seen in this country since the Great Depression.

But the chairman did not seem to think his black constituents were learning the character lesson well enough when it came to the school lunch and new school breakfast programs. Out of work and out of money, few Mississippi Negroes could afford to give their children 25 cents a day for a school lunch, and few schools provided the free lunches that the law technically required for the poor. Agriculture officials virtually begged that the special school lunch assistance budget be raised from $2 million to $10 million annually to give meals to an added 360,000 children in poor areas. Whitten expressed concern only about the impact of civil rights sanctions as he slashed the request by two-thirds.

When another project—a requested million dollars for a pilot school break-fast program to help the neediest youngsters—came up, Whitten's patience wore thin. "Do you contemplate having a pilot dinner program—evening meals—called supper where I grew up?" Whitten asked sarcastically.

When Agriculture Department officials explained that "a hungry child in the morning is not able to take full advantage of the schooling that is offered," Whitten wanted to know why the government should be supplying what the family should have supplied before the child left home.

"We all recognize that the type of home from which some children come affects them in many, many ways, but there is a problem always as to whether the federal government should start doing everything for the citizens. You may end up with a certain class of people doing nothing to help themselves. To strike a happy medium is always a real problem."

In this case, Whitten struck it by cutting all $6.5 million requested for breakfast funds from the budget.

Each time a group of doctors, team of reporters, or other investigators produced firsthand reports of hunger in the South, Whitten launched his own "investigation" and announced that parental neglect is largely responsible for any problems. In 1968, when the drive for a bigger food program began to gather steam nationally, Whitten sent out the FBI to disprove the evidence of the problem. The FBI men, who are assigned to the House Appropriations Committee, in effect intimidated people who had provided evidence of hunger.

When a private group investigating hunger, the Citizens' Board of Inquiry, reported after a lengthy investigation that "we have found concrete evidence of chronic hunger and malnutrition in every part of the United States where we have held hearings or conducted hearings," even the Pentagon rallied to the defense of Jamie Whitten's system. The Pentagon-financed Institute for Defense Analyses published an attack on the book *Hunger USA*,[1] which contained the Board of Inquiry report. The author of the defense document, Dr. Herbert Pollack, took the position that ignorance was at the root of any hunger problems in the United States—the same position taken by Whitten and his congressional allies.

---

[1]Citizen's Board of Inquiry. *Hunger USA* (Boston: Beacon Press, 1968).

The Mississippi Congressman demands that the poor, if they are to get any benefits, must prove they are hungry on a case-by-case basis. "The doctors have not submitted any names," he wrote one concerned Northern lady, assuring her that he would be "most sympathetic and helpful in trying to work this matter out."

Time after time, Whitten has requested names and addresses of the poor who complain of ill-treatment in his home state. Yet in Jamie Whitten's home county, the thought of having their names known strikes terror among those who have had dealings with the local officials.

A news team from television's Public Broadcast Laboratory (PBL), interviewing a black housewife in Whitten's home town of Charleston, felt the danger involved in "naming names." As Mrs. Metcalf began to explain why the food stamp and school lunch programs were not helping her family, a task force of sedans and panel trucks began to cruise back and forth on the U.S. highway about fifty yards from her plantation shack. Suddenly the trucks lunged off the highway into the shack's front yard, surrounding the television crew's two station wagons. A rifle or shotgun was mounted in the rear window of each truck.

"You're trespassing. Git!" growled the plantation manager as he pushed his way past the TV reporter and ordered Mrs. Metcalf to get outside the shack if she knew what was good for her.

"You were trespassing when you crossed the Mississippi state line," shouted Deputy Sheriff Buck Shaw as he ordered the PBL crew to clear out.

In an attempt to ensure Mrs. Metcalf's safety from the local "law," the reporter phoned Congressman Whitten in Washington.

"You remember when Martin Luther King went through my town!" the Congressman answered. "You read the *Wall Street Journal?* It said that he went through there and everybody turned out to look at him. And as soon as he left, they just turned over and went back to sleep. I just know, I live down there and I know, Good God, Chicago, Washington, Detroit. Every one of them would give any amount of money if they could go to sleep feeling as safe—both races—as my folks will!"

It wasn't so peaceful about three o'clock that afternoon with those hard-eyed men threatening Mrs. Metcalf, the reporter explained.

"I suspect Deputy Shaw's like I am," Whitten snapped. "They recognized when you crossed that state line you had no good intention in your mind. I'm no kingfish. I just know my people and my people get along. Unfortunately, you folks and the folks up here don't know how to get along. I bet you money if I ran tomorrow, and nobody voted except the colored people, I'd get the majority. I grew up where five or six of my closest neighbors were Negroes. We played together as kids. We swapped vegetables. Why, I grew up hugging my Momma, and my Momma hugging them."

There were as many Negroes as whites at his father's funeral, Whitten asserts—and he keeps on his desk a yellowed 1936 newspaper editorial that praised District Attorney Jamie Whitten for successfully prosecuting the white man who burned some Mississippi Negroes to death.

Against Whitten's statements about how he is respected by Negroes and would get their vote, about how close his relationship and understanding with Negroes has been, about how quiet and peaceful life is in Charleston, another point of view appeared, as one of his black constituents spoke on the same subject—rambling much as Jamie Whitten does. An eloquent, middle-aged woman told Dr. Robert Coles about the plantation owner for whom her husband works, about his wife, about food, and about life in America:

> He [the plantation owner] doesn't want us trying to vote and like that—and first I'd like to feed my kids, before I go trying to vote.
>
> His wife—the boss man's—she'll come over here sometimes and give me some extra grits and once or twice in the year some good bacon. She tells me we get along fine down here and I says "yes" to her. What else would I be saying, I ask you?
>
> But it's no good. The kids aren't eating enough, and you'd have to be wrong in the head, pure crazy to say they are. Sometimes we talk of leaving; but you know it's just no good up there either, we hear. They eat better, but they have bad things up there I hear, rats as big as raccoons I hear, and they bit my sister's kid real bad.
>
> It's no kind of country to be proud of, with all this going on—the colored people still having it so bad, and the kids being sick and there's nothing you can do about it.[2]

AFFECTION, NOT CASH

Whitten's affection for black constituents like this woman does not extend to federal measures to assist their lot in life. Of the 24,081 residents of Tallahatchie County, 18,000 have family incomes less than $3,000 a year, and 15,197 make less than $2,000. Of these thousands legally defined as poor, only 2,367 qualify for public assistance, and 6,710 receive food stamps. Only a few blocks from Whitten's own white frame home, Negroes live in shacks without toilets, running water, electricity—or food.

Whitten and his fellow white Mississippians point with great pride to the economic progress their state has made in recent years. Improved farming methods, conversion of marginal cropland to timber and other uses, and a strong soil bank program have greatly enriched the commercial farmer in Mississippi. Other government programs, including state tax inducements, have promoted wide industrialization, and rural white workers have found a new affluence in the hundreds of factories and small shops that have sprung up.

But the new farming has eliminated thousands of jobs for Negro plantation workers while the segregated social system denies them factory jobs. The able-

---

[2]Robert Coles and Harry Hughe, "We Need Help," *New Republic*, March 8, 1969.

bodied usually head north, leaving the very young, the very old, and the un-skilled to cope with "progress." The rural black does not share in the new prosperity of Mississippi, and some Negroes are worse off than at any time since the Depression. Indeed, in many parts of the Deep South the black man is literally being starved out by the new prosperity.

Perhaps the white Southern politician is no more to blame than are whites anywhere. But the white in the South could not afford to see the truth of the Negro's suffering, because to feel that truth would have shattered a whole way of life.

Jamie Whitten truly believes in his own fairness, his idea of good works, and the imagined affection he receives from Negroes back home. For fifty-nine years, he has anesthetized his soul to the human misery and indignity only a few yards from his own home and has refused to believe that the responsibility for that indignity lies on his white shoulders. His belief in the basic laziness, indifference, and unworthiness of the black poor is as strong as his belief in the virtues of a way of life that for three centuries has denied these same black poor any avenues of pursuing ambition, self-respect, or a better future for their children.

That Jamie Whitten should suffer from blindness to human need is one thing. But that he can use this blindness as an excuse to limit the destiny of millions of Americans is another matter, one which should concern anyone who believes in the basic strengths of this country's constitutional guarantees. The checks and balances of a reasonable democratic republic have gone com-pletely awry when a huge bureaucracy and the top officials of an Administration base their actions concerning deepest human need on their fearful perception of what one rather limited man seems to want.

The system of seniority and temerity that gives a man such as Jamie Whit-ten such awesome power must come under more serious public scrutiny if the American system of government is ever to establish itself on the basis of moral concern about the individual human being.

Congressmen as Political Entrepreneurs

Congress can be viewed from many perspectives. People elect Congress to serve their interests. Viewed from the outside, Congress is supposed to be a representative body responsive to popular demands. Another perspective is that of the separation of powers, which requires Congress to check the president.

From the perspective of Capitol Hill itself, Congress serves the incen-tives of its members. These are reelection, internal power and influence, and good public policy that motivate members in different ways. The framers of the Constitution were not the first to recognize that while politics *may* involve statesmanship it *always* reflects the quest for personal power. The constitutional system attempts to harness and channel political power in support of the national interest. But, argues a congressional scholar in the following selection, the perennial pursuit of personal power by members of Congress detracts from the ability of Congress as a whole to fulfill its institutional responsibilities.

53

Lawrence C. Dodd
CONGRESS AND THE QUEST FOR POWER

The postwar years have taught students of Congress a very fundamental lesson: Congress is a dynamic institution. The recent congressional changes picture an institution that is much like a kaleidoscope. At first glance the visual images and structural patterns appear frozen in a simple and comprehensible mosaic. Upon closer and longer inspection the realization dawns that the picture is subject to constant transformations. These transformations seem to flow naturally from the prior observations, yet the resulting mosaic is quite different and is not ordered by the same static principles used to interpret and understand the earlier one. The appreciation and understanding of the moving image requires not only comprehending the role of each colorful geometric object in a specific picture, nor developing a satisfactory interpretation of the principles underlying a specific picture or change in specific aspects of the picture, but grasping the dynamics underlying the structural transformations themselves. So it is with Congress. To understand and appreciate it as an institution we must focus not only on particular aspects of internal congressional structure and process, nor on changes in particular patterns. We must seek to understand the

From Lawrence C. Dodd and Bruce Oppenheimer (eds.), *Congress Reconsidered* (New York: Praeger Publishers, 1977), pp. 269–283. Reprinted by permission.

Author's Note: For critical assistance at various stages in the writing of this essay, I would like to thank Arnold Fleischmann, Michael N. Green, Bruce I. Oppenheimer, Diana Phillips, Russ Renka, Terry Sullivan, and numerous graduate and undergraduate students who shared with me their questions and insights.

more fundamental dynamics that produce the transformations in the congressional mosaic. This essay represents an attempt to explain the dynamics of congressional structure. . . .

I

As with politicians generally, members of Congress enter politics in a quest for personal power. This quest may derive from any number of deeper motives: a desire for ego gratification or for prestige, a search for personal salvation through good works, a hope to construct a better world or to dominate the present one, or a preoccupation with status and self-love. Whatever the source, most members of Congress seek to attain the power to control policy decisions that impose the authority of the state on the citizenry at large.

The most basic lesson that any member of Congress learns on entering the institution is that the quest for power by service within Congress requires reelection. First, reelection is necessary in order to remain in the struggle within Congress for "power positions." Staying in the struggle is important not only in that it provides the formal status as an elected representative without which an individual's influence on national legislative policy lacks legal authority; the quest for power through election and reelection also signals one's acceptance of the myth of democratic rule and thus one's acceptability as a power seeker who honors the society's traditional values. Second, reelection, particularly by large margins, helps create an aura of personal legitimacy. It indicates that one has a special mandate from the people, that one's position is fairly secure, that one will have to be "reckoned with." Third, long-term electoral success bestows on a member of Congress the opportunity to gain the experience and expertise, and to demonstrate the legislative skill and political prescience, that can serve to justify the exercise of power.

Because reelection is so important, and because it may be so difficult to ensure, its pursuit can become all-consuming. The constitutional system, electoral laws, and social system together have created political parties that are weak coalitions. A candidate for Congress normally must create a personal organization rather than rely on her or his political party. The "electoral connection" that intervenes between the desire for power and the realization of power may lead members to emphasize form over substance, position taking, advertising, and credit claiming rather than problem solving. In an effort to sustain electoral success, members of Congress may fail to take controversial and clear positions, fail to make hard choices, fail to exercise power itself. Yet members of Congress generally are not solely preoccupied with reelection. Most members have relatively secure electoral margins. This security stems partially from the fact that members of Congress *are* independent of political parties and are independent from responsibility for selecting the executive, and thus can be judged more on personal qualities than on partisan or executive affiliations. Electoral security is further reinforced because members of Congress personally control financial and casework resources that can help them build a loyalty from their constituents independent of policy or ideological considerations. The existence of secure electoral margins thus allows members to devote considerable effort toward capturing a "power position" within Congress and generating a mystique of special authority that is necessary to legitimize a select decision-making role for them in the eyes of their nominal peers.

The concern of members of Congress with gaining congressional power, rather than just securing reelection, has had a considerable influence on the structure and life of Congress. Were members solely preoccupied with reelection, we would expect them to spend little time in Washington and devote their personal efforts to constituent speeches and district casework. One would expect Congress to be run by a centralized, efficient staff who, in league with policy-oriented interest groups, would draft legislation, investigate the issues, frame palatable solutions, and present the members with the least controversial bills possible. Members of Congress would give little attention to committee work, and then only to committees that clearly served reelection interests. The primary activity of congresspeople in Congress, rather, would be extended, televised floor debates and symbolic roll call votes, all for show. Such a system would allow the appearance of work while providing ample opportunity for the mending of home fences. Alternatively, were only a few members of Congress concerned about power, with others concerned with reelection, personal finances, or private lives, one might expect a centralized system with a few leaders exercising power and all others spending their time on personal or electoral matters.

Virtually all members of the U.S. Congress are preoccupied with power considerations. They are unwilling—unless forced by external events—to leave the major decisions in either a centralized, autonomous staff system or a central leadership. Each member wants to exercise power—to make the key policy decisions. This motive places every member in a personal conflict with every other member: to the extent that one member realizes her or his goal personally to control all key decisions, all others must lose. Given this widespread power motive, an obvious way to resolve the conflict is to disperse power—or at least power positions—as widely as possible. One logical solution, in other words, is to place basic policy-making responsibility in a series of discrete and relatively autonomous committees and subcommittees, each having control over the decisions in a specified jurisdictional area. Each member can belong to a small number of committees and, within them, have a significant and perhaps dominant influence on policy. Although such a system denies every member the opportunity to control all policy decisions, it ensures that most members, particularly if they stay in Congress long enough to obtain a subcommittee or committee chair, and if they generate the mystique of special authority necessary to allow them to activate the power potential of their select position, can satisfy a portion of their power drive.

Within Congress, as one would expect in light of the power motive, the fundamental structure of organization is a committee system. Most members spend most of their time not in their district but in Washington, and most of their Washington time not on the floor in symbolic televised debate but rather in the committee or subcommittee rooms, in caucus meetings, or in office work devoted to legislation. While the staff, particularly the personal staff, may be relegated to casework for constituents, the members of Congress sit through hearing after hearing, debate after debate, vote after vote seeking to shape in subcommittee, committee, and floor votes the contours of legislation. This is not to suggest, of course, that members of Congress do not engage in symbolic action or personal casework and do not spend much time in the home district; they do, in their effort at reelection. Likewise, staff do draft legislation, play a strong role in committee investigations, and influence the direction of public policy; they do this, however, largely because members of Congress just do not have enough time in the day to fulfill their numerous obligations. Seen in this perspective, Congress is not solely, simply, or primarily a stage on which individuals intentionally and exclusively engage in meaningless charades. Whatever the end product of their effort may be, members of Congress have actively sought to design a congressional structure and process that would maximize their ability to exercise personal power within Congress and, through Congress, within the nation at large.

The congressional committee structure reflects rather naturally the various dimensions that characterize the making of public policy. There are *authorization* committees that create policies and programs, specify their duties and powers, and establish absolute funding levels. There are *appropriations* committees that specify the actual funding level for a particular fiscal year. There are *revenue* committees that raise the funds to pay for the appropriations necessary to sustain the authorized programs. In addition, since Congress itself is an elaborate institution that must be serviced, there are *housekeeping* committees—those that provide for the day-to-day operation of Congress. In the House of Representatives there is also an *internal regulation* committee, the House Rules Committee, that schedules debate and specifies the rules for deliberation on specific bills.

These committees vary greatly in the nature and comprehensiveness of their impact on national policy making. The housekeeping committees tend to be *service* committees and carry little national weight except through indirect influence obtained from manipulating office and staff resources that other members may want so desperately as to modify their policy stances on other committees. A second set of committees, authorization committees such as Interior or Post Office, have jurisdictions that limit them to the concerns of fairly narrow constituencies; these are *reelection* committees that allow members to serve their constituencies' parochial interests but offer only limited potential to effect broad-scale public policy. A third group of committees are *policy* committees, such as Education and Labor or International Relations, that consider fairly broad policy questions, though questions that have fairly clear and circumscribed jurisdictional limits. A fourth set of committees are the *"power"* committees, which make decisions on issues such as the scheduling of rules (the House Rules Committee), appropriations (House and Senate Appropriations committees), or revenues (House Ways and Means or Senate Finance) that allow them to affect most or all policy areas. Within a pure system of committee government, power committees are limited in the comprehensiveness of their control over the general policy-making process. No overarching control committee exists to coordinate the authorization, appropriations, or revenue process.

Because an essential type of legislative authority is associated with each congressional committee, members find that service on any committee can offer some satisfaction of their power drive. There are, nevertheless, inherent differences in the power potential associated with committees, differences that are tied to the variation in legislative function and in the comprehensiveness of a committee's decisional jurisdiction. This variation between committees is sufficient to make some committees more attractive as a place to gain power. Because members are in a quest for power, not simply reelection, they generally will seek to serve on committees whose function and policy focus allow the broadest personal impact on policy.

Maneuvering for membership on the more attractive committees is constrained by two fundamental factors. First, there are a limited number of attractive committee slots, and much competition will exist for these vacancies. Most members cannot realize their goal to serve on and gain control of these committees. For this reason, much pressure exists to establish norms by which members "prove" themselves deserving of membership on an attractive committee. Such norms include courtesy to fellow members, specialization in limited areas of public policy, a willingness to work hard on legislation, a commitment to the institution, adherence to the general policy parameters seen as desirable by senior members of Congress who will dominate the committee nominations process, and a willingness to reciprocate favors and abide by the division of policy domains into the set of relatively independent policy-making entities. Members who observe these norms faithfully will advance to the more desirable committees because they will have shown themselves worthy of special privilege, particularly if they also possess sufficient congressional seniority.

Seniority is particularly important because of the second constraint on the process—the fact that service on the more powerful committees may limit one's ability to mend electoral fences. On the more comprehensive committees, issues often can be more complex and difficult to understand, necessitating much time and concentration on committee work; members may not be able to get home as often or as easily. Issues will be more controversial and will face members with difficult and often unpopular policy choices; members will be less able to engage in the politics of form over substance. The national visibility of the members will be greater, transforming them into public figures whose personal lives may receive considerable attention. Indiscretions that normally might go unreported will become open game for the press and can destroy careers. Thus, although it is undoubtedly true that service on the more comprehensive committees may bring with it certain attributes that can help reelection (campaign contributions from interest groups, name identification and status, a reputation for power that may convince constituents that "our member can deliver"), service on the more attractive committees does thrust members into a more unpredictable world. Although members generally will want to serve on the most powerful committees, it will normally be best for them to put off such service until they have a secure electoral base and to approach their quest for power in sequential steps.

Because of the constraints operating within a system of committee government, congressional careers reflect a set of stages. The first stage entails an emphasis on shoring up the electoral base through casework, service on constituent-oriented reelection committees, and gaining favor within Congress by serving on the housekeeping committees. Of course, the first stage is never fully "completed": there is never a time at which a member of Congress is "guaranteed" long-term reelection or total acceptance within Congress, so both constituent and congressional service are a recurring necessity. But a point is normally reached—a point defined by the circumstances of the member's constituency, the opportunities present in Congress, and the personality and competence of the member—when he or she will feel secure enough, or perhaps unhappy enough, to attempt a move to a second stage. In the second stage members broaden their horizons and seek service on key policy committees that draft important legislation regulating such national policy dimensions as interstate commerce, education, or labor. In this stage, representatives begin to be "legislators," to preoccupy themselves with national policy matters. Because of the limited number of positions on power committees, many members will spend most, perhaps the rest, of their career in this stage, moving up by committee seniority to subcommittee and committee chairs on the policy committees. As they gain expertise in the specific policy area, and create a myth of special personal authority, they will gain power in some important but circumscribed area of national policy. For members who persist, however, and/or possess the right attributes of electoral security and personal attributes, a third stage exists: service on a power committee—Rules, Ways and Means, or Finance, Appropriations, and, in the Senate, Foreign Relations. Service on these committees is superseded, if at all, only by involvement in a fourth stage: service in the party leadership as a floor leader or Speaker. Few individuals ever have the opportunity to realize this fourth and climactic step; in a system of committee government, in fact, this step will be less sought and the battles less bitter than one might expect, considering the status associated with them, because power will rest primarily in committees rather than in the party. Although party leadership positions in a system of committee government do carry with them a degree of responsibility, particularly the obligation to mediate conflicts between committees and to influence the success of marginal legislation on the house floor, members will generally be content to stay on a power committee and advance to subcommittee and committee chair positions rather than engage in an all-out effort to attain party leadership positions.

This career path, presented here in an idealized and simplified fashion, is a general "power ladder" that members attempt to climb in their quest for power within Congress. Some members leave the path voluntarily to run for the Senate (if in the House), to run for governor, to serve as a judge, or to serve as president. Some for special reasons bypass one or another stage, choose to stay at a lower rung, are defeated, or retire. Despite exceptions, the set of stages is a very real guide to the long-term career path that members seek to follow. Implicit within this pattern is the very real dilemma discussed earlier: progress up the career ladder brings with it a greater opportunity for significant personal power, but also greater responsibility. As members move up the power ladder, they move away from a secure world in which reelection interest can be their dominant concern and into a world in which concerns with power and public policy predominate. They take their chance and leave the security of the re-election stage because of their personal quest for power, without which reelection is a largely meaningless victory.

The attempt to prove oneself and move up the career ladder requires enormous effort. Even after one succeeds and gains a power position, this attainment is not in itself sufficient to guarantee the personal exercise of power. To utilize fully the power prerogatives that are implicit in specific power positions, a member must maintain the respect, awe, trust, and confidence of committee and house colleagues; he or she must sustain the aura of personal authority that is necessary to legitimize the exercise of power. Although the norm of seniority under a system of pure committee government will protect a member's possession of a power position, seniority is not sufficient to guard personal authority. In order to pass legislation and dominate policy decisions in a committee's jurisdictional area, a committee chair must radiate an appearance of special authority. The member must abide by the norms of the house and the committee, demonstrate legislative competence, and generate policy decisions that appear to stay within the general policy parameters recognized as acceptable by the member's colleagues. Among reelection efforts, efforts to advance in Congress to power positions, efforts to sustain and nurture personal authority, and efforts to exercise power, the members of Congress confront an incredible array of crosscutting pressures and internal dilemmas—decisions about how to balance external reelection interests with the internal institutional career, how to maximize the possibility of power within Congress by service on particular committees, how to gain and nurture authority within committees by specific legislative actions. The world of the congressman or congresswoman is complicated further, however, by a very special irony.

II

As a form of institutional organization, committee government possesses certain attributes that recommend it. By dividing policy concerns among a variety of committees it allows members to specialize in particular policy areas; this division provides a congressional structure through which the members can be their own expert advisers and maintain a degree of independence from lobbyists or outside specialists. Specialization also provides a procedure whereby members can become acquainted with particular programs and agencies and follow their behavior over a period of years, thus allowing informed oversight of the implementation of public policy. The dispersion of power implicit in committee government is important, furthermore, because it brings a greater number of individuals into the policy-making process and thus allows a greater range of policy innovation. In addition, as stressed above, committee government also serves the immediate power motive of congresspeople by creating so many power positions that all members can seek to gain power in particular policy domains.

Despite its assets, committee government does have severe liabilities, flaws that undermine the ability of Congress to fulfill its constitutional responsibilities to make legislative policy and oversee the implementation of that policy. First, committee government by its very nature lacks strong, centralized *leadership*, thereby undermining its internal decision-making capacity and external authority. Internally, Congress needs central leadership because most major questions of public policy (such as economic or energy policy) cut across individual committee jurisdictions. Since each committee and subcommittee may differ in its policy orientation from all others, and since the support of all relevant committees will be essential to an overall program, it is difficult, if not impossible, to enact a coherent general approach to broad policy questions. A central party leader or central congressional steering committee with extensive control over the standing committees could provide the leadership necessary to assist the development and passage of a coherent policy across the various committees, but committee government rejects the existence of strong centralized power. The resulting dispersion of power within Congress, and the refusal to allow strong centralized leadership, ensures that congressional decisions on major policy matters (unless aided and pushed by an outside leader) will be incremental at best, immobilized and incoherent as a norm. And to the extent that a Congress governed by committees can generate public policy, it faces the external problem of leadership, the inability of outside political actors, the press, or the public to identify a legitimate spokesperson for Congress on any general policy question. The wide dispersion of power positions allows numerous members to gain a degree of dominance over specific dimensions of a policy domain; all of these members can speak with some authority on a policy question, presenting conflicting and confusing approaches and interpretations. In cases where Congress does attempt to act, Congress lacks a viable mechanism through which to publicize and justify its position in an authoritative manner. Should

Congress be in a conflict with the president, who can more easily present a straightforward and publicized position, Congress almost certainly will lose out in the eyes of public opinion. Lacking a clearly identifiable legislative leader in its midst, Congress is unable to provide the nation with unified, comprehensible, or persuasive policy leadership.

Closely related to the lack of leadership is a lack of *fiscal coordination*. Nowhere within a system of committee government is there a mechanism to ensure that the decisions of authorization, appropriations, and revenue committees have some reasonable relationship tó one another. The authorization committees make their decisions about the programs to authorize largely independent of appropriations committee decisions about how much money the government will spend. The appropriations committees decide on spending levels largely independent of revenue committee decisions on taxation. Since it is always easier to promise (or authorize) than to deliver (or spend), program goals invariably exceed the actual financial outlays and thus the actual delivery of services. And since it is easier to spend money than to make or tax money, particularly for politicians, expenditures will exceed the revenues to pay the bills. Moves to coordinate the authorization, appropriations, and revenue processes are inconsistent with committee government, since such an effort would necessarily create a central mechanism with considerable say over all public policy and thus centralize power in a relatively small number of individuals. Committee government thus by its very nature is consigned to frustration: the policies that it does produce will invariably produce higher expectations than they can deliver; its budgets, particularly in periods of liberal, activist Congresses, will produce sizable and unplanned deficits in which expenditures far exceed revenues. The inability of committee government to provide realistic program goals and fiscal discipline will invite the executive to intervene in the budget process in order to provide fiscal responsibility and coordination. The result, of course, will be a concomitant loss of the congressional control over the nation's purse strings.

A third detriment associated with committee government, and one that is exacerbated by the absence of leadership and committee coordination, is the lack of *accountability* and *responsibility*. A fundamental justification of congressional government is that it allows political decision making to be responsive to the will of a national majority. Committee government distributes this decision-making authority among a largely autonomous set of committees. Since seniority protects each committee's membership from removal and determines who will chair each committee, a committee's members can feel free to follow their personal policy predilections and stop any legislation they wish that falls within their committee's jurisdiction, or propose any that they wish. Within a system of committee government, resting as it does on the norm of seniority, no serious way exists to hold a specific committee or committee chair accountable to the majority views of Congress or the American people, should those views differ from the views held within a particular committee. Because of the process whereby members are selected to serve on major committees—a process that emphasizes not their compatibility with the majority's policy sentiment but rather their adherence to congressional norms, general agreement with the policy views of senior congresspeople, and possession of seniority—the top committees (especially at the senior ranks) are quite likely to be out of step with a congressional or national majority. This lack of representativeness is particularly likely if patterns of electoral security nationwide provide safe seats (and thus seniority) to regions or localities that are unrepresentative of the dominant policy perspectives of the country. Responsiveness is further undermined because the absence of strong central leaders, and a widespread desire among members for procedural protection of their personal prerogatives, require reliance on rigid rules and regulations to govern the flow of legislation and debate, rules such as the Senate's cloture rule that allows the existence of filibusters. Under a system of party government, where limiting rules may exist on the books, strong party leaders can mitigate their effects. In a system of committee government, rules become serious hurdles that can block the easy flow of legislation, particularly major, controversial legislation, thereby decreasing the ability of Congress to respond rapidly to national problems. Committee government thus undermines the justification of Congress as an institution that provides responsive, representative government. Since institutions derive their power not solely from constitutional legalisms but from their own mystique of special authority that comes from their legitimizing myths, committee government undercuts not only Congress's ability to exercise power but also the popular support that is necessary to maintain its power potential.

The lack of accountability and the damage to Congress's popular support are augmented by a fourth characteristic of committee government—a tendency toward *insulation* of congressional decision making. This insulation derives from three factors. First, members of committees naturally try to close committee sessions from public purview, limiting thereby the intrusion of external actors such as interest groups or executive agencies and thus protecting committee members' independent exercise of power within committees. Second, the creation of a multiplicity of committees makes it difficult for the public or the press to follow policy deliberations even if they are open. Third, it is difficult if not impossible to create clear jurisdictional boundaries between committees. The consequent ambiguity that exists between jurisdictional boundaries will often involve committees themselves in extensive disputes over the control of particular policy domains, further confusing observers who are concerned with policy deliberations. By closing its committee doors, creating a multiplicity of committees, and allowing jurisdictional ambiguities, a system of committee government isolates Congress from the nation at large. Out of sight and out of mind, Congress loses the attention, respect, and understanding of the nation and becomes an object of scorn and derision, thus further undermining the authority or legitimacy of its pronouncements and itself as an institution.

Finally, committee government undermines the ability of Congress to perform that one function for which committee government would seem most suited—aggressive oversight of administration. According to the classic argument, the saving grace of committee government is that the dispersion of power and the creation of numerous policy experts ensure congressional surveillance of the bureaucracy. Unfortunately, this argument ignores the fact that the individuals on the committees that pass legislation will be the very people least likely to investigate policy implementation. They will be committed to the program, as its authors or most visible supporters, and will not want to take actions that might lead to a destruction of the program. The impact of publicity and a disclosure of agency or program shortcomings, after all, is very unpredictable and difficult to control and may create a public furor against the program. The better part of discretion is to leave the agency largely to its own devices and rely on informal contacts and special personal arrangements, lest the glare of publicity and the discovery of shortcomings force Congress to deauthorize a pet program, casting aspersions on those who originally drafted the legislation. Members of Congress are unwilling to resolve this problem by creating permanent and powerful oversight committees because such committees, by their ability to focus attention on problems of specific agencies and programs, would threaten the authority of legislative committees to control and direct policy in their allotted policy area. Committee government thus allows a *failure of executive oversight.*

In the light of these five problems, the irony of committee government is that it attempts to satisfy members' individual desires for personal power by dispersing internal congressional authority so widely that the resulting institutional impotence cripples the ability of Congress to perform its constitutional roles, thereby dissipating the value of internal congressional power. Members of Congress thus are not only faced with the daily dilemma of balancing re-election interests with their efforts at upward power mobility within Congress; their lives are also complicated by a cruel paradox, the ultimate incompatibility of widely dispersed power within Congress, on the one hand, and a strong role for Congress in national decision making, on the other. This inherent tension generates an explosive dynamic within Congress as an organization and between Congress and the executive.

In the short run, as members of Congress follow the immediate dictates of the personal power motive, they are unaware of, or at least unconcerned with, the long-term consequences of decentralized power; they support the creation of committee government. The longer committee government operates, the more unhappy political analysts and the people generally become with the inability of Congress to make national policy or ensure policy implementation. With Congress deadlocked by immobilism, political activists within Congress and the nation at large turn to the president (as the one alternative political figure who is popularly elected and thus should be responsive to popular sentiments) and encourage him (or her, if we ever break the sex barrier) to provide policy leadership and fiscal coordination, to open up congressional decision making to national political forces and ensure congressional responsiveness, and to oversee the bureaucracy. Presidents, particularly those committed to activist legislation, welcome the calls for intervention and will see their forthright role as an absolute necessity to the well-being of the Republic. Slowly at first, presidents take over the roles of chief legislator, chief budgetary officer, overseer of the bureaucracy, chief tribune, and protector of the people. Eventually the president's role in these regards becomes so central that he feels free to ignore the wishes of members of Congress, even those who chair very important committees, and impose presidential policy on Congress and the nation at large.

The coming of a strong, domineering, imperial president who ignores Congress mobilizes its members into action. They see that their individual positions of power within Congress are meaningless unless the institution can impose its legislative will on the nation. They search for ways to regain legislative preeminence and constrain the executive. Not being fools, members identify part of the problem as an internal institutional one and seek to reform Congress. Such reform efforts come during or immediately following crises in which presidents clearly and visibly threaten fundamental power prerogatives of Congress. The reforms will include attempts to provide for more centralized congressional leadership, fiscal coordination, congressional openness, better oversight mechanisms, clarification of committee jurisdictions, procedures for policy coordination, and procedures to encourage committee accountability. Because the quest for personal power continues as the underlying motivation of individual members, the reforms are basically attempts to strengthen the value of internal congressional power by increasing the power of Congress vis-à-vis the executive. The reform efforts, however, are constrained by consideration of personal power prerogatives of members of Congress. The attempt to protect personal prerogatives while centralizing power builds structural flaws into the centralization mechanisms, flaws that would not be present were the significance of congressional structure for the national power of Congress itself the only motive. The existence of these flaws provides the openings through which centralization procedures are destroyed when institutional crises pass and members again feel free to emphasize personal power and personal careers. In addition, because policy inaction within Congress often will be identified as the immediate cause of presidential power aggrandizement, and because policy immobilism may become identified with key individuals or committees that have obstructed particular legislation, reform efforts also may be directed toward breaking up the authority of these individuals or committees and dispersing it among individuals and committees who seem more amenable to activist policies. This short-term dispersal of power, designed to break a legislative logjam (and, simultaneously, to give power to additional individuals), will serve to exacerbate immobilism in the long run when the new mechanisms of centralization are destroyed.

Viewed in a broad historical perspective, organizational dynamics within Congress, and external relations of Congress to the president, have a "cyclical" pattern. At the outset, when politicians in a quest for national power first enter Congress, they decentralize power and create committee government. Decentralization is followed by severe problems of congressional decision making, presidential assumption of legislative prerogatives, and an eventual presidential assault on Congress itself. Congress reacts by reforming its internal structure: some reform efforts will involve legislation that attempts to circumscribe presidential action; other reforms will attempt to break specific points of deadlock by further decentralization and dispersal of congressional authority; eventually, however, problems of internal congressional leadership and coordination will become so severe that Congress will be forced to undertake centralizing reforms. As Congress moves to resolve internal structural problems and circumscribe presidential power, presidents begin to cooperate so as to defuse the congressional counterattack; to do otherwise would open a president to serious personal attack as anticongressional and thus antidemocratic, destroying the presidency's legitimizing myth as a democratic institution and identifying presidential motivations as power aggrandizement rather than protection of the Republic. As the immediate threat to congressional prerogatives recedes, members of Congress (many of whom will not have served in Congress during the era of institutional crisis) become preoccupied with their immediate careers and press once again for greater power dispersal within Congress and removal of centralizing mechanisms that inhibit committee and subcommittee autonomy. Decentralization reasserts itself and Congress becomes increasingly leaderless, uncoordinated, insulated, unresponsive, unable to control executive agencies. Tempted by congressional weakness and hounded by cries to "get the country moving," the executive again reasserts itself and a new institutional crisis eventually arises. A review of American history demonstrates the existence of this cycle rather clearly, particularly during the twentieth century. . . .

Congressional Staff: The Surrogates of Power

Both the committee and personal staffs of Capitol Hill are important forces in the legislative process. Astute senators and congressmen know that their effectiveness in Congress largely depends upon the caliber of their staff. Each member of Congress has a personal staff, and the committee chairmen control staffs that are usually far greater in number than those in congressional and senatorial offices.

Although an embryo congressional staff began to develop in the nineteenth century, the origins of today's professional staff are found in the Legislative Reorganization Act of 1946, which increased the staffs of committees and their members. More important than the actual numbers of professional aides provided by the Act was the fact that Congress, for the first time, officially recognized the need for expert assistance, not only to cope with the increasingly complex problems confronting government but also to counterbalance the growing dominance of a highly expert executive branch.

Since the passage of the Legislative Reorganization Act in 1946 there has been a vast increase in congressional staff to approximately 14,000 aides in 1989. The greatest increment in staff occurred during the period from 1970 to 1980, as subcommittees expanded at an unprecedented rate. Moreover, as committee staffs grew, members who were not committee chairmen, noting how effective chairmen used their staffs to boost their power on Capitol Hill, demanded more personal staff. Over 10,000 professional staffers now serve in the offices of members, and approximately 4,000 are employed by the close to 300 committees and subcommittees of Congress.

To what extent does congressional staff constitute an invisible government, exercising power and responsibility that the Constitution has delegated to the elected members of Congress? While senators and congressmen nominally exert control over their staffs, in actual fact, staffers often control their bosses. The time constraints upon members alone make it impossible for them to exercise more than cursory control of staff, and, usually, this increases their dependence upon staff. Members rely upon their aides to set their daily schedules, keep them abreast of important issues, and determine what should be on their legislative agenda. Members often become the surrogates of the staffers, rather than vice versa.

Congressional staff have been called the "unelected representatives." They operate behind the scenes and often hold the reins of power. The committee and personal staffs serve members, and one of the most important emoluments of a committee chairman is control over the committee's staff. "Committees," write Rochelle Jones and Peter Woll in *The Private World of Congress*, "are mere symbols of power, not power itself, unless they are accompanied by adequate staff."[1] Staff is particularly important in the Senate, which has to deal with the same workload as the House but with far fewer members.

That congressional aides often become key power surrogates on Capitol Hill is illustrated in the following selection.

---

[1]Rochelle Jones and Peter Woll, *The Private World of Congress* (New York: Free Press, 1979), p. 128.

54

Hedrick Smith
STAFF AS POLICY
ENTREPRENEURS

. . . [S]taff sometimes leads officeholders, not vice versa. For among the modern congressional staff, there is a culture of activism, a spirit of entrepreneurship, a highly charged sense of competition. Most legislative staffers are bright, young, aggressive, ambitious, full of ideas, and canny enough to know that their own ambitions are best served by expanding the power and turf of their bosses. Their relentless energy and initiative cause some members to complain of "staf-flation."

Michael Malbin, the scholar, contends that the 1970s were the heyday of staff activism because many new government programs were being generated, whereas more recent budget cutbacks have curbed legislative entrepreneurship. But I believe that social issues, foreign policy, defense, tax legislation, and congressional oversight have left ample room for aggressive staffers, even without new programs. In my experience, staff rivalries are rampant in Congress, as in the executive branch. Staffers often generate battles for visibility, turf, agenda, and political credit on Capitol Hill.

For example, when the nuclear accident occurred at Three-Mile Island, Pennsylvania, in March 1979, a dozen congressional committees and subcommittees scurried to claim jurisdiction over that hot item, angling to hold hearings, write reports, draft legislation. But Senator Edward Kennedy, who then deployed the largest staff network on Capitol Hill—120 strong, working for him on three different committees— got the jump. His legions scored a publicity coup by being the first to organize a hearing on the accident.

In the mid-eighties, John Dingell of Michigan, chairman of the House Energy and Commerce Committee, exerted great power not only because of his personal force and position, but also because of his aggressive staff. Pete Stockton, a bird-dog congressional investigator, repeatedly helped Dingell get the press limelight for hearings on the questionable practices of defense contractors such as General Dynamics or lobbyists such as Michael Deaver. Not only did Stockton cross oceans to smoke out boondoggles and scandals but he pump-

From *The Power Game: How Washington Works*, by Hedrick Smith. Copyright © 1988 by Hedrick Smith. Reprinted by permission of Random House, Inc.

primed media coverage by leaking juicy tidbits to selected reporters just before scheduled hearings, generating extra publicity for his boss.

Stockton's activism and Dingell's own bulldog style gave the Michigan Democrat visibility and added to his political turf. It enabled him to rampage into the military-affairs terrain of the Armed Services Committee. For protecting and expanding turf is a vital function of legislative staffs. They know that gaining jurisdiction over the most controversial and important issues is central to the power game in Congress, for despite the established committee structure, jurisdictions overlap, and lines of authority are often unclear. So staffers elbow, scrap, and scramble to extend the political empires of their bosses and to build up their own importance.

One of the most stunning and crucial turf maneuvers in the Reagan presidency was engineered by Steve Bell, staff director of the Senate Budget Committee. It enabled Senator Pete Domenici, the Budget Committee chairman, to gain long-term control over congressional handling of the Reagan economic program, against rival efforts by Mark Hatfield, Senate Appropriations Committee chairman, and Bob Dole, Finance Committee chairman. The decisive gambit was an idea for which David Stockman, Reagan's budget director, was widely credited with devising; Stockman told me that it was actually Bell's brainchild.

Bell, a brash, intense, hard-charging former reporter for the El Paso *Times* and an English-literature major who learned budget economics from legislative economists, epitomizes the modern staff chief. He came out of New Mexico as part of Domenici's inner political family, a strategist in all of Domenici's campaigns, starting in 1972. Domenici and Bell are think-alike Republican conservatives with a passion for budget balancing and the same blunt-spoken drive to confront deficit spenders, whether liberal Democrats or the Reagan Pentagon. Bell, a muscular blond in his early forties, can enthrall or intimidate other staffers with theatrical outbursts of profanity, but shift quickly to "yessir" for senators. He possesses the crucial talents of the best staffers: technical mastery of legislation, political savvy, and a close, personal relationship with his boss.

"No one ever thought he would become a numbers man because he's a journalist, but he's as bright as could be," Domenici told me. "He's also a great writer, a great user of words. And to say he's politically astute is an understatement. Obviously, he has an instant fix on my state, but he understands the politics of the U.S. Senate, the politics of the Senate versus the presidency. We shared the leadership role there. . . . He and I together just pushed stuff down their [other senators'] throats and rolled them over and did a lot of partisan stuff where they had to go along."

In late 1980, Bell, as Budget Committee staff chief, came up with a parliamentary technique that helped pass Reagan's economic program; it also gave Domenici's Budget Committee preeminent legislative control of the Reagan program. Bell's notion—quickly bought by Majority Leader Howard Baker and by Budget Director Stockman—was to employ a rarely used maneuver known as budget reconciliation. It was ideal for ramming Reagan's budget cuts through Congress in one package.

Normally, Congress passes thirteen separate appropriations bills without a central blueprint. A reconciliation bill would provide the blueprint; it would require a single up-or-down vote on the whole Reagan budget, and then its provisions would dictate that other committees bring the cost of their programs in line. It was written into law in 1974, and rarely used because established committee chairmen disliked the budget committee butting into their business. Reconciliation was designed to come at the end of the budget process, after the competing committees failed to agree. But Bell proposed using it at the start of the budget process to discipline all committees at once. Democrats howled that this was railroading the budget. But it pleased Republicans, in their early pro-Reagan enthusiasm. This strategy made Domenici a preeminent figure. And it was crucial to Reagan's first-year success—a dramatic illustration of how a staff man's understanding of procedure critically affected major national policy. On his wall, Bell has letters of thanks from both President Reagan and Howard Baker.

In this case, Bell was implementing Reagan's and Domenici's agenda. But in other cases, staff aides have initiated policy agendas for their bosses. In 1977, staff aides, for example, were the catalysts for the Republican Kemp-Roth proposal to cut marginal tax rates by thirty percent, which later became the nucleus of President Reagan's 1981 tax bill. The initial sponsors were Representative Jack Kemp and Senator William Roth of Delaware, both of whom favored sharp cuts in tax rates. Kemp became the plan's prime public salesman, but its real architects were Paul Craig Roberts, a supply-side economist close to Kemp and then serving on the House Budget Committee staff; Bruce Bartlett, a Kemp staffer; and Bruce Thompson, an aide to Roth.

In a different field—Soviet violations of arms agreements—David Sullivan, a burly, crewcut ex-Marine and former Central Intelligence Agency analyst, was the force behind a relentless campaign by Idaho's two conservative Republican senators, Jim McClure and Steven Symms, for whom Sullivan served as a staffer. Often working with highly classified information slipped to him by friends inside the government or planted in friendly newspapers, Sullivan ghost-wrote speeches and letters of protest urging Reagan to revoke the 1972 and 1979 Strategic Arms Limitation Treaties. Senate pressures, stimulated by Sullivan, helped push Reagan to adopt this policy. On the other side, Leon Fuerth, a quiet, pipe-smoking, high-powered specialist on arms control, spent a year teaching then-Democratic Congressman, now-Senator Albert Gore the intricacies of the nuclear-arms race. Then he helped Gore formulate the rationale for a new single-warhead missile to reduce the doomsday threat of multiwarhead missiles. Gore and others sold that idea to Reagan in 1983.

In none of these cases were the senators or congressmen unwitting dupes. They wanted to move in the direction the staff was pushing. But sometimes staffers steal the ball on policy, and members complain of being at the mercy of staffs, often forced to fight fires started by overly aggressive staff aides.

"There are many senators who feel that all they were doing is running around and responding to the staff: my staff fighting your staff, your staff competing with mine," Senator Fritz Hollings, a South Carolina Democrat, bleated in protest. "It is sad. I heard a senator the other day tell me another senator hadn't been in his office for three years; it is just staff. Everybody is working for the staff, staff, staff, driving you nutty, in fact. It has gotten to the point where the senators never actually sit down and exchange ideas and learn from the experience of others and listen. Now it is how many nutty whiz kids you get on the staff, to get you magazine articles and get you headlines and get all of these other things done."

BIRD-DOGGING THE EXECUTIVE BRANCH

Yet whatever the complaints, no one in Congress is prepared to give up any staff. All too clearly, members of Congress understand that staff is essential for competing with each other and especially for confronting the executive branch. Normally, when this confrontation occurs, staff and members work hand in hand with the congressional member leading the way—but not always. Some exceptional staffers are outchallenging the executive branch, bird-dogging it more aggressively than members. In other cases, congressional staff agencies operate almost as a third force, as referees between Congress and the White House.

For example, the Congressional Budget Office (CBO), set up in 1974, technically has no power; it passes no legislation. Unlike committee staffs, it cannot actually supervise the promoting, revising, or funding of programs. Its power derives purely from the intangible elements of information and credibility. Yet the CBO represents the most important institutional shift of power on domestic issues between the executive branch and Congress in several decades.

Before the CBO was created, the president's budget was, as scholar Hugh Heclo put it, "the only game in town for taking a comprehensive look" at government. The presidency, through the Council of Economic Advisers and the Office of Management and Budget (OMB), had a monopoly on the government's economic forecasting. Congress, like the president, used CEA and OMB forecasts of economic growth, inflation, and budget deficits.

Now, CBO gives Congress an independent perspective on those crucial matters, setting the framework of policy debate. CBO's deficit forecasts can differ from the administration's by $30 billion to $40 billion and that influence has a major impact on a whole session of Congress, because Congress is forced to cut more or may cut less than the president proposed. In the Reagan years,

CBO's capabilities enabled Congress largely to ignore Reagan budgets after 1981 and to develop its own budgets—something inconceivable without CBO.

By December 1985, when Congress passed the six-year deficit-reduction plan (the Gramm-Rudman bill) CBO was put on the political hot seat. To protect itself from politically tilted administration estimates, Congress gave CBO joint responsibility with the administration's OMB to set deficit estimates that would trigger automatic cutting of government programs, if the deficit targets were not met. Having that much political responsibility troubled Rudolph Penner, a Republican economist who was then head of CBO.

"It's hard to think of other instances where unelected officials have such power to do good or evil," said Penner, a bland, balding technocrat. He warned Congress that "substantial errors are possible" in economic forecasting and alerted it to the "disadvantages of conveying so much power to mere technicians." But Congress had more faith in CBO than in OMB and put Penner in the middle.

In early 1986, Rudy Penner got caught in a political crossfire. Pete Domenici, the Budget Committee chairman, was angry at Penner for making relatively optimistic forecasts on the economy and the deficit. House Democrats were happy with Penner's optimism because that meant less pressure to cut programs. Domenici likes to use gloomy forecasts to impose discipline on Congress to cut programs, and he felt Penner's estimates were undermining his strategy. As it turned out, the economy worsened, and the deficit estimates rose naturally, pleasing Domenici without forcing Penner to give in.

Penner had even sharper clashes with the Reagan administration on defense spending in the 1987 budget. Penner said the adminstration had understated the Pentagon's actual spending by $14.7 billion. (Administration figures, I was reliably told, were dictated by Weinberger rather than being economically calculated by Budget Director Miller.) Realizing that Penner's numbers would incite Congress to cut more from defense, the administration attacked Penner, and so did Senator Ted Stevens of Alaska, the hawkish chairman of the Defense Appropriations Subcommittee. At a hearing in July, Stevens raged at Penner, threatening to cut CBO's own budget if Penner did not change his estimate on the Pentagon. "That really rocks this defense bill," Stevens bellowed at Penner. "I am going to cut your money. You cannot put me in this position." But Penner stood his ground. Later, the administration had to change its numbers, tacitly acknowledging that CBO had been right.

The CBO is a special example of congressional staff power. Its estimates are required by law, and that forces its opinions into full view. CBO cannot escape a high profile. But normally, success in the staff power game against the executive branch dictates a low profile. If information is power, anonymity is protection. The basic technique for staffers is to develop substantive mastery, to work contracts inside the administration to feed critical information to key legislators, and then let them take the heat and get the publicity for battling the White House or the Pentagon. Only a few staffers voluntarily go against the grain and play risky, high-visibility tactics.

One of the most powerful in recent years is a blunt-talking weapons expert named Tony Battista, who struck me initially as a white-collar Fonzie (the TV sitcom character), with his jaunty, high-wave hairstyle and the accent of a Staten Island tough. A youthful-looking fifty, Battista looks as if he belongs in a garage, with his head popping out from under a car hood or wiping grease off his hands. That is where he would usually rather be, for Battista is an antique car buff who spends his weekends restoring such prestige models as a Bentley, a Lotus, and several old Cadillacs, when he is not working overtime for the Research and Development (R and D) Subcommittee of the House Armed Services Committee. His engineering skills are definitely hands on. One of his frequent reactions to outrageous military parts prices is to tell the Pentagon, "I could make it for a fraction of that in my own garage." More than once, he has actually done so. Battista was trained as an engineer, worked a couple of years for the space agency and nine more at the Naval Surface Weapons Center before becoming a congressional staffer in 1974.

Battista may be unknown to the public, but he is respected and feared by Pentagon officials and defense contractors. "Tony's got a lot of power and he uses it," said Dave McCurdy, a rising Democratic star on defense issues. Defense lobbyists say he is as powerful as a subcommittee chairman because his technical expertise, hard work, and tenacity carry the day nine times out of ten with committee members. "If Tony wants a certain program to succeed in his committee, chances are it will, and if he wants it not to succeed, chances are it won't," one defense lobbyist told me. Another bluntly told Richard Halloran of *The New York Times:* "If he's against you, you're in trouble. He'll fight a bear with a buggy whip." Having Battista on your side, added Tom Downey, a liberal New York Democrat, "is like the old days when you got into a fight—you took the toughest guy in town with you."

Knowing Battista's clout but attacking his effort to cut spending on Star Wars space defense in 1985, a *Wall Street Journal* editorial blasted Battista as "an antidefense staffer" with "a line-item veto." (Pentagon budgets, like all others, come with each program or weapons procurement item as an entry on a single line, hence the term *line item.* The Pentagon's research and development budget is broken down into some eight hundred line items, embracing 3,400 projects. A real "line-item veto" would give Battista the ability to kill some of those individual items. It is a significant power, one that Congress has refused to give to Reagan. The *Journal* meant that Battista had that kind of power in practice, not in law.)

To call Battista antidefense is inaccurate. Congressional hawks on defense such as Samuel Stratton, a New York Democrat, or Bob Dornan, a hard right California Republican, praise Battista's commitment to defense. Battista has backed the MX missile and favored research on space-based defenses, though he is sharply critical of portions of Reagan's program, which he insists were junked as unworkable or ridiculously expensive before Reagan enshrined SDI in 1983. During the Carter years, Battista quietly helped save research-and-development funding for the B-1 bomber. "Members trust him, both sides of the aisle," Dornan told me. "When he sinks his teeth into something, you know you're going to get a fair bipartisan assessment. He's got an excellent scientific grasp of all the R and D stuff. Tony alone, I believe, prevented the junking of the B-1 R and D program. I think SAC ought to name one plane *The Battista.*" Significantly, one defense contractor whose firm has large business with all three military services told me: "Battista's not in anyone's pocket. If you disagree with him, you'd better reexamine your position, because he's very smart and he does not take his position without good reasons."

In person, Battista is friendly, outgoing, almost casual, not pugnacious—but sure of himself in all things technical. He is good at reading the mood of Congress, and for a Congress that has grown skeptical of Pentagon procurement practices, he is ideal. He believes in both strong defense and efficient spending of tax dollars. At hearings, he grills generals mercilessly, more like a senior member of Congress than a staff aide. He will challenge an administration weapons system and get his subcommittee chairman to invite a bevy of top Pentagon brass to come debate him. In one hearing during the Carter years, Battista went toe-to-toe with Deputy Defense Secretary Graham Claytor, Defense Undersecretary William Perry, General P. X. Kelley, then chief of the Readiness Command, and two other generals, and he carried the day. The subcommittee bought his recommendation to kill funding for research on a new cargo plane. In the Reagan years, he challenged Donald Hicks, once Pentagon research-and-development chief, on three issues: the Star Wars space defense program, a new single-warhead mobile missile, and research into hardening concrete silos around American ICBMs. Hicks went away bristling; Battista was unperturbed, and the committee took his advice on all three issues. Later, with committee support, Battista forced the Navy to drop a duplicate radio communications system and use a similar system being developed by the Air Force, a move that saved taxpayers several hundred million dollars.

"I'll debate anybody at the witness table," Battista told me. "I could be wrong. I have been wrong because I didn't have all the data and the facts on a few occasions. If I'd never been wrong, I haven't been doing my job. I'm not so pompous and cavalier to sit there and say I've never been wrong."

What grates the Pentagon, some contractors, and quite a few House members is that Battista presses his favorites quite openly, such as fiber-optics guided missiles and other high technology. He is a tireless foe of duplication and wasteful rivalry among the services. He insists that new weapons be run through combat-realistic tests. Experience makes him especially valuable to Congress. He has been around long enough to know which contractors are good during the research phase but inefficient on production. He has a keen sense of smell when things are going wrong. He is a bird dog. With the help of longtime contacts inside the Pentagon, he sniffs out weapons systems headed for trouble and huge cost overruns. And he barks very publicly.

Another thing that makes Battista so effective is thorough homework: ferreting out phony Pentagon reports and faulty weapons. Several years ago, for example, the Air Force had contracted with Hughes Aircraft for an air-to-surface missile called the Maverick. It was supposed to be a long-range tank killer using an infrared heat seeker to find the tanks. When an Air Force colonel told Battista that it could lock onto tanks at nearly thirteen miles (65,000 feet slant range, in technical jargon), Battista became suspicious. When the colonel threw technical jargon at Battista, he threw it right back. Their conversation, he recalled, went this way:

" 'Hold on, hold on,' I said, 'What's the minimum resolution of that seeker?' And he told me. And I said, 'What's the minimum resolvable temperature?' And I went through a list of parameters with him and I said, 'Well, I'll tell you what. I don't have a computer here, but I just did a rough calculation in my head and, Colonel, that's pure bullshit.' And he said, 'Oh, no, no, no. I've got it here on tape.' And I said, 'I don't care what you've got on that tape.' So he proceeded to show me this tape, and I said I didn't believe it. So the Air Force said, 'What will it take to make you a believer?' And I said, 'Let's go fly.'

"I hate to fly," Battista confessed to me. "I'm a white-knuckle flyer. So they stuck me in the back seat of an F-4 with a [Maverick] seeker on it. We went out looking for tanks. Only I did something that I didn't give them any advance warning of. I set up a bunch of little charcoal fires out there to simulate thermal clutter."

Translated, that means that Battista took steps to make sure that the Maverick test was realistic. A normal battlefield has many things that generate heat, in addition to tanks; that is known as thermal clutter. Battista figured—quite correctly—that the Air Force had a clear, sandy test range with only one or two tanks, easy conditions for the Maverick heat seeker to find its target—no clutter. So Battista had a colleague, Tom Hahn, set charcoal fires out around the test range to simulate the normal thermal clutter of a battlefield.

"We had a lot of hot spots out there," Battista recalled with a grin. "So I said to the pilot, 'Okay, point me to the tank.' And when we came buzzing in, he found the tank. But at a very small fraction of sixty-five thousand feet slant range. He found the tank when he was practically inside the gun barrel." In short, the heat seeker had been confused by decoy fires and had to get so close to find the tank that the tank would have destroyed the fighter plane before it could have fired its Maverick-guided missile. When Battista reported that to his subcommittee, it slowed approval of the Maverick program.

About a year later, some Air Force brass brought in videotapes of planes using the Maverick system. The film seemed pretty impressive until Battista, tipped off by a Pentagon mole, told Representative Tom Downey, "Make'em play the sound track." When Downey made the request, the Air Force generals got flustered. "They're hiding something," Downey charged. Finally the sound track was played.

"The reason they didn't want to play the sound was because it was hard to make out what was being destroyed," Downey recalled. "In a couple of instances they were blowing up burning bushes and trucks instead of tanks. You could tell from the sound track because you had the pilots talking to one another, saying such things as, 'Holy shit, you just blew up a truck!' One guy was very clever. In the tape he was talking about blowing up burning bushes, and he was glad he wasn't there in Moses' time, because he would have been responsible for killing God."

Again, Battista's bird-dogging slowed the Maverick program and forced improvements. Battista later lamented, however, that the program was eventually pushed through by heavy lobbying on the Senate side. Battista had bird-dogged a wounded bird, but the political hunters did not choose to kill the program.

"Big constituency," Battista explained. "Program worth several billion dollars. It's a production item now."

Battista defies other axioms of the staff game. One such axion claims that staff directors gain clout from powerful committee chairmen. Battista is an exception. He has been powerful for years, but never more powerful than when the R and D Subcommittee was chaired by Mel Price, a feeble, almost absentee boss in his late seventies. Battista stepped into the vacuum. "Tony runs that subcommittee; there's no question about that," veteran New York Democrat Samuel Stratton declared with gruff respect.

Battista also leads with his chin, colliding with senior congressmen such as Stratton. Once he stormed into a hearing of the R and D Subcommittee to protest that Battista was invading the turf of Stratton's Procurement Subcommittee by investigating the Army's Bradley Fighting Vehicle. Since the Bradley was already being bought (procured, in Pentagon jargon), Stratton considered it his worry, not Battista's. But Battista was not intimidated; he insisted the R and D Subcommitttee was investigating how the Bradley was tested. Stratton furiously stalked out.

More broadly, Battista has for years virtually set the R and D Subcommittee's agenda with his personal report to the subcommittee on the Pentagon's R and D budget. Normally, the weapons that he says are in trouble get close scrutiny, ones he says are okay pass easily. In 1985, Battista recommended killing twenty-two proposed weapons systems, and the House Armed Services Committee went along on every item, though in conference with the Senate, it backed down on most—but not before imposing restrictions urged by Battista.

Pentagon officials bristle over what they consider Battista's micromanagement of their programs. "What I object to is that Battista runs his own empire," one thirty-year Pentagon official turned lobbyist angrily told me. "He's like his own Department of Defense without accountability. Thousands of people put the defense budget together, generals and civilians. It's a consensus opinion. So it's sent up there, and here's one guy, Tony Battista, who hasn't been elected, who doesn't have anyone to answer to except the members, and he sits down and says, 'I don't like the way they're doing it.' In a few months, this one guy changes hundreds of things that thousands of people have worked on for a year. Mind you, he may be right on some items. He's intelligent. He's able. But it's not the right way to run a railroad."

But in Congress, some members compare Battista to Ken Dryden, the legendary ice hockey goal tender of the Montreal Canadiens; Battista does not let the Pentagon get things past him. "Day in and day out, Battista's the most honest, most knowledgeable staff guy around, and he's not afraid to jam some general," commented Thomas Downey, a Long Island Democrat. "In the Pentagon, officers get rotated in and out of these jobs as often as the Yankees change relief pitchers. That always gave Battista an enormous competitive advantage. I mean, he's a hawk on defense. No two ways about it. But, he doesn't play favorites. He goes after people who he knows are notoriously ripping off the government."

Congress and the Electoral Connection

Throughout the 1970s public opinion polls consistently revealed the Congress was held in low esteem by the American people. The book *Who Runs Congress?*, published by the Ralph Nader Congress Project, reflected and at the same time helped to crystallize public disenchantment with Capitol Hill.[1] The book emphasized the need for citizens to take on Congress to prevent a further flagging of the institution. In his introduction, Ralph Nader summarized the contents of the book by stating that "the people have indeed abdicated their power, their money, and their democratic birthright to Congress. As a result, without the participation of the people, Congress has surrendered its enormous authority and resources to special interest groups, waste, insensitivity, ignorance, and bureaucracy."[2] The 1972 theme of the Nader project that Congress was in crisis continues to be accepted by the vast majority of people.

While Ralph Nader and his colleagues feel that the major cause of the demise of Congress is its detachment from the people, Richard Fenno in the following selection adopts a different viewpoint. He feels that people fault the *institution* of Congress, not their individual representatives on Cap-

---

[1] Mark J. Green et al. (editors), *Who Runs Congress?* (New York: Bantam/Grossman, 1972).
[2] *Ibid.*, p. 1.

itol Hill. In fact, he points out that there is a close connection between legislators and constituents, and often, a feeling of affection by voters for their representatives. Fenno feels that we apply different standards in judging individual members of Congress than we do in assessing the institution, being far more lenient in the former than the latter case. The individual is judged for his personality, style, and representativeness, while the institution is judged by its ability to recognize and solve the nation's problems. But, the institution cannot be thought of apart from the members that compose it. It is they who have given it its unique character. It is the individual member who, more often than not, has supported a decentralized and fragmented legislature because of the members' incentive to achieve personal power and status on Capitol Hill.

55

Richard F. Fenno, Jr.
IF, AS RALPH NADER SAYS, CONGRESS IS "THE BROKEN BRANCH," HOW COME WE LOVE OUR CONGRESSMEN SO MUCH?

Off and on during the past two years, I accompanied ten members of the House of Representatives as they traveled around in their home districts. In every one of those districts I heard a common theme, one that I had not expected. Invariably, the representative I was with—young or old, liberal or conservative, Northerner, Southerner, Easterner, or Westerner, Democrat or Republican—was described as "the best congressman in the United States." Having heard it so often, I now accept the description as fact. I am even prepared to believe the same thing (though I cannot claim to have heard it with my own ears) of the members of the Senate. Each of our 435 representatives and 100 senators is, indeed, "the best congressman in the United States." Which is to say that each enjoys a great deal of support and approbation among his or her constituents.

Judging by the election returns, this isn't much of an exaggeration. In the recent election, 96 percent of all House incumbents who ran were reelected; and 85 percent of all Senate incumbents who ran were reelected. These convincing figures are close to the average reelection rates of incumbents for the past ten elections. We do, it appears, love our congressmen.

On the other hand, it seems equally clear that we do not love our Congress. Louis Harris reported in 1970 that only one-quarter of the electorate gave Congress a positive rating on its job performance—while nearly two-thirds expressed themselves negatively on the subject. . . . There [is] considerable concern—dramatized recently by the critical Nader project—for the performance of Congress as an institution. On the evidence, we seem to approve of our legislators a good deal more than we do our legislature. And therein hangs something of a puzzle. If our congressmen are so good, how can our Congress be so bad? If it is the individuals that make up the institution, why should there be such a disparity in our judgments? What follows are a few reflections on this puzzle.

A first answer is that we apply different standards of judgment, those that we apply to the individual being less demanding than those we apply to the institution. For the individual, our standard is one of representativeness—of personal style and policy views. Stylistically, we ask that our legislator display a sense of identity with us so that we, in turn, can identify with him or her—via personal visits to the district, concern for local projects and individual "cases," and media contact of all sorts, for example. On the policy side, we ask only that his general policy stance does not get too frequently out of line with ours. And, if he should become a national leader in some policy area of interest to us, so much the better. These standards are admittedly vague. But because they are locally defined and locally applied, they are consistent and manageable enough so that legislators can devise rules of thumb to meet them. What is more, by their performance they help shape the standards, thereby making them easier to meet. Thus they win constituent recognition as "the best in the United States." And thus they establish the core relationship for a representative democracy.

For the institution, however, our standards emphasize efforts to solve national problems—a far less tractable task than the one we (and he) set for the individual. Given the inevitable existence of unsolved problems, we are destined to be unhappy with congressional performance. The individual legislator knows when he has met our standards of representativeness; he is reelected. But no such definitive measure of legislative success exists. And, precisely because Congress is the most familiar and most human of our national institutions, lacking the distant majesty of the Presidency and the Court, it is the easy and natural target of our criticism. We have met our problem solvers, and they are us.

Furthermore, such standards as we do use for judging the institutional performance of Congress are applied inconsistently. In 1963, when public dissatisfaction was as great as in 1970, Congress was criticized for being obstructionist, dilatory and insufficiently cooperative with regard to the Kennedy programs. Two years later, Congress got its highest performance rating of the decade when it cooperated completely with the executive in rushing the Great Society program into law. But by the late 1960s and early 1970s the standard of judgment had changed radically—from cooperation to counterbalance in Congressional relations with the Executive. Whereas, in 1963, Harris had found "little in the way of public response to the time-honored claim that the Legislative Branch is . . . the guardian against excessive Executive power," by 1968 he found that three-quarters of the electorate wanted Congress to act as the watchdog of the Executive and not to cooperate so readily with it. The easy passage of the Tonkin Resolution reflects the cooperative standards set in the earlier period; its repeal reflects the counterbalancing standards of the recent period. Today we are concerned about Ralph Nader's "broken branch" which, we hear, has lost—and must reclaim from the Executive—its prerogatives in areas such as war-making and spending control. To some degree, then, our judgments on Congress are negative because we change our minds frequently concerning the kind of Congress we want. A Congress whose main job is to cooperate with the Executive would look quite different from one whose main job is to counterbalance the Executive.

Beneath the differences in our standards of judgment, however, lies a deeper dynamic of the political system. Senators and representatives, for their own reasons, spend a good deal more of their time and energy polishing and worrying about their individual performance than they do working at the institution's performance. Though it is, of course, true that their individual activity is related to institutional activity, their first-order concerns are individual, not institutional. Foremost is their desire for reelection. Most members of Congress like their job, want to keep it, and know that there are people back home who want to take it away from them. So they work long and hard at winning reelection. Even those who are safest want election margins large enough to discourage opposition back home and/or to help them float further political ambitions. No matter what other personal goals representatives and senators wish to accomplish—increased influence in Washington and helping to make good public policy are the most common—reelection is a necessary means to those ends.

We cannot criticize these priorities—not in a representative system. If we believe the representative should mirror constituency opinion, we must acknowledge that it requires considerable effort for him to find out what should be mirrored. If we believe a representative should be free to vote his judgment, he will have to cultivate his constituents assiduously before they will trust him with such freedom. Either way we will look favorably on his efforts. We come to love our legislators, in the *second* place, because they so ardently sue for our affections.

As a courtship technique, moreover, they re-enforce our unfavorable judgments about the institution. Every representative with whom I traveled criticized the Congress and portrayed himself, by contrast, as a fighter against its manifest evils. Members run *for* Congress by running *against* Congress. They refurbish their individual reputations as "the best congressman in the United States" by attacking the collective reputation of the Congress of the United States. Small wonder the voters feel so much more warmly disposed and so much less fickle toward the individuals than toward the institution.

One case in point: the House decision to grant President Nixon a spending ceiling plus authority to cut previously appropriated funds to maintain that ceiling. One-half the representatives I was with blasted the House for being so spineless that it gave away its power of the purse to the President. The other half blasted the House for being so spineless in exercising its power of the purse that the President had been forced to act. Both groups spoke to supportive audiences; and each man enhanced his individual reputation by attacking the institution. Only by raising both questions, however, could one see the whole picture. Once the President forced the issue, how come the House didn't stand up to him and protect its crucial institutional power over the purse strings? On the other hand, if economic experts agreed that a spending ceiling was called for, how come the House didn't enact it and make the necessary budget cuts in the first place? The answer to the first question lies in the proximity of their reelection battles, which re-enforced the tendency of all representatives to think in individualistic rather than institutional terms. The answer to the second question lies in the total absence of institutional machinery whereby the House (or, indeed, Congress) can make overall spending decisions.

Mention of the institutional mechanisms of Congress leads us to a *third* explanation for our prevailing pattern of judgments. When members of Congress think institutionally—as, of course they must—they think in terms of a structure that will be most congenial to the pursuit of their individual concerns—for reelection, for influence, or for policy. Since each individual has been independently designated "the best in the United States," each has an equal status and an equal claim to influence within the structure. For these reasons, the members naturally think in terms of a very fragmented, decentralized institution, providing a maximum of opportunity for individual performance, individual influence, and individual credit.

The 100-member Senate more completely fits this description than the 435-member House. The smaller body permits a more freewheeling and creative individualism. But both chambers tend strongly in this direction, and representatives as well as senators chafe against centralizing mechanisms. Neither body is organized in hierarchical—or even in well-coordinated—patterns of decision-making. Agreements are reached by some fairly subtle forms of mutual adjustment—by negotiation, bargaining, and compromise. And interpersonal relations—of respect, confidence, trust—are crucial building blocks. The members of Congress, in pursuit of their individual desires, have thus created an institution that is internally quite complex. Its structure and processes are, therefore, very difficult to grasp from the outside.

In order to play out some aspects of the original puzzle, however, we must make the effort. And the committee system, the epitome of fragmentation and decentralization, is a good place to start. The performance of Congress as an institution is very largely the performance of its committees. The Nader project's "broken branch" description is mostly a committee-centered description because that is where the countervailing combination of congressional expertise and political skill resides. To strengthen Congress means to strengthen its committees. To love Congress means to love its committees. Certainly when we have not loved our Congress, we have heaped our displeasure upon its committees. The major legislative reorganizations, of 1946 and 1970, were committee-centered reforms—centering on committee jurisdictions, committee democracy, and committee staff support. Other continuing criticisms—of the seniority rule for selecting committee chairmen, for example—have centered on the committees.

Like Congress as a whole, committees must be understood first in terms of what they do for the individual member. To begin with, committees are relatively more important to the individual House member than to the individual senator. The representative's career inside Congress is very closely tied to his committee. For the only way such a large body can function is to divide into highly specialized and independent committees. Policy-making activity funnels through these committees; so does the legislative activity and influence of the individual legislator. While the Senate has a set of committees paralleling those of the House, a committee assignment is nowhere near as constraining for the career of the individual senator. The Senate is more loosely organized, senators sit on many more committees and subcommittees than representatives, and they have easy access to the work of committees of which they are not members. Senators, too, can command and utilize national publicity to gain influence beyond the confines of their committee. Whereas House committees act as funnels for individual activity, Senate committees act as facilitators of individual activity. The difference in functions is considerable—which is why committee chairmen are a good deal more important in the House than in the Senate and why the first modifications of the seniority rule should have come in the House rather than the Senate. My examples will come from the House.

Given the great importance of his committee to the career of the House member, it follows that we will want to know how each committee can affect such careers. . . .

Where a committee's members are especially interested in pyramiding their individual influence, they will act so as to maintain the influence of their committee (and, hence, their personal influence) within the House. They will adopt procedures that enhance the operating independence of the committee. They will work hard to remain relatively independent of the Executive Branch. And they will try to underpin that independence with such resources as specialized expertise, internal cohesion, and the respect of their House colleagues. Ways and Means and Appropriations are committees of this sort. By contrast, where a committee's members are especially interested in getting in on nationally controversial policy action, they will not be much concerned about the independent influence of their committee. They will want to ally themselves closely with any and all groups outside the committee who share their policy views. They want to help enact what they individually regard as good public policy; and if that means ratifying policies shaped elsewhere—in the Executive Branch particularly—so be it. And, since their institutional independence is not a value for them, they make no special effort to acquire such underpinnings as expertise, cohesion, or chamber respect. Education and Labor and Foreign Affairs are committees of this sort.

These two types of committees display quite different strengths in their performance. Those of the first type are especially influential. Ways and Means probably makes a greater independent contribution to policy making than any other House committee. Appropriations probably exerts a more influential overview of executive branch activities than any other House committee. The price they pay, however, is a certain decrease in their responsiveness to noncommittee forces—as complaints about the closed rule on tax bills and executive hearings on appropriations bills will attest. Committees of the second type are especially responsive to noncommittee forces and provide easy conduits for outside influence in policymaking. Education and Labor was probably more receptive to President Johnson's Great Society policies than any other House committee; it successfully passed the largest part of the program. Foreign Affairs has probably remained as thoroughly responsive to Executive Branch policies, in foreign aid for instance, as any House committee. The price they pay, however, is a certain decrease in their influence—as complaints about the rubber-stamp Education and Labor Committee and about the impotent Foreign Affairs Committee will attest. In terms of the earlier discussions of institutional performance standards, our hopes for a cooperative Congress lie more with the latter type of committee; our hopes for a counterbalancing Congress lie more with the former.

So, committees differ. And they differ to an important degree according to the desires of their members. This ought to make us wary of blanket descriptions. Within the House, Foreign Affairs may look like a broken branch, but Ways and Means does not. And, across chambers, Senate Foreign Relations (where member incentives are stronger) is a good deal more potent than House Foreign Affairs. With the two Appropriations committees, the reverse is the case. It is not just that "the broken branch" is an undiscriminating, hence inaccurate, description. It is also that blanket descriptions lead to blanket prescriptions. And it just might be that the wisest course of congressional reform would be to identify existing nodes of committee strength and nourish them rather than to prescribe, as we usually do, reforms in equal dosages for all committees.

One lesson of the analysis should be that member incentives must exist to support any kind of committee activity. Where incentives vary, it may be silly to prescribe the same functions and resources for all committees. The Reorganization Act of 1946 mandated all committees to exercise "continuous watchfulness" over the executive branch—in the absence of any supporting incentive system. We have gotten overview activity only where random individuals have found an incentive for doing so—not by most committees and certainly not continuously. Similarly, I suspect that our current interest in exhorting all committees to acquire more information with which to combat the executive may be misplaced. Information is relatively easy to come by—and some committees have a lot of it. What is hard to come by is the incentive to use it, not to mention the time and the trust necessary to make it useful. I am not suggesting a set of reforms but rather a somewhat different strategy of committee reforms—less wholesale, more retail.

Since the best-known target of wholesale committee reform is the seniority rule, it deserves special comment. If our attacks on the rule have any substance to them, if they are anything other than symbolic, the complaint must be that some or all committee chairmen are not doing a good job. But we can only find out whether this is so by conducting a committee-by-committee examination. Paradoxically, our discussions of the seniority rule tend to steer us away from such a retail examination by mounting very broad, across-the-board kinds of arguments against chairmen as a class—arguments about their old age, their conservatism, their national unrepresentativeness. Such arguments produce great cartoon copy, easy editorial broadsides, and sitting-duck targets for our congressmen on the stump. But we ought not to let the arguments themselves, nor the Pavlovian public reactions induced by our cartoonists, editorial writers, and representatives, pass for good institutional analysis. Rather, they have diverted us from that task.

More crucial to a committee's performance than the selection of its chairman is his working relationship with the other committee members. Does he agree with his members on the functions of the committee? Does he act to facilitate the achievement of their individual concerns? Do they approve of his performance as chairman? Where there is real disagreement between chairman and members, close analysis may lead us to fault the members and not the chairman. If so, we should be focusing our criticisms on the members. If the fault lies with the chairman, a majority of the members have the power to bring him to heel. They need not kill the king; they can constitutionalize the monarchy. While outsiders have been crying "off with his head," the members of several committees have been quietly and effectively constitutionalizing the monarchy. Education and Labor, Post Office, and Interior are recent examples where dissatisfied committee majorities have subjected their chairmen to majority control. Where this has not been done, it is probably due to member satisfaction, member timidity, member disinterest, or member incompetence. And the time we spend railing against the seniority rule might be better spent finding out, for each congressional committee, just which of these is the case. If, as a final possibility, a chairman and his members are united in opposition to the majority part or to the rest of us, the seniority rule is not the problem. More to the point, as I suspect is usually the case, the reasons and the ways individual members get sorted onto the various committees is the critical factor. In sum, I am not saying that the seniority rule is a good thing. I am saying that, for committee performance, it is not a very important thing.

What has all this got to do with the original puzzle—that we love our congressmen so much more than our Congress? We began with a few explanatory guesses. Our standards of judgment for individual performance are more easily met: the individual member works harder winning approval for himself than for his institution; and Congress is a complex institution, difficult for us to understand. The more we try to understand Congress—as we did briefly with the committee system—the more we are forced to peel back the institutional layers until we reach the individual member. At that point, it becomes hard to separate, as we normally do, our judgments about congressmen and Congress. The more we come to see institutional performance as influenced by the desires of the individual member, the more the original puzzle ought to resolve itself. For as the independence of our judgments decreases, the disparity between them ought to grow smaller. But if we are to hold this perspective on Congress, we shall need to understand the close individual-institution relationship—chamber by chamber, party by party, committee by committee, legislator by legislator.

This is not a counsel of despair. It is a counsel of sharper focus and a more discriminating eye. It counsels the mass media, for example, to forego "broken branch" type generalizations about Congress in favor of examining a committee in depth, or to forego broad criticism of the seniority rule for a close look at a committee chairman. It counsels the rest of us to focus more on the individual member and to fix the terms of our dialogue with him more aggressively. It counsels us to fix terms that will force him to think more institutionally and which will hold him more accountable for the performance of the institution. "Who Runs Congress," asks the title of the Nader report, "the President, Big Business or You?" From the perspective of this paper, it is none of these. It is the members who run Congress. And we get pretty much the kind of Congress they want. We shall get a different kind of Congress when we elect different kinds of congressmen or when we start applying different standards of judgment to old congressmen. Whether or not we ought to have a different kind of Congress is still another, much larger, puzzle.

❖❖ The previous selection defines one dimension of the relationship between congressmen and their constituencies. A commonly held assumption about members of Congress is that their primary incentive is to engage in activities that strengthen their prospects for reelection. David Mayhew, one proponent of this theory, argues in his book *Congress: The Electoral Connection* that both the formal and informal organizations of Congress are oriented principally toward the reelection of its members. For example, the dispersion of committees, which numbered close to three hundred in the 101st Congress (1989–1990), maximizes the opportunities of committee chairmen to use their power to distribute benefits directly to their districts and states and to take positions on issues that will be appealing to their constituents. Moreover, the weak party structure of Capitol Hill allows individual members to go their own ways in dealing with their diverse constituencies. Unified congressional parties, argues Mayhew, would not allow congressmen the necessary flexibility to advertise, claim credit, and take positions to gain electoral support. In the following selection Mayhew illustrates the kinds of activities congressmen engage in to maximize their electoral support.

56

David Mayhew
CONGRESS:
THE ELECTORAL
CONNECTION

Whether they are safe or marginal, cautious or audacious, congressmen must constantly engage in activities related to reelection. There will be differences in emphasis, but all members share the root need to do things—indeed, to do things day in and day out during their terms. The next step here is to present a typology, a short list of the *kinds* of activities congressmen find it electorally useful to engage in. The case will be that there are three basic kinds of activities. It will be important to lay them out with some care . . .

One activity is *advertising*, defined here as any effort to disseminate one's name among constituents in such a fashion as to create a favorable image but in messages having little or no issue content. A successful congressman builds what amounts to a brand name, which may have a generalized electoral value for other politicians in the same family. The personal qualities to emphasize are experience, knowledge, responsiveness, concern, sincerity, independence, and the like. Just getting one's name across is difficult enough; only about half the electorate, if asked, can supply their House members' names. It helps a congressman to be known. "In the main, recognition carries a positive valence; to be perceived at all is to be perceived favorably." A vital advantage enjoyed by House incumbents is that they are much better known among voters than their November challengers. They are better known because they spend a great deal of time, energy, and money trying to make themselves better known. There are standard routines—frequent visits to the constituency, nonpolitical speeches to home audiences, the sending out of infant care booklets and letters of condolence and congratulation. Of 158 House members questioned . . . 121 said that they regularly sent newsletters to their constituents; 48 wrote separate news or opinion columns for newspapers; 82 regularly reported to their constituencies by radio or television; 89 regularly sent out mail questionnaires. Some routines are less standard. Congressman George E. Shipley (D., Ill.) claims to have met personally about half his constituents (i.e. some 200,000 people). For over twenty years Congressman Charles C. Diggs, Jr. (D., Mich.) has run a radio program featuring himself as a "combination disc jockey-commentator and minister." Congressman Daniel J. Flood (D., Pa.) is "famous for appearing unannounced and often uninvited at wedding anniversaries and other events." Anniversaries and other events aside, congressional advertising is done largely at public expense. Use of the franking privilege has mushroomed in recent years; in early 1973 one estimate predicted that House and Senate members would send out about 476 million pieces of mail in the year 1974, at a public cost of $38.1 million—or about 900,000 pieces per member with a subsidy of $70,000 per member. By far the heaviest mailroom traffic comes in Octobers of even-numbered years. There are some differences between House and Senate members in the ways they go about getting their names across. House members are free to blanket their constituencies with mailings for all boxholders; senators are not. But senators find it easier to appear on national television—for example, in short reaction statements on the nightly news shows. Advertising is a staple congressional activity, and there is no end to it. For each member there are always new voters to be apprised of his worthiness and old voters to be reminded of it.

A second activity may be called *credit claiming*, defined here as acting so as to generate a belief in a relevant political actor (or actors) that one is personally responsible for causing the government, or some unit thereof, to do something that the actor (or actors) considers desirable. The political logic of this, from the congressman's point of view, is that an actor who believes that a member can make pleasing things happen will no doubt wish to keep him in office so that he can make pleasing things happen in the future. The emphasis here is on individual accomplishment (rather than, say, party or governmental accomplishment) and on the congressman as doer (rather than as, say, expounder of constituency views). Credit claiming is highly important to congressmen, with the consequence that much of congressional life is a relentless search for opportunities to engage in it.

Where can credit be found? If there were only one congressman rather than 535, the answer would in principle be simple enough. Credit (or blame) would attach in Downsian fashion to the doing of the government as a whole. But there are 535. Hence it becomes necessary for each congressman to try to peel off pieces of governmental accomplishment for which he can believably generate a sense of responsibility. For the average congressman the staple way of doing this is to traffic in what may be called "particularized benefits." Particularized governmental benefits, as the term will be used here, have two properties: (1) Each benefit is given out to a specific individual, group, or geographical constituency, the recipient unit being of a scale that allows a single congressman to be recognized (by relevant political actors and other congressmen) as the claimant for the benefit (other congressmen being perceived as indifferent or hostile). (2) Each benefit is given out in apparently ad hoc fashion (unlike, say, social security checks) with a congressman apparently having a hand in the allocation. A particularized benefit can normally be regarded as a member of a class. That is, a benefit given out to an individual, group, or constituency can normally be looked upon by congressmen as one of a class of similar benefits given out to sizable numbers of individuals, groups, or constituencies. Hence the impression can arise that a congressman is getting "his share" of whatever it is the government is offering. (The classes may be vaguely defined. Some state legislatures deal in what their members call "local legislation.")

In sheer volume the bulk of particularized benefits come under the heading of "casework"—the thousands of favors congressional offices perform for supplicants in ways that normally do not require legislative action. High school students ask for essay materials, soldiers for emergency leaves, pensioners for location of missing checks, local governments for grant information, and on and on. Each office has skilled professionals who can play the bureaucracy like an organ—pushing the right pedals to produce the desired effects. But many benefits require new legislation, or at least they require important allocative decisions on matters covered by existent legislation. Here the congressman fills the traditional role of supplier of goods to the home district. It is a believable role; when a member claims credit for a benefit on the order of a dam, he may well receive it. Shiny construction projects seem especially useful. . . .

The third activity congressmen engage in may be called *position taking*, defined here as the public enunciation of a judgmental statement on anything likely to be of interest to political actors. The statement may take the form of a roll call vote. The most important classes of judgmental statements are those prescribing American governmental ends (a vote cast against the war; a statement that "the war should be ended immediately") or governmental means (a statement that "the way to end the war is to take it to the United Nations"). The judgments may be implicit rather than explicit, as in: "I will support the president on this matter." But judgments may range far beyond these classes to take in implicit or explicit statements on what almost anybody should do or how he should do it: "The great Polish scientist Copernicus has been unjustly neglected"; "The way for Israel to achieve peace is to give up the Sinai." The congressman as position taker is a speaker rather than a doer. The electoral requirement is not that he make pleasing things happen but that he make pleasing judgmental statements. The position itself is the political commodity. Especially on matters where governmental responsibility is widely diffused it is not surprising that political actors should fall back on positions as tests of incumbent virtue. For voters ignorant of congressional processes the recourse is an easy one. The following comment [by a Congressman] is highly revealing: "Recently, I went home and began to talk about the——act. I was pleased to have sponsored that bill, but it soon dawned on me that the point wasn't getting through at all. What was getting through was that the act might be a help to people. I changed the emphasis: I didn't mention my role particularly, but stressed my support of the legislation."

The ways in which positions can be registered are numerous and often imaginative. There are floor addresses ranging from weighty orations to mass-produced "nationality day statements." There are speeches before home groups, television appearances, letters, newsletters, press releases, ghostwritten books, *Playboy* articles, even interviews with political scientists. On occasion congressmen generate what amount to petitions; whether or not to sign the 1956 Southern Manifesto defying school desegregation rulings was an important decision for southern members. Outside the roll call process the congressman is usually able to tailor his positions to suit his audiences. A solid consensus in the constituency calls for ringing declarations. . . .

Probably the best position-taking strategy for most congressmen at most times is to be conservative—to cling to their own positions of the past where possible and to reach for new ones with great caution where necessary. Yet in an earlier discussion of strategy the suggestion was made that it might be rational for members in electoral danger to resort to innovation. The form of innovation available is entrepreneurial position taking, its logic being that for a member facing defeat with his old array of positions it makes good sense to gamble on some new ones. It may be that congressional marginals fulfill an important function here as issue pioneers—experimenters who test out new issues and thereby show other politicians which ones are usable. An example of such a pioneer is Senator Warren Magnuson (D., Wash.), who responded to a surprisingly narrow victory in 1962 by reaching for a reputation in the area of consumer affairs. Another example is Senator Ernest Hollings (D., S.C.), a servant of a shaky and racially heterogeneous southern constituency who launched "hunger" as an issue in 1969—at once pointing to a problem and giving it a useful nonracial definition. One of the most successful issue entrepreneurs of recent decades was the late Senator Joseph McCarthy (R., Wis.); it was all there—the close primary in 1946, the fear of defeat in 1952, the desperate casting about for an issue, the famous 1950 dinner at the Colony Restaurant where suggestions were tendered, the decision that "Communism" might just do the trick.

The effect of position taking on electoral behavior is about as hard to measure as the effect of credit claiming. Once again there is a variance problem; congressmen do not differ very much among themselves in the methods they use or the skills they display in attuning themselves to their diverse constituencies. All of them, after all, are professional politicians. . . .

There can be no doubt that congressmen believe positions make a difference. An important consequence of this belief is their custom of watching each other's elections to try to figure out what positions are salable. Nothing is more important in Capitol Hill politics than the shared conviction that election returns have proven a point. . . .

These, then, are the three kinds of electorally oriented activities congressmen engage in—advertising, credit claiming, and position taking. . . .

❖❖   David Mayhew's thesis, part of which is presented in the preceding selection, is that the Washington activities of congressmen are, with few exceptions, geared toward reelection. In contrast, Richard Fenno argues that the Washington careers of congressmen may or may not be related to reelection. In his early work on Congress, Fenno pointed out that the *incentives* of members of Congress fall generally into three categories: (1) reelection, (2) internal power and influence on Capitol Hill, and (3) good public policy. While the incentives of congressmen cannot always be placed neatly into one of these categories, Fenno's research suggested that the behavior of members *in Congress* tends to be dominated by one of these incentives.[1]

Committee selection, in particular, is made to advance reelection, increase power and status on Capitol Hill, or make a good public policy. For example, such committees as Interior and Insular Affairs in the House serve the reelection incentives of their members by channeling specific benefits, such as water and conservation projects, into their districts. Members seeking influence in the House prefer such committees as Ways and Means and Appropriations, both of which reflect the role of the House in the constitutional system and represent it in the outside world. Congressmen on the Ways and Means and the Appropriations committees, particularly the chairmen and ranking minority members, can use their positions effectively to bolster their reputations for power in the House. "Good public policy" committees are those that are used to reflect ideological viewpoints, such

---

[1]Richard F. Fenno, Jr., *Congressmen in Committees* (Boston: Little, Brown and Co., 1973).

as the House Education and Labor Committee, rather than to give particular benefits to constituents or to augment internal influence.

While congressmen have varying degrees of success in their pursuit of internal power and good public policy, they are overwhelmingly successful in achieving reelection. The power of incumbency is truly formidable. Over ninety-five percent of House incumbents are regularly reelected, usually by margins in excess of fifty-five percent and frequently without opposition. Senators are somewhat more vulnerable than representatives, for Senate seats are attractive targets of opportunity for political parties, interest groups, and ambitious politicians. Nevertheless Senate incumbents, too, have great advantages over challengers and normally well over eighty percent of them are easily reelected. Certainly, as David Mayhew points out in selection 56, congressmen have shaped the legislative environment to enhance their re-election prospects. Incumbents have all sorts of advantages, as the following selection illustrates.

57

George Hackett and Eleanor Clift
THE POWER OF INCUMBENCY

Pity John Dingell, Michigan Democrat. The congressman from suburban De-troit raised a modest $507,000 for his re-election campaign. With TV costs as high as they are, half a million dollars doesn't go very far—unless you take into account the fact that Dingell is unopposed. Dingell is not unique. This year 59 congressmen facing either token opposition or none at all amassed a total of $14.8 million in campaign contributions. Of the remaining "races" involving incumbents, the vast majority will be runaways for the officeholder. According to a survey by *Congressional Quarterly*, fewer than 10 of the 435 House seats are seriously contested.

Thanks largely to special-interest PAC money, incumbents stockpile vast war chests that effectively scare off potential challengers. While the fight for the Oval Office has remained a lively contest, the House has virtually become a "permanent Congress"—a closed club open to new members only when old

From *Newsweek*, November 14, 1988, pp. 20–23. © 1988, Newsweek, Inc. All rights reserved. Reprinted by permission.

ones die or move on. In the election two years ago, an astonishing 98.5 percent of the representatives won re-election—making for a turnover rate lower than that of the Soviet Central Committee of the Communist Party, where all "candidates" are unopposed. This year re-election of incumbents promises to be equally automatic. Only one officeholder was rejected during a primary: California Republican Ernie Konnyu, a conservative who lost voters' confidence after women staffers charged him with sexual harassment.

ACCESS AND INFLUENCE

The Founding Fathers created the House as a "people's body," thinking the two-year terms would make it more responsive to voter attitudes. But the modern-day powers of incumbency serve as a shield for congressmen. Officeholders enjoy easy access to the stuff that votes are made of: money. Fully 50 percent of the campaign cash collected by the 59 unchallenged incumbents this year comes from PAC's. Critics say the relationship between the special-interest funding and senior House members, many of whom chair influential committees, amounts to little more than legalized bribery. "That these PAC's feel compelled to contribute to lawmakers who have no opponent shows that what is being sought is access and influence," says Joan Claybrook, president of Public Citizen, a public-interest group founded by Ralph Nader.

According to another public-interest group, Common Cause, PAC's donate far more generously to incumbents than to outsiders. As of Sept. 30, senators running for re-election this year had raised $102 million in PAC funds, compared with $38 million for challengers. The same 3-1 ratio applies to the House. "The PAC-rigged system for financing congressional elections is creating a challenger-proof House of Representatives," says Common Cause president Fred Wertheimer. "When House incumbents can't lose, regardless of performance, and House challengers can't win, regardless of talent, then we don't have real elections and we don't have representative government." Ironically, generous donations from big-business PAC's are largely responsible for perpetuating the current Democratic Congress.

Other factors work to keep Congress an exclusive club. Incumbents benefit from constant media visibility and have the means to please constituents by channeling federal money back home. Pork-barrel politics go a long way in explaining why the same voters who reject Michael Dukakis as being "too liberal" repeatedly re-elect senators with liberal voting records. "[Constituents] don't care how [their representatives] vote, as long as the street lights work, the curbs are fixed and the sewer grants come in," says Mark Helmke, a former top aide to Sen. Richard Lugar of Indiana.

House Democrats sponsor an Incumbents Protection Program, which includes instruction on fund raising, attracting media coverage and sending a winning image back to their districts. Aides fax press releases to local newspapers, which all too often print the hype as news stories. Scores of congressmen pipe self-serving cable-TV programs to their districts. Another favorite scheme is to videotape committee meetings, then transmit by satellite craftily edited 30-second sound bites to the local "Eyewitness News" program. This technique works particularly well for the more than 150 subcommittee heads on Capitol Hill, who can show themselves being addressed impressively as "Mr. Chairman." "Short of scandalous senility, incumbents can easily persuade local unscrutinizing media that they're little Sam Rayburns," says Mark Green, director of the liberal think-tank Democracy Project and coauthor of the 1984 book *Who Runs Congress?*

Despite all these advantages, congressmen think they need bulging war chests to protect themselves against unforeseen challenges. Martin Frost of Texas, for example, says he raised most of his $524,000 in 1987, before he knew his only opponent would be a Libertarian candidate with virtually no chance of winning. Because he was elected before 1980, Frost benefits from a loophole that allows him to keep for personal use any leftover campaign money when he leaves office. (He says he will give the money to the Democratic Party.) Michigan's Dingell is also stuffing a personal piggy bank with donated cash, as are Jim Wright, Claude Pepper and Sam Gibbons—all of whom raised hundreds of thousands of dollars while running unopposed (chart).

Some congressmen use excess war chests to become political barons. The three contenders for the Senate Democratic leadership have been distributing cash to the campaigns of colleagues whose votes they hope to get later on. Sens. Daniel Inouye of Hawaii and Bennett Johnston of Louisiana have formed PAC's of their own to make the distributions. George Mitchell of Maine solicits checks from his supporters for other senators' campaigns, then passes them along with a note to let them know he was the benefactor.

Thanks to loose campaign-financing laws (legislated by Congress), almost anything goes when it comes to spending donated funds. House Speaker Jim Wright is currently dipping into his $413,000 cash bag to pay for his defense against alleged ethics violations. Three years ago Missouri Rep. Bill Clay asked for and received a ruling from the Federal Election Commission that allowed him to purchase a tuxedo with campaign funds. Paying catering bills for dinner parties for constituents is routine. "If you're going to go out and break bread with voters, technically the campaign can pick up the tab," says Jan W. Baran, a Washington lawyer who specializes in election law. "It's all legal." Some members have stumbled. Former California representative John Rousselot was embarrassed after he bought his wife Spanish lessons with campaign money. Another former congressman, James Weaver of Oregon, overstepped the bounds when he used campaign funds to invest in the bond market. He argued—unsuccessfully—that he was merely borrowing the cash, and intended to repay it with interest. Unfortunately, he lost money.

Money to Burn

Even when running unopposed, congressmen raise big campaign chests. 1988's Top 10 list:

NAME, STATE	AMOUNT RAISED*
Martin Frost D-Texas	**$524,000** ($267,723 from PAC's)
John Dingell D-Michigan	**$506,872** ($379,842 from PAC's)
Sam Gibbons D-Florida	**$503,340** ($309,537 from PAC's)
Charles Rangel D-New York	**$499,939** ($301,400 from PAC's)
Vic Fazio D-California	**$490,672** ($277,683 from PAC's)
Jack Fields R-Texas	**$456,695** ($239,975 from PAC's)
Lamar Smith R-Texas	**$427,405** ($74,680 from PAC's)
Ed Markey D-Mass.	**$415,594** (no PAC money)
Jim Wright D-Texas	**$412,535** ($128,923 from PAC's)
Claude Pepper D-Florida	**$402,222** ($225,862 from PAC's)

*FROM JAN, 1, 1987 TO SEPT. 30, 1988.
SOURCE: PUBLIC CITIZEN'S CONGRESS WATCH

'A permanent Congress'? *Rangel*
AL STEPHENSON—PICTURE GROUP

Chart Campaign contributions collected for unopposed incumbents in the U.S. House of Representatives.

TUNNEL VISION

Defenders of the permanent Congress, and its creative money rules, argue that job security frees congressmen to cast votes in the national interest instead of hewing to the narrow interests of their districts. But there is little evidence to support that theory. If anything, long-term congressmen tend to develop tunnel vision focused on perpetuating themselves in office. Stu Eizenstat, domestic policy chief during the Carter administration, says congressmen are so insulated from national political trends that they show little concern about who becomes president—a phenomenon evident in the lukewarm support for Dukakis among Capitol Hill Democrats. With their majority assured, says Eizenstat, Democratic congressmen "can go about their merry way without being concerned about the presidential side." As long as their rule—and the cash flow that comes with it—remains permanent, why, indeed, would congressmen trouble themselves with matters as trifling as who becomes leader of the government they were elected to serve?

❖❖   Generally, as congressmen gain seniority, their Washington careers become separated from their constituency activities. The incumbency effect, buttressed by an effective organization within their constituency, leaves them free to pursue goals on Capitol Hill that are not specifically for the purpose of gaining votes. In the following selection Richard Fenno discusses the linkage between the constituency and Washington activities of congressmen.

58

Richard F. Fenno, Jr.
HOME STYLE AND WASHINGTON CAREER

. . . When we speak of constituency careers, we speak primarily of the pursuit of the goal of reelection. When we speak of Washington careers, we speak primarily of the pursuit of the goals of influence in the House and the making of good public policy. Thus the intertwining of careers is, at bottom, an intertwining of member goals.

So long as they are in the expansionist stage of their constituency careers, House members will be especially attentive to their home base. They will pursue the goal of reelection with single-minded intensity and will allocate their resources disproportionately to that end. . . . [F]irst-term members go home more frequently, place a larger proportion of their staff in the district, and more often leave their families at home than do their senior colleagues. Building a reelection constituency at home and providing continuous access to as much of that constituency as possible requires time and energy. Inevitably, these are resources that might otherwise be allocated to efforts in Washington. "The trouble is," said one member near the end of his second term,

> I haven't been a congressman yet. The first two years, I spent all of my time getting myself reelected. That last two years, I spent getting myself a district so that I could get reelected. So I won't be a congressman until next year.

By being "a congressman" he means pursuing goals above and beyond that of reelection (i.e., power in the House and good public policy).

In a House member's first years, the opportunities for gaining inside power and policy influence are limited. Time and energy and staff can be allocated to home without an acute sense of conflict. At rates that vary from congressman to congressman, however, the chances to have some institutional or legislative effect improve. As members stretch to avail themselves of the opportunity, they may begin to experience some allocative strain. It requires time and energy to develop a successful career in Washington just as it does to develop a successful career in the district. Because it may not be possible to allocate these resources to House and home, each to an optimal degree, members may have to make allocative and goal choices.

A four-term congressman with a person-to-person home style described the dilemma of choice:

> I'm beginning to be a little concerned about my political future. I can feel myself getting into what I guess is a natural and inevitable condition—the gradual erosion of my local orientation. I'm not as enthused about tending my constituency relations as I used to be and I'm not paying them the attention I should be. There's a natural tension between being a good representative and taking an interest in government. I'm getting into some heady things in Washington, and I want to make an input into the government. It's making me a poorer representative than I was. I find myself avoiding the personal collisions that arise in the constituency—turning away from that one last handshake, not bothering to go to that one last meeting. I find myself forgetting people's names. And I find myself caring less about it than I used to. Right now, it's just a feeling I have. In eight years I have still to come home less than forty weekends a year. This is my thirty-sixth trip this year. What was it Arthur Rubinstein said? "If I miss one practice, I notice it. If I miss two practices, my teacher notices it. If I miss a week of practice, my audience notices it." I'm at stage one right now—or maybe stage one and stage two. But I'm beginning to feel that I could be defeated before long. And I'm not going to change. I don't want the status. I want to contribute to government.

The onset of a Washington career is altering his personal goals and his established home style. He is worried about the costs of the change; but he is willing to accept some loss of reelection support in exchange for his increased influence in Congress.

This dilemma faces every member of Congress. It is built into the twin requirements that Congress be a representative and a legislative institution. Some members believe they can achieve reelection at home together with influence or policy in Washington without sacrificing either. During Congressman O's first year as a subcommittee chairman, I asked him whether his new position would make it more difficult to tend to district matters. He replied,

> If you mean, am I getting Potomac fever, the answer is, no. If you mean, has the change in my official duties here made me a better congressman, the answer is, yes. If you mean has it taken away from my activity in the constituency, the answer is no.

Congressman O, we recall, has been going home less; but he has been increasing the number and the activity of his district staff. Although he speaks confidently of his allocative solution, he is not unaware of potential problems. "My staff operation runs by itself. They don't need me. Maybe I should worry about that. You aren't going back and say I'm ripe for the plucking are you? I don't think I am."

A three-term member responded very positively when I paraphrased the worries of the congressman friend of his who had quoted Arthur Rubinstein:

> You can do your job in Washington and in your district if you know how. My quarrel with [the people like him] of this world is that they don't learn to be good politicians before they get to Congress. They get there because some people are sitting around the table one day and ask them to do it. They're smart, but they don't learn to organize a district. Once you learn to do that, it's much easier to do your job in Washington.

This member, however, has not yet tasted the inside influence of his friend. Moreover, he does not always talk with such assurance. His district is not so well organized that he has reduced his personal attentiveness to it.

> Ralph Krug [the congressman in the adjacent district] tells me I spoil my constituents. He says, "You've been elected twice; you know your district; once a month is enough to come home." But that's not my philosophy. Maybe it will be someday. . . . My lack of confidence is still a pressure which brings me home. This is my political base. Washington is not my political base. I feel I have to come home to get nourished, to see for myself what's going on. It's my security blanket—coming home.

For now, he feels no competing pulls; but he is not unaware of his friend's dilemma.

Members pose the dilemma with varying degrees of immediacy. No matter how confident members may be of their ability to pursue their Washington and their constituency careers simultaneously, however, they all recognize the potentiality of conflict and worry about coping with it. It is our guess that the conflict between the reelection goal on the one hand and the power or policy goals on the other hand becomes most acute for members as they near the peak of influence internally. For, at this stage of their Washington career, the resource requirements of the Washington job make it nearly impossible to meet established expectations of attentiveness at home. Individuals who want nothing from their Washington careers except the status of being a member of Congress will never pursue any other goal except reelection. For these people, the dilemma of which we speak is minimal. Our concern is with those individuals who find, sooner or later, that they wish to pursue a mix of goals in which reelection must be weighed along with power or policy.

One formula for managing a mix of goals that gives heavy weight to a Washington career is to make one's influence in Washington the centerpiece of home style. The member says, in effect, "I can't come home to present myself in person as much as I once did, because I'm so busy tending to the nation's business; but my seniority, my influence, my effectiveness in Washington is of great benefit to you." He asks his supportive constituents to adopt a new set of expectations, one that would put less of a premium on access. Furthermore, he asks these constituents to remain sufficiently intense in their support to discourage challengers—especially those who will promise access. All members do some of this when they explain their Washington activity—especially in connection with "explaining power." And, where possible, they quote from favorable national commentary in their campaign literature. But [very few Congressmen] have made Washington influence the central element of [their] home style.

One difficulty of completely adopting such a home style is that the powerful Washington legislator can actually get pretty far out of touch with his supportive constituents back home. One of the more senior members of [Congress], and a leader of his committee, recounted the case when his preoccupation with an internal legislative impasse affecting Israel caused him to neglect the crucial Jewish element of his primary constituency—a group "who contribute two-thirds of my money." A member of the committee staff had devised an amendment to break the deadlock.

> Peter Tompkins looked at it and said to me, "Why don't we sponsor it?" So we put it forward, and it became known as the Crowder-Tompkins Amendment. I did it because I respected the staff man who suggested it and because I wanted to get something through that was reasonable. Well, a member of the committee called people back home and said, "Crowder is selling out." All hell broke loose. I started getting calls at two and three in the morning from my friends asking me what I was doing. So I went back home and discussed the issue with them. When I walked into the room, it made me feel sad and shocked to feel their hostility. They wanted me to know that they would clobber me if they thought I was selling out. Two hours later, we walked out friends again. I dropped the Crowder-Tompkins Amendment. That's the only little flare up I've ever had with the Jewish community. But it reminded me of their sensitivity to anything that smacks of discrimination.

The congressman survived. But he would not have needed so forceful a reminder of his strongest supporters' concerns were he nearer the beginning of his constituency career. But, of course, neither would he have been a committee leader, and neither would the imperatives of a House career bulked so large in his mix of goals.

Another way to manage conflicting reelection and Washington career goals might be to use one's Washington influence to alter support patterns at home. That is, instead of acting—as is the normal case—to reenforce home support, to keep what he had "last time," the congressman might act to displace that old support with compensating new support. He might even accomplish this inadvertently, should his pursuit of power or policy attract, willy-nilly, constituents who welcome his new mix of goals. The very Washington activity that left him out of touch with previously supportive constituents might put him in touch with newly supportive ones. A newly acquired position of influence in a particular policy area or a new reputation as an effective legislator might produce such a feedback effect. . . .

. . . [There is] a tendency for successful home styles to harden over time and to place stylistic constraints on the congressman's subsequent behavior. The pursuit of a Washington career helps us explain this constituency phenomenon. That is, to the degree that a congressman pursues power or policy goals in the House, he will have that much less time or energy to devote to the consideration of alternative home styles. His predisposition to "do what we did last time" at home will be further strengthened by his growing preoccupation with Washington matters. Indeed, the speed with which a congressman begins to develop a Washington career will affect the speed with which his home style solidifies. . . .

In all of this speculation about career linkages, we have assumed that most members of Congress develop, over time, a mix of personal goals. We particularly assume that most members will trade off some of their personal commitment to reelection in order to satisfy a personal desire for institutional or policy influence. It is our observation . . . that House members do, in fact, exhibit varying degrees of commitment to reelection. All want reelection in the abstract, but not all will pay any price to achieve it; nor will all pay the same price. . . .

One senior member contemplated retirement in the face of an adverse redistricting but, because he had the prospect of a committee chairmanship, he decided to run and hope for the best. He wanted reelection because he wanted continued influence; but he was unwilling to put his present influence in jeopardy by pursuing reelection with the same intensity that marked his earlier constituency career. As he put it,

> Ten years ago, I whipped another redistricting. And I did it by neglecting my congressional duties . . . Today I don't have the time, and I'm not going to neglect my duties . . . If I do what is necessary to get reelected and thus

become chairman of the committee, I will lose the respect and confidence of my fellow committee members because of being absent from the hearings and, occasionally, the votes.

He did not work hard at reelection, and he won by his narrowest margin ever. But he succeeded in sustaining a mix of personal goals very different from an earlier one. . . .

The congressman's home activities are more difficult and taxing then we have previously recognized. Under the best of circumstances, the tension involved in maintaining constituency contact and achieving legislative competence is considerable. Members cannot be in two places at once, and the growth of a Washington career exacerbates the problem. But, more than that, the demands in both places have grown recently. The legislative workload and the demand for legislative expertise are steadily increasing. So is the problem of maintaining meaningful contact with their several constituencies. Years ago, House members returned home for months at a time to live among their supportive constituencies, soak up the home atmosphere, absorb local problems at first hand. Today, they race home for a day, a weekend, a week at a time. [Few] maintain a family home in their district. [Many] stay with relatives or friends or in barely furnished rooms when they are at home. The citizen demand for access, for communication, and for the establishment of trust is as great as ever. So members go home. But the quality of their contact has suffered. "It's like a one-night stand in a singles bar." It is harder to sustain a genuine two-way communication than it once was. House member worries about the home relationship—great under any circumstances, but greater now—contribute to the strain and frustration of the job. Some cope; but others retire. It may be those members who cannot stand the heat of the home relationship who are getting out of the House kitchen. If so, people prepared to be more attentive to home . . . are likely to replace them.

The interplay between home careers and Washington careers continues even as House members leave Congress. For, in retirement or in defeat, they still face a choice—to return home or to remain in Washington. The subject of postcongressional careers is too vast to be treated here. But students of home politics can find, in these choices, indications of the depth and durability of home attachments in the face of influential Washington careers. It is conventional wisdom in the nation's capital that senators and representatives "get Potomac fever" and that "they don't go back to Pocatello" when their legislative careers end. Having pursued the goals of power and policy in Washington with increasing success, they prefer, it is said, to continue their Washington career in some nonlegislative job rather than to go back home. In such a choice, perhaps, we might find the ultimate displacement of the constituency career with the Washington career.

An examination of the place of residence of 370 individuals who left the House between 1954 and 1974, and who were alive in 1974, sheds considerable doubt on this Washington wisdom. It appears that most House members do, indeed, "go back to Pocatello." Of the 370 former members studied, 253 (68 percent) resided in their home states in 1974; 91 lived in the Washington, D.C., area; and 26 resided someplace else. Of those 344 who chose either Washington or home, therefore, nearly three-quarters chose home. This simple fact underscores the very great strength of the home attachments we have described in this book.

No cross section of living former members will tell us for sure how many members lingered in Washington for a while before eventually returning home. Only a careful tracing of all individual cases, therefore, will give us a full and accurate description of the Washington-home choice. Even so, among the former members most likely to be attracted to Washington—those who left Congress from 1970 to 1974—only 37 percent have chosen to remain there. A cursory glance at all those who have chosen to prolong their Washington careers, however, tells us what we might expect—that they have already had longer congressional careers than those who returned home. Our data also tell us that these members are younger than those who choose to return home. Thus, we speculate, the success of a member's previous career in Congress and the prospect that he or she still has time to capitalize on that success in the Washington community are positive inducements to stay. And these inducements seem unaffected by the manner of his or her leaving Congress—whether by electoral defeat (for renomination or reelection) or retirement. Those who were defeated, however, had shorter congressional careers and were younger than those who had voluntarily retired.

A Day in the United States Senate

The environments of the Senate and the House differ rather significantly. Election to the United States Senate means that one has arrived politically. With the exception of the White House, the Senate is the most prestigious body in Washington. Rarely does a senator resign to take another post, as did Maine Senator Edmund Muskie in 1980 to become Secretary of State, considered to be the highest ranking job in the Cabinet. Senators are statesmen in their own right, and they often act as sovereign bodies. They may be involved in international as well as national politics. The six-year term of office and the broad constituencies of senators make them less directly dependent upon the people, and as the framers of the Constitution intended, more capable of independent, deliberative action than members of the House.

Although the Senate is no longer dominated by an inner club of senior members, as described by William S. White in *The Citadel* in 1956, a spirit of collegiality prevails and some past traditions do linger. Norms of hard work, expertise, courtesy, and respect for the institution and its ways continue to characterize those senators who have achieved power and status in the body. A long apprenticeship is no longer required of junior senators before they can make their voice heard on Capitol Hill, but it still behooves them to respect the informal rules governing the way in which the Senate operates.

In the following selection, Elizabeth Drew, Washington correspondent for *The New Yorker* magazine and a freelance writer on politics, describes a day in the life of Senator John Culver of Iowa. Culver first arrived at Capitol Hill in 1964, when he was elected to the House. He was an influential member of the Democratic Study Group and was a leading proponent of House reform. He ran for the Senate in 1974 and won with 52 percent of the vote. He became an active member of the Senate, leading his Democratic colleagues on a number of issues, including arms control and the SALT treaty. As a member of the Armed Services Committee he developed a reputation for hard work, expertise, and an aggressive stance on reviewing defense expenditures that did not always conform to the hawkish views of the committee. He did not hesitate to fight what he considered to be unwarranted increases in defense expenditures. He was an active chairman of the Research and Development Subcommittee of Armed Services. In another policy sphere, he was a member of the Environment and Public Works Committee and chairman of its Resource Protections Subcommittee, which he used to sponsor the endangered-species legislation for which he was the floor-manager.

While Culver was building his profile in the Senate, he was defeated in 1980 in a state that was shifting to the Republican party. To what extent was the senator's day, described in the following selection and largely devoted to floor-managing his endangered-species bill, helpful to reelection? Was Culver striving for power and status in the Senate and in the broader world of Washington? Was the senator's visibility on Capitol Hill useful to him back home?

59

Elizabeth Drew
A DAY IN THE LIFE OF A
UNITED STATES SENATOR

Wednesday, July 19th: Culver has gone to the White House for the eight-o'clock breakfast meeting on lifting the embargo on the sale of arms to Turkey (he asked the President to what extent the policy of lifting the embargo, in the interests of strengthening NATO, had anticipated a negative reaction in Greece, which could have consequences that would weaken NATO); at nine-thirty, he met on the Senate steps with 4-H Clubs from three counties in Iowa; at nine-forty-five, he met with Charles Stevenson to go over some questions he had on the material, which he had read early this morning, for the press conference on Soviet civil defense; and then he met with George Jacobson and Kathi Korpon on amendments that will come up today on the endangered-species bill.

Now, at ten o'clock, the Senate resumes debate on the bill. S. I. Hayakawa, Republican of California, offers a minor amendment, which Culver accepts, in accordance with his policy of accepting as many as he can in order to build a consensus behind the bill. Representatives of the Fish and Wildlife Service are stationed in the Vice President's Capitol Hill office, off the Senate floor, and amendments that Culver is giving consideration to accepting are sent out to them for their opinion. He turns the floor over to [Senator Malcolm] Wallop [R., Wy.] so that Wallop can engage Hayakawa in a colloquy to establish the legislative history of the amendment. Culver is giving Wallop a larger role than the majority manager usually affords the minority—also in the interest of building a consensus.

Shortly before ten-thirty, Culver leaves the floor to go to the Dirksen Office Building for his press conference on Soviet civil defense. Just before the press conference begins, he goes over again with Charles Stevenson the points he wants to stress. A fair number of newspaper reporters are here, along with reporters from two television networks and one television station in Iowa. Culver enters the room and sits behind a table that has several microphones on it. He is wearing a navy-blue suit, a blue shirt, and a navy-blue tie with small white dots. He reads a statement explaining that "for the past two years I have sought an official but unclassified assessment of Soviet civil defense which could be made available for a better-informed public debate on this issue." The report he has received, and is releasing today, he says, "represents the first comprehensive and authoritative analysis of this crucial topic in unclassified form." He says that "the study indicates that the Soviet civil-defense system, while representing a significant national effort, is by no means sufficiently effective to encourage the Soviets to risk starting a nuclear war."

He continues, "While crediting the Soviet Union with a major, ongoing civil-defense program, this report demonstrates that those efforts are not sufficient to prevent millions of casualties and massive industrial damage in the event of a nuclear war. In short, Soviet programs are not enough to tip the strategic balance against us." He is addressing himself to recent alarms that the Soviets are engaged in a new civil-defense effort of sufficient proportions that the strategic balance might indeed be tipped, and to arguments that therefore the United States should also engage in a new, enlarged civil-defense program. Now, also addressing himself to the arguments of critics of SALT, and pursuing his goal, about which he spoke to me earlier, of achieving more understanding in both the United States and the Soviet Union concerning the consequences of a nuclear exchange, he says, "Despite the widespread claims that Soviet leaders might launch a nuclear attack because they expect to suffer only moderate damage and few casualites—and we hear that suggested today in a number of quarters—the professional judgment of our intelligence community is that they would not be emboldened to expose themselves and their country to a higher risk of nuclear attack. Even under the 'worst case' assumptions of this study, nuclear war would be a disaster for the Soviet Union." He takes questions, and answers earnestly and with a large number of facts. He says that the estimates of each side's losses in a nuclear attack vary with the targeting plan and the warning time—that the Soviet Union could lose well over a hundred million people, but that figure could be cut by more than fifty per cent if it had two to three days' warning. "I guess the bottom line in all this," he says, "is that even in the worst case the casualties would be awesome."

When one of the reporters questions his conclusions, Culver becomes annoyed. "We do have a great deal of speculation. It's rampant," he says, referring to the alarms about the nature of the Soviet threat. His voice rises. "We don't need to panic," he says. "There is no surge planning. Since they can't have high confidence—and that's what this report is about—the Soviet Union would not be emboldened to risk a nuclear war." Culver is getting involved, and he just keeps going, making his argument, ranging into the way he thinks about the whole subject. He may have a bill pending on the Senate floor, but now he gives this his all, takes the opportunity to present his case. He says, "We talk so much about military doctrine—that General So-and-So says this, that General So-and-So says that. Soldiers in every country all the time talk about victory. They're not paid to talk about defeat. They are trained with the can-do spirit, and the can-do spirit can lead to nuclear war—holocaust, believe it or not." The passion has come to the surface again. "The political leadership on both sides believe that nuclear war would be a disaster," he says. "Now, whether the troops have got the message is another question." Addressing himself to his questioner, he continues, "The Soviet civil-defense effort, I beg your pardon, is not the coördinated, effective system that some so-called experts have claimed, according to the judgment of the people who wrote this report." He goes on—as he did with me in his office, as he did with the constituents in Des Moines—about both sides having civil-defense signs in their subways, both sides having pamphlets. He says, "If you just like to embrace rumor and innuendo and fear, fine. Some people make a lifetime career of it."

He then tries to turn to someone else, but the reporter follows up with a question based on a statement by a Soviet general.

"I could probably provide you with some statements by our highest military or some article they've written," Culver replies. "In that context, everyone's talking about, quote, winning a war, unquote."

He goes on for a while, talking about Soviet history. "I'm not minimizing their effort, and it may be comfortable to characterize my position as 'weak on civil defense,' " he says, "but what I want to do is to get objective information before the public."

In answer to a question about whether he thinks that the United States should proceed to spend substantially increased funds on civil defense over the next few years, Culver says, "I think that we're just going to have to carefully look at it and review it." He adds that he thinks this is an area that should be explored in future SALT talks. "It seems to me that before we all pour a lot of money along this line," he says, "why don't we get together and try to agree, in the spirit of the A.B.M. agreement"—in 1972, the United States and the Soviet Union agreed to limit substantially their deployment of anti-ballistic missiles—"and try to find a way to minimize the threat." This is how he argued in opposing construction of a military base on Diego Garcia, and later there were talks on demilitarizing the Indian Ocean; this is how he argued about conventional-arms sales, and later there were talks on that subject. However fruitful the talks may or may not be, Culver considers such efforts worth a try.

Culver concludes the press conference at eleven-fifteen.

In an anteroom, Don Brownlee is waiting with a tape-recording machine, so that Culver can record "actualities" to send out to the Iowa radio stations. As Brownlee holds a microphone, Culver reads two excerpts from his statement. Charles Stevenson tells Culver that he has some questions about provisions that Culver backed which might come up in the House-Senate conference on the military-procurement bill this afternoon—questions about which provisions he might want to trade for what. "We'll have to talk about that more, Charlie," Culver says.

When Culver returns to the Senate floor, an amendment by [Gaylord] Nelson [D., Wis.] is pending. This one would limit projects that could be exempted to those for which "a substantial and irretrievable commitment of resources had been made." Culver speaks in opposition, saying that the amendment "does have some superficial appeal" but could have undesirable results—that it could have the effect of discouraging agencies from confronting the problem until a project was well along. He does an imitation, in a prissy voice, of an imagined, unrealistic statement by a representative of the Fish and Wildlife Service in the course of a discussion over whether a project should proceed. He draws an analogy—perhaps because of what he was dealing with in his press conference—between such discussions and the bargaining over SALT. "This amendment could have the force and effect of accelerating the move toward construction," he says. "This amendment says the only way you can have any hope for receiving an exemption is to get in there and build." He cites Nelson's proposed language—"a substantial and irretrievable commitment of resources." He bellows, "What on earth is that? Is there a lawyer in the house? Substantial to whom? Irretrievable to whom?" He returns to the defense analogy, referring now to the current controversy over whether and what sort of a mobile-missile system should be built. "We may have to dig a hole where the Furbish lousewort lives," he says, and he goes on to say that we should not get into a situation where it would be like saying to the Defense Department, " 'Go ahead and build the damn thing, and if you build it enough to spend thirty million dollars, then we will tell you you should not have done it in the first place.' " Nelson's amendment is defeated by a vote of twenty-five to seventy.

During the roll call, Culver goes over to the Republican side to confer with Scott.

Now [William] Scott [R., Va.] offers an amendment to exempt a project that might prevent the recurrence of a natural disaster, and Culver accepts it. Scott previously referred several times in the debate to a flood in Virginia that took the lives of four people, and yesterday afternoon Culver decided to try to reach agreement with him on an amendment to cover natural disasters. Next, he accepts an amendment by Scott to provide that five rather than all seven members of the interagency committee will constitute a quorum. Culver's hope is that if he accommodates Scott, Scott may reciprocate by withholding some of the several amendments he still has pending. "It's like a negotiating situation," Culver has explained to me. "You have twelve amendments, but there are only three or four you care about." Scott, however, is unpredictable. And though Scott has little influence within the Senate, Culver still has to be concerned that, as the day goes on, the Senate might accept something that Scott proposes or an atmosphere might be created in which some surprise amendment would be adopted. When Senate sessions go on until late in the day or into the evening, matters can get increasingly out of hand: tempers rise, a few drinks may have been consumed, and a certain "what the hell?" attitude can take over. "Late in the day gets to be the silly season," Culver has explained to me. "It gets harder and harder to control what happens."

For that reason, Culver has persuaded Scott to bring up now the amendment that Culver most fears: the one to require a majority vote, rather than a vote of five of the seven members, of the interagency committee in granting an exemption. He is worried that his proposal is vulnerable here. And he is concerned that if the number of votes required to exempt a project should be reduced to a simple majority many more projects might be exempted. Scott was not enthusiastic about offering the amendment at this point, but Culver has talked him into it. The theory behind having Scott bring up the amendment now is that it is better to have such a proposal come up in the morning—a time when many senators are in committee meetings or in their offices and are more distracted than usual from the business that is taking place on the floor. Also, Culver figures that most of his colleagues will assume that at this point, especially after a long day of taking up amendments—and major ones—yesterday, only routine, "housekeeping" amendments are being considered, and that they will pay less attention to the issue, be less eager to join the fray, than they might be later on.

These are the sorts of calculations that managers of bills must make. Culver figures, further, that if an amendment is to be offered on the voting of the new committee he would prefer that it be offered by Scott. And, by a prior arrangement that Culver has made with Nelson, Nelson will ask for a roll-call vote on the amendment. Scott does not want a roll call on it. Culver's idea is to beat the amendment, and beat it good, burying the issue in the Senate once and for all, and also putting him in a position to tell a Senate-House conference on the bill that the proposal was resoundingly defeated in the Senate. "It's a judgment call," Culver has said, explaining to me the considerations behind whether or not to put something to a roll-call vote. Sometimes, as happened when [John] Stennis, as chairman of the Armed Services Committee and floor manager of the military-procurement bill, accepted Culver's amendment on aircraft carriers, a senator will decide not to press for a roll-call vote, to—as Culver puts it—"God, take it and run."

So now Scott calls up his amendment to require that the votes of only four of the seven members of the interagency committee are necessary in order to exempt a project. Culver, speaking in opposition to the amendment, offers some precedents for requiring a "super-majority" vote. Culver wasn't sure there were any precedents, but his staff has been imaginative: he uses the example of jury trials in criminal cases—which require unanimity—and he cites the Senate rule that a filibuster can be cut off only by the votes of sixty members, or three-fifths, of the Senate. Scott's amendment is defeated on a roll-call vote, twenty-three to sixty-nine.

Now Culver accepts a number of other amendments offered by Republicans. He has told me, "You can take a couple of amendments you know you are going to drop in a spittoon on the way to the conference." Nelson had some other amendments, too, but by one-thirty he and the environmentalists backing him have decided to give up.

Off the Senate floor, a Democratic senator talks to me about Culver. "He's doing a real good job of managing the bill," the senator says. "It's a controversial issue; he's picking his way through the amendments, and working some out, and fighting and defeating others, and establishing his control over the floor. That's very important: others will follow your lead if they feel that you're being sensible and you have control."

This afternoon, Culver—he has skipped lunch again—works to keep that control. He quickly moves against a senator who has asked for more time than was permitted under the unanimous-consent agreement and who wants to offer a non-germane amendment.

While another senator is speaking, Culver leaves the floor briefly; he has received a card of the sort that visitors send in when they want to see senators, this one telling him that a delegation of forty-one Catholics from Dubuque would like to see him. (He has turned down a number of other requests today to meet with people off the Senate floor.) He goes over to the Rotunda of the Capitol and meets with the group for five minutes, explaining to them that he is managing a bill on the Senate floor, and adding, "I figured if I didn't come out to see you, you'd fire me, but if I don't get back in there the Majority Leader will fire me."

When Culver returns to the Senate, Wallop is sitting next to Scott's seat, in the second-to-last row, talking to Scott, and Culver goes back to join them. After he accepted Scott's amendments this morning, Culver told him that he hoped that that would take care of matters and that Scott would offer no further amendments. Scott said then that he wanted to go back to his office and look over his other amendments. This afternoon, he returned to say that he had four more he wanted to offer, and Culver asked Wallop to go back and talk to Scott and see what he could do. Now Culver finds that they haven't got very far; Scott is insisting that either he be allowed to offer four amendments or he will ultimately offer twelve. Culver has asked for a quorum call—a device used from time to time during a debate in order to gain time to get a senator to the floor, or to regroup, or to work out an amendment, or to negotiate—and the clerk calls the roll, slowly. At one point during the negotiations, Culver puts his head in his hands, seeming very weary.

Finally, at five minutes to three, Culver comes back to his desk and asks that the quorum call be ended. He has talked Scott into offering just one more amendment. Now Scott offers one providing that if the National Security Council determines that any interference with a critical military installation on behalf of an endangered species "would have an adverse effect on the security of the United States," it is authorized to notify the interagency committee in writing and that "the committee shall give immediate consideration to such determination." In the preceding negotiations, Culver has succeeded in getting Scott to modify this amendment; in its original form, it would have allowed the National Security Council to grant an automatic exemption, and it would have been invoked to prevent an adverse effect on any installation, not just one deemed essential to the national security. Culver's objections were that anything might be found adverse to an installation and that granting an automatic exemption was contrary to the spirit of the bill.

Now Scott says, "Suppose a bird or some endangered species was in front of an intercontinental ballistic missile. They could not release that missile." He goes on to say that he thinks "any commander worth his salt" would go ahead and fire the missile, but that, under the Endangered Species Act, the commander would then "be subject to a fine of twenty thousand dollars and imprisonment for up to a year."

Culver, who appears to be struggling to keep a straight face, commends Scott, saying that his amendment "is extremely important and is acceptable."

Then, just as the debate is nearing its end, the Senate sets aside the endangered-species bill to take up the Quiet Communities Act of 1978—the noise-control bill that Culver had talked about in Des Moines, and that he must also manage. Culver is waiting for a certain senator to reach the floor to offer an amendment to the endangered-species bill, and he knows that the noise-control bill is noncontroversial and will take little time, so he and [Marjority Leader Robert] Byrd have decided to bring it up now. Arrangements of this sort are made from time to time, both to accommodate senators and to move legislation along. After Culver reads a statement explaining the provisions of the noise-control bill, it is adopted by voice vote, and the Senate returns to the endangered-species bill, and the last pending amendment is offered and withdrawn.

Now Wallop and Culver commend each other, and their own staffs, on the work on the bill, a few other senators make brief statements, and the roll is called on final passage.

It is clear that the bill will pass, so during the roll call Culver leaves the floor. Don Brownlee has asked him to meet on a grassy spot in front of the Capitol with Dean Norland, a television correspondent from Cedar Rapids. Norland has to have his film at the airport by four o'clock in order to get it on tonight's news.

It is one of those hot, humid Washington summer afternoons. "Hi, Dean," Culver says to Norland. "Can we do this before your subject melts?"

Norland asks him what this bill will do for Iowa, and makes specific reference to the problem of the Dubuque bridge and the Higgins' eye clam.

Culver explains that the bill would require a consultation process. He stands with his hands folded in front of him, and has his somber look; he talks firmly and with composure. There is no sign of how hot and tired he is. The bill, he says, "represents a responsible and rational balance of competing needs, with a strong presumption in favor, whenever there is doubt, of the endangered species." He talks a bit longer, says, "Thank you, Dean, 'preciate it," and then says, "I think I'll go see how my vote is."

On the way back, he glances at his schedule card and notices that he was to meet a constituent for a handshake at three o'clock. He asks Brownlee, "What happened to that constituent?" Brownlee isn't sure. Culver reads a memorandum Brownlee has given him about phone calls that have come in for him: James Schlesinger, the Secretary of Energy, has called him, and so has Patricia Harris, the Secretary of Housing and Urban Development.

When Culver reaches the Senate floor, the roll call is just about completed, and in a few moments Adlai Stevenson, who is presiding, gives the final tally. "On this vote," he says, "the yeas are ninety-four and the nays are three." Culver allows himself a smile of satisfaction, but quickly suppresses it and accepts the congratulations of his colleagues.

It is now shortly after four, and, after going into the cloakroom to talk with some of his colleagues and unwind for a few minutes, Culver goes to the President's Room, a small room behind the Senate floor, to meet Bill Griffee, an Iowa state representative from Nashua, who has been attempting to obtain funds from the Department of Energy to revitalize an old power-dam system. "What would you like me to do at this stage, Bill?" Culver asks.

Griffee replies, "I would like you to keep track of the people in the Department of Energy." Jim Larew, who has accompanied Griffee here, takes notes. Griffee continues, "It just helps if they know a United States senator is darned interested."

Culver offers to make calls when Griffee thinks it would be helpful, and Griffee asks whether he has any objections if when he talks to the press he says that he has spoken with Senator Culver about this project. Culver says, "No, that's all right," and he adds, "I'm not familiar with all the feelings about the project." Don Brownlee takes a picture of the two men standing together.

It is now four-twenty. Jim Larew gives Culver a memorandum from Mike Naylor, Culver's legislative director, telling him that tomorrow the Administration will announce its position on product-liability insurance for small businesses, and that it will fall short of what Culver has proposed. He suggests that Culver get ready to respond to the Administration's announcement, and asks whether, if Culver does not have time to receive a briefing on it this afternoon— he doesn't—Naylor may tell Commerce Department staff members that Culver has asked that Naylor be briefed on the details. Culver writes "Yes" on the memorandum. An aide sends word that today the Agriculture Appropriations Subcommittee has approved one hundred million dollars for Culver's soil-conservation, clean-water program. Brownlee gives him a note saying that a certain part of the military-procurement bill is coming up in conference at four-thirty. Culver decides that if it is important enough one of his colleagues will send word asking him to come.

Now Culver proceeds to the Radio and Television Gallery to talk about the endangered-species bill. This is routine for major figures in a legislative battle. Culver goes into a room containing a set that consists of a mock office. He sits at a desk, with rows of maroon-bound volumes of the *Congressional Record* behind him. There are blue drapes on either side, and Culver pops a cigar that he has been smoking—the cigar is one small way to relieve the tension—on a shelf behind one of the drapes. ABC and CBS are here, and so are several radio reporters.

The first question is "Senator Culver, why did you find it necessary to weaken this act?"

Culver replies carefully—and evenly, under the circumstances—"I don't think we've weakened this act. I think we effected a compromise that would enable it to continue at all. Our subcommittee's hearings indicated that either it would be compromised or it wouldn't be reauthorized at all or it would be emasculated." He explains the bill. This is his best opportunity to explain publicly what it is about. He hasn't had lunch, and he's very tired—he hasn't stopped going all day—but now he states clearly and with energy why the bill was necessary. He draws on his capacity for discipline one more time. He tells how the inflexibility of the existing law had inhibited the Fish and Wildlife Service in carrying it out, and says, "So if you're really concerned about endangered species you've got to be concerned about inflexibility in the law." He stresses the point that through the requirement for five out of seven votes in the committee "the presumption is heavily in favor of the species."

A reporter says that he has had trouble with his tape recorder, and asks Culver if he will explain it all again.

Culver's eyes roll upward, but he coöperates. Then he says, "I hope what we've done is get out ahead of this problem a little bit."

He takes a few more questions, and ends the press conference and retrieves his cigar.

Over coffee in the Senate dining room, Culver talks about the day and goes over some of the messages he has been given. A State Department official is trying to reach him in connection with the proposal to lift the embargo on the sale of arms to Turkey; Howard Metzenbaum is trying to reach him in connection with a torts bill that is pending before the Judiciary Committee. Culver looks at a memorandum about the torts bill. "Doesn't it all just defy belief?" he says to me.

It is now six o'clock. The Senate has taken up the authorization bill for the Department of Housing and Urban Development and is still in session. Later, Culver will go to a fund-raiser for a friend of his who is running for attorney general of Iowa. Tomorrow, he is scheduled to go at eight o'clock to a breakfast seminar on SALT; and then attend a hearing of the Environmental Pollution Subcommittee; and meet with Dr. Norman Borlaug, who is from Iowa, and who received a Nobel Peace Prize for his development of high-yield grain (the "green revolution"); and then meet with Josy Gittler about bills pending before his Juvenile Delinquency Subcommittee; and then have lunch with his two daughters who are in Washington (this weekend, he will go back to McGregor); and then attend the House-Senate conference on the military-procurement bill and also a meeting of the Environment and Public Works Committee on a bill that is part of the President's economic stimulus program (these two meetings will overlap); and meet with a constituent for a handshake; and, of course, go to the Senate floor to vote.

The Contemporary Congress: A Perspective

The twentieth century has been witness to important but infrequent changes in the way Congress carries out its business. The "Revolt of 1910" deposed a powerful House Speaker and reduced the influence of party leaders, resulting in a decentralized Congress dominated by committee chairmen. Those chairmen, who were soon to be almost universally chosen by the seniority rule under which the most senior committee member of the majority party becomes chairman, ruled the roost on Capitol Hill until the early 1970s.

Both the House and the Senate enacted a variety of "reforms" in the 1970s that continue to have an impact as the decade of the 1990s begins. Generically, reform simply means change. Proponents of reform always consider proposed changes to be for the better, while opponents, of course, take the opposite view. Members of Congress who advocate reform often want to change the distribution of power on Capitol Hill to their benefit. The congressional reform camp usually consists of the more junior members who are outside the power loop because they do not possess committee chairmanships or seats on the more powerful committees. To increase their tenuous power, congressional party leaders also may join the cry for reform. The perennial target of the reformers is always the powerful committee system dominated by senior members of the House and the Senate.

During the 1970s House reforms helped to disperse power by strengthening subcommittees, giving them under a Subcommittee Bill of Rights independent authority over legislation initially within their jurisdiction, as well as over their budgets and staffs. Under the Subcommittee Bill of Rights standing-committee chairmen could not unilaterally interfere with their subcommittees in specified areas without the approval of a majority of standing-committee members.

On another front, House reforms in the 1970s voted by congressional Democrats gave rank-and-file party members far more power than they had in the past to influence the legislative process. Senior Democrats on the House Ways and Means Committee no longer controlled the assignment of members to committees when that power was transferred to the Steering and Policy Committee. The Democrats also voted to make the House Rules Committee an adjunct of the Speaker, virtually eliminating the power that the panel and its senior members had in the past over the flow of legislation to the floor. The House reforms helped to democratize the body.

Several years after the House "reformed" itself in 1973 and 1974 the Senate, in 1977, culminated its reform effort by reducing the number of its standing committees, in the interest of increasing legislative efficiency. Moreover, senators were limited to one committee or subcommittee chairmanship, which helped to distribute power to more junior members.

Both the House and the Senate also adopted reforms to strengthen Congress as an institution in relation to the president and the executive branch. The Budget and Impoundment Control Act of 1974 attempted to integrate the decentralized and often chaotic congressional budget process. New Budget committees were supposed to coordinate, integrate, and make some sense of the profligate proposals of the sovereign authorization and appropriations committees. Finally, Congress voted to increase its staff to give it more expertise in dealing with the executive.

The following selection assesses the consequences of the 1970s reforms on the House and the Senate, pointing out important changes that have occurred in both bodies.

60

Norman Ornstein
THE HOUSE AND THE
SENATE IN A NEW
CONGRESS

It is natural to think and write about "Congress" as a unified body. . . . But one of the most interesting aspects of change in Congress is how it has affected the two houses of Congress in the same or different ways. . . .

THE DIFFERENT NATURE OF
THE HOUSE AND THE SENATE

In the 1950s and 1960s, the accepted wisdom about Congress suggested that the House and the Senate were very different institutions. Lewis Froman in 1967 described in outline form the major differences in internal structure, style, and behavior:

From Thomas E. Mann and Norman Ornstein, editors, *The New Congress* (Washington, D.C.: American Enterprise Institute, 1981), pp. 364–371. Reprinted with the permission of the American Institute for Public Policy Research.

House	Senate
Larger (435 members)	Smaller (100 members)
More formal	Less formal
More hierarchically organized	Less hierarchically organized
Acts more quickly	Acts more slowly
Rules more rigid	Rules more flexible
Power less evenly distributed	Power more evenly distributed
Longer apprentice period	Shorter apprentice period
More impersonal	More personal
Less "important" constituencies	More "important" constituencies
Less prestige	More prestige
More "conservative"	More "liberal"

Froman emphasized these differences in analyzing the operation of the two houses, focusing especially on two underlying factors: the size difference and the differing bases of representation (states versus districts).[1]

"Perhaps the most striking difference noticed by most visitors to the Capitol," he wrote, "is the apparent confusion and impersonality in the House chamber as contrasted with the relatively more informal and friendly atmosphere in the Senate." He emphasized the greater insulation of House leaders from their colleagues, the greater friction and more frequent violation of the spirit of comity in the House than in the Senate.

Froman went on to underscore the marked difference in efficiency of operation between the two houses; he commented, "the 'normal' business of the House proceeds quickly. . . . It is rare, for example, for any but major bills in the House to take longer than one day for consideration," while the Senate "is a much more leisurely body." He also discussed the difference between the two chambers in the internal distribution of power, with power dispersed and democratized in the Senate and more narrowly controlled in the House. Senators, on occasion, were even able to chair a subcommittee in their first year, while House members had to wait for a long, long time and had difficulty developing any base of power from which to operate. With all these differences, and especially because of the different constituencies (those of the House being narrower and less diverse), Froman noted that the House tended to be more conservative in its policy predilections than the Senate.

Some three years after Froman's work, Nelson Polsby articulated the broader policy implications of the structural and behavioral differences between the House and Senate. In "Strengthening Congress in National Policy-making," Polsby wrote,

> As institutions, the House and Senate differ markedly in their contemporary characters. The House is a highly specialized instrument for processing legislation. Its great strength is its firmly structured division of labor. This provides

---

[1] Lewis A. Froman, *The Congressional Process: Strategies, Rules, and Procedures* (Boston: Little, Brown, 1967).

the House with a toehold in the policy-making process by virtue of its capacity to specialize . . . this is a consequence of the strong division of labor that the House maintains: members are generally assigned to one or two committees only. Floor debate is normally limited to participation by committee members. There is an expectation that members will concentrate their energies rather than range widely over the full spectrum of public policy.[2]

Specialization in the House, said Polsby, was encouraged by the lack of publicity accorded House members vis-à-vis senators, who preened before the media as presidential hopefuls. The House built in not presidential ambitions but *career* incentives; namely, the possibility down the road of being one of the fifth or tenth of the membership to chair a committee or subcommittee or sit on a key committee like Ways and Means or Rules. With a long-term, career orientation and specialization came experience and expertise. On the other hand, wrote Polsby,

> The essence of the Senate is that it is a forum, an echo chamber, a publicity machine. Thus, passing bills, which is central to the life of the House, is peripheral to the Senate. In the Senate, the three central activities are cultivating national constituencies, formulating questions for debate and discussion on a national scale (especially in opposition to the President), and incubating new policy proposals that may at some future time find their way into legislation.

Thus, two of our most astute students of Congress identified a range of institutional differences between our two legislative houses, which led to formal and informal contrasts in internal operation and to different styles and roles in national policy making.

Froman and Polsby were right, by and large. But, it is worth re-examining their insights in light of the enormous changes which . . . occurred during the 1970s inside Congress and in the broader polity.

I would suggest that one consequence of the changes has been to make the House more like the Senate, and the Senate more like the House. As a result, the unique policy roles Polsby ascribed to the two chambers have been blurred— leading to less consistent and more erratic policy outcomes.

Consider, for a moment, Froman's list of House/Senate differences, beginning on the House side. Size is one constant: the House is still larger than the Senate. But all of the other characteristics have changed during the past decade. The House, to Froman, was more formal and impersonal, more hierarchically organized, with more rigid rules. It acted more quickly than the Senate, had power less evenly distributed, and its members served a longer apprentice period. The House dealt with less "important" constituencies, had less prestige than the Senate, and was more conservative.

---

[2]Nelson Polsby, "Strengthening Congress in National Policy-making," *Yale Review* (Summer 1970), pp. 485–86.

Since Froman wrote, the House has become *less* formal and impersonal, *less* hierarchically organized and with *more* fluid rules and procedures. The House has also become *less* able to act—much less act quickly—on policy matters. It has spread out its power and, like the Senate before it, has abandoned the notion of apprenticeship altogether. The House and House members have become better known (or, at least, more notorious) and are noticed and paid heed to by broader and more important, often national constituencies. And on most issues, even with the changes wrought by the 1980 elections, The House has become much more "liberal" than it was in the 1950s and 1960s. There are some issues, especially the social issues like abortion and busing, where the Senate (at least the 96th) remained more liberal than the House. But on balance, in 1979–1980, and in 1981–1982, the House was and is clearly the more liberal chamber of Congress.

More and more, the House is an ad hoc institution, without firm control over its own schedule or priorities—much like the Senate. With the expansion of subcommittees and chairmanships, many more individuals hold formal positions of importance in the House. Moreover, hierarchical positions, whether in the formal party leadership or at the top of committees, mean much less today than they did in the 1960s; "leadership" on specific issues can come from any of 400 or more different sources.

The Senate has changed, too—becoming in several respects more like the House. Since Froman wrote, the Senate has become much less leisurely. An average in the 1950s of 150 or so roll calls a year has more than quadrupled; so too have the number of meetings and hearings. Indeed, a crushing workload and frenetic pace have changed interpersonal relations (senators see much less of one another, for shorter periods of time) and behavior. The Senate has become *more* formal and impersonal, *more* tightly organized, through its "reformed" committee system, and has developed *more* rigid floor rules and procedures, such as the use of detailed and limiting unanimous consent agreements. The Senate has tried—albeit less than successfully—to develop ways of acting *more* quickly on policy; the tighter filibuster procedures of the late 1970s are an example. While many senators remain celebrities the rapid turnover of members—both the departure of long-time veteran powers and the influx of freshmen—have created a greater anonymity among Senate ranks. Thomas P. "Tip" O'Neill, Morris "Mo" Udall, and several other recent House members rank with Senate celebrities in public recognition and/or acclaim. (Unfortunately for Congress, so do "Ozzie" Myers, John Jenrette, and Charles Diggs.[3]) Clearly, too, the Senate has become more conservative in the late 1970s and early 1980s and, at least since 1978, has been more conservative than the House on many or most policy questions.

---

[3]This is not a function of more scandal in Congress either. As Robinson clearly demonstrates—by contrasting a 1960s scandal involving a *senator* with a 1970s scandal involving a *congressman*—media coverage is much heavier now and especially for the House.

The Senate and House are not now identical, by any means. The size differences and unique constitutional powers ensure that we will continue to have two distinct legislative houses. But the blurring of House-Senate differences in the 1970s has significant implications for their roles in national policy making.

Recall Polsby's distinctions. The House of the 1960s, he wrote, was "a highly specialized instrument for processing legislation," with its strength being its "firmly structured division of labor," giving it the "capacity to specialize" through the committee system. Assignments were limited, only committee members could participate in debate, specialization was encouraged by the lack of public attention given to members' work (compared with senators) and by the various career incentives inside the House. The Senate, on the other hand, was a forum, not a body concerned with the details of legislation. It served as a place to formulate questions for national debate and to incubate new policy approaches for future consideration.

What of the "new" House and Senate? The contemporary House is no longer a "highly specialized instrument." Committee and subcommittee assignments have proliferated, spreading House members much thinner. It is difficult to think of House members now with a reputation for command of, say, the internal revenue code, or the details of the budget, or the ins and outs of the Pentagon approaching that of Wilbur Mills, Clarence Cannon, or Carl Vinson twenty years ago. Reforms weakening committees and encouraging floor amendments, the expansion and decentralization of staff, the influx of new members, the erosion of reciprocity and specialization norms—all have combined to erase the hegemony of committees and committee members in floor debate.

Now the House floor is often a free-for-all, rarely a ratification point for decisions pre-structured by one or two specialists. Carefully crafted legislation is not the only, or the highest, priority of the House. During the floor debate and amendment process, making ideological points for national groups or constituencies, protecting the interests of particular groups, asserting an individual prerogative, or altering a broader policy direction (without deep regard for the specific piece of legislation under consideration) are all competing priorities of significant rank.

It is now possible for an individual House member to become a celebrity profiled in national magazines and featured on national news shows (as Bruce Caputo, George Hansen, Henry Hyde, and Millicent Fenwick, among others, have done in recent years) or to make a credible run for the presidency— witness Mo Udall, John Anderson, and Phil Crane. With the exceptions of Udall and Anderson, all of the above have made their mark through flashy, extralegislative, extra- or anti-committee activity that has captured a national constituency or captivated the networks. None has faced sanctions inside the House for their perfidy.

Career incentives have changed or disappeared, too. Polsby wrote of the incentive for members to accept the House system, biding their time for a decade or two until they, too, could achieve the hefty power of a subcommittee chairmanship or, with a little more patience, the even greater power of a full committee gavel. Reforms, turnover, and subcommittee inflation have changed all that. These days, a subcommittee chairmanship is easy to come by and often quickly achieved—in the 96th Congress, a *freshman* even chaired an Appropriations subcommittee! There is no need or incentive to wait patiently; "those who stand and wait" get no more or better internal rewards than those who do not. Large staffs, which give House members independence, expertise, and the opportunity for notoriety—and which once were the exclusive perquisite of senior leaders and committee honchos—come automatically to all, even the lowliest minority freshmen. Many in the current House—many more than in the past—see their position not as the *capstone* of their careers, but as a *steppingstone* to a Senate seat or state house, to a national political career, to a lucrative position in law, lobbying, or business. The incentive thus is to establish an independent name and reputation as quickly as possible in as many policy areas as possible, with little regard for committee boundaries or subject matter experience. While this incentive existed for the ambitious in the past, the atmosphere and opportunities did not. As the incentive for quick recognition has broadened and been encouraged by new opportunities, the formerly widespread pride in legislative craftsmanship has steadily declined.

Sounds like the "old" Senate, doesn't it? Indeed, the House, as its structures, members, and norms have become more like the Senate's, has seen its policy behavior move in that direction as well.

As the TV cameras blink red, the House floor is a passable forum for discussing national policy, tilting with the president, cultivating national constituencies. The lengthy debate in the House in 1979 over the fiscal 1980 budget—replete with histrionics, bitter rhetoric, and a plethora of amendments—was a good example. The concern in the House was not with passing a tight and consistent budget—not with passing a budget at all. The House instead wanted to put on a national debate over policy choices and priorities.

The "new" House has other Senate-like features. Legions of aggressive and ambitious House subcommittee leaders, with savvy, aggressive, and ambitious staffs, searching for new areas or initiatives to call their own, serve as marvelous incubators for policy proposals that are before their time.

THE SENATE

What of the "new" Senate? It too has changed its policy role. As Senate activity in the past ten years has mushroomed,[4] steps have been taken to bring more coherence and regularity to Senate behavior and scheduling. As these steps—such as more disciplined rules for amendment offering and floor debate—have

---

[4]See John F. Bibby, Thomas E. Mann, and Norman J. Ornstein, *Vital Statistics on Congress, 1980* (Washington, D.C.: American Enterprise Institute, 1980), chap. 8.

been taken, the essential character of the Senate, as a deliberative body, has disappeared. A sharp increase in workload is difficult for a small institution based on comity and informal, flexible procedures to handle. It has the same effect as a substantial increase in membership size. More formal and rigid floor procedures cause tension and shift some legislative activity to other arenas that remain flexible—like subcommittees. Staffs expand to cope with additional work but often serve to provide new work—more bills, more ideas for hearings, more amendments. As Michael Malbin has shown, when staffs become bargaining agents for senators, the informal senator-to-senator relationship changes, becoming less significant, less informal, less close. Expanding committee and subcommittee obligations exacerbate this trend—senators are always on the run, from one subcommittee hearing to another, to the floor to vote (quickly so as to make another meeting or hearing), back to the office, over to another hearing . . . and have fewer and fewer opportunities to socialize or "schmooze" with their colleagues. "I haven't exchanged six words with half these guys," one veteran senator confided to me in 1977, referring to his colleagues on the floor. With more and more bills, amendments, and other votes coming up, little time remains on the Senate floor for debate and deliberation. The "morning hour" is frequently a forum for canned speeches on constituency notables or problems. The rare biting policy speech is largely ignored.

An ironic consequence of these changes—in particular of the tremendous expansion of Senate professional staff—is that the Senate has become increasingly occupied with legislative detail. Several hundred legislative professionals in the Senate have become the "specialists" of the legislative process. They scrutinize the finest details of each piece of legislation, down to the very commas and semicolons, and draft scores of amendments in committee and on the Senate floor. They enable senators to battle the House, line item by line item, in conference committees. They force senators, busy and preoccupied with balancing their overloaded schedules, away from the sustained time necessary to focus on broader, global policy concerns or alternatives. The only option remaining is to haggle over details.

Thus, the House has become less identified with legislative carpentry and more noted for grappling with the larger issues in policy debates. The Senate has moved away from its focus on debate and deliberation, and toward a preoccupation with the legislative nitty-gritty. But neither chamber has moved wholeheartedly to embrace the other's basic policy-making role or to defer to "the other body" in its new incarnation. (Indeed, intra-cameral resentment has grown, if anything.) And, most important, neither the House nor the Senate is *capable* of executing its new role adequately. The modern, 435-member House is inherently too unwieldy, too rigid, and too fractious to be the basic forum for national policy debate. The modern, 100-member Senate is inherently too small and informal to be *the* repository of legislative expertise, and staff cannot compensate for long.

The result is that neither chamber is comfortable with its contemporary role. Both chambers are undergoing identity crises, groping to find policy roles that can accommodate their institutional strengths and limitations, in the context of a greatly changed legislature and society. . . .

Chapter 9

The Judiciary

An independent judicial system is an important part of constitutional government. The United States Supreme Court was created with this view, and its members were given life tenure and guaranteed compensation to maintain their independence. However, Congress was given power to structure the entire subordinate judicial system, including control over the appellate jurisdiction of the Supreme Court. Regardless of any initial lack of power and various attempts made by and through Congress to curb its power, the Supreme Court today occupies a predominant position in the governmental system. The evolution of the Court, its present powers, and their implications are analyzed in this chapter.

Constitutional Background: Judicial Independence and Judicial Review

The Supreme Court and the judicial system play important roles in the intricate separation-of-powers scheme. Through judicial review, both legislative and executive decisions may be overruled by the courts for a number of reasons. To some extent, then, the judiciary acts as a check upon arbitrary action by governmental departments and agencies.The intent of the framers of the Constitution regarding the role of the judiciary, particularly the Supreme Court, in our governmental system is examined in *Federalist 78*.

61

Alexander Hamilton
FEDERALIST 78

We proceed now to an examination of the judiciary department of the proposed government.

In unfolding the defects of the existing confederation, the utility and necessity of a federal judicature have been clearly pointed out. It is the less necessary to recapitulate the considerations there urged; as the propriety of the institution in the abstract is not disputed; the only questions which have been raised being relative to the manner of constituting it, and to its extent. To these points, therefore, our observations shall be confined.

The manner of constituting it seems to embrace these several objects: 1st. The mode of appointing the judges; 2nd. The tenure by which they are to hold their places; 3rd. The partition of the judiciary authority between different courts, and their relations to each other.

First. As to the mode of appointing the judges: This is the same with that of appointing the officers of the union in general, and has been so fully discussed . . . that nothing can be said here which would not be useless repetition.

Second. As to the tenure by which the judges are to hold their places: This chiefly concerns their duration in office; the provisions for their support; the precautions for their responsibility.

According to the plan of the convention, all the judges who may be appointed by the United States are to hold their offices *during good behavior;* which is conformable to the most approved of the state constitutions. . . . The standard of good behavior for the continuance in office of the judicial magistracy is certainly one of the most valuable of the modern improvements in the practice of government. In a monarchy, it is an excellent barrier to the despotism of the prince; in a republic, it is a no less excellent barrier to the encroachments and oppressions of the representative body. And it is the best expedient which can be devised in any government, to secure a steady, upright, and impartial administration of the laws.

Whoever attentively considers the different departments of power must perceive, that, in a government in which they are separated from each other, the judiciary, from the nature of its functions, will always be the least dangerous to the political rights of the constitution; because it will be least in a capacity to annoy or injure them. The executive not only dispenses the honors, but holds the sword of the community. The legislature not only commands the purse, but prescribes the rules by which the duties and rights of every citizen are to be regulated. The judiciary, on the contrary, has no influence over either the sword or the purse; no direction either of the strength or of the wealth of the society; and can take no active resolution whatever. It may truly be said to have neither FORCE NOR WILL, but merely judgment; and must ultimately depend upon the aid of the executive arm for the efficacious exercise even of this faculty.

This simple view of the matter suggests several important consequences: It proves incontestably, that the judiciary is beyond comparison, the weakest of the three departments of power, that it can never attack with success either of the other two; and that all possible care is requisite to enable it to defend itself against their attacks. It equally proves, that, though individual oppression may now and then proceed from the courts of justice, the general liberty of the people can never be endangered from that quarter; I mean so long as the judiciary remains truly distinct from both the legislature and executive. For I agree, that "there is no liberty, if the power of judging be not separated from the legislative and executive powers." It proves, in the last place, that as liberty can have nothing to fear from the judiciary alone, but would have everything to fear from its union with either of the other departments; that, as all the effects of such a union must ensue from a dependence of the former on the latter, notwithstanding a nominal and apparent separation; that as, from the natural feebleness of the judiciary, it is in continual jeopardy of being overpowered, awed or influenced by its coordinate branches; that, as nothing can contribute so much to its firmness and independence as PERMANENCY IN OFFICE, this quality may therefore be justly regarded as an indispensable ingredient in its constitution; and, in a great measure, as the CITADEL of the public justice and the public security.

The complete independence of the courts of justice is peculiarly essential in a limited constitution. By a limited constitution, I understand one which contains certain specified exceptions to the legislative no ex post facto laws, and the like. Limitations of this kind can be preserved in practice no other way than through the medium of the courts of justice, whose duty it must be to declare all acts contrary to the manifest tenor of the constitution void. Without this, all the reservations of particular rights or privileges would amount to nothing.

Some perplexity respecting the right of the courts to pronounce legislative acts void, because contrary to the constitution, has arisen from an imagination that the doctrine would imply a superiority of the judiciary to the legislative power. It is urged that the authority which can declare the acts of another void, must necessarily be superior to the one whose acts may be declared void. As this doctrine is of great importance in all the American constitutions, a brief discussion of the grounds on which it rests cannot be unacceptable.

There is no position which depends on clearer principles than that every act of a delegated authority, contrary to the tenor of the commission under which it is exercised, is void. No legislative act, therefore, contrary to the constitution, can be valid. To deny this would be to affirm, that the deputy is greater than his principal; that the servant is above his master; that the representatives of the people are superior to the people themselves; that men, acting by virtue of powers, may do not only what their powers do not authorize, but what they forbid.

If it be said that that legislative body are themselves the constitutional judges of their powers, and that the construction they put upon them is conclusive upon the other departments, it may be answered, that this cannot be the natural presumption, where it is not to be collected from any particular provisions in the constitution. It is not otherwise to be supposed that the constitution could intend to enable the representatives of the people to substitute their *will* to that of their constituents. It is far more rational to suppose that the courts were designed to be an intermediate body between the people and the legislature, in order, among other things, to keep the latter within the limits assigned to their authority. The interpretation of the laws is the proper and peculiar province of the courts. A constitution is, in fact, and must be, regarded by the judges as a fundamental law. It must therefore belong to them to ascertain its meaning, as well as the meaning of any particular act proceeding from the legislative body. If there should happen to be an irreconcilable variance between the two, that which has the superior obligation and validity ought, of course, to be preferred; in other words, the constitution ought to be preferred to the statute, the intention of the people to the intention of their agents.

Nor does this conclusion by any means suppose a superiority of the judicial to the legislative power. It only supposes that the power of the people is superior to both; and that where the will of the legislature declared in its statutes, stands in opposition to that of the people declared in the constitution, the judges ought to be governed by the latter, rather than the former. They ought to regulate their decisions by the fundamental laws, rather than by those which are not fundamental. . . .

It can be no weight to say, that the courts, on the pretense of a repugnancy, may substitute their own pleasure to the constitutional intentions of the legislature. This might as well happen in the case of two contradictory statutes; or it might as well happen in every adjudication upon any single statute. The courts must declare the sense of the law; and if they should be disposed to exercise WILL instead of JUDGMENT, the consequence would equally be the substitution of their pleasure to that of the legislative body. The observation, if it proved anything, would prove that there ought to be no judges distinct from the body.

If then the courts of justice are to be considered as the bulwarks of a limited constitution, against legislative encroachments, this consideration will afford a strong argument for the permanent tenure of judicial officers, since nothing will contribute so much as this to that independent spirit in the judges, which must be essential to the faithful performance of so arduous a duty.

This independence of the judges is equally requisite to guard the constitution and the rights of individuals, from the effects of those ill-humors which the arts of designing men, or the influence of particular conjunctures, sometimes disseminate among the people themselves, and which, though they speedily give place to better information, and more deliberate reflection, have a tendency, in the meantime, to occasion dangerous innovations in the government, and serious oppression of the minor party in the community. . . . Until the people have, by some solemn and authoritative act, annulled or changed the established form, it is binding upon themselves collectively, as well as individually; and no presumption, or even knowledge of their sentiments, can warrant their representatives in a departure from it, prior to such an act. But it is easy to see, that it would require an uncommon portion of fortitude in the judges to do their duty as faithful guardians of the constitution, where legislative invasions of it had been instigated by the major voice of the community.

But it is not with a view to infractions of the constitution only, that the independence of the judges may be an essential safeguard against the effects of occasional ill-humors in the society. These sometimes extend no farther than to the injury of the private rights of particular classes of citizens, by unjust and partial laws. Here also the firmness of the judicial magistracy is of vast importance in mitigating the severity, and confining the operation of such laws. It not only serves to moderate the immediate mischiefs of those which may have been passed, but it operates as a check upon the legislative body in passing them; who, perceiving that obstacles to the success of an iniquitous intention are to be expected from the scruples of the courts, are in a manner compelled by the very motives of the injustice they mediate, to qualify their attempts. . . .

That inflexible and uniform adherence to the rights of the constitution, and of individuals, which we perceive to be indispensable in the courts of justice, can certainly not be expected from judges who hold their offices by a temporary commission. Periodical appointments, however regulated, or by whomsoever made, would, in some way or other, be fatal to their necessary independence. If the power of making them was committed either to the executive or legislature, there would be danger of an improper compliance to the branch which possessed it; if to both, there would be an unwillingness to hazard the displeasure of either; if to the people, or to persons chosen by them for the special purpose, there would be too great a disposition to consult popularity to justify a reliance that nothing would be consulted but the constitution and the laws.

There is yet a further and a weighty reason for the permanency of judicial offices, which is deducible from the nature of the qualifications they require. It has been frequently remarked, with great propriety, that a voluminous code of laws is one of the inconveniences necessarily connected with the advantages of a free government. To avoid an arbitrary discretion in the courts, it is indispensable that they should be bound down by strict rules and precedents, which serve to define and point out their duty in every particular case that comes before them; and it will readily be conceived, from the variety of controversies which grow out of the folly and wickedness of mankind, that the records of those precedents must unavoidably swell to a very considerable bulk, and must demand long and laborious study to acquire a competent knowledge of them. Hence it is, that there can be but few men in the society, who will have sufficient skill in the laws to qualify them for the stations of judges. And making the proper deductions for the ordinary depravity of human nature, the number must be still smaller, of those who unite the requisite integrity with the requisite knowledge. . . .

❖❖   From *Federalist 78* students can observe that the intent of the framers of the Constitution, at least as expressed and represented by Hamilton, was to give to the courts the power of judicial review over legislative acts. Students should note that this concept was not explicitly written into the Constitution. Although the cause of this omission is not known, it is reasonable to assume that the framers felt that judicial power implied judicial review. Further, it is possible that the framers did not expressly mention judicial review because they had to rely on the states for adoption of the Constitution; judicial power would extend to the states as well as to the coordinate departments of the national government.

The power of the Supreme court to invalidate an act of Congress was stated by John Marshall in *Marbury v. Madison*, 1 Cranch 137 (1803). At issue was a provision in the Judiciary Act of 1789 which extended the *original jurisdiction* of the Supreme Court by authorizing it to issue writs of mandamus in cases involving public officers of the United States and private persons, a power not conferred upon the Court in the Constitution. Marbury had been appointed a justice of the peace by President John Adams under the Judiciary Act of 1801, passed by the Federalists after Jefferson and the Republican party won the elections in the fall of 1800 so that President Adams could fill various newly created judicial posts with Federalists before he left office in March 1801. Marbury was scheduled to receive one of these commissions, but when Jefferson took office on March 4, with Madison as his Secretary of State, it had not been delivered. Marbury filed a suit with the Supreme Court requesting it to exercise its original jurisdiction and issue a writ of mandamus (a writ to compel an official to perform his or her duty) to force Madison to deliver the commission, an act which both Jefferson and Madison were opposed to doing. In his decision, Marshall, a prominent Federalist, stated that although Marbury had a legal right to his commission, and although mandamus was the proper remedy, the Supreme

Court could not extend its original jurisdiction beyond the limits specified in the Constitution; therefore, that section of the Judiciary Act of 1789 permitting the court to issue such writs to public officers was unconstitutional. Incidentally, the Republicans were so outraged at the last-minute appointments of Adams that there were threats that Marshall would be impeached if he issued a writ of mandamus directing Madison to deliver the commission. This is not to suggest that Marshall let such considerations influence him; however, politically his decision was thought to be a masterpiece of reconciling his position as a Federalist with the political tenor of the times.

62

PRESIDENT
JEFFERSON'S
← SEC. OF STATE

PRESIDENT
JOHN →
ADAMS
appointee

MARBURY v. MADISON
1 Cranch 137 (1803)

Mr. Chief Justice Marshall delivered the opinion of the Court, saying in part:
. . . The authority, therefore, given to the Supreme Court, by the [Judiciary Act of 1789] . . . establishing the judicial courts of the United States, to issue writs of mandamus to public officers, appears not to be warranted by the Constitution [because it adds to the original jurisdiction of the Court delineated by the framers of the Constitution in Article III; had they wished this power to be conferred upon the Court it would be so stated, in the same manner that the other parts of the Court's original jurisdiction are stated]; . . . it becomes necessary to inquire whether a jurisdiction so conferred can be exercised.

The question whether an act repugnant to the Constitution can become the law of the land, is a question deeply interesting to the United States; but, happily, not of an intricacy proportioned to its interest. It seems only necessary to recognize certain principles supposed to have been long and well established, to decide it.

That the people have an original right to establish, for their future government, such principles as, in their opinion, shall most conduce to their own happiness, is the basis on which the whole American fabric has been erected. The exercise of this original right is a very great exertion; nor can it nor ought it to be frequently repeated. The principles, therefore, so established, are deemed fundamental. And as the authority from which they proceed is supreme, and can seldom act, they are designed to be permanent.

This original and supreme will organizes the government, and assigns to different departments their respective powers. It may either stop here, or establish certain limits not to be transcended by those departments.

The government of the United States is of the latter description. The powers of the legislature are defined and limited; and that those limits may not be mistaken, or forgotten, the Constitution is written. To what purpose are powers limited, and to what purpose is that limitation committed to writing, if these limits may, at any time, be passed by those intended to be restrained? The distinction between a government with limited and unlimited powers is abolished, if those limits do not confine the persons on whom they are imposed, and if acts prohibited and acts allowed, are of equal obligation. It is a proposition too plain to be contested, that the Constitution controls any legislative act repugnant to it; or, that the legislature may alter the Constitution by an ordinary act.

Between these alternatives there is no middle ground. The Constitution is either a superior paramount law, unchangeable by ordinary means, or it is on a level with ordinary legislative acts, and, like other acts, is alterable when the legislature shall please to alter it.

If the former part of the alternative be true, then a legislative act contrary to the Constitution, is not law; if the latter part be true, then written constitutions are absurd attempts, on the part of the people, to limit a power in its own nature illimitable.

Certainly all those who have framed written constitutions contemplate them as forming the fundamental and paramount law of the nation, and, consequently, the theory of every such government must be, that an act of the legislature, repugnant to the constitution, is void.

This theory is essentially attached to a written constitution, and is consequently to be considered, by this court, as one of the fundamental principles of our society. It is not, therefore, to be lost sight of in the further consideration of this subject.

If an act of the legislature, repugnant to the Constitution, is void, does it, notwithstanding its invalidity, bind the courts, and oblige them to give it effect? Or, in other words, though it be not law, does it constitute a rule as operative as if it was a law? This would be to overthrow in fact what was established in theory; and would seem, at first view, an absurdity too gross to be insisted on. It shall, however, receive a more attentive consideration.

It is emphatically the province and duty of the judicial department to say what the law is. Those who apply the rule to particular cases, must of necessity expound and interpret that rule. If two laws conflict with each other, the courts must decide on the operation of each.

So if the law be in opposition to the Constitution; if both the law and the Constitution apply to a particular case, so that the court must either decide that case conformably to the law, disregarding the Constitution, or comformably to the Constitution, disregarding the law, the court must determine which of these conflicting rules governs the case. This is of the very essence of judicial duty.

If, then, the courts are to regard the Constitution, and the Constitution is superior to any ordinary act of the legislature, the Constitution, and not such ordinary act, must govern the case to which they both apply.

Those, then, who controvert the principle that the Constitution is to be considered, in court, as a paramount law, are reduced to the necessity of maintaining that courts must close their eyes on the Constitution, and see only the law.

This doctrine would subvert the very foundation of all written constitutions. It would declare that an act which, according to the principles and theory of our government, is entirely void, is yet, in practice, completely obligatory. It would declare that if the legislature shall do what is expressly forbidden, such act, notwithstanding the express prohibition, is in reality effectual. It would be giving to the legislature a practical and real omnipotence, with the same breath which professes to restrict their powers within narrow limits. It is prescribing limits, and declaring that those limits may be passed at pleasure.

That it thus reduces to nothing what we have deemed the greatest improvement on political institutions, a written constitution, would of itself be sufficient, in America, where written constitutions have been viewed with so much reverence, for rejecting the construction. But the peculiar expressions of the Constitution of the United States furnish additional arguments in favor of its rejection.

The judicial power of the United States is extended to all cases arising under the Constitution.

Could it be the intention of those who gave this power, to say that in using it the Constitution should not be looked into? That a case arising under the Constitution should be decided without examining the instrument under which it arises?

This is too extravagant to be maintained.

In some cases, then, the Constitution must be looked into by the judges. And if they can open it at all, what part of it are they forbidden to read or obey?

There are many other parts of the Constitution which serve to illustrate this subject.

It is declared that "no tax or duty shall be laid on articles exported from any State." Suppose a duty on the export of cotton, of tobacco, or of flour; and a suit instituted to recover it. Ought judgment to be rendered in such a case? Ought the judges to close their eyes on the Constitution, and only see the law?

The Constitution declares "that no bill of attainder or ex post facto law shall be passed."

If, however, such a bill should be passed, and a person should be prosecuted under it, must the court condemn to death those victims whom the Constitution endeavors to preserve?

"No person," says the Constitution, "shall be convicted of treason unless on the testimony of two witnesses to the same overt act, or on confession in open court."

Here the language of the Constitution is addressed especially to the courts. It prescribes, directly for them, a rule of evidence not to be departed from. If the legislature should change that rule, and declare one witness, or a confession out of court, sufficient for conviction, must the constitutional principle yield to the legislative act?

From these, and many other selections which might be made, it is apparent that the framers of the Constitution contemplated that instrument as a rule for the government of courts, as well as of the legislature.

Why otherwise does it direct the judges to take an oath to support it? This oath certainly applies in an especial manner to this conduct in their official character. How immoral to impose it on them, if they were to be used as the instruments, and the knowing instruments, for violating what they swear to support!

The oath of office, too, imposed by the legislature, is completely demonstrative of the legislative opinion on this subject. It is in these words: "I do solemnly swear that I will administer justice without respect to persons, and do equal right to the poor and to the rich; and that I will faithfully and impartially discharge all the duties incumbent on me as _____, according to the best of my abilities and understanding, agreeably to the Constitution and laws of the United States."

Why does a judge swear to discharge his duties agreeably to the Constitution of the United States, if that Constitution forms no rule for his government—if it is closed upon him, and cannot be inspected by him?

If such be the real state of things, this is worse than solemn mockery. To prescribe, or to take this oath, becomes equally a crime.

It is also not entirely unworthy of observation, that in declaring what shall be the supreme law of the land, the Constitution itself is first mentioned; and not the laws of the United States generally, but those only which shall be made in pursuance of the Constitution, have that rank.

Thus, the particular phraseology of the Constitution of the United States confirms and strengthens the principle, supposed to be essential to all written constitutions, that a law repugnant to the Constitution is void; and that courts, as well as other departments, are bound by that instrument.

The rule must be discharged.

Powers and Limitations
of the Supreme Court

Paul A. Freund, in his book *On Understanding the Supreme Court* (1949), notes that the Supreme Court has a definite political role. He asks:

"Is the law of the Supreme Court a reflection of the notions of 'policy' held by its members? The question recalls the controversy over whether judges 'make' or 'find' the law. A generation or two ago it was thought rather daring to insist that judges make law. Old Jeremiah Smith, who began the teaching of law at Harvard after a career on the New Hampshire Supreme Court, properly deflated the issue. 'Do judges make law?' he repeated. 'Course they do. Made some myself.' Of course Supreme Court Justices decide cases on the basis of their ideas of policy."

To emphasize this point today is to repeat the familiar. The Court makes policy. It would be difficult to conceive how a Court having the power to interpret the Constitution could fail to make policy, i.e., could fail to make rulings that have *general* impact upon the community as a whole. The essential distinction between policy making and adjudication is that the former has a general effect while the latter touches only a specifically designated person or group.

If the Supreme Court has this power of constitutional interpretation, how is it controlled by the other governmental departments and the community? Is it, as some have claimed, completely arbitrary in rendering many of its decisions? Is it potentially a dictatorial body? The Supreme Court and lower courts are limited to the consideration of cases and controversies brought before them by outside parties. Courts cannot initiate law. Moreover, all courts, and the Supreme Court in particular, exercise judicial self-restraint in certain cases to avoid difficult and controversial issues and to avoid outside pressure to limit the powers of the judiciary. John P. Roche, in the next selection, deals with the background, the nature, and the implications of judicial doctrines of self-restraint.

63

John P. Roche
JUDICIAL SELF-RESTRAINT

Every society, sociological research suggests, has its set of myths which incorporate and symbolize its political, economic, and social aspirations. Thus, as
medieval society had the Quest for the Holy Grail and the cult of numerology,
we, in our enlightened epoch, have as significant manifestations of our collective hopes the dream of impartial decision-making and the cult of "behavioral
science." While in my view these latter two are but different facets of the same
fundamental drive, namely, the age-old effort to exorcise human variables from
human action, our concern here is with the first of them, the pervasive tendency
in the American political and constitutional tradition directed toward taking
the politics out of politics, and substituting some set of Platonic guardians for
fallible politicians.

While this dream of objectivizing political Truth is in no sense a unique
American phenomenon, it is surely true to say that in no other democratic
nation has the effort been carried so far and with such persistence. Everywhere
one turns in the United States, he finds institutionalized attempts to narrow
the political sector and to substitute allegedly "independent" and "impartial"
bodies for elected decision-makers. The so-called "independent regulatory commissions" are a classic example of this tendency in the area of administration,
but unquestionably the greatest hopes for injecting pure Truth-serum into the
body politic have been traditionally reserved for the federal judiciary, and particularly for the Supreme Court. The rationale for this viewpoint is simple:
"The people must be protected from themselves, and no institution is better
fitted for the role of chaperone than the federal judiciary, dedicated as it is to
the supremacy of the rule of law."

Patently central to this function of social chaperonage is the right of the
judiciary to review legislative and executive actions and nullify those measures
which derogate from eternal principles of truth and justice as incarnated in the
Constitution. Some authorities, enraged at what the Supreme Court has found
the Constitution to mean, have essayed to demonstrate that the framers did
not intend the Court to exercise this function, to have, as they put it, "the
last word." I find no merit in this contention; indeed, it seems to me undeniable

From John P. Roche, "Judicial Self-Restraint," *The American Political Science Review*, 49 (September 1955). Reprinted by permission.

not only that the authors of the Constitution intended to create a federal government, but also that they assumed *sub silentio* that the Supreme Court would have the power to review both national and state legislation.

However, since the intention of the framers is essentially irrelevant except to antiquarians and polemicists, it is unnecessary to examine further the matter of origins. The fact is that the United States Supreme Court, and the inferior federal courts under the oversight of the high Court, have enormous policy-making functions. Unlike their British and French counterparts, federal judges are not merely technicians who live in the shadow of a supreme legislature, but are fully equipped to intervene in the process of political decision making. In theory, they are limited by the Constitution and the jurisdiction it confers, but, in practice, it would be a clumsy judge indeed who could not, by a little skillful exegesis, adapt the Constitution to a necessary end. This statement is in no sense intended as a condemnation; on the contrary, it has been this perpetual reinvigoration by reinterpretation, in which the legislature and the executive as well as the courts play a part, that has given the Constitution its survival power. Applying a Constitution which contains at key points inspired ambiguity, the courts have been able to pour the new wine in the old bottle. Note that the point at issue is not the legitimacy or wisdom of judicial legislation; it is simply the enormous scope that this prerogative gives to judges to substitute their views for those of past generations, or, more controversially, for those of a contemporary Congress and President.

Thus it is naive to assert that the Supreme Court is limited by the Constitution, and we must turn elsewhere for the sources of judicial restraint. The great power exercised by the Court has carried with it great risks, so it is not surprising that American political history has been sprinkled with demands that the judiciary be emasculated. The really startling thing is that, with the notable exception of the McCardle incident in 1869, the Supreme Court has emerged intact from each of these encounters. Despite the plenary power that Congress, under Article III of the Constitution, can exercise over the appellate jurisdiction of the high Court, the national legislature has never taken sustained and effective action against its House of Lords. It is beyond the purview of this analysis to examine the reasons for Congressional inaction; suffice it here to say that the most significant form of judicial limitation has remained self-limitation. This is not to suggest that such a development as statutory codification has not cut down the area of interpretive discretion, for it obviously has. It is rather to maintain that when the justices have held back from assaults on legislative or executive actions, they have done so on the basis of self-established rationalizations. . . .

The remainder of this paper is therefore concerned with two aspects of this auto-limitation: first, the techniques by which it is put into practice; and, second, the conditions under which it is exercised. . . .

TECHNIQUES OF JUDICIAL SELF-RESTRAINT

The major techniques of judicial self-restraint appear to fall under the two familiar rubrics: procedural and substantive. Under the former fall the various techniques by which the Court can avoid coming to grips with substantive issues, while under the latter would fall those methods by which the Court, in a substantive holding, finds that the matter at issue in the litigation is not properly one for judicial settlement. Let us examine these two categories in some detail.

Procedural Self-Restraint

Since the passage of the Judiciary Act of 1925, the Supreme Court has had almost complete control over its business. United States Supreme Court *Rule 38*, which governs the certiorari policy, states, (§ 5) that discretionary review will be granted only "where there are special and important reasons therefor." Professor Fowler Harper has suggested in a series of detailed and persuasive articles on the application of this discretion [*University of Pennsylvania Law Review*, vols. 99–101; 103] that the Court has used it in such a fashion as to duck certain significant but controversial problems. While one must be extremely careful about generalizing in this area, since the reasons for denying certiorari are many and complex, Harper's evidence does suggest that the Court in the period since 1949 has refused to review cases involving important civil liberties problems which on their merits appeared to warrant adjudication. As he states at one point: "It is disconcerting when the Court will review a controversy over a patent on a pin ball machine while one man is deprived of his citizenship and another of his liberty without Supreme Court review of a plausible challenge to the validity of government action.". . .

Furthermore, the Supreme Court can issue certiorari on its own terms. Thus in *Dennis* v. *United States*, appealing the Smith Act convictions of the American communist leadership, the Court accepted the evidential findings of the Second Circuit as final and limited its review to two narrow constitutional issues. This, in effect, burked the basic problem: whether the evidence was sufficient to demonstrate that the Communist Party, U.S.A., was *in fact* clear and present danger to the security of the nation, or whether the communists were merely shouting "Fire!" in an empty theater.

Other related procedural techniques are applicable in some situations. Simple delay can be employed, perhaps in the spirit of the Croatian proverb that "delay is the handmaiden of justice.". . . However, the technique of procedural self-restraint is founded on the essentially simple gadget of refusing jurisdiction, or of procrastinating the acceptance of jurisdiction, and need not concern us further here.

Substantive Self-Restraint

Once a case has come before the Court on its merits, the justices are forced to give some explanation for whatever action they may take. Here self-restraint can take many forms, notably, the doctrine of political questions, the operation of judicial parsimony, and—particularly with respect to the actions of administrative officers of agencies—the theory of judicial inexpertise.

The doctrine of political questions is too familiar to require much elaboration here. Suffice it to say that if the Court feels that a question before it, e.g., the legitimacy of a state government, the validity of a legislative apportionment, or the correctness of executive action in the field of foreign relations, is one that is not properly amenable to judicial settlement, it will refer the plaintiff to the "political" organs of government for any possible relief. The extent to which this doctrine is applied seems to be a direct coefficient of judicial egotism, for the definition of a political question can be expanded or contracted in accordion-like fashion to meet the exigencies of the times. A juridical definition of the term is impossible, for at root the logic that supports it is circular: political questions are matters not soluble by the judicial process; matters not soluble by the judicial process are political questions. As an early dictionary explained, violins are small cellos, and cellos are large violins.

Nor do examples help much in definition. While it is certainly true that the Court cannot mandamus a legislature to apportion a state in equitable fashion, it seems equally true that the Court is without the authority to force state legislators to implement unsegregated public education. Yet in the former instance the Court genuflected to the "political" organs and took no action, while in the latter it struck down segregation as violative of the Constitution.

Judicial parsimony is another major technique of substantive self-restraint. In what is essentially a legal application of Occam's razor, the court has held that it will not apply any more principles to the settlement of a case than are absolutely necessary, e.g., it will not discuss the constitutionality of a law if it can settle the instant case by statutory construction. Furthermore, if an action is found to rest on erroneous statutory construction, the review terminates at that point: the Court will not go on to discuss whether the statute, properly construed, would be constitutional. A variant form of this doctrine, and a most important one, employs the "case of controversy" approach, to wit, the Court, admitting the importance of the issue, inquires as to whether the litigant actually has standing to bring the matter up. . . .

A classic use of parsimony to escape from a dangerous situation occurred in connection with the evacuation of the Nisei from the West Coast in 1942. Gordon Hirabayashi, in an attempt to test the validity of the regulations clamped on the American-Japanese by the military, violated the curfew and refused to report to an evacuation center. He was convicted on both counts by the district court and sentenced to three months for each offense, the sentences to run *concurrently*. When the case came before the Supreme Court, the justices sustained his conviction for violating the *curfew*, but refused to examine the validity of the evacuation order on the ground that it would not make any difference to Hirabayashi anyway; he was in for ninety days no matter what the Court did with evacuation.

A third method of utilizing substantive self-restraint is particularly useful in connection with the activities of executive departments or regulatory agencies, both state and federal. I have entitled it the doctrine of judicial *inexpertise*, for it is founded on the unwillingness of the Court to revise the findings of experts. The earmarks of this form of restraint are great deference to the holdings of the expert agency usually coupled with such a statement as "It is not for the federal courts to supplant the [Texas Railroad] Commission's judgment even in the face of convincing proof that a different result would have been better." In this tradition, the Court has refused to question *some* exercises of discretion by the National Labor Relations Board, the Federal Trade Commission, and other federal and state agencies. But the emphasis on *some* gives the point away; in other cases, apparently on all fours with those in which it pleads its technical *inexpertise*, the Court feels free to assess evidence de novo and reach independent judgment on the technical issues involved. . . .

In short, with respect to expert agencies, the Court is equipped with both offensive and defensive gambits. If it chooses to intervene, one set of precedents is brought out, while if it decides to hold back, another set of equal validity is invoked. Perhaps the best summary of this point was made by Justice Harlan in 1910, when he stated bluntly the "the Courts have rarely, if ever, felt themselves so restrained by technical rules that they could not find some remedy, consistent with the law, for acts . . . that violated natural justice or were hostile to the fundamental principles devised for the protection of the essential rights of property."

This does not pretend to be an exhaustive analysis of the techniques of judicial self-restraint; on the contrary, others will probably find many which are not given adequate discussion here. The remainder of this paper, however, is devoted to the second area of concern: the conditions under which the Court refrains from acting.

THE CONDITIONS OF
JUDICIAL SELF-RESTRAINT

The conditions which lead the Supreme Court to exercise auto-limitation are many and varied. In the great bulk of cases, this restraint is an outgrowth of sound and quasi-automatic legal maxims which defy teleological interpretation. It would take a master of the conspiracy theory of history to assign meaning, for example, to the great majority of certiorari denials; the simple fact is that these cases do not merit review. However, in a small proportion of cases, purpose does appear to enter the picture, sometimes with a vengeance. It is perhaps unjust to the Court to center our attention on this small proportion, but it should be said in extenuation that these cases often involve extremely significant political and social issues. In the broad picture, the refusal to grant certiorari in 1943 to the Minneapolis Trotskyites convicted under the Smith Act is far more meaningful than the similar refusal to grant five hundred petitions to prison "lawyers" who have suddenly discovered the writ of habeas corpus. Likewise, the holding that the legality of Congressional apportionment is a "political question" vitally affects the operation of the whole democratic process.

What we must therefore seek are the conditions under which the Court holds back *in this designated category of cases.* Furthermore, it is important to realize that there are positive consequences of negative action; as Charles Warren has implied, the post-Civil War Court's emphasis on self-restraint was a judicial concomitant of the resurgence of states' rights. Thus self-restraint may, as in wartime, be an outgrowth of judicial caution, or it may be part of a purposeful pattern of abdicating national power to the states.

Ever since the first political scientist discovered Mr. Dooley, the changes have been run on the aphorism that the Supreme Court "follows the election returns," and I see no particular point in ringing my variation on this theme through again. Therefore, referring those who would like a more detailed explanation to earlier analyses, the discussion here will be confined to the bare bones of my hypothesis.

The power of the Supreme Court to invade the decision-making arena, I submit, is a consequence of that framentation of political power which is normal in the United States. No cohesive majority, such as normally exists in Britain, would permit a politically irresponsible judiciary to usurp decision-making functions, but, for complex social and institutional reasons, there are few issues in the United States on which cohesive majorities exist. The guerrilla warfare which usually rages between Congress and the President, as well as the internal civil wars which are endemic in both the legislature and the administration, give the judiciary considerable room for maneuver. If, for example, the Court strikes down a controversial decision of the Federal Power Commission, it will be supported by a substantial bloc of congressmen; if it supports the FPC's decision, it will also receive considerable congressional support. But the important point is that *either* way it decides the case, there is no possibility that Congress will exact any vengeance on the Court for its action. A disciplined majority would be necessary to clip the judicial wings, and such a majority does not exist on this issue.

On the other hand, when monolithic majorities do exist on issues, the Court is likely to resort to judicial self-restraint. A good case here is the current tidal wave of anti-communist legislation and administrative action, the latter particularly with regard to aliens, which the Court has treated most gingerly. About the only issues on which there can be found cohesive majorities are those relating to national defense, and the Court has, as Clinton Rossiter demonstrated in an incisive analysis [*The Supreme Court and the Commander-in-Chief,*

Ithaca, 1951], traditionally avoided problems arising in this area irrespective of their constitutional merits. Like the slave who accompanied a Roman consul on his triumph whispering "You too are mortal," the shade of Thad Stevens haunts the Supreme Court chamber to remind the justices what an angry Congress can do.

To state the proposition in this brief compass is to oversimplify it considerably. I have, for instance, ignored the crucial question of how the Court knows when a majority *does* exist, and I recognize that certain aspects of judicial behavior cannot be jammed into my hypothesis without creating essentially spurious epicycles. However, I am not trying to establish a monistic theory of judicial action; group action, like that of individuals, is motivated by many factors, some often contradictory, and my objective is to elucidate what seems to be one tradition of judicial motivation. In short, judicial self-restraint and judicial power seem to be opposite sides of the same coin: it has been by judicious application of the former that the latter has been maintained. A tradition beginning with Marshall's *coup* in *Marbury* v. *Madison* and running through *Mississippi* v. *Johnson* and *Ex Parte Vallandigham* to *Dennis* v. *United States* suggests that the Court's power has been maintained by a wise refusal to employ it in unequal combat.

Judicial Decision-making

Judicial decision-making is not quasi-scientific, always based clearly upon legal principles and precedent, with the judges set apart from the political process. The interpretation of law, whether constitutional or statutory, involves a large amount of discretion. The majority of the Court can always read its opinion into law if it so chooses.

Justice William J. Brennan, Jr., a current member of the Supreme Court, discusses below the general role of the Court and the procedures it follows in decision-making.

64

William J. Brennan, Jr.
HOW THE SUPREME COURT
ARRIVES AT DECISIONS

Throughout its history the Supreme Court has been called upon to face many of the dominant social, political, economic and even philosophical issues that confront the nation. But Solicitor General Cox only recently reminded us that this does not mean that the Court is charged with making social, political, economic or philosophical decisions.

Quite the contrary, the Court is not a council of Platonic guardians for deciding our most difficult and emotional questions according to the Justices' own notions of what is just or wise or politic. To the extent that this is a government function at all, it is the function of the people's elected representatives.

The Justices are charged with deciding according to law. Because the issues arise in the framework of concrete litigation they must be decided on facts embalmed in a record made by some lower court or administrative agency. And while the Justices may and do consult history and the other disciplines as aids to constitutional decisions, the text of the Constitution and relevant precedents dealing with that text are their primary tools.

It is indeed true, as Judge Learned Hand once said, that the judge's authority

> depends upon the assumption that he speaks with the mouth of others: the momentum of his utterances must be greater than any which his personal reputation and character can command; if it is to do the work assigned to it— if it is to stand against the passionate resentments arising out of the interests he must frustrate—he must preserve his authority by cloaking himself in the majesty of an over-shadowing past, but he must discover some composition with the dominant trends of his times.

ANSWERS UNCLEAR

However, we must keep in mind that, while the words of the Constitution are binding, their application to specific problems is not often easy. The Founding Fathers knew better than to pin down their descendants too closely.

Enduring principles rather than petty details were what they sought.

Thus the Constitution does not take the form of a litany of specifics. There are, therefore, very few cases where the constitutional answers are clear, all one way or all the other, and this is also true of the current cases raising conflicts between the individual and governmental power—an area increasingly requiring the Court's attention.

Ultimately, of course, the Court must resolve the conflicts of competing interests in these cases, but all Americans should keep in mind how intense and troubling these conflicts can be.

Where one man claims a right to speak and the other man claims the right to be protected from abusive or dangerously provocative remarks the conflict is inescapable.

Where the police have ample external evidence of a man's guilt, but to be sure of their case put into evidence a confession obtained through coercion, the conflict arises between his right to a fair prosecution and society's right to protection against his depravity.

Where the orthodox Jew wishes to open his shop and do business on the day which non-Jews have chosen, and the Legislature has sanctioned, as a day of rest, the Court cannot escape a difficult problem of reconciling opposed interests.

Finally, the claims of the Negro citizen, to borrow Solicitor General Cox's words, present a "conflict between the ideal of liberty and equality expressed in the Declaration of Independence, on the one hand, and, on the other hand, a way of life rooted in the customs of many of our people."

SOCIETY IS DISTURBED

If all segments of our society can be made to appreciate that there are such conflicts, and that cases which involve constitutional rights often require difficult choices, if this alone is accomplished, we will have immeasurably enriched our common understanding of the meaning and significance of our freedoms. And we will have a better appreciation of the Court's function and its difficulties.

How conflicts such as these ought to be resolved constantly troubles our whole society. There should be no surprise, then, that how properly to resolve them often produces sharp division within the Court itself. When problems are so fundamental, the claims of the competing interests are often nicely balanced, and close divisions are almost inevitable.

Supreme Court cases are usually one of three kinds: the "original" action brought directly in the Court by one state against another state or states, or between a state or states and the federal government. Only a handful of such cases arise each year, but they are an important handful.

A recent example was the contest between Arizona and California over the waters of the lower basin of the Colorado River. Another was the contest between the federal government and the newest state of Hawaii over the ownership of lands in Hawaii.

The second kind of case seeks review of the decisions of a federal Court of Appeals—there are eleven such courts—or of a decision of a federal District Court—there is a federal District Court in each of the fifty states.

The third kind of case comes from a state court—the Court may review a state court judgment by the highest court of any of the fifty states, if the judgment rests on the decision of a federal question.

When I came to the Court seven years ago the aggregate of the cases in the three classes was 1,600. In the term just completed there were 2,800, an increase of 75 percent in seven years. Obviously, the volume will have doubled before I complete ten years of service.

How is it possible to manage such a huge volume of cases? The answer is that we have the authority to screen them and select for argument and decision only those which, in our judgment, guided by pertinent criteria, raise the most important and far-reaching questions. By that device we select annually around 6 percent—between 150 and 170 cases—for decision.

PETITION AND RESPONSE

That screening process works like this: when nine Justices sit, it takes five to decide a case on the merits. But it takes only the votes of four of the nine to put a case on the argument calendar for argument and decision. Those four votes are hard to come by—only an exceptional case raising a significant federal question commands them.

Each application for review is usually in the form of a short petition, attached to which are any opinions of the lower courts in the case. The adversary may file a response—also, in practice usually short. Both the petition and response identify the federal questions allegedly involved, argue their substantiality, and whether they were properly raised in the lower courts.

Each Justice receives copies of the petition and response and such parts of the record as the parties may submit. Each Justice then, without any consultation at this stage with the others, reaches his own tentative conclusion whether the application should be granted or denied.

The first consultation about the case comes at the Court conference at which the case is listed on the agenda for discussion. We sit in conference almost every Friday during the term. Conferences begin at ten in the morning and often continue until six, except for a half-hour recess for lunch.

Only the Justices are present. There are no law clerks, no stenographers, no secretaries, no pages—just the nine of us. The junior Justice acts as guardian of the door, receiving and delivering any messages that come in or go from the conference.

ORDER OF SEATING

The conference room is a beautifully oak-paneled chamber with one side lined with books from floor to ceiling. Over the mantel of the exquisite marble fireplace at one end hangs the only adornment in the chamber—a portrait of Chief Justice John Marshall. In the middle of the room stands a rectangular table, not too large but large enough for the nine of us comfortably to gather around it.

The Chief Justice sits at the south end and Mr. Justice Black, the senior Associate Justice, at the north end. Along the side to the left of the Chief Justice sit Justices Stewart, Goldberg, White, and Harlan. On the right side sit Justice Clark, myself and Justice Douglas in that order.

We are summoned to conference by a buzzer which rings in our several chambers five minutes before the hour. Upon entering the conference room each of us shakes hands with his colleagues. The handshake tradition originated when Chief Justice Fuller presided many decades ago. It is a symbol that harmony of aims if not of views is the Court's guiding principle.

Each of us has his copy of the agenda of the day's cases before him. The agenda lists the cases applying for review. Each of us before coming to the conference has noted on his copy his tentative view whether or not review should be granted in each case.

The Chief Justice begins the discussion of each case. He then yields to the senior Associate Justice and discussion proceeds down the line in order of seniority until each Justice has spoken.

Voting goes the other way. The junior Justice votes first and voting then proceeds up the line to the Chief Justice, who votes last.

Each of us has a docket containing a sheet for each case with appropriate places for recording the votes. When any case receives four votes for review, that case is transferred to the oral argument list. Applications in which none of us sees merits may be passed over without discussion.

Now how do we process the decisions we agree to review?

There are rare occasions when the question is so clearly controlled by an earlier decision of the Court that a reversal of the lower court judgment is inevitable. In these rare instances we may summarily reverse without oral argument.

EACH SIDE GETS HOUR

The case must very clearly justify summary disposition, however, because our ordinary practice is not to reverse a decision without oral argument. Indeed, oral argument of cases taken for review, whether from the state or federal courts, is the usual practice. We rarely accept submissions of cases on briefs.

Oral argument ordinarily occurs about four months after the application for review is granted. Each party is usually allowed one hour, but in recent years we have limited oral argument to a half-hour in cases thought to involve issues not requiring longer arguments.

Counsel submit their briefs and record in sufficient time for the distribution of one set to each Justice two or three weeks before the oral argument. Most of the members of the present Court follow the practice of reading the briefs before the argument. Some of us often have a bench memorandum prepared before the argument. This memorandum digests the facts and the arguments of both sides, highlighting the matters about which we may want to question counsel at the argument.

Often I have independent research done in advance of argument and incorporate the results in the bench memorandum.

We follow a schedule of two weeks of argument from Monday through Thursday, followed by two weeks of recess for opinion writing and the study of petitions for review. The argued cases are listed on the conference agenda on the Friday following argument. Conference discussions follow the same procedure I have described for the discussions of certiorari petitions.

OPINION ASSIGNED

Of course, it is much more extended. Not infrequently discussion of particular cases may be spread over two or more conferences.

Not until the discussion is completed and a vote taken is the opinion assigned. The assignment is not made at the conference but formally in writing some few days after the conference.

The Chief Justice assigns the opinions in those cases in which he has voted with the majority. The senior Associate Justice voting with the majority assigns the opinion in the other cases. The dissenters agree among themselves who shall write the dissenting opinion. Of course, each Justice is free to write his own opinion, concurring or dissenting.

The writing of an opinion always takes weeks and sometimes months. The most painstaking research and care are involved.

Research, of course, concentrates on relevant legal materials—precedents particularly. But Supreme Court cases often require some familiarity with history, economics, the social and other sciences, and authorities in these areas, too, are consulted when necessary.

When the author of an opinion feels he has an unanswerable document he sends it to a print shop, which we maintain in our building. The printed draft may be revised several times before his proposed opinion is circulated among the other Justices. Copies are sent to each member of the Court, those in the dissent as well as those in the majority.

SOME CHANGE MINDS

Now the author often discovers that his work has only begun. He receives a return, ordinarily in writing, from each Justice who voted with him and some-times also from the Justices who voted the other way. He learns who will write the dissent if one is to be written. But his particular concern is whether those who voted with him are still of his view and what they have to say about his proposed opinion.

Often some who voted with him at conference will advise that they reserve final judgment pending the circulation of the dissent. It is a common experience that dissents change votes, even enough votes to become the majority.

I have had to convert more than one of my proposed majority opinions into a dissent before the final decision was announced. I have also, however, had the more satisfying experience of rewriting a dissent as a majority opinion for the Court.

Before everyone has finally made up his mind a constant interchange by memoranda, by telephone, at the lunch table continues while we hammer out the final form of the opinion. I had one case during the past term in which I circulated ten printed drafts before one was approved as the Court opinion.

UNIFORM RULE

The point of this procedure is that each Justice, unless he disqualifies himself in a particular case, passes on every piece of business coming to the Court. The Court does not function by means of committees or panels. Each Justice passes on each petition, each time, no matter how drawn, in long hand, by typewriter, or on a press. Our Constitution vests the judicial power in only one Supreme Court. This does not permit Supreme Court action by committees, panels, or sections.

The method that the Justices use in meeting an enormous caseload varies. There is one uniform rule: Judging is not delegated. Each Justice studies each case in sufficient detail to resolve the question for himself. In a very real sense, each decision is an individual decision of every Justice.

The process can be a lonely, troubling experience for fallible human beings conscious that their best may not be adequate to the challenge.

"We are not unaware," the late Justice Jackson said, "that we are not final because we are infallible; we know that we are infallible only because we are final."

One does not forget how much may depend on his decision. He knows that usually more than the litigants may be affected, that the course of vital social, economic and political currents may be directed.

This then is the decisional process in the Supreme Court. It is not without its tensions, of course—indeed, quite agonizing tensions at times.

I would particularly emphasize that, unlike the case of a Congressional or White House decision, Americans demand of their Supreme Court judges that they produce a written opinion, the collective expression of the judges subscribing to it, setting forth the reason which led them to the decision.

These opinions are the exposition, not just to lawyers, legal scholars and other judges, but to our whole society, of the bases upon which a particular result rests—why a problem, looked at as disinterestedly and dispassionately as nine human beings trained in a tradition of the disinterested and dispassionate approach can look at it, is answered as it is.

It is inevitable, however, that Supreme Court decisions—and the Justices themselves—should be caught up in public debate and be the subjects of bitter controversy.

An editorial in *The Washington Post* did not miss the mark by much in saying that this was so because

> one of the primary functions of the Supreme Court is to keep the people of the country from doing what they would like to do—at times when what they would like to do runs counter to the Constitution. . . . The function of the Supreme Court is not to count constituents; it is to interpret a fundamental charter which imposes restraints on constituents. Independence and integrity, not popularity, must be its standards.

FREUND'S VIEW

Certainly controversy over its work has attended the Court throughout its history. As Professor Paul A. Freund of Harvard remarked, this has been true almost since the Court's first decision:

> When the Court held, in 1793, that the state of Georgia could be sued on a contract in the federal courts, the outraged Assembly of that state passed a bill declaring that any federal marshal who should try to collect the judgment would be guilty of a felony and would suffer death, without benefit of clergy, by being hanged. When the Court decided that state criminal convictions could be reviewed in the Supreme Court, Chief Justice Roane of Virginia exploded, calling it a "most monstrous and unexampled decision. It can only be accounted for by that love of power which history informs us infects and corrupts all who possess it, and from which even the eminent and upright judges are not exempt."

But public understanding has not always been lacking in the past. Perhaps it exists today. But surely a more informed knowledge of the decisional process should aid a better understanding.

It is not agreement with the court's decisions that I urge. Our law is the richer and the wiser because academic and informed lay criticism is part of the stream of development.

CONSENSUS NEEDED

It is only a greater awareness of the nature and limits of the Supreme Court's function that I seek.

The ultimate resolution of questions fundamental to the whole community must be based on a common consensus of understanding of the unique responsibility assigned to the Supreme Court in our society.

The lack of that understanding led Mr. Justice Holmes to say fifty years ago:

> We are very quiet there, but it is the quiet of a storm center, as we all know. Science has taught the world skepticism and has made it legitimate to put everything to the test of proof. Many beautiful and noble reverences are impaired, but in these days no one can complain if any institution, system, or belief is called on to justify its continuance in life. Of course we are not excepted and have not escaped.

PAINFUL ACCUSATION

> Doubts are expressed that go to our very being. Not only are we told that when Marshall pronounced an Act of Congress unconstitutional he usurped a power that the Constitution did not give, but we are told that we are the representatives of a class—a tool of the money power.
>
> I get letters, not always anonymous, intimating that we are corrupt. Well, gentlemen, I admit that it makes my heart ache. It is very painful, when one spends all the energies of one's soul in trying to do good work, with no thought but that of solving a problem according to the rules by which one is bound, to know that many see sinister motives and would be glad of evidence that one was consciously bad.
>
> But we must take such things philosophically and try to see what we can learn from hatred and distrust and whether behind them there may not be a germ of inarticulate truth.
>
> The attacks upon the Court are merely an expression of the unrest that seems to wonder vaguely whether law and order pay. When the ignorant are taught to doubt they do not know what they safely may believe. And it seems to me that at this time we need education in the obvious more than investigation of the obscure.

Interpreting the Constitution

Justice William J. Brennan, Jr., in his discussion of how the Supreme Court arrives at decisions in the preceding selection, points out that inevitably Supreme Court decisions and the justices are the subjects of public debate and often bitter controversy. It is not surprising that when Supreme Court justices and lower-court judges as well follow the early dictum of Chief Justice John Marshall, which he stated in *Marbury* v. *Madison* in 1803, that "It is emphatically the province and duty of the judicial department to say what the law is," they will become the center of political storms stirred up by those who feel the Court has overstepped its bounds.

While the Supreme Court may not enter unequal political combat, as John Roche contends in selection 63, it has made many highly controversial decisions since Roche wrote his article in 1955. (For example, see selections Nos. 17–22.) One conservative law scholar has gone so far as to state, "In the years since *Brown* v. *Board of Education* (1954) nearly every fundamental change in domestic social policy has been brought about not by the decentralized democratic (or, more accurately, republican) process contemplated by the Constitution, but simply by the Court's decree."[1]

Conservatives, clearly unhappy with the trend in Supreme Court decision-making not only during the Warren era (1953 to 1969) but under the Chief Justiceship of Warren Burger (1969–1986), charged that the Court's "loose" constitutional interpretations have been contrary to the wishes of the majority of the people and have made a mockery of the Constitution itself. Responding to their conservative constituencies, Republican presidential candidates Richard M. Nixon in 1968 and Ronald Reagan in 1980 promised to take action to reverse the Supreme Court's alleged liberalism by appointing conservative justices.

Ironically, one of Nixon's appointees, Harry Blackmun, authored the Court's controversial abortion decision in 1973 (see selection No. 20). Another Nixon appointee, Lewis Powell, joined the more liberal justices in the *Bakke* case (see selection No. 22) to allow universities and the colleges to take race into account in their admissions processes, a tacit although far from direct support for the affirmative-action programs conservatives so strongly opposed. Nixon found, as had Dwight D. Eisenhower who appointed Earl Warren to be Chief Justice in 1953, that presidents have no control over their appointees once they are on the Court.

For his part in the conservative cause, President Ronald Reagan, while choosing Sandra Day O'Connor as the first woman Supreme Court justice, tried to make certain beforehand that she would support conservative positions on such issues as abortion. Reagan added three conservative Su-

---

[1]Lino A. Graglia, "How the Constitution Disappeared," *Commentary*, February 1986, p. 19.

preme Court justices and had an even greater impact upon the lower federal judiciary, which he "stacked" with conservative judges.

Debate over the role of the Supreme Court intensified during Reagan's second term. His attorney general, Edwin Meese, in a speech given before the American Bar Association, attacked the Supreme Court for interpreting the Constitution according to its own values rather than the intent of the Founding Fathers. In response, Associate Justice William J. Brennan, speaking to a Georgetown University audience, called the attorney general "arrogant" and "doctrinaire," stating that it is impossible to "gauge accurately the intent of the framers on the application of principle to specific, contemporary questions." Another Supreme Court justice, John Paul Stevens, joined the attack on Meese.

The arguments in the 1980s over the proper role of the Supreme Court recalled the debate in the early days of the Republic between proponents of "strict" construction of the Constitution on the one hand and "loose" construction on the other. No less an intellectual and political giant than Thomas Jefferson favored the former approach, arguing that judges should not interpret the Constitution to reflect their own political values. He particularly opposed Chief Justice John Marshall's "loose" construction of congressional authority under Article I and the implied powers clause, which supported an expansion of national power over the states. Prior to Marshall's historic decisions in *McCulloch* v. *Maryland* (1819) and *Gibbons* v. *Ogden* that flexibly interpreted the Constitution to support broad congressional powers over the states (see selection No. 9), Alexander Hamilton had provided the rationale for loose construction in *The Federalist*. He suggested that Congress should be able to carry out its enumerated powers by whatever means it considered to be necessary and proper.

An old adage states that where one stands on political issues depends upon whose ox is being gored. Liberal supporters of Franklin D. Roosevelt attacked the conservative Supreme Court during the early New Deal when it was systematically declaring the core of FDR's program to be unconstitutional. After his overwhelming 1936 electoral victory Roosevelt attempted to "pack" the Court by seeking congressional approval of legislation that would give him the authority to appoint one new justice for each justice over seventy years of age. The legislation would have given him at the time the authority to appoint a Supreme Court majority because there were seven septuagenarian justices on the Court. Conservatives attacked Roosevelt's plan, charging that it was an unconstitutional and even un-American attempt to undermine the Supreme Court's independence. They wanted the Court to continue acting as a super-legislature as long as it advocated conservative views. However, when the tables were turned, and the Court became the advocate of "liberal" views during the Warren era, conservatives were quick to attack it for acting as a super-legislature against the will of the majority, which was the same argument liberals had used against the Court in the 1930s.

The Contemporary Debate over Constitutional Interpretation

The Federalist Society labeled it "The Great Debate." President Ronald Reagan's Attorney General Edwin Meese, in an address before the American Bar Association, attacked the Supreme Court for straying from constitutional principles. He represented the views of President Ronald Reagan and of conservatives throughout the country. They had attacked Supreme Court decisions ranging from *Engel* v. *Vitale* (1962), which prohibited prayers in public schools, to *Roe* v. *Wade* (1973), which upheld the right of a woman to have an abortion during the first trimester of her pregnancy under an implied constitutional right to privacy.

In the following selection, Meese reinforces the views of his president, who at the investiture of his appointees, Chief Justice William H. Rehnquist and Associate Justice Antonin Scalia, both conservatives, told the small audience that had gathered for the ceremony that the Founding Fathers were on the side of strict constitutional construction. "They settled on a judiciary," said Reagan, "that would be independent and strong, but one whose power would also, they believed, be confined within the boundaries of a written constitution and laws. In the convention and during the debates on ratification, some said that there was a danger of the courts making laws rather than interpreting them. . . . The judicial branch interprets the laws, while the power to make and execute those laws is balanced in the two elected branches." Reagan might well have added that under the Constitution, state legislatures, too, were to make policy unencumbered by federal judicial intervention based upon loose construction.

65

Edwin Meese III
FOR STRICT CONSTRUCTION

Welcome to our Federal City. It is, of course, entirely fitting that we lawyers gather here in this home of our government. We Americans, after all, rightly pride ourselves on having produced the greatest political wonder of the world—a government of laws and not of men. Thomas Paine was right: "America has no monarch: Here the law is king."

Perhaps nothing underscores Paine's assessment quite as much as the eager anticipation with which Americans await the conclusion of the term of the Supreme Court. Lawyers and laymen alike regard the Court not so much with awe as with a healthy respect. The law matters here and the business of our highest court—the subject of my remarks today—is crucially important to our political order.

In reviewing a term of the Court, it is important to take a moment and reflect upon the proper role of the Supreme Court in our constitutional system. The intended role of the judiciary generally and the Supreme Court in particular was to serve as the "bulwarks of a limited constitution." The judges, the Founders believed, would not fail to regard the Constitution as "fundamental law" and would "regulate their decisions" by it. As the "faithful guardians of the Constitution," the judges were expected to resist any political effort to depart from the literal provisions of the Constitution. The text of the document and the original intention of those who framed it would be the judicial standard in giving effect to the Constitution.

You will recall that Alexander Hamilton, defending the federal courts to be created by the new Constitution, remarked that the want of a judicial power under the Articles of Confederation had been the crowning defect of that first effort at a national constitution. Ever the consummate lawyer, Hamilton pointed out that "laws are a dead letter without courts to expound and define their true meaning."

The Anti-Federalist *Brutus* took him to task in the New York press for what the critics of the Constitution considered his naivete. That prompted Hamilton to write his classic defense of judicial power in *The Federalist*, No. 78. An independent judiciary under the Constitution, he said, would prove to be the

---

Address before the American Bar Association, July 9, 1985, Washington, D.C.

"citadel of public justice and the public security." Courts were "peculiarly essential in a limited constitution." Without them, there would be no security against "the encroachments and oppressions of the representative body," no protection against "unjust and partial" laws.

Hamilton, like his colleague Madison, knew that all political power is "of an encroaching nature." In order to keep the powers created by the Constitution within the boundaries marked out by the Constitution, an independent—but constitutionally bound—judiciary was essential. The purpose of the Constitution, after all, was the creation of limited but also energetic government, institutions with the power to govern, but also with structures to keep the power in check. As Madison put it, the Constitution enabled the government to control the governed, but also obliged it to control itself.

But even beyond the institutional role, the Court serves the American republic in yet another, more subtle way. The problem of any popular government, of course, is seeing to it that the people obey the laws. There are but two ways: either by physical force or by moral force. In many ways the Court remains the primary moral force in American politics. Tocqueville put it best:

> The great object of justice is to substitute the idea of right for that of violence,
> to put intermediaries between the government and the use of its physical
> force. . . .

> It is something astonishing what authority is accorded to the intervention of
> a court of justice by the general opinion of mankind. . . .

> The moral force in which tribunals are clothed makes the use of physical force
> infinitely rarer, for in most cases it takes its place; and when finally physical
> force is required, its power is doubled by his moral authority.

By fulfilling its proper function, the Supreme Court contributes both to institutional checks and balances and to the moral undergirding of the entire constitutional edifice. For the Supreme Court is the only national institution that daily grapples with the most fundamental political questions—and defends them with written expositions. Nothing less would serve to perpetuate the sanctity of the rule of law so effectively.

But that is not to suggest that the justices are a body of Platonic guardians. Far from it. The Court is what it was understood to be when the Constitution was framed—a political body. The judicial process is, at its most fundamental level, a political process. While not a partisan political process, it is political in the truest sense of that word. It is a process wherein public deliberations occur over what constitutes the common good under the terms of a written constitution.

As a result, as Benjamin Cardozo pointed out, "the greatest tides and currents which engulf the rest of men do not turn aside in their course and pass the judges by." Granting that, Tocqueville knew what was required. As he wrote:

> The federal judges therefore must not only be good citizens and men of education and integrity, . . . [they] must also be statesmen; they must know how to understand the spirit of the age, to confront those obstacles that can be overcome, and to steer out of the current when the tide threatens to carry them away, and with them the sovereignty of the union and obedience to its laws.

On that confident note, let's consider the Court's work this past year. As has been generally true in recent years, the 1984 term did not yield a coherent set of decisions. Rather, it seemed to produce what one commentator has called a "jurisprudence of idiosyncracy." Taken as a whole, the work of the term defies analysis by any strict standard. It is neither simply liberal nor simply conservative; neither simply activist nor simply restrained; neither simply principled nor simply partisan. The Court this term continued to roam at large in a veritable constitutional forest.

I believe, however, that there are at least three general arenas that merit close scrutiny: Federalism, Criminal Law, and Freedom of Religion.

FEDERALISM

In *Garcia v. San Antonio Metropolitan Transit Authority*, [105 S.Ct. 1005 (1985),] the Court displayed what was in the view of this Administration an inaccurate reading of the text of the Constitution and a disregard for the Framers' intention that state and local governments be a buffer against the centralizing tendencies of the national Leviathan. Specifically, five Justices denied that the Tenth Amendment protects States from federal laws regulating the wages and hours of state or local employees. Thus the Court overruled—but barely—a contrary holding in *National League of Cities v. Usery* [426 U.S. 833 (1976)]. We hope for a day when the Court returns to the basic principles of the Constitution as expressed in *Usery*; such instability in decisions concerning the fundamental principle of federalism does our Constitution no service.

Meanwhile, the constitutional status of the States further suffered as the Court curbed state power to regulate the economy, notably the professions. In *Metropolitan Life Insurance Co. v. Ward*, [105 S.Ct. 1676 (1985),] the Court used the Equal Protection Clause to spear an Alabama insurance tax on gross premiums preferring in-state companies over out-of-state rivals. In *Supreme Court of New Hampshire v. Piper*, [105 S.Ct. 1272 (1985),] the Court held that the Privileges and Immunities Clause of Article IV barred New Hampshire from completely excluding a nonresident from admission to its bar. With the apparent policy objective of creating unfettered national markets for occupations before its eyes, the Court unleashed Article IV against any State preference for residents involving the professions or service industries. *Hicklin* v. *Orbeck*, [437 U.S. 518 (1978),] and *Baldwin* v. *Montana Fish and Game Commission*, [435 U.S. 371 (1978),] are illustrative.

On the other hand, we gratefully acknowledge the respect shown by the Court for state and local sovereignty in a number of cases, including *Atascadero State Hospital* v. *Scanlon*, [105 S.Ct. 3142 (1985)].

In *Atascadero*, a case involving violations of §504 of the Rehabilitation Act of 1973, the Court honored the Eleventh Amendment in limiting private damage suits against States. Congress, it said, must express its intent to expose States to liability affirmatively and clearly.

In *Haille* v. *Eau Claire*, [105 S.Ct. 1713 (1985),] the Court found that active state supervision of municipal activity was not required to cloak municipalities with immunity under the Sherman Act. And, States were judged able to confer Sherman Act immunity upon private parties in *Southern Motor Carrier Rate Conference, Inc.* v. *United States*, [105 S.Ct. 1721 (1985)]. They must, said the Court, clearly articulate and affirmatively express a policy to displace competition with compelling anticompetitive action so long as the private action is actively supervised by the State.

And, in *Oklahoma City* v. *Tuttle*, [105 S.Ct. 2427 (1985),] the Court held that a single incident of unconstitutional and egregious police misconduct is insufficient to support a Section 1983 [42 U.S.C. §1983] action against municipalities for allegedly inadequate police training or supervision.

Our view is that federalism is one of the most basic principles of our Constitution. By allowing the States sovereignty sufficient to govern, we better secure our ultimate goal of political liberty through decentralized government. We do not advocate States' rights; we advocate States' responsibilities. We need to remember that state and local governments are not inevitably abusive of rights. It was, after all, at the turn of the century the States that were the laboratories of social and economic progress—and the federal courts that blocked their way. We believe that there is a proper constitutional sphere for state governance under our scheme of limited, popular government.

CRIMINAL LAW

Recognizing, perhaps, that the nation is in the throes of a drug epidemic which has severely increased the burden borne by law enforcement officers, the Court took a more progressive stance on the Fourth Amendment, undoing some of the damage previously done by its piecemeal incorporation through the Fourteenth Amendment. Advancing from its landmark *United States* v. *Leon*, [468 U.S. 897 (1984),] . . . which created a good-faith exception to the Exclusionary Rule when a flawed warrant is obtained by police, the Court permitted warrantless searches under certain limited circumstances.

The most prominent among these Fourth Amendment cases were:

- *New Jersey v. T.L.O.*, [105 S.Ct. 733 (1985),] which upheld warrantless searches of public school students based on reasonable suspicion that a law or school rule has been violated; this also restored a clear local authority over another problem in our society, school discipline;

- *California v. Carney*, [105 S. Ct. 2066 (1985),] which upheld the warrantless search of a mobile home;

- *United States v. Sharpe*, [105 S.Ct. 1568 (1985),] which approved on-the-spot detention of a suspect for preliminary questioning and investigation;

- *United States v. Johns*, [105 S.Ct. 881 (1985),] upholding the warrantless search of sealed packages in a car several days after their removal by police who possessed probable cause to believe the vehicle contained contraband;

- *United States v. Hensley*, [105 S.Ct. 675 (1985),] which permitted a warrantless investigatory stop based on an unsworn flyer from a neighboring police department which possessed reasonable suspicion that the detainee was a felon;

- *Hayes v. Florida*, [105 S.Ct. 1643 (1985),] which tacitly endorsed warrantless seizures in the field for the purpose of finger-printing based on reasonable suspicion of criminal activity;

Similarly, the Court took steps this term to place the *Miranda v. Arizona* [384 U.S. 436 (1966),] ruling in proper perspective, stressing its origin in the Court rather than in the Constitution. In *Oregon v. Elstad*, [105 S.Ct. 1285 (1985),] the Court held that failure to administer *Miranda* warnings and the consequent receipt of a confession ordinarily will not taint a second confession after *Miranda* warnings are received.

The enforcement of criminal law remains one of our most important efforts. It is crucial that the state and local authorities—from the police to the prosecutors—be able to combat the growing tide of crime effectively. Toward that end we advocate a due regard for the rights of the accused—but also a due regard for the keeping of the public peace and the safety and happiness of the people. We will continue to press for a proper scope for the rules of exclusion, lest truth in the fact finding process be allowed to suffer.

I have mentioned the areas of Federalism and Criminal Law, now I will turn to the Religion cases.

RELIGION

Most probably, this term will be best remembered for the decisions concerning the Establishment Clause of the First Amendment. The Court continued to apply its standard three-pronged test. Four cases merit mention.

In the first, *City of Grand Rapids v. Ball*, [105 S.Ct. 3248 (1985),] the Court nullified Shared Time and Community Education programs offered within parochial schools. Although the programs provided instruction in non-sectarian subjects, and were taught by full-time or part-time public school teachers, the Court nonetheless found that they promoted religion in three ways: the state-paid instructors might wittingly or unwittingly indoctrinate students; the symbolic union of church and state interest in state-provided instruction signaled support for religion; and, the programs in effect subsidized the religious functions of parochial schools by relieving them of responsibility for teaching some secular subjects. The symbolism test proposed in *Ball* precludes virtually any state assistance offered to parochial schools.

In *Aguilor v. Felton*, [105 S.Ct. 3232 (1985),] the Court invalidated a program of secular instruction for low-income students in sectarian schools, provided by public school teachers who were supervised to safeguard students against efforts of indoctrination. With a bewildering Catch-22 logic, the Court declared that the supervisory safeguards at issue in the statute constituted unconstitutional government entanglement: "The religious school, which has as a primary purpose the advancement and preservation of a particular religion, must endure the ongoing presence of state personnel whose primary purpose is to monitor teachers and students in an attempt to guard against the infiltration of religious thought."

In *Wallace v. Jaffree*, [105 S.Ct. 2479 (1985),] the Court said in essence that states may set aside time in public schools for meditation or reflection so long as the legislation does not stipulate that it be used for voluntary prayer. Of course, what the Court gave with one hand, it took back with the other; the Alabama moment of silence statute failed to pass muster.

In *Thornton v. Caldor*, [105 S.Ct. 2914 (1985),] a 7–2 majority overturned a state law prohibiting private employers from discharging an employee for refusing to work on his Sabbath. We hope that this does not mean that the Court is abandoning last term's first but tentative steps toward state accommodation of religion in the Creche case.

In trying to make sense of the religion cases—from whichever side—it is important to remember how this body of tangled case law came about. Most Americans forget that it was not until 1925, in *Gitlow v. New York*, [268 U.S. 652 (1925),] that *any* provision of the Bill of Rights was applied to the states. Nor was it until 1947 that the Establishment Clause was made applicable to the states through the 14th Amendment. This is striking because the Bill of Rights, as debated, created and ratified was designed to apply *only* to the national government.

The Bill of Rights came about largely as the result of the demands of the critics of the new Constitution, the unfortunately misnamed Anti-Federalists. They feared, as George Mason of Virginia put it, that in time the national authority would "devour" the states. Since each state had a bill of rights, it was only appropriate that so powerful a national government as that created by the Constitution have one as well. Though Hamilton insisted a Bill of Rights was not necessary and even destructive, and Madison (at least at first) thought a Bill of Rights to be but a "parchment barrier" to political power, the Federalists agreed to add a Bill of Rights.

Though the first ten amendments that were ultimately ratified fell far short of what the Anti-Federalists desired, both Federalists and Anti-Federalists agreed that the amendments were a curb on national power. When this view was questioned before the Supreme Court in *Barron* v. *Baltimore*, [32 U.S. 243 (1833),] Chief Justice Marshall wholeheartedly agreed. The Constitution said what it meant and meant what is said. Neither political expediency nor judicial desire was sufficient to change the clear import of the language of the Constitution. The Bill of Rights did not apply to the states—and, he said, that was that.

Until 1925, that is.

Since then a good portion of constitutional adjudication has been aimed at extending the scope of the doctrine of incorporation. But the most that can be done is to expand the scope; nothing can be done to shore up the intellectually shaky foundation upon which the doctrine rests. And nowhere else has the principle of federalism been dealt so politically violent and constitutionally suspect a blow as by the theory of incorporation.

In thinking particularly of the use to which the First Amendment has been put in the area of religion, one finds much merit in Justice Rehnquist's recent dissent in *Jaffree*. "It is impossible," Justice Rehnquist argued, "to build sound constitutional doctrine upon a mistaken understanding of constitutional history." His conclusion was bluntly to the point: "If a constitutional theory has no basis in the history of the amendment it seeks to interpret, it is difficult to apply and yields unprincipled results."

The point, of course, is that the Establishment Clause of the First Amendment was designed to prohibit Congress from establishing a national church. The belief was that the Constitution should not allow Congress to designate a particular faith or sect as politically above the rest. But to have argued, as is popular today, that the Amendment demands a strict neutrality between religion and irreligion would have struck the founding generation as bizarre. The purpose was to prohibit religious tyranny, not to undermine religion generally.

In considering these areas of adjudication—Federalism, Criminal Law, and Religion—it seems fair to conclude that far too many of the Court's opinions were, on the whole, more policy choices than articulations of constitutional principle. The voting blocs, the arguments, all reveal a greater allegiance to what the Court thinks constitutes sound public policy than a deference to what the Constitution—its text and intention—may demand. It is also safe to say that until there emerges a coherent jurisprudential stance, the work of the Court will continue in this ad hoc fashion. But that is not to argue for *any* jurisprudence. In my opinion a drift back toward the radical egalitarianism and expansive civil libertarianism of the Warren Court would once again be a threat to the notion of limited but energetic government.

What, then, should a constitutional jurisprudence actually be? It should be a Jurisprudence of Original Intention. By seeking to judge policies in light of principles, rather than remold principles in light of policies, the Court could avoid both the charge of incoherence *and* the charge of being either too conservative or too liberal.

A jurisprudence seriously aimed at the explication of original intention would produce defensible principles of government that would not be tainted by ideological predilection. This belief in a Jurisprudence of Original Intention also reflects a deeply rooted commitment to the idea of democracy. The Constitution is the fundamental will of the people; that is why it is the fundamental law. To allow the courts to govern simply by what it views at the time as fair and decent, is a scheme of government no longer popular; the idea of democracy has suffered. The permanence of the Constitution has been weakened. A constitution that is viewed as only what the judges say it is, is no longer a constitution in the true sense.

Those who framed the Constitution chose their words carefully; they debated at great length the most minute points. The language they chose meant something. It is incumbent upon the Court to determine what that meaning was. This is not a shockingly new theory; nor is it arcane or archaic.

Joseph Story, who was in a way a lawyer's Everyman—lawyer, justice, and teacher of law—had a theory of judging that merits reconsideration. Though speaking specifically of the Constitution, his logic reaches to statutory construction as well.

> In construing the Constitution of the United States, we are in the first instance to consider, what are its nature and objects, its scope and design, as apparent from the structure of the instrument, viewed as a whole and also viewed in its component parts. Where its words are plain, clear and determinate, they require no interpretation. . . . Where the words admit of two senses, each of which is conformable to general usage, that sense is to be adopted, which without departing from the literal import of the words, best harmonizes with the nature and objects, the scope and design of the instrument.

A Jurisprudence of Original Intention would take seriously the admonition of Justice Story's friend and colleague, John Marshall, in *Marbury* that the Constitution is a limitation of judicial power as well as executive and legislative. That is what Chief Justice Marshall meant in *McCulloch* when he cautioned judges never to forget it is a constitution they are expounding.

It has been and will continue to be the policy of this administration to press for a Jurisprudence of Original Intention. In the cases we file and those we join as *amicus*, we will endeavor to resurrect the original meaning of constitutional provisions and statutes as the only reliable guide for judgement.

We will pursue our agenda within the context of our written Constitution of limited yet energetic powers. Our guide in every case will be the sanctity of the rule of law and the proper limits of governmental power.

It is our belief that only "the sense in which the Constitution was accepted and ratified by the nation," and only the sense in which laws were drafted and passed provide a solid foundation for adjudication. Any other standard suffers the defect of pouring new meaning into old words, thus creating new powers and new rights totally at odds with the logic of our Constitution and its commitment to the rule of law.

❖❖   Justice William J. Brennan, Jr., argues in the next selection that strict construction is a myth. Many constitutional provisions, by their very nature, are vague and require judicial interpretation. "It is arrogant to pretend," writes Brennan, "that from our vantage we can gauge accurately the intent of the Framers on application of principle to specific, contemporary questions." The Supreme Court must apply the Constitution in a contemporary context, and adapt it to present needs. "Our Constitution was not intended to preserve a preexisting society," concludes Brennan, "but to make a new one, to put in place new principles that the prior political community had not sufficiently recognized."

66

William J. Brennan, Jr.
FOR "LOOSE" CONSTRUCTION

I am deeply grateful for the invitation to participate in the "Text and Teaching" symposium. This rare opportunity to explore classic texts with participants of such wisdom, acumen and insight as those who have preceded and will follow me to this podium is indeed exhilarating. But it is also humbling, Even to approximate the standards of excellence of these vigorous and graceful intellects is a daunting task. I am honored that you have afforded me this opportunity to try.

It will perhaps not surprise you that the text I have chosen for exploration is the amended Constitution of the United States, which, of course, entrenches the Bill of Rights and the Civil War amendments, and draws sustenance from the bedrock principles of another great text, the Magna Carta. So fashioned, the Constitution embodies the aspiration to social justice, brotherhood, and human dignity that brought this nation into being. The Declaration of Independence, the Constitution and the Bill of Rights solemnly committed the United States to be a country where the dignity and rights of all persons were equal before all authority. In all candor we must concede that part of this egalitarianism in America has been more pretension than realized fact. But we are an aspiring people, a people with faith in progress. Our amended Constitution is the lodestar for our aspirations. Like every text worth reading, it is not crystalline. The phrasing is broad and the limitations of its provisions are not clearly marked. Its majestic generalities and ennobling pronouncements are both luminous and obscure. This ambiguity of course calls forth interpretation, the interaction of reader and text. The encounter with the constitutional text has been, in many senses, my life's work.

My approach to this text may differ from the approach of other participants in this symposium to their texts. Yet such differences may themselves stimulate reflection about what it is we do when we "interpret" a text. Thus I will attempt to educidate my approach to the text as well as my substantive interpretation.

Perhaps the foremost difference is the fact that my encounters with the constitutional text are not purely or even primarily introspective; the Consti-

---

Address to the Text and Teaching Symposium, Georgetown University, October 12, 1985, Washington, D.C.

tution cannot be for me simply a contemplative haven for private moral reflection. My relation to this great text is inescapably public. That is not to say
that my reading of the text is not a personal reading, only that the personal
reading perforce occurs in a public context, and is open to critical scrutiny from
all quarters.

The Constitution is fundamentally a public text—the monumental charter
of a government and a people—and a Justice of the Supreme Court must apply
it to resolve public controversies. For, from our beginning, a most important
consequence of the constitutionally created separation of powers has been the
American habit, extraordinary to other democracies, of casting social, economic, philosophical and political questions in the form of lawsuits, in an
attempt to secure ultimate resolution by the Supreme Court. In this way, important aspects of the most fundamental issues confronting our democracy may
finally arrive in the Supreme Court for judicial determination. Not infrequently,
these are the issues upon which contemporary society is most deeply divided.
They arouse our deepest emotions. The main burden of my twenty-nine terms
on the Supreme Court has thus been to wrestle with the Constitution in this
heightened public context, to draw meaning from the text in order to resolve
public controversies.

Two other aspects of my relation to this text warrant mention. First, constitutional interpretation for a federal judge is, for the most part, obligatory.
When litigants approach the bar of court to adjudicate a constitutional dispute,
they may justifiably demand an answer. Judges cannot avoid a definitive interpretation because they feel unable to, or would prefer not to, penetrate to the
full meaning of the Constitution's provisions. Unlike literary critics, judges
cannot merely savor the tensions or revel in the ambiguities inhering in the
text—judges must resolve them.

Second, consequences flow from a Justice's interpretation in a direct and
immediate way. A judicial decision respecting the incompatibility of Jim Crow
with a constitutional guarantee of equality is not simply a contemplative exercise in defining the shape of a just society. It is an order—supported by the
full coercive power of the State—that the present society change in a fundamental aspect. Under such circumstances the process of deciding can be a
lonely, troubling experience for fallible human beings conscious that their best
may not be adequate to the challenge. We Justices are certainly aware that we
are not final because we are infallible; we know that we are infallible only
because we are final. One does not forget how much may depend on the decision. More than the litigants may be affected. The course of vital social,
economic and political currents may be directed.

These three defining characteristics of my relation to the constitutional
text—its public nature, obligatory character, and consequentialist aspect—cannot help but influence the way I read that text. When Justices interpret the
Constitution they speak for their community, not for themselves alone. The
act of interpretation must be undertaken with full consciousness that it is, in a

very real sense, the community's interpretation that is sought. Justices are not platonic guardians appointed to wield authority according to their personal moral predilections. Precisely because coercive force must attend any judicial decision to countermand the will of a contemporary majority, the Justices must render constitutional interpretations that are received as legitimate. The source of legitimacy is, of course, a wellspring of controversy in legal and political circles. At the core of the debate is what the late Yale Law School Professor Alexander Bickel labeled "the counter-majoritarian difficulty." Our commitment to self-governance in a representative democracy must be reconciled with vesting in electorally unaccountable Justices the power to invalidate the expressed desires of representative bodies on the ground of inconsistency with higher law. Because judicial power resides in the authority to give meaning to the Constitution, the debate is really a debate about how to read the text, about constraints on what is legitimate interpretation.

There are those who find legitimacy in fidelity to what they call "the intentions of the Framers." In its most doctrinaire incarnation, this view demands that Justices discern exactly what the Framers thought about the question under consideration and simply follow that intention in resolving the case before them. It is a view that feigns self-effacing deference to the specific judgments of those who forged our original social compact. But in truth it is little more than arrogance cloaked as humility. It is arrogant to pretend that from our vantage we can gauge accurately the intent of the Framers on application of principle to specific, contemporary questions. All too often, sources of potential enlightenment such as records of the ratification debates provide sparse or ambiguous evidence of the original intention. Typically, all that can be gleaned is that the Framers themselves did not agree about the application or meaning of particular constitutional provisions, and hid their differences in cloaks of generality. Indeed, it is far from clear whose intention is relevant—that of the drafters, the congressional disputants, or the ratifiers in the states—or even whether the idea of an original intention is a coherent way of thinking about a jointly drafted document drawing its authority from a general assent of the states. And apart from the problematic nature of the sources, our distance of two centuries cannot but work as a prism refracting all we perceive. One cannot help but speculate that the chorus of lamentations calling for interpretation faithful to "original intention"—and proposing nullification of interpretations that fail this quick litmus test—must inevitably come from persons who have no familiarity with the historical record.

Perhaps most importantly, while proponents of this facile historicism justify it as a depoliticization of the judiciary, the political underpinnings of such a choice should not escape notice. A position that upholds constitutional claims only if they were within the specific contemplation of the Framers in effect establishes a presumption of resolving textual ambiguities against the claim of constitutional right. It is far from clear what justifies such a presumption against claims of right. Nothing intrinsic in the nature of interpretation—if there is such a thing as the "nature" of interpretation—commands such a passive approach to ambiguity. This is a choice no less political than any other; it expresses antipathy to claims of the minority rights against the majority. Those who would restrict claims of right to the values of 1789 specifically articulated in the Constitution turn a blind eye to social progress and eschew adaptation of overarching principles to changes of social circumstance.

Another, perhaps more sophisticated, response to the potential power of judicial interpretation stresses democratic theory: because ours is a government of the people's elected representatives, substantive value choices should by and large be left to them. This view emphasizes not the transcendant historical authority of the Framers but the predominant contemporary authority of the elected branches of government. Yet it has similar consequences for the nature of proper judicial interpretation. Faith in the majoritarian process counsels restraint. Even under more expansive formulations of this approach, judicial review is appropriate only to the extent of ensuring that our democratic process functions smoothly. Thus, for example, we would protect freedom of speech merely to ensure that the people are heard by their representatives, rather than as a separate, substantive value. When, by contrast, society tosses up to the Supreme Court a dispute that would require invalidation of a legislature's substantive policy choice, the Court generally would stay its hand because the Constitution was meant as a plan of government and not as an embodiment of fundamental substantive values.

The view that all matters of substantive policy should be resolved through the majoritarian process has appeal under some circumstances, but I think it ultimately will not do. Unabashed enshrinement of majority will would permit the imposition of a social caste system or wholesale confiscation of property so long as a majority of the authorized legislative body, fairly elected, approved. Our Constitution could not abide such a situation. It is the very purpose of a Constitution—and particularly of the Bill of Rights—to declare certain values transcendent, beyond the reach of temporary political majorities. The majoritarian process cannot be expected to rectify claims of minority right that arise as a response to the outcomes of that very majoritarian process. As James Madison put it:

> The prescriptions in favor of liberty ought to be levelled against that quarter where the greatest danger lies, namely, that which possesses the highest prerogative of power. But this is not found in either the Executive or Legislative departments of Government, but in the body of the people, operating by the majority against the minority. (I Annals 437).

Faith in democracy is one thing, blind faith quite another. Those who drafted our Constitution understood the difference. One cannot read the text without admitting that it embodies substantive value choices; it places certain values beyond the power of any legislature. Obvious are the separation of powers; the privilege of the Writ of Habeas Corpus; prohibition of Bills of Attainder and *ex post facto* laws; prohibition of cruel and unusual punishments; the requirement of just compensation for official taking of property; the prohibition of laws tending to establish religion or enjoining the free exercise of religion; and, since the Civil War, the banishment of slavery and official race discrimination. With respect to at least such principles, we simply have not constituted ourselves as strict utilitarians. While the Constitution may be amended, such amendments require an immense effort by the People as a whole.

To remain faithful to the content of the Constitution, therefore, an approach to interpreting the text must account for the existence of these substantive value choices, and must accept the ambiguity inherent in the effort to apply them to modern circumstances. The Framers discerned fundamental principles through struggles against particular malefactions of the Crown; the struggle shapes the particular contours of the articulated principles. But our acceptance of the fundamental principles has not and should not bind us to those precise, at times anachronistic, contours. Successive generations of Americans have continued to respect these fundamental choices and adopt them as their own guide to evaluating quite different historical practices. Each generation has the choice to overrule or add to the fundamental principles enunciated by the Framers; the Constitution can be amended or it can be ignored. Yet with respect to its fundamental principles, the text has suffered neither fate. Thus, if I may borrow the words of an esteemed predecessor, Justice Robert Jackson, the burden of judicial interpretation is to translate "the majestic generalities of the Bill of Rights, conceived as part of the pattern of liberal government in the eighteenth century, into concrete restraints on officials dealing with the problems of the twentieth century." *Board of Education* v. *Barnette*, [319 U.S. 624, 639 (1943),].

We current Justices read the Constitution in the only way that we can: as Twentieth Century Americans. We look to the history of the time of framing and to the intervening history of interpretation. But the ultimate question must be, what do the words of the text mean in our time? For the genius of the Constitution rests not in any static meaning it might have had in a world that is dead and gone, but in the adaptability of its great principles to cope with current problems and current needs. What the constitutional fundamentals meant to the wisdom of other times cannot be their measure to the vision of our time. Similarly, what those fundamentals mean for us, our descendants will learn, cannot be the measure to the vision of their time. This realization is not, I assure you, a novel one of my own creation. Permit me to quote from one of the opinions of our Court, *Weems* v. *United States*, [217 U.S. 349,] written nearly a century ago:

> Time works changes, brings into existence new conditions and purposes. Therefore, a principle to be vital must be capable of wider application than the mischief which gave it birth. This is peculiarly true of constitutions. They are not ephemeral enactments, designed to meet passing occasions. They are, to use the words of Chief Justice John Marshall, 'designed to approach immortality as nearly as human institutions can approach it.' The future is their

care and provision for events of good and bad tendencies of which no prophesy can be made. In the application of a constitution, therefore, our contemplation cannot be only of what has been, but of what may be.

Interpretation must account for the transformative purpose of the text. Our Constitution was not intended to preserve a preexisting society but to make a new one, to put in place new principles that the prior political community had not sufficiently recognized. Thus, for example, when we interpret the Civil War Amendments to the charter—abolishing slavery, guaranteeing blacks equality under law, and guaranteeing blacks the right to vote—we must remember that those who put them in place had no desire to enshrine the status quo. Their goal was to make over their world, to eliminate all vestige of slave caste.

Having discussed at some length how I, as a Supreme Court Justice, interact with this text, I think it time to turn to the fruits of this discourse. For the Constitution is a sublime oration on the dignity of man, a bold commitment by a people to the ideal of libertarian dignity protected through law. Some reflection is perhaps required before this can be seen.

The Constitution on its face is, in large measure, a structuring text, a blueprint for government. And when the text is not prescribing the form of government it is limiting the powers of that government. The original document, before addition of any of the amendments, does not speak primarily of the rights of man, but of the abilities and disabilities of government. When one reflects upon the text's preoccupation with the scope of government as well as its shape, however, one comes to understand that what this text is about is the relationship of the individual and the state. The text marks the metes and bounds of official authority and individual autonomy. When one studies the boundary that the text marks out, one gets a sense of the vision of the individual embodied in the Constitution.

As augmented by the Bill of Rights and the Civil War amendments, this text is a sparkling vision of the supremacy of the human dignity of every individual. This vision is reflected in the very choice of democratic self-governance: the supreme value of a democracy is the presumed worth of each individual. And this vision manifests itself most dramatically in the specific prohibitions of the Bill of Rights, a term which I henceforth will apply to describe not only the original first eight amendments, but the Civil War amendments as well. It is a vision that has guided us as a people throughout our history, although the precise rules by which we have protected fundamental human dignity have been transformed over time in response to both transformations of social condition and evolution of our concepts of human dignity.

Until the end of the nineteenth century, freedom and dignity in our country found meaningful protection in the institution of real property. In a society still largely agricultural, a piece of land provided men not just with sustenance but with the means of economic independence, a necessary precondition of political independence and expression. Not surprisingly, property relationships formed the heart of litigation and of legal practice, and lawyers and judges tended to think stable property relationships the highest aim of the law.

But the days when common law property relationships dominated litigation and legal practice are past. To a growing extent economic existence now depends on less certain relationships with government—licenses, employment, contracts, subsidies, unemployment benefits, tax exemptions, welfare and the like. Government participation in the economic existence of individuals is pervasive and deep. Administrative matters and other dealings with government are at the epicenter of the exploding law. We turn to government and to the law for controls which would never have been expected or tolerated before this century, when a man's answer to economic oppression or difficulty was to move two hundred miles west. Now hundreds of thousands of Americans live entire lives without any real prospect of the dignity and autonomy that ownership of real property could confer. Protection of the human dignity of such citizens requires a much modified view of the proper relationship of individual and state.

In general, problems of the relationship of the citizen with government have multiplied and thus have engendered some of the most important constitutional issues of the day. As government acts ever more deeply upon those areas of our lives once marked "private," there is an even greater need to see that individual rights are not curtailed or cheapened in the interest of what may temporarily appear to be the "public good." And as government continues in its role of provider for so many of our disadvantaged citizens, there is an even greater need to ensure that government act with integrity and consistency in its dealings with these citizens. To put this another way, the possibilities for collision between government activity and individual rights will increase as the power and authority of government itself expands, and this growth, in turn, heightens the need for constant vigilance at the collision points. If our free society is to endure, those who govern must recognize human dignity and accept the enforcement of constitutional limitations on their power conceived by the Framers to be necessary to preserve that dignity and the air of freedom which is our proudest heritage. Such recognition will not come from a technical understanding of the organs of government, or the new forms of wealth they administer. It requires something different, something deeper—a personal confrontation with the wellsprings of our society. Solutions of constitutional questions from that perspective have become the great challenge of the modern era. All the talk in the last half-decade about shrinking the government does not alter this reality or the challenge it imposes. The modern activist state is a comcomitant of the complexity of modern society; it is inevitably with us. We must meet the challenge rather than wish it were not before us.

The challenge is essentially, of course, one to the capacity of our constitutional structure to foster and protect the freedom, the dignity, and the rights of all persons within our borders, which it is the great design of the Constitution to secure. During the time of my public service this challenge has largely taken shape within the confines of the interpretive question whether the specific guarantees of the Bill of Rights operate as restraints on the power of State government. We recognize the Bill of Rights as the primary source of express information as to what is meant by constitutional liberty. The safeguards enshrined in it are deeply etched in the foundation of America's freedoms. Each is a protection with centuries of history behind it, often dearly bought with the blood and lives of people determined to prevent oppression by their rulers. The first eight amendments, however, were added to the Constitution to operate solely against federal power. It was not until the Thirteenth and Fourteenth Amendments were added, in 1865 and 1868, in response to a demand for national protection against abuses of state power, that the Constitution could be interpreted to require application of the first eight amendments to the states.

It was in particular the Fourteenth Amendment's guarantee that no person be deprived of life, liberty or property without process of law that led us to apply many of the specific guarantees of the Bill of Rights to the States. In my judgment, Justice Cardozo best captured the reasoning that brought us to such decisions when he described what the Court has done as a process by which the guarantees "have been taken over from the earlier articles of the federal bill of rights and brought within the Fourteenth Amendment by a process of absorption . . . [that] has had its source in the belief that neither liberty nor justice would exist if [those guarantees] . . . were sacrificed." *Palko* v. *Connecticut,* [302 U.S. 319, 326 (1937),]. But this process of absorption was neither swift nor steady. As late as 1922 only the Fifth Amendment guarantee of just compensation for official taking of property had been given force against the states. Between then and 1956 only the First Amendment guarantees of speech and conscience and the Fourth Amendment ban of unreasonable searches and seizures had been incorporated—the latter, however, without the exclusionary rule to give it force. As late as 1961, I could stand before a distinguished assemblage of the bar at New York University's James Madison Lecture and list the following as guarantees that had not been thought to be sufficiently fundamental to the protection of human dignity so as to be enforced against the states: the prohibition of cruel and unusual punishments, the right against self-incrimination, the right to assistance of counsel in a criminal trial, the right to confront witnesses, the right to compulsory process, the right not to be placed in jeopardy of life or limb more than once upon accusation of a crime, the right not to have illegally obtained evidence introduced at a criminal trial, and the right to a jury of one's peers.

The history of the quarter century following that Madison Lecture need not be told in great detail. Suffice it to say that each of the guarantees listed above has been recognized as a fundamental aspect of ordered liberty. Of course, the above catalogue encompasses only the rights of the criminally accused, those caught, rightly or wrongly, in the maw of the criminal justice system. But it has been well said that there is no better test of a society than how it treats those accused of transgressing against it. Indeed, it is because we recognize that incarceration strips a man of his dignity that we demand strict adherence to fair procedure and proof of guilt beyond a reasonable doubt before taking such a drastic step. These requirements are, as Justice Harlan once said, "bottomed on a fundamental value determination of our society that it is far worse to convict an innocent man than to let a guilty man go free." *In re Winship*, [397 U.S. 358, 372 (1970),] (concurring opinion). There is no worse injustice than wrongly to strip a man of his dignity. And our adherence to the constitutional vision of human dignity is so strict that even after convicting a person according to these stringent standards, we demand that his dignity be infringed only to the extent appropriate to the crime and never by means of wanton infliction of pain or deprivation. I interpret the Constitution plainly to embody these fundamental values.

Of course the constitutional vision of human dignity has, in this past quarter century, infused far more than our decisions about the criminal process. Recognition of the principle of "one person, one vote" as a constitutional one redeems the promise of self-governance by affirming the essential dignity of every citizen in the right to equal participation in the democratic process. Recognition of so-called "new property" rights in those receiving government entitlements affirms the essential dignity of the least fortunate among us by demanding that government treat with decency, integrity and consistency those dependent on its benefits for their very survival. After all, a legislative majority initially decides to create governmental entitlements; the Constitution's Due Process Clause merely provides protection for entitlements thought necessary by society as a whole. Such due process rights prohibit government from imposing the devil's bargain of bartering away human dignity in exchange for human sustenance. Likewise, recognition of full equality for women—equal protection of the laws—ensures that gender has no bearing on claims to human dignity.

Recognition of broad and deep rights of expression and of conscience reaffirm the vision of human dignity in many ways. They too redeem the promise of self-governance by facilitating—indeed demanding—robust, uninhibited and wide-open debate on issues of public importance. Such public debate is of course vital to the development and dissemination of political ideas. As importantly, robust public discussion is the crucible in which personal political convictions are forged. In our democracy, such discussion is a political duty, it is the essence of self government. The constitutional vision of human dignity rejects the possibility of political orthodoxy imposed from above; it respects the right of each individual to form and to express political judgments, however far they may deviate from the mainstream and however unsettling they might be to the powerful or the elite. Recognition of these rights of expression and conscience also frees up the private space for both intellectual and spiritual development free of government dominance, either blatant or subtle. Justice Brandeis put it so well sixty years ago when he wrote: "Those who won our independence believed that the final end of the State was to make men free to develop their faculties; and that in its government the deliberative forces should prevail over the arbitrary. They valued liberty both as an end and as a means." *Whitney* v. *California* [274 U.S. 357, 375 (1927),] (concurring opinion).

I do not mean to suggest that we have in the last quarter century achieved a comprehensive definition of the constitutional ideal of human dignity. We are still striving toward that goal, and doubtless it will be an eternal quest. For if the interaction of this Justice and the constitutional text over the years confirms any single proposition, it is that the demands of human dignity will never cease to evolve.

Indeed, I cannot in good conscience refrain from mention of one grave and crucial respect in which we continue, in my judgment, to fall short of the constitutional vision of human dignity. It is in our continued tolerance of State-administered execution as a form of punishment. I make it a practice not to comment on the constitutional issues that come before the Court, but my position on this issue, of course, has been for some time fixed and immutable. I think I can venture some thoughts on this particular subject without transgressing my usual guideline too severely.

As I interpret the Constitution, capital punishment is under all circumstances cruel and unusual punishment prohibited by the Eighth and Fourteenth Amendments. This is a position of which I imagine you are not unaware. Much discussion of the merits of capital punishment has in recent years focused on the potential arbitrariness that attends its administration, and I have no doubt that such arbitrariness is a grave wrong. But for me, the wrong of capital punishment transcends such procedural issues. As I have said in my opinions, I view the Eighth Amendment's prohibition of cruel and unusual punishments as embodying to a unique degree moral principles that substantively restrain the punishments our civilized society may impose on those persons who transgress its laws. Foremost among the moral principles recognized in our cases and inherent in the prohibition is the primary principle that the State, even as it punishes, must treat its citizens in a manner consistent with their intrinsic worth as human beings. A punishment must not be so severe as to be utterly and irreversibly degrading to the very essence of human dignity. Death for whatever crime and under all circumstances is a truly awesome punishment. The calculated killing of a human being by the State involves, by its very nature, an absolute denial of the executed person's humanity. The most vile murder does not, in my view, release the State from constitutional restraints on the destruction of human dignity. Yet an executed person has lost the very right to have rights, now or ever. For me, then, the fatal constitutional infirmity of capital punishment is that it treats members of the human race as non-humans, as objects to be toyed with and discarded. It is, indeed, "cruel and unusual." It is thus inconsistent with the fundamental premise of the Clause that even the most base criminal remains a human being possessed of some potential, at least, for common human dignity.

This is an interpretation to which a majority of my fellow Justices—not to mention, it would seem, a majority of my fellow countrymen—does not subscribe. Perhaps you find my adherence to it, and my recurrent publication of it, simply contrary, tiresome, or quixotic. Or perhaps you see in it a refusal to abide by the judicial principle of *stare decisis,* obedience to precedent. In my judgment, however, the unique interpretive role of the Supreme Court with respect to the Constitution demands some flexibility with respect to the call of *stare decisis.* Because we are the last word on the meaning of the Constitution, our views must be subject to revision over time, or the Constitution falls captive, again, to the anachronistic views of long-gone generations. I mentioned earlier the judge's role in seeking out the community's interpretation of the Constitutional text. Yet, again in my judgment, when a Justice perceives an interpretation of the text to have departed so far from its essential meaning, that Justice is bound, by a larger constitutional duty to the community, to expose the departure and point toward a different path. On this issue, the death penalty, I hope to embody a community striving for human dignity for all, although perhaps not yet arrived.

You have doubtless observed that this description of my personal encounter with the constitutional text has in large portion been a discussion of public developments in constitutional doctrine over the last century. That, as I suggested at the outset, is inevitable because my interpretive career has demanded a public reading of the text. This public encounter with the text, however, has been a profound source of personal inspiration. The vision of human dignity embodied there is deeply moving. It is timeless. It has inspired Americans for two centuries and it will continue to inspire as it continues to evolve. That evolutionary process is inevitable and, indeed, it is the true interpretive genius of the text.

If we are to be as a shining city upon a hill, it will be because of our ceaseless pursuit of the constitutional ideal of human dignity. For the political and legal ideals that form the foundation of much that is best in American institutions—ideals jealously preserved and guarded throughout our history— still form the vital force in creative political thought and activity within the nation today. As we adapt our institutions to the ever-changing conditions of national and international life, those ideals of human dignity—liberty and justice for all individuals—will continue to inspire and guide us because they are entrenched in our Constitution. The Constitution with its Bill of Rights thus has a bright future, as well as a glorious past, for its spirit is inherent in the aspirations of our people.

Appendix 1

The Declaration of Independence[1]

IN CONGRESS, JULY 4, 1776

**The unanimous Declaration of the
thirteen united States of America**

When in the Course of human events it becomes necessary for one people to dissolve the political bands which have connected them with another, and to assume among the Powers of the earth, the separate and equal station to which the Laws of Nature and of Nature's God entitle them, a decent respect to the opinions of mankind requires that they should declare the causes which impel them to the separation.

We hold these truths to be self-evident, that all men are created equal, that they are endowed by their Creator with certain unalienable Rights, that among these are Life, Liberty and the pursuit of Happiness. That to secure these rights, Governments are instituted among Men, deriving their just powers from the consent of the governed. That whenever any Form of Government becomes destructive of these ends, it is the Right of the People to alter or to abolish it, and to institute new Government, laying its foundation on such principles and

---

[1]This text retains the spelling, capitalization, and punctuation of the original.

organizing its powers in such form, as to them shall seem most likely to effect their Safety and Happiness. Prudence, indeed, will dictate that Governments long established should not be changed for light and transient causes; and accordingly all experience hath shown, that mankind are more disposed to suffer, while evils are sufferable, than to right themselves by abolishing the forms to which they are accustomed. But when a long train of abuses and usurpations, pursuing invariably the same Object evinces a design to reduce them under absolute Despotism, it is their right, it is their duty, to throw off such Government, and to provide new Guards for their future security.—Such has been the patient sufferance of these Colonies; and such is now the necessity which constrains them to alter their former Systems of Government. The history of the present King of Great Britain is a history of repeated injuries and usurpations, all having in direct object the establishment of an absolute Tyranny over these States. To prove this, let Facts be submitted to a candid world.

He has refused his Assent to Laws, the most wholesome and necessary for the public good.

He has forbidden his Governors to pass Laws of immediate and pressing importance, unless suspended in their operation till his Assent should be obtained; and when so suspended, he has utterly neglected to attend to them.

He has refused to pass other Laws for the accommodation of large districts of people, unless those people would relinquish the right of Representation in the Legislature, a right inestimable to them and formidable to tyrants only.

He has called together legislative bodies at places unusual, uncomfortable, and distant from the depository of their Public Records, for the sole purpose of fatiguing them into compliance with his measures.

He has dissolved Representative Houses repeatedly, for opposing with manly firmness his invasions on the rights of the people.

He has refused for a long time, after such dissolutions, to cause others to be elected; whereby the Legislative Powers, incapable of Annihilation, have returned to the People at large for their exercise; the State remaining in the mean time exposed to all the dangers of invasion from without, and convulsions within.

He has endeavored to prevent the population of these States; for that purpose obstructing the Laws for Naturalization of Foreigners; refusing to pass others to encourage their migration hither, and raising the conditions of new Appropriations of Lands.

He has obstructed the Administration of Justice, by refusing his Assent to Laws for establishing Judiciary Powers.

He has made Judges dependent on his Will alone, for the tenure of their offices, and the amount and payment of their salaries.

He has erected a multitude of New Offices, and sent hither swarms of Officers to harass our People, and eat out their substance.

He has kept among us, in times of peace, Standing Armies without the Consent of our Legislature.

He has affected to render the Military independent of and superior to the Civil Power.

He has combined with others to subject us to a jurisdiction foreign to our constitution, and unacknowledged by our laws; giving his Assent to their acts of pretended Legislation:

For quartering large bodies of armed troops among us:

For protecting them, by a mock Trial, from Punishment for any Murders which they should commit on the Inhabitants of these States:

For cutting off our Trade with all parts of the world:

For imposing taxes on us without our Consent:

For depriving us in many cases, of the benefits of Trial by Jury:

For transporting us beyond Seas to be tried for pretended offenses:

For abolishing the free System of English Laws in a neighboring Province, establishing therein an Arbitrary government, and enlarging its Boundaries so as to render it at once an example and fit instrument for introducing the same absolute rule into these Colonies:

For taking away our Charters, abolishing our most valuable Laws, and altering fundamentally the Forms of our Government:

For suspending our own Legislature, and declaring themselves invested with Power to legislate for us in all cases whatsoever.

He has abdicated Government here, by declaring us out of his Protection and waging War against us.

He has plundered our seas, ravaged our Coasts, burnt our towns, and destroyed the lives of our people.

He is at this time transporting large armies of foreign mercenaries to compleat the works of death, desolation and tyranny, already begun with circumstances of Cruelty & perfidy scarcely paralleled in the most barbarous ages, and totally unworthy the Head of a civilized nation.

He has constrained our fellow Citizens taken Captive on the high Seas to bear Arms against their Country, to become the executioners of their friends and Brethren, or to fall themselves by their Hands.

He has excited domestic insurrections amongst us, and has endeavored to bring on the inhabitants of our frontiers, the merciless Indian Savages, whose known rule of warfare, is an undistinguished destruction of all ages, sexes and conditions.

In every stage of these Oppressions We have Petitioned for Redress in the most humble terms: Our repeated Petitions have been answered only by repeated injury. A Prince, whose character is thus marked by every act which may define a Tyrant, is unfit to be the ruler of a free People.

Nor have We been wanting in attention to our British brethren. We have warned them from time to time of attempts by their legislature to extend an unwarrantable jurisdiction over us. We have reminded them of the circumstances of our emigration and settlement here. We have appealed to their native justice and magnanimity, and we have conjured them by the ties of our common kindred to disavow these usurpations, which, would inevitably interrupt our connections and correspondence. They too have been deaf to the voice of justice and consanguinity. We must, therefore, acquiesce in the necessity, which denounces our Separation, and hold them, as we hold the rest of mankind, Enemies in War, in Peace Friends.

We, therefore, the Representatives of the united States of America, in General Congress, Assembled, appealing to the Supreme Judge of the world for the rectitude of our intentions, do, in the Name, and by Authority of the good People of these Colonies, solemnly publish and declare, That these United Colonies are, and of Right ought to be Free and Independent States; that they are Absolved from all Allegiance to the British Crown, and that all political connection between them and the State of Great Britain, is and ought to be totally dissolved; and that as Free and Independent States, they have full Power to levy War, conclude Peace, contract Alliances, establish Commerce, and to do all other Acts and Things which Independent States may of right do. And for the support of this Declaration, with a firm reliance on the Protection of Divine Providence, we mutually pledge to each other our Lives, our Fortunes and our sacred Honor.

JOHN HANCOCK

New Hampshire

JOSIAH BARTLETT,
WM. WHIPPLE,

MATTHEW THORNTON.

Massachusetts Bay

SAML. ADAMS,
JOHN ADAMS,

ROBT. TREAT PAINE,
ELBRIDGE GERRY.

Rhode Island

STEP. HOPKINS

WILLIAM ELLERY.

Connecticut

ROGER SHERMAN,
SAM'EL HUNTINGTON,

WM. WILLIAMS
OLIVER WOLCOTT

New York

WM. FLOYD,
PHIL. LIVINGSTON,

FRANS. LEWIS,
LEWIS MORRIS.

New Jersey

RICHD. STOCKTON,
JNO. WITHERSPOON,
FRAS. HOPKINSON,

JOHN HART,
ABRA. CLARK.

Pennsylvania

ROBT. MORRIS,
BENJAMIN RUSH,
BENJA. FRANKLIN,
JOHN MORTON,
GEO. CLYMER,

JAS. SMITH,
GEO. TAYLOR
JAMES WILSON,
GEO. ROSS.

Delaware

CAESAR RODNEY,
GEO. READ,

THO. M'KEAN.

Maryland

SAMUEL CHASE,
WM. PACA,

THOS. STONE,
CHARLES CAROLL
of Carrollton.

Virginia

GEORGE WYTHE,
RICHARD HENRY LEE,
TH. JEFFERSON,
BENJA. HARRISON,

THOS. NELSON, jr.,
FRANCIS LIGHTFOOT
LEE,
CARTER BRAXTON.

North Carolina

WM. HOOPER,
JOSEPH HEWES,

JOHN PENN.

South Carolina

EDWARD RUTLEDGE,
THOS. HEYWARD, Junr.,

THOMAS LYNCH, jnr.,
ARTHUR MIDDLETON.

Georgia

BUTTON GWINNETT,
LYMAN HALL,

GEO. WALTON.

The Constitution of the United States

We the People of the United States, in Order to form a more perfect Union, establish Justice, insure domestic Tranquility, provide for the common defence, promote the general Welfare, and secure the Blessings of Liberty to ourselves and our Posterity do ordain and establish this CONSTITUTION for the United States of America.

ARTICLE I

Section 1. All legislative Powers herein granted shall be vested in a Congress of the United States, which shall consist of a Senate and House of Representatives.

Section 2. [1] The House of Representatives shall be composed of members chosen every second Year by the People of the several States, and the Electors in each State shall have the Qualifications requisite for Electors of the most numerous Branch of the State Legislature.

[2] No Person shall be a Representative who shall not have attained to the Age of twenty-five Years, and been seven Years a Citizen of the United States, and who shall not, when elected, be an Inhabitant of that State in which he shall be chosen.

[3] [Representatives and direct Taxes[1] shall be apportioned among the several States which may be included within this Union, according to their respective Numbers, which shall be determined by adding to the whole Number of free Persons, including those bound to Service for a Term of Years, and excluding Indians not taxed, three fifths of all other Persons.][2] The actual Enumeration shall be made within three Years after the first Meeting of the Congress of the United States, and within every subsequent Term of ten years, in such Manner as they shall by Law direct. The Number of Representatives shall not exceed one for every thirty Thousand, but each State shall have at Least one Representative; and until such enumeration shall be made, the State of New Hampshire shall be entitled to choose three, Massachusetts eight, Rhode-Island and Providence Plantations one, Connecticut five, New York six, New Jersey four, Pennsylvania eight, Delaware one, Maryland six, Virginia ten, North Carolina five, South Carolina five, and Georgia three.

[4] When vacancies happen in the Representation from any State, the Executive Authority thereof shall issue Writs of Election to fill such Vacancies.

[5] The House of Representatives shall choose their Speaker and other Officers; and shall have the sole Power of Impeachment.

Section 3. [1] The Senate of the United States shall be composed of two Senators from each State, [chosen by the Legislature][3] thereof, for six Years; and each Senator shall have one Vote.

[2] Immediately after they shall be assembled in Consequence of the first Election, they shall be divided as equally as may be into three Classes. The Seats of the Senators of the first Class shall be vacated at the Expiration of the second Year, of the second Class at the Expiration of the fourth Year, and of the third Class at the Expiration of the sixth Year, so that one-third may be chosen every second Year; [and if Vacancies happen by Resignation, or otherwise, during the Recess of the Legislature of any State, the Executive thereof may make temporary Appointments until the next Meeting of the Legislature, which shall then fill such Vacancies].[4]

[3] No person shall be a Senator who shall not have attained to the Age of thirty Years, and been nine Years a Citizen of the United States, and who shall not, when elected, be an Inhabitant of that State for which he shall be chosen.

[4] The Vice President of the United States shall be President of the Senate, but shall have no Vote, unless they be equally divided.

---

[1]The Sixteenth Amendment replaced this with respect to income taxes.
[2]Repealed by the Fourteenth Amendment.
[3]Repealed by the Seventeenth Amendment, Section 1.
[4]Changed by the Seventeenth Amendment.

[5] The Senate shall choose their other Officers, and also a President pro tempore, in the absence of the Vice President, or when he shall exercise the Office of President of the United States.

[6] The Senate shall have the sole Power to try all Impeachments. When sitting for that Purpose, they shall be on Oath or Affirmation. When the President of the United States is tried, the Chief Justice shall preside: And no Person shall be convicted without the Concurrence of two thirds of the Members present.

[7] Judgment in Cases of Impeachment shall not extend further than to removal from Office, and disqualification to hold and enjoy any Office of honor, Trust or Profit under the United States: but the Party convicted shall nevertheless be liable and subject to Indictment, Trial, Judgment and Punishment according to Law.

Section 4. [1] The Times, Places and Manner of holding Elections for Senators and Representatives, shall be prescribed in each State by the Legislature thereof; but the Congress may at any time by Law make or alter such Regulations, except as to the Places of Choosing Senators.

[2] The Congress shall assemble at least once in every Year, and such Meeting shall [be on the first Monday in December,]⁵ unless they shall by Law appoint a different Day.

Section 5. [1] Each House shall be the Judge of the Elections, Returns and Qualifications of its own Members, and a Majority of each shall constitute a Quorum to do Business; but a smaller number may adjourn from day to day, and may be authorized to compel the Attendance of absent Members, in such Manner, and under such Penalties as each House may provide.

[2] Each House may determine the Rules of its Proceedings, punish its Members for disorderly Behavior, and, with the Concurrence of two thirds, expel a Member.

[3] Each House shall keep a Journal of its Proceedings, and from time to time publish the same, excepting such Parts as may in their Judgment require Secrecy; and the Yeas and Nays of the Members of either House on any question shall, at the Desire of one fifth of those Present, be entered on the Journal.

[4] Neither House, during the Session of Congress, shall, without the Consent of the other, adjourn for more than three days, nor to any other Place than that in which the two Houses shall be sitting.

Section 6. [1] The Senators and Representatives shall receive a Compensation for their Services, to be ascertained by Law, and paid out of the Treasury of the United States. They shall in all Cases, except Treason, Felony and Breach of the Peace, be privileged from Arrest during their Attendance at the Session of

---

⁵Changed by the Twentieth Amendment, Section 2.

their respective Houses, and in going to and returning from the same; and for any Speech or Debate in either House, they shall not be questioned in any other Place.

[2] No Senator or Representative shall, during the Time for which he was elected, be appointed to any civil Office under the Authority of the United States, which shall have been created, or the Emoluments whereof have been increased during such time; and no Person holding any Office under the United States, shall be a Member of either House during his Continuance in Office.

Section 7. [1] All Bills for raising Revenue shall originate in the House of Representatives; but the Senate may propose or concur with Amendments as on other Bills.

[2] Every Bill which shall have passed the House of Representatives and the Senate, shall, before it become a Law, be presented to the President of the United States; If he approve he shall sign it, but if not he shall return it, with his Objections to that House in which it shall have originated, who shall enter the Objections at large on their Journal, and proceed to reconsider it. If after such Reconsideration two thirds of that House shall agree to pass the Bill, it shall be sent, together with the Objections, to the other House, by which it shall likewise be reconsidered, and if approved by two thirds of that House, it shall become a Law. But in all such Cases the Votes of both Houses shall be determined by Yeas and Nays, and the Names of the Persons voting for and against the Bill shall be entered on the Journal of each House respectively. If any Bill shall not be returned by the President within ten Days (Sundays excepted) after it shall have been presented to him, the Same shall be a Law, in like Manner as if he had signed it, unless the Congress by their Adjournment prevent its Return, in which Case it shall not be a Law.

[3] Every Order, Resolution, or Vote to which the Concurrence of the Senate and House of Representatives may be necessary (except on a question of Adjournment) shall be presented to the President of the United States; and before the Same shall take Effect, shall be approved by him, or being disapproved by him, shall be repassed by two thirds of the Senate and House of Representatives, according to the Rules and Limitations prescribed in the Case of a Bill.

Section 8. [1] The Congress shall have Power To lay and collect Taxes, Duties, Imposts and Excises, to pay the Debts and provide for the common Defense and general Welfare of the United States; but all Duties, Imposts and Excises shall be uniform throughout the United States;

[2] To borrow money on the credit of the United States;

[3] To regulate Commerce with foreign Nations, and among the several States, and with the Indian Tribes;

[4] To establish an uniform Rule of Naturalization, and uniform Laws on the subject of Bankruptcies throughout the United States;

[5] To coin Money, regulate the Value thereof, and of foreign Coin, and fix the Standard of Weights and Measures;

[6] To provide for the Punishment of counterfeiting the Securities and current Coin of the United States;

[7] To establish Post Offices and post Roads;

[8] To promote the Progress of Science and useful Arts, by securing for limited Times to Authors and Inventors the exclusive Right to their respective Writings and Discoveries;

[9] To constitute Tribunals inferior to the supreme Court;

[10] To define and punish Piracies and Felonies committed on the high Seas, and Offences against the Law of Nations;

[11] To declare War, grant Letters of Marque and Reprisal, and make Rules concerning Captures on Land and Water;

[12] To raise and support Armies, but no Appropriation of Money to that Use shall be for a longer Term than two Years;

[13] To provide and maintain a Navy;

[14] To make rules for the Government and Regulation of the land and naval Forces;

[15] To provide for calling forth the Militia to execute the Laws of the Union, suppress Insurrections and repel Invasions;

[16] To provide for organizing, arming, and disciplining the Militia, and for governing such Part of them as may be employed in the Service of the United States, reserving to the States respectively, the Appointment of the Officers, and the Authority of training the Militia according to the discipline prescribed by Congress;

[17] To exercise exclusive Legislation in all Cases whatsoever, over such District (not exceeding ten Miles square) as may, by Cession of particular States, and the acceptance of Congress, become the Seat of the Government of the United States, and to exercise like Authority over all Places purchased by the Consent of the Legislature of the State in which the Same shall be, for the Erection of Forts, Magazines, Arsenals, dock-Yards, and other needful Buildings;—And

[18] To make all Laws which shall be necessary and proper for carrying into Execution the foregoing Powers, and all other Powers vested by this Constitution in the Government of the United States, or in any Department or Officer thereof.

Section 9. [1] The Migration or Importation of such Persons as any of the States now existing shall think proper to admit, shall not be prohibited by the Congress prior to the Year one thousand eight hundred and eight, but a tax or duty may be imposed on such Importation, not exceeding ten dollars for each Person.

[2] The privilege of the Writ of Habeas Corpus shall not be suspended, unless when in Cases of Rebellion or Invasion the public Safety may require it.

[3] No Bill of Attainder or ex post facto Law shall be passed.

[4] No capitation, or other direct, Tax shall be laid, unless in Proportion to the Census or Enumeration herein before directed to be taken.[6]

[5] No Tax or Duty shall be laid on Articles exported from any State.

[6] No Preference shall be given by any Regulation of Commerce or Revenue to the Ports of one State over those of another: nor shall Vessels bound to, or from, one State, be obliged to enter, clear, or pay Duties in another.

[7] No Money shall be drawn from the Treasury, but in Consequence of Appropriations made by Law; and a regular Statement and Account of the Receipts and Expenditures of all public Money shall be published from time to time.

[8] No Title of Nobility shall be granted by the United States: And no Person holding any Office of Profit or Trust under them, shall, without the Consent of the Congress, accept of any present, Emolument, Office, or Title, of any kind whatever, from any King, Prince, or foreign State.

Section 10. [1] No State shall enter into any Treaty, Alliance, or Confederation; grant Letters of Marque and Reprisal; coin Money; emit Bills of Credit; make any Thing but gold and silver Coin a Tender in Payment of Debts; pass any Bill of Attainder, ex post facto Law, or Law impairing the Obligation of Contracts, or grant any Title of Nobility.

[2] No State shall, without the Consent of the Congress, lay any Imposts or Duties on Imports or Exports, except what may be absolutely necessary for executing its inspection Laws: and the net Produce of all Duties and Imposts, laid by any State on Imports or Exports, shall be for the Use of the Treasury of the United States; and all such Laws shall be subject to the Revision and Control of the Congress.

[3] No State shall, without the Consent of Congress, lay any duty of Tonnage, keep Troops, or Ships of War in time of Peace, enter into any Agreement or Compact with another State, or with a foreign Power, or engage in War, unless actually invaded, or in such imminent Danger as will not admit of delay.

ARTICLE II

Section 1. [1] The executive Power shall be vested in a President of the United States of America. He shall hold his Office during the Term of four Years, and, together with the Vice-President, chosen for the same Term, be elected, as follows

[2] Each State shall appoint, in such Manner as the Legislature thereof may direct, a Number of Electors, equal to the whole Number of Senators and Representatives to which the State may be entitled in the Congress; but no

---

[6]Changed by the Sixteenth Amendment.

Senator or Representative, or Person holding an Office of Trust or Profit under the United States, shall be appointed an Elector.

[The Electors shall meet in their respective States, and vote by Ballot for two persons, of whom one at least shall not be an Inhabitant of the same State with themselves. And they shall make a List of all the Persons voted for, and of the Number of Votes for each; which List they shall sign and certify, and transmit sealed to the Seat of the Government of the United States, directed to the President of the Senate. The President of the Senate shall, in the Presence of the Senate and House of Representatives, open all the Certificates, and the Votes shall then be counted. The Person having the greatest Number of Votes shall be the President, if such Number be a Majority of the whole Number of Electors appointed; and if there be more than one who have such Majority, and have an equal Number of Votes, then the House of Representatives shall immediately choose by Ballot one of them for President; and if no Person have a Majority, then from the five highest on the List the said House shall in like Manner choose the President. But in choosing the President, the Votes shall be taken by States, the Representation from each State having one Vote; A quorum for this Purpose shall consist of a Member or Members from two-thirds of the States, and a Majority of all the States shall be necessary to a Choice. In every Case, after the Choice of the President, the Person having the greatest Number of Votes of the Electors shall be the Vice-President. But if there should remain two or more who have equal Votes, the Senate shall choose from them by Ballot the Vice-President.][7]

[3] The Congress may determine the Time of choosing the Electors, and the Day on which they shall give their Votes; which Day shall be the same throughout the United States.

[4] No person except a natural born Citizen, or a Citizen of the United States, at the time of the Adoption of this Constitution, shall be eligible to the Office of President; neither shall any Person be eligible to that Office who shall not have attained to the Age of thirty-five Years, and been fourteen Years a Resident within the United States.

[5] In case of the Removal of the President from Office, or of his Death, Resignation, or Inability to discharge the Powers and Duties of the said Office, the same shall devolve on the Vice-President, and the Congress may by Law provide for the Case of Removal, Death, Resignation or Inability, both of the President and Vice-President, declaring what Officer shall then act as President, and such Officer shall act accordingly, until the Disability be removed, or a President shall be elected.[8]

[6] The President shall, at stated Times, receive for his Services, a Compensation, which shall neither be increased nor diminished during the Period

---

[7]This paragraph was superseded in 1804 by the Twelfth Amendment.
[8]Changed by the Twenty-fifth Amendment.

for which he shall have been elected, and he shall not receive within that Period any other Emolument from the United States, or any of them.

[7] Before he enter on the Execution of his Office, he shall take the following Oath or Affirmation:—"I do solemnly swear (or affirm) that I will faithfully execute the Office of President of the United States, and will to the best of my Ability, preserve, protect and defend the Constitution of the United States."

Section 2. [1] The President shall be Commander in Chief of the Army and Navy of the United States, and of the Militia of the several States, when called into the actual Service of the United States; he may require the Opinion in writing, of the principal Officer in each of the executive Departments, upon any subject relating to the Duties of their respective Offices, and he shall have Power to Grant Reprieves and Pardons for Offenses against the United States, except in Cases of Impeachment.

[2] He shall have Power, by and with the Advice and Consent of the Senate, to make Treaties, provided two-thirds of the Senators present concur; and he shall nominate, and by and with the Advice and Consent of the Senate, shall appoint Ambassadors, other public Ministers and Consuls, Judges of the supreme Court, and all other Officers of the United States, whose Appointments are not herein otherwise provided for, and which shall be established by Law: but the Congress may by Law vest the Appointment of such inferior Officers, as they think proper, in the President alone, in the Court of Law, or in the Heads of Departments.

[3] The President shall have Power to fill up all Vacancies that may happen during the Recess of the Senate, by granting Commissions which shall expire at the End of their next Session.

Section 3. He shall from time to time give to the Congress Information of the State of the Union, and recommend to their Consideration such Measures as he shall judge necessary and expedient; he may, on extraordinary Occasions, convene both Houses, or either of them, and in Case of Disagreement between them, with Respect to the Time of Adjournment, he may adjourn them to such Time as he shall think proper; he shall receive Ambassadors and other public Ministers; he shall take Care that the Laws be faithfully executed, and shall Commission all the Officers of the United States.

Section 4. The President, Vice President and all civil Officers of the United States, shall be removed from Office on Impeachment for, and Conviction of, Treason, Bribery, or other high Crimes and Misdemeanors.

ARTICLE III

Section 1. The judicial Power of the United States, shall be vested in one supreme Court, and in such inferior Courts as the Congress may from time to time ordain and establish. The Judges, both of the supreme and inferior Courts, shall hold their Offices during good Behavior, and shall, at stated Times, receive for their Services a Compensation which shall not be diminished during their Continuance in Office.

Section 2. [1] The judicial Power shall extend to all Cases, in Law and Equity, arising under this Constitution, the Laws of the United States, and Treaties made, or which shall be made, under their Authority;—to all Cases affecting Ambassadors, other public Ministers and Consuls;—to all Cases of admiralty and maritime Jurisdiction;—to Controversies to which the United States shall be a Party;—to Controversies between two or more States;—[between a State and Citizens of another State];[9]—between Citizens of different States;—between Citizens of the same State claiming Lands under Grants of different States, and [between a State, or the Citizens thereof, and foreign States, Citizens or Subjects].[10]

[2] In all Cases affecting Ambassadors, other public Ministers and Consuls, and those in which a State shall be Party, the supreme Court shall have original Jurisdiction. In all the other Cases before mentioned, the supreme Court shall have appellate Jurisdiction, both as to Law and Fact, with such Exceptions, and under such Regulations as the Congress shall make.

[3] The trial of all Crimes, except in Cases of Impeachment, shall be by Jury; and such Trial shall be held in the State where the said Crimes shall have been committed: but when not committed within any State, the Trial shall be at such Place or Places as the Congress may by Law have directed.

Section 3. [1] Treason against the United States, shall consist only in levying War against them, or in adhering to their Enemies, giving them Aid and Comfort. No Person shall be convicted of Treason unless on the Testimony of two Witnesses to the same overt Act, or on Confession in open Court.

[2] The Congress shall have power to declare the Punishment of Treason, but no Attainder of Treason shall work Corruption of Blood, or Forfeiture except during the Life of the Person attained.

---

[9]Restricted by the Eleventh Amendment.
[10]Restricted by the Eleventh Amendment.

ARTICLE IV

Section 1. Full Faith and Credit shall be given in each State to the public Acts, Records, and judicial Proceedings of every other State. And the Congress may by general Laws prescribe the Manner in which such Acts, Records and Proceedings shall be proved, and the Effect thereof.

Section 2. [1] The Citizens of each State shall be entitled to all Privileges and Immunities of Citizens in the several States.

[2] A Person charged in any State with Treason, Felony, or other Crime, who shall flee from Justice, and be found in another State, shall on demand of the executive Authority of the State from which he fled, be delivered up, to be removed to the State having Jurisdiction of the Crime.

[3] [No Person held to Service or Labor in one State, under the Laws thereof, escaping into another, shall, in Consequence of any Law or Regulation therein, be discharged from such Service or Labor, but shall be delivered up on Claim of the Party to whom such Service or Labor may be due.][11]

Section 3. [1] New States may be admitted by the Congress into this Union; but no new State shall be formed or erected within the Jurisdiction of any other State; nor any State be formed by the Junction of two or more States, or parts of States, without the Consent of the Legislatures of the States concerned as well as of the Congress.

[2] The Congress shall have Power to dispose of and make all needful rules and Regulations respecting the Territory or other Property belonging to the United States; and nothing in this Constitution shall be so construed as to Prejudice any Claims of the United States, or of any particular State.

Section 4. The United States shall guarantee to every State in this Union a Republican Form of Government, and shall protect each of them against Invasion; and on Application of the Legislature, or of the Executive (when the Legislature cannot be convened) against domestic Violence.

ARTICLE V

The Congress, whenever two-thirds of both Houses shall deem it necessary, shall propose Amendments to this Constitution, or, on the Application of the Legislatures of two-thirds of the several States, shall call a Convention for proposing Amendments, which, in either Case, shall be valid to all Intents and Purposes, as part of this Constitution, when ratified by the Legislature of three-fourths of the several States, or by Conventions in three-fourths thereof, as the one or the other Mode of Ratification may be proposed by the Congress; Pro-

---

[11]This paragraph has been superseded by the Thirteenth Amendment.

vided that no Amendment which may be made prior to Year One thousand eight hundred and eight shall in any Manner affect the first and fourth Clauses in the Ninth Section of the first Article; and that no State, without its Consent, shall be deprived of its equal Suffrage in the Senate.

ARTICLE VI

[1] All Debts contracted and Engagements entered into, before the Adoption of this Constitution, shall be as valid against the United States under this Constitution, as under the Confederation.

[2] This Constitution, and the Laws of the United States which shall be made in Pursuance thereof; and all Treaties made, or which shall be made, under the Authority of the United States, shall be the supreme Law of the Land; and the Judges in every State shall be bound thereby, any Thing in the Constitution or Laws of any State to the Contrary notwithstanding.

[3] The Senators and Representatives before mentioned, and the Members of the several State Legislatures, and all executive and judicial Officers, both of the United States and of the several States, shall be bound by Oath or Affirmation, to support this Constitution; but no religious Test shall ever be required as a Qualification to any Office or public Trust under the United States.

ARTICLE VII

The Ratification of the conventions of nine States, shall be sufficient for the Establishment of this Constitution between the States so ratifying the Same.

DONE   in Convention by the Unanimous Consent of the States present the Seventeenth Day of September in the Year of our Lord one thousand seven hundred and Eighty seven and the Independence of the United States of America the Twelfth. In Witness whereof We have hereunto subscribed our Names,

GO WASHINGTON
President and deputy from Virginia

Articles in Addition to, and Amendment of, the Constitution of the United States of America, Proposed by Congress, and Ratified by the Legislatures of the Several States, Pursuant to the Fifth Article of the Original Constitution.

ARTICLE I[12]

Congress shall make no law respecting an establishment of religion, or prohibiting the free exercise thereof; or abridging the freedom of speech, or of the press; or the right of the people peaceably to assemble, and to petition the Government for a redress of grievances.

ARTICLE II

A well regulated Militia, being necessary to the security of a free State, the right of the people to keep and bear Arms, shall not be infringed.

ARTICLE III

No Soldier shall, in time of peace be quartered in any house, without the consent of the Owner, nor in time of war, but in a manner to be prescribed by law.

ARTICLE IV

The right of the people to be secure in their persons, houses, papers, and effects, against unreasonable searches and seizures, shall not be violated, and no Warrants shall issue, but upon probable cause, supported by Oath or affirmation, and particularly describing the place to be searched, and the persons or things to be seized.

ARTICLE V

No person shall be held to answer for a capital, or otherwise infamous crime, unless on a presentment or indictment of a Grand Jury, except in cases arising in the land or naval forces, or in the Militia, when in actual service in time of War or public danger; nor shall any person be subject for the same offence to be twice put in jeopardy of life or limb; nor shall be compelled in any criminal case to be witness against himself, nor be deprived of life, liberty, or property, without due process of law; nor shall private property be taken for public use, without just compensation.

ARTICLE VI

In all criminal prosecutions, the accused shall enjoy the right to a speedy and public trial, by an impartial jury of the State and district wherein the crime shall have been committed, which district shall have been previously ascertained by law, and to be informed of the nature and cause of the accusation;

---

[12]The first ten amendments were adopted in 1791.

to be confronted with the witnesses against him; to have compulsory process for obtaining witnesses in his favor, and to have the Assistance of Counsel for his defence.

ARTICLE VII

In suits at common law, where the value in controversy shall exceed twenty dollars, the right of trial by jury shall be preserved, and no fact tried by a jury, shall be otherwise reexamined in any Court of the United States, than according to the rules of the common law.

ARTICLE VIII

Excessive bail shall not be required, nor excessive fines imposed, nor cruel and unusual punishments inflicted.

ARTICLE IX

The enumeration in the Constitution, of certain rights, shall not be construed to deny or disparage others retained by the people.

ARTICLE X

The powers not delegated to the United States by the Constitution, nor prohibited by it to the States, are reserved to the States respectively, or to the people.

ARTICLE XI[13]

The Judicial power of the United States shall not be construed to extend to any suit in law or equity, commenced or prosecuted against one of the United States by Citizens of another State, or by Citizens or Subjects of any Foreign State.

ARTICLE XII[14]

The Electors shall meet in their respective states and vote by ballot for President and Vice-President, one of whom, at least, shall not be an inhabitant of the same state with themselves; they shall name in their ballots the person voted for as President, and in distinct ballots the person voted for as Vice-President, and they shall make distinct lists of all persons voted for as President, and of

---

[13]Adopted in 1798.
[14]Adopted in 1804.

all persons voted for as Vice-President, and of the number of votes for each, which lists they shall sign and certify, and transmit sealed to the seat of the government of the United States, directed to the President of the Senate;— The President of the Senate shall, in presence of the Senate and House of Representatives, open all the certificates and the votes shall then be counted;— The person having the greatest number of votes for President, shall be the President, if such number be a majority of the whole number of Electors appointed; and if no person have such majority, then from the persons having the highest numbers not exceeding three on the list of those voted for as President, the House of Representatives shall choose immediately, by ballot, the President. But in choosing the President, the votes shall be taken by states, the representation from each state having one vote; a quorum for this purpose shall consist of a member or members from two-thirds of the states, and a majority of all the states shall be necessary to a choice. [And if the House of Representatives shall not choose a President whenever the right of choice shall devolve upon them, before the fourth day of March next following, then the Vice-President shall act as President, as in the case of the death or other constitutional disability of the President.][15]—The person having the greatest number of votes as Vice-President, shall be the Vice-President, if such number be a majority of the whole number of Electors appointed, and if no person have a majority, then from the two highest numbers on the list, the Senate shall choose the Vice-President; a quorum for the purpose shall consist of two-thirds of the whole number of Senators, and a majority of the whole number shall be necessary to a choice. But no person constitutionally ineligible to the office of President shall be eligible to that of Vice-President of the United States.

ARTICLE XIII[16]

Section 1. Neither slavery nor involuntary servitude, except as a punishment for crime whereof the party shall have been duly convicted, shall exist within the United States, or any place subject to their jurisdiction.

Section 2. Congress shall have power to enforce this article by appropriate legislation.

ARTICLE XIV[17]

Section 1. All persons born or naturalized in the United States, and subject to the jurisdiction thereof, are citizens of the United States and of the State wherein they reside. No state shall make or enforce any law which shall abridge the privileges or immunities of citizens of the United States; nor shall any State

---

[15]Superseded by the Twentieth Amentment, Section 3.

[16]Adopted in 1865.

[17]Adopted in 1868.

deprive any person of life, liberty, or property, without due process of law; nor deny to any person within its jurisdiction the equal protection of the laws.

Section 2. Representatives shall be apportioned among the several States according to their respective numbers, counting the whole number of persons in each State, excluding Indians not taxed. But when the right to vote at any election for the choice of electors for President and Vice-President of the United States, Representatives in Congress, the Executive and Judicial officers of a State, or the members of the Legislature thereof, is denied to any of the male inhabitants of such State, being twenty-one years of age, and citizens of the United States, or in any way abridged, except for participation in rebellion, or other crime, the basis of representation therein shall be reduced in the proportion which the number of such male citizens shall bear to the whole number of male citizens twenty-one years of age in such State.

Section 3. No person shall be a Senator or Representative in Congress, or elector of President and Vice-President, or hold any office, civil or military, under the United States, or under any State, who, having previously taken an oath, as a member of Congress, or as an officer of the United States, or as a member of any State legislature, or as an executive or judicial officer of any State, to support the Constitution of the United States, shall have engaged in insurrection or rebellion against the same, or given aid or comfort to the enemies thereof. But Congress may by a vote of two-thirds of each House, remove such disability.

Section 4. The validity of the public debt of the United States, authorized by law, including debts incurred for payment of pensions and bounties for services in suppressing insurrection or rebellion, shall not be questioned. But neither the United States nor any State shall assume or pay any debt or obligation incurred in aid of insurrection or rebellion against the United States, or any claim for the loss or emancipation of any slave; but all such debts, obligations and claims shall be held illegal and void.

Section 5. The Congress shall have power to enforce, by appropriate legislation, the provisions of this article.

ARTICLE XV[18]

Section 1. The right of citizens of the United States to vote shall not be denied or abridged by the United States or by any State on account of race, color, or previous condition of servitude—

Section 2. The Congress shall have power to enforce this article by appropriate legislation.

ARTICLE XVI[19]

The Congress shall have power to lay and collect taxes on incomes, from whatever source derived, without apportionment among the several States, and without regard to any census or enumeration.

ARTICLE XVII[20]

The Senate of the United States shall be composed of two Senators from each State, elected by the people thereof, for six years; and each Senator shall have one vote. The electors in each State shall have the qualifications requisite for electors of the most numerous branch of the State legislatures.

When vacancies happen in the representation of any State in the Senate, the executive authority of such State shall issue writs of election to fill such vacancies: *Provided*, That the legislature of any State may empower the executive thereof to make temporary appointments until the people fill the vacancies by election as the legislature may direct.

This amendment shall not be so construed as to affect the election or term of any Senator chosen before it becomes valid as part of the Constitution.

ARTICLE XVIII[21]

Section 1. After one year from the ratification of this article the manufacture, sale, or transportation of intoxicating liquors within, the importation thereof into, or the exportation thereof from the United States and all territory subject to the jurisdiction thereof for beverage purposes is hereby prohibited.

Section 2. The Congress and the several States shall have concurrent power to enforce this article by appropriate legislation.

---

[18]Adopted in 1870.
[19]Adopted in 1913.
[20]Adopted in 1913.
[21]Adopted in 1919. Repealed by Section 1 of the Twenty-first Amendment.

Section 3. This article shall be inoperative unless it shall have been ratified as an amendment to the Constitution by the legislatures of the several States, as provided in the Constitution, within seven years from the date of the submission hereof to the States by the Congress.

ARTICLE XIX[22]

The right of citizens of the United States to vote shall not be denied or abridged by the United States or by any State on account of sex.

Congress shall have power to enforce this article by appropriate legislation.

ARTICLE XX[23]

Section 1. The terms of the President and Vice-President shall end at noon on the 20th day of January, and the terms of Senators and Representatives at noon on the 3d day of January, of the years in which such terms would have ended if this article had not been ratified; and the terms of their successors shall then begin.

Section 2. The Congress shall assemble at least once in every year, and such meeting shall begin at noon on the 3d day of January, unless they shall by law appoint a different day.

Section 3. If, at the time fixed for the beginning of the term of the President, the president elect shall have died, the Vice-President elect shall become President. If a President shall not have been chosen before the time fixed for the beginning of his term, or if the President elect shall have failed to qualify, then the Vice-President elect shall act as President until a President shall have qualified; and the Congress may by law provide for the case wherein neither a President elect nor a Vice-President elect shall have qualified, declaring who shall then act as President, or the manner in which one who is to act shall be selected, and such person shall act accordingly until a President or Vice-President shall have qualified.

Section 4. The Congress may by law provide for the case of the death of any of the persons from whom the House of Representatives may choose a President whenever the right of choice shall have devolved upon them, and for the case of the death of any of the persons from whom the Senate may choose a Vice-President whenever the right of choice shall have devolved upon them.

---

[22]Adopted in 1920.
[23]Adopted in 1933.

Section 5. Section 1 and 2 shall take effect on the 15th day of October following the ratification of this article.

Section 6. This article shall be inoperative unless it shall have been ratified as an amendment to the Constitution by the legislatures of three-fourths of the several States within seven years from the date of its submission.

ARTICLE XXI[24]

Section 1. The eighteenth article of amendment to the Constitution of the United States is hereby repealed.

Section 2. The transportation or importation into any State, Territory, or possession of the United States for delivery or use therein of intoxicating liquors, in violation of the laws thereof, is hereby prohibited.

Section 3. This article shall be inoperative unless it shall have been ratified as an amendment to the Constitution by conventions in the several States, as provided in the Constitution, within seven years from the date of the submission hereof to the States by the Congress.

ARTICLE XXII[25]

Section 1. No person shall be elected to the office of the President more than twice, and no person who has held the office of President, or acted as President, for more than two years of a term to which some other person was elected President shall be elected to the office of the President more than once. But this Article shall not apply to any person holding the office of President when this Article was proposed by the Congress, and shall not prevent any person who may be holding the office of President, or acting as President, during the term within which this Article becomes operative from holding the office of President or acting as President during the remainder of such term.

Section 2. This article shall be inoperative unless it shall have been ratified as an amendment to the Constitution by the legislatures of three-fourths of the several States within seven years from the date of its submission to the States by the Congress.

---

[24]Adopted in 1933.
[25]Adopted in 1951.

ARTICLE XXIII[26]

Section 1. The District constituting the seat of Government of the United States shall appoint in such manner as the Congress may direct:

A number of electors of President and Vice-President equal to the whole number of Senators and Representatives in Congress to which the District would be entitled if it were a State, but in no event more than the least populous State; they shall be in addition to those appointed by the States, but they shall be considered, for the purposes of the election of President and Vice-President, to be electors appointed by a State; and they shall meet in the District and perform such duties as provided by the twelfth article of amendment.

Section 2. The Congress shall have power to enforce this article by appropriate legislation.

ARTICLE XXIV[27]

Section 1. The right of citizens of the United States to vote in any primary or other election for President or Vice-President, for electors for President or Vice-President, or for Senator or Representative in Congress, shall not be denied or abridged by the United States or any state by reasons of failure to pay any poll tax or other tax.

Section 2. The Congress shall have power to enforce this article by appropriate legislation.

ARTICLE XXV[28]

Section 1. In case of the removal of the President from office or of his death or resignation, the Vice-President shall become President.

Section 2. Whenever there is a vacancy in the office of the Vice-President, the President shall nominate a Vice-President who shall take office upon confirmation by a majority vote of both Houses of Congress.

Section 3. Whenever the President transmits to the President pro tempore of the Senate and the Speaker of the House of Representatives his written declaration that he is unable to discharge the powers and duties of his office, and until he transmits to them a written declaration to the contrary, such powers and duties shall be discharged by the Vice-President as Acting President.

---

[26]Adopted in 1961.
[27]Adopted in 1964.
[28]Adopted in 1967.

Section 4. Whenever the Vice-President and a majority of either the principal officers of the Executive departments or of such other body as Congress may by law provide transmit to the President pro tempore of the Senate and the Speaker of the House of Representatives their written declaration that the President is unable to discharge the powers and duties of his office, the Vice-President shall immediately assume the powers and duties of the office as Acting President.

Thereafter, when the President transmits to the President pro tempore of the Senate and the Speaker of the House of Representatives his written declaration that no inability exists, he shall resume the powers and duties of his office unless the Vice-President and a majority of either the principal officers of the Executive departments or of such other body as Congress may by law provide transmit within four days to the President pro tempore of the Senate and the Speaker of the House of Representatives their written declaration that the President is unable to discharge the powers and duties of his office. Thereupon Congress shall decide the issue, assembling within forty-eight hours for that purpose if not in session. If the Congress, within twenty-one days after receipt of the latter written declaration, or, if Congress is not in session, within twenty-one days after Congress is required to assemble, determines by two-thirds vote of both houses that the President is unable to discharge the powers and duties of his office, the Vice-President shall continue to discharge the same as Acting President; otherwise, the President shall resume the powers and duties of his office.

ARTICLE XXVI[29]

Section 1. The right of citizens of the United States, who are 18 years of age or older, to vote shall not be denied or abridged by the United States or any state on account of age.

Section 2. The Congress shall have power to enforce this article by appropriate legislation.

---

[29]Adopted in 1971.